W. R. Strong

W. R. Strong & Co. materials

W. R. Strong

W. R. Strong & Co. materials

ISBN/EAN: 9783741138812

Manufactured in Europe, USA, Canada, Australia, Japa

Cover: Foto ©Thomas Meinert / pixelio.de

Manufactured and distributed by brebook publishing software
(www.brebook.com)

W. R. Strong

W. R. Strong & Co. materials

ESTABLISHED 1852.

IFORNIA SEEDS

TREES AND NURSERY STOCK

1889 Catalogue

W. R. STRONG & CO.

SACRAMENTO, CAL.

To Our Customers.

We shall continue our efforts to supply the increasing demand for **Seeds,** and will be constantly supplied with those that are true to name, pure, fresh and reliable. We have these grown for us in California, the Eastern States and in Europe.

Our stock in store, and facilities for procuring and handling all classes of **Seeds** is equal to any house in California or the East, whether **Garden, Flower, Herb, Tree or Field Seeds.** All orders for Seeds, if in packets or ounces will be forwarded, prepaid, by mail. If ordered in bulk, if to go by mail, add ten cents per pound to cover the extra cost.

Send Money with Order at our expense, in Registered Letters, Money Orders, Express or Bank Exchange, as most convenient. Postage Stamps will be received for small sums if carefully protected from dampness. **We make a Specialty of Grass, Clover, and all Field Seeds.** Those wanting Seeds in large quantity will please write for special quotations.

Seedsmen do not **guarantee** the growth of Seeds, and that they will invariably produce perfect crops, there being so many contingencies that are beyond their control, owing to the character of the weather, soil, improper treatment, want of knowledge of when and how to plant, cultivate, etc., which often result in a failure. But we take every precaution, and will not allow any seed to leave our establishment till we are assured that they are reliable and first-class.

NURSERY DEPARTMENT.

This is under the especial management and supervision of our Mr. Williamson, the oldest and most experienced Nurseryman on the Coast. We have over three hundred acres in cultivation in nursery and fruit tree growth. **We know our stock to be True, Clean, Thrifty and Well Grown, and Free from all Insect Pests and Scale,** which is making such ravages in our State

Besides our nursery grounds in this State, we have established a branch department, under the charge of Gillet Bros., in Florida, for the growing of **Orange, Lemon, Magnolia, and other Evergreen Trees and Shrubs** that can be grown to better perfection there, and we believe we can give better satisfaction in quality and price than any other establishment.

Write Plainly, Name, Postoffice, County and State.

Make orders apart from your letter, and for **Trees and Nursery Stock, separate from Seed Orders,** as the departments are separate.

INDEX.

VEGETABLE SEEDS.

	PAGE.
Artichoke	2, 5
Asparagus	2, 5
Beans	1, 6
Beets	2, 7
Broccoli	2, 6
Borecole, or Kale	3, 12
Brussels Sprouts	2, 8
Cabbage	2, 8
Carrots	2, 9
Corn	2, 10
Cucumber	3, 11
Endive	3, 12
Kohl Rabi	3, 12
Leek	3, 13
Lettuce	3, 13
Melon	3, 13, 14
Okra, or Gumbo	3, 14
Onions	3, 15

	PAGE.
Peas	1, 16
Pepper	4, 17
Pumpkin	4, 17
Radish	4, 17
Rhubarb	4, 18
Salsify	4, 19
Squash	4, 19
Tomato	4, 20, 21
Turnip	4, 19, 20
Clover, Grass and Lawn Seeds	21-26
Miscellaneous and Field Seeds	27

FLOWER SEEDS.

Pages 28 to 36.

	PAGE.
Bulbs, etc	36
Herb Seeds	21
Tree seeds	22

	PAGE.
Vegetable, Plant and Esculent Roots	54

NURSERY DEPARTMENT.

Pages 37 to 53.

Plants for transplanting	54
Useful Tables	3d page Cover

ADVERTISEMENTS.

Imperial Egg Food	55
A. C. Sweetser & Co	55
W. P. Coleman	59
J. F. Cooper	56
Paker & Hamilton	57
W. D. Comstock	58
Booth & Co	58
Friend & Terry Lumber Co	56
Western Hotel	56
W. R. Strong & Co	60

Print of H. S. Crocker & Co., Sacramento, Cal.

W. R. Strong & Co.'s

CATALOGUE AND

Price List of Vegetable Seeds

FOR 1889.

Where Seeds are quoted in this catalogue by the pound (if forwarded by mail), add ten cents per pound to pay for postage. When quoted by the ounce or in packets, the postage will be paid by us.

Vegetable **Seeds** in packets, 5c. each or 50c. per dozen.

Peas, Beans and Corn in half pound boxes, 10c. or $1.00 per dozen.

Peas, Beans and Corn in one pound boxes, 15c. or $1.50 per dozen.

PEAS.

EXTRA EARLY.

	Per lb.	Per 100 lb
Cleveland's Alaska, earliest of all, 20 inches.........	$0 15	$10 00
Cleveland's R. N. Y., 2 feet, prolific ; ripens at one time, fine flavor.........	15	9 00
Cleveland's, first, best, 2 ft.,	15	7 00
Premium Tom Thumb, 8 in.,	15	9 00
Premium Gem, wrinkled, sweet, 2 feet	15	8 00
Carter's First Crop........	15	9 00
American Wonder, 10 in...	15	9 00
Laxton Alpha, 3 feet......	15	9 00
Bliss' Abundance, 18 inches,	15	9 00
Bliss' everlasting, 24 inches,	15	9 00
McLean's Advancer, 36 in.,	15	9 00

GENERAL CROP.

	Per lb.	Per 100 lbs
Yorkshire Hero, 2½ feet..	$0 15	$8 00
Telephone, 3 feet..........	15	9 00
Champion of England, 5 ft.,	15	7 50
Blue Imperial, 2 feet......	10	6 00
Royal Dwarf Marrow, 2½ ft.	10	6 00
Large White Marrowfat, 5 feet.....................	10	6 00
Black Eye Marrowfat, 4 ft.,	10	5 00

EDIBLE PODS.

	Per lb.	Per 100 lbs
Tall and Dwarf White Seed,	$0 20	$12 50
Tall and Dwarf Gray Seed,	20	12 50

Field Peas in quantity and variety, at lowest market rates.

BEANS.

DWARF SNAPS OR GREEN STRING.

	Per lb.	Per 100 lbs
Early Refugee............	$0 15	$7 50
Early Pinkeye China......	15	6 00
Early Red Valentine......	15	8 00
Cleveland's Round Pod, earliest, best and most prolific of all............	15	9 00
Early White Valentine....	15	9 00
Early Mohawk............	15	8 00
Early Yellow Six Weeks...	15	6 00
Green Flageolet, fine......	15	10 00
Wax Flageolet, yellow pod, large, fine..............	15	10 00
Early Golden Wax, yellow pod.....................	15	8 00
Ivory Wax, yellow pod....	15	10 00
White Seeded Wax, yellow pod.....................	15	10 00
Black Seeded Wax, yellow pod.....................	15	8 00
Dwarf White Kidney......	15	6 00
Dwarf Cranberry..........	15	7 50
Broad Windsor...........	10	6 00

POLE OR RUNNING BEANS.

	Per lb.	Per 100 lbs
Lima, King of the Garden.	$0 15	$10 00
Lima, selected hand picked,	15	8 00
London Horticultural.....	15	8 00
Dutch Case Knife.........	15	8 00
Giant Wax, red seed......	15	10 00

Two pounds for 25 Cents of Peas, Beans and Corn, when quoted at 15 cents per single pound.

TWENTY-FIVE POUNDS AND OVER WILL BE SOLD AT 100 POUND RATES.

	Per oz.	Per lb
Scarlet and White Runners,	$0 25	$15 00
Asparagus, or Yard Long Pod	50	....

Field Beans of all varieties in quantity at the lowest market rates.

SWEET CORN, FOR TABLE.

	Per lb.	Per 100 lbs
Extra Early Tom Thumb.	$0 15	$9 00
Extra Early Marblehead	15	9 00
Extra Early Cory	15	9 00
Extra Early Minnesota	15	8 00
Extra Early Crosby	15	8 00
Extra Early Moore's Concord	15	8 00
Extra Early Mammoth Sugar	15	8 00
Later, Stowell's Evergreen,	15	9 00
Later, Washington Market,	15	9 00
Amber Cream	15	9 00
Black Mexican	15	9 00
Adams' Extra Early	15	9 00

FIELD CORN.

	Per oz.	Per lb
Early King Philip	$0 10	$7 50
Early White Flint	10	6 00
Early Yellow Canada	10	6 00
Early Tuscarora	10	7 50

Pop Corn, Rice and Common, of all descriptions, for Field Planting and for Feed, furnished in quantities, at lowest market rates.

ARTICHOKE.

	Per oz.	Per lb
Green Globe	$0 30	$3 00

Jerusalem Tubers, $5 per 100 pounds.

ASPARAGUS.

	Per oz.	Per lb
Colossal, largest and best	$0 10	$0 60

Two-year-old roots, $1 50 per 100.

BEETS.

	Per oz.	Per lb
Extra Early Eclipse, new and fine	$0 10	$0 75
Extra Early Egyptian	10	75
Extra Early Bassano	10	60
Dewing's Early Blood Turnip	10	60
Early Blood Turnip	10	60
Early Long Dark Blood	10	60
Bastian's Half Long Dark Blood	10	60
Mangel Wurzel, or Stock Beet	....	25
Improved Long Red Mangel Wurzel	9 10	35
Norbiten Giant Mangel	10	35
Yellow Globe Mangel	13 10	35
Red Globe Mangel	10	35
Imperial White Sugar	9 10	25

BRUSSELS SPROUTS.

	Per oz.	Per lb
Improved Dwarf	$0 20	$2 00

BROCCOLI.

	Per oz.
Early Purple Cape	$0 40
Early White Cape	40

CABBAGE.

	Per oz.	Per lb
Early Etampes	$0 15	$1 50
Early York, Dwarf	15	1 50
Early Large York	15	1 50
Early Oxheart, finest	15	1 50
Henderson's Early Summer	20	2 00
Jersey Early Wakefield	20	2 00
Early Bloomsdale Market	20	2 00
Early Schweinfurth	20	2 50
Early Winingstadt	15	1 50
Early Dwarf Dutch	15	1 50
Early Drumhead or Batterson	15	1 50
Premium Flat Dutch	20	2 00
Premium Drumhead	20	2 00
Stone Mason	20	2 50
Mammoth Marblehead	20	2 50
Improved Brunswick	20	2 00
German Filderkraut	20	2 00
Savoy Drumhead	20	2 00
Savoy Early Dwarf	20	2 00
Red Dutch Pickling	20	2 00

CARROT.

	Per oz.	Per lb
Early Scarlet Horn	$0 10	$1 00
Earliest Short Horn, for forcing	10	1 25
Danvers Orange, Half Long	10	75
Early Half Long Scarlet, Stump Rooted	10	75
Improved Long Orange	10	75
Large White Belgian	10	60
Large Yellow Belgian	..	60

CAULIFLOWER.

	Per oz.	Per lb
Henderson's Early Snowball,	$2 00	$. ..
Extra Early Dwarf Erfurt selected	1 50	....
Early London	60	7 00
Early Paris, best	75	8 00
Large White French	75	8 00
Lenormand's Short Stem	75	8 00
Large Asiatic	50	6 00
Veitch's Autumn Giant	50	6 00
Large Late Algiers	75	....

CELERY.

	Per oz.	Per lb
Henderson's White Plume	$0 25	$3 00
Henderson's Dwarf	15	1 50
Golden Heart	15	1 25
Large White Solid	15	1 25
Dwarf White Solid	15	1 50
Boston Market	15	1 50
Celeriac or Turnip Rooted	15	1 50
Celery Seed, for flavoring	10	35

	Per oz.	Per lb
Chicory, large rooted (coffee),	$0 10	$1 00
Corn Salad	10	1 00

CRESS, or PEPPERGRASS.

	Per oz.	Per lb
Broad Leaf	$0 10	$0 75
Fine Curled	10	75
Fine Water Cress	40	....

CUCUMBERS.

	Per oz.	Per lb
Extra Long White Spine	$0 10	$1 00
Early Russian	10	1 00
Improved Early White Spine	10	1 00
Early Frame	10	1 00
Early Short Green	10	1 00
Nichols' Medium Green	10	1 00
Early Green Cluster	10	1 00
Early Boston Pickling	10	1 00
Improved Long Green	10	1 00
Burr Small Gherkins	20	2 00
Tailby's Hybrid	10	1 00
Dandelion	40	4 00

EGG PLANT.

	Per oz.	Per lb
Early New York Purple	$0 50	$5 00
Early Long Purple	30	3 00

ENDIVE.

	Per oz.	Per lb
Green Curled	$0 15	$1 50
Moss Curled	15	2 00
Batavian	15	2 00

GARLIC.

The price of Garlic is variable.

KALE, or BORECOLE.

	Per oz.	Per lb
Green Curled Scotch	$0 10	$1 50
Dwf. German Green & Purple	10	1 50
Sea Kale	25	3 00

KOHL RABI.

	Per oz.	Per lb
Early White Vienna	$0 20	$2 00
Early Purple Vienna	20	2 00
Large Green	20	2 00

LEEK.

	Per oz.	Per lb
Best London Flag	$0 15	$1 50
Monstrous Carentan	15	1 50
Musselburg or Scotch	20	2 00

LETTUCE.

	Per oz.	Per lb
Hanson	$0 10	$1 25
Simpson's Early Curled	10	1 25
Early Prize Head	10	1 25
White Paris Cos. Romaine Lettuce	10	1 25
San Francisco Market Satisfaction	10	1 25
Philadelphia Butter	10	1 25
Early White Head Cabbage	10	1 25
Early Curled Silesia	10	1 25
Large Drumhead or Ice Cabbage	10	1 25
Simpson's Black Seeded	10	1 25
Boston Market—for forcing	10	1 25
Tennis Ball, Black Seeded—for forcing	10	1 25
Salamander — for hot, dry weather	10	1 25
Passion	10	1 25
Large India	10	1 25

MARTYNIA.

	Per oz.	Per lb
For making pickles	$0 25	$3 00

Mushroom Spawn, in bricks, 15 cents each.

MUSK MELON.

	Per oz.	Per lb
California Large Netted	$0 10	$1 00
Hackensack	10	1 00
Early Yellow Cantaloupe	10	1 00
Montreal Market	10	1 00
Bay View	10	1 00
Skillman's Fine Netted	10	1 00
Large Green Nutmeg	10	1 00
Cassaba, or Green Persian	10	1 00
Montreal Nutmeg, very large	10	1 00

WATER MELON.

	Per oz.	Per lb
Mammoth Iron Clad	$0 10	$0 75
Kolb's Gem	10	75
Scaly Bark	10	75
Black Spanish	10	75
Icing, or Ice Cream, Peerless	10	75
Mountain Sweet, or Gray Seeded Ice Cream	10	75
Mountain Sprout	10	75
Cuban Queen	10	75
Imperial Lodi, or California	10	75
Gypsy or Rattlesnake	10	75
Orange Rind	10	1 25
Citron Melon, for preserves	10	1 00
Pride of Georgia	10	75

NASTURTIUM.

	Per oz.	Per lb
Tall Sorts	$0 15	$1 50
Dwarf	15	1 50

OKRA or GUMBO.

	Per oz.	Per lb
Early Dwarf	$0 10	$1 00
Tall Green	10	1 00

ONIONS.

	Per oz.	Per lb
Early Large Red	$0 15	$1 50
Large Red Wethersfield	15	1 50
Yellow Danvers	15	1 50
Yellow Dutch	15	1 50
White Portugal, Silver Skin	25	2 50
White Globe	25	2 50
Early Bermuda	20	2 00
Giant Yellow Rocca	20	2 00
Early Queen	20	2 00

Onion Sets—Prices variable ; lowest market rates.

PARSNIPS.

	Per oz.	Per lb
Hollow Crown or Sugar	$0 10	$0 75
Long White	10	75

PARSLEY.

	Per oz.	Per lb
Triple Curled	$0 10	$0 75
Plain Curled	10	75
Fern Leaf, Moss Curled	10	75

PEPPER.

	Per oz.	Per lb
Golden Dawn	$0 25	$2 50
Long Red Cayenne	25	2 50
Chili, very small, for pepper sauce	25	2 50
Cherry Red	25	2 50
L'ge Squash, or Tomato-sh'p	25	2 50
Large Bell, or Bull-nose	25	2 50
Sweet Spanish, or Mountain.	25	2 50

PUMPKIN.

	Per oz.	Per lb
Large Yellow, or Conn. F'ld.	$0 10	$ 35
Large Cheese, for table use	10	50
Cashaw, or Crookneck	10	50
Mammonth Tours	10	1 00

RADISH.

	Per oz.	Per lb
Early Long Scarlet	$0 10	$ 75
Early Scarlet Turnip rooted	10	75
Early Sc'l't Turnip White tip	10	75
Early White Turnip-rooted	10	75
Olive shaped, or half-long Scarlet	10	75
French breakfast, or Half-l'ng Scarlet, White Tip	10	75
Beck's Chartier	10	1 00
Black Spanish, Fall or Wint'r	10	75
Scarlet China Winter	10	1 00
Mammoth White China, or California	..	1 00

RHUBARB, or PIE PLANT.

	Per oz.	Per lb
Linnœus, Giant	$0 20	$2 00
Victoria, Giant	20	2 50

Two-year roots, $2 50 per dozen; 25 cents each. One-year roots, $1 50 per dozen, or 15 cents each.

SALSIFY, or VEGETABLE OYSTER.

	Per oz.	Per lb
Best White	$0 15	$1 50
Scorzonera, or Black Salsify.	20	2 00

SQUASH.

	Per oz.	Per lb
Pineapple	$0 10	$1 00
Perfect Gem	10	1 00
Early Yellow Bush Scallop	10	1 00
Early White Bush Scallop	10	1 0u
Yellow Summer Crookneck	10	1 00
American Turban, or Essex	10	1 00
Marblehead	10	75
Boston, or Vegetable Marrow	10	75
Hubbard	10	75
Mammoth, Chili	10	75

Field Squash, for stock feeding, market price, 30 to 50 cents.

SPINACH.

	Per oz.	Per lb
Round Summer, or Large Dutch	$0 10	$0 35
Extra L'ge Prickly, Winter	11	35
Improved Thick Leaved	10	35
Monstrous Viroflay, extra l'rg	10	35
Long Standing, Late Seeding	10	35

SUNFLOWER.

	Per oz.	Per lb
Mammoth Russian	$0 10	$0 50

TOBACCO.

	Per oz.	Per lb
Connecticut Seed Leaf	$0 40	$4 00
Virginia	40	5 00
Havana	50	6 00

TOMATO.

	Per oz.	Per lb
Early Conquerer	$0 20	$2 00
Acme	20	2 00
Livingston's Perfection	20	2 50
Paragon	20	2 50
Hathaway's Excelsior	20	2 00
General Grant	20	2 50
Sacramento Favorite, fine	20	2 50
Mayflower	20	2 50
Fejee	20	2 50
Trophy	20	2 00
Large Yellow	20	2 50
Red Cherry	20	2 50
Cardinal	20	2 50
Mikado	20	2 50

TURNIP.

	Per oz.	Per lb
Early Snowball	$0 10	$0 75
White Egg	10	75
Early Yellow Stone	10	60
Early White Flat Dutch, Strap Leaved	10	60
Early Purple Top, Strap Leaved	10	60
Early Purple Top Munich	10	60
Large White Flat Norfolk	10	60
Yellow Aberdeen Purple Top	10	60
Purple Top, White Globe	10	60
Orange Yellow, or Golden Ball	10	60
Yellow, or Amber Globe	10	60
Pomeranian White Globe	10	60
Long White, or Cowhorn	10	60

RUTA BAGA.

	Per oz.	Per lb
Large White French	$0 10	$0 60
Sweet Russian, White	10	60
Sweet German, White	10	60
Improved Purple Top Yellow	10	60
Improved American Yellow Purple Top	10	60
Skirving's Purple Top	10	60

☞ For prices of Herb Seeds, Grass, Clover and Miscellaneous Field Seeds, see under those headings in the Descriptive part of this Catalogue.

VEGETABLE SEEDS

We examine all new varieties of vegetables, etc., but do not include them in our list unless they are proved, after thorough test, to be of superior excellence. We have no hesitation in saying that our Seeds cannot be excelled in quality and freshness by any other collection.

The following list will cover all varieties needed for successful gardening:

ARTICHOKES.

Green Globe—Sow the seed early in the season in drills 1 inch deep, 12 inches apart, and thin to 4 inches in good rich soil. When one year old transplant to rows 3 feet by 2. They will remain in bearing for years. The portion used is the flower head in its undeveloped state.

Jerusalem—Are tuberous roots, like Potatoes. They are grown mainly for hog and sheep food. They are also used for pickling and the table. Plant same as potatoes.

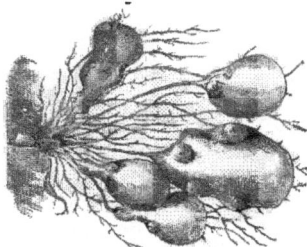

Globe Artichoke.

Jerusalem Artichoke.

ASPARAGUS.

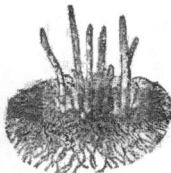

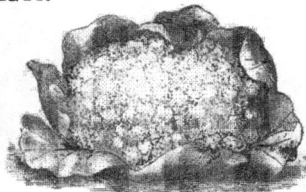

Asparagus.

Broccoli.

Colossal Giant—This is the best variety—unrivalled for productiveness, size and quality. Sow seeds in drills thinly, 1 inch deep; rows at least 1 foot apart. Keep the soil mellow and free from weeds. When one year old transplant into beds about 1 foot apart in deep loamy soil, and cover 4 inches above the crown. Salt is excellent for manuring.

BROCCOLI.

This is allied to the Cauliflower, but is much hardier. It is not suitable for hot Summers, and should be sown later to transplant in the Fall months, succeeding best in moist and cool atmospheres, and arrives at perfection from January to April in the climates of the Pacific Coast.

BEANS.

One pound will plant 75 feet of drill ; 125 pounds one acre in drill.

DWARF SNAPS OR STRINGLESS.

All varieties of this class are tender, and do best in rather dry, light soil, and should not be planted till the ground is warm and can continue at intervals throughout the season. Plant 2 inches deep, in rows 2 feet apart. Keep well hoed, drawing the earth up to the stems while dry.

Early Improved Red Valentine—Is one of the very best leading sorts. Pods are round, fleshy and tender, and remain longer in a green state than most varieties. (Fig. 8.)

Cleveland's Improved Round Red Valentine—Is ten days earlier than the Red Valentine and much more prolific and combines all its good qualities.

White Valentine—Is a good short snap, and also desirable as a shell bean.

Red Eye, or Early China—Is largely cultivated in California by market gardeners, and is good either as a snap or dry shell bean.

Early Mohawk—Is one of the hardiest varieties and will endure some frost. It is a good string bean, and is also desirable for pickling. (Fig. 4.)

Early Dutch Case-Knife—One of the earliest and most prolific. Long, flat pods with white seeds. Good green or dry.

Early Refugee—Is very productive and fine for spring snaps or for pickling. (Fig. 2.)

Yellow Six Weeks—Is very early, productive and excellent for snap or shell.

White Kidney, or Royal Dwarf—Is an excellent green shell bean, and one of the best for baking. (Fig. 6.)

Golden Wax—This variety is quite early. Pods are long, brittle, and entirely stringless, and of rich buttery flavor, and one of the very best. (Fig. 3.)

German, or Black Wax—Is one of the best. Pods are of rich, waxy yellow when fit for use, and very tender and delicious. (Fig. 13.)

Ivory Pod Wax—Are a white bean and earlier than the Black Wax. Pods are tender and stringless, and of a rich creamy flavor, and are ivory white.

Crystal White Wax—Are similar to the above—crisp, tender, and of the richest flavor The pods develop quickly and retain their tenderness longer than other sorts.

English Dwarf, or Broad Windsor—Is a very hardy kind and can be planted very early in the season, in good soil, in drills 3 feet apart. Pinch off tops as soon as the lower pods begin to fill. They are used only as shell beans.

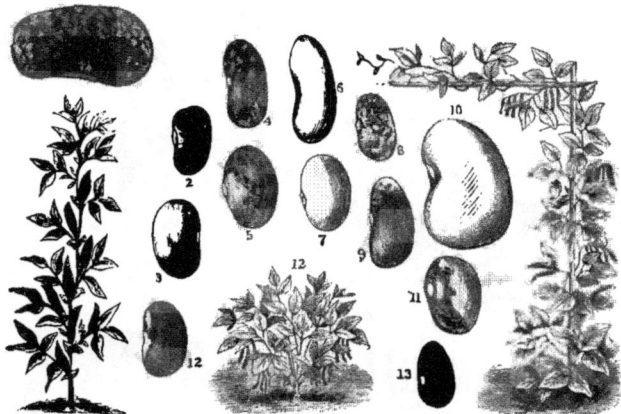

Beans.
POLE, OR RUNNING.—1 pound to 100 hills.

These are generally more tender than dwarf kinds and should not be planted till the ground becomes warm. Set poles about 4 feet apart, and pinch off the tops when they grow higher than the poles, They succeed best in sandy loam mixed with well rotted compost to each hill.

Large Lima—Are the most buttery and delicious of all, and are a universal favorite, green or dry. (Fig. 10.)

Giant Wax (Red Seed)—Make pods 6 to 9 inches long, thick and fleshy, of yellow waxy color, and is very productive and tender. (Fig. 12.)

Horticultural, or Speckled Cranberry—Is an old favorite and is equally good as a snap or as a shell bean, either green or dry. (Fig. 5.)

White Dutch Runners—Are very ornamental, large white seed, and beautiful clusters of white flowers, and is a good shell bean.

Scarlet Runners—Are a great favorite, producing clusters of beautiful scarlet flowers, which are very ornamental. This is very fine for use as a green shell bean. (Fig. 14.)

TABLE BEETS.

One ounce will plant 50 feet in drill; five pounds 1 acre.

Require rich, mellow, deep soil. Plant in rows or drills 1 foot apart for early sorts. Place seed 2 and 4 inches apart and cover 2 inches. While growing, thin out and use, giving room for development. For field culture, the rows should be further apart, to admit the horse cultivator, and the plants thinned to 1 foot in the rows. The Mangels grow to a very large size and are wonderfully productive.

Early Eclipse—Remarkable for rapid growth, smallness of top, and extra fine quality; smooth, round, skin and flesh bright red; very fine grained and sweet.

Egyptian Blood Turnip—One of the earliest; medium size, good quality and small top.

Early Bassano—Very early flat variety; tender and juicy; flesh rosy and white.

Early Blood Turnip—Good quality; blood red; tender and good keeper.

Bastian's Half Long—This is one of the very best for family use and the market gardener; of bright color and of excellent quality.

Pine Apple—Excellent half long; foliage dark red; roots of a dark crimson color.

Long Blood—A good late variety; sweet and tender; popular sort.

Swiss Chard, or Sea Kale—The leaves are used as Spinach, and the mid-rib stewed and served as Asparagus.

Orange Globe Mangel.　　　Egyptian Blood Turnip.

Long Red Mangel.

Long Blood.

Henderson's Pineapple.

Imperial Sugar.

Early Blood Turnip.　　　Bassano.

MANGEL AND SUGAR, FOR FIELD CULTURE.

White Sugar, or Imperial—The sweetest and most desirable for sugar, and one of the best for field use and cattle food.

Golden Tankard Mangel—Valuable variety; fine form and sweet; bright yellow, and heavy cropper.

Yellow Globe Mangel--Roots large and globe-shaped; very productive; better keeper than the Long Red and will grow in shallower soil.

Red Globe Mangel—Large, red, oval; keeps well, and produces better crops in shallow soils than the long varieties.

Mammoth Red Mangel—Is grown most extensively for agricultural purposes: produces very large roots, partly above ground.

BRUSSELS SPROUTS

Produces from the stem small heads resembling Cabbage in miniature. It is very tender, and of mild excellent flavor, and is used as greens.

CABBAGE.

One ounce for about 2,000 plants.

Cabbages require a deep rich soil and thorough working. The seed for the early crops can be sown in hot beds When of size to transplant, place the earlier kinds from 12 to 18 inches apart. The largest and later kinds 2 feet or more. The plants should be set down to first leaf, so that the stem is all below the surface of the ground, and hoe often. Our seed is from the finest and purest selected strains of American growth.

Newark Early Flat Dutch.   Brussels Spouts.

"True" Jersey Early Wakefield.

Early Large York—Is a popular known variety, superior, robust and endures the heat well.
Early French Oxheart—Is quite a favorite, heads early, tender and fine flavor.
Early Jersey Wakefield—Is highly prized, very early, following the Oxheart, and of fine quality.

Premium Flat Dutch.   Ston - M ison Marblehead.   Drumhead Savoy.

Henderson's Early Summer—Is considered one of the best early sorts; large head and sure crop, and good keeper.
Early Winningstadt—Is considered one of the best early for general use; heads large size.
Early Schweinfurt—Large and early, fine for Summer and Fall Cabbage for family garden.

Dwarf Curley Savoy.   Large French Oxheart.

Filderkraut—Similar to Winningstadt, only larger and more pointed and with fewer outside leaves and sure to make firm, solid heads.
Improved Brunswick—An excellent medium and late variety, being the best Early Flat Dutch variety ; short stem and good sized solid heads.

Improved **Premium Late Flat Dutch**—This is the best strain of this standard variety and more largely grown than any other for market and long-keeping quality.

Excelsior Flat Dutch—Is an improved California-grown variety, highly esteeme l by all for its keeping quality.

Stone Mason—An improved variety of Mason Drumhead, of sweet and tender quality.

Mammoth Marblehead—One of the latest and largest of all the cabbage tribe. Solid, tender and freely heading.

Large Late Drumhead—A little later than the Flat Dutch. Large solid heads.

Red Dutch Erfurt—Used mostly for pickling. Solid heads.

Drumhead Savoy—The Savoy Cabbages are the finest flavor of all; finely crimpled and netted and yet makes a compact, solid head. Dark green.

Early Dwarf Ulm Savoy—This is earlier and dwarfer than the Drumhead and of very fine flavor.

Fottler's Improved Brunswick.　　　Filderkraut, or Pomeranean.

CARROTS.

One ounce for 100 foot drill.　Three pounds for an acre.

This, like all root crops, delights in rich sandy loam, well tilled. For early crop, sow as early as the ground can be put in good condition and follow on for later through the season. Sow in drills one foot apart and thin plants four inches in a row. For field culture, increase the distance between the rows to allow use of the cultivator.

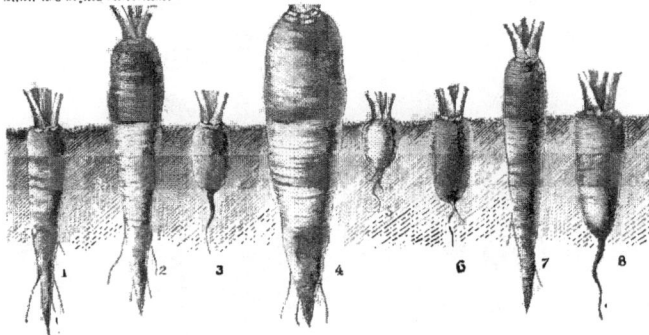

Carrots.

Early Scarlet Short Horn—Earliest forcing variety; small roots and excellent flavor.

Early Horn—A favorite, and best for early Summer use.

Half Long Red, Stump Root—This is an intermediate in size and maturity and is of good quality.

Danvers Half Long—Orange red, smooth and handsome and producing very large crops.

Improved Long Orange—The Standard Sort. Roots large size; of good quality and adapted for garden or farm culture.

Red Altringham—Large and good flavor; for the field and stock feeding.

Large White Belgian—This grows one-third above the ground; white roots, green top and very large. Used for cattle feed.

CAULIFLOWER.

One ounce for about 2,000 plants.

The Cauliflower delights in a rich soil and abundance of water. Sow the early varieties in the spring, in a hotbed or in an open border. For late, sow seed in a cool, moist place. Do not allow the plants to become crowded in the seed-bed. Transplant in moist weather, or shade the newly-set plants. Keep well hoed, bringing the earth up to the stems, water freely and protect from hot summer sun.

Early Dwarf Erfurt—Extra Early Dwarf, small leaf, solid, pure white heads, best quality.

Early Snowball—The earliest and best heading variety cultivated; dwarf habit and short outer leaves.

Early Paris—A popular French variety. White, and sure to head, and standard sort for early or late crop.

Late Asiatico—Large, white and compact, but later than the preceding.

Lenormand—Short Stem.—A superior sort and quality; large, well formed heads, and late.

Walcheren—A good variety, with large white heads.

Large Late Algiers—New, and much prized for late sort.

Veitch's Autumn Giant—This is one of the best late varieties grown. Robust habit, large heads, compact and thoroughly protected by leaves.

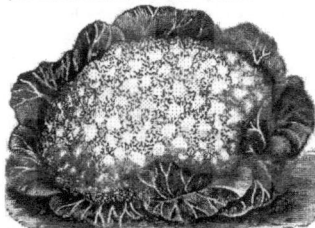 

Cauliflower.   Celery.

CELERY.

One ounce will make about 7,000 plants.

Should be sown in open ground, as early as it will be fit to work, and be kept clear of weeds until fit for planting. Cut tops once or twice before planting, to insure stocky plants. When ground is well prepared, set in rows three feet apart and six inches from each other, and see that the soil is well packed around the roots by pressing with the foot. Run the cultivator or hoe between the rows to destroy the weeds, and when grown to sufficient size draw up the earth for blanching and pressing with the hand to keep the leaf upright from spreading, and banking up to the top on each side.

White Plume, Henderson's—This requires less labor for blanching, is crisp, solid, and of nutty flavor and valuable for family use.

Henderson's Half Dwarf—Solid, crisp, and nutty flavor and very desirable.

Boston Market Dwarf—Short, bushy, white, solid and excellent flavor.

Dwarf Golden Heart—The heart of this variety is waxy and showy, and for market use desirable. It is very solid and of excellent flavor and a good keeper.

Giant White Solid—Large size, solid, crisp, and good market variety.

Celeric, or Turnip-Rooted Celery—A variety with turnip-shaped roots which may be cooked and sliced and used with vinegar, making an excellent salad. It is hardy and otherwise treated as other celery.

Soup Celery—Is old seed used for flavoring soups, stews, etc., and is sold for this purpose at a low price.

CORN.

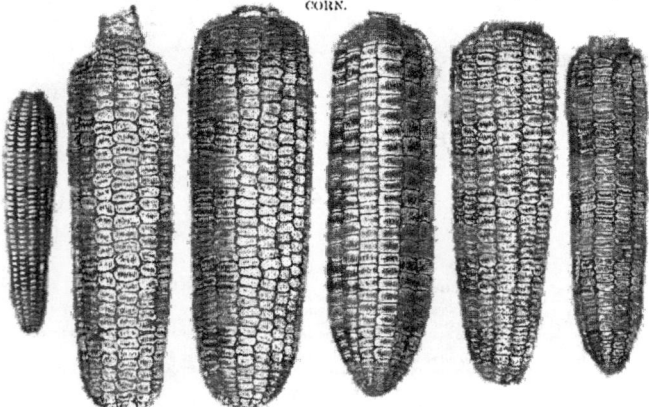

Parching.   Crosby's Early.   Evergreen.   Concord.   Russell's Prolific.   Minnesota.

CORN—SWEET.

All varieties should be planted in hill, 3 to 4 feet apart, after the ground becomes warm; cover half an inch deep and when well up, thin out to 3 plants to the hill; for succession, continue planting at intervals of two or three weeks during the Summer.

Extra Early Marblehead—Certainly as early if not a little earlier than any other Sweet Corn. The stalk is dwarf and it sets its ears very low down, which are of fair market size.

Extra Early Tom Thumb—A very early medium-sized eight-rowed variety. Kernels of fair size, white and sweet. Height about three feet, and is already popular in the market.

Early Minnesota—Is one of the earliest and best. Dwarf in habit, very productive and very sweet.

Crosby's Early—Is excellent and a great favorite market variety; one of the best.

Moore's Early Concord—Ears large and well filled, and of rich, delicate flavor.

Amber Cream—Is a vigorous grower, stalks seven feet long; well filled ears, deep kernel, sugary and tender. Kernel, when dry, amber color, but beautifully white when fit for table.

Egyptian—Is deemed one of the very best. Ears quite large, and for table use and for canning it cannot be surpassed, being particularly rich and sweet.

Black Mexican—Black grain when ripe, and the sweetest of all.

Early Mammoth—Is one of the largest and most productive of all; fine flavor and much in demand by market gardeners.

Stowell's Evergreen—Is a late kind of excellent quality, and remains in green state a long time.

Field Corn—For variety, etc., see Farm Seeds.

COLLARDS

Is used in place of Cabbage, and grown where it is difficult to make Cabbage head. Cultivate same as Cabbage.

CHICORY.

This is grown to mix with or as a substitute for coffee. It requires the same cultivation as Carrots.

Chicory.   Cress.   Long Green Cucumber.

CRESS or PEPPERGRASS.

Well known as a pungent salad. It should be sown thickly and at frequent intervals for succession; it quickly runs to seed. Cover very slightly in planting.

Double and Triple Curled—Is very fine and can be cut two or three times.

Water Cress—Is a perennial and will grow in and alongside of streams and ponds. It has a very pleasant, pungent taste.

CUCUMBERS.

One ounce will plant sixty hills; three pounds one acre.

Cucumbers should be planted in open ground, after the weather is warm and settled, and must be protected from frosts and cold storms. Plant hills six feet apart in good rich mellow soil, covering half an inch. When up and danger is over from insects, thin to three or four plants to the hill.

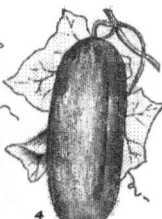

Early Russian.   Early Frame.   Early Green Cluster.   Early White Spine,

Eraly Cluster—Is well adapted for forcing.

Early Frame—Popular variety; medium size, straight and handsome; fine for pickling.

Tallby's Hybrid—An excellent variety for family use.

Early Boston Pickling—Largely used about Boston by market gardeners. A very productive kind, of superior quality.

Early Russian—Very early, fruits in pairs; small, hardy and productive.

Early White Spine—A favorite market variety; medium size, crisp and fine flavor.

Extra Long White Spine—Largely used by market gardeners and quite a favorite.

Long Green Turkey—A most desirable variety of excellent quality. Dark green, firm and crisp.

Nichols' Medium Green—An excellent market variety; dark green, crisp and tender.

Short Green, or English Gherkin—Similar to Early Frame, and fine for pickling.

West India Gherkin, or Burr—Small; used only for pickles.

EGG PLANT.

One ounce will produce about 1,000 plants.

This plant is quite tender, but will thrive in any good garden soil. Seeds should be sown in hot-bed or warm green house. When one inch high transplant into two inch pots. Plant out two and a half feet apart when weather is warm and settled.

New York Improved—Large, fine, and the leading market variety.
Early Long Purple—Longer than the preceding, but early, hardy and productive.
Black Pekin—Handsome, jet black, round and solid. It is quite early and very superior.

  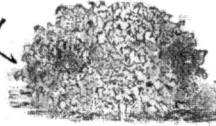

Egg Plant.   Endive.

ENDIVE.

One ounce for 75 feet of drill.

This makes a very fine salad for late and Winter use. Sow seeds during the Summer months in drills, fourteen inches apart; when established, thin to one foot apart in rows. When nearly full grown, tie leaves together over the center to blanch the inside or heart of the plant, which will be done in two weeks or more, according to the temperature. This may also be done by covering with boards, etc., to exclude the light.

Green Curled—This variety is quite hardy, tender and crisp.
Moss Curled—Is a beautiful curled variety of fine quality.
Batavian Broad Leaf—Is a good sort and much used in soups and stews.

KALE, or BORECOLE.

One ounce for 2,0'0 plants.

This is used mainly for greens. It is of the cabbage species, but does not run to head. It is very hardy and will continue growing through the cold and wet months.

Dwarf Curled—This is usually sown in the fall months for winter greens, in rows one foot apart, and is treated same as spinach.

 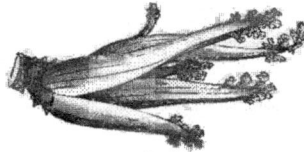

Kale, or Borecole.   Sea Kale.

Green Scotch Curled—Is a dwarf spreading variety often covering three feet in diameter, leaves bright green and beautifully curled.

Cottagers' Kale—Is a valuable kind; excellent flavor and an immense cropper, grows one foot high, leaves rich green, curled, and feathered to the ground.

Sea Kale—This is quite a favorite with many; its young shoots are blanched for use. It is trained and treated like the cabbage.

KOHL RABI.

One ounce for 2,0'0 plants.

This is an intermediate between the Cabbage and Turnip. Sow in drills 12 to 18 inches apart and thin out to eight inches between the plants. Kohl Rabi is a great favorite with Europeans and is rapidly gaining in favor here. It is a superior feed for cows giving milk.

Kohl Rabi.   Cos Lettuce.   Cabbage Lettuce.

Early White Vienna—White and tender. The best market sort and for table use.
Early Purp'e—Differing in color, being of a blueish purple, beautiful and excellent.

LETTUCE.

One ounce for 3,000 plants.

Lettuce succeeds best in good, rich, moist ground. It should be sown thinly in rows, one foot apart, and when plants are well up, thin to stand one foot in each row, transplanting the surplus. It is well also to sow every two or three weeks for a succession, thus furnishing lettuce in perfection the whole season.

Early Curled Silesia—A superior variety and strong grower; highly esteemed for first spring sowing.
Early Curled Simpson—This variety does not head, yet forms a compact mass of leaves and is the leading and earliest market sort.
Black Seeded Simpson—Is a very desirable variety. While similar to the White Seeded the leaves are almost white. It stands the heat of Summer well and attains nearly double the size of the White Simpson.
Early Prize Head—Is of mammoth size. The leaves are crisp and tender, remaining so through the season. It is of fine flavor, hardy and slow to run to seed.
Salamander—Is of good size and one of the best to endure the heat, and is consequently of great merit. It also remains longer in head than other varieties.
Boston Market—This is a good curled variety; early heading; crisp and hardy.
Early Cabbage, or White Butter—A favorite for late sowing, producing fine, well formed heads and hardy.
San Francisco Market, or Satisfaction—Very desirable; firm heads.
Hanson—A fine curled head variety; large, sweet, tender and crisp. Excellent for early Summer use.
Ice Drumhead, or Malta—Heads large, crisp and tender, and good flavor. Stands Summer heat well.
Philadelphia Butter, Spotted—Fine large heads of excellent quality for market sales: stands Summer heat well.
Large India—Immense solid heads, and withstands the heat better than most kinds.
Tennis Ball—Makes a close hard head and is a favorite early and forcing variety.
Paris Cos—(Romaine).—Fine, tender and crisp. Should be tied up to blanch before cutting.

Leek. Martynia. Okra.

LEEK.

One ounce for 100 feet of drill.

The Leek is a very hardy plant and easily cultivated. Succeeds best in a light enriched soil. Sow early in drills one foot apart and one inch deep. When 6 or 8 inches high thin out and transplant to 10 inches apart, and deep as possible that the roots may be blanched.
American Flag—Is large and a great market favorite.
London Flag—Is also a good market variety and broad leaf.
Musselburgh, or Scotch—Is very large with broad fan like leaves, and is hardy and excellent.

MARTYNIA.

Used much for pickling, when gathered while green and tender. Sow in open ground and transplant to two feet apart.

Watermelon. Watermelon.

MELONS.

One ounce for forty hills; three pounds for an acre.

Melons thrive best in good sandy loam. Plant as soon as the ground becomes warm, in hills six feet apart; a little well rotted manure in each hill will be of great benefit. Put twelve to fifteen seeds to a hill, and after they are up and all danger from bugs is over, thin out to three plants to the hill. If the growth is too rapid, pinch off the top and leading shoots, and thin out the fruit, which will increase the size of those remaining. Pumpkins, Squashes or Cucumbers should not be grown near them, as they would be apt to hybridize.

WATERMELON.

One ounce to 40 hills, or about four pounds to acre.

Mammoth Ironclad—This variety grows very large and solid. Rind thin but very tough and best for shipping, flesh deep red and delicious.

Scaly Back—Is also very tough, thin rind, and bears rough usage without breaking, and is a long keeper, flesh light crimson and excellent flavor and good shipping variety.

Gipsy, or Rattlesnake—A very desirable variety, large, oblong, green mottled and striped, thin rind, crimson flesh, sweet and delicious, and one of the best for market and shipping.

Kolb Gem—This is pronounced one of the largest and best keeping melons grown, bringing one-third more in market than any other. Their quality and appearance is superior.

Imperial Lodi—This is now the most popular of all the California-grown varieties. Large, oblong, skin light pea-green in color, and thin. Red flesh, very sweet and fine in flavor and one of the very best for cultivation for market sales.

Cuban Queen—Large, solid and very heavy for its size, often weighing 80 pounds. Skin marking light and dark green. Sweet and fine flavor.

Peerless—White-Seeded Ice Cream.—One of the very best of early sorts. Skin smooth, light green, oblong in shape. Scarlet flesh and most delicious; fine for market or family garden.

Mountain Sweet—Oblong, thin rind and dark green; red solid flesh; sweet and very desirable.

Mountain Sprout—Fruit large, long, oval; skin dark green, marbled; red flesh, of excellent quality.

Black Spanish—Fruit large, almost round; skin dark green; red flesh; delicious; early.

Orange—So called as the rind will peel off from flesh when ripe. Flesh red and good.

Pride of Georgia—This new melon from Georgia is decidedly better in quality than the Sealy Bark, while the rind is equally as hard; is an excellent shipping variety, perfectly round, striped light and dark green; flesh bright red ripening up well and of good quality.

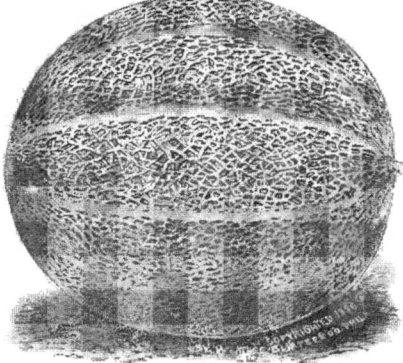

Musk Melon.   Musk Melon.

MUSK MELON.

California Netted Cantaloupe—This is the most popular and best market variety grown in this State; large, deeply ribbed and netted; green flesh and of delicious flavor and a good keeper.

Skillman's Netted—Round oval; flesh deep green; sweet, early and delicious and highly perfumed.

Hackensack—An Eastern variety, similar to California Netted, and fine.

Montreal Nutmeg—This is one of the largest fruiting kind. Round, flattened at the ends and deeply ribbed, similar to California Nutmeg, and highly esteemed.

Bayview—Large, prolific and fine flavor; green flesh; desirable for shipping.

Green Citron—Is green flesh, medium size, deeply netted, and of a very rich and delicious flavor.

Pine Apple—Of medium size, flesh green, firm, juicy and very sweet.

Casaba—Large and delicious. This is one of the best late oval varieties and highly prized.

Large Yellow Musk—A deeply ribbed, salmon flesh variety; thick flesh and very sweet.

MUSHROOM SPAWN.

Mushrooms may be cultivated much easier than is generally supposed. They may be grown in a cellar or shed, or in beds prepared in the open air, in the same manner as hot-beds. Per lb., 20c.; 10 lbs., $1.50. If by mail, add 10c per pound to prepay postage. For full directions for planting, see Henderson's Handbook of Plants.

MUSTARD.

Makes a pungent salad. Sow thickly in rows and cut for use when two inches high. White London is the best for salads. The Brown or Black, is, however, more pungent.

NASTURTIUM.

The seeds, while young and succulent, are pickled for capers. The plants are quite ornamental and make excellent screens in the garden.

OKRA, or GUMBO.

This vegetable is grown for its pods which are used in soups, stews, etc. It is very nutritious and of easy culture. Sow when the ground has become warm, three feet apart and one inch deep, and thin out to ten inches in the row. The pods are dried for winter use.

ONIONS.

Onions thrive best in a deep, rich loamy soil, which should be clean and well cultivated and in good order, level and well pulverized. Sow thinly in drills, one foot apart and one-quarter of an inch deep. Cover with fine soil and press with the foot or a light roller. When the young plants are strong enough, thin out and transplant to three or four inches apart. Hoe shallow but frequently, and keep clear of weeds. One ounce will plant 100 feet of drill; four pounds for an acre.

Early Red

Garlic

Red Wethersfield.

New Pearl, or Early Queen—Is the earliest of all. Color pearly white and very mild in flavor; large; showy.

Extra Early Red—This variety is not as large as the Wethersfield but ten days earlier. It is close grained and heavy and of mild flavor.

Large Red Wethrrsfield—This is a popular variety; large size, deep red and good keeper; very productive.

Yellow Globe Danvers—This is probably more grown for market than other kinds. Mild flavor, early, productive and fine keeper.

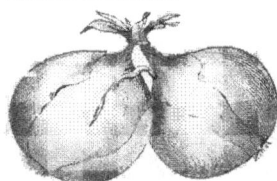
White Globe.

Globe Danvers.

Yellow Strasburg, or SILVER SKIN—An old variety; good keeper and mild flavor. Best for raising Onion Sets.

White Portugal, or SILVER SKIN—Mild flavor and handsome; much grown for pickling, poor keeper for market but good for White Sets.

White Globe—Is one of the best; mild flavor and good keeping quality and of large size

Giant Rocca—Is globe shape, very large, brown skin and delicate flavor.

Yellow Dutch.

Top Onions.

Onion Sets.

ONION SETS.

These are produced from seeds sown thickly in beds or drills. When the tops die down the small bulbs are gathered and spread out and kept in a cool, dry place for future planting, and should be set, when the ground is in condition, in rows one foot apart and three or four inches distant.

Top Onion Sets—Are raised from the bulbs and are gathered, kept and planted in the same manner.

PARSNIP.

Sow early in season as the weather will permit, in drills 15 inches apart and cover half inch deep. When well up, thin out to five or six inches in rows. They can remain in the ground after maturity, to be taken up for future use if desired. One ounce will sow 100 feet drill, or five pounds for an acre.

Long Smoth (HOLLOW CROWN)—Is the kind in general use.

The Student—Is also a fine flavored variety

PARSLEY.

This seed germinates slowly, often taking four or five weeks to come up. They should be sown in a rich mellow soil thickly, ¼ inch deep in rows one foot apart and thin, to stand 6 inches in the row. It will aid germination to soak the seed a few hours in warm water before sowing.

Parsnip.

Parsley.

Parsnip.

Extra Trible Curled—Is perhaps the best. Dwarf, beautifully curled, fine for garnishing.
Fern, or Moss-leaf—Crested like a fern and mossy; valuable for table decoration.

PEAS.

One pound to 75 feet of drill. One hundred and fifty pounds to acre.

For very early crop a light rich soil is best; for general crop a deep rich heavy loam is better. For market crop plant in rows from two to three feet apart covering from two to three inches as to strength of soil. For family use they may be planted in double rows and the taller varieties staked with brush.

EXTRA EARLY.

Cleveland's Alaska Peas—We consider this the earliest, most prolific and finely flavored variety grown. We planted in our grounds and had peas fit for the table in 45 days. Height 2½ feet. See cut.
American Wonder—Is one of the earliest wrinkled peas in cultivation; of the finest flavor and are very productive; compact and dwarf, about ten inches high.
Cleveland's Rural New Yorker—Is considered the earliest and most prolific of all. They are of fine flavor and ripen at one time; two feet high.

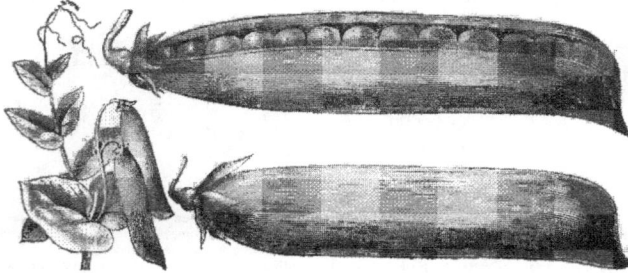

Peas.

Tom Thumb—Is remarkably dwarf, very early, of excellent quality, and a good yielder.
Lexton Alpha—Is one of the earliest wrinkled varieties. Pods good size, well filled and fine quality and prolific; three feet.
Premium Little Gem—A dwarf, green, wrinkled marrow; very prolific and desirable.
Bliss' Abundance—A second early variety; height 15 to 18 inches; pods 3 to 3½ inches long, roundish and well filled; wrinkled, and excellent quality. It has a tendency for branching directly from the roots, forming a bush. Sow the seeds six to eight inches apart, as near as the plants should stand

Bliss' Ever-Bearing—18 inches to 2 feet; foliage large; the pods 3 to 4 inches in length; peas very large and in quality unsurpassed; constant bearer and of especial value for late Summer and Autumn use. Sow thinly or the vines will become crowded.

McLean's Advancer—A second early variety and a great favorite with growers. It is often known as the Early Champion. A green, wrinkled variety of excellent flavor.

GENERAL CROP.

Yorkshire Hero—This is one of the largest and best of the wrinkled Marrows and most now in demand for planting by the market gardeners of this State; branching habit, abundant bearer and fine flavor. 2½ feet.

Champion of England—Is one of the best varieties: delicious in flavor and a profuse bearer. 4 feet.

Telephone—Immensely productive, excellently sweet, of the finest quality. Strong vines, pods large size, well filled with delicious peas. 4 feet.

Blue Imperial—Is a fine market variety; a good bearer and of fine flavor. 3 feet.

Royal Dwarf Marrowfat—This is a favorite with many; pods are well filled with large peas, ripening at one time, so as to be easily gathered at one picking, and of good quality. 2½ feet.

White Marrowfat—A favorite; pods large and well filled. 5 to 6 feet.

Black Eyed Marrowfat—Hardy and productive, and with the White extensively grown for field peas. Four feet.

Edible Pod Sugar Peas—Can cook the pod as Snap Beans or as shelled; very tender and sweet. Varieties: Dwarf and Tall White, and Dwarf and Tall Gray Seed, all desirable. 2½ to 5 feet.

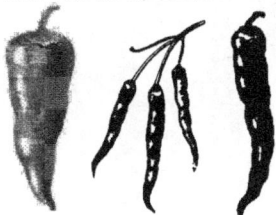 

Peppers.　　　　　Peppers.

PEPPER.

This vegetable is largely grown for pickles and for seasoning for soups, meats, etc. Sow in hot-bed or in a warm sheltered spot, and transplant into rich, warm, mellow soil, in rows 2 feet apart and 18 inches in the row, hoe frequently and earth up a little. One ounce will produce over 1,000 plants.

Sweet Spanish—One of the earliest and largest; flesh sweet and mild.

Sweet Mammoth, or Mountain—Like the preceding in shape and color, but larger and milder.

Bell, or Bull Nose—Early, and mild flavor; rind thick and fleshy.

Squash, or Tomato Shape—Generally grown for pickling; very productive.

Long Red Cayenne—Fruit three to four inches long, bright red; quite productive.

Long Yellow Cayenne—Similar to the preceding, except in color.

Red Cherry—Very ornamental; fruit round, glossy, and of rich scarlet color.

Chili—Red, conical, two inches long; very hot and prolific; used for seasoning.

PUMPKIN.

Plant three to five pounds on an acre.

This is grown for agricultural purposes and planted in the field with corn and potatoes. Plant in hills at least eight feet apart.

Large Cheese—Is one of the best for cooking.

Cushaw—Is quite a favorite, resembling the Winter Crook-neck Squash. White, striped and mottled with green; salmon flesh.

Connecticut Field—Is most largely grown for feeding stock, and very productive.

Mammoth Tours—Very productive; large size, often weighing from 100 to 150 pounds.

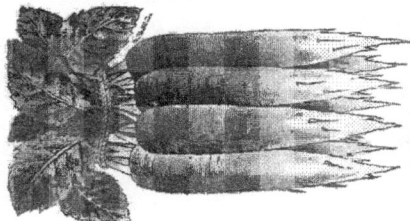 

Chartier Radish.　　　　　Pumpkin.

RADISH.

One ounce to 100 feet of drill; 8 to 10 pounds for an acre.

Becket's Chartier—Is a new variety; crimson at the top, but running downward to fine waxy white. It grows to a large size and of superior quality.

2

Early Long Scarlet, Short Top—The standard sort for the family and market gardeners. (No. 5.)
Early Scarlet Turnip—Nearly round, delicate flavor, and fine for summer use. (No. 1.)
Early White Tipped Scarlet Turnip—A little larger than the preceding; handsome and fine flavor.
White Strasburg—New; claimed the quickest growing of all. Pure white, firm and brittle; large size; fine for hot weather. (No. 4.)
White Summer Turnip—Mild flavor and excellent.
French Breakfast—Oblong, scarlet, tipped with white; rapid grower, mild and tender. (No. 9.)
Olive Shape Scarlet—Rose-colored flesh, tender and excellent; early and good for forcing or general crop; oblong in shape. (No. 2.)

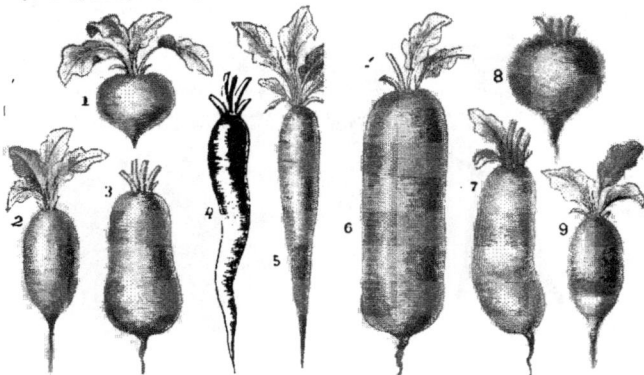

Radishes.

China Rose Winter—Rose color, firm flesh, piquant and most excellent for winter use. (No. 3.)
Black Spanish, (Round and Long)—Both are quite hardy and good for late and Winter use. (No. 8.)
White Spanish—Is milder in flavor than the Black, and good late sort.
California Mammoth, or White China—Is very highly esteemed. White flesh, firm, and excellent quality and of large size, often more than 12 inches long. (No. 6.)

RHUBARB.

One ounce will make about 500 plants.

Stalks are used for pies, tarts and sauce. Sow seeds early, in drills one foot apart, when four inches high, thin out to ten or twelve inches distance; early in the ensuing season transplant into deep, rich soil, three feet apart. It is better for most persons to procure the roots, which can be set out as desired.

Linnæus is the earliest, **Victoria** the latest and largest and best cooking variety; both are tender and fine.

Rhubarb.   Spinach.

SPINACH.

One ounce will make 75 feet of drill; 10 pounds for an acre, in drill.

This is very essential for all market gardens and requiring but little culture. Sow either in drills or broadcast, covering about one inch, as early as the ground can be worked, and every two weeks for succession during the season. It is best developed and tender when grown in rich soil.

Bloomsdale Savoy Leaf—very valuable for market gardens.
Round Thick Leaf Is the main sort, and fine for early or late sowing.
Viroflay—Has large, thick leaves, and fine for market culture, standing a long time before going to seed.
Long Standing—Is like the Round Savoy Leaf, but remains longer before running to seed than other kinds.
Prickly, or Fall - Is quite hardy and stands the cold well; used more in Fall planting.

SALSIFY.

Salsify, or Vegetable Oyster. Used for soups, also boiled, fried, etc., and possesses the flavor of the Oyster, for which it is sometimes used as a substitute. The culture is the same as for Carrots and Parsnips. Sow early, in drills, a foot or more apart, covering the seed not more than two inches in depth. Thin out to six inches apart. Put seed in the ground as early as possible in the Spring. A portion of the crop may remain in the ground all Winter, like the Parsnip.

Bush Scallop Squash.

Sum. Crook-neck.

Salsify.   Winter Crook-neck

SQUASH.

Squash seed should never be planted till the soil is quite warm. Rich, light, open soils are the best Treatment the same as for melons. One ounce for 25 to 40 hills, as to size of seed; four to six pounds for an acre.

BUSH AND EARLY VARIETIES.

Early Scallop Bush—The White and the Golden are the two best early for market, and are abundant bearers.
Yellow Crook-neck—Is early and very productive and of fine quality. All of the above are for Summer use and should be used when young and tender.
Perfect Gem—Is a new variety and is most excellent for Summer use or for a late keeper.

LATE AND LONG-KEEPING VARIETIES.

Pine Apple—A Fall and Winter variety; the color of the skin creamy white; good when quite young and keeps well all Winter; very prolific; flesh creamy white, fine grain and rich cocoanut flavor.
American Turban—Flesh bright orange, thick, fine grained and good flavor. For Fall or late use.
Hubbard—Is a general favorite; one of the very best; fine grained, dry and excellent.
Marblehead—Is like the Hubbard but of lighter color; very sweet, dry and delicious, and good keeper.
Boston Marrow—Is well known as of fine flavor, good keeper and fine Fall market variety.
Cocoanut—Is very prolific; color light yellow; quality very superior.
Winter Crook-neck—Is sweet, close grain and most excellent flavor.
Chili, or Valparaiso—Grows to enormous size (often weighing 200 pounds) and is most excellent for the table or for field or cattle feed; deep orange flesh and splendid keeper.
Mammoth Stock Squash—Are very large and valuable for cattle feed, being immensely productive and good keepers.

TURNIP.

One ounce for 150 feet of drill; or two pounds for an acre.

Turnips succeed best in highly enriched sandy or gravelly soil. Sow in drills 12 to 18 inches apart, cover half inch, and when plants are well up thin to 5 or 6 inches apart, for early kind, and Rutalaga and large sorts to 10 inches. Best always to sow just before a rain, or water well, as success depends upon quick germination and rapid growth.

Extra Early Purple-Top Munich—This is considered the earliest of all; bright purple top, mouse-tail root; distinct and valuable.
Early Flat Dutch—Standard sort; good size, small top, pure white; good market variety.
Long White, or Cow-Horn—Matures very quickly; roots shaped like a Carrot, about half of which is found above ground; flesh white, fine grained and sweet; fine for table use.
White Egg—A quick-growing Fall Turnip; oval shape; flesh firm, fine grained, mild and sweet.
Redtop Strap-Leaf—A most popular variety for early use; rapid grower and mild flavor; good for the table or for stock feed; smooth, handsome and tender.
Early Snowball—Very quick growth; small, solid, sweet and crisp.
White Globe (Strap-Leaf)—Valuable for the table or stock; not as early as the flat sorts.
Large Norfolk—Large grower; globe shape, coarse grain but sweet, and one of the best early for stock feed.

Golden Ball Robertson—Bright yellow, rapid grower, excellent flavor, good keeper, and nothing better for table use.

Early Yellowstone—Medium size, firm, excellent flavor and fine keeper; very popular for growing for table use for yellow varieties; equally good for stock feed.

Yellow Aberdeen—Hardy productive, and fine keeper; globe shape; pale yellow with purple top; good for the table or stock.

Green-Top Swede.   White Swede.   Early Flat Dutch.   White Norfolk.

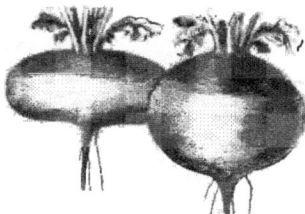

RUTABAGA, OR SWEDISH VARIETIES.

These are more generally grown as farm crops. The roots are hard, close grained, and endure cold without injury. They are excellent for storing for late use : for table or stock.

American Purpletop—Very hardy and productive; solid, sweet and fine; one of the best of yellow kinds.

Skirving's Purpletop—Is good for table or stock ; very large, sweet and firm flesh and fine keeper.

Amber Globe (Strap-Leaf)—This is milder than the common Rutabaga, and one of the best of yellow sorts.

Strap-Leaf Redtop.   Yellow Aberdeen.   Yellow Globe.

Greentop—Similar to Purpletop, except in color.

Sweet German—White; very popular in many parts; should be sown early; flesh white, hard, firm and sweet ; keeps as well as the yellow sorts, and fine for Winter use.

Russian, or White Rutabaga—Grows very large, and is excellent for table or stock feed ; a splendid keeper and fine quality.

TOMATOES.

One ounce will produce over 1,000 plants.

The seed should be sown in a hot-bed, or the house, where the temperature is above 60 degrees. When two inches high, transplant to 4 or 5 inches apart into boxes or pots, where they are to remain till ready to set out in the open ground, which must not be till safe from frost. They do best on good light or open soils. Should be set three or four feet apart and watered freely till plants are established.

Sacramento Favorite—Is one of the very best ; large size, smooth as an apple, firm and hard some ; dark red and fine for market and shipping.

The Eureka, or Perfection—Is similar to the above, but thought to be superior.

Cardinal—Is a very brilliant red in skin and flesh, almost round, solid and first quality.

Mayflower—Is the earliest large variety grown; glossy red, ripens evenly, yields well, and a good market variety.

The Acme—Is quite early an 1 handsome; fruit solid, smooth and regular, and a good bearer; color crimson pink.

Paragon—Is similar to the Acme, except of darker color.

The Trophy—Is a later variety and one of the best; large, fine flavor, productive, solid, and fine for market and canning.

Hubbard Squash.

Tomato—Livingston, or Sacramento Favorite.

General Grant—Is very superior, large and good; ripens early.

Fiji Island, or Lester Perfected—Fruit large; light red or pink; solid and good flavor.

Pear Shape, Yellow Plum and Red Cherry—Are all small varieties; used for pickling.

Hathaway's Excelsior—Early; medium size, smooth, very solid and of excellent quality.

The Conqueror—One of the earliest; large size and uniform in shape.

The Mikado—(New.) This is the largest Tomato in cultivation, often weighing 24 ounces; grows in immense clusters; perfectly solid and usually smooth; excellent for slicing or cooking.

Aromatic, Sweet and Medicinal Herbs.

A few Herbs should have a place in every vegetable garden. A small space will give all that are needed in any family. The culture is simple. Make a little seed-bed in the early spring, and set the plants out as soon as large enough.

	Oz.	Lb.		Oz.	Lb.
Anise	$0 10	$1 00	Henbane	$0 40	$....
Angelica	25	....	Hyssop	25	3 00
Arnica	2 00	....	Hoarhound	30	....
Balm	50	....	Lavender	25	3 00
Belladonna	75	....	Marjoram, Sweet	25	3 00
Borage	10	1 00	Marigold, Pot	25	3 00
Basil (Sweet)	25	3 00	Opium Poppy	25	3 00
Boneset	1 00	....	Pennyroyal	75	....
Bene	20	....	Rosemary	40	....
Chervill	10	1 50	Rue	40	....
Caraway	10	50	Savory, Summer	25	2 50
Catnip	75	....	Savory, Winter	25	2 50
Coriander	10	50	Saffron	15	1 50
Cumin	10	1 00	Sage, Common	20	2 00
Dandelion	25	3 00	Sorrel, Broad-leaved	15	1 50
Dill	10	75	Tansy	50	....
Elecampane	50	75	Thyme, English	40	4 00
Fennel, Large Sweet	10	1 00	Wormwood	40	....
Fenngreek	10	1 00			

The above also put up in Five Cent packages, or Fifty Cents per dozen.

Evergreen, Tree and Shrub Seeds.

Abies Douglasii (Spruce). This tree grows from 200 to 300 feet high, of pyramidal shape; good timber ....Per oz. 50c, per lb. $5.00

Abies Mertensiana (Hemlock Spruce). 150 to 200 feet high; thick brown bark and hardy ; growing from California up and in Alaska...............................

Abies Menziesii. Grows in wet, sandy soil and near the mouths of streams. An excellent timber and the tallest of spruce.............Per oz. 50c, per lb. $5.00

Abies Excelsor (Norway Spruce.) This is quite ornamental and very desirable for timber and windbreaks. It will grow in almost any soil and climate.
....Per oz. 25c, per lb. $2.00

Cupressus Macrocarpa (Monterey Cyprus). Grows from 40 to 60 feet high ; rough bark and spreading branches, and rich, green foliage. Ornamental for lawns, parks, etc...Per oz. 25c, per lb. $2.00

Cupressus McNabiana. A small cyprus 6 to 10 feet high, found in high altitudes; leaves small and of deep green.........................Per oz. 50c, per lb. $4.00

Cyprus Lawsoniana. This is a handsome tree, found in moist grounds and Coast. Range to the north. Wood, white, fragrant and close grain, and very durable. Known also as Oregon cedar.........................Per oz. 50c, per lb. $4 00

Cyprus Italian. Very erect in growth, making a striking appearance. Much used to form arches and gate entrances ....Per oz. 25c, per lb. $3.00

American Arborvitæ. Useful for windbreaks and hedges..Per oz. 25c, per lb $3 00

Red Cedar. This grows in all sections, and is a valuable timber and a fine ornamental tree, and requires but little attention in growing. Very durable in the ground for posts, etc...Per oz. 20c, per lb. $1.50

Giant Arborvitæ. A tall graceful tree 250 feet high, 5 to 12 feet diameter Pyramidal, with spreading branches ; native of Oregon. Wood is fine grain, soft and light color ....Per oz 60c, per lb. $5.00

Chinese Arborvitæ. Small, elegant with erect branches and dense light green foliage ....Per oz. 25c, per lb. $2.50

Golden Arborvitæ. A beautiful variety, spherical outline, with bright yellow-tinged foliage. Very ornamental.............................Per oz. 50c, per lb. 4.00

Silver Fir. This is a tall symmetrical and valuable timber tree...................

Balsam Fir. Grows rapidly in rich, moist soils to 200 to 300 feet high, and is a valuable timber tree ....Per oz. 50c, per lb. $5.00

Red Fir. This is a magnificent tree and makes a fine timber. Said to be superior to other firs ....Per oz. 50c, per lb. $5.00

Monterey Pine (Incignis). Quite ornamental for parks and lawns, and for hedges. Rapid grower and fine green foliage...................Per oz. 25c, per lb. $2.00

Fremont's Pine. A small tree 20 to 30 feet in height. Known also as the Nut Pine. ....Per oz. 25c, per lb. $2.50

Lambertiana or Sugar Pine. A hardy tree of giant size, growing often to 300 feet high and 20 feet diameter, and very valuable timber....Per oz. 25c, per lb. $3.00

Mountain or White California Pine. Grows 60 to 100 feet high and 3 feet diameter. Desirable for timber ....Per oz. 50c, per lb. $5.00

Yellow, or Oregon Pine. One of the largest varieties of pines. Heavy, close grain and hardy. Very valuable timber...................Per oz. 50c, per lb. $5.00

Sequoia Gigantea or Mammoth Tree of California. This is the largest growth tree known, often growing to over 30 feet in diameter and over 300 feet high, with the bark 20 inches thick.................................Per oz. 60c, per lb. $6.00

Sequoia Sempervirens or California Redwood. This is the most valuable timber of California forests. Wood rich brownish red, light, strong and durable.
....Per oz. 50c, per lb. $4.00

California Nutmeg. Found in the mountain districts at height of 60 feet. Light-colored wood and close grained......................Per oz. 30c, per lb. $3 00

Mountain Laurel or Spice Tree. Grows from 30 to 70 feet high. The timber is very valuable and handsome, and used in finishing, ornamentation, etc.
....Per oz. 25c, per lb. $2.00

Pepper Tree (handsome ornamental evergreen), graceful habit, light green foliage with bright scarlet berries; desirable for lawns and parks. . Per oz. 25c, per lb. $2.50

Madrone Tree. A native of California, of deep green foliage and white flowers, moderate size.

Acer Macrophyllum (Maple). Found in Coast Range of California; wood white and hard, taking a fine polish; 50 to 90 feet high...........Per oz. 25c, per lb. $2.50

Sugar Maple. Valauble for its sugar product, makes a rapid growth for hard wood and highly prized in manufactures, as well as for fuel...per oz. 15c, per lb. $1.00

Silver Leaf, or Soft Maple. This is a beautiful tree and of quite rapid growth; soft, light wood..Per oz. 15c, per lb. $1.00

Norway Maple. This is most desirable for ornamental planting, etc
....Per oz. 10c, per lb. $1.00.

Box Elder. This will grow rapidly, attaining a height of 70 feet. It is fine for planting along the highway. It endures drouth.............Per oz. 15c, per lb. $1.00

White Ash. Will grow almost anywhere. Makes one of the best of timbers and rapid grower. Largely used in wagon making, etc.....Per oz. 25c, per lb. $2.00

Catalpa. This is a rapid growing tree; straight, tall and desirable
....Per oz. 15c, per lb. $1.00.

Elm, European. Fine for ornamental and city planting......Per oz. 15c, per lb. 1.00

Linden, or Basswood. Light wood; makes fine paper pulp, and used in manufactures, etc..Per oz. 15c, per lb. $1.00

Alanthus (Tree of Heaven). This is a very rapid grower and attains a large size. The foliage has a rich tropical appearance...................Per oz. 15c, per lb. $1.00

Magnolia Grandiflora. One of the most beautiful and majestic of American trees; perfectly hardy in this climate.......................Per oz. 25c, per lb. $2.00

Mulberry. White and Black...............................Per oz. 25c, per lb. 2.50

Russian Mulberry. This is most desirable on account of its fruit as well as for its timber, which makes valuable posts, etc. It is hard, elastic, close-grained, and being susceptible of fine polish, is largely used in manufactures.

Grevilla Robusta. A beautiful tree, with fern-like foliage, it withstands drouth and grows rapidly. When up to 20 feet it is covered with bright orange flowers and a splendid sight. Will grow to 100 feet in height................Per oz. $1.50.

Eucalyptus, or Australian Gum Trees.......................................

Blue Gum (Globulus). This is a rapid growing variety, and most generally grown. Height 200 feet.......................................Per oz. 50c, per lb. $5.00

Red Gum (Rostrata). Not as rapid grower as the blue, but a hardier tree......

Australian Trees (Eucalyptus, or Gum Trees) are rapid growers, and make valuable timber, attaining about 200 feet in height. There are many varieties...........

Globulus, or Blue Gum, is mostly grown in this State.......Per oz. 50c, per lb. $5.00

Rostrata, or Red Gum, is a fine and hardy variety.........Per oz. 50c, per lb. $6.00

There is also the Stringy Bark, Black Box, Lemon Scented, Bloodwood Crimson Flowered, White Gum, Blackbutt, Peppermint Gum, Ironbark, etc.................
....Per oz. 50c, per lb. 6.00

Accacia (Black Wattle), Golden Wattle, Crested Wattle, Floribunda, etc...........
....Per oz. 25c, per lb. $2.00

Black, or Timber Locust...Per lb. 60c

Honey Locust..Per lb. 60c

Osage Orange ....Per lb. 60c

FRUIT TREE SEEDS.

	Per lb.		Per lb.
Apple Seed	$0 50	Mahaleb Cherry Pits	$0 50
Pear Seed	2 50	Mazzard Cherry Pits	30
Quince Seed	3 00	Myrobolum Plum Pits	20
Peach Pits		5c per lb.; $3.00 per 100 lbs.	

Lawn Grass, Clover and Other Field Seeds.

These we keep in very large stock, and of unsurpassed quality. We import heavily of Eastern and European varieties, and make a specialty of Alfalfa and other California grown Seed.

Nothing is more desirable for comfort and to beautify a home than *a good lawn*. And nothing is more easily made and kept in order if given a little well directed attention. A good, well mellowed and even ground is important. The best time to sow the seed, after the soil is prepared, is just before the early rains set in. It is better to wait than sow in hot weather. The best single variety for a lawn is the Kentucky Blue Grass, but a little White Clover and Sweet Vernal will add much to its fragrance.

DIRECTIONS FOR A FINE LAWN.

The ground should be spaded deeply and thoroughly, and a good compost of decomposed and finely pulverized manure or rich loam spread over the ground. It would be well, also to give a sprinkling of bone dust. Then use a slanted tooth harrow and a light or medium roller till the soil is smooth, even and firm. Then sow the seed and harrow again and smooth off with a common garden rake. When the grass has grown to two or three inches in height use the lawn mower gauged to cut full one inch above the ground; repeat the same as often as it grows to that height. The weeds and foul grass are in the soil and can be kept down and destroyed by the repeated mowing. If this is neglected they will spread and take possession of the soil, but being constantly clipped the leaf and seed stalks are destroyed and the foul vegetation disappears.

To Renew the Lawn.—When the old growth is well clipped, scatter the seed thickly in the cool of the season and give the ground a good dressing of rich loam or well rotted manure and a little bone dust as at first, and as the season advances a strong and beautiful turf will be assured.

LAWN AND FIELD GRASSES.

Mixed Lawn Grass—Is made up of the finest Evergreen Grasses, intermixed in proper proportions, for a fine, permanent and velvety lawn, and best adapted to our hot and dry climate; 60 to 70 pounds should be applied per acre.

Kentucky Blue Grass—Is the finest and best of all grasses when used separately or in mixtures for general lawn purposes; for this purpose 60 to 80 pounds are necessary.

Meadow Fescue, or English Blue Ghass—Is said to do well on poor soils, the roots penetrating more deeply and better resisting the dry weather, and is valuable for a pasturage ; sow 30 to 40 pounds per acre.

English, or Australian Rye Grass—Is also a perennial, much like the preceding, and is very valuable for either lawns, pasturage or for hay ; sow for lawns 60 pounds, hay 30 pounds per acre.

Perennial Rye Grass—Makes a fine lawn, and is also desirable for a permanent pasture. It produces a large amount of nutritious hay, but succeeds best on moist grounds. It is very desirable in mixtures for the lawn ; sow 40 to 60 pounds per acre.

Italian Rye Grass—Is more of an annual, and is also good in mixtures for the lawn or for hay crop. It is of quick growth and valuable for sheep pasturage.

Sweet Vernal Grass—Produces a strong, pleasant fragrance, and is very desirable in lawn mixtures, for pleasure grounds or pasture when used in small quantity. It produces but little feed.

Wood Meadow Grass—Is very desirable in moist locations and in shaded places among trees, but is not adapted to dry lands ; sow 30 pounds per acre.

Crested Dog's Tail—Is very fine for dry lands ; its foliage is fine and small, and therefore good for lawn mixtures ; for pasturage sow 30 pounds per acre.

Meadow Foxtail—A valuable pasture grass of rapid growth and much relished by all kinds of stock. Adapted for rich, moist soils. Sow 20 pounds per acre.

Bromus, or Rescue Grass—This grass is recommended for its drouth-resisting quality. Will thrive on any soil where it is not too wet. Sow 35 pounds per acre.

Tall Meadow Oat-Grass.—This grass is early and very luxuriant. It makes fine pasturage and good hay. Can be cut often. It is also valuable to plough under for soiling. Sow 30 to 40 pounds per acre.

Hard Fescue—Is also noted for its drouth-resisting quality, and well adapted for awn mixtures and valuable for sheep pasture. Sow 30 poun ls to the acre.

Fine Leaf Fescue—Is similar to above in its qualities and adaptation.

Herd, Red Top Grass (or Bent Grass)—Is most largely used for wet lands, but does well in almost any soil, moist or dry. It makes good hay or pasture and much used in mixture with timothy and clover. Sow 30 pounds per acre.

Timothy—Is very largely grown for hay crop in northern climates, and is fine when sown with Red Top and Clover. Sow 15 pounds per acre.

Mesquit Grass—Is very desirable for dry lands. It resists the drouth well and makes a good crop for hay or pasturage. Sow 30 pounds per acre.

Orchard, or Rough Cocksfoot Grass—Well adapted to sow under trees and in shaded situations ; also valuable for hay or grazing. Sow 20 to 25 pounds per acre.

Johnson Grass (Evergreen Millet)—This is a perennial, having strog, vigorous roots, and produces an immense amount of large nutritious leaves. It can be often cut, growing rapidly, and will thrive where other grasses perish from drouth and heat. Sow early in Autumn that it may get a good root, or in the Spring; 30 pounds to the acre ; cover lightly.

Egyptian, or Pearl Millet—Produces an enormous amount of green feed. It can be cut repeatedly, growing very rapidly after cutting, and is equal to Sweet Corn for feed. Sow in drills two to three feet apart; four pounds will sow an acre.

Millet (German)—Can be sown broadcast in the Spring of the year for hay; 30 to 40 pounds per acre. If for seed, sow in drills 20 pounds to the acre. It produces largely as an annual early crop.

Golden Millet—Is not quite as early as the above, but yields more largely.

Hungarian Grass—Is a very valuable forage plant for light, dry soils. It withstands drouth and remains green when most vegetation is parched. Sow and cultivate as for Millet.

Amber Cane (Sorghum)—Is the earliest variety, and being rich in sacharine matter is grown for making sugar and syrup. It makes a large amount of forage for stock feed.

African Cane, or Sorghum—Is also a fine forage plant, and in large demand for Spring planting.

Egyptian Corn (White and Red Varieties)—Both produce an immense crop of both seed and stalks for forage to the acre and mature without rain. The white is more cultivated, and, perhaps, the earliest. The seed is quite valuable to feed stock or poultry.

Bermuda Grass. The roots of this grass are very tenacious of life, outrooting other vegetation. It grows in almost any soil and spreads rapidly, making a good pasturage. The seed is hard to save and is worth $3.00 per pound. The roots can be furnished for $2.00 per barley sack or $3.00 per barrel. Cut up into short lengths and sown broadcast and cover with a roller. One barrel will thus plant an acre.

CLOVER SEED.

Alfalfa. Is cultivated above all other clover in California. It produces enormous crops, and is cut many times in the season for hay. It roots deeply, keeping fresh and green through our long dry season, and is the most valuable and profitable of all crops for abundance of feed. Sow 20 to 25 pounds to the acre. It in the fall sow early enough to get a little root before a frost, it can be sown again in February and Spring months.

Red Clover. Two varieties—large and medium. Both succeed well in California, especially in our bottom lands and deep soils ; 25 pounds to the acre.

Alsyke or Swedish Clover. Is very hardy and valuable for hay, yielding largely. Its roots are fibrous, and it is very desirable for hillsides and levees liable to wash; 10 to 15 pounds to the acre.

White Dutch Clover. Grows low, spreading and very fragrant, and is most excellent for lawns and lawn mixture ; 10 pounds to the acre.

Crimson Trefoil, or Scarlet Clover. Grows about one foot high, dark roots, long leaves and blossoms of deep red. It makes good hay and will give four or five cuttings each season. Sow 15 pounds to the acre.

Bokhara Clover. This is a tall shrubbery plant, growing to height of four to six feet. It produces an abundance of small white flowers of great fragrance. Sow 10 pounds to the acre.

Burr Clover. This makes a good fodder. Creeping stem, which spreads over a large surface. It is fine for dry lands. The seeds is in burr pods ; 8 to 10 pounds per acre.

Espersette (French Sanfoin). This plant is of a lignumvinus character, having many stems two and three feet long. Smooth and tapering, with many long oblate leaflets in pairs, and spikes of variegated crimson flowers. The root is a perennial of a hard, woody nature. The plant flowers early and can be repeatedly cut, thus furnishing a great abundance of most nutritious food through the long dry and heated seasons, and requiring no irrigation. Stock will eat it with impunity, without danger of bloat as in alfalfa. The seed and seed pods are said to be more nutritious than oats. The plant does best in calcareous and gravelly soils, and elevated slopes and arid regions, where other vegetation fails. It will, however, not succeed in wet or low lands where there is no drainage. From 30 to 40 pounds are required for an acre.

Carolina, or Cow Pea. This makes a valuable fodder and is a good fertilizer. The pods can be harvested or all cut green for fodder, or it can be ploughed under for a fertilizer.

Vetches. Are much used for stock feed. Sow and cultivate same as for peas.

Lentils. Are similar to Vetches, and are cultivated in like manner.

Broom Corn. Many farmers make this a profitable crop, an acre producing about 500 cwt. of broom and forty bushels of seed ; plant and cultivate same as for corn.

Buckwheat. Can be sown late as in July at the rate of 30 to 40 pounds per acre. It should be thrashed as soon as dry, as if left standing in mass it will quickly gather moisture.

Field Beans. Should be planted after all danger from frost is past. Does best in rich, dry, light soil. Hoe frequently while the plant is dry, but not otherwise. The Medium White, White Navy and the Bayo, or Chile, varieties are mostly used for marketing in this country.

Field Peas. Should be sown on good cultivated soil at the rate of about one hundred and fifty pounds to the acre, in drills or broadcast. They are often sown in less quantity with oats and cut and cured together for hay, or threshed and bound together.

Sun Flower Seed. Is growing to be a valuable farm crop. The seed is very desirable for planting, while the leaves make excellent fodder. The plant is said to be an excellent protection from malaric, and should be grown for hedges about the house where this disease prevails.

FIELD GRAIN.

☞ SEED WHEAT, BARLEY, OATS, CORN and OTHER GRAINS of every variety, will be furnished to our customers in quantities as may be desired ; also, SEED POTATOES, at LOWEST MARKET RATES. Prices given on application.

GRASS AND CLOVER SEEDS.

Price List.

Clover Seed.

	Per lb			Per lb
Alfalfa, variable, about	$0 10 $0 12½		Alsyke, or Sweedish Clover	$0 25
Mammcth, or Sapling			Crimson Trefoil	50
Clover	12½ 15		Yellow "	50
Common, or Red Clover	11 15		Espersett, per 100, $20 00	30
White Dutch Clover	20 30			

Grass Seed.

	Per lb.	Per 100 lbs			Per lb.	Per 100 lbs
Lawn Grass, Best Mixed	$0 20	$15 00		Burmuda Grass	$2 00	$....
Lawn Grass, Extra Fancy				Timothy Grass Seeds	10	7 00
Blue	20	12 50		Red Top " "	15	8 00
Lawn Grass, Kentucky Ex.		10 00		Mesquite " "	10	8 00
Cl. Blue	15	....		Orchard " "	20	14 00
Sweet Vernal Grass	50	....		Evergreen Millet "	20	15 00
Perennial Rye "	15	10 00		German or Golden Millet	10	6 00
Australian "	15	10 00		Egyptian, or Pearl "	50	....
Italian "	15	10 00		Hungarian	10	6 00
Fine Fescue "	50	....		Burr Clover	15	10 00
Meadow Fescue	50	....				

Bermuda Grass Roots—price on application.

Miscellaneous and Field Seeds.

	Per lb.	Per 100 lbs			Per lb.	Per 100 lbs
Kaffir Corn	$0 50	$....		Lupins	$0 25	$....
Amber Sugar Cane Seed	10	6 00		Castor Oil Beans	25	15 00
African Seed	10	6 00		Hemp Seed	10	6 00
Egyptian Corn, White	5	2 50		Flax Seed	10	5 00
" " Red	5	2 00		Canary Seed	10	6 00
Buckwheat (market rates)	5	....		Mixed Bird Seed	10	6 00
Sun Flower Seed	40	25 00		Rape Seed	10	6 00
Vetches, or Tares	10	8 00		Bird Leituce	25	....
Leutils	10	....		Cuttle Fish Bone	50	....
Broom Corn	5	....		Maw, or Poppy Seed	30	....

Ramie Roots, price on application.

When ordered in quantity, reduced rates and subject to market fluctuations. Prices on application.

Express or Freight charges must be paid by the purchaser, and when small quantities are wanted to be forwarded by mail, to send money extra to cover cost of postage.

Bird Seed.

Canary, Hemp, Rape, Millet and Mixed Bird Seeds, 6 lbs. for 50 cents.

Vegetable Plants and Roots

Will be supplied in their proper season, and in quantities to suit.

Cabbage Plants	40c per 100 ;	$2.50 per 1000
Cauliflower Plants	40c per 100 ;	2.50 per 1000
Celery Plants	$1.00 per 100 ;	7.50 per 1000
Egg Plants	3.00 per 100 ;	50c per doz.
Tomato Plants	1.25 per 100 ;	20c per doz.
Sweet Potato Plants	50 per 100;	$4.00 per 1000
Asparagus Roots	1.50 per 100;	$10 per 1000.
Rhubarb Roots	25 each ;	$2.00 per doz.
Jerusalem Artichoke Tubers	10 per lb.;	$5.00 per 100 lbs.

We refer you to circular for more particular description and prices on large orders.

These require a good sandy soil, enriched with good fertilizers and well pulverized, loose and moderately moist. Sow the seed in usual way in boxes or warm seed bed, covering lightly, and keep in total darkness till the plant begins to show above ground, when gradually expose to the light. By pursuing this plan, uniform temperature and moisture is secured, and all seeds possessing life will be sure to grow. When the plants have grown to say two inches in height, they are ready to transplant. Give plenty of room, according to habit of growth of the plant. Crowding destroys the vigor and beauty of the flower.

We offer the following liberal inducements to those who wish to purchase Flower Seeds in quantity. These rates apply only to seeds in packets, but the seeds will be sent by mail, post-paid :

Send us $1.00, and select Packets to the value of $1.15.
Send us $2.00, and select Packets to the value of $2.35.
Send us $3.00, and select Packets to the value of $3.60.
Send us $4.00, and select Packets to the value of $5.00.

ABBREVIATIONS MADE IN FLOWER SEED LIST.

A.—For Annuals that grow, bloom and die the first year. **B.**—For Biennials blooming and dying the second year. **P.**—For Perennials that usually bloom the first or second year from seed, but continue to grow and bloom for many years thereafter. **H.**—Indicates Hardy. **H.H.**—Half hardy. **T.**—Tender.

The hardy can be sown in open ground early, or almost any time not requiring protection. Half hardy cannot be sown in open ground until the weather becomes warm, unless sown in greenhouse or with good protection.

ABOBRA (Climbers). H. H. P., 10 feet.	**ABUTILON.** H. H. P., 2 to 4 feet.
Rapid growing, with dazzling scarlet flowers. 10c	Chinese Bellflower. Flowers freely in house in Winter and Spring, and a good bedding Summer
ABRONIA. H. A. 9 to 18 in.	plant 15c
Trailing and prostrate habit, like the Verbena, and quite fragrant; natives of California.	WHITE- YELLOW AND CRIMSON MIXED.................. 15c
	ADLUMIA (Mountain Fringe). H. B., 18 feet.
UMBELLATA. rosy....................... .... 10c	CLIMBER, graceful foliage, light pink, tubular
ARENARIA. yellow 10c	flowers................................ .... 5c

FLOWER SEEDS SENT FREE BY MAIL ON RECEIPT OF PRICE.

ACERATUM. H. A.

Bears a great many flowers, and keeps in bloom a long time, and is, therefore, desireable for bouquet making. It is well to start the seed under glass and transplant

ACERATUM CONSPICUM. white; 18 inches......... 5c
MEXICANUM ALBIFLORUM NANUM, six inches......... 5c
CŒLESTINUM. TOM THUMB, light blue; 8 inches high, and of compact habit; mixed varieties 5c

AGROSTEMMA (ROSE CAMPION). H. A., 1 to 2 feet.

Annual, very pretty, free blooming and hardy; always makes desirable beds and useful for cutting; 12 inches in height.

NEW SCARLET, bright............................ 5c
CELIA ROSEA, deep rose....................... 5c
PICTA, dark crimson, white margin............ 5c
FINEST MIXED.................................. 5c

ALYSSUM. H. A., 1 foot.

Pretty little white flowers, useful in making up all kinds of small bouquets. Its fragrance is very delicate. The Alyssum grows freely from seed and makes a pretty border.

ALYSSUM. SWEET, hardy annual, flowers small in clusters, 6 inches............................ 5c
WIERCZBECKII, hardy perennial, yellow, 1 foot high....................................... 5c

ALONSOA. H. H. A.

Young plants removed to the house or greenhouse in the autumn, will continue to flower during the winter. The flowers are small but of remarkably brilliant colors.

ALONSOA WARSZEWICZI, bright scarlet, forming a very pretty spike, 18 inches high; set plants 8 to 10 inches apart............................ 5c
GRANDIFLORA. large-flowered, scarlet, 2 feet in height.................................... 5c

AMARANTHUS. H. H. A., 2 to 5 feet.

Valuable for their ornamental foliage, the leaves of most varieties being highly colored.

SALICIFOLIUS, fountain plant, beautiful both in habit and color; plant pyramidal; 3 feet.... 5c
BICOLOR RUBER, the lower half of the leaf a fiery red, the upper half maroon; splendid bedding plant.................................. 5c
TRICOLO (JOSEPH'S COAT), red, yellow and green foliage............................... 5c
MELANCHOLICUS RUBER, of compact habit, with striking blood red foliage; 18 inches....... 5c
CAUDATUS (LOVE LIES BLEEDING), long drooping "chains" of flowers, pretty for decoration.. 5c
CRUENTUS (PRINCE'S FEATHER), flowers somewhat similar to A. Caudatus, but in erect masses. 5c

AMMOBIUM (EVERLASTING FLOWER). H. A.

Fine white, showy and hardy annual......... 5c

AMPELOPSIS (VEITCHII, JAPAN WOODBINE, CLIMBER).

Very hardy and rapid grower; attaches to buildings, fences, etc., as closely as English Ivy; leaves olive green, changing to scarlet. Easy to cultivate and ornamental; 50 feet.

ANAGALLIS.

Anagallis is remarkable for the beauty of its flowers, useful for borders or baskets. Should be sown under glass. 6 inches.

ANAGALLIS GRANDIFLORA SUPERBA, mixed colors....... 5c

ANCHUSA.

This plant is fine for shaded places and city yards where the sun reaches only at intervals; hardy perennial.

BLUE, 2 feet................................. 5c

ACCONITUM (MONKSHOOD). H. P. 3 to 4 feet.

This plant loves a shady place under trees, and is a hardy perennial; 2 feet............. 5c

ACROLINIUM (EVERLASTING). H. H. P., 1 foot.

Fine for Winter bouquets; pure white and rose colors...................................... 5c

ADONIS. H. A., 1 foot.

The Adonis has pretty, narrow leaves, and are very brilliant. It will flourish almost anywhere, in the shade or under trees.

ADONIS ÆSTIVALIS. Summer, scarlet; 1 foot........ 5c
AUTEMALIS. Autumn, blood red; 1 foot.......... 5c

ANEMONS (WIND FLOWER).

A pleasing flower of various shades, blooming early and fine for bouquets, mixed colors, 1 ft 10c

ANTIRRHINUM (SNAPDRAGON.) H. A., 2 to 3 feet.

One of the very best of our perennials, blooms abundantly the first Summer until after frost, and flowers well the second Summer and even longer. By removing a portion of the flowers, the plants will become strong.

BRILLIANT, scarlet and yellow................ 5c
FIREFLY, orange and scarlet, with white throat.. 5c
CALATHE, crimson, throat white; large........ 5c
TOM THUMB, mixed colors...................... 5c

AQUILICA (COLUMBINE OR WILD HONEYSUCKLE). H. P. 2 feet.

Showy and one of the best early bloomers; herbaceous; hardy perennial.

CŒRULEA HYBRICA, porcelain blue, white and yellow; 2 feet.............................. 5c
CALIFORNIA HYBRICA, flowers large, golden yellow petals and orange red lepals and spurs...... 5c
DOUBLE AND SINGLE VARIETIES, mixed.......... 5c

ARCEMONE. H. H. P., 2 feet.

Handsome, large growing plant for flower beds; white and yellow flowers resembling Poppies................................... 5c

ASPERULA (WOODRUFF). H. A. 1 foot

AZUREA, a profuse flowering little annual, with numerous clusters of small lavender blue, sweet-scented flowers, fine for bouquets...... 5c

AURICULE. H. P. 6 inches.

A beautiful, favorite hardy perennial. The ALPINE is the most hardy.................... 10c

ASTERS.

Are one of the most popular and effective garden favorites, producing in abundance flowers of great richness and variety. They make elegant borders and showy beds; hardy annual.

TRUFFAUTS LARGE PÆONY-FLOWER, beautiful in perfection, size and fullness of flowers, mixed colors; 2 feet............................. 10c
LA SUPERBE, large flowers, 4 inches in diameter; 2 feet in height; three colors mixed........ 10c
NEW ROSE, 2 feet in height, robust, large flowers, petals finely imbricated; one of the very best; mixed colors........................ 10c
IMBRIQUE POMPON, very perfect, almost a globe and beautifully imbricated; mixed colors....... 10c
COCARDEAU OR NEW CROWN, two colored flowers, the central petals being of pure white, sometimes small and quilled, surrounded with large, flat petals of a bright color, 18 inches; mixed colors........................ 10c
NEW PÆONY-FLOWERED GLOBE, the earliest of the Asters, flowers very large, plant branching and strong; does not require support........ 10c
WASHINGTON, the largest Aster, 5 inches in diameter and perfect; mixed colors........... 10c
HEDGEHOG OR NEEDLE, petals long, quilled and sharply pointed; 2 feet; mixed colors....... 10c
CRYSANTHEMUM-FLOWERED DWARF WHITE, a superb variety every flower usually perfect; fine mixed varieties................................. 10c
DWARF BOUQUET, splendid for edging and small beds..................................... 10c
Six separate colors, variety................ 50c

AZALEA.

Shrubyplant, produces large heads of beautiful flowers; finest mixed ; tender perennial; 2 ft. 25c

BALSAM (LADY SLIPPER, OR TOUCH-ME-NOT).

This is one of the most beautiful and popular annuals. They are sown in beds or frames, and if growing too thick, thin out and prune as desired. They transplant readily. Among the many varieties we name:

DOUBLE CAMELIA-FLOWER, DOUBLE ROSE-FLOWER, DOUBLE DWARF. CARNATION—striped ; SOLFERINO—white ; striped, all fine............................ 10c
EXTRA DOUBLE MIXED of above and others.......... 10c

BALOON VINE (CARDIOSPERMUM).

CLIMBER, a half hardy annual with inflated capsules, very pretty; rapid grower; 10 feet 5c

BAPTISEA.   H. P. 4 to 5 feet.

A handsome perennial,bright blue, pea-shaped flower in spikes 6 inches long............... 5c

BELLIS (DOUBLE DAISY).   H. H. P., 6 inches.

Beautiful for edging, dwarf groups and beds; earliest and prettiest of the spring flowers.
Finest mixed and pure white............... ... 10c

BEGONIA.   T. P., 1 foot.

TUBEROUS ROOT, fine for bedding out in Summer or for pot culture ; scarlet, crimson, white and yellow; fine mixed..................... 25c

BARTONIA.   H A.

A succulent plant with large golden flowers expanding in the middle of the day.
AUREA, or Golden Yellow; 2 feet............... 5c
NANA, or Dwarf; 9 inches,..................... 5c

BRACHYCOME (SWAN RIVER DAISY).   H. A., ¼ foot.

A dwarf plant covered all summer with Cineraria-like blossoms; annual; blue, white and mixed colors................... 5c

BROWALLIA.   H. H. A., 1½ feet.

The Browallias are excellent, free-flowering, and valuable for Winter house plants. The flowers are beautiful and delicate. Seeds grow freely and give abundance of bloom ; set a foot apart. Varieties
CERVIAKOWSKI, blue, with white center.... ...... 5c
ELATA, white........................... 5c
GRANDIFLORA, blue mixed..................... 5c

CACALIA.   H. A., 1½ feet.

Pretty free-flowering plant, often called Flora's Paint Brush. Set plants six inches apart. They bloom early in Summer until Autumn; mixed colors................... 5c

CALAMPELIS (CLIMBER).   H. H. A., 10 feet.

SCABRA, blooms in racemes of bright orange flowers, Start in hotbed. 10 feet.......... 5c

CALENDRINIA.   H. H. A., 1 foot.

Beautiful dwarf plant; succeed best in light rich soil.
Mixed colors, large and showy............... 5c

CALCEOLARIA (GREENHOUSE PLANT).   T. P. 1½ feet.

A highly decorative plant for conservatory. Sow the seed in pots in light loam and sand.
HYBRIDA CORONATA—Bears dense heads of most brilliant colored flowers................ 25c

CALENDULA.   H. A. 1 foot.

English Marigold; a showy free-flowering annual, fine for beds and mixed borders...... 5c
PE MARICOLD, white, large flowers............... 5c
NCE OF ORANGE, very fine double, orange striped................... 5c

CALLIOPSIS (COREOPSIS).   H. A., 2 feet.

Showy, free-flowering and beautiful annual; the tall are fine for beds and mixed borders, and dwarf for bedding. Crimson, yellow, brown and marbled, mixed colors. 5c

CALLIRRHOE.

Beautiful annual ; violet, purple and crimson flowers; white center; attractive, and blooms through the summer................ 5c

CAMPANULA (CANTERBURY BELL).   H. A. and P. 6 to 12 in.

Beautiful and popular for the garden; annual and perennial; varieties.
CARPATICA DWARF—Blue; ALBA white, both fine for beds or edging; mixed or separate...... 5c
GRANDIFLORA—Blue and white; large and handsome................... 5c
PYRAMIDALIS—Blue and white,fine for greenhouse; P. 3 feet................... 5c
SPECULUM (Venus' Looking-glass)—Hardy annual; blue and white, fine for edging, etc... 5c

CANARY BIRD FLOWER (CLIMBER).   H. H. A. 10 to 15 feet.

TROPÆOLUM—Popular and pretty, rapid grower and abundant bloomer of rich yellow-fringed flowers................... 10c

CANDYTUFT.   H. A. 6 to 12 inches.

Popular and useful, blooming long and freely and perfectly hardy. The flowers are quite a treasure for making bouquets and for massing or ribbon gardening. Varieties and shades are numerous
WHITE, PURPLE, ROSE, CRIMSON, ROCKET—Pure white and fragrant, separate or mixed............ 5c

CANNA (INDIAN SHOT).   H. H. P.

Stately and ornamental plants, desirable in groups or background ; annual; soak seed in hot water before sowing ; varieties.
INDIAN—Red; WARCZWICZII, red striped ; COMPACTA, yellowish red ; 2 feet; mixed or separate colors................... 5c

CARNATION (DIANTHUS).   H. H. P. 1 to 2 feet.

Magnificent and popular, very fragrant, and beautiful colors; hardy perennial.
Finest strains of German and Italian seed.... 20c
Good Mixed................... 10c

CASSIA.

Hardy perennial, with yellow flowers; 18 inches high; good border flower........... 10c

CATCHFLY (SILENE).   H. A., 1½ feet.

Showy and great favorite; annual; bright, dense heads of flowers; blooms freely and of easy culture; colors, red and white......... 5c

CENTRANTHUS.   H. A. 1½ feet.

Pretty, free flowering annual, effective in beds and borders; transparent stems and glaucous leaves; rose colored and white............. 5c

CENTAUREA.   H. A.

Showy border plant, succeeding in almost any soil; hardy annual and perennial; varieties.
BACHELOR'S BUTTON OR CORN BOTTLE—2 feet; quite showy................... 5c
SWEET SULTAN—Hardy annual; 1 foot........... 5c
BASKET FLOWER (Americana), large-growing; 3 feet; pink................... 5c

CHRYSANTHEMUM.   H. A. and P. 12 to 18 inches.

Very showy and effective favorites; colors have the appearance of being laid ou with a brush; annual and perennial; varieties.
CRIMSON, white center; WHITE, crimson center; DOUBLE WHITE and DOUBLE YELLOW, separate or mixed ; annuals................... 5c

W. R. Strong & Co., Sacramento, Cal.   31

FRUTESCENS CRANDIFLORUM (Marguerite or Paris Daisy), H. P.; now so fashionable and popular; large white star-like flowers, growing freely and profusely........................ 10c

CLARKIA. H. A. 1 to 2 feet.
Hardy annual plant, blooming profusely, with handsome flowers.
DOUBLE AND SINGLE—Mixed colors 5c

CINERARIA (GREENHOUSE PLANT). H. H. P., 1 foot.
Free flowering, blooming most of the year; rich and diversified colors.
HYBRIDA, Mixed.. 25c
MARITIMA AND ACANTHIFOLIA are ornamental foliage plants; large silvery leaves.............. ... 10c

CLEMATIS (CLIMBER). H. P., 6 to 12 feet
Handsome and hardy; seed germinates slowly; 15 feet.
FLAMULA, white and fragrant.................... 10c

CLEOME.
Annual; free-flowering and handsome.
PURPLE AND ROSE.............................. 10c

CLIANTHUS. H. H. P., 2 feet.
GLORY PEA OF AUSTRALIA, magnificent plant; should be grown in light, rich soil.
DAMPIERI has brilliant scarlet flowers, with intense black spots in center; beautiful; 4 ft.. 25c

CLINTONIA. H. A., 6 inches.
Annual, pretty and neat; has blue, white and yellow flowers, like Lobelia............... 5c

COBÆA (SCANDENS). H. H. P., 20 to 30 feet.
Climbing plant; rapid grower and large bell-shaped flowers; fine for Summer; plant seed edge wise 10c

COCCINEA. H. H. P., 10 feet.
CLIMBING PLANT. Smooth, glossy leaves, and showy white flowers; deep scarlet fruit..... 10c

COCKSCOMB (CELOSIA).
Annual plant, showy and attractive; half hardy.
CHRISTATA- Dwarf, crimson, fine; VARIEGATA, new, brilliant, combs of crimson and gold........ 10c
JAPAN, branching variety of great beauty; scarlet and crimson combs, like ruffled lace, in pyramidal masses 10c
Tall and dwarf varieties mixed............... 10c

COLEUS. T. P., 1 to 3 feet
Ornamental foliage plant; leaves of all shapes and colors, of velvety appearance and great beauty. Splendid flower for garden decoration. Finest hybrid, mixed............... 25c

COLLINSIA. H. H. A., 1 to 2 feet.
California annual; marbled or many colored, for beds and borders........................ 5c

COMELINA.
Tender perennial, tuberous root; rich and beautiful; flowers of blue and white; roots can be taken up and planted like Dahlias; 2 feet high...................................... 5c

COLLOMIA.
Hardy annual; fine for borders and baskets; buff flowers 5c

CONVOLVULUS MAJOR (MORNING GLORY). H. A., 30 to 50 ft.
Varieties and colors too well known for description; white, dark blue, blood red, rose and striped, growing 20 feet high; mixed colors or separate............................ 5c

CONVOLVULUS MINOR. H. A., 1 foot.
Hardy annual, largely used for bedding and borders, their brilliant colored flowers producing a fine effect. Colors: violet, striped blue and white, pure white, etc.
Separate or mixed 5c

MAURITANICUS,
Is a fine creeper, blue flowers and splendid for basket and rock work................. 5c
COWSLIP. H. P., 9 inches.
Hardy perennial; useful for borders.
ENGLISH MIXED.............. .... 5c

CREPIS (HAWKWEED).
Annual of easy culture and abundant bloomer; red, white and yellow..................... 5c

CUPHEA (CIGAR PLANT).
Tender perennial, 3 to 4 feet high; a profuse bloomer; fine for ornamentation of garden or greenhouse.................. .... 10c

CYCLAMEN.
Greenhouse plant of rich bloom and much esteemed for making bouquets and baskets; half-hardy perennial; mixed varieties..... 25c

CYCLANTHERA.
Climbing plant, 10 feet high; half-hardy annual; bears oval shaped fruit, which explodes when ripe............................ 10c

CYPRUS VINE (Ipomœ Quamaoclit). H. H. A., 15 ft.
Climbing Annual, popular, elegant and graceful; different colors, scarlet, white and rose..... 5c

DAHLIA. H. H. P., 4 to 6 feet.
Tuberous root, hardy perennial; seed of finest mixed colors.............................. 10c

DATURA (Trumpet Flower). H. A., 3 feet.
Ornamental plant; flowers trumpet-shaped, large and sweet-sented; purple and white...

DIANTHUS. H. P. and A., 1 foot.
The most popular flower cultivated, the varieties of which are Pinks, Carnations, Picotees and Sweet Williams, the last three described elsewhere.
Chinensis (Chinese Pink), hardy annual; brilliant garden flowers; double mixed........ 5c
Double Imperialis, annual, finest mixed........ 5c
Japanese Pink (Heddewigii), annual; flowers large and brilliant 5c
Diadem Pink, annual; dwarf, compact, luxuriant and dense double flowers of all shades 5c
Laciniatus Pink—Annual; one foot; beautifully fringed, various colors; mixed.......... 5c
Gardenarianus—Perennial, 1½ feet, various colors; mixed........................... 5c

DIDISCUS.
Didiscus Cœruleus—Annual, half hardy; very pretty blue border plant................. 5c

DIGITALIS (Foxglove). H. P. 3 to 5 feet.
Hardy perennials, three feet, handsome ornamental plant of stately growth and varied colors; mixed or separate colors............. 5c

DICTAMNUS.
Hardy perennial, 2 feet, lemon scented flowers white and blue..................... 5c

DOLICHOS (Hyacinth Bean). T. A. 10 feet.
A beautiful climber, flowers in clusters, purple and white, 10 feet................... 5c

EGG PLANT (Solanum). H. H. A., 1½ feet.
Ornamental and handsome egg-shaped fruit; white and scarlet...................... 5c

ERYSIMUM.   H. A. 1 foot.

Annual 1½ feet. free-flowering and showy for beds or border, sulphur yellow and deeper orange shades.. 5c

ERYTHINIA (Coral Tree).   H. H. P. 3 to 5 feet.

This shrub bears large spikes of pea-shaped blossoms, deep scarlet...................... 25c

ESCHSCHOLTZIA (California Poppy).   H. A. 1 foot.

A hardy annual, profuse bloomer, with rich and beautiful colors; continues in bloom until frost; varieties.

EUCHARIDIUM.   H. A. 1 foot.

Showy dwarf, spreading Summer plant, for flowering in masses; purple, rose and white, 10c

EUPATORIUM.   H. P. 2 to 3 feet.

Herbaceous plant, hardy; showy flowers in beautiful bunches, fine for bouquets......... 5c

EUPHORBIA.   H. A. 18 to 24 in.

Ornamental annual, leaves edged with white; very pretty in bouquets...................... 5c

EUTOCA.

Annual; desirable for cut flowers; blue and lilac; 6 inches 5c

FENZLIA.

Hardy annual, dwarf plant, suited for rustic baskets, etc.; flowers rosy lilac and orange.. 5c

FERNS.   T. P. 1 to 3 feet.

A graceful class of plants; choice mixed seed, 10c

FUCHSIA.   T. P. 1 to 3 feet.

A beautiful plant blooming all the season; mixed...................................... 25c

FORGET-ME-NOT (Myosotis.)   H. P., 6 to 12 inches.

Very popular and beautiful; will grow in any moist situation.

Palustris, blue; Alba, white.................. 10c
Azorica, flowers rich blue, shaded with purple 10c
Semperflorus, a charming dwarf of fine growth 10c

GAILLARDIA.   H. A., 1 foot.

Easy culture, thriving in any garden soil, fine for masses; diversified colors, mixed....... 10c

GAUREA.   H. A.

Spikes of white flowers, profuse bloomer and fine for bouquets.......................... 5c

GERANIUM (Pelargonium.)   H. H. P., 12 to 18 in.

Beautiful plants for pot culture or flower garden.

Finest Mixed.. .... 25c
Lady Washington and other fancy varieties.... 25c

GEUM.   H. P., 1½ feet.

A hardy perennial, with bright scarlet flowers...................................... 5c

GLADIOLIAS.   H. H. P., 2 to 4 feet.

Bulbous; choice flowers of many colors; a beautiful summer flowering plant.......... 5c

GLAUCIUM (Horn Poppy).   H. P., 1 to 2 feet

Showy plant, silvery leaves, deeply cut and curved, bell-shaped, orange flowers......... 10c

GLOBE AMARANTH (Everlasting Flower).

Batchelor Buttons, white, purple, variegated and mixed.................................. 5c

GLOXINIA.   T. P., 1 foot.

Hothouse plant, produces flowers of richest colors, thrives best in loamy soils; fine hybrid.................................... 25c

GODETIA.   H. A., 1 foot.

A hardy annual, a profuse bloomer of delicate tints of color, and a universal favorite. Choicest varieties, separate or mixed...... 15c

GRAPHALIUM,   H. P., 6 inches

The Edelweiss of the Alps. Flowers pure white, star-shaped, downy and greatly fringed...................................... 25c

GYSOPHILA.   H. A.

Annual, elegant and free flowering, fine for rustic work and edging or bouquets......... 5c

GOURDS (Climbers.)   T. A., 10 to 30 feet.

Very desirable for trellis work, arbors, etc.; being of rapid growth. They are of varied forms. Bottle Shaped, Pear Shaped, Egg Shaped, Club Shaped, Orange, Turban, Dipper, Powder Horn, etc., separate............................ 10c
Fine mixed varieties....................... 5c

HELIOTROPE.   P., 18 inches

A deliciously fragrant plant, fine for bedding and pot culture; choice mixed............. 10c

HELICHRISUM (Everlasting Flower).   H. A., 1 to 2 ft.

Ornamental and admired for beauty of flower; when dried retain their color for years; hardy annual............................... 5c

HIBISCUS.   H. H. P., 2 to 4 feet.

Hardy annual, showy and ornamental.
Africanus, rich, cream-brown center.......... 5c
California, herbaceous, gives a mass of pure white flowers............................. 5c

HOLLYHOCK.   H. B., 4 to 8 feet.

A grand Autumn-flowering plant and an old favorite; magnificent improved varieties... 5c

HONESTY.   H. B., 2 feet.

Lunaria or Satin Flower, an interesting plant; seed vessels look like transparent silver; handsome for bouquets or dried flowers; hardy perennial............................ 5c

HUMEA   H. H. H. B., 5 to 6 feet.

Makes a beautiful decoration in gardens or pleasure grounds; flowers ruby red, in drooping racemes.................................. 10c

ICE PLANT (Mesembryanthemum).   H. H. A., 6 in.

Dwarf trailer, with thick fleshy leaves, having the appearance of being covered with ice crystals................................. 5c

IPOMŒA (Convolvulus).

A beautiful climber, useful in covering trellises, arbors, etc.
Bona Nox, or Evening Glory, flowers white and and fragrant, blooming in the evening; 10 feet...................................... 5c
Buridgi, rose and crimson; Coccinea, scarlet; Limbata, blue and white; 10 feet; either separate or mixed....................... 5c

IPOMOPSIS.   H. H. B., 3 to 6 feet.

A beautiful plant with long spikes of orange and scarlet............................... 5c

KAULFUSSIA.   H. A., 6 inches.

Dwarf annual, like an aster; pretty branching and free flowering; mixed colors.......... 5c

PANSY.

LARKSPUR (Delphinum). II. A.

Desirable and beautiful; flowers mostly blue.
Dwarf Rocket, fine double, 1 foot............... 5c
Tall Rocket, finest mixed double, 2 feet 5c
Branching Stockflower, blooms all the season.. 5c

LATHYRUS (Perennial Peas). II. II. A.

Ornamental and useful climbers; crimson,
white and mixed varieties.................. 5c

LAVENDER. II. P., 1 to 2 feet.

Prized for its fragrant violet flowers; does best
in a dry, gravelly soil; hardy perennial.... 5c

LAVETERA. II. A., 3 feet.

Showy and profuse bloomer; rose and white;
mixed colors............................. 5c

LEPTOSIPHON. II. A., 8 inches.

Beautiful dwarf for lines and ribbon beds;
white and yellow; mixed.................. 5c

LIMNAPTHES DOUGLASII. II. A., 8 inches.

Dwarf, yellow and white; fragrant.......... 5c

LINARIA.

Annual; handsome for rock work, ribbon
lines, etc.; white and purple............. 5c

LINUM (Flowering Flax. II. A, 1 foot.

Conspicuous for its brilliant colors

Flavum, yellow; perennial................. 5c
Grandiflorum, scarlet; annual............. 5c

LOASA (Climber). II. P., 6 feet.

Flowers profusely through the season........ 10c

LOBELIA.

Annuals. An elegant dwarf of easy culture;
fine for borders and ribbon beds and for vases and
hanging baskets.
Erinus Alba, pure white; Paxtonia, white with blue
belt; both splendid.
Crystal Palace and Gracilea, blue; fine bedding.
Erinus and above, finest mixed............ 10c
Fulgens, perennial, 2 feet; of brilliant scarlet. 10c
Cardinalis, or Cardinal Flower, is perfectly hardy, growing to four feet; flower spikes long
and of intense vermilion.................. 10c

LOPHOSPERMUM (Climber).

Very ornamental, with large handsome flowers; rosy carmine; 10 feet............. 10c

LUPINUS. II. A., 1 to 3 feet.

Desirable in every garden; colors rich and
varied; valuable for mixed flower borders
or for bedding; colors blue, white and purple, violet, brown and yellow, scarlet, etc.;
separate or in mixed varieties............. 5c

LYCHNIS. II. P., 1 to 3 feet.

A handsome ornamental plant for flower and
shrubbery borders; scarlet and scarlet and
orange, mixed............................. 5c

MALOPE. II. A., 3 to 4 feet.

Handsome plant of branching habit, flowering profusely; crimson, rose and white..... 5c

MARIGOLD. II. II. A.

Showy and brilliant.
African, is the tallest, 2 feet; quilled orange,
brown and yellow, mixed................. 5c
French, is of dwarf habit and more compact.. 5c

MARVEL OF PERU (Four O'clock). II. A., 2 feet.

One of the most ornamental flowering plants;
they are quite fragrant, flowers expanding in the
evening.

3

Longifolia, long flower, pure white and fragrant.................................... 5c
Mixed varieties, white, yellow and violet..... 5c

MARTYNIA. II. A., 3 to 4 feet.

Free flowering, of easy culture and hardy,
sweet-scented; yellow and purple.......... 5c

MATRICARIA (Feverfew).

Perennial; 1 to 2 feet.
Eximia, double white, beautifully extra curled. 15c
Alba Plenissima, is a fine double white....... 15c

MAURANDIA (Climber). T. A., 6 to 10 feet.

Very graceful for training on trellis work, verandas, etc.; perennial, flowers the first season from seed; violet, pink, purple, white
and mixed................................ 10c

MIGNONETTE.

A hardy annual, well known and esteemed for
its fragrance.
Sweet. Large flower; is very fragrant; per
ounce, 25c............................... 5c
Parsons' New White, is very desirable........ 5c
Hybrid Spiral, is different, producing long spikes
of most abundant bloom and deliciously fragrant................................... 5c
Machet, are dwarf but vigorous growth, with
thick, dark green leaves and highly fragrant red flowers........................ 5c

MIMULUS (Monkey Flower).

A perennial, brilliant free flowering plant; luxuriates in damp, shady spots, but adapted to pots
or open culture.
Scarlet, rose-color and spotted.............. 10c

MOSCHATUS (Musk Plant).

Yellow, strong musk flavor................. 10c

MORNING GLORY.

See Convolvulus.

MOMONDICA. T. A., 10 feet.

A trailing plant, ornamental foliage and singular fruit.
Balsam Apple, fine orange color............ 5c
Balsam Pear, golden yellow............... 5c

NASTURTIUM (Minor). II. A., 1 foot.

Dwarf, excellent for beds, masses and groups, or
planting in ribbon style with other bedding plants;
stand heat and drouth wonderfully.
Scarlet, Red, Yellow, White, Spotted and Tom
Thumb varieties......................... 5c

NASTURTIUM (Major). II. A., 8 to 10 feet.

Tall, valuable and desirable climbers; handsome and pleasing; all colors, separate or
mixed.................................... 5c

NEMOPHILA. II. A., 1 foot.

A charming dwarf annual, neat, compact and
of uniform growth, adapted for beds and
borders; fine mixed varieties............. 5c

NEMESIA.

Pretty dwarf annual of various colors........ 5c

NEREMBERGIA.

A pretty half hardy plant for flower beds, of a
shrubby character; flowers, white, blue and
purple................................... 5c

NIGELLA. II. A., 6 inches.

A curious and interesting annual of easy culture
and free bloomers; handsome foliage.

Hispanica (Love in a Mist). Pure white and
blue 5c

Damascena (Devil in a Bush). Double, blue
and white 5c

NOLANO.   H. A., 6 inches.

Very pretty trailing plant, excellent for hanging baskets and rustic work 5c

NYCTERINIA.   H. H. A., 6 inches.

A sweet-scented little plant with large head of
star flowers, white and pink with yellow
center, suited for rock work and edgings.... 5c

ŒNOTHERA (Evening Primrose). H. A., 1 to 2 feet.

Beautiful, free growing and useful, flowering in
long spikes, fine for beds or borders.

Odorata, true Evening Primrose, hardy annual,
yellow and sweet-scented ; 1 foot 5c
Acaulis, large flowers ; blossoms silver white.. 10c
Vetchii, large, yellow, with crimson spots...... 10c
Lamarkiana, flowers bright yellow, 3 to 4 inches
in diameter, in great profusion 10c
Fine mixed varieties 5c

OXALIS.   H. H. A., 6 to 9 inches.

Perennial A beautiful plant, with rich colored flowers, fine for decorations, basket work,
etc 10c

PASSION FLOWER (Climber).

Handsome rapid grower, fine for decoration and
open ground.
Cerulea, large violet and light blue, fragrant.. 20c

PANSY (Viola Tricolor.)

This is a great favorite for all flower gardens. It
is biennial and can be perpetuated by division of
the roots. Seeds sown in the autumn produce
earlier and better flowers the coming season.
They require good rich soil.

Colors, rich **Golden Yellow, Intense Blue, Azure
Blue, Bronze, Pure White, Striped and Blotched,
Violet, Gold Margin, King of the Blacks,** etc.
all fine varieties, separate 10c
Extra fine mixed German 10c

PENTSTEMON.

Perennial, herbaceous plant, with long spikes
of rich colored flowers, scarlet, purple, blue,
rose, white and striped ; separate or mixed.. 20c

PERILLA.   T. A., 1½ feet

Annual, ornamental, leaf broad and serrated,
of mulberry color 5c

PETUNIA.

A hardy annual, unequaled for out door decoration for borders or bedding.

Hybrida grandiflora, rich crimson, large flower.. 20c
Fimbrata, new ; finely fringed and blotched,
and mixed colors 20c
Double Dwarf, compact and beautiful ; desirable for pots or masses 20c
Fine mixed varieties 10c
Yellow-Throated. These Petunias form a class
of rare beauty and come true from seed ; flowers of large size, with broad, deep yellow
throat, veined very much like the Salpiglos-
sis 25c

PHASŒLOS.

An ornamental climbing bean ; 10 feet.

Scarlet Runner, dazzling scarlet flower 5c
White Runner, white 5c
Painted Lady, flowers red and white 5c

PHLOX.   H. A., 1½ feet.

A magnificent hardy annual of great brilliancy
and variety of colors, long bloomers and splendid
bedding flowers.

**Drummondii, Pure White, Brilliant Scarlet, Blue
and White, Blood Purple, Black Warrior,** (deep
purple,) **Pure Rose,** etc., separate 10c
Mixed Drummondii, finest varieties 10c
Mixed Drummondii Grandiflora, larger than the
above 15c
Perennial Phlox, mixed, very hardy, splendid
sorts 15c

PINKS
See Dianthus.

POPPY.

An annual with brilliant and showy flowers.

Carnation, double fringed, mixed colors.... 5c
Pæony flowered, large and fine, double.... 5c
Ranunculus flowered, African rose, mix'd, 5c
Orientale, brilliant scarlet 5c
Somniferum (Opium Poppy), perennial,
large double flowers 5c

PORTULACCA.   H. A , 6 inches.

This is one of the most charming annuals, of
easy culture and luxuriating in any sunny spot.
Flowers of almost every shade in great profusion.
Splendid, mixed, or colors separate 5c
Double Rose flowered. extra selected,
mixed 10c

PRIMULA (Chinese Primrose). H. P.

Beautiful plant for parlor or greenhouse.
Most charming flowers for Winter or Spring.
Sinensis fimbriata, very choice mixed.... 25c
Coccinea, flower large and beautiful crim-
son 25c
Double-flowered, mostly double, various
colors, mixed 25c

POLYANTHUS.   H. P., 1 foot.

A hardy Spring flower and great favorite ; extra mixed colors 10c

PYRETHREUM (Feverfew). H. P., 1½ ft.

Free flowering and handsome ; fine for flower
borders, etc.; herbaceous plant.
Hybridum, beautiful form, double flowers.. 10c
Golden Feather, dwarf, gold leaf, fine for
beds or ribbon planting 10c
Double White, very fine double 10c
Carneum (Cineraifolium). The true insect Powder flower of Persia and California ;
25 cts. per ounce, or. 5c

RHODANTHE (Everlasting Flower)
    H. H. A., 1 foot.

Very valuable for Winter bouquets, and also
desirable for pot plants or for the garden.... 10c

RHODODENDRON.   H. H., 3 to 4 feet.

Handsome shrub for lawns ; flowers large and
luxuriant foliage 25c

RICINUS (Castor Oil Plant). H. H A ,6 to 15 ft

This is a rapid grower with fine palm-like foliage, giving a fine effect on lawns or large beds.
In variety 5c

ROCKET (Hesperis).   H. P., 2 to 3 feet.

Well known, free flowering and very fragrant ;
purple and white 5c

SALPIGLOSSIS.   H H. A., 1½ feet.

Autumn-blooming annual, funnel-shaped flowers, varied and mottled, scarlet and blue ;
finest mixed 10c

SALVIA (Flowering Sage). H. H. P., 3 ft.

Scarlet and blue ; a most gorgeous plant.
Patten's, splendid deep blue ; the best...... 20c
Splendens, Scarlet sage, very bright 10c

SANVITALIA. H. H. A., ½ foot.

Annual, dwarf and compact; golden yellow flowers; fine in beds and masses............ 10c

SAPONARIA. H. A., ½ foot.

Dwarf annual, long bloomer, rose and white flowers; beautiful........ .... 10c

SCABIOSA (Mourning Bride). H. A., 1 foot.

Very showy and excellent for beds or cut flowers. White, rose and purple shades.
Dwarf varieties, separate or mixed........ 5c
Tall varieties, separate or mixed.... ...... 5c

SENSITIVE PLANT (Mimosa Pudica).

Leaves close when slightly touched; suitable for pots and borders; 1 foot................. 10c

SCHIZANTHUS. H. H. A., 1½ feet.

Butterfly Flower. Elegant foliage; flowers rich color and beautiful...................... 5c

SUNFLOWER.

This stately plant, so universally known, with many very fine double varieties that are very magnificent.
Mixed..................... 5c

SEDUM. H. A., ½ foot.

Grows freely on rocks, and desirable for rustic work; bright blue............................ 10c

SENECIO. H. H. P., 1 foot.

Free flowering, blooming all the season in the garden, and greenhouse in the Winter...... 10c

SILENE. H. A, 6 in.

An attractive flower, adapted for summer beds, ribbon and rock work............... .... 5c

SMILAX (Myrsiphyllum). T. P., 6 feet.

This is the most popular and graceful evergreen vine in cultivation, adapted for hanging baskets and pot culture, floral wreaths, etc.................................. 10c

STATICE (Everlasting).

An interesting, free flowering plant of easy culture, long-blooming, and valuable for Winter bouquets, perennial; fine mixed.... 10c

STOCK (Gilliflower, Mathiola).

One of the most valuable garden plants, and highly esteemed for their beauty, fragrance and brilliant, showy beds.
German Ten Weeks, all colors; Pure White, Scarlet, Purple, etc; Dwarf, separate colors or finest mixed............ 10c
Large-Flowered Pyramidal, very fine.. 10c

INTERMEDIATE STOCKS.

Valuable for late flowering and for pots for Spring bloom; scarlet, white, purple or mixed varieties................................ 10c
Emperor, or perpetual bloomer, mixed...... 10c
Brompton or Winter Stock, finest mixed................................ 10c

SWEET PEAS. H. A., 4 to 6 feet.

Fragrant and beautiful climbers; bloom all the season and admirable for screens and trailing.
Scarlet Invincible, Striped, Painted Lady, Purple, White, etc, separate or mixed, per ounce, 15c ... 5c
Perennial Pea, mixed colors, 15c per ounce, 5c

SWEET SULTAN. H. A., 1½ feet.

Very fragrant and effective in flower beds or border, and valuable for bouquets; mixed colors... 5c

SWEET WILLIAM. H. A., 1½ feet.

A well known perennial, perfectly hardy, easily grown, and of extreme richness and diversity of color.
Auricula Flowered. Trusses of immense size and beautiful colors; finest mixed..... 5c
Double flowers, from choice collections....... 10c
Fine mixed 5c

TRITOMA (Red-Hot Poker). H. P., 4 feet.

Herbaceous plant; flower spikes 1 foot; colors yellow to deep scarlet; blooms through the season and gives a striking effect........... 5c

THUNBERGIA (Climber). H. H. A., 4 feet.

Very ornamental and of rapid growth; the flowers are very much admired; colors, red, white, buff and bright orange, separate or mixed..................... 5c

TROPÆOLUM (Minor and Major

See Nasturtium

VALERIANA. H. P., 1½ feet.

A handsome, hardy plant with long heads of fragrant flowers, scarlet and white 5c

VERBENA. H. H. P., 1 foot.

A universally admired plant, blooming freely the first year.
Hybrida Finest colors, mixed............. 10c
Scarlet. White and striped, separate.... 10c
Montana. A hardy variety from the Rocky Mountains; rose and lilac 10c

VERONICA. H. A., 5 inches.

Handsome herbaceous plant; blue and rose.. 10c

VINCA (Periwinkle). T. P., 1½ feet.

A beautiful greenhouse plant; rosy and pure white.................... 10c

VIRGINIA STOCK. H. A., 6 inches.

A beautiful little plant for beds, baskets or edging, growing freely in any soil........... 10c

VIOLET (Viola). H. P., 1½ feet.

A great favorite from its beauty, long-continued bloom and delightful fragrance.
Blue Sweet.............................. 10c
Alba, white.................. .... 10c
Lutea, yellow................................ 10c

VISCARIA. H. A, 1 foot.

Handsome brilliant crimson, pink and white. 5c

WALLFLOWER.

A plant well known and much esteemed for its fragrance and bright, showy yellow and blood-colored flowers.
Single, mixed............................. 5c
Double, mixed.................. .... 10c

WHITLAVIA. H. A., 1 foot.

A dwarf, growing in clumps. The flowers are bell-shaped and beautiful; grows in any soil; violet, blue, and white with blue lips....... 5c

WAITZIA (Everlasting).

Yellow flowers, borne in clusters; fine for dried flowers................................ 10c

ZINNIA ELEGANS. H. A., 2 to 3 feet

Few plants have improved as much as the Zinnin, and we have now dazzling scarlet, yellow, orange, rose, lilac, crimson and white, rivaling the Dahlia in symmetry.
Zinnia Elegans, fl pl. Extra choice double mixed.............................. 5c
Zinnia Alba, fl. pl. White.............. 5c
Zinnia Coccinea, fl. pl. Scarlet....... 5c
Zinnia Striata, fl. pl. Double Striped..... 5c
Zinnia Haageana, fl. pl. The flower is of a deep orange-yellow color, keeping its color when dried............................ 5c

ORNAMENTAL GRASSES.

Nearly all the Ornamental Grasses are very showy and beautiful, and when dried and tastefully arranged in connection with the Everlasting Flowers, make exceedingly attractive Winter bouquets.

Ornamental Grasses—A collection of eight different varieties, our own selection................ 30c

Agrostis pulchella—Feathery, very delicate; 1 foot................................... 5c
Avena scirilis (Animated Oats)—2½ feet ... 5c
Briza maxima (Quaking Grass)—Very ornamental; 1 foot............................ 5c
Briza gracilis (Slender Quaking Grass)—Very pretty; 1 foot.......................... 5c
Brizopyrum siculum—Shining green leaves 8 inches.. 5c
Bromus brizæformis—A beautiful hanging grass; 1 foot,.............................. 5c
Chrysurus cynosuroides—Yellow feathery spikes; 1 foot................................ 5c
Eragrostis elegans—Graceful habit; 1 ft.. 5c

Coix lacrimæ (Job's Tears)—Broad corn-like leaves; 2 feet............................ 5c
Gynerium argentium (Pampas Grass)-The most noble grass in cultivation: 10 feet..... 10c
Hordeum jubatum (Squirrel Tail Grass)—Lovely; purplish plum; 3 feet 5c
Lagurus ovatus (Hare's Tail Grass)—Very pretty; 1 foot............................ 5c
Pennisetum longistylum—Graceful and interesting; 18 inches....................... 10c
Stipa pinnata (Feather Grass)—A beautiful variety................................ 10c
Tricholæna rosea—Beautiful rose-tinted grass; 2 feet................................ 10c

FLOWER BULBS, ROOTS, PLANTS, ETC.

IN THEIR SEASON.

Holland Bulbs—Hyacinths, Tulips, Narcissus, Anemones, Ranunculus, Crocus, Iris, Snowdrops, etc.

These should be planted from September to January, and later in season.

Lilies, in variety ; Tuberoses, Pæonies, Bleeding Heart, Gladiolus, in variety ; Lily of the Valley, Dahlias, named and unnamed.

For description and price list we refer you to our Bulb Catalogue.

Greenhouse and Ornamental Pot Plants.

These we do not grow but are prepared to fill all orders from the Conservatories and Greenhouse establishments in our vicinity, as also

Cut Flowers for Bouquets, Designs for Funerals,

And other special occasions.

Roses and Other Choice Shrubbery

AND ORNAMENTAL TREES

Of out-door culture, will be found and described in the Nursery department of this Catalogue.

ROBERT WILLIAMSON.   **W. R. STRONG.**   **P. E. PLATT.**

W. R. STRONG & CO.'S

Descriptive Catalogue of Trees and Nursery Stock

FOR 1888-89.

THE CAPITAL NURSERIES.

ROBERT WILLIAMSON, the original founder and manager of these Nurseries, still has the management thereof. With his long experience, and the increased facilities of the present firm, we feel warranted in saying that we can compete with any Nursery on the Coast, and hope for a continuance of the liberal patronage so long enjoyed by these well known and popular Nurseries.

Our headquarters and chief office is at our store, Nos. 102 to 110 J Street, Sacramento, Cal.

We have greatly increased our facilities for carrying on this branch of our business by the purchase of 320 acres of the very best land on the Mokelumne River in the celebrated Lodi District. This, added to our 210 acres at Sacramento and our large orchard and experimental grounds near Penryn, in Placer County, gives us unrivaled advantages for growing good stocks, and testing varieties on different soils and in different climates. Add to this our thirty years experience in handling and shipping fruit, we certainly are in better position for supplying the planter with trees that will give the very best satisfaction than any other nursery firm on the Coast or elsewhere.

Our stock this season is unusually large; trees very large and healthy, most of them trained low so as to protect themselves from the hot rays of the sun. For the past six years our buds and grafts have been taken from bearing trees fruited under our own observation, and we think they cannot fail to give satisfaction, especially when planted in similar climates and soils to that of Sacramento Valley and adjacent foothills. The great diversity of climates in this State makes it impossible to get the same results in all localities with the same fruit. For instance, some of our best fruits here are worthless in San Jose, and some of the best kinds there are of no value here.

READ WITH CARE THE FOLLOWING:

(1.) Persons planting should try to find out what succeeds best in their particular climate.

(2.) Different persons know fruits by different names, which sometimes causes planters to think they have been swindled, when they have actually got exactly what they ordered.

We regard fruit culture in California as being yet in its infancy; we think it is destined to become the paramount interest of the State. People generally are using more fruit than in former years, and as a proof of the success of the fruit interest in California, fruits of all kinds have brought better prices of late years than formerly. Our fruits are being sent to all parts of the world, and find a ready market. We are in the center of the commercial world, and from present indications we are to be the world's great fruit center. The low freights recently secured, and the lower rates which we still expect to get, will enable us to find market for all we can raise.

☞ Those varieties which we consider most valuable we have cultivated in larger quantities, and are indicated by an asterisk, thus (*).

We are also extensively engaged in Fruit Packing and Shipping, and flatter ourselves that we are competent to judge of the best kinds of fruit to grow for profit. We make it a point not to recommend or send out any new varieties until we have fully tested them ourselves, and proved them worthy of cultivation. Our Nurseries, so far, have been kept clear of the Scale Bug pest, and we are determined by constant vigilance to keep them so.

READ CAREFULLY THE TERMS OF SALE.

First—The articles in the following list will be furnished at the annexed prices only, when the quantities specified are taken. Moreover, these prices are intended for a reasonable assortment of varieties. When parties order long lists of only one or two trees of a kind, for such bills extra charge will be made.

☞ Second—When parties order specific varieties we will follow their instructions so far as practicable. But as it often occurs that we have run out of certain varieties, or may not have of the age and size ordered, we reserve the right to substitute in such cases other varieties equally good, unless positively instructed not to do so.

☞ Third—We will use every effort to avoid mistakes in varieties, for we fully realize that our success in the nursery business depends upon the reliability of our labels; but as there is such a margin for mistakes and misunderstanding (as above indicated), we will not warrant against errors or apparent mistakes in varieties, only to this extent, we will replace, free of charge, all trees that do not prove true to name, or we will refund in cash the original cost of such trees, with 10 per cent. interest per annum on said amount. (See fig. 2 on 1st page.)

Fourth—All trees are carefully labeled and packed in the best manner for shipping, for which a charge will be made sufficient to cover the cost of material and labor. As trees are often delayed in transit and roughly handled, it is much better to pay a small sum to have them securely packed than to have them poorly packed for nothing.

Fifth—All orders should be made in a separate list, and not mixed up with the body of the letter.

Write in a plain, legible hand, the name of the person and the place to which the goods are to go; also the route by which they are to be shipped. In the absence of such directions we will ship according to our best judgment, and will deliver to railroad or boat, all goods free of charge, but will not be responsible for accidents or delays which may occur in transit.

☞ TERMS OF PAYMENT.—CASH, or sufficient guarantee that the money will be forwarded on receipt of trees

For extra large trees and plants above the sizes mentioned, extra prices will be charged, and smaller ones lower in proportion.

Money may be sent by Express, Draft or Post-office Order, at our risk; but if sent in any other way, at sender's risk.

☞ Agents wanted in every community, to whom a liberal commission will be paid. Correspondence solicited.

☞ Any error of ours in filling orders will be cheerfully rectified on receiving notice, provided such notice be given within ten days from the receipt of goods.

CATALOGUE.

☞ In selecting varieties to propagate, we have endeavored to select only such varieties as can be profitably cultivated on this Coast, though all may not succeed well in any one locality. Experience and observation have taught us that the most profitable orchards are those containing but a few choice kinds. It is a great mistake to plant a long list of kinds in one orchard.

☞ A long list of varieties with a very few trees of a kind, is a provoking curse to the nurseryman, and a perpetual curse to the planter.

APPLE TREES.

☞ Our stock of Trees comprises all the leading and popular sorts, and is unsurpassed in vigor, thrift and hardiness. There is so much variation in climate on this Coast that the time of ripening of the several fruits can only be approximately named, and some apples that are classed as fall apples would be winter fruit in some localities. We would call special attention to our one-year extra apple trees; they are one year from bud, on strong roots, and are as large as two-year-old trees. We should prefer them to two-year trees to plant. A one-year tree has buds all along the body, hence a good head can be secured at any desired height.

Apples—Leading Varieties.	Each	10	100	1000
2 year, No. 1—4 to 6 feet, branched	$0 25	$2 00	$18 00	$150
1 year, No. 1—4 to 5 feet	20	1 75	15 00	120
1 year, No. 2—3 to 4 feet	18	1 40	12 00	100
1 year from bud—extra	25	2 00	18 00	150
Special varieties, 2 year, 4 to 6 feet, branched	35	3 00	25 00	...
Special varieties, 1 year, 4 to 5 feet—the Violett	30	2 50	20 00	...

SUMMER APPLES.

Red June--Small to medium, deep red, juicy and good. Ripens about the 20th of June.

Early Harvest—Large, pale yellow, flavor mild, sub-acid. Ripens about the 20th of June.

*Red Astrachan—Large, roundish, striped with deep crimson, thick bloom, very juicy and acid, good bearer; ripens in June.

*Williams' Favorite—Large, oblong, light red, juicy and good; ripens early in July.

AUTUMN APPLES.

*Alexander—Very large and beautiful, striped with red, one of the most profitable varieties for market; ripens about the 20th of July.

*White Astrachan—Large, oblate, skin very smooth and white, with faint red stripes, juicy, acid, valuable for market; ripens 10th to 20th of July.

*Gravenstein--Large, roundish, striped, very productive and good for market; ripens last of July to 1st of August.

*Santa Clara King—Large, roundish, skin yellow with red blush on exposed side, flesh crisp and juicy, good for all purposes; ripens 10th to 20th of August.

*Yellow Bellflower--Large, oblong, pale yellow, flesh tender, sub-acid, very good; ripens in September.

*Rhode Island Greening--Large, roundish, a little flattened, skin green, yellow flesh, tender, crisp, acid, juicy; ripens in October.

*King of Tompkins County--Large, conical shaped, skin yellowish, striped with red, flesh juicy, tender, vinous flavor, very good; November to February.

WINTER APPLES.

*Esopus Spitzenberg--Large, oblong, skin smooth, yellowish, covered with red stripes, flesh crisp and juicy, one of the best keepers; November to March.

Baldwin—Beautiful, large red apple, flesh white, crisp, very good; October to February.

Yellow Newton Pippin—Medium size, skin greenish yellow, flesh crisp, sub-acid; one of the very best, but does best in the Coast Counties; November to March.

Green Geneting, or Virginia Greening—A large, late, green-colored apple, conical shape, smooth oily skin, flesh crisp and juicy, fine for cooking, a good shipper; October to March.

Swaar—Large, pale yellow, with exceedingly rich, aromatic flavor, good; November to March. Does best in the mountains.

*Wine Sap—Medium, roundish, deep red, tree hardy and good bearer; November to March. One of the best for the mountains.

White Winter Pearmain—Above medium size, skin pale yellow, flesh yellow, crisp and juicy, very good; ripens in October to February. Best in the Coast Counties.

*Nickajack--Large, roundish, skin striped with crimson, flesh yellow, sub-acid flavor; November to February. A Southern apple.

Jonathan--Above medium size, conical shape, red striped, sometimes quite red; a good keeper, especially in the Coast Counties.

Hoover--A large, deep red apple, good flavor, good bearer and fine keeper, one of the best; November to March. Does splendidly near the Coast.

*Merkley's Red—A seedling variety of great promise. Original tree growing in the orchard of R. J. Merkley, on the Riverside road. Fruit large size, dark red, excellent flavor, crisp and juicy; a superior market variety.

Twenty Ounce Pippin—A very large, conical shaped apple, covered with dull red stripes, has a fine crisp sub-acid flavor, will cook well when only half grown, a very profitable market kind, tree a strong vigorous grower with upright habit.

CRAB APPLES.

Yellow Siberian—Fruit about an inch in diameter, fine rich yellow; good for jelly,

Transcendent--A beautiful variety of large size, yellow flesh, with red cheek; very productive.

Hyslop—A large, beautiful red crab, one of the best.

SPECIAL VARIETY.

☞ **The Violett**—This is a new apple, raised by J. W. Violett, of Ione. It is one of the largest apples grown, averaging nearly as large as the Gloria Monda ; conical shape, a beautiful red nearly all over, solid, firm and crisp, good flavor, fine shipper ; September to January. Tree strong grower with upright habit ; bark, on new wood' smooth, glossy and light, chestnut color, leaves quite peculiar—a rich glossy green.

PEARS.

The following list includes most of the kinds that have proved valuable in our locality. A succession of good bearing varieties is all that is needed.

PRICE OF TREES—Leading sorts.

2 year, No. 1—4 to 6 feet, branched	$0 30	$2 50	$20 00	$160
1 year, No. 1—4 to 5 feet	20	1 75	14 00	110
1 year, extra—4 to 6 feet	25	2 00	16 00	140
1 year 4 to 6 feet, special varieties	40	3 50	30 00	...

SUMMER PEARS.

Madeline—Medium size, pale yellowish green, flesh white, melting, juicy ; 20th of June.

Dearborn's Seedling—Small to medium, light yellow, flesh white, very juicy and melting ; ripens 20th of June.

*Bartlett—This pear is too well known to need any description from us.

AUTUMN PEARS.

Le Count—A new pear, recommended highly East, but we do not think much of it, though many still recommend it.

Kieler's Hybrid—A large roundish pear, recommended highly, but we have not tested it sufficiently to judge of its merits.

Chinese Pear—Fruit large, flavor not good, but tree highly ornamental, foliage large, rich green till late in Fall, when they turn red and hang a ong time. The Chinamen will pay 12 to 15 cents a pound for the fruit ; trees 1 year, No. 1, $1 each.

Beurre Hardy—Fruit large, skin greenish, covered with light russet, flesh buttery, melting and juicy, one of the best, ships well ; August.

Seckel—Small to medium, skin dull yellowish brown, with russet red cheek, flesh white, very juicy, perfection of flavor ; last of August.

Beurre d'Anjo—Large round pear, one of the best, good shipper.

Louis Bon De Jersey—A very sweet, delicious Autumn pear ; shaped much like the Bartlett only more elongated, greenish yellow with bright red cheeks ; flesh fine-grained and exceedingly fine flavored, good for drying, canning or shipping.

WINTER PEARS.

Beurre Clargeau—Fruit very large, skin yellow, covered with russet dots, flesh yellowish, good flavor, good shipper ; September to December.

Easter Beurre—Fruit large, skin yellowish green, with russety dots, flesh white, rich flavor, long keeper.

Winter Nelis—Medium size, greenish, russet, melting and juicy, rich flavor, good shipper ; October to December.

Beurre Boss—Large long russet pear, good flavor and good shipper, one of the very best ; October to April.

Winter Seckel—Above medium size, shaped much like the Bartlett and nearly as large, color and flavor much like the Fall Seckel, long keeper, good shipper.

P. Barry—A California seedling, originated by the late B. S. Fox, of San Jose ; a very large elongated russet pear, quite late, and a long keeper, can be kept till March ; an excellent pear for Eastern shipping, fine texture and excellent flavor when fully ripe.

Santa Ana—A new pear, originated at Santa Ana, in Los Angeles County. It is a large conical shaped pear, a bright golden yellow covered with russet ; it is an exceedingly handsome fruit, flesh fine-grained and free from all woody substance, with a flavor equal to the finest Winter Nelis or the famous Seckel ; it will eat well when picked from the tree, and yet will keep all Winter ; it is a very remarkable pear in this respect ; its shipping and keeping qualities cannot be excelled. We consider it a very valuable accession to our list of pears. The tree is a moderately strong grower, with upright habit, forming a close, compact head, makes a very handsome tree.

Special Varieties the P. Barry and Santa Ana.

PEACHES.

In order to secure healthy and vigorous trees it is necessary to prune severely. Their tendency in this State is to develop an immense number of fruit buds, and as they are not destroyed by frost, they produce more fruit than the tree can mature. The consequence is it is small and inferior. The tree should be trained low and pruned regularly every year. By this practice the breaking of limbs is avoided, and the fruit grows much larger and finer. Many new varieties have been produced in the past few years, so that the fruiting season has been materially lengthened. The following list contains most of the valuable kinds, but the period of ripening varies so much in different localities that the time given can only be considered approximate. *Good peach trees are scarce this season.*

PRICE OF TREES—Leading Varieties.

1 year, No. 1—4 to 6 feet...$0 25 $2 00 $18 00 $150
1 year, No. 1—4 to 6 feet, new and rare kinds................ 35 3 00 25 00 ...

JUNE BUDS.

1st class, 2 to 3 feet... 20 1 75 15 00 120
2d class, 1½ to 2 feet............ .... 12 1 00   9 00   80

Only have June buds of Early Crawford, Tuscan Cling and Stilson. Dormant buds of all the kinds on list.

Dormant buds in quantity at special rates ; prices on application.

FREESTONES.

Yellow St. Johns—A fine yellow freestone, very much like the Early Crawford, and ripens a little earlier. Shipping qualities not yet tested by us.

Brigg's Red May—Fruit medium to large, deep red cheek, flesh firm, good market variety ; 1st June.

Waterloo—Medium size, deep red, curly.

Alexander—Medium size, white flesh, with clear red cheek ; ripens here 10th, June.

Early Rivers—Large early peach, white with red cheeks, half cling, tender and juicy, good flavor.

***Hale's Early**—Medium to large, white with red check, one of the best market varieties ; ripens here 10th to 20th June.

Foster—A magnificent large, yellow peach, red cheek, good flavor ; July.

***Early Crawford**—A magnificent large, yellow peach, too well known to need any description from us : 1st July.

Late Crawford—Much the same as Early Crawford, but ripening two weeks later.

Jones' Seedling—Origin, Sacramento ; large, yellow flesh, with red cheek, excellent flavor ; 10th of August.

***Susquehanna**—Very large yellow peach, red check, of best quality ; July.

Keyport White—A large white peach, with red cheek, good for shipping, canning or drying; last of August.

Ward's Late Free—Large white flesh peach, good for canning ; September.

***Salway**—Large yellow peach, dull red check, good flavor, superior market variety ; 1st September.

***Bilyeu's Late October**—Large, white flesh, red cheek, very fine flavor, good shipper ; ripens 20th October, tree strong grower, doesn't curl, freestone, does best in foot-hills.

Wheatland—A large yellow free, bright red cheek, ripening a little later than Late Crawford ; bids fair to be one of our best peaches.

Wager—A large yellow tree, with pale red cheek, flesh quite dry, one of the best for drying, probably as good as the Muir.

Muir—Almost a fac-simile of the Wager, a little higher color ; an excellent peach for drying.

Stilson (California Seedling)—A very large, yellow fleshed peach, bright red cheeks, with dark crimson stripes, one of the very best market sorts ; ripens two weeks later than Late Crawford.

Boquier (California Seedling)—A very large yellow peach, with bright red cheeks excellent flavor, good shipper, freestone ; 1st September.

Salway--A large, late yellow tree, with faint red cheeks : ripens 10th to 20th September ; good shipper.

CLINGSTONES.

Day's Yellow Cling (California Seedling--A very large, yellow flesh, with red cheek good market variety ; August.

***Orange Cling**--A very large yellow flesh, with red cheek, a well known variety ; August.

Heath Cling--Large, white flesh, superior flavor ; 1st September.

***George's Late Cling** (California Seedling)--Very large, white flesh, with bright red cheek, superior quality ; September.

Lemon Cling--Large, yellow, with bright red cheek, a fine market peach, good shipper.

Edwards' Cling (The same called by C. W. Reed, the California)--A California Seedling, produced by the late Mr. Edwards, near this city. It is a large, yellow fleshed peach, highly colored, a fine market or shipping fruit.

Twenty Ounce Cling--A very large yellow fleshed cling, bright red cheek, one of the best clings, but does not usually bear heavy crops.

Albright Cling (California Seedling)--A very large, yellow peach, with bright red cheek. A fine shipper and good peach in every particular.

NEW AND RARE PEACHES.—SPECIAL VARIETIES.

Blood Leaved Peach--Leaves blood red, very beautiful as an ornamental tree; trees $1 00 each.

Tuscan Cling--A very large yellow cling, ripens same time as Early Crawford, a fine shipper, and its early ripening makes it very valuable.

Winter's Cling (a Seedling from the Heath Cling)--Original tree raised by C. H. Wolfskill, of Winters. The old tree is now 32 years old and still bearing good crops of fruit, and Mr. Wolfskill says it has never curled or mildewed, while the Heath Cling does both. The Winters is almost a fac simile of the Heath, except it is slightly larger, and much better shaped. It possesses all the excellent qualities of the Heath, is larger, color a beautiful creamy white, with red blush on exposed side ; is white to the pit, and therefore a fine canning peach It is very solid and a fine shipper.

McDevit Cling (a California seedling, raised by Neal McDevit, of Placer County) --This is one of the largest peaches we have ever seen, many of them weighing one pound each ; peaches very uniform in size, rich golden yellow, becoming quite red when ripe, flesh very solid and firm, an excellent shipper, superior flavor ; tree a good and regular bearer.

Tuscany Cling--An exceedingly large yellow cling peach (from Italy), deep yellow with bright red cheek, very late, good shipper, tree hardy and strong grower, don't curl or mildew, and consequently good for the Coast Counties.

French Cling--A large, late, yellow fleshed cling, very large firm fruit, good shipper. One of the best of our new peaches ; tree hardy and strong grower.

NECTARINES.—Leading Varieties.

1 year, No. 1—4 to 6 feet.................................$0 25 $2 00 $18 00

New White--Large, creamy white, freestone : very superior for drying.

Stanwick--Large, greenish white, splashed with red ; freestone.

Boston--Medium to large red freestone, fine flavor ; good for drying.

Clement's Nectarine--A large red nectarine, good flavor ; will make a good shipper ; tree a good and regular bearer.

APRICOTS.

This fruit is produced in large quantities, and seems to be profitable to the growers. As all varieties seem to be equally hardy, and the limit of the season is short, it is proper to grow only such as are large and productive. The following varieties are considered the most profitable:

PRICE OF TREES—Leading varieties.

1 year, No. 1—4 to 6 feet on peach root.................	$0 30	$2 50	$25 00	$200
1 year, No. 1—4 to 6 feet, on Myrobolan.................	35	3 00	25 00	200
New and rare kinds, 4 to 6 feet.......................	40	3 50	30 00	...
JUNE BUDS.				
1st class, 2 to 3 feet, on peach root.....................	20	1 75	15 00	140
2d class, 1½ to 2 feet.................................	15	1 25	11 00	120

Store and Principal Office, 102 to 110 J Street, Sacramento, Cal.

Routier's Peach Apricot—A new kind from Mr. Routier's orchard. Large size, skin yellow in the shade, deep orange mottled, or splashed with red in the sun; flesh rich and juicy, very high flavor; good market variety.

Early Royal—Medium size, good flavor, very productive.

Moorpark—Large, orange color, moderate bearer, but of the highest flavor.

Hemskirk—Very much like the Moorpark; one of the best; tree good bearer.

SPECIAL VATIETY.—Newcastle Early—A new variety originated by M. C. Silva & Son, of Newcastle, California. Medium size, round, well shaped, a shade smaller than the Royal; two weeks earlier than the Royal; very valuable on account of its earliness; tree a good and regular bearer; fruit ships well.

PLUMS.

The Plum and Prune succeeds admirably in this State, and we can and should not only produce for home consumption, but export large quantities instead of importing. Many varieties of Plums and Prunes have a tendency to over-bear, and, to secure a good article, the fruit should be carefully thinned out. This should be done when it is one-third or one-half grown. Those who are willing to take these pains will be amply repaid by a superior quality of fruit, and a more remunerative price.

PRICE OF TREES—Leading varieties.

1 year, 6 to 7 feet, extra, on peach root	$0 25	$2 00	$18 00	$150
1 year, No. 1—4 to 6 feet	20	1 80	15 00	135
1 year, 5 to 6 feet, extra, on Myrobol root	30	2 50	18 00	175
1 year, No. 1—4 to 5 feet, on Myrobol root	25	2 00	16 00	150
Special sorts, 1 year from bud, extra	35	3 00	25 00	...

Peach Plum—Fruit very large, round, greenish white, with red cheek; flesh yellow, sweet and firm; early; good for shipping.

*Columbia—Fruit large size; skin brownish purple, with fawn colored specks; flesh yellow, sugary; excellent; one of the best for shipping.

Duane's Purple—Large, reddish purple; flesh juicy and moderately sweet; good shipper.

Victoria (or Oakshade Prune)—Medium size, beautiful red plum; good shipper, and superior for drying, being very free and quite a dry meated plum; very prolific.

Coe's Golden Drop—Fruit large, oval, flesh yellow, firm, rich and sweet; adheres to stone; good for canning and ships well.

*Gros Prune D'Agen (Hungarian Prune)—Very large, oval, violet red; very prolific, often growing double; good flavor; a valuable market kind; best shipper.

Yellow Egg—A very large elongated plum; golden yellow; adheres to the stone; quite juicy, rich sub-acid flavor; the best known canning variety and ships well.

Washington—Large, round, greenish yellow; good for canning or drying.

*Japanese Plum (known as the Kelsey Plum)—Fruit very large, as large as an ordinary peach; roundish, or inclined to be conical; color greenish yellow, with faint red cheek; adheres closely to the pit, which is very small; flesh firm and juicy; it is the best keeper known. We have kept them this year in a perfect state of preservation for thirty days after being picked from the tree. We know of no plum that can be shipped so long a distance; sold readily this season in the East for $4 00 per box; tree hardy, but a slow grower, inclined to dwarf; a heavy and regular bearer. Trees, 1 year, No. 1, 4 to 6 feet, 35 cents each; $30 per 100. No. 2, 3 to 4 feet, 25 cents each; $20 per 100.

NEW JAPANESE PLUMS.

Prunis Pissardi—A medium size plum; red, fine flesh, good flavor, long keeper; the tree is very ornamental, foliage blood red. Trees, 1 year, No. 1, $1 00 each.

Prunis Simoni—Quite large, somewhat elongated, bright yellow, red cheek; very fine fruit; good for shipping or drying; tree a strong grower; bears heavily. Price of trees, 1 year, No. 1 (on Myrobolan), 40 cents each; $30 per 100.

Blood Plum—A fine, handsome, strong growing tree; fruit above medium size, blood red both outside and inside, very handsome and fine flavor. Trees, 1 year, No. 1 (on Myrobolan), 50 cents each; $40 per 100.

PRUNES.

PRICE OF TREES.

Common sorts, on peach root, 1 year, No 1—4 to 6 feet......$0	25	$2 00	$16 00	$150
French prune, on peach root, 1 year, No 1—4 to 5 feet......	30	2 50	20 00	180
French prune, on peach root, 1 year, extra, 5 to 7 feet	30	2 50	22 00	200
French prune, on Myrobolan root, 1 year, 4 to 5 feet........	30	2 50	22 00	200
French prune, on Myrobolan root, 1 year, extra, 5 to 7 feet..	35	3 00	25 00	200
French prune De Ent, on Myrobolan root, 1 year, No. 1—4 to 6 feet...	30	2 50	25 00	200
French prune, June buds, on peach root ; 1st class, 2½ to 3 ft.	20	1 75	15 00	140
French prune, June buds, on peach root ; 2d class, 1½ to 2 ft	15	1 25	12 00	100
French prune, on peach, spring buds, 3 to 5 feet.............	25	2 00	18 00	150
French prune, June buds, or Myrobolan ; 1st class, 2 to 3 ft.	20	1 75	15 00	125
French prune, June buds, on Myrobolan; 2d class, 1½ to 2 ft	15	1 25	12 00	110

Tragedy prune, June buds; see Tragedy prune below. Same prices as French prune.

VARIETIES.

*Petit Prune D'Agen (French Prune)- Small to medium, reddish purple, very sweet, parts freely from stone ; one of the best varieties for drying as a prune.

*Silver Prune—Originated in Oregon. The fruit is a fac simile of Coe's Golden Drop, except it is a darker green, and it is yet a question whether it should be called a prune or a plum. It is a very superior shipper, and it certainly makes an excellent dried fruit, either pitted or unpitted ; makes a splendid prune.

Bul arian Prunes—A very prolific, dark colored prune, larger than the French Prune, and by some considered a very valuable prune, but we have not yet tested it sufficient to judge of its value.

Prune D'Agen (or Prune d'Ent) –Very like the Petit or French Prune, only larger and more desirable. It is now demonstrated that this Prune will bear as heavy crops as the French or Petite Prune, and as it is so much larger and of equally as good a quality, it is of course the most valuable of the two. There has been some fears that it might not be a good bearer, but that doubt has been dispelled. Many trees are now bearing heavy crops in this State. Price of trees same as the Petite Prune on Myrobolan root. It will not grow on peach root, but must be grown on plum root. This is the same prune recommended by Felix Gillet, of Nevada City, as the true Gros Prune.

German Prune—A large purple prune, flesh greenish yellow, very sweet, always brings fancy prices as a fresh fruit ; it is a good shipper and makes an excellent dried prune, tree a strong grower and a good and regular bearer.

Tragedy Prune—A new prune originated by Mr. Runyon, near Courtland, in this county. It would seem to be a cross between the German Prune and Purple Duane. Fruit medium size, nearly as large as the Duane Purple Plum ; looks much like it, only it is more elongated ; skin dark purple, flesh yellowish green, very rich and sweet, frees readily from the pit. Its early ripening (in June) makes it very valuable as a shipping fruit. Coming as it does before any other good plum, it will always bring fancy prices, both in the local and Eastern market. So far it has no rival. We believe we are the first to work it. The first to get orchards of this fruit will make fortunes out of it.

CHERRIES.

As a pleasant and refreshing dessert fruit the cherry is everywhere highly esteemed. The early season at which it ripens, its juiciness, delicacy and richness render it always acceptable. It thrives best in rich dry loam. The trees should be trained low, that the foliage may protect the trunk, which should never be exposed to the sun. We cultivate only a few of the leading kinds, a brief description of which may be found below :

PRICE OF TREES.

2 year, No. 1—4 to 6 feet, branched........................$0	35	$2 50	$20 00	$150
1 year, No. 1—4 to 6 feet.................................	25	2 00	18 00	150
1 year, No. 2—3 to 4 feet.................................	20	1 80	15 00	125
1 year, No. 1—4 to 6 feet—Schmidt, Bigarreau & Centennial.	35	3 00	25 00	...

VARIETIES.

Knight's Early Black—Large, black, tender, juicy, rich and high flavored; early. This is the earliest good variety.

Early Purple—Guigne, medium size, black; quite early.

*Black Tartarian—Very large, purplish black, rich and juicy; one of the best varieties.

Governor Wood—A fine, early cherry, white, shaded with red, tender, juicy and delicious.

Royal Ann (or Napoleon Bigarreau)—Very large, pale yellow, with bright red cheek; flesh very firm, juicy and sweet; good shipper.

Black Oregon—Sometimes called Lewelling or Black Republican; a large, late black cherry; good flavor, long keeper and ships well.

Rochport Bigarreau—A large, early, flesh colored cherry; valuable for canning or drying; it is also a good shipper; its very early ripening makes it very valuable; it will always command a good price.

QUINCE.

Orange—Large, roundish; bright golden yellow; the best for general use.

Portugal—Fruit of largest size, oblong, skin bright yellow, mild flavor.

Apple—Shaped much like the orange, color a little darker.

PRICE OF TREES.

2 year, No. 1—4 to 6 feet	$0 35	$3 00	$25 00	....
1 year, No. 1—3 to 4 feet	30	2 50	20 00	....

FIGS.

The fig is one of the most valuable plants ever cultivated by man. It is more nutritious and contains more medicinal properties than any other fruit (excepting possibly the olive). Its cultivation has been sadly neglected, and such neglect would seem almost criminal in a country like California, where the soil and climate is peculiarly adapted to its successful cultivation. All that is wanted is the right varieties and proper attention to make this fruit exceedingly profitable, and a great source of wealth to the State. A great many varieties have been imported from different countries, and quite a number of them are good; but we still have doubts about our having the best kind of the true fig of commerce. It is now thought by some that the Verdoni (or the so-called White Adriatic) is the genuine, but this may yet prove a mistake. While we have the trees for sale, we would hesitate to guarantee it to be the right kind until we can see it further tested and demonstrated. Most of the white figs we have will crack open and sour in process of drying, when dried in the sun, and we have noticed the same trait in this fig, though not so bad as some other white kinds, and we regard it as one among our best white figs. By recent experiments we have demonstrated that any of the kinds can be successfully dried by artificial heat. Even the San Pedro, when dried in a dryer, makes an exceedingly fine product equal if not superior to the imported fig.

PRICE OF TREES.

2 year, No. 1—4 to 6 feet, branched	$0 25	$2 00	$15 00	$120
1 year, No. 1—3 to 4 feet	18	1 50	12 00	100

WHITE ADRIATIC.

2 year, 4 to 6 feet	40	3 50	30 00	250
1 year, 3 to 4 feet	30	2 50	23 00	180

VARIETIES.

We cultivate only a few of our best known varieties, as follows:

Large Purple—One of the most fruitful sorts; large size; dark purple, very sweet, good flavor; drys well.

Brown Ischia—Very large, skin light or chestnut brown, very sweet and excellent.

Pacific White—Fruit medium size, fine grained, very sweet, seeds very small; very white and exceedingly fine flavored when dry; but the skin when dry is thicker and more tough than the imported; that and its small size is the only objection to it. It never cracks and sours in drying. The tree is a strong grower, very hardy, and always good shaped, a fine shade or avenue tree. A good, regular bearer.

San Pedro (usually called **White Smyrna**)--A very large, dirty or rusty white fig ; good flavor ; one of the best as a green or fresh fruit ; valuable for that purpose, but does not dry well if dried in the sun, as it cracks and sours in drying, but makes a very superior product when dried by artificial heat. We regard it as one of the best figs for profit we have if properly handled ; the tree is rather a slow grower, but a great bearer ; exceedingly prolific.

Verdoni (White Adriatic)—Above medium size, greenish white, skin thin, rather coarse grained ; quite red inside ; seeds large, flavor fair to good. We have not tested it as a drying fig, and consequently cannot say more than above mentioned.

ALMONDS.

Nut growing should be carried on far more extensively in this State than it now is. Almonds are a sure crop over a large area of the State. They can be raised to profit at lower rates than the usual current prices. Our foothill lands seem to be peculiarly adapted to their culture. We know of no district in the State where they do better than in the foothills, at an altitude of from 600 to 2,000 feet above the sea level.

PRICE OF TREES.

Almond, on almond, Spring buds, 3 to 5 feet	$0 25	$2 00	$18 00	$150
1 year, No. 1--4 to 6 feet, branched	30	2 50	22 00	200
Special kinds, 1 year, No. 1--4 to 6 feet ; Hatch's I. X. L., Nonpariel and Drake's Seedling	35	3 00	25 00	200
Almonds, June buds on peach, I. X. L., Nonpariel and Drake's Seedling ; 1st class, 2 to 3 feet	20	1 75	15 00	140
Almonds, June buds on peach, I. X. L., Nonpariel and Drake's Seedling ; 2d class, 1½ to 2 feet	15	1 40	12 00	110

VARIETIES.

Languedoc—A well-known old standard variety.

Routier's New Languedoc--A new seedling from Joseph Routier's orchard. A fac-simile of the Languedoc, except the shell is a little softer ; tree moderately strong grower, and very prolific.

Routier's Soft Shell--From same orchard as above. Shell quite soft, but not soft enough to crumb'e ; tree moderately strong grower, very prolific.

Blower's Languedoc--A Languedoc grown by R. B. Blower, of Woodland. It is a fine nut and a good and regular bearer.

Twin Almond--A new seedling originated by J. Routier. A very large smooth nut, all with double kernels. Shell soft as the Languedoc ; tree hardy and good bearer.

A. T. Hatch's New Seedling Almonds, I. X. L. Nonpariel and Drake's Seedling.

Texas Prolific -A new seedling variety originated at Dalis, Texas. Nut full as large as the Languedoc, but softer shell, very smooth and bright color, well filled with a very sweet meat ; tree full as strong grower, and very much resembles the Languedoc tree. It is a very heavy and regular bearer. It is the only variety that will fruit well at Dalis, Texas. We consider it by all odds the finest and most desirable almond we have ever seen. We have but a very few trees this year,we h old them at $1 each. They are very cheap at that to any one who wants to get a start of them.

OTHER NUT TREES.

Eastern Black Walnuts--A well known tree, valuable for timber. Two-year trees, 50 cents each.

California Black Walnuts—A native specie, valuable for shade and nuts. Very productive. 2 year trees, 5 to 7 feet, well branched, 30c each, per hundred $25. 1 year trees, 3 to 5 feet, 20 each, per hundred $15.

English Walnuts—Good shade and profitable nut tree. 2 year trees, 5 to 8 feet, 50c each, $40 per hundred ; small trees 20 to 30 cents each.

Praeparturien Walnut –A very fine table nut, trees of dwarfish habit, bears quite young and heavy crop. Trees 2 to 3 feet, 30c each, $25 per hundred ; 3 to 4 feet, 40c each, $35 per hundred ; 4 to 5 feet, 50c each, $40 per hundred.

Pecan Nut--A fine nut, does well on deep soil. Tree 1 year, 1 to 1½ feet, 12½c each, $10 per hundred. 2 year, 2 to 3 feet, 25c each, $20 per hundred. 2 year, 3 to 4 feet, 40c each, $35 per hundred.

Chestnuts (Italian or Spanish)--Trees 1 to 1½ feet, 15c each, $10 per hundred. 2 to 3 feet, 25c each, $20 per hundred. 3 to 4 feet, 40c each, $35 per hundred.

Chestnut (American Sweet)--Same sizes, same prices as the Italian.

GRAPES.

As most kinds of foreign grapes thrive well and produce fruit in abundance, we have only to choose such as suit our wants and fancies. We will name a few of the best in their season.

PRICE OF ASSORTED VARIETIES.	EACH.	PER 100.	PER M
2 year—No. 1	$0 08	$6 00	$40 00
1 year—No. 1	04	3 00	25 00
1 year—No. 2	03	2 00	15 00

Grape vines or cuttings in large lots at special rates, very low. Price on application.

VARIETIES.

*White Muscat (Muscat of Alexandria)--Fine, large, white grape, musk flavored, good market variety, either for shipping or raisins.

*Muscatelle Gordo Blanco—Resembling the Muscat; berries large, less musky flavor ; good raisin variety.

Black Hamburg—A very fine, large black grape, good quality and productive.

Black Prince—A splendid large black grape, good market variety, good shipper.

*Flame Tokay--A magnificent large, red grape ; very firm, vigorous grower and productive ; good shipper.

Zinfandel--A medium size, black grape, close compact bunches, very productive, valuable for wine.

Seedless Sultana—Small white grape, clusters large. It makes a fine raisin for culinary purposes, at the same time it is a fine wine grape. It is the only grape we know of that is good for both raisins and wine.

Emperor--A large red grape, resembling the Tokay, ripens quite late, is an excellent shipper, its lateness and long keeping qualities makes a very valuable grape; does splendidly on our granite soils in the foothills ; the vines of this variety should be staked up to get the best results.

Black Morocco--A very large late black grape, a splendid shipping variety.

Cornischon--The largest and latest grape we cultivate, berries quite elongated, firm, solid, and skin thick and tough, which will enable it to carry farther than any other grape. Sells well in the East.

Berger--A large white wine grape, very productive, makes an excellent wine, is a very profitable grape to raise.

Mattaro--A medium sized black grape, close compact bunches, an abundant bearer, makes a superior wine. This grape is always in good demand as a wine grape, brings good price, is a very profitable grape to grow.

Vites Cal.fornica--The wild grape of California, used for stock to graft on. Good 1 year plant, $1 50 per 100 ; $12 00 per 1000.

CURRANTS.

PRICE.	EACH.	PER 100.
2 year—No. 1	$0 12½	$10 00
1 year—No. 1	8	6 00

The only varieties of any value here are the **Cherry** and **Fertile de Palneu**, though we keep a few of several other kinds to please the fancies of our customers.

GOOSEBERRIES.

AMERICAN.	EACH.	PER 100.
Houghton's Seedling, 2 year	$0 20	$15 00
Houghton's Seedling, 1 year	15	10 00
Mountain Seedling	Same price,	

ENGLISH.		
Large English Crown Bob, Smith's White, Klee Variety, Birkley and Oregon Champion	25	15 00

BLACKBERRIES.

Price..........4 cents each | $3 00............per 100 | $10 00............per 1,000

Wilson's Early—Fruit large, productive and early.

Dorchester—A fine sweet berry.

Kittatinny—Good market variety ; large and good flavor.

Lawton—Good market variety for this locality ; large and late.

Crandall's Early—This berry was brought from Texas some years ago and planted on the place of Dr. J. R. Crandall, of Auburn, Placer County. (The origin of this berry is not known to us.) Here it was discovered that it was not only an excellent berry and prolific bearer, but was also found to ripen three weeks earlier than the Lawton, and continues to blossom and bear fruit until late in the Fall. We have often picked good, ripe, well developed berries as late as the last days of December. The wood of the vine is light colored, resembling the Wilson's Early, but is a much stronger grower. The berry is as large as the Lawton, fine flavor, firm and solid. It is an excellent shipper. Price, $1 per dozen, 85 per 100, $15 per 1,000. Fifty plants at 100 rates ; 500 at 1,000 rates.

RASPBERRIES.

Price..........4 cents each | $3 00............per 100 | $15 00............per 1,000

Fastolff, Franconia, Red Antwerp, Naomi, Hudson River Antwerp and Cuthbert.

The **Hansel**—A fine early berry. Its early ripening makes it very valuable. It is a good bearer and ships well. Price of plants, 6 cents each, $4 00 per 100, $20 00 per 1,000.

The **Barter Raspberry**—This berry was produced, or at least first cultivated, by Mr. Wm. Barter, of Penryn, Placer County. Some years ago a friend gave Mr. B. two raspberry plants. One of them died, and he, having discovered the living plant to be a berry of superior variety, propagated it as rapidly as possible and it has proved to be one of the most profitable berries we have. Price of plants, 4 cents each, $3 00 per 100, $20 00 per 1,000.

Herstine—A very large red raspberry, much like the Barter in all respects, but is a stronger grower. Price of plants, 4 cents each, $3 00 per 100, $20 00 per 1,000.

STRAWBERRIES.

Price.........50 cents per doz. | $1 00..........per 100 | $6 00...........per 1,000

Triomphe de Gand, Sharpless, Forest Rose, Monarch of the West, Captain Jack, Champion, and many other new varieties not fully tested.

ESCULENT ROOTS.

Asparagus..2 cents each; $10 00 per 1,000
Rhubarb...20 to 50 cents each
Hop Roots..................... 50 cents per doz.; $1 50 per 100; $10 00 per 1,000
(Large lots at special rates, very low.)

OLIVES.

Many localities in California are peculiarly adapted to the cultivation of the Olive, and we think there are none more favorable for its culture than the foothills, at an altitude of from 500 to 1,200 feet above the sea level. We have tested them thoroughly at our place near Penryn, Placer County, and they grow and bear splendidly, with or without irrigation. As to varieties, we believe the old Mission, or Spanish Olive, is the best for general use. It is good for both oil and pickles. It is harder to propagate than some other kinds, but the tree is hardy and long-lived, and not subject to disease.

The Picolene is more easily propagated, tree a rapid grower when young, but will never grow as large as the Spanish. It bears very young and is a constant and good bearer. The fruit is small but very rich in oil and makes a fine quality of light (mild) oil, preferred (by amateurs) to the heavier oil, and the tree is such an abundant bearer that an acre of them will yield a very large amount of fine oil. Some experiments we witnessed lately have raised this Olive very much in our estimation. In fact it now bids fair to become the favorite Olive in this country.

There are some new kinds being introduced of late. We have a few of them, but have not seen them fruited enough to judge of their merit.

☞ Olive trees are very scarce this season, and parties desiring to secure them will do well to order early.

PRICE OF TREES.	Each.	Per 100.	Per M
Spanish (or Mission)—4 to 5 feet	$1 00	$60 00	......
" " 3 to 4 feet	75	40 00	......
" " 2 to 3 feet	50	40 00	......
Picolene—3 to 4 feet, fine stocky trees	50	......	......
" 2 to 3 feet (stocky)	40	35 00	......
" 12 to 14 inches	20	18 00	......
" 10 to 12 inches	18	15 00	$140 00

Olive trees in propagating boxes 4 to 12 inches in length; prices given on application. At this writing prices have not been established on that class of stock, the same is true to a great extent on all kinds of Box plants, but we will be in position during the selling season to give as good terms as other nurserymen.

ORANGE AND LEMON TREES.

In view of the great scarcity of Orange trees in this State, and our inability to get California-grown trees, we (early in the spring of 1887) sent buds to Florida (of the genuine Washington Navel from Riverside, Cal.), and had a large lot buded to order. Later in the season our nurseryman, Mr. Williamson, went to Florida and bought a large lot of the best known Florida kinds. We shipped out and sold last winter all of these that were large enough, and the smaller ones and others grown to order for us, will be brought out this season, and we do not hesitate to say that we shall bring out for sale this season the finest lot of Orange and Lemon trees that was ever offered in this State. Our trees are not only fine trees but they are all of the very best varieties in America. Below we give a brief description of kinds. All are true to name, having been buded to our order; also trained or shaped especially to suit the California demand. Our success in handling these Florida trees exceeded our most sanguine expectations last season. With the exception of one car that arrived late in the season and got heated in transit, there was not to exceed 2 per cent. that failed to grow when planted—the smallest per cent. of failure we've ever knew with Orange trees. We will take contracts to plant large lots of these Orange and Lemon trees on reasonable terms and guarantee them to grow, thus showing our faith in this stock.

☞ Most of these trees are budded on the Florida Sour Stock, and we believe that to be the hardiest and best root, but we have trees worked on the Sweet root and can furnish them to parties preferring that stock. We can also furnish large Sweet seedlings for planting in orchard ; also large Sour orange trees for avenue planting. There is no finer avenue or street tree than the sour orange.

·PRICE OF TREES.

Leading varieties, budded on Florida sour and sweet stocks, naked roots :

2 year buds on 4 and 5 year roots	$1 50	$12 50 $100 00	$800
1 year buds on 3 and 4 year roots	1 25	10 00	80 00	700

Genoa and Sicily lemons same price as orange trees.

VILLA FRANCA LEMON.

2 year buds on 4 and 5 year old roots	$1 50	$12 00 $110 00	$1000
Large 1 year buds on 3 and 4 year roots	1 35	11 00	100 00	900
Mandarin and Tangarine 2 year buds on 4 to 5 year roots			$1 50 each
Mandarin and Tangarine 1 year buds on 3 to 4 year roots			$1 30 each

We can furnish any of the above trees, well bagged, at an additional cost of 15 cents for one year, and 20 cents each for 2 year buds. This is to cover cost of bagging and extra freight, but we know from past experience that bagging orange trees is a useless expense.

Sweet (Indian River) seedlings, 4 to 5 years old, ¾ to 1¼ inch
    in diameter ....60c each, $45 00 per 100

Sour orange trees for street planting, 4 to 6 years old, ¾ to
    1¼ inch in diameter ....60c each, $50 00 per 100

4

We will give special rates to dealers, nurserymen or parties buying in large lots to plant.

Parties asking for special rates should state varieties and number of trees wanted.

BRIEF DESCRIPTION OF VARIETIES (All Hardy).

Parson Brown—Fruit medium size, oblong in shape, smooth, high color, very sweet, ripens early, is sweet as soon as it begins to turn, grand bearer ; tree has some thorns.

Homosassa--Fruit medium size, very heavy, skin quite thin and smooth, high color, rich and glossy in appearance, exceedingly fine flavor, one of the best market oranges known, good keeper, always brings fancy prices, good bearer, tree thorny.

Magnum Bonum—A very large orange, a little flattened, skin smooth and glossy, fruit heavy and of excellent quality, ripens early, tree very prolific, thorny.

Peerless—Fruit large and round, smooth skin, one of the best market sorts, tree a heavy and regular bearer and strong grower.

Hart's Tardiff—A large round orange of good quality, its chief excellence consisting in its lateness ; it does not ripen till May or June, and will hang on the tree in good eating condition till August ; tree strong grower and good bearer.

Jaffa—Imported from the city of Joppa, in Syria, a very fine medium size orange of superior quality, tree nearly thornless.

Mandarin—A very small orange, always brings fancy prices ; is called a kid-glove variety.

Tangerine—Much like the Mandarin, only larger, leaf of tree is broader and the fruit is a dark red color ; generally brings double the price of other oranges.

Mediterrenean Sweet and Washington Navel—Both too well known in this State to need describing.

Beache's No. 1—A very fine sweet orange ; ripens very early ; brings fancy prices.

Beache's No. 5—A large fine late orange, much of the same type of the Hart's Tardiff, valuable on account of its very late ripening.

Nonpareil—A large handsome and good flavored orange ; a fine market variety ; tree strong grower and hardy.

LEMONS.

Sicily—The common lemon of commerce ; an old standard variety.

Genoa—Much like the Sicily, but rather larger ; a good market kind, tree hardy and a good bearer.

Villa Franba (a new variety)—This lemon has become the favorite in Florida ; the fruit is of a very superior quality, tree a strong grower, a heavy and regular bearer, excelling all other varieties in productiveness. The tree is exceedingly hardy ; it withstood the heavy freeze in Florida in January, 1886, in the same orchards where all other kinds, and also orange trees, were killed. It ripens in July and August, thus coming in the hot season when lemons are most needed and when the market is bare of other citrus fruits. It is emphatically the lemon for profit.

Deciduous Shade and Ornamental Trees.

POPLARS AND LOCUSTS.

	Each	Per 100
No. 1—2 to 2½ inches diameter	$1 00	$60 00
No. 2—1½ to 2 inches diameter	50	40 00
No. 3—1 to 1½ inches diameter	25	20 00
No. 4—¾ to 1 inch diameter, 7 to 9 feet high	15	10 00

(Large orders at special rates, very low.)

Carolina Poplar—A magnificent tree for street planting, forming a beautiful head ; large leaf and spreading habit ; rapid grower.

Lombardy Poplar—Erect and upright grower.

Black Locust—Strong grower, valuable for timber ; same prices as Poplar.

Cork Bark Elm—Rapid grower ; symmetrical in shape ; 50 cents to $1 25 each.

American Elm—A magnificent tree with drooping branches ; 25 to 75 cents each.

Soft or Silver Maple—Fine for street planting, handsome foliage ; 25 to 50 cents each ; large trees 75 cents to $1 each.

Weeping Willow—A beautiful weeping tree, with slender, drooping branches ; 50 cents to $1 00 each.

Our stock of both Maple and American Elm is very large, and on large lots we will make very low prices.

MULBERRIES.

The Mulberry is a very valuable family of trees. Most of them make beautiful, well shaped and clean shade trees. All make very valuable timber and make it very quick, being rapid growers. The fruit is excellent for fowls, as well as man, and it will serve an excellent purpose in keeping birds from cherries and other fruits, as the birds will eat that in preference to any other fruit. Besides the above, millions of dollars is made out of the leaves by feeding them to silk worms. It should receive more attention in this country than it does.

VARIETIES.

Downing's Everbearing—A rapid growing tree, valuable for its fruit, as it remains in fruit for three months; 50 cents to $1 00 each.

Persian—Largest fruit, but slow grower; 50 to 75 cents each.

New American—This is a large, strong growing, beautiful shaped tree; one of the best shade trees that grows; it also produces large crops of very fine berries, very sweet and delicious; 30 cents to $1 00 each. Fine.

Russian Mulberry—This also makes a fine tree, and the fruit is said to be very large and fine; we have not fruited it yet; 25 to 75 cents each.

Circassian Mulberry—This is a very fine, strong growing variety, makes a splendid shade tree, fruit of little value; 30 to 70 cents.

Morus Alba or White Mulberry—Fine shade tree, but fruit of no value; 25 to 50 cents each.

Morus Multicolus—Only valuable for the foliage, which is used to feed silk worms; 10 to 25 cents. Large lots for silk culture very cheap.

Dyospyros Kaki, or Japanese Persimmons.

Hyakume, Kuro Kume, Zemon, Dai Dai Marn, Zanji Marn Hachija, Tane Nashi—The two last named are nearly or quite seedless. We have several other varieties, but have not space to name or describe them. Most of our people are familiar with this fruit.

PRICE OF BUDDED OR GRAFTED TREES.	EACH.	PER DOZ.	PER 100.
2 to 3 feet	$0 20	$1 80	$12 00
3 to 4 feet	30	2 50	15 00

ORNAMENTAL DEPARTMENT.

☞ Our limited space will not admit of a full description of every shrub or flower, neither can we give the exact price for each particular size and style of plant. They vary so much in size, shape and condition that a minute description would occupy too much space. But we can guarantee satisfaction if you will, in ordering articles where the price ranges from one figure to another, simply give the price you wish to pay, and we will send articles to correspond with the price given.

☞ We do not Grow Greenhouse Plants, but carry them in stock during the selling season and can furnish anything in that line at regular florists' prices. So we can fill orders for anything in that line, though it may not be named in the Catalogue. In the item of Roses we can furnish over 100 varieties not mentioned in this Catalogue.

Roses.

Price, in pots..60 cts. to $1 00 each.
Price, naked roots..30 to 40 cents each.

Marechal Neil, Lamarque, Gold of Ophir, John Hopper, Giant of Battle, Cloth of Gold, James Sprunt, President Lincoln, Auguste Mie. Cardinal Patrizzi, Duchess of Norfork, General Jacqueminot, Louis Van Houtte, Pauline Saboute, Paul Naynon, Reive D' Orr, Salfaterre, Amelie Vibert, Celine Farester, White Cluster, Banksian (White), Baltimore Belle, Greville (or Seven Sisters), Bon Seline, Isabella Sprunt, Mad. Falcot, Duchess of Edinburgh, Anna Oliver, Bella, Catharine Merment, Homer Hermosa, Madam Stella.

Moss Roses—Captain Ingraham, Glory of Mosses, Henry Martin, Luxembaury, Black Morean, James Veitch, and many others too numerous to mention. A few choice new kinds at 75 cents to $1 50 each.

Deciduous Shrubs.

Pomegranate, fruiting...35 to 50 cts.
Pomegranate, flowering...35 to 50 cts.
Dwarf Pomegranate, flowering, very ornamental.......................75 cts.
Lilacs..25 to 75 cts.
Spirea, or Bridal Wreath..25 to 50 cts.
Deutzia, Crenate ....50 to 75 cts.
Snow Ball...50 to 75 cts.
Spirea Balardi..50 to 75 cts.

Rare and Choice Shrubbery.

Flowering Almond..$0 75
Pyrus Japonica.. 75
Purple Fringe... 75
Weigelia Rosea.. 75
Bottle Brush..1 00
Golden Dwarf Peach..1 00

Rare and Choice Ornamental Trees.

Golden Weeping Ash...$1 00
Mountain Ash—hangs full of red berries all Winter................ 1 00
Kilmarnock Willow...$1 50 to 2 00
New American Weeping Willow....................................... 1 50
Gravelia Robusti, Evergreen...........................60c to 1 00
Umbrella Tree—A most beautiful shaped tree, very handsome.....$1 to $1 50 each.

Evergreen Trees.

Eucalyptus—Globulus (Blue Gum), in variety, in pots or bagged, 2½ to 10 feet, 20c to $1. Blue Gum and other varieties of Eucalyptus, in seed boxes, 3 to 12 inches, $1 to $4 per 100. Transplanted in boxes so as to cut with balls of earth, 2 to 12 inches, $2 to $6 per 100.

☞ In large quantities for forest planting at special rates.

Acacia—Native of Australia, rapid growth, beautiful foliage and masses of yellow and orange-colorerd flowers ; in pots or bagged, 3 to 5 feet, 30 to 50 cents.

Acacia Melonoxelon, or Blackwood Acacia, a very fine hardy kind.

Acacia floribunda, or fragrans, long lance-like leaves.

Acacia molissima, fine elegant species ; light green leaves.

Pepper Trees (California Schinn Molle), 3 to 6 feet, 40 cents to $1.

Palms, in variety, $1 to $5, as per size and variety.

Cupressus (Cypress), most popular and very ornamental ; perfectly hardy, and thrives well in most localities and soils.

Cupressus Lawsoniana (Port Orford Cedar), very fine ; branches curve like green plums ; 50 cents to $1.

Cupressus Funebrus, elegant drooping foliage, adapted for planting in cemeteries; 75 cents to $1.

Cupressus macrocarpa (Monterey Cypress), 15 cents to $1 each.

Cupressus pyramidalis (Italian Cypress), very erect, close pressing branches ; 50 cents to $1.

Pinus macrocarpa (Monterey Pine), 3 to 7 feet ; 30 cents to 75 cents.

Arbor Vitæ, golden, beautiful compact plants ; 75 cents to $2 50.

Sequoia gigantea (California Mammoth Tree), $1 to $2 50.

Laurel, English, good plants ; 75 cents to $1.

Magnolia Grandiflora, 50 cents to $2 50.

☞ Surplus stock, which we will sell at special rates in quantity. Price on application—

500,000 Strawberry plants, leading sorts.
50,000 Raspberry plants.
50,000 Blackberry plants.
10,000 Carolina and Lombardy Poplar Trees, for shade, 1 to 2 years old.
500,000 Grape cuttings, leading sorts, free from insect pests.

Quantity of Seed Required to Sow an Acre of Ground.

	Pounds.		Pounds.
Grass, Timothy	20	Vetches—broadcast	150
Grass, Mesquit, in the chaff	35	Hemp—broadcast	40 to 50
Grass, Hungarian	40	Flax, when wanted for the seed	50
Grass, Millet	40	Flax, when wanted for the fiber	80
Grass, Mixed Lawn	75	Beans, Dwarf or Bush—hills or drills	80
A much larger quantity of seed is required to make a close, fine lawn than for other purposes.		Beans, tall or pole—hills	20
		Beets—drills	5 to 6
		Broom Corn—drills	15
Grass, mixture for mow-) Clover	8	Buckwheat—broadcast	45
ing or grazing ....) Timothy	15	Cabbage, in beds to cover an acre after	
Redtop	15	transplanting	¼
Grass, Kentucky Blue, for pasture	30	Carrots—drills	3 to 4
Grass, Kentucky Blue, for lawn	75	Melon, Water—hills	2 to 3
Grass, Orchard	40	Melon, Cantaloupe—hills	4
Grass, English or Australian Rye, for meadow	50	Onions, black seed—drills	5 to 6
		Onions, top set—drills	200
Grass, English or Australian Rye, for lawn	75	Onions, black seed, for bottom sets	40
		Parsnips—drills	6
Grass, Italian Rye	30 to 40	Peas—drills	100
Grass, Redtop	30	Peas—broadcast	180
Alfalfa or Lucerne	20 to 25	Potatoes—hills	500 to 600
Clover, Red alone—broadcast	15 to 20	Pumpkins—hills	5
Clover, White alone—broadcast	12	Radishes—drills	8
Clover, Alsike—broadcast	10	Sage—drills	8
Barley—broadcast	125 to 150	Spinach—drills	15
Oats—broadcast	80	Squash, bush varieties—hills	6
Rye—broadcast	100	Squash, running varieties—hills	3
Wheat—broadcast	125	Tomato, in beds to transplant	¼
Wheat—drills	90	Turnip and Rutabaga—drills	1½
Corn, Sweet or Field—hills	15	Turnip and Rutabaga—broadcast	3
Corn, to cut green for fodder—drills or broadcast	150	Cucumber—hills	2

Quantity of Seed Required to Produce a Given Number of Plants, or Sow a Certain Quantity of Ground.

Artichoke	1 oz. to 500 plants	
Asparagus	1 oz. to 60 feet of drill or 500 plants	
Beans, dwarf	1 lb. to 50 feet of drill	
Beans, tall	1 lb. to 75 hills	
Beet	1 oz. to 50 feet of drill	
Broccoli	1 oz. to 2,000 plants	
Brussels Sprouts	1 oz. to 2,000 plants	
Cabbage	1 oz. to 2,000 plants	
Carrots	1 oz. to 150 feet of drill	
Cauliflower	1 oz. to 2,000 plants	
Celery	1 oz. to 3,000 plants	
Chicory	1 oz. to 100 feet of drill	
Corn	1 lb. to 100 hills	
Cress	1 oz. to 100 feet of drill	
Cucumber	1 oz. to 75 hills	
Egg Plant	1 oz. to 1,000 plants	
Endive	1 oz. to 150 feet of drill or 3,000 plants	
Kale	1 oz. to 2,000 plants	
Kohl Rabi	1 oz. to 2,000 plants	
Leek	1 oz. to 150 feet of drill	
Lettuce	1 oz. to 3,000 plants	
Melon, Water	1 oz. to 50 hills	
Melon, Musk	1 oz. to 50 hills	
Okra	1 oz. to 50 feet of drill	
Onion Seed	1 oz. to 100 feet of drill	
Onion, top sets	1 lb. to 20 feet of drill	
Parsnips	1 oz. to 200 feet of drill	
Parsley	1 oz. to 150 feet of drill	
Peas	1 lb. to 50 feet of drill	
Pepper	1 oz. to 1,000 plants	
Pumpkin	1 oz. to 40 hills	
Radish	1 oz. to 100 feet of drill	
Salsify	1 oz. to 70 feet of drill	
Sage	1 oz. to 150 feet of drill	
Spinach	1 oz. to 100 feet of drill	
Squash, early	1 oz. to 50 hills	
Squash, winter	1 oz. to 10 hills	
Tomato	1 oz. to 3,000 plants	
Tobacco	1 oz. to 10,000 plants	

Table Showing Number of Plants or Trees to the Acre at Given Distances.

Dis. apart each way.	No. Plants.	Dis. apart each way.	No. Plants.	Dis. apart each way.	No. Plants.	Dis. apart each way.	No. Plants.
½ foot	174240	3 feet	4,840	8 feet	680	15 feet	193
1 foot	43,560	4 feet	2,722	9 feet	537	18 feet	134
1½ feet	19360	5 feet	1,742	10 feet	435	20 feet	108
2 feet	10,890	6 feet	1,210	11 feet	360	25 feet	69
2½ feet	9,696	7 feet	888	12 feet	302	30 feet	48

RULE.—Multiply the distance in feet between the rows by the distance the plants are apart in the rows, and the product will be the number of square feet for each plant or hill, which, divided into the number of feet in an acre (43,560), will give the number of plants or trees to the acre.

ESTABLISHED 1852.

W.R. STRONG & CO. PROPRIETORS OF CAPITAL NURSER

WHOLESALE DEALERS, PACKERS, SHIPPERS
IN CAR LOAD LOTS OF
CALIFORNIA FRUIT & PRODUCE.

CATALOGUE

1890

Established 1852

W·R·STRONG & CO.

CALIFORNIA SEEDS
TREES & NURSERY STOCK

SACRAMENTO, CAL.

W. R. STRONG COMPANY,

J and Front Sts. Sacramento, Cal.

To Our Friends and Customers:

IN ISSUING OUR CATALOGUE FOR 1890, we would thank our many customers and friends for their confidence and patronage in past years. It shall ever be our aim to supply you with the purest and best seed obtainable, and that will produce the perfect type of vegetation and crop desired.

That we have been successful in the past, we are assured by the many testimonials we have received and from our constantly increasing trade. We shall continue to use every effort in the future to give our patrons satisfaction.

Our strains of seed this season are of unusual excellence, and our prices will compare favorably with those of any other house on this coast or of Eastern cities.

WARRANTY. No Seedsman can sell Seeds and guarantee and be responsible for the crop. Our Seeds are selected with the greatest care to secure the best, and from the most careful and reliable growers. When it is considered that there are many contingencies upon which depend the success of a crop, which are beyond our control, the propriety of this must be conceded by all.

SUGGESTIONS.

ORDER EARLY AS POSSIBLE, while stock is complete, that you may be sure of getting what you send for, and so you will have them to plant when wanted.

USE OUR ORDER SHEETS and Envelopes when you have them ; it will be more convenient and there will be less danger of miscarrying or of mistakes. FOR ORDERS FOR TREES AND NURSERY STOCK use separate sheet, as this department is quite distinct and has a separate office and management.

BE VERY PARTICULAR. WRITE YOUR NAME, POST OFFICE, COUNTY AND STATE, IN FULL AND PLAINLY. We often receive orders without name or address, and it is often impossible to trace them up.

STATE HOW YOUR ORDER IS TO BE FORWARDED, otherwise we are compelled to use our own judgment.

SEND CASH with your order (at our risk—if sent by Postal or Express Order, or Draft on any good Banking House). Small sums may be sent in Postage Stamps if proper care is taken to prevent adhesion together.

MAIN PLACE OF BUSINESS—J, NEAR FRONT ST, SACRAMENTO.

Nursery Department.

This is under the management of our MR. WILLIAMSON and his son, who have had the largest practical experience of any Nurserymen in the State.

We have over four hundred acres now in cultivation on our ground in this county, and San Joaquin and Placer counties, in Nursery and Fruit Tree growth.

Our stock is absolutely true, clean, thrifty and well grown, and free from all scale and insect pests. We have also a branch in Florida for the growing of the Orange, Lemon, Magnolia, and various other evergreens that can be propagated to better advantage in that State. We sold over 100,000 of these trees last year in California, and not 2 per cent. have failed, and they are giving universal satisfaction.

Please make your orders for TREES AND ALL NURSERY STOCK separate from Seed Orders, as our Departments and Offices are entirely distinct.

Office, Yards and Packing Houses, next to Passenger Depot on Second St, Sacramento.

GENERAL PRICE LIST OF SEEDS
FOR 1889-90.

Our Vegetable Seeds are also put up in small packets at Five Cents each or Fifty Cents per dozen.

PEAS, BEANS and CORN in half-pound boxes at Ten Cents each, or One Dollar per dozen, and in one pound boxes at 15 cents each.

ALL SEEDS QUOTED BY THE OUNCE AND IN SMALL PACKETS WILL BE FORWARDED BY MAIL POSTAGE PREPAID BY US.

SEEDS QUOTED AT POUND RATES (if to be sent by mail), add TEN CENTS PER POUND TO COVER COST OF POSTAGE.

Assortments of Seeds for Family Garden.

To accommodate those not familiar with selection of the choicest varieties, we have prepared boxes of THOSE KINDS MOST DESIRABLE. Three sizes; price, one dollar, two dollars, and five dollars each, and which are at least one-fourth less than catalogue rates, and which we are sure will give satisfaction.

Peas.

EXTRA EARLY.

	Per hun.	Per lb
Cleveland's Alaska, earliest of all, 20 inches	$9 00	$0 15
Cleveland's R. N. Y., 2 feet, prolific; ripens at one time, fine flavor	8 00	15
Extra Early, first and best, 2feet	7 00	15
Premium Tom Thumb, 8 inches	9 00	15
Premium Gem, wrinkled, sweet, 2 feet	8 00	15
Carter's Stratagem	9 00	15
American Wonder, 10 inches	9 00	15
Laxton Alpha, 3 feet	9 00	15
Bliss Abundance, 18 inches	9 00	15
Bliss Everbearing 24 inches	9 00	15
McLean's Advancer, 36 inches	8 00	15

GENERAL CROP.

	Per hun.	Per lb
Yorkshire Hero, 2½ feet	$8 00	$0 15
Telephone, 3 feet	8 00	15
Champion of England, 5 feet	7 00	15
Bliss Imperial, 2 feet	6 00	10
Royal Dwarf Marrow, 2½ feet	6 00	10
Large White Marrowfat, 5 feet	6 00	10
Black Eye Marrowfat, 4 feet	5 00	10

EDIBLE PODS, SUGAR PEAS

	Per hun.	Per lb
Tall and Dwarf White Seed	$12 50	$0 20
Tall and Dwarf Gray Seed	12 50	20

Field Peas in quantity and variety, at lowest market rates.

Beans.

DWARF SNAPS OR GREEN STRING.

	Per hun.	Per lb
Early Refugee	$ 8 00	$0 15
Early Pinkeye China	6 00	15
Early Red Valentine	8 00	15
Cleveland's Round Pod, earliest, best and most prolific of all	9 00	15
Early White Valentine	9 00	15
Early Mohawk	8 00	15
Early Yellow Six Weeks	6 00	15
Green Flageolet, fine	10 00	15
Early Case Knife	9 00	15
Southern Prolific	9 00	15
Wax Flageolet, yellow pod, large, fine	10 00	15
Early Golden Wax, yellow pod	8 00	15

	Per hun.	Per lb
Ivory Wax, yellow pod	$10 00	$0 15
White Seeded Wax, yellow pod	10 00	15
Black Seeded Wax, yellow pod	8 00	15
Dwarf White Kidney	6 00	15
Dwarf Cranberry	7 00	15
Broad Windsor	5 00	10

POLE OR RUNNING.

	Per hun.	Per lb
London Horticulture	$ 8 00	$0 15
Large White Lima Hand Picked	10 00	15
King of the Garden Lima	10 00	15
Giant Wax, red seed	10 00	15
Dutch Caseknife	8 00	15
Scarlet Runners	12 50	20
White Runners	12 50	20
Asparagus, or Yard Long	15 00	25

All varieties of Field Beans in quantity at the very lowest market rates.

Sweet Corn, Etc.

CORY

	Per hun.	Per lb
Extra Early	$9 00	$0 15
Extra Early Marblehead	9 00	15
Early Pee and Kay	9 00	15
Early Minnesota	8 00	15
Early Crosby, very early	8 00	15
Early Moore's Concord	8 00	15
Early Mammoth Sugar	8 00	15
Black Mexican	8 00	15
Amber Cream	8 00	15
Stowell's Evergreen	8 00	15
Egyptian or Washington Market	8 00	15
Adams' Extra Early	7 00	15
Improved King Philip	7 00	10
Early Canada	6 00	10
Early White Flint	5 00	10
Large Yellow Eight-rowed	5 00	10
Pop Corn (Rice and Common)		10

Sweet corn for fodder and common Yellow and White Field Corn, or any of the above in quantity, at lowest market rates.

Artichoke.

	Per oz.	Per lb.
Green Globe	$0 30	$3 00
Jerusalem Tubers, $5 per 100 pounds.		

Two pounds for 25 cents of Peas, Beans and Corn, when quoted at 15 cents per single pound.

TWENTY-FIVE POUNDS AND OVER WILL BE SOLD AT 100 POUND RATES.

Asparagus.

	Per oz.	Per lb
Colossal, largest and best..................	$0 10	$0 60

Two-year-old roots, $1 50 per 100.

Beets.

	Per oz.	Per lb
Extra early Eclipse, new and fine..........	$0 10	$0 60
Extra Early Egyptian...............	10	60
Extra Early Bassanno...............	10	60
Dewing's Early Blood Turnip....	10	60
Early Blood Turnip................	10	60
Early Long Dark Blood.............	10	60
Bastian's Half Long Dark Blood..........	10	60
Mangel Wurzel, or Stock Beet..........	10	25
Improved Long Red Mangel Wurzel.......	10	35
Norbiton Giant Mangel.................	10	35
Yellow Globe Mangel...............	10	35
Red Globe Mangel...................	10	35
Improved White Sugar........	10	25
Imperial White Sugar..................	10	25
Swiss Chard..................	10	75

Brussels Sprouts.

	Per oz	Per lb
Improved Dwarf..................	$0 15	$1 50

Brocoli.

	Per oz.
Early Purple Cape..................	$0 40
Early White Cap..................	40

Cabbage.

	Per oz.	Per lb
Early York Dwarf..........	$0 15	$1 50
Early Large York...........	15	1 50
Early Oxheart, finest........	15	1 50
Henderson's Early Summer....	15	1 50
Jersey Early Wakefield.......	15	1 50
Early Bloomsdale Market.......	15	1 50
Early Winingstadt...........	15	1 50
Early Dwarf Dutch...........	15	1 50
Early Drumhead or Battersea....	15	1 50
Premium Flat Dutch..........	15	1 50
Premium Drumhead........	15	1 50
Stone Mason..............	15	1 50
Mammoth Marblehead....	15	1 50
Improved Brunswick..........	15	1 50
German Filderkraut..........	15	1 50
Savoy Drumhead...........	15	1 50
Savoy Early Dutch...........	15	1 50
Red Dutch Pickling..........	15	1 50

Carrot.

	Per oz	Per lb
Early Scarlet Horn..........	$0 10	$1 00
Earliest Short Horn, for forcing..........	10	1 00
Danvers Orange, Half Long...........	10	75
Early Half Long Scarlet, Stump Rooted.....	10	75
Improved Long Orange...........	10	75
Large White Belgian...............	10	60
Large Red Altringham..............	10	60

Cauliflower.

	Per oz.	Per lb
Henderson's Early Snowball..........	$2 50	$....
Extra Early Dwarf Erfurt selected..........	1 00	...
Early London.................	60	6 00
Early Paris, best..................	75	7 00
Large White French...........	75	7 00
Lenormand's Short Stem..........	75	7 00
Large Asiatic...............	50	5 00
Veitch's Autumn Giant........	50	5 00
Half Early Paris or Nonpareil..........	75	7 00
Large Late Algeriers..........	75	7 00

Celery.

	Per oz	Per lb
Henderson's White Plume.........	$0 25	$3 00
Henderson's Dwarf.........	15	1 50
Golden Heart............	15	1 50

	Per oz.	Per lb
Large White Solid...............	15	1 25
Dwarf White Solid...............	15	1 50
Boston Market.................	15	1 50
Celeriac or Turnip Rooted...........	15	1 50
Celery Seed, for flavoring..........	10	50

	Per oz.	Per lb
CHERVILL..................	$0 10	$1 00
COLLARDS..................	10	1 00
CHICORY (large rooted).........	10	1 00
CORN SALAD..................	10	1 00

Cress or Peppergrass.

	Per oz.	Per lb
Broad Leaf..................	$0 10	$0 75
Fine Curled..................	10	75
Fine Water Cress..................	40	....

Cucumbers.

	Per oz.	Per lb
Extra Long White Spine............	$0 10	$1 00
Early Russian..................	10	1 00
Improved Early White Spine..........	10	1 00
Early Frame..................	10	1 00
Early Short Green...............	10	1 00
Nichols' Medium Green..........	10	1 00
Early Green Cluster..................	10	1 00
Early Boston Pickling...........	10	1 00
Improved Long Green..........	10	1 00
Burr Small Gherkins..........	20	2 00

Egg Plant.

	Per oz.	Per lb
Early New York Purple.........	$0 50	$5 00
Early Long Purple..........	30	3 00
Early Black Peakin..........	50	5 00

Endive.

	Per oz.	Per lb
Green Curled..................	$0 15	$1 50
Moss Curled..................	15	2 50

Garlic.

The price of Garlic is variable.

Kale, or Borecole.

	Per oz.	Per lb
Green Curled Scotch............	$0 10	$1 00
Dwf. German Green and Purple..........	10	1 00
Sea Kale..................	25	3 00

Kohl Rabi.

	Per oz.	Per lb
Early White Vienna..........	$0 20	$2 00
Early Purple Vienna..........	20	2 00
Large Green..................	20	2 00

Leek.

	Per oz	Per lb
Best London Flag..........	$0 15	$2 50
Monstrous Carentan..........	15	2 50

Lettuce.

	Per oz.	Per lb
Hanson..................	$0 10	$1 00
Simpson's Early Curled..........	10	1 00
Early Prize Head..........	10	1 00
White Paris Cos. Romaine Lettuce........	10	1 00
San Francisco Market Satisfaction....	10	1 00
Philadelphia Butter..........	10	1 00
Early White Head Cabbage...........	10	1 00
Early Curled Silesia..........	10	1 00
Large Drumhead or Ice Cabbage..........	10	1 00
Simpson's Black Seeded..........	10	1 00
All the Year Round..........	10	1 00
Boston Market—for forcing....	10	1 00
Tennis Ball, Black Seeded—for forcing.... ..	10	1 00
Salamander—for hot, dry weather..........	10	1 00
Bird Lettuce........		30

Martynia.

	Per oz.	Per lb
For making Pickles	$0 25	$3 00

MUSHROOM SPAWN, in bricks, 15 cents each.

Musk Melon.

	Per oz.	Per lb
Surprise	$0 10	$1 00
California Large Netted	10	1 00
White Japan	10	1 00
Hackensack	10	1 00
Early Yellow Cantaloupe	10	1 00
Golden Gem	10	1 00
Montreal Market very large	10	1 00
Bay View	10	1 00
Skillman's Fine Netted	10	1 00
Large Green Nutmeg Citron	10	1 00
Cassaba, or Green Persian	10	1 00

Watermelon.

	Per oz.	Per lb
Mammoth Iron Clad	$0 10	$ 75
Kolb's Gem	10	75
Scaly Bark	10	75
Black Spanish	10	75
Icing, or Ice Cream, Peerless	10	75
Mountain sweet, or Gray Seeded Ice Cream	10	75
Mountain Sprout	10	75
Cuban Queen	10	75
Imperial Lodi, or California	10	75
Gypsy, or Rattlesnake	10	75
Orange Rind	10	1 25
Citron Melon, for preserves	10	1 00
Pride of Georgia	10	75

Nasturtium.

	Per oz.	Per lb
Tall Sorts	$0 15	$1 50
Dwarf	15	1 50

Okra, or Gumbo.

	Per oz.	Per lb
Early Dwarf	$0 10	$1 00
Tall Green	10	$1 00

Onions.

	Per oz.	Per lb
Early Large Red	$0 15	$1 50
Large Red Wethersfield	15	1 50
Yellow Danvers	15	1 50
Yellow Dutch Strasburg	15	1 50
White Portugal, Silver Skin	25	2 50
White Globe	25	2 50
Tripili, White and Red	20	2 00
Giant Yellow Rocca	20	2 00
Early Queen	20	2 00

ONION SETS—Prices variable; lowest market rates.

Parsnips.

	Per oz.	Per lb
Hollow Crown	$0 10	$0 75
Half Long Student	10	75

Parsley.

	Per oz.	Per lb
Triple Curled	$0 10	$0 75
Plain Curled	10	75
Fern Leaf	10	75
Moss Curled	10	75

Pepper.

	Per oz.	Per lb
Golden Dawn	$0 25	$2 50
Long Red Cayenne	25	2 50
Chili, very small for pepper sauce	25	2 50
Cherry Red	25	2 50
Large Squash, or Tomato-sh'p	25	2 50
Large Bell, or Bull-nose	25	2 50
Sweet Spanish, or Mountain	25	2 50

Pumpkin.

	Per oz.	Per lb
Large Yellow, or Conn. F'ld	$0 10	$ 35
Large Cheese, for table use	10	50
Casnaw, or Crookneck	10	50
Mammoth Tours	15	1 00

Radish.

	Per oz.	Per lb
Early Long Scarlet	$0 10	$ 75
Early Scarlet Turnip rooted	10	75
Early Scarlet Turnip White tip	10	75
Early White Turnip rooted	10	75
Olive shaped, or Half-long Scarlet	10	75
French Breakfast, or Half-long Scarlet, White Tip	10	75
Beck's Chartier	10	1 00
Scarlet China Winter	10	1 75
Black Spanish, Fall or Winter	10	75
White Strasburg Radish	10	1 00
Mammoth White China, or California	10	1 00

Rhubarb, or Pie Plant.

	Per oz.	Per lb
Linnaeus, Giant	$0 20	$2 00
Victoria, Giant	20	2 00

Two year roots, $2 50 per dozen, 25 cents each; one-year roots, $1 50 per dozen, or 15 cents each.

Salsify, or Vegetable Oyster.

	Per oz.	Per lb
Best White	$0 15	$1 50
Scorzonera, or Black Salsify	20	2 00

Squash.

	Per oz.	Per lb
Pineapple	$0 10	$1 00
Perfect Gem	10	1 00
Early Yellow Bush Scallop	10	75
Early White Bush Scallop	10	75
Yellow Summer Crookneck	10	75
American Turban	10	75
Marblehead	10	75
Boston or Vegetable Marrow	10	75
Hubbard	10	75
Mammoth, fine for exhibition	10	1 00

Field squash, for stock feeding, 30 cents.

Spinach.

	Per oz.	Per lb
Round Summer, or Large Dutch	$0 10	$ 35
Extra Large prickly, Winter	10	35
Improved Thick Leaved	10	35
Monstrous Viroflay, extra large	10	35
Long Standing, Late Seeding	10	35

Sunflower.

	Per oz.	Per lb
Mammoth Russian	$0 10	$0 50

Tobacco.

	Per oz.	Per lb
Connecticut Seed Leaf	$0 40	$4 00
Virginia	40	5 00
Havana	50	6 00

Tomato.

	Per oz.	Per lb
Early Conqueror	$0 20	$2 00
Acme	20	2 00
Livingston's Perfection	20	2 00
Paragon	20	2 00
Hathaway's Excelsior	20	2 00
General Grant	20	2 00
Sacramento Favorite	20	2 00
Mayflower	20	2 00
Fejee	20	2 00
Trophy	20	2 00
Large Yellow	20	2 00
Red Cherry	20	2 00

Tomato.

	Per oz.	Per lb		Per oz.	Per lb
Cardinal	20	2 00	Purple Top White Globe	10	60
Livington's Favorite	20	2 00	Orange Yellow, or Golden Ball	10	60
Livingston's Beauty	20	2 50	Yellow or Amber Globe	10	60
Mikado	20	2 50	Pomeranian White Globe	10	60
Optimus	20	2 50	Long White or Cowhorn	10	60

Turnip.

	Per oz.	Per lb
Early Snowball	$0 10	$ 75
White Egg	10	75
Early Yellow Stone	10	60
Early White Flat Dutch, Strap Leaved	10	60
Early Purple Top, Strap Leaved	10	60
Early Purple Top, Munich	10	60
Large White Norfolk	10	60
Yellow Aberdeen Purple Top	10	60

Ruta Baga.

	Per oz.	Per lb
Large White French	$0 10	$0 60
Sweet Russian, White	10	60
Sweet German White	10	60
Improved Purple Top Yellow	10	60
Skirving's Swede, Purple Top Yellow	10	60
Laing's Improved Yellow Early	10	60
Improved American Yellow Purple Top	10	60

Sweet and Medicinal Herbs, Etc.

A few herbs should have a place in every vegetable garden. A very small space will give all that are needed in any family. The culture is simple. Make a little seed-bed in the early spring, and set the plant out in a bed as soon as large enough.

	Oz.	Lb.		Oz.	Lb.
Anise	$0 10	$1 00	Henbane	$0 40	$....
Angelica	25	....	Hyssop	25	3 00
Arnica	2 00	....	Hoarhound	30	....
Balm	50	....	Lavender	25	2 50
Belladonna	75	....	Marjoram, Sweet	25	2 50
Borage	10	1 00	Marigold Pot	25	2 50
Basil (Sweet)	25	3 00	Opium Poppy	20	2 50
Boneset	1 00	....	Pennyroyal	75	....
Bene	20	....	Rosemary	40	....
Caraway	10	50	Rue	40	....
Catnip	75	....	Savory, Summer	25	2 50
Coriander	10	50	Savory, Winter	25	2 50
Cumin	10	1 00	Saffron	15	1 50
Dandelion	25	2 50	Sage, Common	20	2 00
Dill	10	50	Sorrel, Broad-leaved	15	1 50
Elecampane	50	....	Tansy	50	....
Fennel, Large Sweet	10	50	Thyme, English	40	4 00
Fenugreek	10	1 00	Wormwood	40	....

The above are also put up in Five Cent packages of Fifty Cents per dozen.

Grass and Clover Seeds.

When sold in quantity, at much reduced rates and being subject to market fluctuations. Prices given on application.

Express or Freight charges must be paid by the purchaser, and when small quantities are wanted to be forwarded by mail, be sure to send money extra to cover postage.

Clover Seed.

	Per lb			Per lb
Alfalfa	$0 10 $ 12½	Alsyke, or Sweedish Clover		$0 25
Mammoth, or Sapling Clover	12½ 15	Crimson Trefoil		50
Common, or Red Clover	12½ 15	Yellow Trefoil		50
White Dutch Clover	25	Sanfoin, or Esparsette		15

Grass Seed.

	Per 100	Per lb		Per 100	Per lb
Lawn Grass, Best Mixed	$15 00	$0 20	Timothy Grass Seeds	$7 00	$0 10
Lawn Grass, Extra Fancy Blue	15 00	20	Red Top Grass Seeds	9 00	15
Lawn Grass, Kent'ky Ex. Cl. Blue	15 00	20	Mesquite Grass Seeds	9 00	15
Sweet Vernal Grass		50	Orchard Grass Seeds	15 00	20
Perennial Rye Grass	12 00	15	Evergreen Millet Grass	14 00	20
Australian Grass	10 00	15	German or Golden Millet Grass	6 00	10
Italian Grass	10 00	15	Egyptian or Pearl Millet		25
Fine Fescue Grass		50	Hungarian Grass	6 00	10
Meadow Fescue		50			

Miscellaneous and Field Seeds.

	Per 100	Per lb		Per lb
Amber Sugar Cane Seed	$6 00	$0 10	Castor Oil Beans	25
African Seed	6 00	10	Hemp Seed	10
Egyptian Corn, White	2 50	5	Flax Seed	10
Egyptian Corn, Red	2 50	5	Canary Seed	10
Buckwheat	2 50	5	Mixed Bird Seed	10
Sun Flower Seed	30 00	50	Rape Seed	10
Vetches	6 00	10	Bird Lettuce	30
Lentils	6 00	10	Cuttle Fish Bone	25
Broom Corn	2 00	5	Maw, or Poppy Seed	30

Bird Seed.

Canary, Hemp, Rape, Millet and Mixed Bird Seeds, 6 pounds for 50 cents.

Early Snowball Cauliflower.

EARLY SNOWBALL CAULIFLOWER.

There is no vegetable in which the quality of the seed is of more vital importance than the Cauliflower, and none in which it is more difficult to secure the best During the past five years we have had samples from the best growers of this country and Europe, planted on our trial grounds, and have carefully studied them and as a result present our stock of Snowball Cauliflower as *the very best in existence.* The plants are dwarf and compact, and with fair treatment every one will form a good head. Our customers can plant this seed with the assurance of getting as good heads and as early as from any sort that is offered, for we have spared no pains to discover and secure the best without regard to cost. Pkt. 20c. oz. $2.50.

NEW GOLD COIN SWEET CORN.

This is a remarkably distinct and handsome variety. Its enormous productiveness is enough to place it in advance of any sort now grown; almost always yielding two, and frequently three, mammoth ears to the stalk. It is sweeter, more delicate in flavor, and ten days earlier than the Stowell's Evergreen. The cob is snowy white, compactly covered with large, deep grains. Perhaps its most valuable characteristic lies in the fact that it is evergreen to an unprecedented degree. Last season the great bulk of the crop could have been gathered at any time during a period of four weeks, and have been found in perfect condition for table use. This is a very important quality to market gardeners. ¼ lb. 15c. lb. 25c.

CORY SWEET CORN.

The earliest of all sweet corns. In general appearance closely resembles the Early Marblehead, but is earlier by at least a week than this variety, which has hitherto always taken the lead. To market men, the Cory is a valuable variety, as the first sweet corn will bring double the price it commands when the supply becomes general. ¼ lb. 10c.; lb. 15c.; 100 lbs. $9.00

CELERY.

(White Plume.) The stalk and inner portions of the leaves and heart *are naturally white,* so that by closing the stalks, either by tying them together or by pressing the soil up against the plant with the hand, and again drawing up the soil with the hoe or plow, so as to keep the soil that has been squeezed against the Celery in place the work of blanching is completed. The great advantage of this over the slow and troublesome process of blanching required by the old sorts is evident. Its eating qualities are equal to the very best of the older sorts, being crisp solid and of a pleasing nutty flavor, while its white feather-like foliage places it ahead of all others as a table ornament. Pkt. 5c. 1 oz. 25c. lb. $3.00

PERRY'S HYBRID. Sweet Corn.

A very fine, new, early variety, fully as early as the Minnesota, and ears much larger, each containing twelve or fourteen rows of kernels, well filled to the end. The grains are very large and pure white, but the cob is red. The ears are about the same length as Crosby's, but larger round, and are ready to market fully a week earlier. The stalks grow 5½ feet high, and the ears (2 to a stalk) are set about 2 feet from the ground. ¼ lb. 15c.; lb. 25c.

NICHOL'S MEDIUM GREEN.

We consider this variety the most valuable sort that has been introduced since the advent of the Green Prolific variety. As a pickle sort, Nichol's Medium Green will be found unequalled, and for early forcing purposes or for slicing, there is no better variety. It is exceedingly productive, of medium size, and always straight and smooth. The color is dark green, the flesh tender and crisp. (*See cut.*) 10 cts. oz. $1.00 lb.

Miller Cream Musk Melon.

This splendid melon was thoroughly tested the past season by many of our best market gardeners, and is pronounced by all, one of the very best they have ever grown. The flesh is of a rich salmon color, very sweet and melting in quality, and is so very thick that the melon is almost solid, the seed cavity being remarkably small. The rind is thin, slightly sutured, but little netted. This vine is a strong grower and very productive, covering the ground with fruit. It is extremely sweet, rich and delicious and very distinct from any other. Seed is very scarce. Per oz., 20c. lb., $2.

Emerald Gem Musk Melon. The Emerald Gem Melon is certainly the most distinct and at the same time the most deliciously flavored Melon we ever came across. It is a very early and prolific variety, with a skin which, while it is ribbed, is perfectly smooth and of a deep emerald green color. The flesh, which is thicker than in most other melons, is of a suffused salmon color, exceedingly sweet and delicious; in fact, the variety is thick meated that it yields but little seed. Those seeking a Musk Melon for quality alone will find all they are looking for in the Emerald Gem. Price, 10c. pkt. oz., 15c. lb., $1.50.

Florida Favorite Watermelon. Finest table melon extant; oblong in shape, growing to very large size; rind dark, with light-green stripes; flesh light-crimson, very crisp and deliciously sweet; seed rather small and of light creamy-white color. Ripened the past season 10 days earlier than the Kolb Gem, Iron Clad, or Rattlesnake. We offer seed grown by originator. Pkt. 5c., oz. 15c., lb. $1.00.

NEW OAK-LEAVED LETTUCE.

A distinct and beautiful new variety which should be in every garden. Our illustration will show the peculiar outline of the leaves, which are shaped like those of the oak. The heads are compact, crisp and tender, and entirely free from that bitter taste peculiar to many sorts. Several of our market gardeners who tried it the past two seasons are much pleased with its many fine qualities. Pkt., 5c.; oz., 15c.; lb., $1.50.

Champion Market.

Champion Market. Is very productive, frequently bearing seven melons on a single vine, while on one vine we counted five melons set within a length of 22 inches. The melons mature early. It is an excellent shipper; and we consider it, unquestionably, the most profitable variety that can be grown for market. Price, 10c., oz. 15c. lb. $1.25.

Burpee's Hungarian Honey. Mr. Burpee says: "This new and superb variety was brought by us from Hungary in the summer of 1884, and after two years' thorough trial on a large scale, having had several acres of them growing the past season, we can positively state that it is decidedly the richest and sweetest flavored of all watermelons. Pkt. 10c., oz. 15c., lb. $1.50.

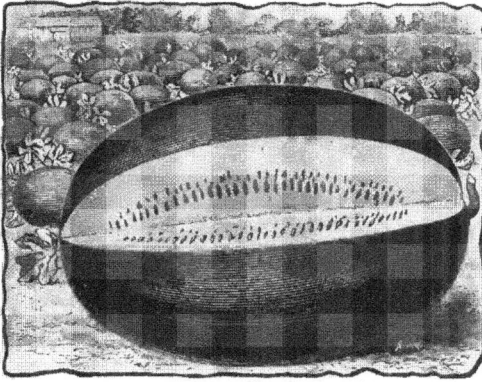

Green and Gold.

Green and Gold. Is the largest early variety in cultivation, melons ranging from 25 to 45 pounds, and its productiveness is equal to any of the red-fleshed sorts, while in delicious flavor it surpasses them all. The rind is the thinnest of any melon, the white being on 3-8 to 1-2 an inch in thickness. The flesh is a beautiful golden-orange color, free from any tinge of white or other color, even immediately around the seeds. The flesh is beautifully granular in appearance, juicy and sweet, and as we have already stated, of unequaled flavor Coupled with the delicious flavor of the Green and Gold Watermelon, its rich golden color will make it most desirable as an ornament for the table, especially if its golden slices are arranged in contrast with the crimson of the other sorts. Pkt, 10c., oz. 15c., lb. $1.50.

Kolb's Gem. Much has been said against this variety and it has been condemned on account of its coarse grained flesh, but we think this complaint comes in part at least from the use of inferior stock grown at the North. It is essentially a southern shipping melon, and as such has no equal. Prominent commission merchants in Sacramento and San Francisco and other cities, report that this is the favorite variety in their markets, always arriving in good condition and selling at an advance of five to ten dollars per hundred over other varieties. Melons from one of our fields were pronounced by good judges to be the best they had ever tasted, and the entire field was said to be the best in a section where the water melon is the principal crop. We can recommend it as

Seminole. This new variety originated in the home of melons,—Florida—and is said to be quite an acquisition. The following description is by the originator: Oblong in shape, smooth, and beautifully proportioned, it is of two colors, gray and light green; the later seems to be just a darker coloring of the former, the gray greatly predominates. Melons of both colors are found on the same vines. Melons of both colors are exactly the same in shape, size, color of seed, flavor, etc.

This melon possesses four qualities which will make it the most popular ever offered to the public. It is *extra early, extra large, enormously productive, and of most delicious flavor.* Pkt. 10c., oz. 15c. lb. $1.50.

of unequalled purity and excellence. Pkt. 5c., oz. 10c., lb. 75c.

The Volga Watermelon. Is cultivated on the lower Volga, near the Caspian Sea, for shipment in barrels to St. Petersburg and Moscow. In solidity and hardness it is remarkable, and therefor carries well. In productiveness it surpasses most sorts, two melons being sometimes borne at adjacent joints of the same vine. In form it is nearly perfectly globular. In color it is so pale green as to be nearly white, with nearly imperceptible stripes. Although so solid and hard, the rind is not thick. The flesh is remarkably crisp, and when fully ripe, very sweet, luscious and red in color. Pkt., 10c., oz. 15c. lb. $1 50.

THE OSAGE MUSK MELON.

No variety of Musk Melon, as far as we are aware, has advanced in popularity and become at once so widely known as this variety. "Skin dark green, slightly netted on the lobes on the upper side, and on the best specimens a rich orange color where the melon lies on the ground, and on this side it is eatable within an eighth of an inch of the surface. The shape is pointed oval—egg shaped most exactly expresses it. Medium sized, and the whole crop is very even and extra heavy owing to the thickness of the meat." Pkt., 10c.; 1 oz., 30c.; 1 lb., $4.00

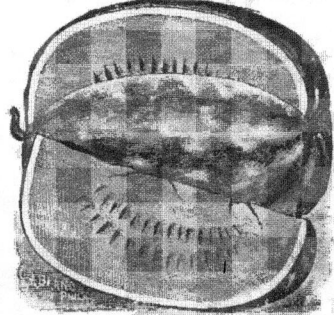

Mammoth Ironclad.

Mammoth Ironclad. This superb Melon acknowledged by all to be unsurpassed, excelling in every good point a Melon should have, ripening early, holding their own until late, and being unexcelled for shipping and market. The dainty red-colored flesh is of rich sugary flavor, ripening to full perfection almost to the rind. This Melon grows to enormous size, 60 to 70 lbs. being the ordinary weight, while extra cultivation will produce them 125 lbs. and over. Per pkt. 5 c., oz. 10 c., lb. 75c.

New Japanese Pie Pumpkin.

After thoroughly testing this remarkable variety, we now offer it for the first time in America. It comes from Japan, and will unquestionably prove a valuable addition to our pie and cooking pumpkins. The flesh is *very thick*, nearly solid, the seed cavity being very small in one end of the pumpkin, unusually *fine-grained dry and sweet*, having much the same taste and appearance as sweet potatoes. They ripen early, keep well and produce largely. The seeds are peculiarly marked and sculptured in Japanese characters. Pkt., 10c.; oz., 20c., lb., $2.00.

True Tennessee Sweet Potato Pumpkin.

Although not entirely new, we think so highly of this splendid pie and cooking pumpkin, that we have made a specialty of it. They grow to medium size, slightly ribbed; skin is screamy-white, lightly striped with green, flesh very thick creamy-white, dry and fine-grained; when cooked resembles sweet potatoes, but much more delicious in taste. The vines are hardy and enormously productive. Pkt., 10c., oz., 15c.; lb., $1.50.

Mammoth Etampes Bright Red Pumpkin

We have imported the seed of this giant variety from France, where it is quite celebrated. It has been grown in this country to enormous size; it is of a bright glossy red color, and makes a splendid variety to grow for exhibition purposes. Pkt. 10c. oz. 15c. lb. $1.50.

Improved Chartier Radish.

It is rare that we have the opportunity to offer a new thing of such decided merit and distinct character as this. We have carefully observed it in our own grounds for three years, and as a result do not hesitate to say it is the most profitable out door radish yet introduced. It is not adapted to forcing, but when planted out of doors it will reach a usable size very nearly as early as the Long Scarlet and it often continues in condition for two months, remaining crisp and tender until it reaches a diameter of two inches. It is so vigorous that in many instances it will outgrow the attacks of the radish maggot and produce good roots when all other sorts fail. We have taken especial pains to secure good stock and to have it well grown. We recommend this as unquestionably the best sort for those who only care to plant one kind. We know that all who tried it last year will plant it again, and we hope every one of our readers will plant at least one packet, feeling sure they will be fully satisfied with the result. 5c. Pkt.; 10c. oz.; $1.00 lb. See cut.

Sibley Squash.

The flesh is solid, thick, a vivid, brilliant orange in color, and is possessed of rare edible qualities. The weight

ranges from 8 to 11 pounds. It ripens its fruit simultaneously with the Hubbard. A good shipper and long keeper. Pkt. 5c. oz., 15c.; lb., $1.50.

Brazil Sugar.

This new variety, originally from South America, has been thoroughly tested in the United States the past two years, and is pronounced by critical growers a most valuable acquisition to our list of summer and autumn squashes. The flesh and skin are of a bright yellow color, slightly varied. As its name indicates, it is one of the sweetest of all squashes, the flesh being unusually fine-grained and tender, so much so that it is palatable even when eaten raw. They reach a weight of three to four pounds each, ripen early, and grow so vigorously that they are but little affected by the squash-bug. Pkt., 5c.; oz., 10c.; lb., $1.00.

New Giant Mammoth Zinnias.

A particularly fine new class of Zinnias, differing from the older ones from its unusually robust habit of growth and the immense size (five to six inches across) of its perfectly formed, very double flowers of various striking colors. The plants rise to a hight of three to three and a quarter feet, are clothed with a luxuriant foliage, and bloom freely during a long period. Being of great consistency, the flowers are uninfluenced by heat and remain in good condition for several weeks. The luxurious growth and the large bright flowers of this novelty make it particularly valuable for large groups, but it will also be found most effective when planted singly or as a border plant in small gardens, and it will undoubtedly soon become a general favorite. All colors mixed. Per Pkt. 15 cents.

New Large Flowering Verbena.

Verbena Hybrida Grandiflora. In our extra fine mixed Verbena we thought we had the finest verbena seed known, but are free to admit that this new strain offered last year for the first time, is superior, both in size of flowers and cluster. In the Grandiflora the flowers are of unusual size, many single flowers being as large as a twenty cent piece, while the clusters of some are magnificent. Plants from seed of the Grandiflora grown alongside of the New Mammoth Verbenas, were pronounced equal in size and beauty of flowers, while the range of color is much more varied. Verbenas are so easily raised from seed that we are sure this new large, flowering strain will immediately become very popular. To place it within the reach of all, we offer it now as low as it can be sold, and are sure that all purchasers will be delighted with it. Per Pkt. 15 cents.

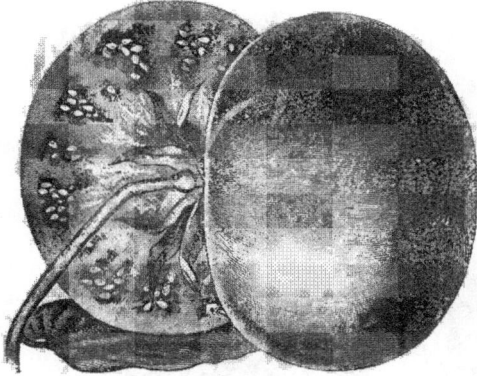

The Mikado Tomato.

The largest early variety in cultivation; certainly no more distinct or valuable Tomato has ever been introduced One of the most remarkable features about this variety is the fact that, notwithstanding that it produces perhaps the largest fruit of any sort in cultivation, it is at the same time one of the very earliest to ripen; generally we find that we secure earliness at the expense of size, but the *Mikado Tomato* seemingly reverses the rule. The *Mikado* differs from all other Tomatoes in its immense size, and the Tomatoes are produced in immense clusters, are perfectly solid, generally smooth, but sometimes irregular. The color is purplish red, like that of the Acme, while the variety has all the solidity that characterizes the Trophy. It is not unusual for single fruits of this variety to weigh from 1 to 1½ *lbs. each.* The foliage of the *Mikado Tomato* alone shows the distinctiveness of the variety, for it is whole or entire, while in all other varieties the leaves are cut or serrated. Whether for slicing or for cooking purposes, the variety is unsurpassed. (*See cut*)

Tomato. Livingston's Beauty.

An excellent variety of large size and beautiful appearance The color is glossy crimson with a slight purplish tinge. It grows in clusters of four and five, retaining its large size late in the season; very solid with a tough skin, making it very desirable for market and shipping. Pkt., 5c., oz., 20c.; lb , $2.50.

Millo Maize or Branching Dhorma.

This variety is from South America. It is much superior to the Egyptian or Rice varieties, being much earlier and producing wonderfully. It has been grown near Sacramento, and from a single seed four and five stalks have been produced averaging five large heads 8 inches long, loaded with seed. It is a valuable forage plant and can be cut at any stage for feed, and shoots up again rapidly; cured when heading for dry fodder and cattle eat it ravenously. Five to eight pounds per acre. 15c. per lb; 10 lbs., $1 00

MELILOTUS. Spike Clover.

A native of Klamath River, California, is found growing on the bars and its banks up to high water mark. The seed having been deposited by the freshets, grows among the cobbles in the gravel, slickens and sand; yields an immense amount of feed for stock, and attains a height of 10 to 12 feet. The first year it keeps green, and grows the entire season. The second year it produces seed, maturing in September and October. It has the clover leaf, white blossoms borne on a spike, a bushy growth, and the characteristic sweet clover fragrance. Per lb. 15cts.; per 100 lbs. $12.50.

Japan Clover. (*Lespedeza Striata*). This highly appreciated species of clover is t y no means a new discovery, but it is only la ely that the seed has been gathered in quantities for sale. It ranks far above red clover in nutritive value, and is by analysis 72 per cent. Being of dwarfish habits on most soils, yet on rich lands it reaches a height of two feet and makes the best kind of hay. Also for the renovating of lan is it equals the best of clovers. For live stock it is almost a complete food. The seed is yet scarce thirty cents per pound in quantity. Ten pounds are sufficient for one acre, as it spreads very rapidly.

Texas Bluegrass Seed. (*Pba Arachnifera*). A new winter grass which is fast being introduced into the Southern States. It is much superior to the Kentucky Bluegrass because of its long roots, which will go four or five times as deep for moisture. It makes a beautiful lawn for winter, and when grown with the Bermuda makes a lawn which lasts the whole year. It is hardy and can be planted at any time of the year, but mid-summer. The price is 50 cts. per oz., $5 per pound. Postage paid.

CLEVELAND'S ALASKA

THE QUICKEST PEA ON RECORD.

Cleveland's Alaska Peas. We consider this the earliest, most prolific and finely flavored variety grown. We planted in our grounds and had peas fit for the table in 45 days. Height 2½ feet.

Cleveland's Improved Round Pod Valentine Beans.

HENDERSON'S NEW BUSH LIMA BEAN.

Thousands have been deterred from cultivating the most delicious of Vegetables, the Lima Bean, from the great trouble and expense of procuring the unsightly poles which were required on which to grow them. This is now a thing of the past, as the HENDERSON'S NEW BUSH LIMA grows without the aid of stakes or poles, in compact bush form, about 18 inches high, and produces enormous crops of delicious Beans, which can be as easily gathered as the common garden Bush Beans. They are at least TWO WEEKS EARLIER than any of the climbing Limas. This fact alone would stamp it as the most valuable novelty of recent years, but when in addition to this, we realize that it is a true BUSH BEAN, requiring no supports, some idea of its great value can be realized. HENDERSON'S BUSH LIMA produces a continuous crop from the time it comes into bearing until frost and being enormously productive, a very small patch will keep a family supplied all summer. Our stock of the NEW BUSH LIMA being quite limited this season, we have decided to offer it in PACKETS only. 12 packets will plant five rows, each fifty feet long, which is ample for an ordinary family. Price, per single packet, 25c ; 5 packets for $1.00; 12 packets for $2.00

Cleveland's Improved Round Pod Valentine Beans is ten days earlier than the Red Valentine and much more prolific and combines all its good qualities. We recommend this as one of the very best for market gardeners and general cultivation.

W. R. STRONG COMPANY,

WHOLESALE FRUIT AND

Produce  Merchants

Packers and Forwarders,

In Carload Lots, to Eastern, Southern and Interior Markets.

Having been engaged in this business for many years, and being the oldest house and largest shippers on the Pacific Coast, our advantages are unrivaled, for the disposal of California Fruits and Products in the great marts of their consumption.

Our arrangements with the leading Fruit and Produce Growers are very extensive, and we know we can be of the largest advantage to both the producer and consumer.

WE KEEP CONSTANTLY ON HAND, IN THEIR SEASON,

A FULL STOCK OF TROPICAL FRUITS,

AS WELL AS OF CALIFORNIA GROWTH. ALSO

Canned Goods, Machine and Sun-Dried Fruits, Butter, Cheese.

NUTS, HONEY, ETC.

Having business connections with the largest and best Canneries of the State, we are able to fill all orders at the lowest rates.

No effort shall be spared to give satisfaction.

By fair dealing and close attention to the wants of our customers, we are determined to merit the confidence of the public in the future, as we believe we have in the past.

COLD STORAGE.

We have the largest Cold Storage House or Refrigerator on the Coast. It is used to preserve consignments of butter, eggs, and other perishable products consigned to us, and we can assure shippers of butter, eggs, cheese, dressed poultry, etc., that the same will be well cared for if sent to us.

W. R. STRONG COMPANY,
SACRAMENTO, CAL.

W. R. STRONG COMPANY
SPECIAL LIST OF
Vegetable Plants AND Esculent Roots.

Several seasons ago we added to our list of specialties, the growing of vegetable plants; with each year our demand has so increased that we have been obliged to put a large area under glass for the purpose of forwarding the plants for the benefit of our customers wishing to plant early.

We think we can safely say, there is no more complete Establishment in California specially constructed for the growing of plants. We shall be prepared to to supply all demands for the varieties listed below in their proper season.

Large York Cabbage.   Perfection Tomato.   Optimus Tomato.   Favorit tomato.   Stone Mass tomato.

Asparagus Roots, Conover's Colossal, 2 years old...$1.50 per 100
Special prices on large lots.
Artichokes, Jerusalem tubers...$5 00 per 100 lbs.
Hop Roots...........................$1.50 per 100, $10.00 per 1,000.

Cabbage Plants.

	Per 100.	Per 1,000.
Early York.	$0 40	$3 00
Early Summer	40	3 00
Early Ox Heart	40	3 00
Large Flat Dutch	40	3 00
Large Late Drumhead	40	3 00

Cauliflower Plants.

	Per 100.
Early Snowball	$1 00
Early Paris	1 00
Late Dutch	1 00

Egg Plants.

	Per doz.	Per 100.
New York Purple	$0 50	$3 00
Black Pekin	50	3 00

Pepper Plants.

	Per doz.	Per 100.
Large Bell	$0 50	$3 00
Sweet Mountain	50	3 00

Rhubarb Roots.

2 and 3 years old.

	Per doz.
Mammoth Linneus	$3 00

Special prices on lots of 100.

Celery Plants.

	Per doz.	Per 100.
Large White Solid	$0 50	$2 00
White Plume	50	2 00

Horse Radish Roots.

Per 100.................................$......

Onion Sets.

Scarce. Prices on application.

Sweet Potato Plants.

	Per 100.	Per 1000.
Yellow Carolina	$0 50	$4 00

We grow immense quantities of these plants and shall be prepared to supply all orders at short notice.

Tomato Plants.

Put up in boxes of 50 to 100 plants each. We make a specialty of tomato plants, and can always supply in their season well grown stalky plants of the best known varieties. Our New Boss tomato has given universal satisfaction, and we can highly recommend it to the trade.

Special New Kinds.

ACME,   MIKADO,   PERFECTION,   NEW DWARF CHAMPION,   NEW BOSS,   LIVINGSTON BEAUTY, SACRAMENTO FAVORITE
Per dozen, 20 cents.   Per 100, $1.00.

Special Prices.

On all kinds of plants furnished on application on all orders aggregating from 1,000 to 10,000 plants.
In all cases we will ship plants by express in small quantities, unless otherwise ordered.

FERTILIZERS.

We are prepared to supply at manufacturer's prices BONE MEAL, GUANO and other fertilizers, price given on application. Also INSECTICIDES, for destruction of insects infesting Fruit Trees and Plants.

W. R. STRONG COMPANY.

W. R. STRONG COMPANY'S

DESCRIPTIVE LIST OF

VEGETABLE SEEDS

We examine all new varieties of vegetables, etc., but do not include them in our list unless they are proved, after thorough test, to be of superior excellence. We have no hesitation in saying that our Seeds cannot be excelled in quality and freshness by any other collection.

The following list will cover all varieties needed for successful gardening :

Artichok .

Culture.—Sow in seed bed early in spring, in drills twelve inches apart. When one-year-old transplant to permanent bed spaded deep, and dressed with rotten manure, ashes and a little salt, then plant them about two feet apart. The edible portion is the undeveloped flower heads, which should be used before they begin to open, and then cut to the ground, for if the flowers expand they weaken the plants. In the fall cover with manure , which should be spaded in the following spring, taking care not to injure the plants. The crop is the largest and

Globe Artichoke.

best the second year, after which the bed should be renewed by seed or suckers.

Large Globe. —The best sort for general use. Buds large nearly round; scales deep green, shading to purple, very thick and fleshy.

Jurusalem.—A hardy and productive plant, used for pickling and feeding stock. Strong tubers. Per 100 lbs. $5 00.

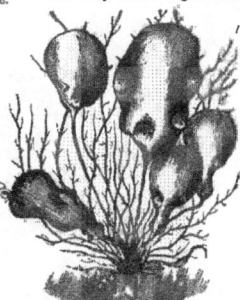

Jerusalem Artichoke.

Asparagus.

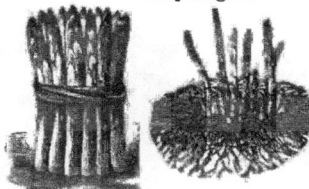

Giant Collossal Asparagus.

Asparagus is one of the earliest spring vegetables and would be in univer-sal use were it not for the prevalent idea that it is diffi-cult to grow it. There is no vegetable on our list that can be produced so cheaply and easily. It delights in a moist, sandy soil, but can be grown in any garden by following the directions. A bed 12x40 feet, requiring 75 to 100 plants, give an abundant supply for an ordinary family.

Culture.—Beds are usually formed by setting plants one or two years old, which can be procured of us. If you wish to grow them yourself, prepare a light, rich spot early in the spring, and after soaking the seed twenty-four hours in warm water, sow in drills one foot apart. When the plants are well up, thin to two or three inches in the row, and give frequent and thorough cultivation during the summer. The plants will be fit to set the next spring. The permanent beds should be prepared by deep spading, working in a large quantity of rotted manure. Dig trenches four feet apart and twelve to eighteen inches deep, and spade in at least four inches of well rotted manure in the bottom. Set the plants two feet apart in this trench and cover with two inches of fine soil. After the plants are well started give frequent and thorough cultivation, and draw a little earth in the trenches at each hoeing until they are filled. Early the next spring spade in a dressing of manure, and one quart of salt to each square rod, and cultivate well until the plants begin to die down. The bed may be cut one two or three times, *all* the short shoots above the surface should be cut, and after final cutting, give a good dressing of manure, ashes and salt. Ever after that, the bed should give a full crop if annually dressed with manure, ashes and salt. As soon as the tops are ripe and yellow they should be cut and burned.

Conover's Colossal.—A mammoth sort, frequently sending up fifteen to thirty sprouts from one to ons and a half inches in diameter from a single plant, and spreading less than most sorts. Color deep green; quality good.

Broccoli.

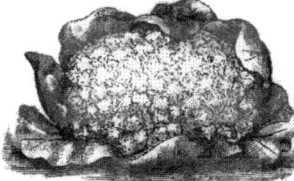

Produces heads in autum like a Cauliflower. Sow about the middle of April; trasplant in rich soil and manage as winter Cabbage. For an early crop

White Cape Broccoli.

sow in a hot-bed and cultivate as early Cauliflower. It succeeds best in a moist soil and cool climate; can be had in perfection from November to April.

Early Purple Cape.—This is the best for the Northern States, producing compact heads, of a brownish purple, and of good flavor.

White Cape.—Not as early as the above; heads large, creamy white; close and certain to head.

Brussels Sprouts.

This is one of the best vegetables for winter use, producing from the axils of the leaves an abundance of sprouts resembling small cabbages, of excellent mild flavor.

Brussels Sprouts.

Early Refugee is very productive and fine for spring snaps or for pickling. Used by market gardeners. (Fig. 2.)

Yellow Six Weeks is very early, productive and excellent for snap or shell.

White Kidney, or Royal Dwarf is an excellent green shell bean, and one of the best for baking. (Fig. 6.)

Golden Wax. This variety is quite early. Pods are long, brittle and entirely stringless, and of rich buttery flavor, and one of the very best for our Market Gardeners. (Fig. 3.)

German, or Black Wax is one of the best. Pods are of rich, waxy yellow when fit for use, and very tender and delicious. (Fig. 18.)

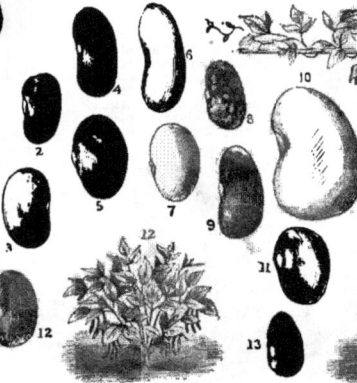

Beans.

One pound will plant 50 feet of drill; 80 pounds one acre in drill.

DWARF SNAPS OR STRINGLESS.

All varieties of this class are tender, and do best in rather dry, light soil, and should not be planted till the ground is warm and can continue at intervals throughout the season. Plant 3 inches deep, in rows 2 feet apart. Keep well hoed, drawing the earth up to the stems while dry.

Early Improved Red Valentine is one of the very best leading sorts. Pods are round, fleshy and tender, and remain longer in a green state than most varieties. (Fig 8.)

Cleveland's Improved Red Pod Valentine is ten days earlier than the Red Valentine and much more prolific and combines all its good qualities. One of the best for market and gardeners.

White Valentine is a good short snap, and also desirable as a shell bean.

Red Eye, or Early China is largely cultivated in California by market gardeners, and is good either as a snap or dry shell bean.

Early Mohawk is one of the hardiest varieties and will endure some frost. It is a good string bean, and is also desirable for pickling. (Fig. 4.)

Ivory Pod Wax are a White bean and earlier than the Black Wax. Pods are tender and stringless, and of a rich creamy flavor, and are ivory white.

Crystal White Wax are similar to the above—crisp, tender, and of the richest flavor. The pods develop quickly and retain their tenderness longer than any other sorts.

English Dwarf, or Broad Windsor is a very hardy kind and can be planted very early in the season, in good soil, in drills 5 feet apart. Pinch off tops as soon as the lower pods begin to fill. They are used only as shell beans.

Beans.

POLE, OR RUNNING. 1 pound to 75 hills.

These are generally more tender than dwarf kinds, and should not be planted till the ground becomes warm. Set poles about 4 feet apart, and pinch off the tops when they grow higher than the poles. They succeed best in sandy loam mixed with well rotted compost to each hill.

Large Lima are the most buttery and delicious of all, and are a universal favorite, green or dry. (Fig. 10.)

Giant Wax (Red Seed) make pods 6 to 9 inches long, thick and fleshy, of yellow waxy color, and is very productive and tender. (Fig. 12.)

Horticultural, or Speckled Cranberry is an old favorite and is equally good as a snap or as a shell bean, either green or dry. (Fig. 5.)

White Dutch Runners are very ornamental, large white seed, and beautiful clusters of white flowers, and is a good shell bean.

Scarlet Runners are a great favorite, producing clusters of beautiful scarlet flowers, which are very ornamental. This is very fine for use as a green shell bean. (Fig. 14.)

Dutch Case-Knife. A very productive variety, and one of the earliest; sometimes used as "snaps," but generally shelled. Next to the Limas the best market sort.

Southern Prolific. Desirable for snap beans, mature in seventy days. Bears its pods in clusters. Popular in the South.

Asparagus, or Yard Long. Pod sometimes grows from two to three feet long; very curious, succulent and tender.

Beets.

The soil best suited for Beet culture is that which is rather light and well enriched. Sow in drills one foot apart and 1 inch deep, as early as the ground can be worked; continue for a succession as late as the middle of July; when the plants are large enough thin out to stand 6 inches apart in the rows. The Sugar and Mangel Wurzel varieties are grown for feeding stock, and should be sown from April to June in drills 2 feet apart, and

afterwards thinned out to stand 1 foot apart in the rows; keep well cultivated. One ounce will sow a drill fifty feet in length; five or six pounds are required for an acre.

Eclipse. A very early, smooth, globe-shaped beet with small top and thin root; its skin an intense deep red, its flesh of very fine texture, earliness and quality it is excelled by none. Many of our Market Gardeners prefer it to the Egyptian.

Early Blood Turnip. An old standard variety of fine form and avor. Next to Eclipse in earliness.

Egyptian Turnip. A standard sort, being from ten to twelve days earlier than the old Blood Turnip. The roots are large in size, and of a rich, deep crimson color. From the smallness of the tops of the Egyptian at least one-fourth more can be grown on the same space than any other variety.

Extra Early or Bassano. Turnip-shaped. An improved early kind, small top, round root, sweet and tender attain a very large size.

Dewing's Improved Blood Turnip. Roots deep blood-red, of fine form and flavor. Very early. An excellent market variety.

Pine Apple. The roots are half long, medium size; well formed and of very dark crimson color. Fine grained, sweet, tender and excellent for table use.

Long Dark Blood. Long, smooth, growing to good size; half out of the ground; color dark blood-red; top small, dark red, and of upright growth; keeps well. It is apt to be tough when sown to early.

Bastian's Half-Long Blood Of bright color and excellent quality; a valuable variety to follow. The early sorts for winter use plant about the middle of July.

Swiss Chard, or Sea Kale. The leaves are used as Spinach, and the mid-rib stewed and served as Asparagus.

Early Blood Turnip.

Dewing's Improved Blood Turnip.

Hendersons Pineapple

Long Blood

Egyptian Blood Turnip.

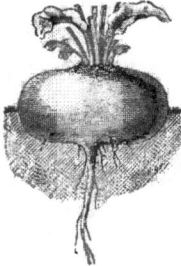

Bassano.

Mangel Wurtzel.—(For Field Culture.)

4 to 6 pounds to the acre. Extensively cultivated in all parts of the country as a field crop for feeding stock in the winter. When grown for this purpose, the distance between the rows should be from two to two and a half feet so that the cultivation can be done with horse tools instead of with hand-hoes.

Norbiton Giant. Ons of the finest quality in cultivation; grows to an enormous size.

Golden Tankard Mangel. Considered indispensable by the best dairymen, owing to its productiveness and richness in saccharine matter. Deep yellow flesh and skin.

Red Globe Mange.

Yellow Ovoid.

Imperial Sugar.   Orange Globe Mangel.   Golden Tankard Mangel.   Long Red Mangel.

Yellow Ovoid. A very nutritious and valuable variety; bulb ovoid; intermediate between the long and globe varieties; flesh solid, vigorous and productive.

Red Globe Mangel. A large red oval variety, which keeps well, and produces better crops on shallow soil than the Long Red.

Orange Globe Mangel. The same as the above, only differing in color.

Mammoth Long Red. Grown extensively for agricultural purposes, producing large roots partly above the ground.

White Sugar Beet. The large amount of saccharine matter contained in this variety makes it very valuable for stock feeding purposes; grows to a large size.

Cabbage.

One ounce for about 2,000 plants.

Cabbages require a deep rich soil and thorough working. The seed for the early crops can be sown in hot beds. When of size to transplant, place the earlier kinds from 12 to 18 inches apart. The largest and later kinds 2 feet or more. The plants should be set down to first leaf, so that the stem is all below the surface of the ground, and hoe often. Our seed is from the finest and purest selected strains of American growth.

" True " Jersey Early Wakefield.

Early Jersey Wakefield. The *best early* Cabbage in cultivation. It possesses the merit of large size of head, small outside foliage, and uniformity in producing a crop.

Early Winningstadt. A second early variety, coming in about three weeks later than the early varieties. It is an excellent sort, as it

Early Winningstadt.

heads uniformly and is of large size, often weighing 20 lbs.; heads pyramidal, the outer leaves spiral and spreading, which necessitates planting it wider than the early sorts.

All Seasons. Similar in form to the Stone Mason; solid, compact; claimed to be as early and larger than the Henderson's Summer; comparatively new; wherever tried has given surprising satisfaction.

Early French Ox-heart. A leading variety among the market gardeners; heads very early, tender, and of fine flavor; our seed is selected from extra fine stock

Improved Premium Late Flat Dutch. This is the best strain of this standard variety and more largely grown than any other for market and long-keeping quality. Short stem and large solid flat heads.

Excelsior Flat Dutch is an improved California-grown variety, highly esteemed by all for its keeping quality.

Large French Oxheart.

Stone Mason. An improved variety of Mason Drumhead, of sweet and tender quality.

Early Large York. Is a popular known variety, superior, robust and endures the heat well.

Marblehead. One of the latest and largest of all the cabbage tribe. Solid, tender and freely heading.

Drumhead Savoy. The Savoy Cabbages are the finest flavor of all; finely crimped and netted and yet makes a compact, solid head. Dark green.

Mammoth Marblehead.

Early Dwarf Ulm Savoy. This is earlier and dwarfer than the Drumhead, and of very fine flavor.

Henderson's Early Summer. Heads about ten days later than the Jersey Wakefield It may be classed as the best *large early* Cabbage In weigh. it is equal to most of the late varieties; its short outer leaves enable it to be planted as close as the Jersey Wakefield.

Filderkraut resembles the well known Winningstadt, but is larger, more pointed, and heads up with fewer outside leaves. Largely grown for making kraut.

Henderson's Early Summer.

Fottler's Improved Brunswick. A second early and late variety grown originally by the Boston gardeners, but which is now cultivated quite generally all over the country

Large Late Drumhead.   Red Dutch,

Large Late Drumhead. A favorite winter variety with the market gardener. It bears extra large solid heads, and is a little later than the Flat Dutch,

Red Dutch. Used almost exclusively for pickling. It is one of the hardiest of all cabbages; will keep later in the season than any of them. Slow to mature, however, and requires a richer soil for its perfect development.

Cauliflower.

CULTURE. Cauliflower ought to receive a similar treatment to Cabbage, except that it requires an extra rich soil, an occasional application of liquid manure and frequent watering, especially when heading. Early sorts are mostly sown in hot beds, and transplanted before setting out in open ground, and finally transplanted in rich deeply worked soil, 2 feet by 15 inches apart. Late sorts are sown and cultivated like late cabbage. When heading tie the top leaves together to protect from exposure to the sun.

Early Dwarf Erfurt. Extra Early Dwarf, small leaf, solid, pure white heads, best quality.

Early Snowball. The earliest and best heading variety cultivated; dwarf habit and short outer leaves. (See among specials.)

Early Paris. A popular French variety. White and sure to head, and standard sort for early or late crop.

Late Asiatic. Large, white and compact, but later than the preceding.

Lenormand. Short stem. A superior sort and quality; large, well-formed heads, and late.

Large Late Algiers. New, and much prized for late sort.

Veitch's Autumn Giant. This is one of the best late varieties grown. Robust habit, large heads, compact and thoroughly protected by leaves.

Celery.

One ounce will make about 2,000 plants.

Should be sown in open ground, as early as it will be fit to work, and be kept clear of weeds until ready for transplanting Cut tops once or twice before to insure stocky plants. When ground is well prepared. set in rows three feet apart and six inches from each other, and see that the soil is well packed around the roots by pressing with the foot Run the cultivator or hoe between the rows to destroy the weeds, and when grown to sufficient size draw up the earth for blanching pressing with the hand to keep the leaf upright and banking up to the top on each side.

Henderson's White Plume. This requires less labor for blanching, is crisp, solid, and of nutty flavor and valuable for family use. (See specials).

Henderson's Half Dwarf. Solid, crisp, and nutty flavor and very desirable.

Boston Market Dwarf. Short, bushy, white, solid and excellent flavor.

Dwarf Golden Heart. The heart of this variety is waxy and showy, and for market use desirable. It is very solid and of excellent flavor and a good keeper.

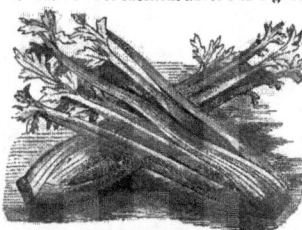

Giant White Solid. Large size, solid, crisp, and good market variety.

Celeriac, or Turnip Rooted Celery. A variety with turnip shaped roots which may be cooked and sliced and used with vinegar, making an excellent salad. It is hardy and otherwise treated as other celery.

Giant White Solid.

Soup Celery. Its seed is used for flavoring soups, stews, etc., and is sold for this purpose at a low price.

Carrot.

The Carrot like other root crops, delights in a sandy loam, richly tilled. For early crop sow in spring, as soon as the ground is in good working order; for later crops they may be sown any time until the middle of June. Sow in rows about fifteen inches apart, thinning out to three or four inches between the plants. In field culture, when grown for horses or cattle, the rows should be two feet apart, so that the crop can be worked by the Horse Cultivator. As Carrot seed is slow to germinate, all precautions must be taken.

Early Scarlet Horn. A favorite sort for early crop, but not large enough for general culture. It is one of the varieties that is sold in the markets bunched up in the green state. It matures earlier than the Long Orange, and is some times used for forcing. No. 3.

Half Long Red (Stump Rooted.) Largely grown for the market. In size and time of maturity it is between the Early Scarlet Horn and the Long Orange. No. 6.

Large White Belgian Grows one-third out of the ground; root pure white, green above ground, with small top; grows to a very large size and is easily gathered; flesh rather coarse; is raised exclusively for stock. No. 4.

Danvers. A very valuable sort; in form midway between the Long Orange and Early Horn class. It is of a rich shade of orange, growing very smooth and handsome. This variety will yield the greatest bulk with the smallest length of root of any now grown. Under the best cultivation it has yielded from twenty-five to thirty tons per acre. No. 8.

Improved Long Orange. The best late, deep orange colored variety, equally adapted for garden or farm culture. An improvement on the Long Orange, by careful selections of the best formed and deepest colored roots. No. 7.

Long Scarlet Altringham. A large, good flavored field variety, for table use or feeding stock. No. 2.

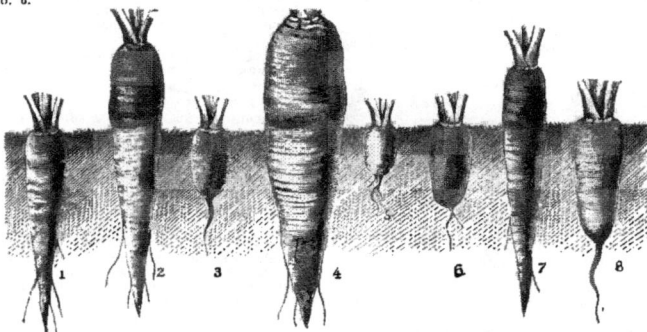

Collard.

Is used in place of Cabbage, and grows where it is difficult to make Cabbage head. Cultivate same as Cabbage.

Chicory.

This is grown to mix with or as a substitute for coffee. It requires the same cultivation as Carrots.

Cress or Pepper Grass.

Well known as a pungent salad. It should be sown thickly and at frequent intervals for succession; it quickly runs to seeds. Cover very slightly in planting.

Double and Triple Curled. Is very fine and can be cut too or three times.

Water Cress. Is a perennial and will grow in and alongside of streams and ponds. It has a very pleasant, pungent taste.

Cucumber·

Cucumbers succeed best in warm, moist, rich, loamy ground. They should not be planted in the open air until there is a prospect of settled warm weather. Plant in the hills about four feet apart each way. The hills should be previously prepared by mixing thoroughly with the soil of each a shovelful of well rotted manure. When all danger from insects is past, thin out the plants, leaving three or four of the strongest to each hill. The fruit should be plucked when large enough, as if left to ripen on the vines, it destroys their productiveness.

Early Frame. Excellent variety for table use; tender and well flavored, and keeps green longer than any other variety; also makes splendid hard, green pickels, comes into use after the Early Cluster.

Early Cluster. Vines vigorous, producing the crop near the root and in clusters. Fruit short, dark green. Good for table use, but not adapted to pickling.

Improved Long Green. Undoubtedly the best variety in cultivation for table or pickling. About one foot in length, firm and crisp; this variety produces seeds sparingly.

Early White Spine. An excellent variety for table use; very early; grows uniformly straight and smooth; light green with white prickels; tender; of excellent flavor.

Long Green Turkey. The leading long green variety for pickling, of excellent quality and productiveness, fruit dark green, firm and crisp.

Nichol's Medium Green. For early forcing, late sowing for pickling, or for ordinary table use this variety will be found useful. It is of a dark green color, pleasant flavor, and very productive.

Extra Long White Spine. A variety used largely for forcing, by market gardeners. They grow ten to twelve inches long and very straight. They make fine, hard, brittle pickels when four to five inches long; dark green and handsome.

Boston Pickling, or Green Prolific. One of the best pickling varieties, dark green, tender, crisp, very productive, of fine flavor, uniform size, and good for table use.

Early Russian. Fruit three to four inches long, an inch and a half in diameter; generally produced in pairs; flesh tender, crisp and well flavored; comes into use about ten days earlier than any other variety, and makes a fine, small pickel.

Gherkin, for Pickling. A very small oval shaped, prickly variety. It is grown exclusively for pickling; is the smallest of all the varieties, and should always be pickled when young and tender The seed is slow to germinate.

Corn, Sweet.

Pee-and-Kay. Crosby's Early. Amber Cream. Mammoth Sugar.

A rich, warm, alluvial soil is the best, and immediately before planting this should be as deeply and thoroughly worked as possible. Plant for a succession of crops every three weeks, in hills three feet apart each way, and six seeds in a hill. Cover about half an inch, thin out to three plants.

Pee-and-Kay. It has a very large, plump sweet ear, and comes nearly as early as the Marblehead. The stalks are from six to seven feet high, with from two to the ears on the stalk, set well down, kernels large, plump, pearly white and sweet. We can recommend it highly.

Cory. The earliest of all sweet corns. It closely resembles the Early Marblehead, but earlier by at least a week. To market men, the Cory is a valuable variety, as the first sweet corn will bring double the price it commands when the supply becomes general. (Specialties.)

Marblehead Early. Early Minnesota. Black Mexican. Egyptian Sweet.

Crosby's Early. Highly prized by market gardeners; very early; ears rather short, averaging from 12 to 16 rows; of a rich sugary flavor.

Amber Cream. 8-rowed; cream colored; height 4 feet; very sweet.

Mammoth Sugar. Very large ears and very sweet.

Marblehead Early. Larger than the Cory and a little later; it is a good early sort for the home garden, and market gardeners.

Early Minnesota. Very early; a decidedly excellent variety; ears fair size and uniform; plant rather dwarf.

Black Mexican. Although the ripe grain is blush-black, the corn, when in condition for the table, cooks remarkably white, and is surpassed by none in tenderness. This by many, is considered the most desirable for family use of any of the second sorts.

Egyptian Sweet. Noted for its productiveness, large ears, and for sweetness and tenderness. It is peculiarly adapted for canning purposes. The superiority of often bringing a half more per can than other sorts. In rich ground the stalks will average 3 ears each. Its season is about the same as the Evergreen.

Stowell's Evergreen. The Standard late variety. If planted at the same time with earlier kinds, will keep the table supplied until October. It is hardy and productive, very tender and sugary, remaining a long time in a fresh condition, suitable for boiling.

Field corn in quantities to suit, at lowest market rates.

Egg Plant.

The Egg Plant will thrive well in any good garden soil; succeeds best in a deep, warm, rich soil and full exposure to the sun. Sow in hot bed very early in Spring; transplant two and one-half feet apart each way after weather becomes settled and warm. If no hot bed is at hand, plants may be started in pots or boxes.

New York Improved Egg Plant.

New York Improved. The leading market sort, very large and smooth; fine dark color; very prolific and of excellent quality.

Early Long Purple. Much smaller than the New York Improved; very early and productive; fruit long, dark, rich purple; good quality.

Black Pekin. The fruit of this variety is jet black, fine grain and delicate flavor; very prolific and desirable for market gardeners.

Endive.

One of the best salads for Fall and Winter use. Sow from late in the Spring to the middle of Summer, in shallow drills fourteen inches apart; thin the plants to one foot in drills, and when fully grown, tie over the onter leaves of a few plants every week or fortnight in dry weather, to blanch, which takes ten days in hot, and twenty days in cool weather. Draw up a little earth to the base of the plant. Rich, mellow soil, in an open situation is most suitable.

Green Curled. Is the hardiest variety, with beautifully curled dark green leaves, which blanch white, and are very crisp and tender.

Green Curled Endive.

Garlic.

This is extensively used for flavoring soups, stews, etc. The sets should be planted early in spring in rich soil in rows one foot apart, and from three to five inches apart in the rows. Cultivate like onions. When the tops die off the crop is ready to gather.

Kohl-Rabi.

This is an intermediate between the Cabbage and Turnip. For an early crop start in hot-bed and treat the same as early cabbage; if for late crop, sow in June or July. Remove the plants early in the Fall and store for Winter use, the same as turnips. This is a favorite with Europeans, and very superior for feeding cows for milk.

Early white Vienna. Best early variety for table; bulbs white, handsome, small, highly esteemed by market gardeners.

White Vienna Kohl Rabi.

Early Purple. Very similar to the last, except in color, which is a bright purple; a desirable sort.

Kale or Borecole.

The Kales are more hardy than Cabbage, make excellent greens for winter and spring use, and are improved by frost. Sow from May to June, in well prepared soil, covering it thinly and evenly and cultivate the same as Cabbage. Half an ounce will sow a bed of twenty square feet.

Dwarf Green Curled. This variety is extensively grown as Winter Greens, sown in the Fall, in rows one foot apart and treated in every way as Spinach, it is ready for use in early Spring.

Green Curled Scotch. Very hardy, and is improved by a moderate frost. Leaves bright green and beautifully curled, It stands the winters in the Middle States without protection.

Green Curled Scotch Kale, or Borecole.

Sea Kale. This is quite a favorite with many; its young shoots are blanched for use. It is trained and treated like the Cabbage.

Sea Kale.

Leek.

The Leek is very hardy and easily cultivated; it succeeds best in a light but well enriched soil. Sow as early in spring as practicable, in drills one inch deep and one foot apart. When six or eight inches high, they may be transplanted in rows ten inches apart each way, as deep as possible, that the neck, being covered, may be blanched. If fine Leeks are desired, the ground can hardly be made too rich.

London Flag Leek.

London Flag. The variety most generally cultivated in this country, hardy, of good quality.

Lettuce.

Lettuce thrives best in rich, moist ground. For successive crops, sowing may be made in the open ground as early as the spring opens, and continuing until July. Always thin out well or the plants will not be strong. When wanted as a cut salad, sow the seed thickly in rows or broadcast.

Early Curled Silesia. A fine early curled variety which does not head, leaves large, tender and of fine flavor.

Early Curled Simpson. This does not head, but forms a close, compact mass of leaves; very early, excellent for forcing.

Early Curled Simpson.

Boston Curled Of superior quality; does not form solid heads; fine for early use.

Boston Curled.

Early Prize Head. Forms a mammoth plant, in which even the outer leaves are crisp and tender, and remains so throughout the season. It is slow to run up to seed, of superb flavor and very hardy, one of the best varieties for family use, but for market gardens it is if too tender to stand much handling.

Hanson. The heads are of very large size, deliciously sweet, tender and crisp, even to the outer leaves. Color green outside and white within.

Black Seeded Simpson. Like the Curled Simpson, this variety does not, properly, form a head; but it differs in the leaves being nearly white, and attaining nearly DOUBLE the size of the Curled Simpson. It stands the summer heat splendidly while it is equally suited for forcing.

Early Summer Cabbage. One of the very best head Lettuces for summer that we know of. The heads are of good size, close and well formed. It is a splendid market variety.

Oak Leaved. A distinct variety due to the peculiar outline of the leaves, which are shaped like those of the oak. The heads are compact, crisp and tender, and it is largely free from that bitter taste peculiar to so many kinds of Lettuce. See specialties.

Tennis Ball. A favorite forcing variety. Well formed heads, hardy and crisp, of excellent quality. One of the earliest of the heading varieties.

Salamander. An excellent summer variety, forming good sized heads that stand drought and heat longer without injury than any other sort.

Salamander.

Phila. Butter or Cabbage.

Phila. Butter or Cabbage. Produces fine, greenish-white, large heads, of extra quality, remarkably crisp, and tender, sure to head; of quick growth. It is one of the best for forcing, and for summer use, as it is slow to shoot to seed, and resists heat well.

Ice Drumhead. Produces a beautiful head, very firm, solid and compact. The head is of an attractive and silvery white, rich, buttery, and most delicious in flavor. It comes early and stands a long while before running to seed; excellent for early spring and summer use.

White Paris Cos. The heads are long, upright, with oblong leaves. It is very hardy, of large size, and long in running to seed; tender, brittle, and high flavored.

All the Year Round. A hardy, crisp eating and compact growing variety, with small, close heads of a dark green color; an excellent summer Lettuce, and valuable for forcing.

White Paris Cos.

Martynia Used much for pickling, when gathered while green and tender. Sow in open ground and transplant to two feet apart.

Musk Melons.

One oz. for 50 hills; three pounds for an acre.

Melons thrive best in good sandy loam. Plant as soon as the ground becomes warm, in hills six feet apart; a little well rotted manure in each hill will be of great benefit. Put twelve to fifteen seeds to a hill, and after they are up and all danger from bugs is over, thin out to three plants to the hill. If the growth is too rapid, pinch off the top and leading shoots, and thin out the fruit, which will increase the size of those remaining. Pumpkins, Squashes or Cucumbers should not be grown near them, as they would be apt to hybridize.

Emerald Gem Melon. This most excellent new musk melon originated in Michigan. It is of superior flavor and quality; the outside skin is an emerald green color and quite smooth; they ripen early and produce well; the flesh is light red or salmon, very thick, juicy and crystalline, and luscious in flavor. See specialties.

California Netted Cantaloupe. This is the most popular and best market variety grown in this State; large, deeply ribbed and netted; green flesh and of delicious flavor and a good keeper.

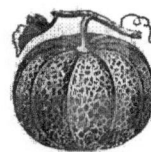

Montreal Improved Green Nutmeg. Nearly round, slightly flattened at the ends, with a densely netted, green skin. They grow to a large, uniform size, averaging from fifteen to twenty pounds in weight, specimens often weighing twenty-five pounds. The flesh is remarkably thick and of good flavor. Owing to its large and handsome appearance, it sells rapidly in the market at very high prices.

Surprise. An excellent variety, having thin, cream-colored skin, thickly netted; of medium size and thick, salmon-colored flesh. The flavor is delicious, and they are very productive.

Surprise.

Champion Market Musk Melon In shape is almost a perfect globe and densely netted; ripens early and grows to a very large, uniform size. The flesh is thick, light green in color, and of a rich, sweet flavor. Vines are vigorous and remarkably healthy. Very productive. See specialties.

Skillman's Fine Netted. This is a small, rough, netted variety, flattened at the ends; flesh green; very thick, firm, sugary, and of delicious flavor. Among the earliest of the green-fleshed melons.

Casaba, or Persian Of good size, very delicious and fine flavor; usual weight from 10 to 15 pounds; the best prolific, late oval, netted green-fleshed variety.

Casaba, or Persian.

Large Hackensack. Very popular with market gardeners in the vicinity of large cities, being of a very large size; very prolific, rich in flavor, thick, juicy flesh, and always commands a ready sale.

Large Hackensack.

Bay View. A large oval Melon of the Persian type, of superior quality, thin rind, flesh green, firm and sugary.

Baltimore. A green-fleshed Melon, which should be largely grown. It is very productive; of good size, flesh thick and of delicious flavor, and is largely grown by leading market gardeners as being in every way a desirable sort.

Miller Cream Nutmeg Melon.

This splendid melon was thoroughly tested the past season by many of our best market gardeners and melon growers, and is pronounced by all one of the very best they have ever grown. The flesh is of a rich salmon color, very thick, sweet and melting in quality. The rind is very thin, slightly sutured and finely netted. Vines grow strong and are very productive, covering the ground with fruit. They retain their bright fresh appearance, and remain solid several days after being pulled. See Specialties.

Green Citron. A very desirable melon either for the table or market; very juicy; honey flavor; thick green flesh; a standard sort.

White Japan. Medium size; flesh thick, skin pale green; one of the earliest; worthy of a place in every family garden.

Green Citron.

Golden Gem. This valuable new cantaloupe, is admitted by prominent melon growers to be the very best early variety now grown. They grow very uniform in shape and size, weighing about two pounds each, skin green and thickly netted. They are very thick-meated, flesh of a light green color, the inside surface, when cut open, being of a beautiful golden color. In quality and flavor they are *superior*, being uniformly *rich, sugary and luscious.* They are *extra early* in ripening, the vines keeping green longer and producing better than any variety we have ever known. They sell in markets, where known, right alongside of other good varieties, at double price.

The Volga. See Specialties.

Green and Gold See Specialties.

Florida Favorite See Specialties.

Watermelon.

One ounce to 50 hills, or about three pounds to an acre.

Mountain Sprout A good market sort, fruit of large size; longish oval; skin dark green, marbled with light shades; red flesh of excellent quality.

Mountain Sprout.   Black Spanish.

Black Spanish. Fruit large of a round shape, color a very dark green, and seeds black.

Mountain Sweet Fruit oblong, dark green, rind thin, flesh red, solid and very sweet.

Ice Cream, or Peerless Fruit of medium size, nearly round; skin pale green, rind very thin, white seeds, flesh solid and delicious.

Ice Cream or Peerless.   Georgia Rattlesnake.

Georgia Rattlesnake. One of the largest varieties, and stands shipment long distances. Fruit cylindrical, square at the ends, smooth, distinctly striped and mottled light and dark green. Flesh bright scarlet, and very sweet.

Pride of Georgia Originated in Monroe County, Georgia. The rind is dark green, shape nearly oval, and ridged like an orange; grows partly on one end, flesh rich scarlet, very sweet and crisp; attains a large size, and a good shipper.

Citron For preserving; flesh white and solid; seed red.

Scaly Bark An excellent variety; of great value to shippers; remains in choice eating condition from ten to fifteen days after being pulled. The flesh is light crimson; solid, tender and of fine flavor. Skin is almost smooth, looks as if covered with fish scales. Rind, though quite thin, is remarkably tough.

Cuban Queen. The largest and one of the best grown; an excellent keeper, skin beautifully striped dark and light green. The flesh is red, solid, delicate in flavor and very sweet; bears transit well.

Orange. Flesh red, tender and sweet, separating from the rind like an orange.

Mammoth Ironclad. A variety of undoubted excellence, of large size and weight, crops of it averaging nearly 50 pounds each. The flesh is deep red and of a delicious rich flavor, holding its fine qualities very close to the skin. In outside appearance it is somewhat like the Gypsy. For shipping and keeping qualities the Ironclad is unsurpassed. The vines are strong growing, and altogether it is a most valuable acquisition. See Specialties.

Kolb Gem. This variety originated in Alabama three years ago, has proven to be a very valuable acquisition. It is uniformly round and grows to a good size, often attaining a weight of twenty-five or fifty pounds; the flesh is a bright red and flavor excellent, rind dark green, striped and very tough. It is unsurpassed as a shipping melon, retaining its freshness and sweetness for a long time after ripening. It is unusually productive and will mature as far north as Chicago. See Specialties.

Imperial Lodi. This is now the most popular of all the California grown varieties. Large, oblong, skin light pea-green in color, and thin. Red flesh, very sweet and fine in flavor, and one of the very best for cultivation for market sales.

Seminole See Specialties.

Hungarian Honey. See Specialties.

Mushrooms.

The Mushroom is an edible fungus, of a white color, changing to brown when old. The gills are loose, of a pinkish red, changing to liver color. It produces no seed, but instead, a white, fibrous substance in broken threads, called spawn, which is preserved in horse manure, being pressed in the form of bricks. Thus prepared it will retain its vitality for years.

CULTURE. Mushrooms can be grown in the cellar, in sheds, or in hot-beds in open air, on shelves, or out-of-the-way places. Fermenting horse manure, at a temperature of about 70 degrees, is made into beds the size required, eighteen inches deep. In this bed plant the broken pieces of spawn six inches apart, covering the whole with two inches of light soil, and protect from cold and severe rains. The mushrooms will appear in about six weeks. Water sparingly and with lukewarm water.

Mustard.

Makes a pungent salad. Sow thickly in rows and cut for use when two inches high. White London is the best for salads. The Brown or Black, is, however, more pungent.

Nasturtium.

The seeds, while young and succulent, are pickled for capers. The plants are quite ornamental and make excellent screens in the garden.

Okra, or Gumbo.

This vegetable is grown for its pods which are used in soups, stews, etc. It is very nutritious and of easy culture, Sow when the ground has become warm, three feet apart and one inch deep, and thin out to ten inches in the row. The pods are dried for winter use.

New Improved Dwarf. This new early variety, has long, green, slender pods, very productive, and grows fourteen inches high.

Long Green. Long ribbed erect pods, sharply tapering to a point; very productive.

Onion.

The value of this crop depends almost solely on the quality of the seed sown. Realizing this, we have taken the greatest care in selecting our stocks, and can confidently recommend them to all our customers, those who use large quantities, as well as those who use small, as being unsurpassed for quality, germination and trueness; being grown for us solely by men of years of experience in raising this important seed. Our seed will produce full-sized Onions the first year of sowing, for which purpose sow four to five lbs. per acre. For growing small sets our seed is equally good, and should be sown for this purpose at the rate of about 60 lbs. to the acre.

Extra Early Red. A medium sized, flat variety; an abundant producer, and very uniform in shape and size; moderately strong flavored, and comes into use nearly two weeks earlier than the Large Red Wethersfield; very desirable for early market use.

Early Red Globe. A comparatively new variety, maturing as early as the flat sort. It is globe shaped; skin deep red; flesh mild and tender. Very handsome in appearance.

Large Red Wethersfield. This is a standard variety. Large size; skin deep purplish red; form round, somewhat flattened; flesh purplish white; moderately fine grained, and stronger flavored than any of the other kinds. Very productive, the best keeper, and one of the most popular for general cultivation.

Yellow Danvers. A fine variety of medium size, globular in form; skin yellowish brown; flesh white, comparatively mild and well flavored, and very productive; requires rich soil and good cultivation to produce heavy crops. By careful selection we have improved the original shape of this variety, so that many seedsmen catalogue it as Yellow Globe Danvers.

White Globe. Yields abundantly, producing handsome and uniformly globe shaped bulbs. The flesh is firm, fine grained, and of mild flavor. Sometimes called Southport White Globe.

Yellow Strasburg (Yellow Dutch). Later, flatter and larger than Yellow Danvers; good keeper.

Giant Rocca. An immense onion. Globular in form; skin light brown; flesh mild and tender. It will produce a large onion from seed the first season, but to attain the largest growth, the smallest bulbs should be set out the next spring, when they will continue increasing in size, instead of producing seed.

Giant White Italian Tripoli. A large, beautiful, pure white,

flat onion of mild and excellent flavor, and will produce a somewhat larger onion from seed than the the White Portugal.

Queen. A silver skinned variety, of quick growth and remarkable keeping qualities. If sown in early spring it will produce onions one to two inches in diameter early in summer, and if sown in July, will with favorable weather be ready to pull late in autumn, and be sound and fit for use until the following summer. Particularly valuable for pickles, as if sown thickly they will mature perfect hard onions from one-half to three-quarters of an inch in diameter.

Large Red Italian Tripoli This has the same characteristics as the White Tripoli; except in color however.

Bulbs.

Top Sets or Buttons Produce on the top of the stalk instead of seed, a number of small bulbs or onions, about the size of acorns, which, if planted, will produce a large onion maturing earlier than from seed. The large onion produces the top onion, and the little top onion produces the large onion.

Bottom Sets. These are produced from seeds sown thickly in beds or drills. When the tops die down the small bulbs are gathered and spread out and kept in a cool dry place for future planting, and should be set, when the ground is in condition, in rows one foot apart and three or four inches distant.

White Portugal, or Silver Skin.

White Portugal or Silver Skin Mild flavor and handsome; much grown for pickling; poor keeper for market but good for White Sets.

Parsnip.

The value of the Parsnip for the table depends solely on the careful selection of the best roots and most thorough cultivation. As the seed is slow to germinate, too much care cannot be taken with planting. The soil must be warm and mellow. The earth should be firmly pressed over the seed. It should be covered to the depth of half an inch. Sow in drills 15 to 18 inches apart and thin out to 6 inches in the row.

Hollow Crown or Long Smooth. Roots oblong, ending somewhat abruptly, with a small tap root; grows mostly below the surface; has a very smooth, clean skin, and is easily distinguished by the leaves arising from a cavity on the top or crown of the root.

Student. A half long variety of delicious flavor.

Pepper.

Grown largely for pickles. Sown in hot bed early and transplanted to the open ground when the weather is favorable. They should be planted in warm, mellow soil, in rows eighteen inches apart. They may also be sown in the open ground when the danger of frost is past, and the soil is warm and weather settled.

Golden Dawn. In size and shape it resembles the Large Bell. It is very productive; color a bright golden yellow; excellent quality, being distinguished from all others, on account of its mild flavor and beautiful appearance.

Red Cayenne. A long, slim pod, rather pointed, and when ripe, of a bright red color. Extremely strong and pungent, and is the sort used for commercial purposes.

Sweet Mountain Plants very vigorous and productive, growing upright with moderately large leaves. Fruit large, long, smooth and handsome, being when green of a bright deep green color, entirely free from purple tinge, and when mature of a rich red. Flesh thick, sweet and mild flavored. Well suited to use as a stuffed pickle.

Large Squash. Fruit large, flat, tomato shaped, more or less ribbed; skin smooth and glossy; flesh mild, thick meated, and pleasant to the taste, although possessing more pungency than the other large sorts; very productive, and the best variety for pickling.

Large Bell, or Bull Nose. A very large sort of inverted bell shape, suitable for filling with cabbage, etc., and for a mixed pickle. Flesh thick, hard and less pungent than most other sorts, and one of the earliest varieties.

Large Bell, or Bull Nose.

Chili. Used in the manufacture of pepper sauce. Pods sharply conical, brilliant scarlet and exceedingly pungent when ripe. Requires a long, warm season, and plants should be started quite early in hot bed.

Parsley.

Used for garnishing and seasoning soups, meats, etc. Succeeds best in a mellow, rich soil. Sow thickly, early, in rows 1 foot apart and ⅓ inch deep; thin out the plants to stand 6 inches apart in the rows. The seed is slow of germination, taking from three to four weeks to make its ap-.

pearance, and often failing to come up in dry weather. To assist its coming up, soak the seed a few hours in warm water, or sprout in damp earth, and sow when it swells or bursts. For winter use protect in a frame or light cellar.

Fern Leaved. Nothing better for garnishing could be desired. As a garden decorative plant it is very ornamental. It will stand the winter if covered before frost.

Dwarf Extra Curled. Leaves tender, crisp and very curly, of a beautiful bright green color, and very ornamental; excellent for garnishing.

Pumpkin.

Sow in good soil, when the ground has become warm, in hills 8 or 10 feet apart each way, or in fields of Corn about every fourth hill; plant at the same time with the Corn; always avoid planting near other vines, as they will hybridize. The Cashaw is generally preferred for cooking or making pies.

Mammoth Tours, or Jumbo. Grows to an enormous size, often weighing 150 pounds, very productive; flesh salmon color; good keeper; desirable for cooking purposes or for stock feeding.

Connecticut Field. One of the best for field culture; can be grown with corn; largely used for stock for winter feeding.

Cashaw. A very prolific variety, resembling in form the Winter-Crook-Neck Squash, although growing to a much larger size, frequently weighing 60 pounds and over; color light cream; flesh salmon color.

Large Cheese. About the most desirable variety for culinary purposes; light yellow, with very thick sweet, brittle flesh, and a most excellent keeper.

Large Cheese.

Sugar. This variety is smaller than the Large ield, but of finer grain, sweeter and very prolific. First rate either for table or for feeding to stock.

New Japanese Pie Pumpkin. See Specialties.

Tennessee Sweet Potato Pumpkin. See Specialties.

Etampes. See Specialties.

Peas.

Peas mature earliest in a light, rich soil; for a general crop, a rich deep loam, or inclining to clay, is the best. When grown for a market crop sow in rows, 1 inch apart and 2 to 3 inches deep, the rows from 2 to 4 feet apart, according to the variety. When grown in gardens sow in double rows, 6 to 8 inches apart, that tall ones requiring brush. Commence sowing the extra early varieties as early as the ground can be worked. They should be kept clean, and earth up twice during growth. The wrinkled varieties are not as hardy as the small hard sorts, and if planted early should have a dry soil; they are, however, the sweetest and best flavored varieties. The dwarf varieties are best suited for small gardens and can be planted in rows 1 foot apart.

Cleveland's Alaska. This is considered to be the earliest, most prolific and finely flavored variety of pea grown. See cut, Specialties.

First and Best. This is one of the best extra early sorts for market planting, and is a very heavy and reliable yielder and of good quality.

Rural New Yorker. Early, productive, and uniform in ripening. It grows about 20 inches high, and is quite similar to Philadelphia Extra Early.

Royal Dwarf White Marrowfat. A large, delicious marrow pea, an excellent cropper, and a favorite with gardeners; height, 2 feet.

American Wonder. It is best suited to the private garden, as it is not productive enough as a market sort. It is very early, and requires no staking. The peas are wrinkled, and extreme dwarf growth, about 10 inches in height. It is of the finest quality.

Carter's Premium Gem.

Carter's Premium Gem. Pods long and of a dark green color. A type of and improvement on the Little Gem; very early and productive; height, 1 foot.

Bliss's Ever-Bearing. Height, eighteen inches to 2 feet; foliage large. Pods, 3 to 4 inches in length, each producing 6 to 8 large wrinkled peas. Half an inch and over in diameter, and in quality unsurpassed. A continous bearing, which gives it especial value. It should be sown thinner than other kinds, else the vines will become too crowded.

Bliss's Ever-Bearing.

Champion of England. This is acknowledged to be the best of the late varieties. It is tall growing, attaining a height of 5 feet, and requires to be staked up. The pods and peas are of the largest size.

Telephone. A tall, wrinkled marrow, enormously productive, and of the best quality. Is a strong grower, averaging 18 pods to the stalk. The pods are of the largest size, and contain from 6 to 7 large peas. A desirable sort for the family garden.

Extra Early Tom Thumb. A remarkably early variety. Very dwarf, growing but nine inches. If planted early in the Spring, three crops can be obtained in a single season.

Bliss's Abundance. A second early variety, attaining a height of from 15 to 18 inches. Pods 3 to 3½ inches long, roundish and well filled, containing 6 to 8 large wrinkled peas of excellent quality. This variety branches directly from the roots forming a veritable bush, making it necessary to sow the seeds much thinner than usual. Six to eight inches apart in the rows is as near as the plants should stand; if the soil is very rich 8 inches is preferable.

Carter's Stratagem.

Carter's Stratagem Seeds green, square, wrinkled, height, 2 feet; vigorous, branching habit; remarkably luxuriant foliage, leaves unusually large sized, under favorable conditions an enormous cropper; pods long, well filled with from seven to nine peas of the largest size, extra fine quality. One of the most elegant and showy peas in cultivation.

Yorkshire Hero A splendid wrinkled green marrow pea of branching habit and abundant bearer. Seedsmen on both sides of the Atlantic find their sales for this variety constantly on the increase; 2½ feet.

Tall White Marrowfat A favorite marrow sort; 6 feet. Mostly grown as a field pea, and very productive.

Black-Eyed Marrowfat This is extensively grown as a field pea; hardy and productive, but not so fine flavored as most other varieties; 4 feet.

Tall Sugar (Edible pods.) Can be used either shelled or cooked in the pods, which when young are very tender and sweet; 5 feet.

Dwarf Sugar (Edible pods.) Similar to the last; height, 3 feet.

RADISH.

Radishes require a sandy loam, made rich and light. A heavy clay soil will not produce good, smooth roots. Sow in 12 inch drills as early as the ground will permit, and once in two weeks for succession.

French Breakfast.   Early Scarlet Turnip.

FRENCH BREAKFAST. A very quick growing variety; brittle; crisp and tender; of oval form, bright scarlet, white tipped, and a very handsome sort.

EARLY SCARLET TURNIP A small, round, scarlet, turnip-shaped, small top variety, of quick growth, mild and crisp when young. Pkt. 5 cts., oz. 10 cts., ¼ lb. 25 cts.

OLIVE-SHAPED SCARLET Very early; handsome rose color, oblong in shape; crisp and tender. (See cut.)

EARLY WHITE TURNIP Like the above, except of a white color.

WHITE TIPPED SCARLET TURNIP An early variety of medium size and excellent flavor, and of very handsome appearance.

LONG WHITE SPANISH Roots long; skin white, slightly wrinkled; solid and pungent; somewhat milder than the Black Spanish.

Long Black Spanish.   Chinese Rose Winter.

LONG BLACK SPANISH Black skin, white flesh, very firm, solid, good keeper, grows long and large.

Chinese Rose Winter. Bright rose color; excellent for winter use; white flesh.

Early Long Scarlet.

Early Long Scarlet Short Top A main variety for outdoor planting for market gardeners or family use; grows 6 to 8 inches long; very crisp and brittle; quick growth; uniformly straight.

Round Black Spanish Globe-shaped, black skin, white flesh, very firm; the flavor is piquant and appetizing.

California White Winter A mammoth variety, growing 12 inches long, white-fleshed, firm, and of excellent quality.

Becker's Chartier Decidedly distinct in appearance from any Radish in cultivation. The color at the top is crimson, running into pink about the middle, and from thence downward it is pure, waxy white. It will attain a very large size before it becomes unfit for the table. (See specialties.)

White Strasburg Though not a new variety, is one that should be more largely grown. The roots are oblong, of a pure white color, very brittle, and of a mild flavor. For summer and fall use this sort will be found very desirable.

White Strasburg.

RHUBARB.

One ounce will sow 50 feet of drill.

Rhubarb succeeds best in deep, rich loam; the richer its condition, and the deeper it is stirred, the better, as it is scarcely possible to cultivate too deeply or to manure too highly. It is propagated by seeds, or by division of the roots—the latter being the usual method. Sow in drills eighteen inches apart, and thin out the plants to nine inches apart in the drills. When the plants are one year old transplant into beds, setting the plants five feet apart each way. Do not cut until the second year, and give a liberal dressing of manure every Fall.

We would advise, for small and family gardens, to procure the roots, which can be set out as desired.

Linnæus. An early and productive variety; skin thin; pulp highly flavored, possessing little acidity; one of the best sorts for family use.

Victoria Leaves large; skin thicker than above; pulp more acid; but a more productive variety; used largely for market.

SPINACH.

One ounce will sow 100 feet of drill; ten pounds required for one acre.

Spinach is very hardy, extremely wholesome, and makes most delicious greens, and is of the easiest culture. Sow in drills one foot apart, and commence thinning out the plants as soon as the leaves are an inch wide. Cut before hot weather, or it will become tough and stringy. For early Spring use, the seed should be sown early in the Autumn; and the plants protected through the winter by a slight covering of leaves or straw.

Round Thick Leaved. Leaves large, thick and fleshy; the variety generally grown for market, and equally good for Spring or Fall sowing..

Round Leaved Viroflay A splendid variety, with leaves long and broad, round, thick and fleshy, dark-green. Young plants transplanted into a rich soil will grow to an enormous size.

Round Leaved Viroflay.

Long Standing Spinach.

Long Standing. An improved strain; stands three weeks longer without going to seed than any variety we know of. This valuable property will be appreciated by market gardeners.

Prickly, or Fall. Best suited for Fall planting, as it is the hardiest variety and will withstand the severest weather with only a slight protection of leaves or straw. The seed is prickly, leaves triangular, oblong or arrow-shaped.

Savoy-Leaved. A very hardy and productive sort; leaves handsomely curled; a valuable variety for market or family use.

SALSIFY OR VEGETABLE OYSTER.

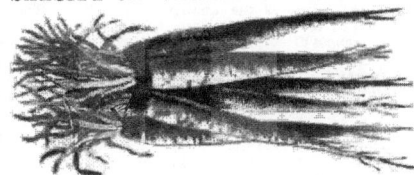

Salsify.

Long, white, tapering roots, resembling somewhat the small white parsnip, and when cooked,

have a flavor similar to oysters. Cultivate same as Parsnips.

Large White The standard variety; tender and very fine.

Scorzonera or Black Oyster Plant. Similar to the White Salsify, save in color.

SQUASHES.

Squashes should be planted in a warm, light, rich soil, after the weather has become settled and warm. Plant in well-manured hills, in the same manner as Cucumbers and Melons—the bush varieties 3 or 4 feet apart each way, and the running kinds from 6 to 8 feet. Eight to ten seeds should be sown in each hill, thinning out, after they have attained their rough leaves, and danger from bugs is over, leaving three or four of the strongest plants per hill.

Early Yellow Bush Scallop. An early, flat, scallop-shaped variety; color yellow; flesh pale yellow and well flavored; very productive; used when young and tender.

Early White Bush Scallop. Similar to the preceding, except in color, which is white.

Summer Crookneck One of the best; very early and productive. It is small, crooked neck, covered with warty excrescences; color bright yellow; shell very hard when ripe.

Boston Marrow. A fall and winter variety, very popular. Of oval form; skin thin; when ripe, bright orange mottled with light cream color; flesh rich salmon yellow, dry, fine grained, and for sweetness and excellence, unsurpassed.

Boston Marrow.

Winter Crookneck. The most certain to produce a crop, he strong growing vines suffering less from insects than those of the other sorts. Color varying from dark green to clear yellow. Flesh variable, affected by soil and weather. If kept from cold and damp, they will keep the entire year.

Winter Crookneck.

Cocoanut. Very prolific, producing six to twelve on a vine. Outer color light yellow, the bottom of the fruit being of a rich green hue. Quality first-class.

Hubbard Squash.

Hubbard This is a superior variety, and the best winter squash known; flesh bright orange yellow, fine grained, very dry, sweet and rich flavored; keeps perfectly good throughout the winter; boils or bakes exceedingly dry, and is esteemed by many to be as good baked as the sweet potato.

Improved American Turban. (Essex Hybrid.) Developed by selection and crossing from the old American Turban, being of a richer color, having a hard shell and in its remarkable keeping qualities. It is of medium size, and the skin is a rich orange red. Flesh deep, rich color, very thick, and of excellent quality. The earliest of the winter varieties

Imp. Am. Turban.

Pine Apple. Vigorous and hardy, coming into bearing late in the season, and then producing fruit at nearly every joint, making it one of the most productive kinds grown. Skin creamy white; flesh very thick and with a peculiar flavor, on which account it is much liked for pies; it is also used green like the summer squashes, and baked or stewed like the winter kinds.

Pine Apple.

Perfect Gem. Vine coming into bearing late, but very productive. Fruit four inches in diameter, nearly round, ribbed white; flesh yellowish white and cooking very sweet and well flavored. This is the best of the intermediate kinds, and many think it fully equal to the winter sorts.

Perfect Gem.

Mammoth Chili.

Mammoth Chili. Rich orange-yellow, flesh thick, and of good quality for making pies. They grow to an enormous size, specimens frequently attaining the weight of 200 lbs. Valuable sort for feeding stock.

Sibley. See Specialties.

Brazil Sugar. See Specialties.

TOMATOES.

1 ounce for 1,500 plants; ¼ lb. (to transplant) for an acre.

This vegetable is now one of the most important of garden and market products. The seed may be sown in a hot-bed, greenhouse, or where a temperature of not less than 60 degrees is kept. When the plants are about two inches high they should be set out in boxes three inches deep. When safe from frosts, plants may be set in the open ground. They are planted for early crops on light, sandy soil, at a distance of 4 feet apart, in hills. Water freely at the time of transplanting, and shelter from the sun a few days until the plants are established. Tomatoes will always produce greater crops and be of better flavor when staked up or when trained against walls or fences.

General Grant. A very early sort; fair sized, but not as smooth as the later sorts.

Hathaway's Excelsior. Vines large and vigorous, fruit medium size, smooth, apple-shaped; dark, rich color when ripe; quite early; a favorite Southern sort.

Early Conqueror. A well-known standard sort, medium in size, irregular in shape, flattened and slightly corrugated; color scarlet-crimson.

Livingston's Perfection. Very large and early; blood-red; perfectly smooth; thick meat; few seeds; a good shipping sort; really one of the best of all the Livingston tomatoes of which we now have so many strains.

Optimus Tomato. A variety that should be placed in the front rank among early Tomatoes. In all trials it is found remarkably early, in that respect being fully the equal of or superior to the "Mikado." Optimus is a very smooth variety, uniform in size and shape, ripens evenly, and is of a bright red color. The flesh is scarlet crimson, very solid, of good flavor and entirely free from core. The fruit is usually produced in clusters of five.

The Mikado.

Mayflower. Very early and productive; very large; splendid shape; perfectly smooth; bright red, and ripens uniformly to the stem.

The Mikado. One of the earliest and of the largest size. Perfectly solid and of unsurpassed quality. The Mikado differs from all tomatoes in its immense size. They are produced in great clusters and are perfectly solid, generally smooth but occasionally irregular. The color is purplish red, like that of the Acme; while it has all the solidity that characterizes the Trophy. It is not unusual for single fruits to weigh from one pound to one and a half pounds each. Its earliness is a remarkable feature in so large a tomato, and adds to its value. Whether for slicing or for cooking purposes the quality is excellent. The foliage of the Mikado Tomato will show the distinctiveness of the variety.

Acme. Very productive; form round; very smooth and uniform; delicious in flavor; possesses good shipping qualities.

Paragon. Medium size; color dark red; ripens evenly; very solid; largely used for canning.

Acme.

Livingston's Favorite. One of the most perfect shaped tomatoes grown; very smooth; darker than the perfection; ripens evenly and quite early; is noted for its good shipping qualities.

Cardinal.

Cardinal. This is a beautiful tomato, being of a brilliant cardinal red, very glossy looking when ripe; the flesh of the same brilliant color; ripens evenly through, having no hard, green core, like many others; in shape it is round and smooth and solid.

Early. Large. Smooth Red. Standard market variety; skin bright scarlet; good size, good quality, ripens early.

Yellow Plum. Bright yellow in color; round and regular in shape; useful for preserves.

Livingston's Beauty. It is extra early, growing in clusters of four or five; glossy crimson, partaking of some of the characteristics of the Acme; solid; retains its color and size until late in the season. See Specialties.

Trophy, selected.

Trophy. Selected. One of the best standard varieties; fruit large, smooth, bright red, solid and good flavor; unsurpassed for all purposes.

Livingston, or Sacramento Favorite.

Sacramento Favorite. Is one of the very best; large size, smooth as an apple, firm and handsome; dark red and fine for market and shipping.

Turnip.

One ounce for 150 feet of drill; or two pounds for an acre

Turnips succeed best in highly enriched sandy or gravelly soil. Sow in drills 12 to 18 inches apart, cover half inch, and when plants are well up thin to 5 or 6 inches apart, for early kind, and

Rutabaga and large sorts to 10 inches. Best always to sow just before a rain, or water well, as success depends upon quick germination and rapid growth.

Extra Early Purple Top Munich.

Extra Early Purple Top Munich. This new variety is two weeks earlier than any other in cultivation. It is of a handsome appearance, somewhat flattened, white, with purlish top; flesh snow white, fine grained, and most delicate.

Early White Flat Dutch. An early, white fleshed, strap-leaved variety, usually sown for early Summer use in the Spring; of quick growth, mild flavor and excellent quality; also grown for a Fall crop.

Early White Flat Dutch.

Early White Egg. A new egg shaped variety, for Spring or Fall sowing, flesh white, firm, fine grained, mild and sweet; an extra keeper, in every respect a first-classed table and market sort.

Golden Ball. A rapid grower of excellent flavor; globe-shaped; bright yellow color; good keeper and a superior table variety.

Yellow Globe. One of the best for a general crop; flesh firm and sweet; grows to a large size; excellent for table use or feeding stock, and keeps well until Spring.

Yellow Aberdeen. or Scotch. Hardy, productive, and a good keeper; globe shaped; yellow; flesh firm; good for table use or feeding stock.

Long White. or Cow Horn. Grows very quickly, partly above ground; very productive; flesh white, fine grained and sweet; of excellent quality.

Early White Egg.   Long White, or Cow Horn.

Early Snowball. Small, solid, sweet and crisp, and also of remarkably quick growth.

Early White Stone. An English garden variety; round in shape; firm, of quick growth, medium size; very desirable.

Improved Purple Top Yellow Ruta Baga. The best variety of Swedish Turnip in cultivation; hardy and productive; flesh yellow, of solid texture; sweet and well flavored; shape slightly oblong, terminating abruptly, with no side or bottom roots; color, deep purple above, and bright yellow under the ground; leaves small, light green, with little or no neck, the most perfect in form, the richest in flavor, and the best in every respect.

Sweet Russian or White Ruta Baga This is a most excellent kind, either for table or stock. It grows to a very large size, flesh white, solid, firm texture, sweet and rich, keeps well.

Skirving's Purple Top Grows to a large size, yellow flesh, solid fine flavored, good keeper; good table or stock variety.

Laing's Improved. One of the large sorts; productive and good size, sweet, firm, very hardy; excellent for table or stock feeding.

Red Top Strap Leaf Rapid grower and of mild flavor; the most popular variety for early use, either for the table or stock.

Sweet German. This variety is very popular in many sections. It partakes largely of the nature of the Ruta Baga, and should be sown a month earlier than the flat turnips The flesh is white, hard, firm and sweet, and it keeps nearly as well as the Ruta Baga. Highly recommended for winter and spring use.

POT, SWEET, AND MEDICAL HERBS.

Herbs, in general, delight in rich, mellow soil. Sow the seeds early in the spring in shallow drills, 1 foot apart; when up a few inches, thin out at proper distances, or transplant. No garden is complete without a few sweet, aromatic or medical herbs for flavoring soups, meats, etc., and care should be taken to harvest them properly. This should be done on a dry day just before they come into full blossom; then dry quickly in the shade, pack close in dry boxes or vessels, so as to exclude the air.

Anise. Used for garnishing and flavoring.

Angelica. Garden. Supposed to have medical virtues.

Arnica. Has medical qualities.

Balm. Used for tea or balm wine; height, 1 foot.

Belladonna Used in medicine.

Boneset. Has medical qualities.

Basil. Sweet. Used for soups, stews and sauces; 1 foot.

Bene. Used medicinally; 18 inches.

Borage. Excellent for bees, etc.; 3 feet.

Caraway For confectionery and medicine, also flavoring; 2 feet.

Catnip. Has medical qualities.

Coriander Grown for its seed, also for garnishing; 2 feet.

Cumin. Good for pigeons, etc.

Dill. The leaves are used in soups, sauces and pickles; also the seed for flavoring; 3 feet.

Elecampane. Has tonic expectorant qualities.

Fennel. Sweet The leaves are ornamental; when boiled they are used in fish sauces; 6 feet.

Hoarhound. Used medicinally; 2 feet.

Lavender. An aromatic medicinal herb; 2 feet.

Marigold. Pot. For flavoring and medicine; 1 foot.

Opium Poppy. (White Seeded.) Used medicinally; 3 feet.

Pennyroyal. Has medicinal qualities.

Rosemary. Yields an aromatic oil and water, and largely in use.

Rue. Said to have medicinal qualities.

Saffron. Used in medicine and also in dyeing.

Sage The tender leaves and tops are used in sausage, stuffing and sauces; 18 inches.

Savory. Summer. For seasoning purposes; 1 foot.

Savory. Winter For same use as the above.

Tansy. For medicinal use; 3 feet.

Thyme. Broad-leaved English. Used as a seasoning.

Wormwood. Used medicinally, beneficial for poultry, and should be planted in poultry yards.

SEEDS FOR FAMILY GARDENS.

These are of the choicest and best varieties for small gardens and home use.
30 packets (sold for $1.50) for $1.00, consisting of

2	best kinds	Snap Beans.	2	best kinds	Cabbage.
2	"	Beets.	1	"	Cauliflower.
2	"	Sweet Corn.	1	"	Celery.
1	"	Carrot.	2	"	Cucumbers.
2	"	Lettuce.	1	"	Musk Melon.
1	"	Onions.	1	"	Water Melon.
1	"	Pepper.	1	"	Pumpkins.
1	"	Parsnip.	1	"	Squash.
2	"	Peas.	3	"	Radish.
1	"	Tomatoes.	2	"	Turnips.

All for the small price of One Dollar.

LAWN GRASS, CLOVER AND OTHER FIELD SEEDS.

These we keep in very large stock, and of unsurpassed quality. We import heavily of Eastern and European varieties, and make a specialty of Alfalfa and other California grown Seed.

A Beautiful Lawn

Is the first thing that attracts one's attention on approaching a residence, consequently this is the first thing to look after, either in arranging a new place or an old established home. A beautiful grass plot is within the reach of every one, and the arrangement of the trees and flowers should be an after consideration, according to the tastes and means of the owner, but when possible, combine both.

How to Secure a Beautiful Lawn.

In establishing a new lawn great care should be taken in preparing the ground before sowing the seed. If at all inclined to be wet, the plot designed for the lawn should be most thoroughly underdrained and carefully graded, and the entire surface made rich and as fine as possible. Bone dust and superphosphate are the most suitable for enriching a lawn, as they are free from the seed of the obnoxious weeds, which cannot be said of stable manure, unless it has been thoroughly composted with the utmost possible care. The ground being ready, sow the seed as early in the Spring as convenient, the earlier the better, if the soil is in good condition. No one kind of grass will make a lawn that will keep beautifully green all through the season, but a mixture of several is essential, as some varieties are most luxuriant in Spring, others in Summer, and again others in the Autumn, and a proper combination of these various sorts is required to create and maintain a perfect carpet-like lawn. Our Fancy Mixture is most admirably adapted to this purpose, and as near perfection as possible to attain.

Old lawns will be greatly benefited, if as early in Spring as the weather will permit, they are carefully raked so as to remove the dead grass and leaves that may be on them; then sprinkle it with our Fancy Mixture, which will renew the thin places and spots that have been killed by the Winter or other causes, then give it a thorough rolling with a heavy roller.

LAWN GRASS Fancy Mixture Is composed of a variety of fine dwarf, close growing grasses, which on properly prepared, finely pulverized ground, will produce a neat, velvety lawn and permanent sod. 80 lbs. to the acre. 20 cts. per lb.

KENTUCKY BLUE GRASS Fancy Lawn Is the finest and best of all grasses when used for general lawn purposes; for this purpose 60 to 80 pounds are necessary. 20 cts. per lb.

SWEET-SCENTED VERNAL. One of the earliest Grasses in Spring and latest in Autumn and more fragrant than any other grass. Valuable to mix in pastures with other grasses on account of its earliness, and it exhales a delightful fragrance when in bloom. About 30 pounds to the acre. 50 cts. per lb.

ORCHARD GRASS or COCK'S FOOT. One of the most valuable grasses on account of its quick growth and valuable aftermath. It is ready for grazing two weeks sooner than most grasses, and when fed off is again ready for grazing in a week, and will continue green when other grasses are withered by dry weather. It is palatable and nutritious, and stock eat it greedily when green. It has a tendency to grow in tufts, and so does better if sown with clovers, and as it ripens at the same time, the mixed hay is of the best quality. For grazing, it has no equal, and should be used more than it is. When sown alone, 25 lbs. per acre; if sown with clover, half that amount. It is perennial, and will last for years. 20 cts. per lb.

ITALIAN RYE GRASS Is more of an annual, and is also good in mixtures for the lawn or for hay crop. It is of quick growth and valuable for sheep pasturage. 15 cts. per lb.

ENGLISH, or AUSTRALIAN RYE GRASS. Is a perennial, much like the English Blue Grass and is very valuable for either lawns, pasturage or for hay; and well adapted for moist land. Sow for lawns 60 pounds, hay 30 pounds per acre. 15 cts. per lb.

WOOD MEADOW GRASS Grows from one and a half to two feet high; has a perennial creeping root, and an erect, slender, smooth stem. Its chief value is in that it will produce a good crop of hay in moist, shady situations, where it frequently grows quite tall. Cattle are fond of it; it is succulent and nutritious, and is perhaps the best variety for sowing in orchards, under trees, and shaded situations, either for hay or pasturage, and for parks and pleasure grounds. About 25 pounds per acre. 40 cts. per lb.

JOHNSON GRASS. This is one of the most valuable forage plants, very popular in the Southern States, and will come into universal use in all parts of the United States when known. It is perennial, a rapid grower, very nutritious, being eagerly devoured by all kinds of stock. Comes early in spring, grows until the frost cuts it down in the fall stands the drought better than any grass, and having long cane-like roots, which penetrate the soil for moisture; superior both as a grazing and hay grass. 30 pounds per acre. 20 cts. per lb.

MEADOW FOXTAIL. A valuable pasture grass of rapid growth and much relished by all kinds of stock. Adapted for rich, moist soils. Sow 20 pounds per acre. 40 cts. per lb.

BROMUS or RESCUE GRASS. This grass is recommended for its drouth-resisting quality. Will thrive on any soil where it is not too wet. Sow 35 pounds per acre. 40 cts. per lb.

TALL MEADOW OAT-GRASS. This grass is early and very luxuriant. It makes fine pasturage and good hay. Can be cut often. It is also valuable to plough under for soiling. Sow 30 to 40 pounds per acre. 30 cts. per lb.

MEADOW, or WOOLLY SOFT GRASS (*Holcus lanatus*) Has the merit of easy culture, and accommodates itself to all descriptions of soil, from the richest to the poorest. Sow 30 lbs. per acre. Weight, 8 pounds per bushel. 30 cts. per lb.

WATER MEADOW GRASS (*Poa aquatica*). This is an excellent pasture grass for very wet situations. Sow twenty pounds to the acre. 40 cts. per lb.

ROUGH STALKED MEADOW GRASS (*Poa trivialis*). This is one of the most valuable of grasses for moist, rich soils and sheltered situations. Sow twenty pounds to the acre. Per lb., 30 cts.

HERD, RED TOP GRASS, (or BENT GRASS) Is most largely used for wet lands, but does well in almost any soil, moist or dry. It makes good hay or pasture and is much used in mixture with timothy and clover. Sow 30 pounds per acre. 15 cts. per lb.

TIMOTHY Is very largely grown for hay crop in northern climates, and is fine when sown with Red Top and Clover. Sow 15 pounds per acre. 10 cts. per lb.

MESQUIT GRASS Is very desirable for dry lands. It resists the drought well and makes a good crop for hay or pasturage. Sow 30 pounds per acre. 15 cts. per lb.

SHEEP FESCUE GRASS (*Festuca ovina*)—This variety grows naturally on light, dry sandy soil, and on elevated mountain pastures. Sow twenty-five to thirty pounds to the acre. 20c. per lb.

MEADOW FESCUE TRUE ENGLISH BLUE GRASS (*Festuca pratensis*)—One of the most valuable pasture grasses, its long and tender leaves are much relished by stock of all kinds. In some Southern States it is called RANDALL GRASS, sometimes EVERGREEN GRASS. Sow in spring or fall, at the rate of thirty to forty pounds per acre. 20c. per lb.

CRESTED DOGSTAIL GRASS. This grass may be sown on lawns and other places to be kept under by the scythe. The roots penetrate deeply, and remain longer green than any other variety. Sow twenty to twenty-four pounds to the acre. 50c. per lb.

HARD FESCUE. Is also noted for its drouth-resisting quality, and well adapted for lawn mixture and valuable for sheep pasture. Sow thirty pounds to the acre. 25c. per lb.

BERMUDA GRASS. The roots of this grass are very tenacious of life, outrooting other vegetation. It grows in almost any soil and spreads rapidly, making a good pasturage. The seed is hard to save and is worth $3 00 per pound. The roots can be furnished for $2 00 per barley sack or $3 00 per barrel. Cut up into short lengths and sown broadcast and cover with a roller. One barrel will thue plant an acre.

EGYPTIAN, OR PEARL MILLET. Produces an enormous amount of green feed. It can be cut repeatedly, growing very rapidly after cutting, and is equal to Sweet Corn for feed. Sow in drills two to three feet apart; four pounds will sow an acre. 40c. per lb.

COMMON MILLET. Can be sown broadcast in the Spring of the year for hay; thirty to forty pounds per acre if for seed, sow in drills twenty pounds to the acre. It produces largely as an annual early crop. 10c. per lb.

HUNGARIAN GRASS. Is a very valuable forage plant for light dry soils. It withstands drouth and remains green when most vegetation is parched. Sow and cultivate as for Millet. 10c. per lb.

GERMAN GOLDEN MILLET. Is not quite as early as the above, but yields more largely. 10c. per lb.

WHITE MILLO MAIZE, OR BRANCHING DHOURA. Of South American origin. Valuable as a forage plant and for its grain, having great capacity to stand drought. It can be cut and fed at any stage, or cured when heading out, for fodder. It bears grain in erect full heads, and it is equal to corn for feeding all sorts of stock; also makes excellent meal. It requires all summer to mature seed. Plant three to five seed in a hill eighteen inches apart four foot rows, and this to two plants and cultivate as Corn. It shoots out greatly and makes a great amount of foliage. Three to five pounds per acre. Can be cut for green feed several times a season. 25c. per pound.

YELLOW MILLO MAIZE, OR YELLOW BRANCHING DHOURA. Tall, nine to ten feet stooling from the ground like the White Millo Maize, but not so much. The seed head grows to great size on good land. These heads are set close and solid, with a large plump grain, double the size of White Millo, and of deep golden yellow color. The Cultivation is like Corn. 20c. per lb.

AMBER CANE (SORGHUM.) Is the earliest variety, and being rich in saccharine matter is grown for making sugar and syrup. It makes a large amount of forage for stock feed.

AFRICAN CANE, OR SORGHUM. Is also a fine forage plant, and in large demand for Spring planting. 10c. per lb.

EGYPTIAN CORN (White and Red Varieties). Both produce an immense crop of both seed and stalks for forage to the acre and mature without rain. The white is more cultivated, and perhaps the earliest. The seed is quite valuable to feed stock or poultry. 5c. per lb.

KAFFIR CORN. A variety of Sorghum, cultivated for both forage and grain, growing from 4½ to 5 feet high, is stocky and erect, and has wide foliage. Kaffir Corn has the quality common to all Sorghums of resisting drought, and in this fact is to be found its peculiar value. It has yielded paying crops of grain and forage even in dry seasons, when corn has utterly failed. Sow in rows three feet apart, five to six pounds to the acre. 25c. per lb.

—— o ——

CLOVER SEEDS.

There are no plants so valuable for fertilizers as the Clovers. They have the faculty of absorbing nitrogen from the air, and also of rendering available much of the inert plant food of the soil. Their long, powerful tap roots penetrate to a great depth, loosen the soil, admit air, and by their decay add immensely to the fertility of the soil. The seed may be sown in fall or spring; which is the best season will depend upon local climate, and method of culture. In any case, it should be evenly distributed on a mellow, well prepared soil. Plaster will increase the growth remarkably, and should be sown broadcast the season following the seeding.

RED CLOVER. Two varieties—large and medium. Both succeed well in California, especially in our bottom lands and deep soils; 25 pounds to the acre.

WHITE DUTCH CLOVER. Grows low, spreading and very fragrant, and is most excellent for lawns and lawn mixture; 10 pounds to the acre.

CRIMSON TREFOIL, OR SCARLET CLOVER. Grows about one foot high, dark roots, long leaves and blossoms of deep red. It makes good hay and will give four or five cuttings each season. Sow 15 pounds to the acre.

ALSIKE, OR SWEDISH CLOVER. This variety is fast gaining great popularity. It is the most hardy of all the clovers; perennial. On rich, moist soils it yields an enormous quantity of hay or pasture, and may be cut several times in a season, but its greatest value is for sowing with other clovers and grasses, as it forms a thick bottom, and greatly increases the yield of hay, and cattle prefer it to any other forage. The heads are globular, very sweet and fragrant, and much liked by bees, who obtain a large amount of honey from them. Sow in spring or fall, at the rate of 10 pounds per acre, where used alone.

ALFALFA. In cultivated above all other clover in California. It produces enormous crops, and is cut many times in the season for hay. It roots deeply, keeping fresh and green through our long dry season, and is the most valuable and profitable of all crops for abundance of feed. Sow 20 to 25 pounds to the acre. If in the fall sow early enough to get a little root before a frost, it can be sown again in February and Spring months.

BOKHARA CLOVER. This is a tall shrubbery plant, growing to height of four to six feet. It produces an abundance of small white flowers of great fragrance. Sow 10 pounds to to the acre. Lb., 25c.

BURR CLOVER. This makes a good fodder. Creeping stem, which spreads over a large surface. It is fine for dry lands. The seeds are in burr pods; 8 to 10 pounds per acre. 15 cts. per lb. $10 00 per 100 lbs.

ESPERSETTE. (French Sanfoin.) This plant is of a lignuminous character, having many stems two and three feet long. Smooth and tapering, with many long oblate leaflets in pairs, and spikes of variegated crimson flowers. The root is a perennial of a hard, woody nature. The plant flowers early and can be repeatedly cut, thus furnishing a great abundance of most nutritious food through the long dry and heated seasons, and requiring no irrigation. Stock will eat it with impunity, without danger of bloat as in alfalfa. The seed and seed pods are said to be more nutritious than oats. The plant does best in calcareous and gravelly soils, and elevated slopes and arid regions, where other vegetation fails. It will, however, not succeed in wet or low lands where there is no drainage. From 30 to 40 pounds are required for an acre. 15c. per lb. $12 50 per 100 lbs.

MELILOTUS. This variety of clover grows on the banks of streams and among cobbles, gravel, slickens and sand. It yields an immense amount of feed for stock, who are very fond of it. The plant attains a height of 10 to 12 feet, keeping green the entire season, producing seed the second year and maturing in October. Price $12 50 per 100 lbs.

TEXAS BLUE GRASS.—"The Texas Blue Grass grows on the roadsides, by fences and hedges; shade does not hurt it any more than Orchard Grass It stands the hot and dry summers of the south very well, better than any other grass." Seed very scarce and difficult to obtain, and cannot be separated from the chaff. Per oz., 40c.; lb., $5 00.

CAROLINA, OR COW PEA. This makes a valuable fodder and is a good fertilizer. The pods can be harvested or all cut green for fodder, or it can be ploughed under for a fertilizer. $5 00 per 100 lbs.

VETCHES. Are much used for stock feed. Sow and cultivate same as for peas. 10 cts. per lb. $6 per 100 lbs.

LENTILS. Are similar to Vetches, and are cultivated in like manner. 15 cts. per lb. $10 00 per 100 lbs.

BROOM CORN. Many farmers make this a profitable crop, producing on an acre about 500 cwt. of broom and forty bushels of seed; plant and cultivate same as for corn.

BUCKWHEAT. Can be sown late as in July at the rate of 30 to 40 pounds per acre. It should be thrashed as soon as dry, as if left standing in mass it will quickly gather moist.

FIELD BEANS. Should be planted after all danger from frost is past. Does best in rich, dry, light soil. Hoe frequently while the plant is dry, but not otherwise. The Medium White, White Navy and the Bayo, or Chile varieties are mostly used for marketing in this country. Prices on application.

FIELD PEAS. Should be sown on good cultivated soil at the rate of about one hundred and fifty pounds to the acre, in drills or broadcast. They are often sown in less quantity with oats and cut and cured together for hay, or threshed and bound together. Prices on application.

SUNFLOWER SEED. Is growing to be a valuable farm crop. The seed is very desirable for planting, while the leaves make excellent fodder. The plant is said to be an excellent protection from malaria, and should be grown for hedges about the house where this disease prevails.

FIELD GRAIN.

☞ *Seed Wheat, Barley, Oats, Corn and other Grains, of every variety, will be furnished to our customers in quantities as may be desired; also Seed Potatoes at Lowest Market Rates. Prices given on application.*

QUOTATIONS MADE IN THIS CATALOGUE are for small quantities, and Liberal Deductions will be made on Large Amounts.

TREE AND SHRUB SEEDS.

HOW TO GROW THEM.

THE growing of trees from seeds is in the case of some varieties a very simple and easy process, requiring but little care or skill on the part of the grower.

Some varieties require special treatment and great care and attention to insure success; others are very difficult to grow, and planters are not very likely to succeed until after having made repeated failures.

One important fact must be kept in view, and that is, IT TAKES TIME FOR THESE SEEDS TO GERMINATE, in some cases only a few days, in others, several weeks; while quite frequently they will lie dormant the whole season before commencing to grow. It often happens that seeds of a given variety, all taken from the tree at one time, sown to-gather and subjected to the same treatment will show great irregularity in time of germinating, some coming up in a few days, others not until the next season, and still others not until the season following.

CONIFERS AND EVERGREEN TREE SEEDS should be kept in perfectly dry sand until the time of sowing; if this cannot be done readily, place them in a cool, dry spot, where mice will not eat them. CHESTNUTS and WALNUTS should be planted in the fall, or kept during the winter in sand or moss; they shrivel up by too long exposure to the air, and many of them lose their power of vegetating entirely. APPLE, PEAR, QUINCE SEED, CHERRY PITS, PEACH PITS, also those with hard shells like the LOCUST, MAGNOLIAS, etc., should be placed in boxes with sand and exposed to frost before planting, otherwise they may not vegetate until a second year, but if too late in the spring to expose them to the action of the frost, they may be put into a vessel of hot water for an hour or so before planting. The seeds of DECIDUOUS TREES and SHRUBS, with few exceptions, can be planted from the end of March to the middle of May with success.

The soil should be deep, mellow and rich; if not so, make it so by deep spading and thoroughly pulverizing the ground. If not rich, apply a good liberal dressing of any old, well-decomposed manure; mix thoroughly with the soil and rake down all smooth and level, and your seed-bed is ready. Now draw a line across one side of the plat, and with the hoe make a shallow trench from a half to one inch deep, according to the size of the seed to be sown; make the trench about six inches wide, scatter the seeds over the bottom, but not too thickly, then draw the soil back and cover to the depth of about the thickness of the seeds as evenly as possible, then press the beds gently with the back of the spade to make firm the earth around the seeds.

Great care must be taken not to give too much water, as the young plants imbibe moisture very easily. Water with a fine hose, but never so that the ground becomes soggy. Some shade must be used to protect the young plants from the hot, drying sun and winds, and also to keep the birds from destroying them.

The trenches or drills are to be two feet apart, so that the hoe or garden cultivator can be employed in cultivation. Keep the soil loose between the rows, and keep them well clear of weeds. Seeds of the rarer sorts may be sown in cold-frames or in boxes; if in cold-frames, the sashes should be shaded and the frame raised at the corner three or four inches to allow the air to circulate freely.

Allow the young plants to remain from one to two years before transplanting.

CALIFORNIA TREE AND SHRUB SEEDS.

Abies Douglasii. Douglas Spruce, A very large timber tree, 200 to 300 feet high, of pyramidal shape. Found throughout the Rocky Mountains, from Oregon to Mexico. Very hardy. Oz., 50c.; lb., $5.00.

Abies Mertensiana. Tsuga M., Hemlock Spruce. A very large tree, 150 to 200 feet high, with rather thick, red-brown bark. Very hardy, ranging from California far into Alaska. Oz., 60c.; lb., $6.00.

Abies Menzeisii. Picea Sitchensis. Peculiar to the Northern Coast, found mostly in wet, sandy soil near the mouth of streams; the tallest spruce known; an exellent timber tree; pyramidal form. Very hardy. Oz. 60c.; lb. $6.

Cupressus Goveniana. Goven's Cypress. Thirty to forty feet high; very ornamental; found in the coast ranges of Monterey. Oz., 60c.; lb. $6.

Cupressus Macrocarpa. Monterey Cypress. A tree forty to sixty feet high, with rough bark, spreading, horizontal branches, with rich, green foliage: very ornamental for lawns or parks; also used extensively for hedges. Oz., 25c.; lb., $2 50.

Cupressus McNabiana. McNab's Cypress. A small tree, six to ten feet high, found about Mt. Shasta, at 5,000 feet altitude. The leaves are small, and of a deep green. Oz., 40c.; lb. $4 00.

Cupressus Lawsoniana. Lawson's Cypress. A handsome tree, found in moist grounds in the Shasta mountains, and in the coast range of Oregon. The wood is white, fragant, fine and close-grained, free from knots, easily worked, and very durable; also known as Oregon Cedar, White Cedar and Ginger Pine. Oz., 40c ; lb. $4.00.

Cupressus Italian. A very erect, close-growing tree; fine for entrances and arches. Oz., 25c.; lb., $3 00.

Cupressus Guadalupensis. Blue Cypress. A new fast-growing variety with beautiful bluish foliage; very ornamental for lawns, parks or cemeteries. Oz. 25c

Libocedrus decurrens. Thuya Craigiana. Found in the coast ranges, from Oregon to San Diego; grows from 100 to 150 feet high; fine, hardy timber tree; known as the White Cedar of California. Oz , 30c.; lb. $3 00.

Madrone. A beautiful native tree of California; the foliage is of a deep green, and feathery; it attains a considerable size, flowers white. Oz., 25c.

Picea amabilis. Silver Fir. Tall, symmetrical, valuable timber tree. Oz., 50c.; lb., $5 00.

Picea grandis. Balsam Fir. Grows 200 to 300 feet high, four to six feet in diameter; grows in rich, moist soils; valuable timber tree. Oz , 50c.; lb. $5 00.

Picea nobilis. California Red Fir. A magnificent tree, with thick, brown bark, making fine timber; forms large forests about the base of Mt. Shasta; timber said to be better than that of other fir. Oz., 50c.; lb. $5 00.

Picea magnifica. 200 to 250 feet high. The Red Fir of the Sierras, found at an altitude of 7,000 feet. Very hardy. Oz., 60c.; lb., $6 00.

Picea Concolor. Abies lasiocarpa. A very ornamental tree; 100 to 200 feet high; very common throughout the Sierras, ranging into Oregon; also found in Arizona, Utah and Colorado. Oz., 50c.; lb., $5 00.

Pinus Benthamiana. A magnificent tree; grows from 200 to 300 feet high: fine timber. Very hardy. Oz., 50c ; lb., $5 00.

Pinus Coulteri. Great Coned Pine. Found in the coast ranges from Mt. Diablo to the Southern part of this State. Oz., 35c.; lb., $3 50.

Pinus contorta. A low tree, five to fifteen feet high, found on the wet, sandy coast of the Pacific, from Mendocino to Alaska. Very hardy. Oz., 70c.; lb., $5 00.

Pinus Fremontiana. Pinus monophylla. A small tree, twenty to twenty-five feet high; frequent in the coast ranges in Nevada, Arizona and Utah; well known as the Nut Pine. Oz., 30c.; lb., $3 00.

Pinns insignis. Monterey Pine. A very ornamental tree for parks or lawns; grows from sixty to seventy feet high, of rapid growth, and has beautiful, green foliage. Oz., 25c.; lb. $2 50.

Pinus Jeffreyi. A magnificent tree, from 100 to 200 feet high; usually found on our mountains at an eleva-

tion of 5,000 feet, ranging from California to Oregon. Very hardy. Oz., 35c.; lb., $3 50.

Pinus Lambertiana. Sugar Pine. A hardy tree of gigantic dimensions, from 250 to 300 feet high, and from fifteen to twenty feet thick, with light brown, smoothish bark; found on both slopes of the Sierras. The wood is like that of the White Pine. Oz., 30c.; lb., $3 00

Pinus monticola. From sixty to eighty feet high, and about three feet in diameter at the base. Found at an altitude from 7,000 to 10,000 feet, known as the white pine of California, and of the North. Oz., 60c.; lb., $6 00.

Pinus Parryana. A small tree, twenty to thirty feet high, found in the vicinity of San Diego, at an altitude of 2,000 feet. Oz., 50c.; lb., $5 00.

Pinus ponderosa. Yellow Pine. One of the largest pines known, 200 to 300 feet high, and twelve to fifteen feet in diameter, with very thick red-brown bark. Found in the Coast Range. Very hardy. Oz , 40c., lb. $4 00.

Pinus tuberculata. California Scrub Pine. A small crooked tree, often found full of cones when only two or three feet high. Oz., 50c., lb., $5 00.

Sequoia gigantea. Wellingtonia gigantea. The mammoth tree of California. This is the largest tree known to exist on the American continent, grows over 300 feet high. The bark is from one to two feet thick. Many of these California trees are over 90 feet in circumference. Oz., 60c.; lb., $6 00.

Sequoia sempervirens. Known as the Redwood of California. The most valuable timber of the California forests. From 200 to 250 feet high, and from eight to twelve feet in diameter. The wood is of a rich, brownish red; light, but strong and durable, making excellent timber. Hardy. Oz., 50c.; lb., $3 00.

Thuya gigantea. Giant Arbor Vitæ. A tall, graceful tree, 200 to 250 feet high, three to twelve feet thick; pyramidal form, with spreading and somewhat drooping branches; frequent in the coast ranges of Oregon. The wood is soft, fine-grained, and of light color. Oz., 60c.; lb., $6 00.

Torreya Californica. California Nutmeg. Found in the mountain districts Grows to the height of 60 feet, the wood is light-colored, close-grained, and small branches being reddish. Oz., 25c.; lb., $2 00

Arctostaphylos glauca. Great berried Manzanita. Oz., 50c.; lb., $2 00.

Mountain Laurel. Spice Tree A handsome shrub or tree, twenty to seventy feet high, the timber very handsome and valuable, for ornamental wainscoting and finishiug. Oz., 25c.; lb. $2 00

Negundo Californicum. Box Elder. Usually a small tree, sometimes reaching a height of seventy feet. Oz., 25c ; lb., $1 50.

Acer Macropyllum Maple. A tree of 50 to 90 ft. high, from coast ranges in California. The wood is white, hard, and takes a fine polish. Oz., 25c.; lb , $2 50.

Cornus Nuttalli. Dogwood. A small showy tree, flowering in May, followed by large clusters of double berries, resembling the eastern Cornus. Wood close-grained and very hard. Oz., 50c.; lb., $5 00.

Azalea occidentalis. Charming California Azalea, the ornament of the wooded districts. Flowers two to three inches long, white, pink variegated. Pkt., 25c

Yellow or Black Locust. Robinia psuedo-accacia. This variety is noted for its rapid growth of hard and durable timber. It is hardy and succeeds well in most soils and climates. Oz., 10c.; lb., 60c.

Honey Locust. Gleditschia Triachanthos. This is a large and handsome tree. The trunk and branches generally beset with long and formidable spines, on which account it has been employed as a hedge. The wood is heavy and affords excellent fuel. Oz., 10c.; lb 60c.

Osage Orange. Maclura Aurantinca. One of the most valuable of hedge plants. The plants will also grow into fine trees, and the wood endures for centuries. Lb., 50c.

Hawthorn. Craiægus oxyacantha. A very handsome thorny hedge plant, which has been grown in various parts of the Northern and Middle States. Oz., 15c.; lb., $1 50.

Buckthorn. Rhamnus cathartica. This makes a strong thorny hedge, adapted to the North and Middle States. Oz., 20c.; lb., $2 00

AUSTRALIAN TREE AND SHRUB SEEDS.

Eucalyptus globulus. Blue Gum. A very rapid growing tree, making valuable timber; height 200 feet. Oz., 50c.; lb., $5 00.

E. Rostrata. Red Gum. Oz., 50c.; lb.. $6 00.

*E. bicolor. Black Box. A valuable timber tree; it is equal to the best Ironbark for all the purposes for which that wood is used, and is more easily wrought. It is sometimes called "Ironbark." 100 to 150 feet. Oz., 75c.

*E. Citriodora. Lemon-scented Gum. A useful timber. The strong lemon scent which is emitted when the leaves are gently rubbed, is equally powerful and agreeable with that of the lemon-scented Verbena. Oz. 75c.

*E. hemipholia. Common Box. A hard but useful timber, strong, tough and durable, but will not last sunk in the ground. It is also a first-class fuel for domestic use or other industrial purposes. 100 to 150 feet.

*E. longifolia. Woollybutt. An average-sized tree. Fair timber for fencing and building purposes; it is a good fuel for domestic use; very durable. 100 to 120 feet. Oz., 75c.

*E. leucoxylon. Crimson Flowered Eucalyptus. This is a very ornamental species of Eucalyptus; having large and very beautiful flowers, color crimson; and as the tree flowers while quite young, it is very desirable as an addition to the the shrubbery or flower border. Oz., 75c.

*E. obliqua. Stringybark. The best wood for flooring boards and rafters. It ls of very quick growth, inferior fuel, but produces the best charcoal. 120 feet. Oz. 75c.

*E. paniculata. Common Ironbark. For most purposes is equal to the last species, and is more easily split into shingles or palings; it is as lasting and as good fuel as other Ironbarks; the wood is not so dark in color. 150 feet.

*E. paniculata var., mycrophylla. Small-leaved Ironbark. The wood of this species is used for fencing and many purposes, the same as the other Ironbarks. But the wood being of a nature much more easy to work, to which the hardness of other sorts offers an obstacle; first-class fuel. 120 feet. Oz., 75c.

*E. robusta. Swamp Mahogany. A good lasting timber for house carpentry and many kinds of turnery, but not durable in the ground. 150 feet. Oz. 75c.

*E. siderophloia. Dark or broad-leaved Ironbark. The most valuable wood for piles, girders, railway sleepers, and for every purpose in which strength and durability are required. This specie is the strongest of all Australian timbers, and superior to most as fuel for steam engines, as it throws off more heat, etc. 150 feet. Oz., 75c.

Acacia decurrens. Black Wattle. Oz., 50c.; lb., $5 00.

Acacia melanoxylon. Lightwood. Oz., 50c.

Acacia mollissima. Oz., 50c.

*Acacia pyenantha. Golden Wattle. Oz., 50c.; lb., $5 00.

Acacia floribunda. Oz., 50c.

Acacia lopantha Crested Wattle. Oz.; 25c. lb., $2 00.

Dracena indivisa A very desirable tree for a garden or a lawn; of graceful habit; makes rapid growth, very hardy; native of New Zealand. Oz., 30c.; lb., $4 00.

Grevillea robusta. Silk Oak of East Australia. Beautiful fern-like foliage; attains a height of 100 feet; withstands drouth; of rapid growth, and flowers when about twenty feet in height, then it is a sight worth seeing, covered from top to bottom with bright orange scarlet flowers. Pkt., 50c.; oz., $2 00.

Pittosporum eugenoides, nigrescens, and undulatum. Valuable evergreens; an ornamental shrub or tree from Southern Australia. Pkt., 25c.; oz, $1 00.

CONIFERS AND EVERGREEN TREE SEED.

Arbor Vitæ, American. Thuja occidentalis. Useful for hedges and wind breaks. Oz., 30c.; lb., $3 00.

Chinese Arbor Vitæ. A small, elegant tree, with erect branches, and dense flat, light green foliage; becomes brown in winter. Oz., 25c.; lb., $ 2 50.

Golden Arbor Vitæ. A variety of the Chinese, nearly spherical in outline. with bright yellow tinged foliage. Beautiful. Oz., 50c.; lb., $5 00.

Fir, Balsam. Balsamea. A small evergreen tree of symmetrical growth, and conical form when young. Of rapid growth, with rich, green foliage. Oz., 30c.; lb., $3 00.

Fir, Silver. A well known evergreen tree, tall symmetrical, very valuable. Oz., 15c.; lb., 1 50.

Larch, European. Larix Europœa. Valuable for forest planting. Oz., 15c.; lb., 1 50.

Magnolia Grandiflora. The most majestic of all American trees; a native of the Southern States; perfectly hardy here. Oz., 25c.; lb., 2 50.

Pine, Scotch. Pinus Sylvestris. One of the most valuable of European varieties. It is hardy, of rapid growth, and adapted to a great variety of soil and climate. Oz., 20c.; lb., $2 00.

Pine, White, or Weymouth. Pinus Strobus. An old, well known and useful tree. Of gigantic proportions and rapid growth. Oz., 30c.; lb., $3 00.

Pepper Tree. Schinus molle. A handsome, ornamental evergreen tree, of graceful habit, light green foliage, and bright, scarlet berries; a desirable tree for parks and lawns. Oz., 25c.; lb., $2 00.

Red Cedar. Juniperus Virginiana. Very valuable timber, and fine ornamental tree. It will stand the dry hot winds, and for wind-breaks, as well as for fence posts, the Red Sedar is invaluable; symmetrical in growth and readily shaped with the shears, it is one of the most useful trees. After properly planting, it will stand more neglect than any other evergreen. Oz., 15c.; lb., $1 50.

Spruce Hemlock Canadensis. An known evergreen tree of high latitudes. It is one of the most graceful of spruces, with a light and spreading, branches almost to the ground. It is a beautiful tree for the lawn and makes a highly ornamental hedge. Oz., 40c.; lb., $4 00.

Spruce Norway. Abies Excelsa. A popular variety from Europe. Extensively planted for ornamental purposes, and for timber and wind-breaks. It is easily transplanted or grown from seed and succeeds in a great variety of soils and climate. Oz., 15c.; lb., $1 50.

FOREST AND DECIDUOUS TREE SEEDS.

Ash-American, White. Fraxinus Americana. Prefers moist soil, but will grow almost anywhere; wood valuable for handles, in wagon-making, etc.; grows rapidly, one of the best of timbers; best when grown on dry land. Oz., 10c.; lt., $1 00.

Ash-European. Fraxinus excelsior. Suitable for warm climates and dry loam soils, wood used in carriage making. Oz., 10c.; lb., $1 00.

Box Elder. Acer Negundo. Thrives on the western plains; grows rapidly, attaining 70 feet in height; excellent for planting along highways; endures drought. Its sap yields sugar. Oz., 10c.; lb., $1 00.

Catalpa Hardy. Catalpa Speciosa. An upright and rapid grower, the trees being remarkably straight and tall, so that even in mild climates, where hardiness is no object, the superior habit of growth of this variety is a matter of the utmost importance in its favor. Oz., 10c.; lb., $1 00.

Elm-European. Ulmus Campestris. The best Elm for ornamental and for city planting. Oz., 10c.; lb., $1 00.

Lime or Linden. Silia Europæa. Makes good paper pulp, the inner bark is used for cordage, matting, etc. Oz., 10c.; lb., $1 00.

Norway Maple. Acer platanoides. A well known ornamental tree. Oz., 10c.; lb., $1 00.

Sugar Maple. Acer saccharinum. It succeeds well in all soils and locations, making a stout, vigorous, rapid growth of hard wood, most valuable for fuel and highly prized for manufacturing purposes. Oz., 10c.; ½ lb. 30c.; lb., $1 00.

Maple Soft, or Silver leaved. Acer dasycarpum. One of the most beautiful of Maples. Is being extensively planted on account of its extremely rapid growth. Its

wood is soft and light, and the branches are often broken by the action of the wind and storm. Oz., 10c.; lb., $1 00.

Mulberry White. Morus alba. Oz., 25c.; lb., $2 50.

Mulberry Black. Morus nigra. Oz. 25c.; ¼ lb., 75c.; lb., $2 50.

Mulberry Russian. Valuable for its fruit, and its timber, which makes valuable posts and stakes, being hard elastic, close grained and susceptible of a fine polish. The Mulberry is also used for hedges, and the leaves for food for silk worms. The berries are often more than an inch long, and one-half inch or more in diameter. They are more acid and sprightly than our American Mulberries, and the fruit is prized by the Russians, for desert, and cooked in various ways; also made into wine. Oz., 40c.; lb., $4 00.

Linden Silver or White-leaved European. A vigorous growing tree, of medium size and pyramidal form. It is noticeable among trees by its white appearance. Its handsome form, growth and foliage render it worthy to be classed among the finest of our ornamental trees. Oz., 25c.; lb., $1 25.

Tree of Heaven. Ailanthus glandulosus. Quite extensively planted in some states, and is noted for its extremely rapid growth. It grows to a large size, and the foliage has a rich tropical appearance. Oz., 10c.; lb., $1 00.

Virginia Creeper. American Ivy. Ampelopsis quinquefolia. This native vine is one of the most ornamental of the climbers, and is much cultivated for covering walls and buildings. It is perfectly hardy, and gives a dense mass of brilliant green throughout the summer, which in the autum changes to the richest shades of crimson and purple. Oz., 25c.; lb., $2 50.

FRUIT TREE SEEDS.

Apple. Pyrus Malus. Apple seeds do not reproduce the same variety. Upon the stock thus used for seed are grafted or budded the varieties desired. The seed can be planted in good soil, any time during the winter, or early in the spring, in rows eighteen inches apart. During their growth they should be well cultivated and kept free from weeds. ¼ lb , 20c.; lb., 50c.

Cherry Mahaleb. Cerasus Mahaleb. The remarks regarding apple seeds are applicable to cherries. This variety is considered the best stock upon which to graft the choicer sorts. ¼ lb., 20c.; lb., 60c.

Cherry Mazzard. Cerasus Communis. The common or ordinary variety of cherry is useful alone for grafting purposes. The stock is hardy, and if properly grafted, fine fruit can be relied on. ¼ lb , 20c.; lb., 50.

Pear. Pyrus Communis. Sow the seed thickly in drills eighteen inches apart. The soil should be rich—a deep, moist loam is most suitable. The value of the stock depends largely on a rapid and vigorous growth the first season. Oz., 25c.; lb., $2 50.

Plum. Prunus Communis. The directions given for planting apples will also apply to plums, except the pits should be planted farther apart in the row. ¼ lb. 20c.; lb. 50c.

Peach. Amygdalis Persica. Peach stocks are raised by planting the stones two or three inches deep. If the stones are cracked they are more sure to grow. The after treatment is about the same as for apples, though budding can be commenced sooner than grafting in apple stocks. Lb., 5c.; 100 lbs., $3 00.

Apricot Pits. Armenia Vulgaris. Planted and cultivated same as peach pits. Lb., 10c.; 100 lbs., $5 00.

Quince. Cydonia Communis. The culture for seed is the same as for apples. Oz., 25c.; lb., $2 50.

Texas Umbrella Tree. This is one of the finest ornamental and attractive trees known. It makes a spreading umbrella shape. Tip of very dense and beautiful foliage, will grow from 20 to 80 feet high. Oz., 30c.; lb., $3 00.

PALM SEEDS.

ORDERS for all Palm Seeds are forwarded as the various species reach us. Their vitality cannot be tested before the sale. Many varieties do not hold their vitality but a short time, and should be planted as soon as received. We cannot warrant this class of seeds, nor will we hold ourselves responsible for the crop; if the purchaser does not accept the seeds on these terms they must be returned at once.

Brahea Filamamentosa. California Fan Palm, A hardy, vigorous growing plant; foliage very regular, of a bright green, deeply and regularly pinnated; the margins being covered with hair-like filaments, giving them a remarkable appearance. They are beautiful decorative plants in all respects, for in or outdoor use. Oz., 30; lb , $3 00.

Washingtonia robusta. Similar in every respect to the preceding, only being more compact, dwarf growth; a great acquisition for many purposes. Oz., 60c.; lb., $6 00.

Brahea glauca. Blue Palm. A very ornamental Fan Palm of robust habit. Oz., 50c.; lb., $3 00.

Areca Lutescens. One of the most valuable and beautiful palms in cultivation; bright glossy green foliage and rich golden-yellow stems. 10 seeds, 50c.

Areca rubra. The foliage a pretty green, deeply and closely pinnated; stems and midribs red, particularly whilst young. 10 seeds, 50c.

Caryota Urens. Very graceful plants, twin pinnate leaflets, with a neat fringe on margin; native of the East Indies. 10 seeds 30c., 100 seeds $1 50.

Chamærop's Excelsa. One of the hardiest of the order; foliage dark green; the segments of the fan deeply cut. This species grows into small trees from fifteen to twenty feet high; very desirable for outdoor decorations. 100 seeds, 50c.

Cocos Australis. Hardy and elegant; foliage plumous, long and slender; pinnate leaflets; leaf-stalks from three to six feet long, of a light, glaucous-green color; compact and symmetrical growth; flowers and matures fruit in this climate, and is readily reproduced for outdoor decoration; one of the best. 19 seeds, 50c.

Corypha Australis. Livistonia. A hardy Australian palm, foliage dark green, symmetrically and regularly slit, the segments partly doubled from the base. 10 seeds, 30c., 100 seeds, $1 50.

Latania Borbonica. Chinese Fan-Palm. The most desirable for general cultivation; especially adapted for centers of baskets, vases, jardinieres, etc. 50 seeds, 50c.

Oreodoxia regia. Royal-Palm. One of the grandest of pinnate-leaved palms. Stands severe frosts. Native of South Florida; The Royal Palms often reach a height of 150 feet; valuable as a decorative palm when small, 10 seeds, 30c.

These require a good sandy soil, enriched with good fertilizers and well pulverized, loose and moderately moist. Sow the seed in usual way in boxes or warm seed bed, covering lightly, and keep in total darkness till the plant begins to show above ground, when gradually expose to the light. By pursuing this plan, uniform temperature and moisture is secured, and all seeds possessing life will be sure to grow. When the plants have grown to say two inches in height, they are ready to transplant. Give plenty of room, according to habit of growth of the plant. Crowding destroys the vigor and beauty of the flower.

We offer the following liberal inducements to those who wish to purchase Flower Seeds in quantity. These rates apply only to seeds in packets, but the seeds will be sent by mail, post-paid:

Send us $1.00 and select Packets to value of $1.20.
Send us $2.00 and select Packets to value of $2.50.
Send us $3.00 and select Packets to value of $4.00.

ABBREVIATIONS MADE IN FLOWER SEED LIST.

A.—For Annuals that grow, bloom and die the first year. **B.**—For Biennials blooming and dying the second year. **P.**—For Perennials that usually bloom the first or second year from seed, but continue to grow and bloom for many years thereafter. **H.**—Indicates Hardy. **H.H.**—Half Hardy. **T.**—Tender.

The hardy can be sown in open ground early, or almost any time, not requiring protection. Half hardy cannot be sown in open ground until the weather becomes warm, unless sown in greenhouse or with good protection.

ABOBRA (Climber.) H. H. P., 10 feet.
Rapid growing, with dazzling scarlet fruit... 10c

ABRONIA. H. A. 9 to 18 in.
Trailing and prostrate habit, like the Verbena, and quite fragrant; natives of California.
Abronia Umbellata, rosy.................... 10c
" Arenaria, yellow.................. 10c

ABUTILON (Chinese Bellflower).
H. H. A., 2 to 4 feet.
Flowers freely in house in Winter and Spring, and a good bedding Summer plant........ 15c
White, Yellow and Crimson mixed........... 15c
ADLUMIA (Mountain Fringe.) H. B., 18 feet.
Climber, graceful foliage, light pink, tubular flowers................................. 5c

---

FLOWER SEEDS SENT FREE BY MAIL ON RECEIPT OF PRICE.

AGERATUM. H. B.

Bears a great many flowers, and keeps in bloom a long time, and is, therefore, desirable for bouquet making. It is well to start the seed under glass transplant.

Ageratum **Conspicum.** White-flowered, blooms until frost. 18 inches.............. 5c
Ageratum **Lasseauxi.** Very fine rose flowers, most valuable for cutting............... 10c
Ageratum **Mexicanum.** (Little Dorritt.) Azure blue, dwarf, splendid for bedding... 5c
Ageratum **Mexicanum.** (Little Dorritt.) Albiflorum, white...................... 5c

AGROSTEMMA (Rose Campion).
H. A., 1 to 2 feet.

Annual, very pretty, free blooming and hardy; always makes desirable beds and useful for cutting; 12 inches in height.
Agrostemma **Coronaria.**
Red and white.......................... 5c
Astrosanquinea; dark blood-red.......... 5c
Alba; white........................... 5c
Finest mixed.......................... 5c

ALYSSUM. H. A., 1 feet.

Pretty little white flowers, useful in making up all kinds of small bouquets. Its fragrance is very delicate. The Alyssum grows freely from seed and makes a pretty border.

Alyssum, Sweet, hardy annual, flowers small in clusters, 6 inches...................... 5c
Wlorczbeckii, hardy perennial, yellow, 1 foot high................................. 5c
Saxatile Compactum. Yellow compact for edgings................................. 5c
Serpyllifolium. Quite dwarf; yellow....... 5c
Procumbens. Very dwarf, white.......... 5c

ALONSOA. H. H. A.

Young plants removed to the house or greenhouse in the autumn, will continue to flower during the winter. The flowers are small but of remarkably brilliant colors.

Alonsoa **Grandiflora.** Large flowered, scarlet, 2 feet in height..................... 5c
Alonsoa **Albiflora.** White................ 5c

AMARANTHUS. H. H. A., 2 to 5 feet.

Valuable for their ornamental foliage, the leaves of most varieties being highly colored.

Tricolor (Joseph's Coat.) Red, yellow and green foliage.......................... 5c
Melancholicus Ruber, of compact habit, with striking blood red foliage; 18 inches...... 5c
Caudatus (Love lies bleeding), long drooping "chains" of flowers, pretty for decoration.. 5c
Cruentus (Prince's Feather), flowers somewhat similar to A. Caudatus, but in erect masses....... .... 5c
Bicolor Ruber. Carmine scarlet; splendid.. 5c
Tricolor Splendens. Very beautiful; new.. 10c

AMMOBIUM (Everlasting Flower).

Ammobium **Alatum Grandiflorum.** A large flowered white, everlasting; fine for dried bouquets with fancy grasses, pick the flowers in the bud to dry................. .... 5c

AMPELOPSIS
(Vetchi, Japan Woodbine, Climber.)

Very hardy and rapid grower; attaches to buildings, fences, etc., as closely as English Ivy; leaves olive green, changing to scarlet. Easy to cultivate and ornamental; 50 feet.

ANAGALLIS.

Anagallis is remarkable for the beauty of its flowers, useful for borders or baskets. Should be sown under glass; 6 inches.
Anagallis **Grandiflora Superba,** mixed colors 5c

ACROLINIUM (Everlasting). H. H. P., 1 foot.
Fine for Winter bouquets; pure white and rose colors............................. 5c
Acrolinium **Flore Plino.** Fine double varieties, mixed.......................... 10c

ADONIS. (Pheasant's Eye.) H. A., 1 foot.
The Adonis has pretty, narrow leaves, and are very brilliant. It will flourish almost anywhere, in the shade or under trees.
Autumnalis. Autumn; blood red; 1 foot.... 5c
Vernalis. Yellow........................ 5c

ANTIRRHINUM MAJUS (Snapdragon.)
H. A., 2 to 3 ft.

One of the very best of our perennials, blooms abundantly the first Summer until after frost, and flowers well the second Summer and even longer. By removing a portion of the flowers, the plants will become strong.
Brilliant, scarlet, golden and white.......... 5c
Luteum, yellow............
Striatum, finest striped................... 5c
Majus, tall varieties; fine mixed............ 5c
Majus Album, pure white................. 5c

Naum (Dwarf varieties).
Album, pure white........................ 5c
Firefly, scarlet........................... 5c
Picturatum, new blotched................. 5c
Dwarf Varieties, fine mixed............... 5c

ARGEMONE. H. H. P.s 2 feet.

Handsome, large growing plant for flower-beds; white and yellow flowers resembling Poppies.
Hunnemanni, dark yellow flowers.......... 5c
Platyceras Grandiflora, large white flowers. 5c

AQUILEGIA.

Ornamental hardy plants known as (Columbine, or Wild Honeysuckle). Showy, and one of the best early bloomers; herbaceous; hardy perennial. Effective in rookeries.
Alpine, blue............................. 5c
Artica, brick-red and green................. 10c
Chrysantha, golden spurred; beautiful, long yellow spurred flowers.................. 5c
Bicolor, fl. pl. Double blue and white...... 10c
Bicolor fl. pl., Rubra, double red.......... 10c
Vulgaris, fl. pl., fine double varieties, mixed. 10c
Vulgaris. fl. pl., Alba, double white........ 10c
Single varieties, mixed.................... 5c

ASPERULA.

A dwarf plant covered all summer with Cineraria-like blossoms; annual, blue, white and mixed colors.
Azurea Letosa, blue, free bloomer, sweet-scented................................ 5c
Adorata (Sweet Woodruff), white......... 5c

ASTERS.

Are one of the most popular and effective garden favorites, producing in abundance flowers of great richness and variety. They make elegant borders and showy beds; hardy annual.

Trufflaut's Large Peony Flower. A favorite class, thrifty, upright growers; flowers large and almost perfectly round, with incurved petals; height 18 inches to 2 feet.... 10c

New Rose, 2 feet in height; robust, large flowers, petals finely imbricated; one of the very best; mixed colors..................... 10c

'mbrique Pompon, very perfect, almost a globe and beautifully imbricated; mixed colors.. 10c

Cocardeau or New Crown, two colored flowers, the central petals being of pure white, sometimes small and quilled, surrounded with large, flat petals of a bright color, 18 inches, mixed colors; beautiful............ 10c

New Peony-flowered Globe, the earliest of the Asters, flowers very large, plant branching and strong; does not require support.. 10c

Hedgehog or Needle. petals long, quilled and sharply pointed; 2 feet; mixed colors...... 10c

Chrysanthemum-flowered Dwarf White, a superb variety, every flower usually perfect; fine mixed varieties............. .... 10c

Dwarf Bouquet. splendid for edging and small beds............................... 10c

Dwarf Bouquet, pyramidal shaped.......... 10c

Dwarf Victoria, flowers very double and round; many extremely delicate, and some gorgeous shades, handsome varieties, mixed colors 10c

Mignon Aster, pure white flowers of beautiful form, resembling the Victoria race...... 15c

Alpinus, alpine aster, perrennial, blue....... 5c

Alpinus Gymnocephalus, perennial, rose.. 5c

BALSAM.
(Lady Slipper or Touch-Me-Not).

This is one of the most beautiful and popular annuals. They are sown in beds or frames, and if growing too thick, thin out and prune as desired. They transplant readily. Among the many varieties we name:

Double Camelia-Flower, Double Rose-Flowered, Double Spotted and Carnation, striped.each 10c
Extra Double Mixed, of above and others.... 10c

BALLOON VINE (Cardiospermum).
H. A., 4 to 8 feet.

A half hardy, rapid growing, handsome climber, having small white flowers, which are followed by seed vessels shaped like balloons..................................... 5c

BELLIS (Double Daisy).
H. H. P., 6 inches.

Beautiful for edging, dwarf groups and beds; earliest and prettiest of the spring flowers.

Finest mixed and pure white................ 10c

Longfellow, new, large, double rose-colored flowers; fine............................. 15c

BEGONIA (Tuberose Rooted).

Magnificent flowering plants for pots, and in Europe is extensively bedded out, flowering in the greatest profusion all Summer.

Single varieties, rooted 15c
Double varieties   " 25c

BARTONIA.   H. A.

A succulent plant with large golden flowers expanding in the middle of the day.

Aure, or golden yellow; 2 feet................ 5c

BRACHYCOME (Swan River Daisy.)
H. A., ½ foot.

A dwarf plant covered all summer with Cineraria-like blossoms, annnal; blue, white and mixed colors..... .... 5c

BIDENS ATROSANGUINEA.
(Dahlia Zimapani).

A large showy free flowering plant, resembling single Dahlias; black purple flowers, fine... 10c

BROWALLIA. H. H. A., 1½ feet.

The Browallias are excellent, free-flowering, and valuable for winter house-plants. When bedded out in Summer, are completely studded with bright, delicate flowers the whole season.

Czerwiakowski, deep blue, very fine........ 10c
Elata Alba, white........ .... 5c
Elata Nana, new, compact, very fine........ 10c

BRYONOPSIS (Ornamental Cue).

A very beautiful climber, bearing green fruits, which change to bright scarlet striped with white; 8 to 10 feet........................ 5c

CACALIA.   H. A., 1¼ feet.

Pretty free-fiowering plant, often called Flora's Paint Brush. Set plant six inches apart, They bloom early in summer until autumn; mixed colors........................... 5c

CALAMPELIS (Climber). H. H. A., 10 feet.

Scabra, blooms in racemes of bright orange flowers; one of the finest climbers......... 5c

CALENDRINIA. H. H. A., 1 foot.

Beautiful dwarf plant; succeed best in light rich soil. The sunshine causes the flowers to expand like portulaca, In a perfect blaze of beauty.

Mixed colors, large and showy.............. 5c

CALENDULA.   H. A.

Remarkably free-flowering plants, producing a fine effect in beds and borders; succeeds in any garden soil; height 1 foot.

Officialis, fl. pl., Le Proust; Nankeen colored, very fine; double, constant................ 5c
Meteor, large doubled striped flowers of light orange............................... 5c
Prince of Orange, similar to meteor but much darker; very beautiful................ 5c

CALCEOLARIA (Greenhouse Plant).
T. P., 1¼ feet.

Gorgeous plants for greenhouse and window decoration; the large pocket-shaped flowers are borne in the greatest profusion through the Spring and Summer months; colors, yellow, maroon crimson, etc.; spotted and blotched in the most unique and beautiful fashion; height, 1¼ feet.

Grandiflora, finest mixed.................. 25c
Pinnata California, yellow.................. 5c
Rugosa. Shrubby or bedding calceolarias, more hardy than the grandiflora variety is, bearing innumerable flowers; beautiful and small.. 25c
Striata, fine striped and mottled........... 25c

CALLIOPSIS (Coreopsis). H. A. 2 ft.

Showy, free-flowering and beautiful annual; the tall are fine for beds and mixed borders, and dwarf for bedding. Crimson, yellow, brown and marbled; mixed colors.

Atkinsoni, yellow and brown; biennial	5c
Cardaminifolia, of pyramidal habit	5c
Cornuta, yellow and large-flowered	5c
Longipes, yellow, perennial	5c
Fine mixture of tall sorts	5c
Fine mixture of dwarf sorts	5c

CALLIRRHOE.

Beautiful annual; violet, purple and crimson flowers; white center; attractive, and blooms through the summer ... 5c

CAMPANULA (Canterbury Bell).
H. A. and P., 6 to 12 inches.

Well-known favorites; bearing large bell and saucer-shaped flowers in profusion.

Medium, fl. pl.; double blue, double white and double rose, each separate	10c
Medium, single, finest mixed	5c
Medium Striata, new; striped, very fine	10c
Calycanthema (Cup and Saucer). The flowers are large, resembling somewhat a cup and saucer; blue, white and lilac; fine mixed	15c
Rosea, single rose	5c
Pyramidalis, very beautiful sorts, fine colors, mixed	5c
Speculum (Venus's Looking-glass). Single, finest mixed	5c
Speculum, double sorts, finest mixed	10c

CANARY BIRD FLOWER (Climber).
H. H. A., 10 to 15 feet.

TROPÆOLUM.

Popular and pretty; rapid grower and abundant bloomer of rich yellow fringed flowers ... 10c

CANNA (Indian Shot). **H. H. P.**

Stately and ornamental plants, desirable in groups or background; soak seed in hot water 12 hours before sowing.

Extra choice mixed	5c
Dark leaved varieties	10c

CANDYTUFT. H. A. 6 to 12 inches.

Popular and useful, blooming long and freely and perfectly hardy. The flowers are quite a treasure for making bouquets and for massing or ribbon gardening. Varieties and shades are numerous.

Armara, pure white	5c
Coromaria, "White Rocket;" large trusses of pure white flowers; much prized by the florists	5c
"Empress", a most beautiful Candytuft, being a series of Candellabra-shaped branches, each producing a large truss of white flowers, thus presenting a pyramid of bloom throughout the season	10c
"Carter's Carmine;" this new variety is of a dwarf compact habit, and bears a mass of fine Carmine bloom, true from seed	10c
Purpurea (Dark Crimson) beautiful	5c
Fine mixed, annual sorts	5c
Sempervirens Perennial, White, blooming and hardy, adapted for rockeries baskets and etc	10c

CARNATION (Dianthus)
H. H. P. 1 to 2 feet.

Magnificent and popular, very fragrant, and beautiful colors; hardy perennial.

Finest strains of German and Italian seed	25c
Good Mixed	10c
Grenadin, A new dwarf compact variety of great value to florists, producing a profusion of large double, brilliant scarlet flowers, three weeks earlier than any other variety	25c
Grenadin, White, new novelty	50c
German Perpetual or tree	25c
Cassia, Hardy perennial, with yellow flowers, 18 inches high; good border flower	5c

CATANANCHE.

Coernlea, coerulea, fl. albo (bicolor). Fine everlasting.

Fine perennials, blue and white mixed ... 5c.

CATCHFLY (Silence). H. A. 1½ feet.

Showy and great favorite; annual; bright dense heads of flowery; blooms freely and of easy culture; colors, red and white ... 5c

Pendula Carnea, double red, new and fine	5c
Compacta Alba, double white new and pretty	5c
Snow King, pure white Globular, new, and a fine novelty	10c

CONVALLARIA MAJALIS (Lily of the Valley).

Clean seed in berries.

LILY OF THE VALLEY.

One of the most charming of our spring flowering plants, its slender stems set with tiny bells diffusing a delicious odor, have rendered it a universal favorite. They are very hardy, and require a shaded situation, soil rich sandy loam ... 10c

Japonica, very fine ... 10c

CENTRANTHUS. H. A. 1¼ feet.

Pretty, free flowering annual, effective in beds and borders; transparent stems and glaucous leaves; rose colored and white ... 5c

CENTAUREA. **H. A.**

Showy border plant, succeeding in almost any soil; hardy annual and perennial; varieties.

Bachelor's Button or Corn Bottle, 2 feet; quite showy	5c
Sweet Sultan, Hardy annual; 1 foot	5c

CLARKIA. H. A. 1 to 2 feet.

Hardy annual plant, blooming profusely with handsome flowers.

Double and Single, mixed colors ... 5c

CINERARIA (Greenhouse Plant).
H. H. P., 1 foot.

Hybrida Grandiflora,, a favorite attractive free flowering plant, blooming during the winter and early spring months. Mixed	25c
Plenissima, new, double, from finest double flowers	40c

CHRYSANTHEMUM.
H. A. and P. 12 to 18 inches.

Very showy and effective favorites; colors have the appearance of being laid on with a brush; annual and perennial; varieties.

Chrysanthemum (Single Annual Varieties).

TricolorCarinatumAlbum, white...........	5c
Burridgi, (Lord Beaconsfield), white and rose.	5c
Coronarium, fl. pl., double yellow..........	5c
Coronarium, fl. pl., double white..........	5c

Chrysatnhemum, (Perennial varieties).

Indicum Majus, large flowering double varities...................................	25c
Indicum, double pom pon mixed	25c
Japenicum, fl. pleno, Japanese	25c
Japenicum Nanum, fl. pl., dwarf double Japanese.................................	25c
Uglinesum, abundant, large white flowers, fine for cutting...........................	50c
Frutescens Grandiflorum, (Marguerite or Paris Daisy), H. P., now so fashionable and popular; large white star-like flowers, growing freely and profusely...................	10c

COBŒA (Scandens).
H. H. P., 20 to 30 feet.

Climbing plant; rapid grower and large bell-shaped flowers; fine for Summer; plant seed edgewise.................................. 10c

COLEUS.   T. P., 1 to 3 feet.

Ornamental foliage plant; leaves of all shapes and colors, of velvety appearance and great beauty. Splendid flower for garden decoration. Finest hybird, mixed................ 25c

COLLINSIA. H. H. A., 1 to 2 feet.

California annual; marbled or many colored, for beds and borders...................... 5c

COCKSCOMB (Celosia).

Annual plant, showy and attractive; half hardy.

Christata, dwarf, crimson, fine; Variegata, new, brilliant, combs of crimson and gold.	10c
Japan, branching variety of great beauty; scarlet and crimson combs, like ruffled lace, in pyramidal masses....................	10c
Tall and dwarf varieties mixed..............	10c
Pyramidalis Plumosa, fine feathered varieties, choice mixed.......................	10c

COMELINA.

Tender perennial, tuberous root; rich and beautiful; flowers of blue and white; roots can be taken up and planted like Dahlias; 2 feet high................................. 5c

CONVOLVULUS MAJOR (Morning Glory).
H. A., 30 to 50 feet.

Varieties and colors too well known for description; white, dark blue, blood red, rose and striped, growing 20 feet high; nothing can equal them for rapidity of growth and profusion of bloom, thriving in almost any situation; tall mixed..................... 5c

Hederacia Grandiflora Superba, Large-flowering, mixed; white edged varieties. Many beautiful sorts.................... 10c

Aureus Superbus. A smaller growing sort, with smaller flowers of golden yellow......	10c
Minor, mixed; including many varieties......	5c

Bedding Varieties (C. Minor).
These grow only about 1 foot high; the flowers are freely borne and remain open all day, if pleasant; splendid for bedding.

Ipomœa Grandiflora. The Moon Flower, "Evening Glory" or "Good Night." Large pure white fragrant flowers in profusion, opening in the evening; rapid and luxuriant summer climber......................... 10c

Cypress Vine (Ipomœa Quamaoclit). H. H. A., 15 feet.

Climbing Annual, popular, elegant and graceful; different colors, scarlet, white and rose; separate colors or mixed................... 5c

Rubro Coerulea Alba, fl. pl., new, double white cyprus; choice novelty.............. 10c

CREPIS (Hawkweed).

Annual of easy culture and abundant bloomer;
| red, white and yellow..................... | 5c |
| Nana Compacta, dwarf, 18 inches........... | 5c |

CYCLAMEN, PERSICUM.

Charming bulbous-rooted plants, with beautiful foliage, and rich-colored orchid-like fragrant flowers; universal favorites for winter and spring blooming. If seed is sown early they make flowering bulbs in one season; they require sandy loam; half hardy perennial; mixed; 6 inches.......... 25c

Persicum giganteum. This new large-flowering variety has beautiful mottled leaves, broad petals, and stout flower-stalks, throwing the flowers well above the foliage; 8 inches 40c

CYCLANTHERA.

A climbing plant of the gourd species, free-growing, handsome foliage and oval-shaped fruit, exploding loudly when ripe; half-hardy annual; explodens; 10 feet.......... 5c

DAHLIA. H. H. P., 4 to 6 feet.

Tuberous root, hardy perennial; seed of finest single mixed colors...................... 10c
Extra choice double mixed, from named flowers 20c

DATURA (Trumpet Flower).
H. A., 3 feet.

Strong growing plants known as "Angel's Trumpets," large showy flowers suitable for borders.

Datura Wrightii, large white and lilac flowers.	5c
Fastuosa, fl. pl., mixed; fine double varities .	5c

DIANTHUS (Pinks).

A magnificent genus, embracing some of the most popular flowers in cultivation, producing a great variety of brilliant colors and profusion of bloom. The hardy biennials, or Chinese and Japanese varieties, bloom the first season, the same as hardy annuals; height, 1 foot. The hardy perennial varieties are very fragrant, and of easy culture for the garden or greenhouse.

Chinensis (China or Indian Pink). Extra double, all colors mixed.................. 5c

Heddewiggi, fl. pl. (Double Japan Pink,) Flowers very large and double, nearly three inches in diameter, of various shades of the most brilliant colors...................... 5c

Heddewiggi diadematus (Double Diadem Pink.) This is of denser growth than the Heddewiggi, and dwarfer habit. Very regular, densely double, and of all shades of color 5c

Laciniatus, fl.pl. (Double fringed Japan Pink.) Large double showy flowers with fringed edges, mixed, various colors and beautifully striped.................................... 5c

Striata, fl. pl. Large double fringed flowers of crimson, rose, white, etc., all beautifully striped.................................... 10c

Laciniatus. very fine, large-flowered, single Japan Pink, mixed...................... 5c

Imperalis, fl. pl. (Double Imperial Pink.) A superb double variety, all colors mixed..... 5c

Pheasant's Eye (Plumarie Simplex.) A beautiful single variety, with fringe-edged white flowers, and a dark center; hardy perennial; 1 foot.................................... 5c

DOLCHIOS (Hyacinth Bean).
T. A., 10 feet.

A beautiful climber, flowers in clusters, purple and white, 10 feet..................... 5c

Giganteus, species from Texas.............. 5c

DIGITALIS (Foxglove).
H. P., 3 to 4 feet.

Hardy perennials, three feet, handsome ornamental plant of stately growth and varied colors; mixed or separate colors........... 5c

Monstrosa (Mammoth Foxglove.) The largest and best type; all colors mixed..... 10c

ERYSIMUM. H. A., 1 foot.

Annual, 1¼ feet, free flowering and showy for beds or border, sulphur yellow and deeper orange shades.................... 5c

ESCHSCHOLTZIA (California Poppy).
H. A., 1 foot.

A hardy annual, profuse bloomer, with rich and beautiful colors; continues in bloom until frost; varieties.

Eschscholzia Californica. Sulphur yellow with orange center...................... 5c

Rose Cardinal. A charming new variety, producing freely beautiful large flowers of intense carmine...................... 10c

Crocea, fl. pl., mixed; a double-flowering, orange, scarlet and white.............. 10c

EUPHORBIA (Snow on the Mountain).

Attractive foliage, with white and green bracts on the tips of each branch, veined and margined with white; 2 feet.

Variegata...................... 5c

EUTOCA.

Annual; desirable for cut flowers; blue and lilac; 6 inches...................... 5c

FUCHSIA. T. P., 1 to 3 feet.

A beautiful plant blooming all the season; mixed; single and double.............. 25c

FORGET-ME-NOT (Myosotis).
H. P., 6 to 12 inches.

Very popular and beautiful; will grow in any moist situation.

Palustris, blue, Alba, white............... 10c
Azorica, flowers rich blue, shaded with purple 10c

Myosotis (Alpestris Victoria).
Of stout and bushy habit of growth, bearing umbels of large bright azure-blue flowers with central double blooms. The plant attains a height of 5 to 7 inches, with a diameter of 8 to ten inches, and when fully grown is quite globular in shape, and perfectly covered with flowers. This beautiful Forget-me-not is the best for carpet bedding, edgings and masses, and for growing in pots for market........ .... 25c

Eliza Fonrobert. New, large-flowering, bright blue, of pyramidal habit; remarkably fine and distinct.................... 15c

Eliza Fonrobert, Alba; white, beautiful..... 15c

GAILLARDIA.

Splendid bedding plants, remarkable for the profusion, size, and brilliancy of their flowers, continuing in beauty during the summer and autumn; half-hardy annuals; 1½ feet.

Grandiflora. mixed single varieties; includes many sorts.................... 5c

Picta Lorenziana. A charming profuse flowering "so-called" double variety, entirely distinct from the single flowering. Fine for massing, and use as a bouquet flower, continuing in bloom until frost.............. 10c

Amblyodon, fine red.................... 5c

GERANIUM. H. H. P.

A popular bedding plant for the house or garden, extensively used for massing; half-hardy perennial; flowering the first season; from 1 to 3 feet.

Zonale, Mixed, a superb strain of the largest and finest varieties; mixed colors........ 25c

Variegated, Mixed, bronze, gold, and silver tri-colored foliage varieties.............. 25c

Double, Mixed. This seed will produce a large percentage of double flowers of extra fine colors.................... 25c

Pelargonium, Mixed, (Lady Washington). From the finest fancy and spotted large flowering.................... 25c

Apple-Scented (Pelargonium odoratissimum). This fragrant favorite variety can only be grown from seed to form five plants. Sow in light soil, and keep moist until they germinate.................... 25c

GLOXINIA HYBRIDA CRASSIFOLIA.

A bulbous-rooted plant, producing in great profusion, during the summer months, large bell-shaped flowers of the richest and most beautiful variety of brilliant colors; the bulbs must be kept warm and dry during the winter; 1 foot.

Grandiflora Erecta, Mixed, rich colored, erect flowers.................... 25c

Grandiflora, New French Tigred and spotted varieties........................ 25c

GLOBE AMARANTH (Everlasting Flower).

"Bachelor's Buttons"; ornamental summer-blooming plants, and fine for "Everlastings." H. A. 2 feet.

Globe Amaranth, white, purple, variegated and mixed.................... 5c

Aurea Superba (Hoagena), fine orange.

GODETIA. H. A.

An attractive hardy annual, deserving more extensive cultivation. The plant blooms profusely, and bear showy flowers of rich and varied colors; 1½ feet.

Bijou, flowers splendid white, with a dark rose spot; very dwarf and dense growing... 5c

Lady Abemarle, flowers large, of carmine crimson shade; the edges of the petals suffused with pale lilac........................ 5c

Grandiflora Maculata, Large white, flowers with crimson spots, fine.................. 5c

New Godetias (Rubicunda Splendens). Double red very brilliant.................... 10c

Lady Satin Rose, Deep rose pink, glossy and satiny, by some thought the most beautiful annual of recent introduction............ 10c

GOURD (Cucurbita). H. A.

Rapid growing, interesting plants with ornamental fringe, and varieties of singular shaped fruit; tender annuals; 15 to 20 feet.

Calabash, the dipper...................... 5c

Hercules' Club, club-shaped; 4 feet long..... 5o

Egg-Shaped, fruit white like an egg........ 5c

Orange-Shaped, or Mock-Orange.......... 5c

Bottle-Shaped........................... 5c

Turk's Turban, red striped........... ..... 10c

Pear-Shaped, striped; very showy.......... 10c

Argyrosperma, Dish Rag, or (Bonnet Gourd). 10c

Augora, black-seeded white-spotted fruits, very useful for arbors etc.................. 10o

Tricosanthes Colubrina (True Serpent Gourd). Striped like a serpent, changing to brilliant carmine when ripe; 5 feet in length................................... 10c

Fine Mixed, from a large collection of large sorts............ .. ..·.............. 5c

Fine Mixed, small ornamental sorts.......... 5o

GYPSOPHILA. H. P.

Delicate, free flowering little plants, covered with a profusion of tiny star-shaped, blossoms, valuable for making bonquets.

Acutifolia, rose-colored delicate and pretty.. 5c

Elegans, white a choice variety............. 5c

Paniculata Compacta, new dwarf compact variety, beautiful for bonquets............ 10c

HELIOTROPE. H. H. P. 18 inches.

A deliciously fragrant plant, fine for bedding and pot culture; choice mixed............. 10c

Fine mixture of dark flowering sorts......... 10c

HELICHRYSUM (Everlasting Flowers).

Very popular Everlastings with globular flowers, useful for borders and beds. When used for dyeing, flowers should be picked before fully expanded. H. A.

H. Monstrosum fl. pl., a mixture of many varieties. 2 feet.......................... 5c

HOLLYHOCK (Althaea Rosea). H. P.

Old fashioned favorites which should be in every garden. Seeds should be sown in June or July to have flowering plants the next summer or if sown in the house early in the spring they will bloom the first year. Height 4 to 6 feet.

Fine Mixed, including many colors.......... 10c

Extra Choice Mixed, From chaters unrivaled collection................................. 15c

HIBISCUS. H. H. 2 to 4 feet.

Hardy annual, showy and ornamental.

Africanus, rich; cream-brown center........ 5c

Roseus Grandiflorus. rose-colored flowers... 5c

Coccineus Speciosus, scarlet; fine..... .... 10c

HONESTY. H. B., 2 feet.

Lunaria or Satan Flower, an interesting plant; seed vessel looks like transparent silver; handsome for bonqnets or dried flowers; hardy perennial................... 5c

ICE PLANT (Mesembryanthemum). H. H. A., 6 inches.

Dwarf trailer, with thick fleshy leaves, having the appearance of being covered with ice crystals.............................. 5c

Tricolor-, (dew plant) 5c

Album. White,............................ 5c

IMPATIENS SULTANI. H. T. A.

One of the most distinct and beautiful plants of recent introduction for the warm greenhouse or summer bedding; owing to its gorgeous coloring and profuse and continuous flowering it is rapidly becoming popular. This plant is of compact, neat habit of growth, with good constitution, and almost a perpetual bloomer. Planted out in the open ground at the end of June it grows luxuriantly, flowers with the greatest profusion, and produces an admirable effect until cut down by frost. The flowers are of a brilliant rosy-scarlet color, about 1¼ inches in diameter.

Sultani...................................... 25c

KAULFUSSIA. H. A., 6 inches.

Dwarf annual, like an aster; pretty branching and free flowering; mixed colors........... 5c

LARKSPUR (Delphinum). H. A. and perennial.

One of our most showy and useful plants, possessing almost every requsite for the adornment of the garden; the hardy perennials producing splendid spikes of flowers in profusion throughout the summer. If sown early they bloom the first year from seed. The hardy annuals are profuse bloomers, and succeed best if sown in the autumn, or very early in the spring.

Tall Rocket. Double Mixed, includes many colors. 2½ feet.......................... 5c

Mixed Dwarf Rocket Varieties, includes many varieties............................ 5c

Double Stock Flowered. a tall branching variety, with beautiful long spikes of flowers of of various colors; fine for cut-flowers; 2 feet. 5c

Larkspur (Delphinum), perennial varieties.

Nudicaule, Dwarf, of compact growth, with spikes of bright scarlet flowers; 18 inches... 10c

Cashmerianum, a beautiful dark blue, blooms in corymbs of six or more; 15 inches........ 20c

Hybridum, many varieties extra fine mixed .. 10c

Delphinium Zalil, a pure sulphur yellow flowering perennial of a lovely and delicate shade, resembling in color the Marechal Neil Rose, a color unknown till now. The plant is of branching habit, 3½ to 4½ feet high, the branches ending in long-spikes of 40 to 50 blossoms, which open almost at the same time. The flowers are one inch in diameter, and last in flower from June till August. Price per packet, ——

LANTANA. H. H. P.

A remarkably handsome free-flowering genus of of plants with brilliantly colored flowers, constantly chaning in hue, very effective either for pot culture or for bedding. Half-hardy perennial.

Finest varieties mixed........................ 10c

LINUM (Flowering Flax). H. A., 1 foot.

Conspicuous for its brilliant colors.

Flavum, yellow; perennial................... 5c
Perennial sorts, fine mixed. 5c

LINARIA.

Cymballaria (Kenilworth Ivy). A very pretty climber.................................... 5c

LEPTOSIPHON. H. A., 8 inches.

Beautiful dwarf for lines and ribbon beds; white and yellow; mixed, French.......... 5c

LOBELIA.

Annuals. An elegant dwarf of easy culture; fine for borders and ribbon beds and for vases and hanging baskets.

Erinus, **Emperor William**. A very compact variety, with fine sky-blue flowers......... 10c
Erinus, **Crytal Palace Compacta**. A new densely compact miniature variety, which, during the summer months, is studded with rich deep blue flowers..................... 10c
Erinus Speciosa, **Crystal Palace**. Of trailing growth; flowers of an ulra-marine blue.. 10c
Crystal Palace Oculata, dark stalks and dark blue flowers, with a distinct white eye; splendid 10c

LUPINUS (Sun Dials). H. A. and P.

Desirable bedding plants with long, graceful flower spikes, bearing richly colored, pea-shaped flowers.

Mixed annual varieties; 1 to 3 feet........... 5c
Mixed perennial varieties. Hardy sorts...... 5c

LAVENDER. H. P., 1 to 2 feet.

Prized for its fragrant violet flowers; does best in a dry, gravelly soil; hardy perennial. 5c

LYCHNIS.

Showy flowering plants for shrubberies and flower beds; flowers strikingly brilliant.

Chalcedonica, dazzling scarlet, hardy perennial; 1 to 3 feet,........................ 5c
Haageana. Brilliant scarlet flowers, 2 inches across; 1 foot......................... 10c
Mixed Haageana Hybrids. Shades of white scarlet, flesh, pink, etc.; annual varieties; 1 foot,.................................... 10c
Haageana Grandiflora Gigantea............. 10c

MARIGOLD (Tagetes). H. H. A.

A class of showy and extremely effective plants with fine double flowers of rich and beautiful colors, very well adapted for large beds and bordering. No garden should be without them

Tall African. Many varieties mixed, 2 feet.. 5c
Sulphurea. sulphur yellow.................. 5c
Aurea Fistulosa Pl. quilled golden yellow.. 5c
Dwarf French. A mixture of many shades; 1 foot..................................... 5c
Dwarf African, all colors mixed............. 5c
Signata Pumila. Splendid for edgings; dwarf plants with fern-like foliage and small brilliant yellow cross-shaped flowers in profusion, which gives it a delicate, airy appearance, making beautiful borders for long beds....................................... 5c
Signata Pumila (New Golden Ring). Foliage same as above; flowers have a deep golden stripe across each petal, which forms a complete golden ring, very showy and pretty.. 5c
Tall French, fine mixed, all shades.......... 5c

MARVEL OF PERU (Four o'clock).
H. H. P., 2 feet.

One of the most ornamental flowering plants; they are quite fragrant, flowers expanding in the evening; half hardy perennial; blooming the first season from seed; the roots can be preserved in winter like Dahlias.

Mixed, beautiful colors.................... 5c
Longifolia, long flower, pure white and fragrant 5c
Dwarf White Tom Thumb. When fully developed this variety does not exceed 10 inches in height, and forms a charming little bush completely studded with pure white flowers; new............................. 10c
Multiflor, large umbels of dark, lilac, red flowers; perennial, fine.................... 15c

MARTYNIA. H. A., 3 to 4 feet.

Free flowering, of easy culture and hardy, sweet-scented; yellow and purple.......... 5c

MATRICARIA (Fever Few).

Handsome free-flowering plants, good for beds and pot culture. H. H. P.
Matricaria Eximia Crispa Fl. Pl. Lovely little plants with double white flowers and prettily curled foliage like parsley. 8 inches................................... 10c
Capensis. Double white flowers; splendid for banquets etc....................... 5c
Grandflora Fl. Pl. Large flowering double white, beautiful...................... 15c

MAURANDIA. (Climber.) T. A.
6 to 10 feet.

Very graceful for training on trellis work, verandas, etc.; perennial, flowers the first season from seed ; violet, pink, purple white and mixed........................... 10c

MIGNONETTE (Reseda Odorata).

A well known annual with spikes of deliciously fragrant flowers. Indispensable in every garden. H. A.

Grandiflora. Large flowered; per oz., 20c. 5c
Ameliorata. Very sweet scented; per oz., 15c. 5c
Parsons' White. A distinct almost white variety, with long spikes. 5c

Gabriele. New, red flowering; very sweet, spikes very thick; one of the best for florists' use 10c

New Hybird Spiral. Is a vigorous grower, with spikes often attaining a length of 10 inches; delightfully fragrant 5c

Giant Pyramidal. Flowers reddish, sweet-scented and very large 10c

Machet. The plants are dwarf and vigorous, of pyramidal growth. They throw up numerous long and broad spikes of deliciously scented red flowers. Entirely distinct..... 10c

Crimson Queen. very fine, robust, excellent for pots, red-flowered 5c

Golden Queen. An entirely distinct sort, with golden yellow flowers, which give it a most attractive appearance; very fragrant.. 10c

Victoria. New dark red, very fine........... 10c

MIMULUS (Monkey Flower.) H. H. P.

A very interesting free-blooming genus of plants with beautiful spotted and blotched flowers of brilliant colors. Succeeds best in shaded and damp situations. Perennials in the greenhouse, annuals in the open air.

Tigrinus Grandiflora. very large flowering, new tigred and spotted varieties, most beautiful; very showy as window plants.... 15c

Nanus. New dwarf varieties, spotted and blotched, fine............................. 10c

Albus. White ground, handsome large-flowering varieties............................ 10c

Hose in Here. Very curious and pretty, one flower sitting in another; fine mixed....... 20c

Moschatus. (Musk Plant.) The thin delicate leaves emit a delicate musk odor.......... 10c

MOMONDICA.

A curious annual climber, with yellow blossoms. The fruit is the chief curiosity, is egg-shaped, and covered with warty excrescences, which, when ripe, bursts suddenly open, scattering its seed, and showing a brilliant carmine interior. Fine for trellises, fences, stumps, etc. Half hardy annual.

Balsamina (Balsam Apple.)................ 6c

Charantia (Balsam Pear) golden yellow...... 5c

TALL NASTURTIUM (Tropaeolum Major). H. H. A.

Elegant profuse flowering plants for verandas, trellises, etc. The seed pods can be gathered while green and tender, for pickling, hardy annuals; 10 feet.

Finest mixed. All colors, of Climbing Nasturtium 5c

Lobb's Nasturtium.   H. H. A. 4 to 6 feet.

Tropaeolum **Lobbianum**, these are distinguished from the Tall Nasturtius above (Tropaeolum Majus) by their longer vines; their leaves and flowers, however, are somewhat smaller, but their greater profusion renders them superior for trellises, arbors, for hanging over vases, rock-work, etc; the flowers are of unusual brilliancy and rich-

ness, and they are also splendid for winter decoration in the green-house and conservatory. Mixed, contains many beautiful sorts.......... 10c

DWARF NASTURTIUM (Tropaeolum Minor.) H. H. A.

The dwarf varieties are all desirable, and are among the most popular plants, standing any amount of heat and drought, growing vigorously and flowering freely all summer and fall; excellent for massing and ribboning, doing well even in poor soil; hardy annuals; 1 foot.

Empress of India, very dwarf habit; flowers brilliant crimson; abundant bloomer..... .... 10c

Tom Thumb King Thedore, flowers almost black.......... .... 5c

Coccineum, scarlet, fine...... .... 5c

Tom Tumb. mixed all colors................ 5c

NEMOPHILA (Love Grove). H. A., 1 foot.

A charming dwarf annual, neat, compact and of uniform growth, adapted for beds and borders, fine mixed varieties.......... 5c

NIEREMBERGIA.   H. H. P.

A half-hardy perennial, slender growing plant, perpetually in bloom, flowering the first year if sown early; desirable for the greenhouse, baskets, vases or bedding out; 1 foot..................................... 5c

NIGELLA.   H. A

(Love in a Mist. or Devil in the Bush.)

A compact, free flowering plant, with finely cut foliage, curious looking flowers and seed pods; of easy culture, growing in any garden soil; hardy annuals; 1 foot.

Damascena (Devil in a bush.) Double, blue and white.................................. 5c

Nana fl. pleno, double dwarf, very beautiful, 6 to 8 inches high........................ 10c

NOLANA.   H. A.

Very pretty annual of trailing habit, with Morning Glory-like flowers, well adapted to rock work. Height 6 inches.

Mixed. All varieties... .... 5c

OENOTHERA (Evening Primrose.) H. P. 1 to 2 feet.

Beautiful, free growing and useful, flowering in long spikes, fine for beds or borders.

Biennis (Evening Primrose.) Yellow flowers opening in the evening and early morning. 5c

Acaulis alba, large white flowers, dwarf, showy and beautiful...................... 5c

Taraxacifolia aurea, golden yellow, large flowered, very fine...................... 5c

Rosea (Mexicana,) 6 inches high, extra fine, true rose colored flowers................. 10c

Passion Flower (Climber.)   H. P.

Handsome rapid grower, fine for decoration and open ground.

Cerulea. large violet and light blue, fragrant. 10c

PERILLA.

The foliage of this plant is exceedingly elegant, of a very dark purple color, and produces a charming contrast with silvery-leaved plants; growing freely in any soil; half-hardy annual; 1½ feet.
Nankinensis Atropurpureus Laciniatis, elegant dark cut foliage...................... 5c

PENTSTEMON.

One of our most beautiful an attractive herbaceous plants; bearing long, graceful spikes of rich-colored flowers; will bloom the first season if sown early in March, and planted out in May; half-hardy perennials; 2 feet.
Hartwegi (gentianoides, hybridus), extra fine mixed, from the handsomest new sorts, which the seed reproduces in great variety. 10c

PANSIES.

Pansy (Viola Tricolor.)
This is a great favorite with all flower gardens. It is biennial and can be perpetuated by division of the roots. Seeds sown in autumn produce earlier and better flowers the coming season. They require good rich soil.

Pansies in Separate Colors.

Odier or Five Blotched. A beautiful strain, perfect in size and form of flower, containing many beautiful colors; each of the 5 petals is marked with a large dark blotch; very effective.............. .... 15c

Emperor William. Large handsome flowers borne in great profusion, well above the foliage, brilliant ultramarine blue with a purple violet eye......................... 10c

Faust (King of the Blacks). Almost black, the darkest pansy known.................. 10c

Lord Beaconsfield. A splendid sort; flowers deep purple violet, shading to white on the upper petals............. .... 10c

Snow Queen. Very large, satiny white, light yellow center........................... 10c

Yellow Gem. Pure yellow, without eye..... 10c

"Non Plus Sultra," offered this year for the first time; very choice mixed fine variety; highly effective........................... 25c

Trimardeau. An altogether distinct and beautiful new race, the flowers of which are larger than any hitherto produced. Each flower is marked with three large blotches or spots; and the plants produce an endless variety of beautiful shades.................. 15c

White, pure black center.................... 10c

Yellow, (golden), pure black center, fine for bedding................................ 10c

Azure Blue, bright sky blue................ 10c

Bronze, dark mahogany, shades fine........ 10c

German Finest Mixed, including many colors.................................. 10c

PETUNIA.　　T. P.

For out-door decoration or house culture few plants are equal to this class. They commence flowering early, and continue a mass of bloom throughout the whole season, until killed by frost; easily cultivated, requiring rich soil and a sunny situation. Of late years the single-striped, mottled and double varieties have been greatly improved.

Single Varieties.

Petunia. fine mixed......................... 5c
Grandiflora Venosa. Large flowering, finest shades of colors beautifully veined......... 10c
Finest Striped and Blotched. Seed saved from magnificent collections of striped and blotched varieties........................ 10c
Large Flowered Yellow Throat. These form a class of rare beauty, and come true from seed. The flowers are very large, and of perfect form, with a deep yellow throat, veined very much like the Salpiglossis..... 25c
Hybrida Grandiflora Fimbriata. Fringed varieties in splendid mixtures............. 25c
Marginata Maculata, green bordered and blotched varieties; very rare............... 25c
Hybrida Grandiflora. Choicest mixed, seed saved from show flowers.................... 20c
Pure White. Single. Desirable for cemetery beds, or where large masses of white are wanted.................................. 10c

PYRETHRUM.　　H. P.

This family contains the well-known "Golden Feather," a low growing plant, with yellow foliage for ribbon beds, edgings, etc.; and also contains some of the handsomest flowering hardy plants for borders that are in cultivation.

Yellow Foliage Sorts For Ribboning.

Aureum. Bright yellow foliage; 1 foot...... 10c
Laciniatus. Yellow foliage, finely fringed; 1 foot 10c
Selaginoides. Handsome fern-like foliage, ½ ft. 15c

Hardy Flowering Varieties.

Valuable for permanent beds, bearing large, bright colored flowers of rose, flesh, pink, white, crimson, etc., which remain in bloom for a long time. H.H.P.
Single Large Flowering Hybride Mixed....... 10c
Double Large Flowering Hybrids Mixed 25c

RHODANTHE (Everlasting Flower.)
H. H. A., 1 foot.

Very valuable for winter bouquets, and also desirable for pot plants or for the garden; red, white and pink, finest mixed.......... 10c

RICINUS (Caster Oil Plant).
H. H. A., 6 to 15 ft.

This is a rapid grower with fine palm-like foliage, giving a fine effect on lawns or large beds.
Fine mixture of all varieties, foliage sorts.... 5c
" 　 " 　 " 　 " 　 dwarf sorts..... 5

ROCKET (Hesperia).
H. P., 2 to 3 feet.

Well known, free-flowering and very fragrant; purple and white........................ 5c

SALPIGLOSSIS.   H. H. A.

Neat and beautiful ornamental autumn blooming plants, with curiously pencilled and marbled funnel-shaped flowers; suitable for the greenhouse or flower border; of easy culture, requiring a light, rich soil; half hardy annual, 1½ feet.

Grandiflora. Large flowered, all colors mixed. 10c

SAZVIA (Flowering Sage).
H. H. P., 3 feet.

One of our handsomest summer and autumn flowering plants, when they are literally ablaze with brilliant flowers; very effective for massing on the lawn or for ribbon beds.

Splendens (Scarlet sage.) Beautiful, Fiery scarlet.................................... 10c

Splendens Coccinea. Nana compacta, dwarf, compact, very free flowering.............. 15c

SAPONARIA (Bouncing Bet).   H. A.

Handsome dwarf growing plants, with pretty star-shaped flowers; excellent for massing and edging.

Multiflora compacta, new, compact, beautiful for borders planted in a sunny situation. 5c

Ocymoides. splendes, very brilliant red, fine. 5c

SENSITIVE PLANT (Mimosa Pudica).

A very interesting plant with fern-like foliage, which is so sensitive that the leaves close up immediately when touched or shaken; suitable for pots or borders. H. A., 1 foot..... 5c

SCHIZANTHUS (Butterfly Flower.)
H. H. A.

A splendid class of plants, combining elegance of growth and profusion of beautiful flowers, valuable in the garden and greenhouse. White, purple, yellow and crimson; half hardy annual; finest mixed colors.......... 5c

Papilionaceous. In this charming variety we have one of the finest annuals in cultivation. The flowers are handsome as some of the orchids............................... 5c

Papilionaceous Pyramidalis, compactus. New, compact, fine...................... 5c

Pinnatus Rossus. new rose, beautiful....... 10c

STATICE (Everlasting).

An interesting, free flowering plant of easy culture, long-blooming, and valuable for Winter bonquets, perennial, fine mixed.... 10c

Suworowi. The branching flower spikes of this new annual Statice are of a bright rose, shaded with crimson. Each plant produces from 10 to 15 spikes, measuring from 12 to 18 inches. One plant will last in flower more than two months, and if sown in succession it may be had in bloom throughout the whole summer and autumn................. 20c

SCABIOSA.   H. P.

The "Mourning Bride" or "Sweet Scabious" of our old gardens, but much improved in size, colors and doubleness. They are very free bloomers, the colors white, carmine, lilac, maroon, etc., excellent for bonquets.

Nana. fl. pl., mixed dwarf, double. 1 foot.... 5c

Maxima Pleno Mixed. New, large flowering, tall double sorts......................... 5c

Minor, fl. pl., cherry red and white, new..... 5c

Candidissima. Double white flowers, useful for bouquets. 1 foot.................... 10c

SMILAX (Madsola asparagoides)
SMILAX (Myrsiphyllum).
T. P., 6 feet.

This is the most popular and graceful evergreen vine in cultivation, adapted for hanging baskets and pot culture, floral wreaths, etc...................... 10c

SUNFLOWER.   H. A.

Stately growing plants, with immense golden yellow flowers; the single varieties are well known, but the double sorts are not; they are perfectly magnificent.

Double Sorts.

Globosus Fistulosus. perfecly round flowers. very double, saffron; 6 feet.............. 5c

Oculatus Viridis. double yellow flowers, with green center; 4 feet.................... 5c

Miniature Sunflower. Of dwarf branching habit, wearing many little flowers only 2 inches across; orange........ 5c

Nanum, fl. pl., (Dwarf Double). Yellow, quite dwarf, fine............................ 5c

Giant Russian. Flowers 18 to 20 inches across; grown principally for the seeds, of which it is very prolific......................... 5c

JACOBÆA (Senicio).

Remarkably pretty, free growing, profuse flowering plants, almost unsurpassed for brilliancy and beauty. Grow freely from seed, and are easily propagated from cuttings, not one in fifty failing. The double are the only ones worth cultivating. Hardy annuals in open border, biennial in greenhouse. Sow in loam mixed with leaf mold. Purple, pink and white flowers.

Senecio Elegans, fl. pl. Tall double Jacobaea. Finest varieties........................... 5c

Nana, fl. pl. Double Dwarf sorts. Finest mixed, 8 inches......................... 5c

SWEET PEAS (Lathyrus Odoratus).

Beautiful fragrant free flowering plants, thriving in any open situation; excellent for screening unsightly objects, will bloom all summer and autumn if the flowers are cut freely and the pods picked off as they appear. They may be sown in autumn in this section; early sowing is necessary, hardy annuals; 6 feet. No garden is complete without them................................... 5

Blue Bird. Bright blue................... 5c
Captain Clarke (Tricolor). White, rose and
  purple...................................... 5c
Crown Princess, of Prussia. Bright blush,
  shading to rose........................... 5c
Invincible, scarlet. Bright scarlet flowers... 5c
Fairy Queen, white and rose............... 5c
Dark Red.................................... 5c
Purple Crown, purple...................... 5c
Snowflake. Pure white..................... 5c
Invincible Red-striped...................... 5c
Light Blue and Purple...................... 5c
Painted Lady. Red and white.............. 5c
Purple-striped.............................. 5c
Rotundifolius, cropper-red, fine.............. 10c
Giganteus, true, very fine................... 10c
Mixed, many colors......................... 5c

LATHYRUS (Everlasting Pea).

Showy, free flowering plants, growing in any common soil. A good climber for covering fences or walls. Hardy perennial,

Latifolius (Everlasting Pea). Red.......... 10c
Albus, white, splendid climber............... 10c
Lathyrus. Mixed colors..................... 10c

TEN WEEKS STOCKS.

The Ten Weeks Stock, "Stock Gilly" or Gillyflower," as they are sometimes called, stands preeminent among annuals for either flower beds, pot culture, cut flowers, and delicious spicy perfume; they have been greatly improved in the past few years, and a large flowering strain has been originated which for size, doubleness and variety of exquisite shades of color is remarkable.

Large Flowering Dwarf Ten Week. The following are the best double varieties and most desirable colors for cultivation; mixed, all choice double large-flowering.......... 10c
Very Dwarf Snowflake. A beautiful small-growing variety, with vigorous main spike and numerous side shoots of very large double snow-white flowers; very early......... 15c
Dwarf Bouquet Ten-week Stock. Finest mixed.................................... 10c
Large-flowering Pyramidal. This variety has compact flower spikes, and throws out many side shoots, excellent for pots........ 10c
New Giant Perfection. This sort produces plants 2½ feet high, with long flower spikes of extra double handsome flowers, and is extremely effective in beds and borders.... 10c
White (Dresden perpetual), very beautiful, large spikes, splendid for cutting.......... 15c
Emperor, or Brompton (Winter or Biennial). These make very bushy and branching plants, with an abundance of choice double flowers. Sow in July or August. Will last several years when protected.
Many Colors. In finest mixture............ 10c
Wallflower-leaved. Large flowering, choice mixed.................................... 10c
The Wallflower-leaved Stocks have quite distinct dark glossy foliage.
Intermediate, or Autumnal. These are prized on account of their flowering late in Autumn or early in Spring. The seeds should be sown in July. Finest mixed.... 10c

Perpetual Dwarf Ten-week Stock, mixed, (Sem perflorens). A double constant blooming sort, with fine double flowers of various colors; 15 inches........................ 10c

SWEET WILLIAM. (Dianthus Barbatus). H. P.

A well known attractive free-flowering plant, which has been greatly improved of late years, producing a splendid effect in beds and shrubbery with their rich and varied flowers; hardy perennial; 1¼ feet.
Double. From choice collections.......... 10c
Single. Choicest mixed.................... 5c

THUNBERGIA (Climber).
H. H. A., 4 feet.

Very ornamental and rapid growth; the flowers are very much admired; colors red, white, buff and bright orange, with variously colored throats; choicest mixed.. 5c

VERBENA.

Georgeous for beds or massing, flowers of the most brilliant colors; flowering continually from Spring until late in the Autumn. Verbenas grown from seed are always thrifty and free bloomers, but flowering the first year from seed; HHP., 1 ft.
Hybrida, finest mixed varieties, from beautiful collection............................... 10c
Defiance, scarlet, extra for bedding; beautiful. 10c
Candidissima, with large trusses of flowers of the purest white...................... 10c
Striata. Italian Carnation-like Striped, saved from a rich collection............... 10c
Lutea, new yellow, distinct, new and pretty.. 15c
Venosa, blue fine for edging................ 15c
Coccinea. fol. auries, golden yellow foliage and dazzling scarlet flowers; strikingly beautiful, especially at the end of the summer................................... 25c

VINCA (Madagascar Periwinkle.) T. P.

Ornamental free-blooming plants; they flower from seed, if sown early, the first season, continuing until frost; or they may be potted and kept in bloom through the winter; 2 feet.
Vinca. Mixed colors...................... 10c

VIRGINIA STOCK. H. A.
(CheiranthusMaritimus).

Beautiful free-flowering little plants, very effective in small beds, edging, or baskets, growing in any soil; hardy annual.
Mixed. All colors; 3 inches................ 5c

VIOLET (Viola Odorata) H. P.

Well known fragrant early spring blooming plants for edging, groups, or borders; thriving best in the summer in a shady situation, in a rich, deep soil; extensively used by florists for forcing for cut flowers during the fall and winter months; hardy perennials; 6 inches.
Single Blue (Odorata Semperflorens). Very sweet-scented blue flowers................ 10c
Single White (Odorata semperflorens) Sweet Violet, very fragrant and free-flowing...... 10c
The Czar, fl. albo, fine double white....... 20c
Lutea, Grandiflora, fine yellow............. 10c
Viola, very fine mixed..................... 10

WALLFLOWER (Cheiranthus Cheiri)
H. H. P.

Well known deliciously fragrant garden plants, blooming early in the spring, with large conspicuous spikes of beautiful flowers; they should be protected in a cold frame in the winter, and planted out in May; are much prized for bouquet flowers; half-hardy perennials.

Single Mixed, all colors 2½ feet..............   5c
Finest Double Mixed, all colors 2 feet........   10c
Waltzia (Everlasting.)
Yellow flowers, borne in cluster; fine for dried
flowers......................................   10c

WHITLAVIA.

Charming hardy annual, with delicate foliage and clusters of beautiful bell-shaped flowers, fine for ribbonning, mixed borders or shady spots; growing freely in any garden soil, also good for baskets, vases, etc.; 1 foot.
Grandiflora. Large, violet-blue..............   5c

ZINNIA ELEGANS. Fl. Pl.
(Youth and Old Age)

Double Zinnias are in acquisition to our list of garden favorites; of branching habit and splendid brilliant colored double flowers, rivalling the Dahlia in beauty and form. The seed can be sown early in the hot-bed and transplanted, or sown later in the open ground; half-hardy annuals; 2 feet.

White. Pure white flowers; fine for florists..   5c
Coccinea Flore Pleno, fine double scarlet...   5c
Kermesina Flore Pleno, bright crimson.....   5c
Alba, Fl. Pl., White...........................   5c
Tall Double, finest mixed, splendid quality.....   5c
Grandiflora Robusta Plenissima (New Giant Zinnias.) A new very large flowering race, differing from the old varieties in their more luxuriant robust growth, and in the larger and more conical-shape of the flowers, which have broader and many more petals. The plant forms a handsome bush, 3 feet in height. and the large perfectly formed double measuring 5 to 6 inches across, are borne in profusion, lasting until killed by frost.
Splendid....................................   10c
Pompone. Excellent Zinnias, differing from the older ones in habit of growth and the immense size of their perfectly formed very double flowers of various striking colors. The plants are dwarf and bloom freely during a long period.............. ....   10c
Zinnia Grandiflora, single, fine mixed........   5c

XERANTHEMUMS.

A showy class of everlastings; the flowers are white, purple and yellow, single and double. If gathered before fully opened, and dried in the shade they will retain their beauty for years. They make fine Winter bouquets. Sow in Spring and thin, to one foot apart. Hardy annual, 1 foot.
Xeranthemum, mixed...........................   10c

ORNAMENTAL GRASSES.

Nearly all the ornamental grasses are very showy and beautiful, and when dried and tastefully arranged in connection with the Everlasting Flowers, make exceedingly attractive Winter bouquets.

Ornamental Grasses. A collection of eight different varieties, our own selection......   30c
Agrostis Nebulosa. Light, feathery and graceful, fine for winter bouquets, hardy annual; 1 foot........................... ....   5c
Avena Sterilis (Animated Oats.) Large drooping graceful heads, for winter bouquets. hardy annual, 2 feet............................   5c
Briza Maxima (Large Quaking Grass.) Large pendent seeds fine for clumps or bouquets, hardy annual, 1 foot........................   5c
Briza Gracilis (Small Quaking Grass.) Smaller graceful variety of above, hardy annual, 1 foot................. ....   5c
Bromus Brizæformis. Splendid variety. with drooping spikes of pendent seeds, hardy annual, 1 foot...............................   5c
Cryptopyrum Richardsoni. very fine and delicate for winter bouquets..... ....   5c

Cynosurus Elegans, for bouquets............   5c
Eragrostis Elegans, (Love Grass.) Elegant and feathery foliage, hardy annual, 1 foot..   5c
Erianthus Ravennæ (South American Pampas.) Handsome, hardy perennial, tall specimens for lawns, 10 feet................   5c
Gynerium Argenteum (True Pampas Grass.) Makes fine clumps for lawns, large silvery plumes, half-hardy perennial, 6 to 10 feet...   10c
Lagurus Ovatus (Hare's Tail Grass.) Woolly cone-shaped heads, fine for Winter bouquets, hardy annual, 1 foot........................   5c
Liplachne Fascicularis, for bouquets, highly interesting from the disposition of the flower spikes................................   5c
Stipa Pennata (Feather Grass.) Delicate long silvery feathers, fine for Winter bouquets, hardy perennials, 2 feet.....................   10c
Tricholaena Rosea. Pretty Rose colored grass, hardy annual, 1 foot 10c
Pennisetum Longistylum. Graceful and interesting; admirable for the composition of bouquets......................................   5c

BULBS

Our Importations are mostly direct from the GROWERS OF HOLLAND, AND ARE OF EXTRA QUALITY. We shall also soon be in receipt from Japan and other Oriental sources, of a large variety of Japonicas, Lilies and other Flowering Plants.

Dutch Bulbs.

One of the first questions that the purchasers of bulbs ask is, "Are they easy to grow?" To this very natural question we reply that with scarcely any exception, bulbs are easily managed, sure to bloom, and require but little labor and care to enable them to produce exquisite flowers.

No class of flowers has gained more rapidly in public favor during the last few years than those produced from bulbs. Many of them are especially desirable, as they afford a profusion of blossoms early in the spring, when few other plants are in bloom out of doors. They are easily cultivated, and are unsurpassed for their beauty and variety of colors. We know of no plant that will give equal satisfaction for out-door culture; and in no other way can the home be so satisfactorily and easily beautified during the winter as with a few Hyacinths, Tulips, Lilies, Narcissus, etc.

It should be be borne in mind that the bulbs must be secured and planted in autumn, whether they are wanted for flowering in the house for the holidays and Easter, or for a display out of doors in the early spring. Do not wait till spring comes, and you see your neighbor's yard the delight of all passers-by, but order at once.

MANAGEMENT.

Bulbs intended for blooming in pots during the winter season should be planted during the months of October and November in pots, and be left in the open air, covered with a few inches of tan or soil, until the earth begins to freeze, and then be placed in a cool greenhouse, cellar or room, at a temperature of 50 degrees, in a very dark place.

They will need, occasionally, moderate watering after they are brought inside. When the top is well grown and the flower stem well out of the bulb, they should be brought to the light and given plenty of water, and exposed as much as possible to the sun, air and light, to prevent the leaves from growing too long or becoming yellow.

The proper compost for Hyacinths, Tulips, Crown Imperials, Iris, Ranunculus, Anemones, Crocus, and many other bulbs is the following: One-third sand, one-third well-rotted cow manure, and one-third good garden soil.

The preferable season for planting all hardy bulbs is from October to December; but they can be set out later if the bulbs remain sound and the ground is not frozen.

The Hyacinth.

Among hardy bulbs the Hyacinth deservedly stands foremost on the list. It is not only a general favorite for the garden, but has become exceedingly popular as a winter flower, from the facility with which it may be forced into bloom, either in pots or glasses.

HYACINTHS IN GLASSES.

For this purpose Single Hyacinths, and such as are designated early among the Double, are to be preferred. Single Hyacinths are generally held in higher estimation than Double ones, their colors are more vivid, and their bells, though smaller, are more numerous. Some of the sorts are exquisitely beautiful. They are preferable for flowering in winter to most of the Double, as they bloom two or three weeks earlier, and are less liable to failure. The bulbs should be placed in glasses during October and November. Fill with pure water, so that the base of the bulb may just touch; then place them in a dark closet, box or cellar, at a temperature of 45 to 50 degrees. When the glasses are well filled with roots, and the flower stem well out of the bulb, gradually expose to the light and sun at a higher temperature. If kept too light and warm at first, and before there is sufficient fibre, they will rarely flower well. They will bloom without any sun, but the colors of the flowers will be inferior. The water should be changed as it becomes impure. draw the roots entirely out of the glasses, rinse off the fibres in clean water, and wash the inside of the glass well. Care should be taken that the water does not freeze, as it would not only burst the glass, but cause the fibres to decay. Avoid a low-water mark in the glasses by keeping it to a level with the base of each bulb. To stimulate and strengthen the growth, dissolve a pinch of sulphate of ammonia occasionally in the water after the bulbs are exposed to light.

When Hyacinths and other bulbs are in bloom it is a good plan to place them in a cold room, free of frost, where they flower for a considerable length of time.

HYACINTHS IN THE OPEN GROUND.

They require a light, rich soil, and it may be necessary to provide this to the depth of a foot or more by removing the natural soil and substituting a proper compost.

One of the most suitable compost is composed of equal parts of sandy loam, well decayed cow manure and sand. Plant the bulbs at any time from the middle of September to the end of November, October being the most preferable. The crowns of the bulbs should be from three to five inches below the surface. After the ground is frozen, cover to depth of three inches with straw, or any material, to prevent constant freezing and thawing. This should be moved early in the spring to prevent drawing the flower stems.

The bulbs should be planted six inches apart. Where large quantities for brilliant effects are wanted, the cheaper grades of Garden Hyacinths will answer all requirements.

The flowers may be cut freely without injury to the bulb. When through flowering remove the tops, and the bulbs can be lifted and kept in a dry place for the next season's planting.

SINGLE HYACINTHS.

We head our list with Single Hyacinths by design, because we consider them more useful and valuable than the double varieties. They are better for forcing, more vigorous in growth, and produce stronger spikes of bloom, which are generally of better substance and are at least as beautiful as those of the double sorts.

NAMED HYACINTHS.

Price, (except as noted) 20 cts. each; per dozen, $1 75.

Single Red and Rose.

Amy. Very fine bright scarlet.
Cosmos. Pink, large bulb and long spike.
Gigantea. Gigantic pink spike.
Le Prophete. Pink, large bulb and spike.
Veronica. Red, fine for forcing.
Robert Steiger. Very fine dark red, large spike.

Single White.

Baron Von Thuill. Pure white, large close spike.
Grandeur a'Merveille. Finest blush white, large spike.
Voltaire. Cream white, a favorite for cutting.
Alba Superbissima. Pure white, large tall spike.
Grand Verdette. Earliest, pure white; large bells, (fine for cutting.) Extra, 25c. each.
Madame Vanderhoop. Pure white, very large bells.

Single Blue.

Argus. Blue, white center.
Baron Von Thuill. Very fine dark blue, large spike.
Charles Dickens. Light blue, large compact spike.
La Peyrouse. Fine porcelain blue, not early.
Marie. Enormous truss and bulb.
Grand Federic. Light blue, large spike.

Single Yellow.

Herman. Orange yellow, very large bulb.
La Plui d'Or. Pale yellow. New extra, 25c.
Ida. Pure yellow, larger truss.

DOUBLE HYACINTHS.

For exhibition purposes and for growing in pots or open ground, the double sorts will be found charming.

Double Red and Rose.

Grootvoorst. Very fine blush pink, large truss and bells.
Noble par Merite. Very fine pink, grand truss; early;
Princess Royal. Scarlet, with brown center; fine.
Dibbitz Sebalkansky. Very Deep Scarlet.
Rejina Victoria. Rosy, large truss; extra.

Double White.

Anna Maria. Blush white, purple center, large spike; extra.
La Virgenite. Very fine, blush white.
Non Plus Ultra. Pure white, extra large; fine spike and bells.
Prince of Waterloo. Pure white, large truss and bells.
Duchess of Bedford. Pure white.

Double Blue.

Bloksberg. The finest of all light blues; large compact spike.
Charles Dickens. Light blue, large compact truss, extra fine, 25c.
King of Wurtemberg. Light blue shaded indigo.
Louis Phillippe. Dark blue, shaded with indigo.
Prince of Saxony Weimar. Dark blue, semi-double.

Double Yellow.

Goethe. Finest yellow.
Ophir d'Or. Pure yellow, with purple eye.

ROMAN HYACINTHS.

The earliest for forcing or spring blooming. The flower spikes are smaller than the Dutch varieties, but the flowers are equally as pretty and fragrant. They force readily in the house, and as the bulbs are of moderate size, several can be grown in one pot. The blooming season is prolonged by the bulbs throwing up three to five spikes of flowers, which do not come to perfection all together.

Single White, 10 cts. each; per doz., 75c. Per hundred $5.

UNNAMED HYACINTHS.

Separate Colors.

Price, 10cts. each; per doz., $1. Per hundred, $7.

These are selected from good forcing varieties, and will give good results. They are unnamed, but comprise different shades of the various colors.

Single Red, all shades.	Double Red, all shades.
" White, "	" White, "
" Blue, "	" Blue, "
" Yellow, "	" Yellow, "

SINGLE SMALL HYACINTHS.

Unnamed Hyacinths—For Forcing.

These varieties are of interest to those who desire to cultivate them. The bulbs, though small, produce fine spikes of flowers of various shades and colors, and are desirable for garden or pot culture.

Price, 5cts. each; per doz., 50 cts.; per 100, $3.

Small Hyacinths.

Single Red,	Single Blue—dark.
Single Rose,	Single Light Blue.
Single White,	Single Cream White.

TULIPS.

It is difficult to conceive of anything more pleasing to the eye than a bed of good tulips. The great variety of colors produced, their intense brilliancy and beautiful shading make them universal favorites. Another great consideration in their favor is the ease with which they can be cultivated, requiring only any good common soil to grow them to perfection; the price, too, as compared with other bulbs, places them within the reach of all.

The Tulip has been so much improved by Dutch cultivators that it ranks high in the floral world. In form, wealth of color, and the variety of its markings, it is one of the most perfect of flowers.

The culture of Tulips is the same as that of Hyacinths, except that the bulbs should be planted three or four inches deep and two to six inches apart. Tulips are perfectly hardy, so only a slight protection from extreme and sharp winds is desirable.

All of the single varieties force readily, and of late have become great favorites in the house in mid-winter. If potted in September, and treated as directed for Hyacinths, they may be had in bloom in December. When they show a tendency to bloom just above the bulbs they must be kept longer in the dark to draw out the flower stems. A splendid effect is obtained by planting from three to a dozen bulbs in a medium sized pot.

MIXED TULIPS.

The following are all first quality bulbs, but are offered without names. Where masses of bloom are wanted; they will be found very serviceable, as they comprise good colors and fine shaped flowers.

5 cents each; per doz., 40 cents; per 100, $2 50.

Early Single Mixed,   Early Double Mixed,   Late Double Mixed.

Bybloemen. White ground flaked with violet, crimson and maroon; 5 cents each; 40 cents dozen.

Bizarres. Yellow ground flaked with crimson, purple and violet. 5 cents each; 40 cents dozen.

Late Show Tulips Bybloome and Bizarres, $2.50 per 100.

EARLY SINGLE NAMED TULIPS.

All suitable for forcing or growing in the garden. These commence flowering two weeks in advance of other sorts of Tulips, and are admirably adapted to culture in pots, borders or beds.

Named Sorts, per doz., 50 cts.; per 100, $3.00.

Brutus. Bright red and yellow. Each, 5 cts.

Cameleon. Creamy white, rosy spotted. Each, 5 cts.

Cardinal's Hat. Scarlet. Each, 5 cts.

Count de Mirabeau. Pure white. Each, 5 cts.

Duchess de Parma. Orange yellow; fine large truss. Each, 5 cts.

Keizerskroon. Red, with broad yellow edge. The largest Tulip. Each, 5 cts.

La Reine. (Queen Victoria). White, fine for forcing. Each, 5 cts.

Pottebaker. White, finest of all white Tulips. Each, 5 cts.

Rose Mundi. (Huikman). Bright pink. Each, 5 cts.

EARLY DWARF DUC VAN THOL TULIPS.

Early red and yellow, violet and carmine. Each, 5 cts., 40 cts. per doz.

EARLY DOUBLE-NAMED TULIPS.

This class of Double Tulips can be forced in pots. Their large, early, fine-colored flowers and dwarf habit, make them very desirable for bedding. The late Double Tulips are best adapted for planting in the garden, and will not bear forcing as well as the early varieties.

EARLY DOUBLE.

Named, 40 cts. per doz., $3.00 per 100.

La Candeur. Pure white. Each, 5 cts.

Le Blazon. Fine rosy pink. Each, 5 cts.

Murillo. (Albano). Pink and white, best double for forcing. Each, 5 cts.

Pæony Gold. Scarlet, feathered yellow. Each, 5 cts.

LATE DOUBLE.

Full Varieties—Named.

Admiral Kingsbergen. Red and yellow.

Blue Flag. (Lord Wellington). Blue.

Brown Imperial. Crimson and white.

Rose Eclatante. Red.

Yellow Rose. (Gecle Roos). Splendid golden yellow large flower.

PARROT TULIPS.

For the Open Ground Only.

Singularly beautiful flowers containing brilliant shades of scarlet, crimson, yellow and green, curiously intermixed and variegated. The edges of the petals are feathered. In masses or in shrubbery border they are very striking and effective.

Parrot Tulips. All shades. Red, variegated, yellow and mixed. Per doz., 30 cents; per 100, $2.

CROCUS.

Among the earliest to blossom in spring is this beautiful little flower, lifting its head almost before the snow has disappeared. Blooming at a time when the ground is destitute of foliage or flower, it is a welcome visitor. The Crocus should be planted in autumn, in October, November or December, in any good garden soil, about three inches deep and about two inches apart if in beds or borders. As they are entirely hardy, they may remain undisturbed for years.

To secure blooms in pots, commence early in October with six or eight bulbs in each pot, using rich soil, and planting about an inch deep. Place the pots on a surface of ashes, cover the top one inch deep with soil, until the leaves appear, when they may be removed to the house.

UNNAMED VARIETIES.

Mixed. Per doz., 15 cts., per 100, $1.00.

SPLENDID NAMED CROCUS.

Cloth of Gold. Large yellow, 10 cts.

Baron Brunnow. Bright purple, large, extra.

Non Plus Ultra. Purple, with white top.

Mont Blanc. Large white.

Madam Mina. Light blue, striped.

Sir Walter Scott. White striped, purple.
   20 cts. per doz., $1.25 per 100.

POLYANTHUS NARCISSUS.

The Flower of Love.

This charming flower has not received its due share of attention, owing, doubtless, to its merits as a winter and spring flower not being fully recognized.

As a ladies' flower, it is taking front rank and lends to beauty an additional charm.

It can be grown in glasses as readily as the Hyacinth, and surpasses in beauty of form, delightful perfume and variety of coloring, all its rivals among winter-flowering bulbs. For planting on the edge of woods, among shrubbery, on rockeries, or for planting in groups on the lawn, the Narcissus is invaluable; it will be found among the chief attractions of the spring garden.

To obtain satisfactory results, the bulbs should remain undisturbed for three years at least; they may then be divided and reset. When desired for forcing, treat same as Hyacinths.

Polyanthus Narcissus. Fine named.

Grand Monarque. Large pure white, white citron cup; fine, 10 cts. each; $1 per dozen.

Paper White (*Totus albus*). Pure white; fine for florists' use. 5 cents each; 50 cents per dozen.

Roman Double White. Orange center; rich. 5 cts. each; 50 cts. per dozen.

The Pearl. Large white, with white cup; beautiful. 15 cts. each; $1.50 per dozen.

DOUBLE NARCISSUS. (Daffodils).

Albus Plenus Odoratus. Pure white, very double, sweet—resembling the Gardenia—delicious odor; fine for cut flowers. 5 cts. each; 50 cts. per dozen.

Double Mixed. Without names, 5 cts. each; 50 cts. per dozen.

SINGLE NARCISSUS. (Daffodils).

Poeticus (*The Poets' Narcissus*). Flower large, snow white, with beautiful cup suffused with bright orange red, early flowering and fragrant. Slow for forcing. Five cts. each; 50 cts. per dozen; 2.50 per hundred.

Poeticus Ornatus. (*Pheasant's Eye*). Pure white, rosy scarlet eye. Blooms earlier than Poeticus. Fine for forcing; sweet scented. Ten cts. each; 40 cts. per dozen.

Narcissus Bulbocodium (*Hoop Petticoat Narcissus*.) A pretty and shapely flower of a rich golden yellow color. Each bulb produces 6 to 12 flowers. A dry and sheltered situation suits it best when planted in the open ground. 5 cts. each; 50 cts. per dozen.

ANEMONES.

These charming hardy spring flowers are becoming better known and more popular as a garden flower; both double and single are equally desirable, and no garden should be without them. They are suitable for pot or border culture, and when planted in masses are most effective. They succeed best in a light, rich, well-drained loam. Plant in October or November, or as soon as the ground can be worked in the spring. If planted in the autumn, they should be covered with leaves, straw or long manure on the approach of winter.

The flowers are very beautiful in form and color and remain perfect a long time.

DOUBLE ANEMONES.

Double Large Scarlet.

40 cts. per dozen; $2.50 per 100.

Grand Monarque. Sky blue; 40 cts. per dozen.

Hamlet. Lilac. Extra large.

Madame Royal. Red variegated.

Sir Walter Scott. Carmine and green.

Double Mixed. Thirty cts. per dozen.

SINGLE ANEMONES.

Coronaria Scarlet. Very brilliant; 30 cts. doz.

"The Bride." Pure white; 40 cts. doz.

Single Varieties. Per dozen, 20 cts.

Ranunculus.

RANUNCULUS.

Strikingly beautiful flowers, well adapted to pot culture, in the house. The individual flowers are about two inches in diameter, as full and double as the finest Camelia or Rose, and as a cut flower, quite as useful as the Rose itself.

Like Anemones, they do best planted in very rich soil, having a northerly exposure to escape our sharp winds and too much sun. The beds should have good drainage, and the soil be light and warm. Plant three inches deep, in October or November, and press the earth close around them. They will amply repay all care bestowed upon them. Ranunculus bulbs are peculiarly shaped and should be handled carefully, but if kept QUITE DRY when out of the ground, they will last almost any length of time.

Ranunculus. French, Persian and Turban, finest mixed varieties, per dozen, 15 cts.; per 100, $1.

RANUNCULUS. (Fine named).

Grootvoorst. Bright crimson; 20 cts. per doz.

Hercules. White; extra; 40 cts. per doz.

Turban Grandiflora. Crimson and yellow; 20 cts. per doz.

Turban Virdiflora. Green center, scarlet and yellow border; 20 cts. per doz.

LILY OF THE VALLEY.

One of the most charming of our spring flowering plants, bearing slender stems set with tiny bells. Fowers freely and powerfully fragrant. They are largely used for forcing in winter.

For pot culture, use the buds or pips, pot them in well-drained pots, covering the bottom with a layer of fibrous moss and filling with sandy soil, slightly mixed with the moss which will hold the moisture, which is essential to success. Cover the bulbs to the depth of half an inch. Cover the top with moss and keep in a cool place till they are thoroughly rooted, then remove most of the moss and bring to light to perfect the flowers. They are perfectly hardy in the open ground if in a cool, shaded situation. Clumps of 50 or more, 75 cts.; single, 5 cts.

Tuberose. PEARL. Each, 10 cts.; per doz., $1.

Dahlia Bulbs. All colors; 25 cts. each; per dozen, $2.

DIELYTRA.

(Bleeding Heart.)

Tuberous-rooted plants, blooming in the early spring; favorably known almost everywhere. They require only the ordinary culture of border plants. The roots should be divided every third year. Roots planted in autumn will flower freely. The flowers are a delicate pink color, graceful; produced continuously from May to July.

Dielytra, Spectabilis. Pink; 25 cts. each; $2.50 per dozen. Alba white, 50 cts. each.

GLADIOLUS.

Per dozen, fifty cents.

Floribundis. Pink, very fine; per dozen, 50 cts.

Large Bulbs. Per dozen, 50 cts.

Gandavensis. Scarlet and yellow; large bulbs; price per dozen, 50 cts.

Seedlings. Mixed; per dozen, 50 cts;

The Bride. A lovely pure white form of the Gladiolus Colvilli. The flowers are freely borne on the long stems and can be forced into bloom at a time when flowers are scarce. Ten cents each; $1 per dozen.

LILIES.

Lilium Auratum (golden rayed Queen of Lilies.) This magnificent variety has become one of the standard favorites of the Flower Garden, and is considered by many, the finest of all Lilies. The immense blooms, measuring nearly a foot in width when fully expanded, are produced in great profusion and are deliciously fragrant. Choice large bulbs, 25 cts. each, per doz. $2.50.

Candidum. A well-known hardy garden lily; commonly called (St. Joseph's.) Snow-white, fragrant blossoms. One of the best varieties for forcing, and an established favorite. 20 cts. each, per dozen $2.00.

Longiflorum. The well-known beautiful snow-white fragrant lily. Fine for forcing and handsome in the garden. 20 cts. each, per dozen $2.50.

Lancifolium Album. Pure white and very fragrant. 25 cts. each; per dozen, $2.50.

Lancifolium Rubrum. White spotted red beautiful. 25 cts. each; per dozen, $2.50.

Lilium Harrisii. (Bermuda Easter Lily.) This beautiful lily was introduced a few years ago from Bermuda. The flowers are large, trumpet-shaped, pure white and very fragrant. This mammoth white trumpet lily with flowers four to five inches long, is pre-eminently the best of all winter lilies for forcing and flowering. As a pot plant it is tall and stately, the spike thickly studded with bloom, which are lovely as cut flowers, and keep a long time in water. 25 cts. each; per doz. $2.50.

Tigrinum. (Tiger Lily.) Orange salmon spotted black. 12½ cts. each; per doz. $1.25.

Humboltii. Flowers golden yellow, spotted with purple.

Pardalinum. Scarlet, shading to rich yellow; spotted with purple brown. 20 cts. each; per doz. $2.00.

Washingtonianum. White with small purple dots; very fragrant and beautiful. 25 cts. each; per dox. $2.50

Atrosanguineum. Rich blood crimson spotted with black. 15 cts. each; per doz. $1.50.

PIONEER BOX CO.

MANUFACTURERS OF ALL KINDS OF

Fruit and Packing Boxes, Trays, etc., Grape and Berry Baskets

OF ALL KINDS.

Having recently put in a new plant, with new and improved machinery, and with greatly enlarged facilities, for manufacturing, we are now prepared to fill all orders promptly on short notice.

Factory, Front and T Sts. Office, Cor. Front and M Sts., Sacramento. Cal.

W. D. COMSTOCK

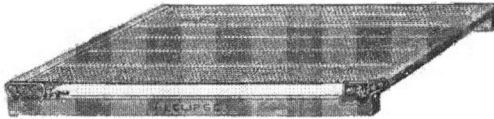

FURNITURE and BEDDING

K Street, Corner Fifth, Sacramento, Cal.

Manufacturer and Importer, Wholesale and Retail.

Specialty of Solid Walnut and Hardwood.

PRICES ALWAYS THE LOWEST.

W. P. COLEMAN

REAL ESTATE

SALESROOM AND INSURANCE OFFICE,

No. 325 J STREET, SACRAMENTO, CAL.

A large list of Farm and City Property for Sale. *Money to Loan.*

P. BOHL. E. A. CROUCH.

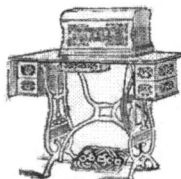

Quantity of Seed Required to Sow an Acre of Ground.

	Pounds.		Pounds.
Grass, Timothy	20	Vetches—broadcast	150
Grass, Mesquit, in the chaff	35	Hemp—broadcast	40 to 50
Grass, Hungarian	40	Flax, when wanted for the seed	50
Grass, Millet	40	Flax, when wanted for the fiber	80
Grass, Mixed Lawn	75	Beans, Dwarf or Bush—hills or drills	80
A much larger quantity of seed is required to make a close, fine lawn than for other purpose.		Beans, tall or pole—hills	20
		Beets—drills	5 to 6
		Broom Corn—drills	15
Grass, mixture for mowing or grazing — Clover	8	Buckwheat—broadcast	45
Timothy	15	Cabbage, in beds to cover an acre after transplanting	¼
Redtop	15	Carrots—drills	. to 4
Grass, Kentucky Blue, for pasture	30	Melon, Water—hills	2 to 3
Grass, Kentucky Blue, for lawn	75	Melon, Cantaloupe—hills	4
Grass, Orchard	40	Onions, black seed—drills	5 to 6
Grass, English or Australian Rye, for meadow	50	Onions, top set—drills	200
		Onions, black seed, for bottom sets	40
Grass, English or Australian Rye, for lawn	75	Parsnips—drills	6
Grass, Italian Rye	30 to 40	Peas—drills	100
Grass, Redtop	30	Peas—broadcast	180
Alfalfa or Lucerne	20 to 25	Potatoes—hills	500 to 600
Clover, Red alone—broadcast	15 to 20	Pumpkins—hills	5
Clover, White alone—broadcast	12	Radishes—drills	8
Clover, Alsike, broadcast	10	Sage—drills	8
Barley—broadcast	125 to 150	Spinach—drills	15
Oats—broadcast	80	Squash, bush varieties—hills	5
Rye—broadcast	100	Squash, running varieties—hills	3
Wheat—broadcast	125	Tomato, in beds to transplant	¼
Wheat—Drills	90	Turnip and Rutabaga—drills	1¼
Corn, Sweet or Field—hills	15	Turnip and Rutabaga—broadcast	3
Corn, to cut green for fodder—drills or broadcast	150	Cucumber—hills	2

Quantity of Seed Required to Produce a Given Number of Plants, or Sow Certain Quantity of Ground.

Artichoke	1 oz. to 500 plants	Lettuce	1 oz. to 3,000 plants
Asparagus	1 oz. to 60 feet of drill of 500 plants	Melon, Water	1. oz. to 50 hills
Beans, dwarf	1 b. to 50 feet of drill	Melon, Musk	1 oz. to 50 hills
Beans, tall	1.. lb. to 75 hills	Okra	1 oz. to 50 feet of drill
Beet	1 oz. to 50 feet of drill	Onion seed	1 oz. to 100 feet of drill
Broccoli	1 oz. to 2,000 plants	Onion, top set	1 lb to 20 feet of drill
Brussels Sprouts	1 oz. to 2,000 plants	Parsnips	1 oz. to 200 feet of drill
Cabbage	1 oz. to 2,000 plants	Parsley	1 oz. to 150 feet of drill
Carrots	1 oz. to 150 feet of drill	Peas	1 lb. to 50 feet of drill
Cauliflower	1 oz. to 2,000 plants	Pepper	1 oz. to 1,000 plants
Celery	1 oz. to 3,000 plants	Pumpkin	1 oz. to 40 hills
Chicory	1 oz. to 100 feet of drill	Radish	1 oz. to 100 feet of drill
Corn	1 lb. to 100 hills	Salsify	1 oz. to 70 feet of drill
Cress	1 oz. to 100 feet of drill	Sage	1 oz. to 150 feet of drill
Cucumber	1 oz. to 75 hills	Spinach	1 oz to 100 feet of drill
Egg Plant	1 oz. to 1,000 plants	Squash, early	1 oz. to 50 hills
Endive	1 oz. to 150 feet of drill or 3,000 plants	Squash, winter	1 oz. to 10 hills
Kale	1 oz. to 2,000 plants	Tomato	1 oz to 3,000 plants
Kohl Rabi	1 oz. to 2,000 plants	Tobaco	1 oz. to 10,000 plants
Leek	1 oz. to 150 feet of drill		

Table Showing Number of Plants or Trees to the Acre at Given Distances.

Dis. apart each way.	No. Plants.	Dis. apart each way.	No. Plants.	Dis. apart each way.	No. Plants.	Dis. apart each way.	No. Plants.
½ foot	174,240	3 feet	4,840	8 feet	680	15 feet	193
1 foot	43,560	4 feet	2,722	9 feet	537	18 feet	134
1½ feet	19,360	5 feet	1,742	10 feet	435	20 feet	108
2 feet	10,890	6 feet	1,210	11 feet	360	25 feet	69
2½ feet	9,696	7 feet	888	12 feet	302	30 feet	48

RULE.—Multiply the distance in feet between the rows by the distance the plants are apart in the rows, and the product will be the number of square feet for each plant or hill, which, divided into the number of feet in an acre (43,560), will give the number of plants or trees to the acre.

W. R. STRONG & CO'S

Descriptive Catalogue of Trees and Nursery Stock

FOR 1889-90.

OF THE CAPITAL NURSERIES

ROBERT WILLIAMSON, the original founder and manager of these Nurseries, still has the management thereof. With his long experience, and the increased facilities of the present firm, we feel warranted in saying that we can compete with any other Nursery on the Coast, and hope for a continuance of the liberal patronage so long enjoyed by these well known and popular Nurseries.

Our headquarters and chief office is at our store, Nos. 102 to 110 J. Street, Sacramento, Cal.

We have greatly increased our facilities for carrying on this branch of our business by the purchase of 320 acres of the very best land on the Mokelumne River in the celebrated Lodi District. This, added to our 210 acres at Sacramento, and our large orchard and experimental grounds near Penryn, in Placer County, gives us unrivaled advantages for growing good stocks, and testing varieties on different soils and in different climates. Add to this our thirty years experience in handling and shipping fruit, we certain-ly are in better position for supplying the planters with trees that will give the very best satisfaction than any other nursery firm on the Coast or elsewhere.

Our stock this season is unusually large; trees very large and healthy, most of them trained low so as to protect themselves from the hot rays of the sun. For the past seven years our buds and grafts have been taken from bearing trees fruited under our own observation, and we think they cannot fail to give satis-faction, especially when planted in similar climates and soils to that of Sacramento Valley and adjacent foothills. The great diversity of climates in this State makes it impossible to get the same results in all localities with the same fruit. For instance, some of our best fruits here are worthless in San Jose, and some of the best kinds there are of no value here.

Read With Care The Following:

(1.) Persons planting should try to find out what succeeds best in their particular climate.

(2.) Different persons know fruits by different names, which sometimes causes planters to think they have been swindled, when they have actually got exactly what they ordered.

We regard fruit culture in California as being yet in its infancy; we think it is destined to become the paramount interest of the State. People generally are using more fruit than in former years, and as a proof of the success of the fruit interest in California, fruits of all kinds have brought better prices of late years than formerly. Our fruits are being sent to all parts of the world, and find a ready market. We are in the center of the commercial world, and from present indications we are to be the world's great fruit center. The low freights recently secured, and the lower rates which we still expect to get, will enable us to find market for all we can raise.

☞ Those varieties which we consider most valuable we have cultivated in larger quantities, and are indicated by an asterisk, thus (*).

We are also extensively engaged in Fruit Packing and Shipping, and flatter ourselves that we are com-petent to judge of the best kinds of fruit to grow for profit. We make it a point not to recommend or send out any new varieties until we have fully tested them ourselves, and proved them worthy of culti-vation. Our Nurseries, so far, have been kept clear of the Scale Bug pest, and we are determined by constant vigilance to keep them so.

Principal Tree Depot, Second and H Sts., near C. P. R. R. Passenger Depot.

Read Carefully The Terms Of Sale.

First—The articles in the following list will be furnished at the annexed prices only, when the quantities specified are taken. Moreover, these prices are intended for a reasonable assortment of varieties. When parties order long lists of only one or two trees of a kind, for such bills extra charge will be made.

Second—When parties order specific varieties we will follow their instructions so far as practicable. But as it often occurs that we have run out of certain varieties, or may not have of the age and size ordered, we reserve the right to substitute in such cases other varieties equally good, unless positively instructed not to do so.

Third—We will use every effort to avoid mistakes in varieties, for we fully realize that our success in the nursery business depends upon the reliability of our labels, but as there is such a margin for mistakes and misunderstanding (as above indicated), we will not warrant against errors or apparent mistakes in varieties, only to this extent, we will replace, free of charge, all trees that do not prove true to name, or we will refund in cash the original cost of such trees, with 10 per cent, interest per annum on said amount. (See fig. 2 on 1st page.)

Fourth—All trees are carefully labeled and packed in the best manner for shipping, for which a charge will be made sufficient to cover the cost of material and labor. As trees are often delayed in transit and roughly handled, it is much better to pay a small sum to have them securely packed than to have them poorly packed for nothing.

Fifth—All orders should be made in a separate list, and not mixed up with the body of the letter.

Write in a plain, legible hand, the name of the person and the place to which the goods are to go; also the route by which they are to be shipped. In the absence of such directions we will ship according to our best judgment, and will deliver to railroad or boat, all goods free of charge, but will not be responsible for accidents or delays which may occur in transit.

TERMS OF PAYMENT.— Cash, or sufficient guarantee that the money will be forwarded on receipt of trees.

For extra large trees and plants above the sizes mentioned, extra prices will be charged, and smaller ones lower in proportion.

Money may be sent by Express, Draft or Post-office Order, at our risk; but if sent in any other way, at sender's risk.

Agents wanted in every community, to whom a liberal commission will be paid. Correspondence solicited.

Any errors of ours in filling orders will be cheerfully rectified on receiving notice, provided such notice be given within ten days from the receipt of goods.

We desire to tender our thanks to the public for the liberal share of patronage they have extended us in the past, and we shall hope to merit a continuation of the same. We shall certainly try by strict integrity and prompt attention to business to retain the public confidence so generously accorded us. Please advise us promptly of any errors or omission on our part that we may have a chance to rectify.

CATALOGUE.

☞In selecting varieties to propagate, we have endeavored to select only such varieties as can be profitably cultivated on this coast, though all may not succeed well in any one locality. Experience and observation have taught us that the most profitable orchards are those containing but a few choice kinds. It is a great mistake to plant a long list of kinds in one orchard.

☞A long list of varieties with a very few trees of a kind, is a provoking curse to the nurseryman, and a perpetual curse to the planter.

APPLE TREES.

Apples are among our most profitable fruits, when proper varieties and locations are secured. Early and autumn varieties should be planted in the valleys and foothills, and winter varieties in the mountains and along the coast.

☞Our stock of trees comprises all the leading and popular sorts, and is unsurpassed in vigor, thrift and hardiness. There is so much variation in climate on this coast that the time of ripening of the several fruits can only by approximately named, and some apples that are classed as fall apples would be winter fruit in some localities. We would call special attention to our one-year extra apple trees; they are one year from bud, on strong roots, and are as large as two-year old trees. We should prefer them to two-year trees to plant. A one-year tree has buds all along the body, hence a good head can be secured at any desired height.

Apples—Leading Varieties.	Each	10	100	1000
2 year, No. 1—4 to 6 feet, branched	$0 25	$2 00	$18 00	$150
1 year, No. 1—4 to 5 feet	20	1 80	16 00	120
1 year, No. 2—3 to 4 feet	18	1 40	12 00	100
1 year from bud—extra, 5 to 7 feet	25	2 20	20 00	150

APPLES.----Summer.

RED JUNE Small to medium, deep red, juicy and good. Ripens about the 20th of June.

EARLY HARVEST Large, pale yellow, mild, sub-acid. Ripens about the 20th of June.

*RED ASTRACHAN Large, roundish, striped with deep crimson, thick bloom, very juicy and acid, good bearer; ripens in June.

*WILLIAMS' FAVORITE Large, oblong, light red, juicy and good; ripens early in July.

APPLES.----Autumn.

*ALEXANDER Very large and beautiful, greenish yellow, striped with red, one of the best and most profitable market varieties. Ripens early in July.

*WHITE ASTRACHAN Large, oblate, skin very smooth and white, with faint red stripes, juicy, acid, valuable for market; ripens 10th to 20th of July.

*GRAVENSTEIN Large, roundish, striped, very productive and good for market; ripens last of July to 1st of August.

*SANTA CLARA KING Large, roundish, skin yellow with red blush on exposed side, flesh crisp and juicy, good for all purposes; ripens 10th to 20th of August.

*YELLOW BELLFLOWER Large, oblong, pale yellow, flesh tender, sub-acid, very good; ripens in September

*RHODE ISLAND GREENING Large, roundish, a little flattened, skin green, yellow flesh, tender, crisp, acid, juicy; ripens in October.

*KING of TOMPKINS COUNTY Large, conical shaped, skin yellowish, striped with red, flesh juicy, tender, vinous flavor, very good; November to February.

APPLES.----Winter.

*ESOPUS SPITZENBERG Large, oblong, skin smooth, yellowish, covered with red stripes, flesh crisp and juicy, one of the best keepers; November to March.

BALDWIN Beautiful, large red apple, flesh white, crisp, very good; October to February

YELLOW NEWTON PIPPIN Medium size, skin greenish yellow, flesh crisp, sub-acid; one of the very best, but does best in the Coast Counties; November to March.

GREEN GENETING A large, late, green-colored apple, conical shape, smooth oily skin, flesh crisp and juicy, fine for cooking, a good shipper; October to March.

SWAAR Large, pale yellow, with exceedingly rich, aromatic flavor, good; November to March. Does best in the mountains.

*WINE SAP Medium, roundish, deep red, tree hardy and good bearer; November to March. One of the best for the mountains.

APPLES. Winter—Continued.

WHITE WINTER PEARMAIN Above medium size, skin pale yellow, flesh yellow, crisp and juicy, very good; ripens in October to February. Best in the Coast Counties.

*NICKAJACK Large, roundish, skin striped with crimson, flesh yellow, sub-acid flavor; November to February. A Southern apple.

JONATHAN Above medium size, conical shape, red striped, sometimes quite red; a good keeper, especially in the Coast Counties.

HOOVER A large, deep red apple, good flavor, good bearer and fine keeper, one of the best; November to March. Does splendidly near the Coast.

*MERKLEY'S RED A seedling variety of great promise. Original tree growing in the orchard of R. J. Merkley, on the Riverside road. Fruit large size, dark red, excellent flavor, crisp and juicy; a superior market variety.

TWENTY OUNCE PIPPIN A very large, conical shaped apple, covered with dull red stripes, has a fine crisp sub-acid flavor, will cook well when only half grown, a very profitable market kind, tree a strong vigorous grower with upright habit.

Crab Apples.

YELLOW SIBERIAN Fruit about an inch in diameter, fine rich yellow; good for jelly.

TRANSCENDENT A beautiful variety of large size, yellow flesh, with red cheek; very productive.

HYSLOP A large, beautiful red crab, one of the best.

Special Variety.

THE VIOLETT This is a new apple raised by J. W. Violett, of Ione. It is one of the largest apples grown, averaging nearly as large as the Gloria Monda; conical shape, a beautiful red nearly all over, solid, firm and crisp, good flavor, fine shipper; September to January. Tree strong grower with upright habit; bark, on new wood, smooth, glossy and light, chestnut color, leaves quite peculiar—a rich glossy green. 30 cts. each. $20 per 100.

PEARS.

We do not propagate a long list of pears. Our experience has been that only a few of the leading varieties are the most profitable. The following list includes most of the kinds that have proven valuable.

PRICE OF TREES—Leading sorts.

	each	10	100	1000
2 year, No. 1—4 to 6 feet, branched	$0 30	$2 50	$20 00	$160
1 year, No. 1—4 to 5 feet	20	1 80	16 00	120
1 year, extra—4 to 6 feet	25	2 00	18 00	140
1 year 4 to 6 feet, special varieties	40	3 50	30 00	...

PEARS—Summer.

MADELINE Medium size, pale yellowish green, flesh white, melting, juicy; 20th of June.

DEARBORN'S SEEDLING Small to medium, light yellow, flesh white, very juicy and melting; ripens 20th of June.

BARTLETT One of the most popular pears; large size, clear yellow skin; flesh fine grained, juicy, buttery and melting, with a rich, musky flavor; the best early pear, and has no competitor as a market and canning fruit. Tree vigorous, bearing early and abundantly. August.

PEARS—Autumn.

KIEFER'S HYBRID A large roundish pear, recommended highly, but we have not tested it sufficiently to judge of its merits.

BEURRE HARDY Fruit large, skin greenish, covered with light russet, flesh buttery, melting and juicy, one of the best, ships well; August.

SECKEL Small to medium, skin dull yellowish brown, with russet red cheek, flesh white, very juicy, perfection of flavor; last of August.

BEURRE D'ANJO Large round pear, one of the best, good shipper.

LOUIS BON DE JERSEY A very sweet, delicious Autumn pear; shaped much like the Bartlett only more elongated, greenish yellow with bright red cheeks; flesh fine-grained and exceedingly fine flavored, good for drying, canning or shipping.

CHINESE PEAR Fruit large, flavor not good, but tree highly ornamental, foliage large, rich green till late in Fall, when they turn red and hang a long time. The Chinamen will pay 12 to 15 cents a pound for the fruit; trees 1 year, No. 1, $1 each.

PEARS—Winter.

BEURRE CLARGEAU Fruit very large, skin yellow, covered with russet dots, flesh yellowish, good flavor, good shipper; September to December.

EASTER BEURRE Fruit large, skin yellowish green, with russety dots, flesh white, rich flavor, long keeper.

WINTER NELIS Medium size, greenish, russet, melting and juicy, rich flavor, good shipper, October to December.

BEURRE BOSS Large long russet pear, good flavor and good shipper, one of the very best, October to April.

WINTER SECKEL Above medium size, shaped much like the Bartlett and nearly as large, color and flavor much like the Fall Seckel, long keeper, good shipper.

P. BARRY A California seedling, originated by the late B. S. Fox, of San Jose; a very large elongated russet pear. quite late, and a long bearer, can be kept till March; an excellent pear for Eastern shipping, fine texture and excellent flavor when fully ripe.

SANTA ANA A new pear, originated at Santa Ana, in Los Angeles County. It is a large conical shaped pear, a bright golden yellow covered with russet; it is an exceedingly handsome fruit, flesh fine-grained and free from all woody substance, with a flavor equal to the finest Winter Nelis or the famous Seckel; it will eat well when picked from the tree, and yet will keep all Winter; it is a very remarkable pear in this respect; its shipping and keeping qualities cannot be excelled. We consider it a very valuable accession to our list of pears. The tree is a moderately strong grower, with upright habit, forming a close, compact head, makes a very handsome tree.

Special Varieties the P. Barry and Santa Ana.

PEACHES.

In order to secure healthy and vigorous trees it is necessary to prune severely. Their tendency in this State is to develop an immense number of fruit buds, and as they are not destroyed by frost, they produce more fruit than the tree can mature. The consequence is it is small and inferior. The tree should be trained low and pruned regularly every year. By this practice the breaking of limbs is avoided, and the fruit grows much larger and finer. Many new varieties have been produced in the past few years, so that the fruiting season has been materially lengthened. The following list contains most of the valuable kinds, but the period of ripening varies so much in different localities that the time given can only be considered approximate.

We have the largest and finest stock of Peach on the Coast.

PRICE OF TREES—Leading Varieties.

	each	10	100	1000
1 year, No. 1—4 to 6 feet	$0 25	$2 00	$18 00	$150
1 year, No. 1—4 to 6 feet, new and rare kinds	35	3 00	25 00	....

JUNE BUDS.

	each	100	1000
1st class, 3 to 4 feet	$0 15	12 50	90
2d class, 2 to 3 feet	10	9 00	70

Freestones.

YELLOW ST. JOHNS A fine yellow freestone, very much like the Early Crawford, and ripens a little earlier. Shipping qualities good.

BRIGG'S RED MAY Fruit medium to large, deep red cheek, flesh firm, good market variety; 1st June.

GOV. GARLAND Fruit large, bright red cheek, ripens with Alexander.

WATERLOO Medium size, deep red, early.

ALEXANDER Medium size, white flesh, with clear red cheek; ripens here 10th June; the earliest shipping peach.

HALE'S EARLY—An early and very profitable market peach; medium size, and nearly round; skin greenish, mostly covered with red when ripe; flesh white, melting, juicy, rich, sweet; 20th of June. Ships well.

FOSTER Very large yellow peach, red cheek, bears well, ripens about same time as Early Crawford.

'EARLY CRAWFORD A magnificent large, yellow peach, heavy bearer, one of the best for shipping and all purposes, ripens last of June.

PEACHES. Freestones—Continued.

LATE CRAWFORD Much the same as Early Crawford, but ripening two weeks latter.

WHEATLAND A large yellow free, bright red cheek, ripening a little later than Late Crawford, one of our most popular peaches.

JONES' SEEDLING Origin, Sacramento; large yellow flesh, with red cheek, excellent flavor, 10th of August.

*SUSQUEHANNA Very large yellow peach, red cheek, of best quality; July. Ripens Aug. 1st.

KEYPORT WHITE A large white peach, with red cheek, good for shipping, canning or drying last of August.

WARD'S LATE FREE Large white flesh peach, good for canning, September.

*SALWAY Large yellow peach, dull red cheek, good flavor, superior market variety; 1st September.

*BILYEU'S LATE OCTOBER Large, white flesh, red cheek, very fine flavor, good shipper; ripens 20th October, tree strong grower, doesn't curl, freestone, does best in foot-hills.

*PICQUET'S LATE Very large, yellow, with a red cheek, flesh yellow, buttery, rich and sweet, nd of the highest flavor.

MUIR Large, yellow peach, flesh very dry and sweet, pitt very small, one of the best for drying and canning, planted more for this purpose than any other peach.

WAGER Almost a fac-simile of the Muir, and supposed by some to be the same.

STILSON (California Seedling) A very large, yellow fleshed peach, bright red cheeks, with dark crimson stripes, one of the very best market sorts, ripens two weeks later than Late Crawford.

LOVELL Well recommended.

Clingstones.

DAY'S YELLOW CLING (California seedling) A very large, yellow flesh, with red cheek good market variety; August.

*ORANGE CLING A very large yellow flesh, with red cheek, a well known variety; August.

HEATH CLING Large, white flesh, superior flavor; 1st September.

*GEORGE'S LATE CLING (California seedling) Very large, white flesh, with bright red cheek, superior quality; September.

LEMON CLING Large, yellow, with bright red cheek, a fine market peach, good shipper.

EDWARDS' CLING (The same called by C. W. Reed, the California) A California Seedling, produced by the late Mr. Edwards, near this city. It is a large, yellow fleshed peach, highly colored, a fine market or shipping fruit.

ALBRIGHT CLING (California seedling) A very large, yellow peach, with bright red cheek. A fine shipper and good peach in every particular.

*TUSCAN CLING A very large yellow cling, ripens same time as Early Crawford, a fine shipper, and its early ripening makes it very valuable.

WINTER'S CLING (a seedling from the Heath Cling) Original tree raised by C. H. Wolfskill, of Winters. The old tree is now 32 years old and still bearing good crops of fruit, and Mr. Wolfskill says it has never curled or mildewed, while the Heath Cling does both. The Winters is almost a fac simile of the Heath, except it is slightly larger, and much better shaped. It possesses all the excellent qualities of the Heath, is larger, color a beautiful creamy white, with red blush on exposed side, is white to the pit, and therefore a fine canning peach. It is very solid and a fine shipper.

McDEVIT CLING (A California seedling, raised by Neal McDevit, of Placer County.) This is one of the largest peaches we have ever seen, many of them weighing one pound each, peaches very uniform in size, rich golden yellow, becoming quite red when ripe, flesh very solid and firm, an excellent shipper, superior flavor; tree a good and regular bearer.

TUSCANY CLING An exceedingly large yellow cling peach (from Italy), deep yellow with bright red cheek, very late, good shipper, tree hardy and strong grower, don't curl or mildew, and consequently good for the Coast Counties.

DIAMOND CLING A large white fleshed peach, bright red cheek, very handsome and very fine shipper, excellent flavor, succeeds well in the mountains.

McKEVITT'S CLING A California seedling, very large, flesh white to the pit, firm and good, stands shipping well, good for canning and drying; 10th September.

Peaches of Recent Introduction.—Special Varieties.

FRENCH CLING A large, late, yellow fleshed cling, very large firm fruit, good shipper. One of the best of our new peaches; tree hardy and strong grower.

PINE APPLE.
  BIDWELLS' EARLY.
    BIDWELLS' LATE.
      BIDWELLS' No. 7.
        POOLS SEEDLING.
          SEMINOLE.
            CHATMAN'S CLING.

New varieties not tested, said to be valuable.

NECTARINES.—Leading Varieties.

	each	10	100
1 year, No. 1—4 to 6 feet	$0 25	$2 00	$18 00

NEW WHITE   Large, creamy white, freestone, very superior for drying.

BOSTON   Medium to large red freestone, fine flavor, good for drying.

CLEMENT'S NECTARINE   A large red nectarine, good flavor, will make a good shipper, tree of good and regular bearer.

VICTORIA   Large, red cling, good shipper.

APRICOTS.

A popular and profitable fruit, and though planted heavily it will always remain so, on account of the increasing demand. The soil and climate of California matures it to perfection. We have only propagated the best and most profitable varieties.

PRICE OF TREES—Leading Varieties.

	each	10	100	1000
1 year, No. 1—4 to 6 feet on peach root	$0 25	$2 20	$20 00	$160
1 year, No. 1—4 to 6 feet, on Myrobolan	30	2 50	22 00	180
New and rare kinds, 4 to 6 feet	40	3 50	30 00	250

JUNE BUDS.

	each	10	100	1000
1st class 3 to 4 feet, branched on peach root	$0 20	1 75	15 00	120
2d class, 2 to 3 feet	15	1 25	11 00	100

ROUTIER'S PEACH APRICOT   A new kind from Mr. Routier's orchard. Large size, skin yellow in the shade, deep orange mottled, or splashed with red in the sun; flesh rich and juicy, very high flavor; good market variety.

EARLY ROYAL   Medium size, good color, very productive, a favorite for canning and drying.

HEMSKIRK   Very much like the Moorpark; one of the best; tree good bearer.

BLENHEIM   A good early variety, above medium oval; orange with deep yellow; juicy and tolerably rich flesh; vigorous grower and a regular prolific bearer. Ripens with the Royal.

MOORPARK   Large, orange color, moderate early bearer, but of the highest flavor.

Special Varieties.

NEWCASTLE EARLY   A new variety originated by M. C. Silva & Son, of Newcastle, California. Medium size, round, well shaped, a shade smaller than the Royal; two weeks earlier than the Royal; very valuable on account of its earliness; tree a good and regular bearer; fruit ships well.

FRENCH APRICOT   Very large; good flavor; firm; ripens evenly on both sides; a good shipper, highly esteemed for canning and drying; a regular and prolific bearer; ripens with the Royal; very popular where it is known.

McCORMACK   Supposed to be a seedling of the Large Early, which it very much resembles, but ten days earlier. Tree a strong grower and very productive, very showy, and fine for shipping. We have only small June buds of this variety 1½ to 3 feet, 25 cents each, $20 per 100.

PRUNES.

PRICE OF TREES.

Our stock of Prunes this season is very large and fine.

Prunes on Peach Root.

	each.	per 100.	per 1000
1 year, No. 1, 4 to 5 ft	.25	$20.00	$170.00
1 year, extra 5 to 7 ft. Branched	.30	25.00	180.00
June Buds, 3 to 4 ft	.20	15.00	120.00
" " 2 to 3 ft	.15	12.00	100.00

Prunes on Myrobolan Root.

	each.	per 100.	per 1000.
1 year, No. 1, 4 to 5 ft	.30	$22.00	$180.00
1 year, extra 5 to 7 ft, Branched	.35	25.00	200.00
June Buds (small) 18 inches to 3 ft		15.00	100.00

PRUNES--Continued.

Varieties.

TRAGEDY PRUNE A new prune originated by Mr. Runyon, near Courtland, in this county. It would seem to be a cross between the German Prune and Purple Duane. Fruit medium size, nearly as large as the Duane Purple Plum; looks much like it, only it is more elongated; skin dark purple, flesh yellowish green, very rich and sweet, frees readily from the pit. Its early ripening (in June) makes it very valuable as a shipping fruit. Coming as it does before any other good plum, it will always bring fancy prices, both in the local and Eastern market. So far it has no rival. We believe we are the first to work it. The first to get orchards of this fruit will make fortunes out of it.

'PETIT PRUNE D'AGEN (French Prune) Small to medium, reddish purple, very sweet, parts freely from stone; one of the best varieties for drying as a prune.

'SILVER PRUNE Originated in Oregon. The fruit is a fac-simile of Coe's Golden Drop, except it is a darker green, and it is yet a question whether it should be called a prune or a plum. It is a very superior shipper, and it certainly makes an excellent dried fruit, either pitted or unpitted; makes a splendid prune.

BULGARIAN PRUNES A very prolific, dark colored prune, larger than the French Prune, and by some considered a very valuable prune, but we have not yet tested it sufficient to judge of its value.

PRUNE D'AGEN (or Prune d'Ent) Very like the Petit or French Prune, only larger and more desirable. It is now demonstrated that this prune will bear as heavy crops as the French or Petit Prune, and as it is so much larger and of equally as good a quality, it is of course the most valuable of the two. There has been some fears that it might not be a good bearer, but that doubt has been dispelled. Many trees are now bearing heavy crops in this State. Price of trees same as the Petit Prune on Myrobolan root. It will not grow on peach root, but must be grown on plum root. This is the same prune recommended by Felix Gillet, of Nevada City, as the true Gros Prune.

PRUNIS PISSARDI A medium size plum; red, fine flesh, good flavor, long keeper; the tree is very ornamental, foliage blood red.

PRUNIS SIMONI Quite large, somewhat elongated, bright yellow, red cheek; very fine fruit; good for shipping or drying; tree a strong grower; bears heavily.

GERMAN PRUNE A large purple prune, flesh greenish yellow, very sweet, always brings fancy prices as a fresh fruit; it is a good shipper and makes an excellent dried prune, tree a strong grower and a good and regular bearer.

PLUMS.

The Plum and Prune succeeds admirably in this State, and we can and should not only produce for home consumption, but export large quantities instead of importing. Many varieties of Plums and Prunes have a tendency to over-bear, and, to secure a good article, the fruit should be carefully thinned out. This should be done when it is one-third or one-half grown. Those who are willing to take these pains will be amply repaid by a superior quality of fruit, and a more renumerative price.

PRICE OF TREES'--Leading varieties.

	each	10	100	1000
1 year, 6 to 7 feet, extra, on peach root	$0 25	$2 00	$18 00	$150
1 year, No. 1—4 to 6 feet	20	1 80	15 00	135
1 year, 5 to 6 feet, extra, on Myrobol root	30	2 50	18 00	175
1 year, No. 1—4 to 5 feet, on Myrobol root	25	2 00	16 00	150
Special sorts, 1 year from bud, extra	35	3 00	25 00	...

PEACH PLUM Fruit very large, round, greenish white, with red cheek; flesh yellow, sweet and firm; early; good for shipping.

'COLUMBIA Fruit large size; skin brownish purple, with fawn colored specks; flesh yellow, sugary; excellent; one of the best for shipping.

DUANE'S PURPLE Large, reddish purple; flesh juicy and moderately sweet; good shipper.

VICTORIA (or Oakshade Prune) Medium size, beautiful red plum; good shipper, and superior for drying, being very free and quite a dry meated plum; very prolific.

COE'S GOLDEN DROP Fruit large, oval, flesh yellow, firm, rich and sweet; adheres to stone; good for canning and ships well.

'GROS PRUNE D'AGEN (Hungarian Prune) Very large, oval, violet red; very prolific, often growing double; good flavor; a valuable kind; best shipper.

YELLOW EGG A very large elongated plum; golden yellow; adheres to the stone; quite juicy, rich sub-acid flavor; the best known canning variety and ships well.

WASHINGTON Large, round, greenish yellow; good for canning or drying.

PLUMS—Continued.

*JAPANESE PLUM (known as the Kelsey Plum) Fruit very large, as large as an ordinary peach; roundish, or inclined to be conical; color greenish yellow, with faint red cheek; adheres closely to the pit, which is very small; flesh firm and juicy; it is the best keeper known.

ROYAL HATIVE Medium size, early, roundish, purple; flesh yellow amber, rich, good, high flavor; parts from the stone when ripe. A favorite in Vaca Valley, where its earliness makes its valuable.

BLOOD PLUM A fine, handsome, strong growing tree; fruit above medium size, blood red both outside and inside, very handsome and fine flavor. Trees, 1 year, No. 1 (on Myrobolan), 50 cents each; $40 per 100.

ICKWORTH'S IMPERATRICE Above medium size; purple, firm, sweet, rich, a valuable variety for market, bears transportation well, will keep a long time after being gathered. Clings to the stone. September to October.

CHERRIES.

As a pleasant and refreshing dessert fruit the cherry is everywhere highly esteemed. The early season at which it ripens, its juiciness, delicacy and richness render it always acceptable. It thrives best in rich dry loam. The trees should be trained low, that the foliage may protect the trunk, which should never be exposed to the sun. We cultivate only a few of the leading kinds, a brief description of which may be found below:

PRICE OF TREES.

	each	10	100	1000
2 year, No. 1—4 to 6 feet, branched	$0 35	$3 00	$25 00	$200
1 year, No. 1—4 to 6 feet	30	2 50	20 00	160
1 year, No. 2—3 to 4 feet	20	1 80	15 00	125

Varieties.

EARLY PURPLE GUIGNE. Medium size, black; quite early.

*ROCHPORT BIGARREAU. A large, early, flesh colored cherry; valuable for canning or drying; it is also a good shipper; its very early ripening makes it very valuable; it will always command a good price.

KNIGHT'S EARLY BLACK. Large, black, tender, juicy, rich and high flavored; early. This is the earliest good variety.

*BLACK TARTARIAN. A very large, purplish black, rich and juicy; one of the best varieties.

GOVERNOR WOOD. A fine, early cherry, white, shaded with red, tender, juicy and delicious.

*ROYAL ANN (or Napolean Bigarreau). Very large, pale yellow, with bright red cheek; flesh very firm, juicy and sweet; good shipper.

BLACK OREGON. Sometimes called Lewelling or Black Republican; a large, late black cherry; good flavor, long keeper and ships well.

CENTENNIAL. A new cherry, seedling from the Royal Ann, which it resembles; a little more oblate in form, and has a higher color; valuable for shipping, being a splendid keeper. Price 1 year, 35 cents each; $30 per 100; $250 per 1000.

SCHMIDT'S BIGARREAU. Very large black cherry; moderate bearer; good shipper; late.

QUINCE.

PRICE OF TREES.

	each	10	100
2 year, No. 1—4 to 6 feet	$0 35	$3 00	$25 00
1 year, No. 1—3 to 4 feet	30	2 50	20 00

ORANGE. Large, roundish; bright golden yellow; the best for general use.

EARLY GOODRICH. Very large, bright yellow; early; good flavor.

FIGS.

It has been thoroughly demonstrated that the Fig will grow most luxuriantly, thrive and bear great crops from one end of the State to the other; the warm, dry alluvial soils, and the dry warm climate of the interior valleys, and foot-hills seem to be peculiarly adapted to its successful culture and caring; it will grow and do well on lands too dry to mature other fruits; it will do well on rich bottom lands, provided they are well drained, so that there is no Fruit that can be more generally grown all over the State; and no other with so little care and risks or that is more profitable in the end. At the same time there is no other Fruit that has been so generally neglected. It is only in the last few years, that the value of this fruit has been recognized. All of the common varieties can be made profitable and with the varieties we are now introducing, there is no fruit that will be more desirable, or more profitable.

PRICE OF TREES.

	each	10	100	1000
2 year, No. 1—4 to 6 feet, branched (common kinds)	$0 25	$2 00	$15 00	$120
1 year, No. 1—3 to 4 feet	15		12 00	100

WHITE ADRIATIC AND VERDONI.

	each	10	100	1000
2 year, 4 to 6 feet	$0 35	$3 00	$25 00	$200
1 year, 3 to 4 feet	30	2 50	20 00	160

Varieties.

LARGE PURPLE One of the most fruitful sorts; large size; dark purple, very sweet, good flavor; drys well.

BROWN ISCHIA Very large, skin light or chestnut brown, very sweet and excellent.

PACIFIC WHITE Fruit medium size, fine grained, very sweet, seeds very small; very white and exceedingly fine flavored when dry; but the skin when dry is thicker and more tough than the imported; that and its small size is the only objection to it. It never cracks and sours in drying. The tree is a strong grower, very hardy, and always good shaped, a fine shade or avenue tree. A good regular bearer.

SAN PEDRO (usually called WHITE SMYRNA) A very large, dirty or rusty white fig; good flavor, one of the best as a green or fresh fruit; valuable for that purpose, but does not dry well if dried in the sun, as it cracks and sours in drying, but makes a very superior product when dried by artificial heat. We regard it as one of the best figs for profit we have, if properly handled; the tree is rather a slow grower, but a great bearer; exceedingly prolific.

VERDONI Called by many White Adriatic, but it differs from the fig which is now generaly called the White Adriatic in the color of the pulp or inside of the fruit. The Verdoni is white inside, while the other is red, otherwise they are very much alike. While they are both excellent figs, we are planting (in orchard) more largely of the Verdoni, mainly on account of its white flesh, but either of them will make a very superior dried product, that will equal if not surpass the best imported article, (where they are well grown and properly cared.)

WHITE ADRIATIC.

ALMONDS.

Nut growing should be carried on far more extensively in this state than it now is. Almonds are a sure crop over a large area of the state. They can be raised to profit at lower rates than the usual current prices. Our foothill lands seem to be peculiarly adapted to their culture. We know of no district in the state where they do better than in the foothills, at an altitude of from 600 to 2,000 feet above the sea, level.

PRICE OF TREES.

1 year, No. 1—4 to 6 feet on peach	$0 20	18 00	150
1 year, No. 1—4 to 6 feet on almond	25	20 00	160
June Buds on almond	20	15 00	125
June Buds on peach	15	12½	100

Varieties.

ROUTIER'S SOFT SHELL A new seedling from the orchard of Hon. J. Routier, shell quite soft good size, a regular and prolific bearer.

BLOWERS' LANGUEDOC Originated and highly recommended, by R. B. Blowers, of Woodland, a fine nut and good and regular bearer.

BYERS' LANGUEDOC A new seedling, one of the best.

TWIN A very large smooth nut, each nut containing a double kernel, shell soft, free, hardy and good bearer.

GOLDEN STATE A large nut, soft shell, full smooth meat; parts readily from the hull; ripens early.

ALMONDS—Continued.

I X L Nuts large, soft shell, good color; recommended by A. T. Hatch.

NONPARIEL An extraordinarly heavy and regular bearer; shell very soft.

DRAKE'S SEEDLING Originated by Mr. Drake Suisun, and recommended by him as being very prolific, and a regular and abundant bearer.

TEXAS PROLIFIC A new seedling variety originated at Dalis, Texas. Nut full as large as the Languedoc, but softer shell, very smooth and bright color, well filled with a very sweet meat; tree full as strong grower, and very much resembles the Languedoc tree. It is a very heavy and regular bearer. It is the only variety that will fruit well at Dalis, Texas. We consider it by all odds the finest and most desirable almond we have ever seen, we sold all we had last season at $1 00 each. Price 50 cents each. $35 00 per 100, $250 per 1,000.

WALNUTS.

EASTERN BLACK WALNUTS A well-known tree; valuable for timber, nut a little larger than the California walnut; price 2 year trees, 50 cents.

CALIFORNIA BLACK WALNUTS A native specie, valuable for shade and nuts. Very productive. 2 year trees, 5 to 7 feet, well branched, 30 cents each, per hundred $25. 1 year trees, 3 to 5 feet, 20 cents each, per hundred $15.

ENGLISH WALNUTS Very popular and profitable nut, makes a very handsome shade, 2 year trees 5 to 8 feet, 50 cents each, $30 per hundred. 1 year 2 to 4 feet, 25 cents each, $20 per hundred We have a large stock of these, and will quote special price on large lots.

PRAEPARTURIEN WALNUT A very fine table nut, trees of dwarfish habit, bears quite young and heavy crop. Trees 2 to 3 feet, 30 cents each, $25 per hundred; 3 to 4 feet 40 cents each, $35 per hundred, 4 to 5 feet, 50 cents each, $40 per hundred.

PECAN NUT A fine nut, does well on deep soil. Tree 1 year, 1 to $1\frac{1}{2}$ feet, $12\frac{1}{2}$ cents each, $10 per hundred. 1 year, 2 to 3 feet, 25 cents each, $20 per hundred. 2 year, 3 to 4 feet, 40 cents each, $35 per hundred.

CHESTNUTS.

These nuts do well in the greater portion of the state, they are among are handsomest shade trees and the nuts bring a fancy price, they should be planted by every one.

Varieties.

ITALIAN CHESTNUT A very large nut, sweet, bears well, tree very ornamental. Trees 1 to $1\frac{1}{2}$ feet, 15 cents each, $10 per hundred. 2 to 3 feet, 25 cents each, $20 per hundred. 3 to 4 feet, 40 cents, each, $35 per hundred.

CHESTNUT (American Sweet) Same sizes, same prices as the Italian.

GRAPES.

Grape growing in California is one of our leading industries, most all varieties thrive well, and produce abundant crops. We have endeavored to select out of the vast number of varieties such as ave proved the most valuable. We have an extra large stock this season, and will quote special price orders.

We only quote prices on 1 year plants, as we find that 1 year vines give the best results. All our lines are extra well grown, well rooted and strictly first class in every respect.

	PRICE.	Each	100	1000
1 year No. 1 (fine roots)		5	$3	$25

Varieties.

*WHITE MUSCAT (Muscat of Alexandria) Fine, large, white grape, musk flavored, good market variety, either for shipping or raisius.

*MUSCATELLE GORDO BLANCO Resembling the Muscat, berries large, less musky flavor, good raisin variety.

*FLAME TOKAY A magnificent large, red grape, very firm, vigorous grower and productive, our most popular shiping grape.

*ZINFANDEL A medium size, black grape, close compact bunches, very productive, valuable for wine.

GRAPES--Continued.

SEEDLESS SULTANA Small white grape, clusters large. It makes a fine raisin for culinary purposes, at the same time is a fine wine grape. It is the only grape we know of that is good for both raisins and wine.

EMPEROR A large red grape, resembling the Tokay, ripens quite late, is an excellent shipper, its lateness and long keeping qualities makes a very valuable grape, does splendidly on our granite soils in the foothills, the vines of this variety should be staked up to get the best results.

CORNISCHON The largest and latest grape we cultivate, berries quite elongated, firm, solid, and skin thick and tough, which will enable it to carry farther than any other grape. Sells well in the East.

ROSE PERU Medium size black grape, ripens quite early, good bearer, one of our best early shipping grapes.

BLUE MALVOISE Large, reddish black, oblong, with faint bloom, good early table grape.

BLACK FARURA Large, oblong, firm black grape, good flavor, one of the best for shipping.

TROSSEAU Bunches medium sized, cylindrical, berries black, covered with a thick bloom, yields a dark colored wine of the best quality for flavor and bouquet.

CARIGNAN Bunches similar to Mataro, berries oblong, black, produces heavy crops, and a highly colored good wine.

BERGER A large white wine grape, very productive, makes an excellent wine, is a very profitable grape to raise.

MATTARO A medium sized black grape, close compact bunches, an abundant bearer, makes a superior wine. This grape is always in good demand as a wine grape, brings good price, is a very profitable grape to grow.

PETITE BOUSCHET Valuable as a coloring for wine.

*WHITE NIECE Wine grapes.

*GRENACHE Wine grapes.

Resistant Stock.

VITES CALIFORNIA We have a fine stock of this valuable resistant stock. Grafts on these stocks make a stronger and more vigorous growth than on their own roots. Price 2 year, $10 per thousand.

CURRANTS.

PRICE.	Each.	Per 100
2 year—No. 1......	$0 12½	$10 00
1 year—No. 1...	8	6 00

CHERRY Fruit of the largest size; bunches short; berries large, deep red; a valuable market sort.

WHITE DUTCH Bunches long; berries yellowish white, nearly transparent; very sweet and agreeable; sometimes used for making currant wine.

GOOSEBERRIES.

PRICE.	Each.	Per 100
American..	$0 20	$15 00
English..	25	20 00

BLACKBERRIES.

PRICE.................4 cents each | $3 00................per 100 | $10 00.................per 1000

WILSON'S EARLY Fruit large, productive and early.

DORCHESTER A fine sweet berry.

KITTATINNY Good market variety; large and good flavor.

LAWTON Good market variety for this locality; large and late.

CRANDALL'S EARLY This berry was brought from Texas some years ago and planted on the place of Dr. S. R. Crandall, of Auburn, Placer County. (The origin of this berry is not known to us.) Here it was discovered that it was not only an excellent berry and prolific bearer, but was also found to ripen three weeks earlier than the Lawton, and continues to blossom and bear fruit until late in the Fall. We have often picked good, ripe, well developed berries as late as the last days of December. The wood of the vine is light colored, resembling the Wilson's Early, but is a much stronger grower. The berry is as large as the Lawton, fine flavor, firm and solid. It is an excellent shipper. Price $1 per dozen, $5 per 100, $15 per 1,000. Fifty plants at 100 rates; 500 at 1,000 rates

RASPBERRIES.

PRICE. ....5 cents each | $3 00...............per 100 | $15 00...............per 1,000

Leading Varieties.

HANSEL Medium size berry, very early and firm; ships well.

BARTER We have cultivated all of the leading varieties, and do not hesitate to recommened the Barter, as being the finest and most profitable berry we have ever seen, it is a very large bright red berry, bears very heavy crops, and trees easily from the stem; a splendid shipper, and has brought the highest price of any berry we ever handled.

HERSTINE Fine large market berry.

STRAWBERRIES.

Price.................50 cents per doz. | $1 00...............per 100 | $6 00.................per 1000

Triomphe de Gand, Sharpless, Forest Rose, Monarch of the West, Captain Jack, Champion, and many other new varieties not fully tested.

ESCULENT ROOTS.

Asparagus..2 cents each; $10 00 per 1000
Rhubarb...... ....20 to 50 cents each
Hop Roots...... ....50 cents per doz.; $1.50 per 100; $10 00 per 1000

(Large lots at special rates, very low.)

OLIVES.

Olive culture in California has of late attracted much attention and it is an established fact that a great many localities especially the foothills are exactly suited to the successful growth of the olive, and the production of an Oil that will have no superior.

Olive growing in California is only in its infancy, but the flattering results that have been obtained, guarantees for Olive growing a perfect success and a most profitable future. There are a great many different varieties of the Olive now being propagated, most of them not yet thoroughly tested, and we only offer those varieties that have been tested and are known to be the most profitable.

PRICE OF MISSION OLIVE TREES.

	each.	100.
14 to 18 inches..............	$ .20	$18 00
18 to 24 inches...	.25	22 00
24 to 30 inches..	.30	25 00

PICHOLINE. Prices on application later.

Varieties.

MISSION. This we believe to be the best Olive for all purposes; it is good for both oil and pickles.

PICHOLINE. A small olive used chiefly for oil; makes fine grade of light oil.

MANZANILLO (Queen Olive). Berries very large, highly prized for pickles; also good for oil.

NEVADILLO. One of the finest olives for oil.

Price of Manzanillo and Nevadillo.

	each.	100.
14 to 18 inches...	$ .25	$ 20 00
18 " 24 "	35	25 00
24 " 30 "	40	30 00

ORANGE and LEMON.

For the last three seasons we have been growing our Orange and Lemon trees in Florida, owing to the high prices of California grown trees, and the superiority of the Florida sour root of the sweet roots. In the spring of 1889, we sent buds of the leading varieties from trees in the best orchards in Riverside, Cal., to Florida and had them budded to our order, and have been propagating from these trees since, it is a thoroughly established and well-known fact that trees grown on the Florida Wild Orange Root are longer lived, more healthy and vigorous, stand our winters far better, can be transplanted with less loss, and are in every respect better than trees grown on sweet seedling roots. We can refer to all our customers who have planted our stock, for the reliability of this statement. Out of 40,000 orange trees sold to one planter in1887, less than 2 per cent failed to grow, a record that can not be equalled by any orchard planted with California grown trees.

Our Florida trees are grown for California trade.

ORANGES—Continued.

We have this season 140,000 budded orange trees mostly Washington Navel, balance Lemon and assorted well-known varieties. We have had them all staked up and grown perfectly straight, most of them running in height from 3½ to 6 ft. They are clean, thrifty and free from all scale, and we can safely say that we will have this season the finest lot of trees ever brought into or grown in California, and we will sell them at prices that will defy competition.

In addition to this we saved out last season about 7,000 orange trees which we planted out in our nursery and salesyard. They are intended for early delivery before we can get trees out from Florida.

These trees have made a most remarkable growth and are especially adapted for yard planting.

We make a specialty of orders for car load lots, and will quote special low prices to any one wanting large orders.

See our trees and get our prices before buying elsewhere.

PRICE OF BUDDED TREES.

	each.	10.	100.	1000.
4 to 6 ft. on 4 and 5 yr. roots	$ 1 50	$ 12 00	$ 90 00	$ 750 00
3½ to 4 ft. on 3 and 4 yr. "	1 25	10 00	75 00	650 00
2 to 3 ft	75		50 00	350 00

Extra large trees, 2.00 each; $150 per 100.

Lemon same sizes and prices of Orange trees.

Sweet (Indian River) seedlings, 4 to 5 years old, ¾ to 1¼ inch in diameter......60c each, $45 00 per 100
Sour orange trees for street planting, 4 to 7 years old, ¾ to 1¼ inch in diameter...75c each, $50 00 per 100

We will give special rates to dealers, nurserymen or parties buying in large lots to plant.

Parties asking for special rates should state varieties and number of trees wanted.

Brief Description of Varieties. (All Hardy).

WASHINGTON NAVEL. Acknowledged by all to be the leading orange; too well known to need any further description. ½ of our trees are budded to this variety.

MEDT SWEET. A popular variety; medium size, very sweet, and good bearer; tree thornless.

BEACH'S No. 1. A large, fine, thin-skinned sweet orange, ripens very early in the season, is a good bearer, tree strong grower and hardy.

BEACH'S No. 5. A large, fine, very late orange of excellent quality; its very late ripening makes it valuable, coming in as it does after most all others are gone (in almost midsummer).

NONPAREIL. A very handsome orange of most excellent quality, a popular sort in the market; tree a strong grower, hardy and a good bearer.

PARSON BROWN. Fruit medium size, oblong in shape, smooth high color, very sweet, ripens early, is sweet as soon as it begins to turn, grand bearer, tree has some thorns.

MAGNUM BONUM. A very large orange, a little flattened, skin smooth and glossy, fruit heavy and of excellent quality, ripens early, tree very prolific, thorny.

PEERLESS. Fruit large and round, smooth skin, one of the best market sorts, tree a heavy and regular bearer and strong grower.

ST. MICHAEL. Fruit medium size, very fine quality, a little flattened, thin skin, tree a good bearer, nearly thornless.

HART'S TARDIFF. A large round orange of good quality, its chief excellence consisting in its lateness; it does not ripen till May or June, and will hang on the tree in good eating condition till August; tree strong grower and good bearer.

JAFFA. Imported from the city of Joppa, in Syria, a very fine, medium size orange of superior quality, tree nearly thornless.

The **VILLA FRAKA LEMON**; the finest lemon ever introduced in California. This lemon has become the favorite in Florida; the fruit is of a very superior quality, tree a strong grower, a heavy and regular bearer, excelling all other varieties in productiveness. The tree is exceedingly hardy; it withstood the heavy freeze in Florida in January, 1886, in the same orchards where all other kinds, and also orange trees, were killed. It ripens in July and August, thus coming in the hot season when lemons are most needed and when the market is bare of other citrus fruits. It is emphatically the lemon for profit.

MILAN LEMON. Very similar to the Villa Franka.

Deciduous Shade and Ornamental Trees.

POPLARS AND LOCUSTS.

	each	per 100
No. 1—2 to 2½ inches diameter	$1 00	$60 00
No. 2—1½ to 2 inches diameter	50	40 00
No. 3—1 to 1½ inches diameter	25	20 00
No. 4—¾ to 1 inch diameter, 7 to 9 feet high	15	10 00

(Large orders at special rates, very low.)

CAROLINA POPLAR. A magnificent tree for street planting, forming a beautiful head; large leaf and spreading habit; rapid grower.

LOMBARDY POPLAR. Erect and upright grower.

BLACK LOCUST. Strong grower, valuable for timber; same price as poplar.

CORK BARK ELM. Rapid grower; symmetrical in shape; 50 cents to $1.25 each.

AMERICAN ELM. A magnificent tree with drooping branches; 25 to 75 cents each.

SOFT OR SILVER MAPLE. Fine for street planting, handsome foliage; 25 to 50 cents each; large trees 75 cents to $1 each.

WEEPING WILLOW. A beautiful weeping tree, with slender, drooping branches; 50 cents to $1 each.

Our stock of both Maple and American Elm is very large, and on large lots we will make very low prices.

MULBERRIES.

The Mulberry is a very valuable family of trees. Most of them make beautiful, well shaped and clean shade trees. All make very valuable timber and make it very quick, being rapid growers. This fruit is excellent, and is recommended by some to plant in orchards for the purpose of attracting the birds from the cherries, as they eat mulberries in preference to any other fruit.

PRICES OF TREES.

1 yr. no. 1—5 to 8 ft..50 cts. each.

1 yr. " 2—3 " 5 " ....35 " "

Varieties.

DOWNING'S EVERBEARING. A rapid growing tree, valuable for its fruit, as it remains in fruit for three months.

PERSIAN. Largest fruit, but slow grower

NEW AMERICAN. This is a large, strong growing, beautiful shaped tree; one of the best shade trees that grows; it also produces large crops of very fine berries, very sweet and delicious. Fine.

RUSSIAN MULBERRY. This also makes a fine tree, and the fruit is said to be very large and fine; we have not fruited it yet.

CIRCASSIAN MULBERRY. This is a very fine, strong growing variety, makes a splendid shade tree; fruit of little value.

MORUS ALBA or WHITE MULBERRY. Fine shade tree, but fruit of no value.

MORUS MULTICOLUS. Only valuable for the foliage, which is used to feed silk worms; 10 to 25 cents. Large lots for silk culture very cheap.

DYOSPYROS KAKI, OR JAPANESE PERSIMMONS.

Hyakume, Kuro, Kunie, Zemon, Dai Dai Marn, Zanji Marn Hachija, Tane Nashi. The two last named are nearly or quite seedless. We have several other varieties, but have not space to name or describe them. Most of our people are familiar with this fruit. Price 35 cents each.

ORNAMENTAL DEPARTMENT.

Our limited space will not admit of a full description of every shrub or flower, neither can we give the exact price for each particular size and style of plant. They vary so much in size, shape and condition that a minute description would occupy too much space. But we can guarantee satisfaction if you will, in ordering articles, where the price ranges from one figure to another, simply give the price you wish to pay, and we will send articles to correspond with the price given.

We do not grow Greenhouse Plants, but carry them in stock during the selling season and can furnish anything in that line at regular florists' prices. So we can fill orders for anything in that line, though it may not be named in the Catalogue. In the item of Roses we can furnish over 100 varieties not mentioned in this Catalogue.

ROSES.

Price, in pots..60 cts. to $1.00 each.

Price, naked roots..30 cts. each.

Marechal Neil, Lamarque, Gold of Ophir, John Hopper, Giant of Battle, Cloth of Gold, James Sprunt, President Lincoln, Auguste Mie, Cardinal Patrizzi, Duchess of Norfork, General Jacqueminot, Louis Van Houtte, Pauline Sabonte, Paul Nanyon, Reive D Orr, Salfaterre, Amelie Vibert, Celine Farester, White Cluster, Banksian (White), Baltimore Belle, Greville (or Seven Sisters), Bon Seline, Isabella Sprunt, Mad. Falcot, Duchess of Edinburgh, Anna Oliver, Bella, Catharine Merment, Homer Hermosa, Madam Stella.

MOSS ROSES. Captain Ingraham, Glory of Mosses, Henry Martin, Luxemaury, Black Morean, James Veitch, and many others too numerous to mention. A few choice new kinds at 75 cents to $1.50 each.

UMBRELLA TREE. One of the most beautiful and ornamental trees grown. It naturally grows in the shape of an umbrella, and is a very rapid grower; makes a dense shade. Price 50 cents each; extra large trees 75 cents each.

EVERGREEN TREES.

EUCALYPTUS. Globulus (Blue Gum), in variety, in pots or bagged, 2½ to 10 feet, 20c to $1. Blue Gum and other varieties of Eucalyptus, in seed boxes, 3 to 12 inches, $1 to $4 per 100. Transplanted in boxes so as to cut with balls of earth, 2 to 12 inches, $2 to $6 per 100.

In large quantities for forest planting at special rates.

ACACIA Native of Australia, rapid growth, beautiful foliage and masses of yellow and orange-colored flowers; in pots or bagged, 3 to 5 feet, 30 to 50 cents.

ACACIA MELONOXELON, or Blackwood Acacia, a very fine hardy kind.

ACACIA floribunda, or fragrans, long lance-like leaves.

ACACIA molissima, fine elegant species; light green leaves.

PEPPER TREES (California Schinn Molle), 3 to 6 feet, 40 cents to $1.

PALMS, in variety, $1 to $5, as per size and variety.

CUPRESSUS (Cypress), most popular and very ornamental; perfectly hardy, and thrives well in most localities and soils.

CUPRESSUS LAWSONIANA (Port Orford Cedar) very fine; branches curve like green plums; 50c. to $1.

CUPRESSUS FUNEBRUS, elegant drooping foliage, adapted for planting in cemeteries; 75 cents to $1.

CUPRESSUS macrocarpa (Monterey Cypress), 15 cents to $1 each.

CUPRESSUS pyramidalis (Italian Cypress), very erect, close pressing branches; 50 cents to $1.

PINUS macrocarpa (Monterey Pine), 3 to 7 feet; 30 cents to 75 cents.

ARBOR VITÆ, golden, beautiful compact plants; 75 cents to $2.50.

SEQUOIA gigantea (California Mammoth Tree), $1 to $2.50.

LAUREL, English, good plants; 75 cents to $1.

MAGNOLIA GRANDIFLORA, 50 cents to $2.50.

Surplus stock, which we will sell at special rates in quantity. Price on application—

MISCELLANEOUS.

Pinks, in variety.....................35c each	Honeysuckle, in variety.................35c each
Lillies (See Seed Catalogue for price of bulbs)	Ivy................................25c "
................................25 to 70c "	Olrander..............................35c "
Chrysanthemums....... ....25c "	Veronica.......... ....25 to 50c "
Fuchsia............................35c "	English Box........................10 to 30c "
Heliotrope....... ....35c "	Euonomous, plain......................40c "
Pampas Grass..........................50c "	Enonomous, Varigated Golden............50c "
Verbenas, per bunch...................20c "	Lauristimus..........................40c "
Pansies, per bunch...................10c "	Camelias, assorted ....50c to $3 00 "
Violets, per bunch...............10 to 25c each	Geraniums........................25 to 75c "

Transplanting Trees.

In the first place see that the ground selected for orchard is thoroughly ploughed and well pulverized. Dig the holes large enough to allow all the roots to spread out in their natural shape, two feet wide and two feet deep will usually do, though the larger and deeper the hole is, the better, as you get the ground more thoroughly worked up. After the holes are all dug take the trees from the bale a few at a time, so that they will not be exposed. Do not expose roots to sun or frost, fill the hole with loose moist soil until the tree will stand about the same depth as it stood in the nursery, trim off all the bruised parts of the roots, place the tree in the hole so that the roots will spread out naturally, throw in moist earth and pack it solid around the roots, after the roots are covered, and the ground packed thoroughly it is an excellent thing to throw in a bucket of water, then fill up the hole. To preserve from borers and other injuries during the first summer, wrap the trunk with cloth, woolen preferred — but burlap will do.

Hints on Pruning.

The best dug tree loses more than half the fibrous roots that act as feeders. Shorten the top to correspond. Don't fail to cut back heavily when you transplant. Don't forget that a half root cannot support a whole top. Never neglect pruning. Trees trained low protect their own trunks from the sun's rays, are less liable to break with the weight of the fruit, and the fruit is easier gathered

Transplanting Potted Plants.

In transplanting potted plants, lift the ball carefully out of the pot, then with a sharp knife cut the circle of roots that encompass the outside of the ball, so as to force a straight and not a crooked root from the plant into the ground, in order that, as the tree or plant increases in size, it will not be so liable to blow over. Thousands of trees are annually blown over and destroyed by reason of this circle of roots, for as the root is shaped when the plant is set, so it will continue to grow. Bagged plants should be planted with the bag on, only cutting the string at the collar or top of the bag.

Anything not mentioned in this Catalogue, or Greenhouse and Florists' specialties, will be furnished at regular florists' prices, provided it can be procured in the market.

Principal Office at Store, Nos. 102 to 110 J street, between Front and Second.

Principal Depot and Sales Yards, Second Street, near Passenger Depot of C. P. R. R.

W. R. STRONG & CO. Proprietors,

SACRAMENTO, CAL.

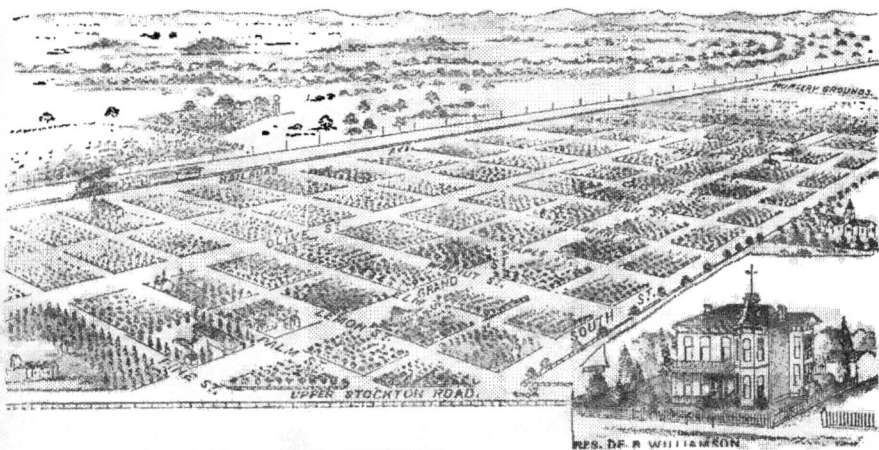

W. R. STRONG COMPANY TRACT, EAST SACRAMENTO.

The above is a cut of a tract of land containing 130 acres adjoining the City on the southeast. This land we formerly had in nursery, but is now all in bearing orchard. We have surveyed this tract in lots and blocks, to correspond with the streets of Sacramento, and are now offering it for sale in lots to suit. No more desirable land can be found for pleasant suburban homes. No land in this vicinity will grow into value faster. Sacramento must extend its limits before long, and it must do so in this direction. A complete map and full particulars relative to this land will be furnished on application to all persons wishing to buy.

FOOTHILL FARMS.

We have a tract of land in the famous Penryn and New Castle Fruit Belt in Placer county. Our tract lies one-half mile from Penryn; it is all planted to fruit trees of the most profitable kinds; orange, peach, etc. We offer it for sale in 5 and 10 acre tracts, and for any one wanting a small profitable place, with a healthy climate and beautiful surrounding, this section has no equal.

We also have a few ten-acre tracts in the new and thriving Orange Vale Colony. Just across the river from Folsom, and the land is sure to become very valuable. These tracts are also planted to fruit trees, which WILL BEGIN BEARING NEXT SEASON.

VALLEY LAND.

We have 320 acres of rich orchard land in the celebrated Lodi watermelon country 3 miles east of Acampo. This is one of the finest bodies of land in the State; it is mostly planted to orchard and nursery stock; the quality and capabilities of this tract of land are too well known to need any recommendation from us. We offer it as a whole; or tracts to suit the purchaser.

A full and complete description of these tracts will be furnished on application.

W. R. STRONG COMPANY,
SACRAMENTO, CAL.

W.R. Strong & Co.

SACRAMENTO

PROPRIETORS

CAPITAL NURSERIES

Wholesale Dealers, Packers & Shippers

of CALIFORNIA
Fruit & Produce

Car Load Lots our Specialty

1890.

BULBS

ONE of the first questions that the purchasers of Bulbs asks is, "Are they easy to grow?" To this very natural question we reply that with scarcely any exception, bulbs are easily managed, sure to bloom, and require but little labor and care to enable them to produce exquisite flowers.

No class of flowers has gained more rapidly in public favor during the last few years than those produced from bulbs. Many of them are especially desirable, as they afford a profusion of blossoms early in the spring, when few other plants are in bloom out of doors. They are easily cultivated, and are unsurpassed for their beauty and variety of colors. We know of no plant that will give equal satisfaction for out-door culture, and in no other way can the home be so satisfactorily and easily beautified during the winter as with a few Hyacinths, Tulips, Lilies, Narcissus, etc.

It should be borne in mind that the BULBS MUST BE SECURED AND PLANTED IN AUTUMN, whether they are wanted for flowering in the house for the holidays and Easter, or for a display out of doors in the early spring. Do not wait till spring comes, and you see your neigibor's yard the delight of all passers-by, but order at once.

MANAGEMENT.

Bulbs intended for blooming in pots during the winter season should be planted during the months of October and November in pots, and be left in the open air, covered with a few inches of tan or soil, until the earth begins to freeze, and then be placed in a cool greenhouse, cellar or room, at a temperature of 50 degrees, in a very dark place. They will need occasionally moderate watering after they are brought inside. When the top is well grown and the flower stem well out of the bulb, they should be brought to the light and given plenty of water, and exposed as much as possible to the sun, air and light, to prevent the leaves from growing too long or becoming yellow.

The proper compost for Hyacinths, Tulips, Crown Imperials, Iris Ranunculus, Anemones, Crocus, and many other bulbs, is the following : One-third sand, one-third well-rotted cow manure, and one-third good garden soil.

The preferable season for planting all hardy bulbs is from October to December ; but they can be set out later if the bulbs remain sound and the ground is not frozen.

If Hyacinths and other bulbs are placed in water for some time before planting, they will root much quicker and insure earlier flowering.

HYACINTHS.

Among hardy bulbs the Hyacinth deservedly stands foremost on the list. It is not only a general favorite for the garden, but has become exceedingly popular as a winter flower, from the facility with which it may be forced into bloom, either in pots or in glasses.

Hyacinths in Glasses.

For this purpose, Single Hyacinths, and such as are designated early among the Double, are to be preferred. Single Hyacinths are generally held in higher estimation than Double ones; their colors are more vivid, and their bells, though smaller, are more numerous. Some of the sorts are exquisitely beautiful. They are preferable for flowering in winter to most of the Double, as they bloom two or three weeks earlier, and are less liable to failure. The bulbs should be placed in glasses during October and November. Fill with pure water, so that the base of the bulb may just touch; then place them in a dark closet, box, or cellar, at a temperature of 45 to 50 degrees. When the glasses are well filled with roots, and the flower stem well out of the bulb, gradually expose to the light and sun at a higher temperature. If kept too light and warm at first, and before there is sufficient fibre, they will rarely flower well. They will bloom without any sun, but the colors of the flowers will be inferior. The water should be changed as it becomes impure. Draw the roots entirely out of the glasses, rinse off the fibres in clean water, and wash the inside of the glass well. Care should be taken that the water does not freeze, as it would not only burst the glass, but cause the fibres to decay. Avoid a low-water mark in the glasses by keeping it to a level with the base of each bulb. To stimulate and strengthen the growth, dissolve a pinch of sulphate of ammonia occasionally in the water after the bulbs are exposed to light.

When Hyacinths and other bulbs are in bloom it is a good plan to place them in a cold room, free of frost, where they flower for a considerable length of time.

Hyacinths in Open Ground.

They require a light, rich soil, and it may be necessary to provide this to the depth of a foot or more by removing the natural soil and substituting a proper compost.

One of the most suitable composts is composed of equal parts of sandy loam, well decayed cow manure and sand. Plant the bulbs at any time from the middle of September to the end of November, October being the most preferable. The crowns of the bulbs should be from three to five inches below the surface. If the ground freezes, cover to the depth of three inches with straw, or any material to prevent freezing and thawing. This should afterwards be removed to prevent drawing the flower stems.

The bulbs should be planted six inches apart. Where large quantities for brilliant effects are wanted, the cheaper grades of Garden Hyacinths will answer all requirements.

The flowers may be cut freely without injury to the bulb. When through flowering remove the tops, and the bulbs can be lifted and kept in a dry place for the next season's planting.

Single Hyacinths.

We head our list with Single Hyacinths by design, because we consider them more useful and valuable than the double varieties. They are better for forcing, more vigorous in growth, and produce stronger spikes of bloom, which are generally of better substance and are at least as beautiful as those of the double sorts.

Named Hyacinths.

Price (except as noted), 20 cts. each; per dozen, $1.75.

Single Red and Rose.

Baron von Thuill.—Pink.
Amy.—Very fine bright scarlet.
Cosmos.—Pink; large bulb and long spike.
Gigantea.—Gigantic pink spike.
Le Prophete.—Pink; large bulb and spike.
Veronica.—Red; fine for forcing.
Robert Steiger.—Very fine dark red; large spike.

Single White.

Baroness von Thuill.—Pure white; large close spike.
Grandeur a'Merveille.—Finest blush white; large spike.
Voltaire.—Cream white; a favorite for cutting.
Alba Superbissima.—Pure white; large tall spike.
Mont Blanc.—Earliest; pure white; large bells. Fine for cutting. Extra, 25c each.
Madame Vanderhoop.—Pure white; very large bells.

Single Blue.

Argus.—Blue; white center.
Charles Dickens.—Light blue; large compact spike.
La Peyrouse.—Fine porcelain blue; not early.
Marie.—Enormous truss and bulb; purple and indigo.
Czar Peter.—Bright blue; large spike; extra, 25 cents.
Lord Byron.—Azure blue; very large spike.

Single Yellow.

Herman.—Orange yellow; very large bulb.
Ida.—Pure yellow; larger truss; new. Extra, 25 cents.
La Citromere.—Citron yellow.

Double Hyacinths.

For exhibition purposes and for growing in pots or open ground, the double sorts will be found charming.

Double Red and Rose.

Grootvoorst.—Very fine blush pink, large truss and bells.
Noble par Merite.—Very fine pink, grand truss, early.
Princess Royal.—Scarlet with brown center, fine.
Lieutenant Wagthorn.—Deep scarlet.
Rejina Victoria.—Rosy, large truss, extra.
Czar Nicolas.—Large spikes and bulbs, fine pink.

Double White.

Anna Maria.—Blush white, purple center, large spike, extra.
La Virginate.—Very fine, blush white.
Non Plus Ultra.—Pure white, extra large, fine spike and bells.
Prince of Waterloo.—Pure white, large truss and bells.
Fleva.—Pure white, large spike.

Double Blue.

Bloksberg.—The finest of all light blues, large compact spikes.
Charles Dickens.—Light blue, large compact truss, extra fine, 25 cents.
Lord Ragland.—Azure blue, dark center, fine.

Prince of Saxony Weimar. — Dark blue, semi-double.
Garrick.—Azure blue, large compact spike.

Double Yellow.

Goethe.—Finest yellow.
Ophir d'Or.—Pure yellow, with purple eye.
Boquet d'Orange.—Orange, extra, 25 cents.

Roman Hyacinths.

The earliest for forcing or spring blooming. The flower spikes are smaller than the Dutch varieties, but the flowers are equally as pretty and fragrant. They force readily in the house, and as the bulbs are of moderate size, several can be grown in one pot. The blooming season is prolonged by the bulbs throwing up three to five spikes of flowers, which do not come to perfection all together.

Single White.—10 cts. each; per doz., 75 cts. Per hundred, $5.

Unnamed Hyacinths.

Separate Colors.

Price, 10 cts. each; per doz., $1.00. Per hundred, $7.00.

These are selected from good forcing varieties, and will give good results. They are unnamed, but comprise different shades of the various colors.

Single Red, all shades.	Double Red, all shades.
" White, "	" White, "
" Blue, "	" Blue, "
" Yellow, "	" Yellow, "

Single Small Hyacinths.

Unnamed Hyacinths—for Forcing.

These varieties are of interest to those who desire to cultivate them. The bulbs, though small, produce fine spikes of flowers of various shades and colors, and are desirable for garden or pot culture.

Price, 5 cts. each ; per doz., 50 cts. ; per 100, $3.

Small Hyacinths.

Single Red,	Single Blue—dark.
Single Rose,	Single Light Blue.
Single White,	Single Cream White.

Tulips.

It is difficult to conceive of anything more pleasing to the eye than a bed of good Tulips. The great variety of colors produced, their intense brilliancy and beautiful shading make them universal favorites. Another great consideration in their favor is the ease with which they can be cultivated, requiring only any good common soil to grow them to perfection; the price, too, as compared with other bulbs, places them within the reach of all.

The Tulip has been so much improved by Dutch cultivators that it ranks high in the floral world. In form, wealth of color, and the variety of its markings, it is one of the most perfect of flowers.

The culture of Tulips is the same as that of Hyacinths, except that the bulbs should be planted three or four inches deep, and two to six inches apart. Tulips are perfectly hardy, so only a slight protection from extreme and sharp winds is desirable.

All of the single varieties force readily, and of late have become great favorites in the house in mid-winter. If potted in September, and treated as directed for Hyacinths, they may be had in bloom in December. When they show a tendency to bloom just above the bulbs they must be kept longer in the dark to draw out the flower stem. A splendid effect is obtained by planting from three to a dozen bulbs in a medium sized pot.

MIXED TULIPS.

The following are all first quality bulbs, but are offered without names. Where masses of bloom are wanted they will be found very serviceable, as they comprise good colors and fine shaped flowers.

Early Single and Double Mixed.

5 cts. each ; per doz., 40 cts.; per 100, $2.50.

Late Single Mixed.

Flowering soon after the early varieties.

Bybloemen. — White ground flaked with violet, crimson and maroon. 5 cents each; 40 cents dozen.

Bizarres.—Yellow ground flaked with crimson, purple and violet. 5 cts. each ; 40 cts. doz.

Late Show Tulips.— Byblooms and Bizarres, $2.50 per 100.

EARLY SINGLE NAMED TULIPS.

All suitable for forcing or growing in the garden. These commence flowering two weeks in advance of other sorts of Tulips, and are admirably adapted to culture in pots, borders, or beds.

Named Sorts.

Per dozen, 50 cents; per 100. $3.00.

Brutus —Bright red and yellow. Each, 5 cts.

Cameleon. — Creamy white, rosy spotted. Each, 5 cts.

De Keiser.—Scarlet. Each, 5 cts.

Count de Mirabeau.—Pure white. Each, 5 cts.

Duchess de Parma.—Orange yellow, fine large truss. Each, 5 cts.

Keizerskroon.—Red, with broad yellow edge. The largest Tulip. Each, 5 cts.

Joost van Vondel.—Glossy, rosy red and white. Each, 5 cts.

Van der Neer.—Finest of all violets. Each, 5 cts.

La Reine (Queen Victoria).—White, fine for forcing. Each, 5 cts.

Pottebaker. — White, finest of all white Tulips. Each, 5 cts.

Rose Mundi (Huikman). — Bright pink. Each 5 cts.

EARLY DWARF DUC VAN THOLL TULIPS.

Early red and yellow, violet and carmine. Each, 5 cts.; 45 cts. per doz.

EARLY DOUBLE NAMED TULIPS.

This class of Double Tulips can be forced in pots. Their large, early, fine-colored flowers and dwarf habit make them very desirable for bedding. The late Double Tulips are best adapted for planting in the garden, and will not bear forcing as well as the early varieties.

EARLY DOUBLE.

Named.

40 cts. per doz.; $3.00 per 100.

Le Candeur.—Pure white. Each, 5 cts.

Le Blazon.—Fine rosy pink. Each, 5 cts.

Murillo (Albano). — Pink and white, best double for forcing. Each, 5 cts.

Peony Gold. — Scarlet, feathered yellow. Each, 5 cts.

Duke of York.—Red, white edged.

LATE DOUBLE.

Fall Varieties—Named.

Admiral Kingsbergen.—Red and yellow.

Blue Flag (Lord Wellington).—Blue. Each, 5 cts.

Crown Imperial.—Crimson and white. Each, 5 cts.

Rose Eclatante.—Red.

Yellow Rose (Geele Roos).—Splendid golden yellow. Each, 10 cts.

La Belle Alliance.—Blue and white feathered. Each 5 cts.

PARROT TULIPS.

For the open ground only. Singularly beautiful flowers, containing brilliant shades of scarlet, crimson, yellow and green, curiously intermixed and variegated. The edges of the petals are feathered. In masses or in shrubbery border they are very striking and effective.

Parrot Tulips.—All shades—red, variegated, yellow, and mixed. Per doz., 30 cts; per 100, $2.

Crocus.

Among the earliest to blossom in spring is this beautiful little flower, lifting its head almost before the snow has disappeared. Blooming at a time when the ground is destitute of foliage or flower, it is a welcome visitor. The Crocus should be planted in autumn, in October, November or December, in any good garden soil, about three inches deep, and two inches apart, if in beds or borders. As they are entirely hardy, they may remain undisturbed for years.

To secure blooms in pots, commence early in October with six or eight bulbs in each pot, using rich soil and planting about an inch deep. Place the pots on a surface of ashes, cover the top one inch deep with soil, until the leaves appear, when they may be removed to the house.

UNNAMED VARIETIES.

Mixed.—Per doz., 15 cts. ; per 100, $1.00.

SPLENDID NAMED CROCUS.

Cloth of Gold.—Large yellow, 25 cts per doz; $1.25 per 100.

Baron Brunnow.—Bright purple, large, extra.

Non Plus Ultra.—Purple, with white top.

Mont Blanc.—Large white.

Madam Mina—Light blue, striped.

Sir Walter Scott.—White striped, purple. 20 cts. per doz., $1.25 per 100.

Pupuria Grandiflora.—Purple, very large flower.

POLYANTHUS NARCISSUS.

(The Flower of Love.)

This charming flower has not received its due share of attention, owing, doubtless, to its merits as a winter and spring flower not being fully recognized.

As a ladies' flower it is taking front rank, and lends to beauty an additional charm.

It can be grown in glasses as readily as the Hyacinth, and surpasses in beauty of form, delightful perfume and variety of coloring, all its rivals among winter flowering bulbs. For planting upon the edge of woods, among shrubbery, on rockeries, or for planting in groups on the lawn, the Narcissus is invaluable. It will be found among the chief attractions of the spring garden.

To obtain satisfactory results, the bulbs should remain undisturbed for three years at least. They may then be divided and reset. When desired for forcing, treat same as Hyacinths.

Polyanthus Narcissus.—Fine named.

Grand Monarque. — Large, pure white, white citron cup, fine. 10 cts. each, $1.00 per dozen.

Grand Primo.—White, extra; 10 cts. each, $1.00 per dozen.

Paper White (Totus Albus).—Pure white, fine for florists' use; 5 cts. each, 50 cts per doz.

Roman Double White.—Orange center, rich; 5 cts. each, 50 cts. per doz.

The Pearl.—Large white, with white cup, beautiful; 15 cts. each, $1.50 per dozen.

DOUBLE NARCISSUS (Daffodils).

Albo Pleno Odorat.—Pure white, very double, sweet—resembling the Gardenia—delicious odor; fine for cut flowers; 5 cts each, 50 cts. per doz.

Double Mixed. — Without names; 5 cts. each, 50 cts. per dozen.

SINGLE NARCISSUS (Daffodils).

Poeticus (The Poet's Narcissus). — Flower large, snow white, with beautiful cup suffused with bright orange red, early flowering and fragrant. Slow for forcing. 5 cts. each, 50 cts. per dozen, $2.50 per hundred.

Poeticus Ornatus (Pheasant's Eye). — Pure white, rosy scarlet eye. Blooms earlier than

Poeticus. Fine for forcing; sweet scented. 10 cts. each; 50 cts. per dozen.

Narcissus Bulbocodium (*Hoop Petticoat Narcissus*).—A pretty and shapely flower of a rich golden yellow color. Each bulb produces six to twelve flowers. A dry and sheltered situation suits it best when planted in the open ground. 5 cts. each, 50 cts. per dozen.

Trumpet Princeps.—Sulphur white, with golden trumpet. 10 cts. each, 75 cts. per dozen.

ANEMONES.

These charming hardy spring flowers are becoming better known and more popular as a garden flower; both double and single are equally desirable, and no garden should be without them. They are suitable for pot or border culture, and when planted in masses are most effective. They succeed best in light, rich, well drained loam. Plant in October or November, or as soon as the ground can be worked in the spring. If planted in the autumn, they should be overed with leaves, straw or long manure on the approach of winter.

The flowers are very beautiful in form and and color, and remain perfect a long time.

DOUBLE ANEMONES.

Double Large Scarlet.
40 cts. per dozen; $2.50 per 100.
Sir Robert Peel.—Sky blue; 40 cts. per doz.
Hamlet (*Lilac*).—Extra large.
Sapho.—Red variegated.
Sir Walter Scott—Carmine and green.
King of Scarlet.—Large scarlet; 50 cts. per dozen.
Double Mixed.—30 cts. per dozen.

SINGLE ANEMONES.

Coronaria Scarlet.—Very brilliant; 30 cts. per dozen.
"The Bride."—Pure white; 40 cts. per doz.
Single Mixed Varieties.—20 cts. per dozen.

English Iris.

Large handsome flowers, with rich purple, blue and lilac colors predominating. Perfectly hardy and growing 18 to 20 inches high.
Finest mixed; 5c each; per dozen, 40c.

Snow Drops

Beautiful little bulbs for early Spring blooming, when planted near the Crocus are very effective.
Single bulbs, 5c each; per dozen, 15c. Double ulbs, 5c each; per dozen, 25c.

RANUNCULUS.

Strikingly beautiful flowers, well adapted to pot culture, in the house. The individual flowers are about two inches in diameter, as full and double as the finest Camelia or Rose, and as a cut flower, quite as useful as the Rose itself.

Like Anemones, they do best planted in very rich soil, having a northerly exposure to escape our sharp winds and too much sun. The beds should have good drainage, and the soil be light and warm. Plant three inches deep, in October or November, and press the earth close around them. They will amply repay all care bestowed upon them. Ranunculus bulbs are peculiarly shaped and should be handled carefully, but if kept QUITE DRY when out of the ground, they will last almost any length of time.

Ranunculus. French, Persian and Turban, finest mixed varieties, per dozen, 15c; per 100, $1.

Ranunculus. (Fine Named).

Grootvoorst. Bright crimson; 20c per dozen.
Hercules. White; extra; 50c per dozen.
Seraphique. Citron yellow, extra; 25c per dozen.
Turban Virdiflora. Green center, scarlet and yellow border; 25c per dozen.
Romano. Bright scarlet, extra; 30c per dozen.
Merveilleuse. Yellow; 20c per dozen.

Tuberose.

Pearl. Each, 10c; per dozen, $1.

Dahlia Bulbs.

All Colors. 25c each; per doz. $2.

LILY OF THE VALLEY.

One of the most charming of our Spring flowering plants, bearing slender stems set with tiny bells. Flowers freely and powerfully fragrant. They are largely used for forcing in winter.

For pot culture, use the buds or pips, pot them in well-drained pots, covering the bottom with a layer of fibrous moss, and filling with sandy soil slightly mixed with the moss, which will hold the moisture, which is essential to success. Cover the bulbs to the depth of half an inch. Cover the top with moss and keep in a cool place till they are thoroughly rooted, then remove most of the moss and bring to light to perfect the flowers. They are perfectly hardy in the open ground if in a cool, shaded situation. Clumps of fifty or more, 75c; single, 5c.

DIELYTRA.

(Bleeding Heart.)

Tuberous-rooted plants, blooming in the early spring; favorably known almost everywhere. They require only the ordinary culture of border plants. The roots should be divided every third year. Roots planted in autumn will flower freely. The flowers are a delicate pink color, graceful; produced continuously from May to July.

Dielytra, Spectabilis. Pink; 25c each; $2.50 per dozen. Alba white, 50c each.

LILIES.

Lilium Auratum (golden rayed Queen of Lilies). This magnificent variety has become one of the standard favorites of the Flower Garden, and is considered by many, the finest of all Lilies. The immense blooms, measuring nearly a foot in width when fully expanded, are produced in great profusion, and are deliciously fragrant. Choice large bulbs, 25c each; per dozen, $2.50c.

Candidum. A well-known hardy garden Lily; commonly called St. Joseph's. Snow-white, fragrant blossoms. One of the best varieties for forcing, and an established favorite. 20c each; per dozen, $2.

Longiflorum. The well-known beautiful snow-white fragrant Lily Fine for forcing and handsome in the garden. 20c each; per dozen, $2.50.

Lancifolium Album. Pure white and very fragrant 25c each; per dozen. $2.50.

Lancifolium Rubrum. White spotted red; beautiful. 25c each; per dozen, $2.50,

Lilium Harrisii. (Bermuda Easter Lily). This beautiful Lily was introduced a few years ago from Bermuda. The flowers are large, trumpet-shaped, pure white and very fragrant. This mammoth white trumpet Lily with flowers four to five inches long, is pre-eminently the best of all winter Lilies for forcing and flowering. As a pot plant it is tall and stately, the spike thickly studded with bloom, which are lovely as cut flowers, and keep a long time in water. 25c each; per dozen $2 50.

Tigrinum. (Tiger Lily). Orange Salmon, spotted black. 15c each; per dozen, $1.25.

Humboltii. Flowers golden yellow, spotted with purple.

Pardalinum. Scarlet, shading to rich yellow; spotted with purple brown. 20c each; per dozen, $2.

Washingtonianum. White with small purple dots; very fragrant and beautiful. 25c each; per dozen, $2.50.

Atrosanguineum. Rich blood crimson, spotted with black. 15c each; per dozen, $1.50.

GLADIOLUS.

Floribundis. Pink, very fine; per dozen, 50c.
Large Bulbs. Per dozen, 50c.
Gandavensis. Scarlet and yellow; large bulbs; price per dozen. 50c.
Formosissimus. Scarlet & white; per dozen, 75c.
Seedlings. Mixed; per doz. 50c.
The Bride. A lovely pure white form of the Gladiolus Colvilli. The flowers are freely borne on the long stems and can be forced into bloom at a time when flowers are scarce. Ten cents each; $1 per dozen.

JAPAN LILIES, GLADIOLUS, DIELYTRAS, DAHLIAS, TUBEROSES, and LILYOF THE VALLEY ready about the first of January.

CATALOGUE

1891.

Established 1852

W·R·STRONG COMPANY

CALIFORNIA SEEDS

TREES & NURSERY STOCK

SACRAMENTO, CAL.

CATALOGUE OF
W. R. Strong Co., Sacramento, Cal.
FOR 1891.

WE again desire to return our thanks to our friends and customers, some of whom have been our patrons for over thirty years. To ALL who have added to our success through their patronage, we would solicit a continuance of their favors.

To ALL who may read this, we would say, that we desire to make your acquaintance and so enroll your names on our books, not only as patrons but also as friends.

Our success in the past and our constantly increasing trade is the best evidence of our success.

We shall use every effort in the future as we have in the past to give satisfaction, and with our increased facilities and knowledge of our business, we are sure our customers will find their wants most perfectly and cheaply supplied.

Our strains of seed this season are of unusual excellence, and our prices will compare favorably with those of any other house on this coast or of Eastern cities.

WARRANTY. No Seedsman can sell Seeds and guarantee and be responsible for the crop. Our Seeds are selected with the greatest care to secure the best, and from the most careful and reliable growers. When it is considered that there are many contingencies upon which depend the success of a crop, which are beyond our control, the propriety of this must be conceded by all.

SUGGESTIONS.

ORDER EARLY AS POSSIBLE, while stock is complete, that you may be sure of getting what you send for, so you will have them to plant when wanted.

USE OUR ORDER SHEETS and Envelopes when you have them; it will be more convenient and there will be less danger of miscarrying or of mistakes. FOR ORDERS FOR TREES AND NURSERY STOCK use separate sheet, as this department is quite distinct and has a separate office and management.

BE VERY PARTICULAR. WRITE YOUR NAME, POST OFFICE, COUNTY AND STATE IN FULL AND PLAINLY. We often receive orders without name or address, and it is often impossible to trace them up.

STATE HOW YOUR ORDER IS TO BE FORWARDED, otherwise we are compelled to use our own judgment.

SEND CASH with your order (at our risk—if sent by Postal or Express Order, or Draft on any good Banking House). Small sums may be sent in Postage Stamps if proper care is taken to prevent adhesion together.

MAIN PLACE OF BUSINESS—J, NEAR FRONT ST., SACRAMENTO.

Nursery Department.

This is under the management of our MR. WILLIAMSON and his son, who have had the largest practical experience of any Nurseryman in the State.

We have over four hundred acres now in cultivation on our ground in this county, and San Joaquin and Placer counties, in Nursery and Fruit Tree growth.

Our stock is absolutely true, clean, thrifty and well grown, and free from all scale and insect pests. We have also a branch in Florida for the growing of the Orange, Lemon, Magnolia, and various other evergreens that can be propagated to better advantage in that State. We sold over 100,000 of these trees last year in California, and not 2 per cent. have failed, and they are giving universal satisfaction.

Please make your orders for TREES AND ALL NURSERY STOCK separate from Seed Orders, as our Departments and Offices are entirely distinct.

Office, Yards and Packing Houses, next to Passenger Depot on Second St., Sacramento.

COLLECTION A. OF STRONG'S CHOICE
FLOWER SEEDS FOR 60 CTS. VALUE 85 CTS.

No. 1. Pansies-Ponsées.
Strong's Very Large-flowering. 25 cts.

No. 2. Cheiranthus Cheiri.
Single Wallflower. 5 cts.

No. 3. Mixed Double Hollyhocks.
10 cts.

No. 4. Silene pendula.
Mixed 5 cts.

No. 5. Dahlia
Single. 10 cts.

No. 6. Primula veris (elatior).
Polyanthus. 10 cts.

No. 7. Single Poppy.
Papaver umbrosum. 5 cts.

No. 8. Lobelia erinus Crystal Palace compacta.
10 cts.

No. 9. Gaillardia Lorenziana
Double. 5 cts.

W. R. STRONG COMPANY
ORDER SHEET.

Name.. O. B. No..... Am't.

Very Plain.

Post Office.

County..

State...

Do not write here.

Express Office..

Railroad...

Forwarded by...

VERY IMPORTANT.—Write your name very plainly, in black ink, and always give your Post Office, County and State in full.

AMOUNT ENCLOSED.

Money Order....... $....

Draft............... $....

Stamps .... $....

Postal Note......... $....

Date 1891

In ordering Seeds by mail in oz. and packets, postage will be paid by us. WHEN IN LARGER QUANTITIES, ADD TEN CENTS PER POUND FOR POSTAGE, ETC. For large orders for Seeds, Trees, etc., please give full directions as to manner of transit.

Pounds.	Ounces.	Packets.	NAMES OF ARTICLES WANTED.	PRICE.	
				Dolls	Cents.

Pounds.	Ounces.	Packets.	NAMES OF ARTICLES WANTED.	PRICE.	
				Dolls	Cents.

GENERAL PRICE LIST OF SEEDS

FOR 1890-91.

It is cheaper and of more advantage to purchase SEEDS in bulk or by weight, but to accomodate small trade our VEGETABLE and FLOWER SEEDS are also put up in small and neat lithographic descriptive packets at Five Cents each or Fifty Cents per dozen.

PEAS, BEANS and CORN in half-pound boxes at Ten Cents each, or One Dollar per dozen, and in one pound boxes at 15 cents each; $1 75 per dozen. These packets are of full weight, and contain more Seed than those offered by Seed Houses generally.

ALL SEEDS QUOTED BY THE OUNCE AND IN SMALL PACKETS WILL BE FORWARDED BY MAIL POSTAGE PREPAID BY US.

SEEDS QUOTED AT POUND RATES (if to be sent by mail), add TEN CENTS PER POUND TO COVER COST OF POSTAGE.

Assortments of Seeds for Family Garden.

To accommodate those not familiar with selection of the choicest varieties, we have prepared boxes of THOSE KINDS MOST DESIRABLE. Three sizes; price, one dollar, two dollars, and five dollars each, and which are at least one-fourth less than catalogue rates, and which we are sure will give satisfaction.

Peas.
EXTRA EARLY.

	Per hun.	Per lb.
Cleveland's Alaska, earliest of all, 20 inches	$9 00	$0 15
Cleveland's K. N. Y., 2 feet, prolific; ripens at one time, fine flavor	8 00	15
Extra Early, first and best, 2 feet	7 00	15
Premium Tom Thumb, 8 inches	8 00	15
Premium Gem, wrinkled, sweet, 12 inches	8 00	15
Carter's Stratagem	9 00	15
American Wonder, 10 inches	9 00	15
Laxton Alpha, 3 feet	9 00	15
Bliss Abundance, 18 inches	9 00	15
Bliss Everbearing, 24 inches	9 00	15
McLean's Advancer, 36 inches	8 00	15

GENERAL CROP.

	Per hun.	Per lb.
Pride of the Market	$8 00	15
Prince of Wales	8 00	15
Yorkshire Hero, 2 feet	8 00	15
Telephone, 3 feet	8 00	15
Champion of England, 5 feet	7 00	15
Royal Dwarf Marrow, 2 feet	6 00	10
Large White Marrowfat, 5 feet	5 00	10
Black Eye Marrowfat, 4 feet	5 00	10

EDIBLE PODS, SUGAR PEAS.

	Per hun.	Per lb.
Tall and Dwarf White Seed	$12 50	20
Tall and Dwarf Gray Seed	12 50	20

Field Peas in quantity and variety, at lowest market rates.

Beans.
DWARF SNAPS OR GREEN STRING.

	Per hun.	Per lb.
Early Refugee	$8 00	$0 15
Early Pinkeye China	8 00	15
Early Red Valentine	8 00	15
Cleveland's Round Pod, earliest, best and most prolific of all	9 00	15
Early White Valentine	9 00	15
Early Mohawk	8 00	15
Early Yellow Six Weeks	7 00	15
Green Flageolet, fine	10 00	15
Early Case Knife	9 00	15
Southern Prolific	9 00	15
Wax Flageolet, yellow pod, large, fine	10 00	15
Early Golden Wax, yellow pod	8 00	15

	Per hun.	Per lb.
Ivory Wax, yellow pod	$10 00	$0 15
White Seeded Wax, yellow pod	10 00	15
Black Seeded Wax	8 00	15
Dwarf White Kidney	8 00	15
Dwarf Cranberry	7 00	15
Broad Windsor	5 00	10

POLE OR RUNNING.

	Per hun.	Per lb.
London Horticulture	$8 00	15
Large White Lima, Hand Picked	10 00	15
King of the Garden Lima	11 00	15
Giant Wax, red seed	10 00	15
Dutch Case knife	8 00	15
Scarlet Runners	12 50	20
White Runners	12 50	20
Asparagus or Yard Long	15 00	25

All varieties of Field Beans in quantity at the very lowest market rates.

Sweet Corn, Etc.

	Per hun.	Per lb.
Extra Early Cory	$9 00	$0 15
Extra Early Marblehead	9 00	15
Early Pee and Kay	9 00	15
Early Minnesota	8 00	15
Early Crosby, very early	8 00	15
Early Moore's Concord	8 00	15
Early Mammoth Sugar	8 00	15
Black Mexican	8 00	15
Amber Cream	8 00	15
Stowell's Evergreen	8 00	15
Egyptian or Washington Market	8 00	15
Adam's Early	7 00	15
Improved King Philip, Eastern grown	7 00	10
Early Canada	6 00	10
Early White Flint " "	5 00	10
Large Yellow Eight-rowed " "	5 00	10
Pop Corn (Rice and Common		10

Sweet Corn for fodder and Common Yellow and White Field Corn, or any of the above in Quantity, at lowest market rates.

Artichoke.

	Per oz.	Per lb.
Green Globe	$0 30	$3 00
Jerusalem Tubers, $5 00 per 100 pounds.		

Two pounds for 25 cents of Peas, Beans and Corn, when quoted at 15 cents per single pound.
TWENTY-FIVE POUNDS AND OVER WILL BE SOLD AT 100 POUND RATES.

Asparagus.

	Per oz.	Per lb.
Palmetto......	$0 15	$1 25
Colossal, largest and best..................	10	60

Two-year-old roots, $1 50 per hundred.

Beets.

	Per oz.	Per lb.
Extra Early Eclipse, new and fine..........	$0 10	$0 60
Extra Early Egyptian......................	10	50
Extra Early Bassano......................	10	50
Dewing's Early Blood Turnip..............	10	60
Early Blood Turnip......................	10	50
Early Long Dark Blood....................	10	50
Bastian's Half Long Dark Blood...........	10	60
Mangel Wurzel, or Stock Beet.............	10	25
Improved Long Red Mangel Wurzel........	10	35
Norbiten Giant Mangel...................	10	35
Yellow Globe Mangel.....................	10	32
Red Globe Mangel.......................	10	35
Improved White Sugar....................	10	25
Swiss Chard............................	10	75

Brussels Sprouts.

	Per oz.	Per lb.
Improved Dwarf........................	$0 15	$1 50

Brocoli.

	Per oz.
Early Purple Cape..................................	$0 40
Early White Cape.................................	40

Cabbage.

	Per oz.	Per lb.
Early York Dwarf......................	$0 15	$1 25
Early Large York.....................	15	1 25
Early Oxheart, finest.................	15	1 25
Henderson's Early Summer.............	15	1 50
Jersey Early Wakefield...............	15	1 50
Early Bloomedale Market..............	15	1 50
Early Winingstadt...................	15	1 50
Early Dwarf Dutch...................	15	1 50
Early Drumhead or Battersea..........	15	1 50
Premium Flat Dutch..................	15	1 50
Premium Drumhead...................	15	1 50
Stone Mason........................	15	1 50
Mammoth Marblehead.................	15	1 50
Improved Brunswick.................	15	1 50
German Fliderkraut.................	15	1 50
Savoy Drumhead....................	15	1 50
Savoy Early Dutch..................	15	1 50
Red Dutch Pickling.................	15	1 50

Carrot.

	Per oz.	Per lb.
Early Scarlet Horn....................	$0 10	$1 00
Earliest Short Horn, for forcing......	10	1 00
Danvers Orange, Half Long....	10	75
Early Half Long Scarlet, Stump Rooted......	10	75
Improved Long Orange..................	10	75
Large White Belgian..................	10	60
Large Red Altingham..................	10	60
St Vallery or Intermediat............	10	1 00
Emerande or Ox Heart.................	10	1 00

Cauliflower.

	Per oz.	Per lb.
Henderson's Early Snowball..........	$2 50	$....
Extra Early Dwarf Erfurt selected.....	1 00	....
Early London........................	60	6 00
Early Parls, best....................	75	7 00
Large White French..................	75	7 00
Lenormand's Short Stem..............	75	7 00
Large Asiatic.......................	50	5 00
Veitch's Autumn Giant...............	50	5 00
Half Early Paris or Nonpareil........	75	7 00
Large Late Algeriers................	75	7 00

Celery.

	Per oz.	Per lb.
Self Blanching........	$0 25	3 00
Henderson's White Plume.............	25	3 00
Henderson's Dwarf...................	15	1 50
Golden Heart.......................	15	1 50

	Per oz.	Per lb.
Large White Solid......................	15	1 50
Dwarf White Solid.....................	15	1 50
Boston Market........................	15	1 50
Celeriac or Turnip Rooted..............	15	1 50
Celery Seed, for flavoring.............	15	1 50
CHERVILL............................	$0 10	$1 00
COLLARDS............................	10	1 00
CHICORY (large rooted)................	10	1 00
CORN SALAD..........................	10	1 00

Cress or Peppergrass.

	Per oz.	Per lb.
Broad Leaf............................	$0 10	$0 75
Fine Curled...........................	10	75
Fine Water Cress......................	40	....

Cucumbers.

	Per oz.	Per lb.
Extra Long White Spine................	$0 10	$1 00
Early Russian.........................	10	1 00
Improved Early White Spine...........	10	1 00
Early Frame..........................	10	1 00
Early Short Green....................	10	1 00
Nichols' Medium Green...............	10	1 00
Early Green Cluster..................	10	1 00
Early Boston Pickling................	10	1 00
Improved Long Green.................	10	1 00
Burr Small Gherkins..................	20	2 00
Giant Pera...........................	15	1 25
Snake or Serpent.....................	25	2 50
Siberian..............................	30	3 00

Egg Plant.

	Per oz.	Per lb.
Early New York Purple..................	$0 50	$5 00
Early Long Purple......................	30	3 00
Early Black Peakin.....................	50	5 00

Endive.

	Per oz.	Per lb.
Green Curled..........................	$0 15	$1 50
Moss Curled...........................	15	2 50

Garlic.

The Price of Garlic is variable.

Kale, or Borecole.

	Per oz.	Per lb.
Green Curled Scotch...................	$0 10	$1 00
Dwf. German Green and Purple..........	10	1 00
Sea Kale..............................	25	3 00

Kohl Rabi.

	Per oz.	Per lb.
Early White Vienna....................	$0 20	$2 00
Early Purple Vienna...................	20	2 00
Large Green..........................	20	2 00

Leek.

	Per oz.	Per lb.
Broad London Flag....................	$0 15	$2 50
Monstrous Carentan....................	15	2 50

Lettuce.

	Per oz.	Per lb.
Hanson................................	$0 10	$1 00
Simpson's Early Curled...............	10	1 00
Early Prize Head.....................	10	1 00
White Paris Cos. Romaine Lettuce.....	10	1 00
Satisfaction.........................	10	1 00
Philadelphia Butter..................	10	1 00
Early White Head Cabbage............	10	1 00
Early Curled Silesia................	10	1 00
Large Drumhead or Ice Cabbage.......	10	1 00
Simpson's Black Seeded..............	10	1 00
All the Year Round..................	10	1 00
Boston Market—for forcing...........	10	1 00
Tennis Ball, Black Seeded—for forcing......	10	1 00
Salamander—for hot, dry weather	10	1 00
Deacon..............................	10	1 00
Bird Lettuce........................		30

Martynia.

	Per oz.	Per lb.
For making Pickles	$0 25	$3 00

Mushroom Spawn.

One Pound Bricks...............................$0 25

Musk Melon.

	Per oz.	Per lb.
Surprise	$0 10	$1 00
California Large Netted	10	1 00
White Japan	10	1 00
Hackensack	10	1 00
Early Yellow Canteloupe	10	1 00
Golden Gem	10	1 00
Montreal Market very large	10	1 00
Bay View	10	1 00
Skillman's Fine Netted	10	1 00
Large Green Nutmeg Citron	10	1 00
Cassaba, or Green Persian	10	1 00
Miller's Cream	15	1 25
Emerald Gem	15	1 25
Champion Market	15	1 25
Osage	25	2 00

Watermelon.

	Per oz.	Per lb.
Mammoth Iron Clad	$0 10	$ 75
Kolb's Gem	10	75
Scaly Bark	10	75
Black Spanish	10	75
Icing, or Ice Cream, Peerless	10	75
Mountain Sweet, or Gray Seeded Ice Cream	10	75
Mountain Sprout	10	75
Cuban Queen	10	75
Imperial Lodi, or California	10	75
Gypsy, or Rattlesnake	10	75
Orange Rind	10	1 25
Citron Melon, for preserves	10	1 00
Pride of Georgia	10	75
Florida Favorite	10	1 00
Hungarian Honey	15	1 50
Seminole	15	1 50
Green and Gold	15	1 50
The Volga	15	1 50

Nasturtium.

	Per oz.	Per lb.
Tall Sorts	$0 15	$1 50
Dwarf	15	1 50

Okra, or Gumbo.

	Per oz.	Per lb.
Early Dwarf	$0 10	$1 00
Tall Green	10	1 00

Onions.

	Per oz.	Per lb.
Early Large Red	$0 15	$1 50
Large Red Wethersfield	15	1 50
Yellow Danvers	15	1 50
Yellow Dutch Strasburg	15	1 50
White Portugal, Silver Skin	25	2 50
White Globe	25	2 50
Tripoli, White and Red	20	2 00
Giant Yellow Rocca	20	2 00
Early Queen	20	2 00

ONION SETS—Prices variable; lowest market rates.

Parsnips.

	Per oz.	Per lb.
Hollow Crown	$0 10	$0 75
Half Long Student	10	75

Parsley.

	Per oz.	Per lb.
Triple Curled	$0 10	$0 75
Plain Curled	10	75
Fern Leaf	10	75
Moss Curled	10	75

Pepper.

	Per oz.	Per lb.
Golden Dawn	$0 25	$2 50
Long Red Cayenne	25	2 50
Chili, very small for pepper sauce	25	2 50
Cherry Red	25	2 50
Large Squash, or Tomato sh'p	25	2 50
Large Bell, or Bull-nose	25	2 50
Sweet Spanish, or Mountain	25	2 50

Pumpkin.

	Per oz.	Per lb.
Large Yellow, or Conn. F'ld	$0 10	$ 35
Large Cheese, for table use	10	50
Cashaw, or Crookneck	10	50
Mammoth Tours	15	1 00
Japanese Pie	15	1 50
Tennessee Sweet Potato	15	1 50
Mammoth Etampes	15	1 50

Radish.

	Per oz.	Per lb.
Early Long Scarlet	$0 10	$ 75
Early Scarlet Turnip rooted	10	75
Early Scarlet Turnip White tip	10	75
Early White Turnip rooted	10	75
Olive shaped, or Half-long Scarlet	10	75
French Breakfast, or Half-long Scarlet, White Tip	10	75
Beck's Chartier	10	1 00
Scarlet China Winter	10	1 75
Black Spanish, Fall or Winter	10	75
White Strasburg Radish	10	1 00
Mammoth White China, or California	10	1 00
Earliest Carmine	10	1 00

Rhubarb, or Pie Plant.

	Per oz.	Per lb.
Linnaeus, Giant	$0 20	$2 00
Victoria, Giant	20	2 00

Two year roots, $2.50 per dozen, 25 cents each; one-year roots, $1.50 per dozen, or 15 cents each.

Salsify, or Vegetable Oyster.

	Per oz.	Per lb.
Best White	$0 15	$1 50
Scorzonera, or Black Salsify	20	2 00
Sandwich Island	20	2 00

Squash.

	Per oz.	Per lb.
Pineapple	$0 10	$1 00
Perfect Gem	10	1 00
Early Yellow Bush Scallop	10	75
Early White Bush Scallop	10	75
Yellow Summer Crookneck	10	75
American Turban	10	75
Marblehead	10	75
Boston or Vegetable Marrow	10	75
Hubbard	10	75
Mammoth, fine for exhibition	10	1 00
Sibley	15	1 50
Brazil Sugar	10	1 00
Field Squash		80

Spinach.

	Per oz.	Per lb.
Round Summer, or Large Dutch	$0 10	$ 35
Extra Large Prickly, Winter	10	35
Improved Thick Leaved	10	35
Monstrous Viroflay, extra large	10	35
Long Standing, Late Seeding	10	35
Bloomsdale	10	35

Sunflower.

	Per oz.	Per lb.
Mammoth Russian	$0 10	$0 50

Tobacco.

	Per oz.	Per lb.
Connecticut Seed Leaf	$0 40	$4 00
Virginia	40	5 00
Havana	50	6 00

Tomato.

	Per oz.	Per lb.
Early Conqueror	$0 20	$2 00
Acme	20	2 00
Livingston's Perfection	20	2 00
Paragon	20	2 00
Hathaway's Excelsior	20	2 00
General Grant	20	2 00
Sacremento Favorite	20	2 00
Mayflower	20	2 00
Fejee	20	2 00
Trophy	20	2 00
Large Yellow	20	2 00
Red Cherry	20	2 00

Tomato.

	Per oz.	Per lb.
Strawberry	40	4 00
Cardinal	20	2 00
Livingston's Favorite	20	2 00
Livingston's Beauty	20	2 50
Mikado	20	2 50
Optimus	20	2 50
Dwarf Champion	20	3 00

Ruta Baga Turnip.

	Per oz.	Per lb
Large White French	$0 10	$0 60
Sweet Russian, White	10	60
Sweet German White	10	60
Improved Purple Top Yellow	10	60
Skirving's Swede, Purple Top Yellow	10	60

Laing's Improved Yellow Early	10	60
Improved American Yellow Purple Toy	10	60

Turnip.

	Per oz.	Per lb.
Early Snowball	$0 10	$ 75
White Egg	10	75
Early Yellow Stone	10	60
Early White Flat Dutch, Strap Leaved	10	60
Early Purple Top, Strap Leaved	10	60
Early Purple Top, Munich	10	60
Large White Norfolk	10	60
Yellow Aberdeen Purple Top	10	60
Purple Top White Globe	10	60
Orange Yellow, or Golden Ball	10	60
Yellow or Amber Globe	10	60
Pomeranian White Globe	10	60
Long White or Cowhorn	10	60

Sweet and Medicinal Herbs, Etc.

A few herbs should have a place in every vegetable garden. A very small space will give all that are needed in any family. The culture is simple. Make a little seed-bed in the early spring, and set the plant out in a bed as soon as large enough.

	Oz.	Lb.		Oz.	Lb.
Anise	$0 10	$1 00	Henbane	$0 40	$
Angelica	25		Hyssop	25	3 00
Arnica	2 00		Hoarhound	30	
Balm	50		Lavender	25	2 50
Belladonna	75		Marjoram, Sweet	25	2 50
Borage	10	1 00	Marigold Pot	25	2 50
Basil (Sweet)	25	3 00	Opium Poppy	20	2 50
Boneset	1 00		Pennyroyal	75	
Bene	20		Rosemary	40	
Caraway	10	50	Rue	40	
Catnip	75		Savory, Summer	25	2 50
Coriander	10	50	Savory, Winter	25	2 50
Cumin	10	1 00	Saffron	15	1 50
Dandelion	25	2 50	Sage, Common	20	2 00
Dill	10	50	Sorrel, Broad-leaved	15	1 50
Elecampane	50		Tansy	50	
Fennel, Large Sweet	10	50	Thyme, English	40	4 00
Fenugreek	10	1 00	Wormwood	40	

The above are also put up in Five Cent packages of Fifty Cents per dozen.

Grass and Clover Seeds.

When sold in quantity, at much reduced rates and being subject to market fluctuations. Prices given on application.

Express or Freight charges must be paid by the purchaser, and when small quantities are wanted to be forwarded by mail, be sure to send money extra to cover postage.

Clover Seed.

	Per lb.			Per lb.
Alfalfa	$0 10	12½	Alsyke, or Sweedish Clover	$0 25
Mammoth or Saplin Clover	12½	15	Crimson Trefoil	50
Common, or Red Clover	12½	15	Yellow Trefoil	50
White Dutch Clover		25	Sanfoin, or Esparsette	15

Grass Seed.

	Per 100	Per lb.		Per 100	Per lb.
Lawn Grass, Best Mixed	$20 00	$0 30	Timothy Grass Seeds	$7 00	$0 10
Lawn Grass, Extra Fancy Blue	25 00	30	Red Top Grass Seeds	9 00	15
Lawn Grass, Kent'ky Ex. Cl. Blue	15 00	20	Masquite Grass Seeds	9 00	15
Sweet Vernal Grass		50	Orchard Grass Seeds	15 00	20
Perennial Rye Grass	12 00	15	Evergreen Millet Grass	14 00	20
Australian Grass	10 00	15	German or Golden Millet Grass	8 00	10
Italian Grass	10 00	15	Egyptian or Pearl Millet		25
Fine Fescue Grass		50	Hungarian Grass	6 00	10
Meadow Fescue		50			

Miscellaneous and Field Seeds.

	Per 100	Per lb.			Per lb.
Amber Sugar Cane Seed	$6 00	$ 10	Castor Oil Beans		25
African Seed	6 00	10	Hemp Seed		10
Egyptian Corn, White	2 50	5	Flax Seed		10
Egyptian Corn, Red	2 00	6	Canary Seed		10
Buckwheat	2 50	5	Mixed Bird Seed		10
Sun Flower Seed	20 00	50	Rape Seed		10
Vetches	6 00	10	Bird Lettuce		30
Lentils	6 00	10	Cuttle Fish Bone		75
Broom Corn	2 00	5	Maw, or Poppy seed		30

Bird Seed.

Canary, Hemp, Rape, Millet and Mixed Bird Seeds, 6 pounds for 50 cents, 14 pounds for $1 00.

SEEDS OF SPECIAL MERIT.

PERFECTION WAX BEANS.

The habit of this plant is clean, uniform and vigorous. Built to produce an immense crop, and able to sustain and perfect the crop to perfection. The pods are long and beautifully filled, color a golden yellow, and free from rust. Tender, stringless and of a rich buttery flavor. Price ½ lb. 15c.; lb. 25c.

Parties wishing this variety should order early as our stock is limited.

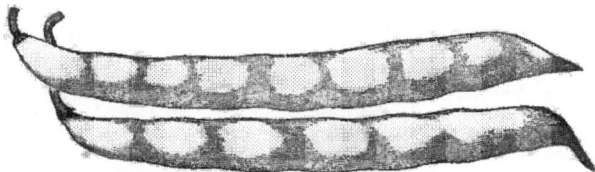

WARDELL'S KIDNEY WAX BEANS

The most valuable point, in its favor, is that it has not yet shown the slightest indication of rust or spot, no matter where or under what condition grown. It is greatly superior to the well-known Drawf German Black Wax or Golden Wax sorts, being nearly a week earlier and yielding a third greater. The vines are remarkably vigorous, hardy and productive; the pods are very large, smooth and showy, and will sell when all other varieties will be refused, they are tender, perfectly stringless and of unusually fine quality. The entire pod assumes a rich golden color at a very early stage of growth—a very important feature which no other sort does. The dry beans are white, with two shades of reddish purple more or less visible, and a distinct kidney shape. Prepared for the table, it has a fine buttery flavor, and is destined to become the leading snap bean, as well as a strongly endorsed winter shelled sort. Price ½ lb., 15 cts.; lb. 25c.

---o---

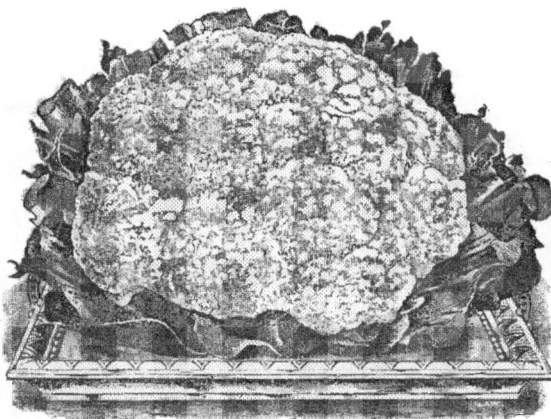

Early Snowball Cauliflower.

EARLY SNOWBALL CAULIFLOWER.

There is no vegetable in which the quality of the seed is of more vital importance than the Cauliflower, and none in which it is more difficult to secure the best. During the past five years we have had samples from the best growers of this country and Europe planted on our trial grounds, and have carefully studied them, and as a result present our stock of Snowball Cauliflower as *the very best in existence.* The plants are drawf and compact, and with fair treatment every one will form a good head. Our customers can plant this seed with the assurance of getting as good heads and as early as from any sort that is offered, for we have spared no pains to discover and secure the best without regard to cost. Pkt. 20c. oz. $2.50.

NEW GOLD COIN SWEET CORN.

This is a remarkably distinct and handsome variety. Its enormous productiveness is enough to place it in advance of any sort now grown; almost always yielding two, and frequently three, mammoth ears to the stalk. It is sweeter, more delicate in flavor, and ten days earlier than the Stowell,s Evergreen. The cob is snowy white, compactly covered with large, deep grains. Perhaps its most valuable characteristics ies in the fact that it is evergreen to an unprecedented degree. Last season the great bulk of the crop could have been gathered at any time during a period of four weeks, and have been found in perfect condition for table use. This is a very important quality to market gardeners. ¼ lb. 15c., lb. 25c.

EDMUND'S BLOOD TURNIP BEET.

This we recommend above all others, for family or market use, as a second early and late variety. Of handsome round shape, skin very deep blood-red; flesh very dark, and exceedingly sweet and tender. Grow regularly, of good marketable size, not over-large and course as many sorts of turnip beets when they have plenty of room. They mature early, give the very best satisfaction as a bunch beet in the markets. Grow with small top, making it very desirable for bunching, and will remain sweet and tender longer than any other sort.

GIANT PERA CUCUMBER.

This is one of the largest and best Long Cucumber in cultivation. The skin is perfectly free from spines, flesh clear, crisp and white. Price, oz. 15c.; lb. $1 25.

CELERY.

(White Plume.) The stalk and inner portions of the leaves and heart *are naturally white*, so that by closing the stalks, either by tying them together or by pressing the soil up against the plant with the hand, and again drawing up the soil with a hoe or plow, so as to keep the soil that has been squeezed against the Celery in place the work of blanching is completed. The great advantage of this over the slow and troublesome process of blanching required by the old sorts is evident. Its eating qualities are equal to the very best of the older sorts, being crisp, solid and of a pleasing nutty flavor, while its white feather-like foliage places it ahead of all others as a table ornament. Pkt. 5c. 1 oz. 25c. 1 lb. $3 00.

PERRY'S HYBRID.
Sweet Corn.

A very fine, new, early variety, fully as early as the Minnesota, and ears much larger, each containing twelve or fourteen rows of kernels, well filled to the end. The grains are very large and pure white, but the cob is rod. The ears are about the same lengths as Crosby's, but larger round, and are ready to market fully a week earlier. The stalks grow 5½ feet high, and the ears (2 to a stalk) are set about 2 feet from the ground. ¼ lb. 15c.; lb. 25c.

GOLDEN SELF-BLANCHING CELERY.

Close compact, handsome; heart beautiful golden-yellow, outer stalks yellowish-white, ribs perfectly solid, crisp, well-flavored and excellent keeper; very fine new celery, highly recommended. Price, oz. 25c., lb. $3 00.

SERPENT OR SNAKE CUCUMBER.

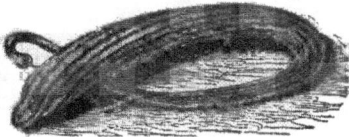

A remarkable and very interesting curiosity. The Cucumbers grow curled up like a snake with the head protruding, and sometimes are six feet in length. The Illustration will represent their shape, and although they attain great size, the quality is only fair; grown more as a curiosity than any thing else, and to exhibit at fairs. Can also be used for picking. Per pkt., 10c., postpaid.

SIBERIAN CUCUMBER.

Absolutely the earliest cucumber known. It is also a splendid free bearing variety, and for early forcing purposes or for slicing it is the most valuable addition ever made to our list of cucumber. Always grows straight and smooth flesh, extraordinary tender and crisp. Price, pkt., 10c. oz. 30c.; lb. $3 00.

NICHOL'S MEDIUM GREEN.

We consider this variety the most valuable sort that has been introduced since the advent of the Green Pro-

lific variety. As a pickle sort, Nichol's Medium Green will be found unequalled. and for early forcing purposes or for slicing, there is no better variety. It is exceedingly productive, of medium size, and always straight and smooth. The color is dark green, the flesh tender and crisp. (See Cut.) Oz. 10c. $1.00 lb

St. Vallery or Intermediate Carrot.

This we consider one of the best varieties grown. The size is about 12 inches long and 2½ inches in diameter. The color is a beautiful rich orange red. The roots grow very smooth and the flesh fine and even. The shape is between the Long Orange and the half long varieties. In light soil they grow especially fine. Price oz. 10c. lb. $1 00.

THE OSAGE MUSK MELON.

No variety of Musk Melon, so far as we are aware, has advanced in popularity and become at once so widely known as this variety. "Skin dark green, slightly netted on the lobes on the upper side, and on the best specimens a rich orange color where the melon lies on the ground, and on this side it is eatable within an eighth of an inch of the surface. The shape is pointed oval—egg shape most exactly expresses it. Medium sized, and the whole crop is very even and extra heavy owing to the thickness of the meat." Pkt., 10c.; 1 oz. 25c.; 1 lb. $2 00.

MILLER CREAM MUSK MELON.

This splendid melon was thoroughly tested the past season by many of our best market gardeners and melon growers, and is pronounced by all, one of the very best they have ever grown. The flesh is of a rich salmon color, very sweet and melting in quality, and is so very thick that the melon is almost solid, the seed cavity being remarkably small.

The rind is thin, slightly entured, but little netted. This vine is a strong grower and very productive, covering the ground with fruit. It is extremely sweet, rich and delicious and very distinct from any other. Seed is very scarce. Per oz. 15c. lb., $1 25.

Florida Favorite Watermelon. Finest table melon extant; oblong in shape, growing to very large size; rind dark, with light-green stripes; flesh light-crimson, very crisp and deliciously sweet; seed rather small and of light creamy-white color. Ripened the past season 10 days earlier than the Kolb Gem, Iron Clad, or Rattlesnake. We offer seed grown by originator. Pkt. 5c., oz. 10c., lb. $1 00.

---o---

Strong's Perfection Cabbage Lettuce.

We are offering this season for the first time our new *Perfection Lettuce*, and we feel certain that no variety ever introduced will give better satisfaction. This lettuce originated in one of the large vegetable gardens near this city. Being in the shipping business the shipment of winter and spring vegetables is a specialty with us. We therefore, have ample opportunity to test the merit of all vegetables, and it is a matter of vast importance to us to secure the best. This new lettuce was the largest, finest and best flavored we have ever seen, measuring 13 inches in diameter, of which 8 inches was solid head. We secured a small quantity of the seed from our market gardener, and have propagated and improved the strain ourselves, and out of numerous standard varieties in our Test Gardens last season, it *proved* itself *perfection*; eclipsing all other kinds for large size, solid crisp heads and delicate flavor. Our supply of seed is quite limited this season, and as we wish all of our customers to try it, we will in no case sell to any one party more than *two ounces*. Price der pkt. 25c., per oz. $1 00, two oz. $1 75.

Emerald Gem Musk Melon. The Emerald Gem Melon is certainly the most distinct and at the same time the most deliciously flavored Melon we ever came across. It is a very early and prolific variety, with a skin which, while it is ribbed, is perfectly smooth and of a deep emerald green color. The flesh, which is thicker than in most other melons, is of a suffused salmon color, exceedingly sweet and delicious; in fact, the variety is thick meated that it yields but little seed. Those seeking a Musk Melon for quality alone will find all they are looking for in the Emerald Gem. Price, 10c. pkt., oz. 15c. lb., $1 25.

CHAMPION MARKET.

Burpee's Hungarian Honey. Mr. Burpee says: "This new and superb variety was brought by us from Hungary in the summer of 1884, and after two years' thorough trial on a large scale, having had several acres of them growing the past season, we can

positively state that it is decidedly the richest and sweetest flavored of all watermelons Pkt. 10c. |oz. 15c., lb. $1 50.

Champion Market. Is very productive, frequently bearing seven melons on a single vine, while on one vine we counted five melons set within a length of 22 inches. The melons mature early. It is an excellent shipper; and we consider it, unquestionably, the most profitable variety that can be grown for market. Price, 10c., oz. 15c. lb. $1 25.

NEW OAK-LEAVED LETIUCE.

A distinct and beautiful new variety which should be in every garden. Our illustrations will show the peculiar outline of the leaves, which are shaped like those of the oak. The heads are compact, crisp and tender, and entirely free from that bitter taste peculiar to many sorts. Several of our market gardeners who tried it the past two seasons are much pleased with its many fine qualities. Pkt., 5c.; oz. 15c.; lb., $1 50.

Sibley Squash.

The flesh is solid, thick, a vivid, brilliant orange in color, and is possessed of rare edible qualities. The weight

ranges from 8 to 11 pounds. It ripens its fruit simultaneously with the Hubbard. A good shipper and long keeper. Pkt. 5c., oz. 15c., lb. $1.50.

New Japanese Pie Pumpkin.

After thoroughly testing this remarkable variety, we now offer it for the first time in America. It comes from Japan, and will unquestionably prove a valuable addition to our pie and cooking pumpkins. The flesh is *very thick*, nearly solid, the seed cavity being very small in one end of the pumpkin, unusually *fine-grained dry and sweet*, having much the same taste and appearance as sweet potatoes. They ripen early, keep well and produce largely. The seeds are peculiarly marked and sculptured in Japanese characters. Pkt. 10c., oz. 15c., lb. $1 50.

Green and Gold.

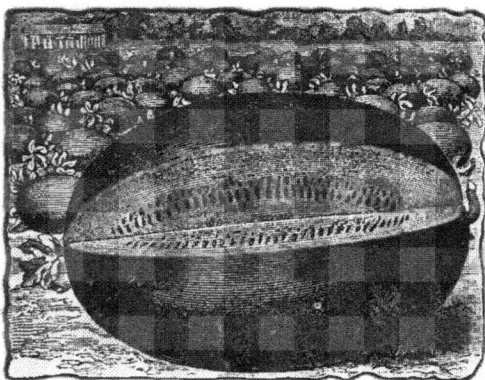

Green and Gold.

Is the largest early variety in cultivation, melons ranging from 25 to 45 pounds, and its productiveness is equal to any of the red-fleshed sorts, while in delicious flavor it surpasses them all. The rind is the thinnest of any melon, the white being only 3-8 to 1-2 an inch in thickness. The flesh is a beautiful golden orange color, free from any tinge of white or other color, even immediately around the seeds. The flesh is beautifully granular in appearance, juicy and sweet, and as we have already stated, of unequalled flavor. Coupled with the delicious flavor of the Green and Gold Watermelon, its rich golden color will make it most desirable as an ornament for the table, especially if its golden slices are arranged in contrast with the crimson of the other sorts. Pkt., 10c., oz. 15c., lb. $1.50.

Seminole. This new variety originated in the home of melons—Florida—and is said to be quite an acquisition. The following description is by the originator; Oblong in shape, smooth, and beautifully proportioned, it is of two colors, gray and light green; the latter seems to be just a darker coloring of the former; the gray greatly predominates. Melons of both colors are found on the same vines. Melons of both colors are exactly the same in shape, size, color of seed, flavor, etc.

This melon possesses four qualities which will make it the most popular ever offered to the public. It is *extra early, extra large, enormously productive, and of most delicious flavor.* Pkt. 10c., oz. 15c., lb. $1 50.

The Volga Watermelon. Is cultivated on the lower Volga, near the Caspian Sea, for shipment in barrels to St. Petersburg and Moscow. In solidity and hardness it is remarkable, and therefore carries well. In productiveness it surpasses most sorts, two melons being sometimes borne at adjacent joints of the same vine. In form it is nearly perfectly globular. In color it is so pale green as to be nearly white, with nearly imperceptible stripes. Although so solid and hard, the rind is not thick. The flesh is remarkably crisp, and when fully ripe, very sweet, luscious and red in color. Pkt. 10c., oz. 15c., lb. $1 50.

New Large Flowering Verbena.

Verbena Hybrida Grandiflora. In our extra fine mixed Verbena we thought we had the finest Verbena seed known, but are free to admit that this new strain offered last year for the first time, is superior, both in size of flowers and cluster. In the Grandiflora the flowers are of unusual size, many single flowers being as large as a twenty-cent piece, while the clusters of some are magnificent. Plants from seed of the Grandiflora grown alongside of the New Mammoth Verbenas, were pronounced equal in size and beauty of flowers, while the range of color is much more varied. Verbenas are so easily raised from seed that we are sure this new large, flowering strain will immediately become very popular. To place it within the reach of all, we offer it as low as it can be sold, and are sure that all purchasers will be delighted with it. Per pkt , 15 cents.

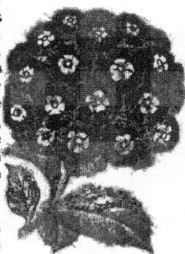

Brazil Sugar.

This new variety, originally from South America, has been thoroughly tested in the United States the past two years, and is pronounced by critical growers a most valuable acquisition to our list of summer and autumn squashes. The flesh and skin are of a bright yellow color, slightly warted. As its name indicates, it is one of the sweetest of all squashes, the flesh being unusually fine-grained and tender, so much so that it is palatable even when eaten raw. They reach a weight of three to four pounds each, ripen early, and grow so vigorously that they are but little affected by the squash-bug. Pkt., 5c., oz., 10c., lb. $1 00.

True Tennessee Sweet Potato Pumpkin.

Although not entirely new, we think so highly of this splendid pie and cooking pumpkin, that we have made a specialty of it. They grow to medium size, slightly ribbed; skin is a creamy white, lightly striped with green, flesh very thick creamy-white, dry and fine grained; when cooked resemble sweet potatoes, but much more delicious in taste. The vines are hardy and enormously productive. Pkt. 10c., oz. 15c., lb. $1 50.

Earliest Carmine Forcing Radish.

The earliest variety in cultivation; valuable alike for forcing or general sowing. It is the earliest strain for forcing or outside planting, and is used extensively around New York for forcing purposes with great success. Pkt. 10c., oz. 15c., lb. $1 00.

Mammoth Etampes Bright Red Pumpkin

We have imported the seed of this giant variety from France, where it is quite celebrated. It has been grown in this country to enormous size; it is of a bright, glossy red color, and makes a splendid variety to grow for exhibition purposes. Pkt. 10c., oz. 15c., lb. $1 50.

New Giant Mammoth Zinnias.

A particularly fine new class of Zinnias, differing from the older ones from its unusually robust habit of growth and the immense size (five to six inches across) of its perfectly formed, very double flowers of various striking colors. The plants rise to a height of three to three and a quarter feet, are clothed with a luxuriant foliage, and bloom freely during a long period. Being of great non-existence, the flowers are un-influenced by heat and remain in good condition for several weeks. The luxurious growth and the large bright flowers of this novelty make it particularly valuable for large groups, but it will also be found most effective when planted singly or as a border plant in small gardens, and it will undoubtedly soon become a general favorite. All colors mixed. Per Pkt., 10c.

Two new varieties of Phlox "Star of Quedlinburg" and 'Fimbriata." These new Phloxes with their sharply fringed and toothed flowers are really great novelties. From the singularity and gracefulness of the flowers, they are ornaments in any garden. Of easy cultivation and beautiful as cut flowers. Both varieties including many colors mixed. Per pkt. 15 cts.

Star of Quedlinburg.

The Mikado Tomato.

The largest early variety in cultivation; certainly no more distinct or valuable Tomato has ever been introduced. One of the most remarkable features about this variety is the fact that, notwithstanding that it produces perhaps the largest fruit of any sort in cultivation, it is at the same time one of the very earliest to ripen; generally we find that we secure earliness at the expense of size, but the *Mikado Tomato* seemingly reverses the rule. The *Mikado* differs from all other Tomatoes in its immense size, and the Tomatoes are produced in immense clusters, are perfectly solid, generally smooth, but sometimes irregular. The color is purplish red, like that of the Acme, while the variety has all the solidity that characterizes the Trophy. It is not unusual for single fruits of this variety to weigh from 1 to 1½ lbs. each. The foliage of the *Mikado Tomato* alone shows the distinctiveness of the variety, for it is whole or entire, while in all other varieties the leaves are cut or serrated. Whether for slicing or for cooking purposes, the variety is unsurpassed. Price, pkts., oz. 20c., 1b , $3 00.

---o---

Dwarf Champion Tomato.

This is without doubt one of the best Tomatoes for market gardeners. It is also a good variety for family use. The plant grows stiff and upright with very thick and short stems, dwarf and compact. It ripens very early and yields enormously. It is of exceedingly fine flavor, smooth and solid. Price, oz. 20c., 1b. $3.

MILLO MAIZE OR BRANCHING DHORMA.

This variety is from South America. It is much superior to the Egyptian or Rice varieties, being much earlier and producing wonderfully. It has been grown near Sacramento, and from a single seed four and five stalks have been produced averaging five large heads 8 inches long, loaded with seed. It is a valuable forage plant and can be cut at any stage for feed, and shoots up again rapidly; cured when heading for dry fodder and cattle eat it ravenously. Five to eight pounds per acre. 10c. per lb., 10 lbs. 50c. Per 100, $3.

Tomato. Livingston's Beauty.

An excellent variety of large size and beautiful appearance. The color is glossy crimson with a slight purplish tinge. It grows in clusters of four and five, retaining its large size late in the season; very solid with a tough skin, making it very desirable for marking and shipping. Pkt., 5c., oz., 20c., 1b. $2 50.

FLOWER NOVELTIES FOR 1891.

THREE NEW ASTERS—HARLEQUIN, TRIUMPH AND COMET.

Harlequin. A peculi r va-ri ty of n oddly spotted and striped flowers of striking beauty, entirely distinct from all o ers. Of upright habit. Medium height and profuse blossoming. Price pkt. 15cts.

Triumph. Deep scarlet changing to a lake crimson. This is without doubt the most beautiful and p r ect of all dwarf asters. Each plant forms an elegant b uquet of itself. 7 o 8 inc as high. The flowers nea ure fro 2½ to 3 inches in diameter, and are of faultile s Paeony form. Pkt. 25cts.

Triumph.

Comet. Differing from all o hers in shape of flo e s, its l ng, w vy and twisted petals are formed into a dense, half globe rese bling the Japanese Chrysanthemums, each pet l a delicate pink margined with white. Pkt. 20 cts.

Ostrowskia. Bokhara Bell Flower. (Ostrowskia Mag nifica.) This new "Bell F ower" is a hardy perennial herbaceous plant (flowering he second season from seed) stately and beautiful. It forms a tall bush 3 to 5 feet igh, surmounted with enormous ell-shaped flowers of an exquisite lave der shade, veined with purple. Every lover of flowers should have it. Pkt. 25 cts.

Comet.

NEW LARGE FLOWERING SWEET PEAS.

Eckford's Hybrid.

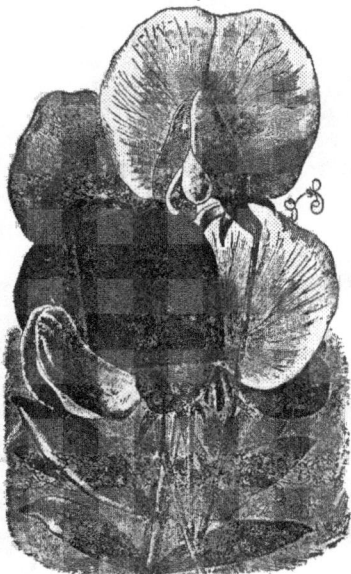

These new varieties produce flowers in prof sion of more perfect form, nearly double the size, of greater substance and brighter colors thau the older sorts. Cut the lossoms freely if you w sh them to bloom ALL summer. If allowed to go to seed they will stop blooming, so cut all the flowers you can. Excellent varieties for keeping in bouque s. Fine mixe . Pkt. 15 cts.

MELILOTUS. Spike Clover.

A native of Klamath River, California, is found growing on the bars and its banks up to high water mark. The seed having been deposited by the freshets, grows among the cobbles in the gravel, slickens and sand; yields an immeuse amount of feed for stock, and attains a height of 10 to 12 feet. The first year it keeps green, and grows the entire season. The second year it produces seed, maturing iu September and October. It has the clover leaf, white blossoms borne on a spike, a bushy growth, and the characteristic sweet clover fragrance. Per lb. 15c , per 100 lbs. $12.50.

Japan Clover. (*Lespedeza Striata.*) This highly appreciated species of clover is by no means a new discovery, but it is only lately that the seed has been gathered in quantities for sale. It ranks far above red clover in nutritive value, and is by analysis 72 per cent. Being of dwarfish habits on most soils, yet on rich lands it reaches a height of two feet and makes the best kind of hay. Also for the renovating of lauds it equals the best of clovers. For live stock it is almost a complete food. The seed is yet scarce, thirty cents per pound in quantity. Ten pounds are sufficient for one acre, as it spreads very rapidly.

Texas B uegrass Seed. (*Poa Arachnifera.*) A new winter grass which is fast being introduced into the Southern States. It is much superior to the Kentucky Bluegrass because of its long roots, which will go four or five times as deep for moisture. It makes a beautiful lawn for winter, and when grown with the Bermuda makes a lawn which lasts the whole year. It is hardy and can be planted at any time of the year, but midsummer. The price is 50cts. per oz., $5 per pound. Postage paid.

PEAS. Pride of the Market.

One of the best sweet peas grown. They are at least one week earlier than the well known Strata-gem, but resembling it in habit of growth; the foliage and pods are however, of a deeper green, the pods are 5 to 7 inches in length fil ed with large and fine peas. Price per ¼ lb. 10c., per lb. 15c.

CLEVELAND'S ALASKA

THE QUICKEST PEA ON RECORD.

Cleveland's Alaska Peas. We consider this the earliest, most prolific and finely flavored variety grown. We planted in our grounds and had peas fit for the table in 45 days. Height 2½ feet.

Cleveland's Improved Round Pod Valentine Beans.

HENDERSON'S NEW BUSH LIMA BEAN.

Thousands have been deterred from cultivating the most delicious of Vegetables, the Lima Bean, from the great trouble and expense of procuring the unsightly poles which were required on which to grow them. This is now a thing of the past, as the HENDERSON'S NEW BUSH LIMA grows without the aid of stakes or poles, in compact bush form, about 18 inches high, and produces enormous crops of delicious Beans, which can be as easily gathered as the common garden Bush Beans. They are at least TWO WEEKS EARLIER than any of the climbing Limas. This fact alone would stamp it as the most valuable novelty of recent years, but when in addition to this, we realize that it is a true BUSH BEAN, requiring no supports, some idea of its great value can be realized. HENDERSON'S BUSH LIMA produces a continuous crop from the time it comes into bearing until frost, and being enormously productive, a very small patch will keep a family supplied all summer. ¼ lb., 15c., lb. 25c.

Cleveland's Improved Round Pod Valentine Beans is ten days earlier than the Red Valentine and much more prolific and combines all its good qualities. We recommend this as one of the very best for market gardeners and general cultivation.

W. R. STRONG COMPANY
SPECIAL LIST OF
Vegetable Plants AND Esculent Roots.

Several seasons ago we added to our list of specialties, the growing of vegetable plants; with each year our demand has so increased that we have been obliged to put a larger area under glass for the purpose of forwarding the plants for the benefit of our customers wishing to plant early.

On most of the varieties listed below we have grown our own seeds realizing the importance to our customers of obtaining the very best to be had, many seeds have been greatly improved by saving seed from the finest specimens of vegetables. We can safely say our plant establishment is the most complete on the Coast.

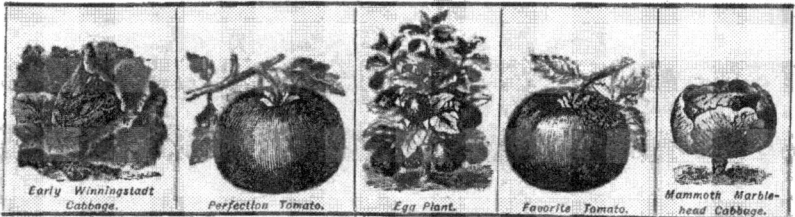

Early Winningstadt Cabbage.   Perfection Tomato.   Egg Plant.   Favorite Tomato.   Mammoth Marblehead Cabbage.

Asparagus Roots, Conovers Colossal, 2 years old...$1.50 per 100.
Special prices on large lots.
Artichokes, Jerusalem tubers...$5 00 per 100 lbs.
Hop Roots....................................$1.50 per 100, $10.00 per 1,000.

Cabbage Plants.
Ready about December 1st.

	Per 100.	Per 1,000.
Early Winningstadt	$0 40	$3 00
Early Summer	40	3 00
Early Ox Heart	40	3 00
Large Flat Dutch	40	3 00
Large Late Drumhead	40	3 00

Cauliflower Plants.
Ready about December 1st.

	Per 100.
Early Snowball	$1 00
Early Paris	1 00
Late Dutch	1 00

Egg Plants.
Ready in March and April.

	Per doz.	Per 100.
New York Purple	$0 25	$2 00
Black Pekin	25	2 00

Pepper Plants.
Ready in March and April.

	Per doz.	Per 100.
Large Bell	$0 25	$2 00
Sweet Mountain	25	2 00

Rhubarb Roots.
2 and 3 years old.

	Per doz.
Mammoth Linneaus	$3 00

Special prices on lots of 100.

Celery Plants.
Ready in March.

	Per doz.	Per 100.
Large White Solid	$0 25	$1 00
White Plume	25	1 00

Horse Radish Roots.
Per 100.....................................$........

Onion Sets.
Scarce. Prices on application.

Sweet Potato Plants.
Ready March 1st.

	Per 100.	Per 1000.
Yellow Carolina	$0 50	$4 00

We grow immense quantities of these plants and shall be prepared to supply all orders at short notice.

Tomato Plants. Ready about March 1st.

Put up in boxes of 50 to 100 plants each. We make a specialty of tomato plants, and can always supply in their season well grown stalky plants of the best known varieties.

All seed of Perfection, Sacramento Favorite, Livingston Beauty, Dwarf Champion, Mikado, New Boss, Etc., grown by ourselves and Seed, is of choicest selection.

Special New Kinds.
ACME, MIKADO, SELECTED, PERFECTION, NEW DWARF CHAMPION, NEW BOSS, LIVINGSTON BEAUTY, SACRAMENTO FAVORITE.
Per dozen, 20 cents. Per 100, $1.00.

Special Prices.
On all kinds of plants furnished on application on all orders aggregating from 1,000 to 10,000 plants.
In all cases we will ship plants by express in small quantities, unless otherwise ordered.

W. R. STRONG COMPANY.

W. R. STRONG COMPANY'S

DESCRIPTIVE LIST OF

VEGETABLE SEEDS

We examine all new varieties of vegetables, etc., but do not include them in our list unless they are proved, after thorough test, to be of superior excellence. We have no hesitation in saying that our Seeds cannot be excelled in quality and freshness by any other collection.

The following list will cover all varieties needed for successful gardening:

Artichoke.

Culture.—Sow in seed bed early in spr'ng, in drills twelve inches apart. When one-year-old transplant to permanent bed spaded deep, and dressed with rotten manure, ashes and a little salt, then plant them about two feet apart. The edible portion is the undeveloped flower heads, which should be used before they begin to open, and then cut to the ground, for if the flowers expand they weaken the plants. In the fall cover with manure which should be spaded in the following spring, taking care not to injure the plants. The crop is the largest and best the second year, after which the bed should be renewed by seed or enokers.

Globe Artichoke.

Large Globe. —the best sort for general use. Buds large nearly round; scales deep green, shading to purple, very thick and fleshy.

Jerusalem.—A hardy and productive plant, used for pickling and feeding stock. Strong tubers. Per 100 lbs. $5 00.

Jerusalem.

Asparagus.

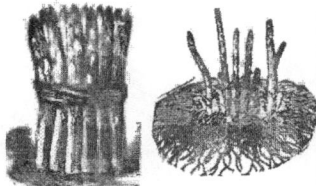

Asparagus is one of the earliest spring vegetables and would be in universal use were it not for the prevalent idea that it is difficult to grow it. There is no vegetable on our list that can be produced so cheaply and easily. It delights in a moist, sandy soil, but can be grown in any garden by following the directions. A bed 12x40 feet requiring 75 to 100 plants, give an abundant supply for an ordinary family.

Culture.—Beds are usually formed by setting plants one or two years old, which can be procured of us. If you wish to grow them yourself, prepare a light, rich spot early in the spring, and after soaking the seed twenty-four hours in warm water, sow in drills one foot apart.

Giant Collossal Asparagus.

When the plants are well up, thin two or three inches in the row, and give frequent and thorough cultivation during the summer. The plants will be fit to eat the next spring. The permanent beds should be prepared by deep spading, working in a large quantity of rotted manure. Dig trenches four feet apart and twelve to eighteen inches deep, and spade in at least four inches of well rotted manure in the bottom. Set the plants two feet apart in this trench and cover with two inches of fine soil. After the plants are well started give frequent and thorough cultivation, and draw a little earth in the trenches at each hoeing until they are filled. Early the next spring spade in a dressing of manure, and one quart of salt to each square rod, and cultivate well until the plants begin to die down. The bed may be cut one two or three times, *all* the short shoots above the surface should be cut, and after final cutting, give a good dressing of manure, ashes and salt. Ever after that, the bed should give a full crop if annually dressed with manure, ashes and salt. As soon as the tops are ripe and yellow they should be cut and burned.

Conover's Colossal.—A mammoth sort frequently sending up fifteen to thirty sprouts from one to one and a half inches in diameter from a single plant, and spreading less than most sorts. Color deep green; quality good.

Palmetto.—It is of very large size, even and regular in growth and appearance. It is a very early sort and highly recommended by Southern market men.

Broccoli.

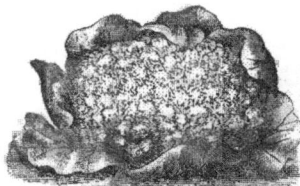

White Cape Broccoli.

Produces heads in autumnlike a Cauliflower. Sow about the middle of April; trans plant in rich soil and manage as winter Cabbage. For an early crop sow in a hot-bed and cultivate as early Cauliflower. It succeeds best in a moist soil and cool climate; can be had in perfection from November to April.

Early Purple Cape.—This is the best for the Northern States, producing compact heads, of a brownish purple, and of good flavor.

White Cape.—Not as early as the above; heads large, creamy white; close and certain to head.

Brussels Sprouts.

This is one of the best vegetales for winter use, producing from the axils of the leaves an abundance of sprouts resembling small cabbages, of excellent mild flavor.

Brussels Sprouts.

Beans.

One pound will plant 50 feet of drill; 80 pounds one acre in drill.

DWARF SNAPS OR STRINGLESS.

All varieties of this class are tender, and do best in rather dry, light soil, and should not be planted till the ground is warm and can continue at intervals throughout the season. Plant 3 inches deep, in rows 2 feet apart. Keep well hoed, drawing the earth up to the stems while dry.

Early Improved Red Valentine is one of the very best leading sorts. Pods are round, fleshy and tender, and remain longer in a green state than most varieties. (Fig 8.)

Cleveland's Improved Red Pod Valentine is ten days earlier than the Red Valentine and much more prolific and combines all its good qualities. One of the best for market and gardeners.

White Valentine is a good short snap, and also desirable as a shell bean.

Red Eye, or **Early China** is largely cultivated in California by market gardeners, and is good either as a snap or dry shell bean.

Early Refugee is very productive and fine for spring snaps or for pickling. Used by market gardeners. (Fig. 2.)

Yellow Six Weeks is very early, productive and excellent for snap or shell.

White Kidney, or **Royal Dwarf** is an excellent green shell bean, and one of the best for baking. (Fig. 6.)

Golden Wax. This variety is quite early. Pods are long, brittle and entirely stringless, and of rich buttery flavor, and one of the very best for our Market Gardeners. (Fig. 3.)

German, or **Black Wax** is one of the best. Pods are of rich, waxy yellow when fit for use, and very tender and delicious. (Fig. 13.)

Early Mohawk is one of the hardiest varieties and will endure some frost. It is a good string bean, and is also desirable for pickling. (Fig. 4.)

Ivory Pod Wax are a white bean and earlier than the Black Wax. Pods are tender and stringless, and of a rich creamy flavor, and are ivory white.

Crystal White Wax are similar to the above—crisp, tender, and of the richest flavor. The pods develop quickly and retain their tenderness longer than any other sorts.

English Dwarf, or **Broad Windsor** is a very hardy kind and can be planted very early in the season, in good soil, in drills 5 feet apart. Pinch off tops as soon as the lower pods begin to fill. They are used only as shell beans.

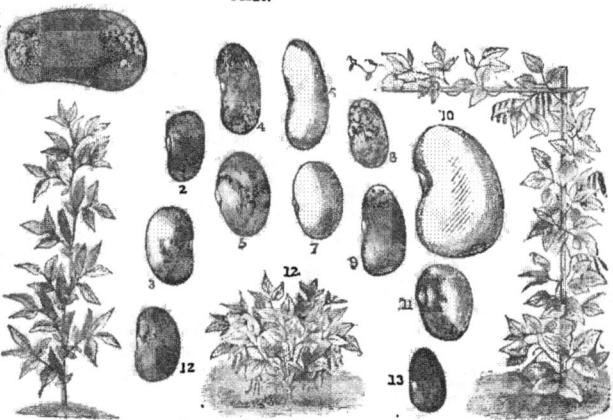

Beans. POLE, OR RUNNING. 1 pound to 75 hills.

These are generally more tender than dwarf kinds, and should not be planted till the ground becomes warm. Set poles about 4 feet apart, and pinch off the tops when they grow higher than the poles. They succeed best in sandy loam mixed with well rotted compost to each hill.

King of the Garden Lima.—When green, much larger in pod and bean than the ordinary Large Lima; vigorous, productive, handsome, popular, excellent; two vines will be sufficient for each pole.

Large Lima are the most buttery and delicious of all, and are a universal favorite, green or dry. (Fig. 10.)

Giant Wax (Red Seed) make pods 6 to 9 inches long, thick and fleshy, of yellow waxy color, and is very productive and tender. (Fig. 12.)

Horticultural, or Speckled Cranberry is an old favorite and is equally good as a snap or as a shell bean, either green or dry. (Fig. 5.)

White Dutch Runners are very ornamental, large white seed, and beautiful clusters of white flowers, and is a good shell bean.

Scarlet Runners are a great favorite, producing clusters of beautiful scarlet flowers, which are very ornamental. This is very fine for use as a green shell bean. (Fig. 14.)

Dutch Case-Knife. A very productive variety, and one of the earliest; sometimes used as "snaps," but generally shelled. Next to the Lima the best market sort.

Southern Prolific. Desirable for snap beans, mature in seventy days. Bears its pods in clusters. Popular in the South.

Asparagus, or Yard Long. Pod sometimes grows from two to three feet long; very curious, succulent and tender.

Perfection Wax.   } See Specialties.
Wardell's Kidney Wax. }

BEETS.

The soil best suited for Beet culture is that which is rather light and well enriched. Sow in drills one foot apart and 1 inch deep, as early as the ground can be worked; continue for a succession as late as the middle of July; when the plants are large enough thin out to stand 6 inches apart in the rows. The Sugar and Mangel Wurzel varieties are grown for feeding stock, and should be sown from April to June in drills 2 feet apart, and afterwards thinned out to stand 1 foot apart in the rows; keep well cultivated. One ounce will sow a drill fifty feet in length; five or six pounds are required for an acre.

Eclipse.

Eclipse. A very early, smooth, globe-shaped beet with small top and thin root; its skin an intense deep red, its flesh of very fine texture, earliness and quality it is excelled by none. Many of our Market Gardeners prefer it to the Egyptian.

Early Blood Turnip. An old standard variety of fine form and flavor. Next to Eclipse in earliness.

Dewing's Improved Blood Turnip. Roots deep blood-red, of fine form and flavor. Very early. An excellent market variety.

Pine Apple. The roots are half long, medium size; well formed and of very dark crimson color. Fine grained, sweet, tender and excellent for table use.

Long Dark Blood. Long, smooth, growing to good size; half out of the ground; color dark blood-red; top small, dark red, and of upright growth; keeps well. It is apt to be tough when sown too early.

Early Blood Turnip.

Dewing's Improved Blood Turnip.

Henderson's Pineapple

Long Blood.

Egyptian Blood Turnip.

Bassano.

☞ Don't forget to send for a package of Strong's Perfection Cabbage Lettuce and other Specialties.

Egyptian Turnip. A standard sort, being from ten to twelve days earlier than the Blood Turnip. The roots are large in size, and of a rich, deep crimson color. From the smallness of the tops of the Egyptian at least one-fourth more can be grown on the same space than any other variety.

Extra Early or Bassano. Turnip-shaped. An improved early kind, small top, round root, sweet and tender, attain a very large size.

Bastian's Half-Long Blood. Of bright color and excellent quality; a valuable variety to follow. The early sorts for winter use plant about the middle of July.

Edmund's Blood Turnip. See Specialties.

Mangel Wurtzel.—(For Field Culture.)

4 to 6 pounds to the acre. Extensively cultivated in all parts of the country as a field crop for feeding stock in the winter. When grown for this purpose, the distance between the rows should be from two to two and a half feet so that the cultivation can be done with horse tools instead of with hand-hoes.

Norbiton Giant. One of the finest quality in cultivation; grows to an enormous size.

Golden Tankard Mangel. Considered indispensable by the best dairymen, owing to its productiveness and richness in saccharine matter. Deep yellow flesh and skin.

Red Globe Mangel.

Yellow Ovoid

Imperial Sugar.   Orange Globe Mangel.   Golden Tankard Mangel.   Long Red Mangel.

Yellow Ovoid. A very nutritious and valuable variety; bulb ovoid; intermediate between the long and globe varieties; flesh solid, vigorous and productive.

Red Globe Mangel. A large red oval variety, which keeps well, and produces better crops on shallow soil than the Long Red.

Orange Globe Mangel. The same as the above, only differing in color.

Mammoth Long Red. grown extensively for agricultural purposes, producing large roots partly above the ground.

White Sugar Beet. The large amount of saccharine matter contained in this variety makes it very valuable for stock feeding purposes; grows to a large size.

Cabbage.

One ounce for about 2,000 plants.

Cabbages require a deep rich soil and thorough working. The seed for the early crops can be sown in hot beds When of size to transplant, place the earlier kinds from 12 to 18 inches apart. The largest and later kinds 2 feet or more. The plants should be set down to first leaf, so that the stem is all below the surface of the ground, and hoe often. Our seed is from the finest and purest selected strains of American growth.

Stone Mason.
An improved variety of Mason Drumhead, of sweet and tender quality.

Early Large York.
Is a popular known variety, superior, robust, and endures the heat well.

Large Late Drumhead.
Large Late Drumhead. A favorite winter variety with the market gardener. It bears extra large solid heads, and is a little later than the Flat Dutch.

Red Dutch.

Early French Oxheart. A leading variety among the market gardeners; heads very early, tender, and of fine flavor; or r seed is selected from extra fine stock.

Improved Premium Late Flat Dutch. This is the best strain of this

Large French Oxheart.

standard variety and more largely grown than any other for market and long-keeping quality. Short stem and large solid flat heads.

Excelsior Flat Dutch. This is a California variety and we consider it one of the best late sorts grown. The heads are large and compact, of a light green foliage. Valuable as a Winter cabbage, also for Fall use by sowing early.

Red Dutch. Used almost exclusively for pickling. It is one of the hardiest of all cabbages; will keep later in the season than any of them. Slow to mature, however, and requires a richer soil for its perfect development.

"True" Jersey Early Wakefield.

Early Jersey Wakefield. The *best early* Cabbage in cultivation. It possesses the merit of large size of head, small outside foliage, and uniformity in producing a crop.

Early Winningstadt. A second early variety, coming in about three weeks later than the early varieties. It is an excellent sort, as it

heads uniformly and is of large size, often weighing 20 lbs.; heads pyramidal, the outer leaves spiral and spreading, which necessitates planting it wider than the early sorts. One of the best for early shipments.

Early Winningstadt.

All Seasons. Similar in form to the Stone Mason; solid, compact; claimed to be as early and larger than the Henderson's Summer; comparatively new; wherever tried has given surprising satisfaction.

Marblehead. One of the latest and largest of the cabbage tribe. Solid, tender, and free heading.

Drumhead Savoy. The Savoy Cabbages are the finest flavor of all; finely crimped and netted and yet makes a compact, solid head. Dark green.

Mammoth Marblehead.

Henderson's Early Summer. Heads about ten days later than the Jersey Wakefield. It may be classed as the best *large early* Cabbage. In weight it is equal to most of the late varieties; its short outer leaves enable it to be planted as close as the Jersey Wakefield.

Filderkraut resembles the wellknown Winningstadt, but is larger, more pointed, and heads up with fewer outside leaves. Largely grown for making kraut.

Fottler's Improved Brunswick. A second early and late variety grown originally by the Boston gardeners, but which is now cultivated quite generally all over the country.

Early Dwarf Ulm Savoy. This is earlier and dwarfer than the Drumhead, and of very fine flavor.

Cauliflower.

CULTURE. Cauliflower ought to receive a similar treatment to Cabbage, except that it requires an extra rich soil, an occasional application of liquid manure and frequent watering, especially when heading. Early sorts are mostly sown in hot beds, and transplanted before setting out in open ground, and finally transplanted in rich deeply tworked soil, 2 ft. by 15 inches apart. Late sorts are sown and cultivated like late Cabbage. When heading tie the top leaves together to protect from exposure to the sun.

Early Dwarf Erfurt. Extra Early Dwarf, small leaf, solid, pure white heads, best quality.

Early Snowball. The earliest and best heading variety cultivated; dwarf habit and short outer leaves. (See among specials).

Early Paris. A popular French variety. White and sure to head, and standard sort for early or late crop.

Late Asiatic. Large, white and compact, but later than the preceding.

Large White French. A superior late sort of fine quality, with short stem and large well-formed heads.

Large Late Algiers. New, and much prized for late sort.

Veitch's Autumn Giant. This is one of the best late varieties grown. Robust habit, large heads, compact and thoroughly protected by leaves.

Celery.

One ounce will make about 2,000 plants.

Should be sown in open ground, as early as it will be fit to work, and be kept clear of weeds until ready for transplanting. Cut tops once or twice before to insure stocky plants. When ground is well prepared, set in rows three feet apart and six inches from each other, and see that the soil is well packed around the roots by pressing with the foot. Run the cultivator or hoe between the rows to destroy the weeds, and when grown to sufficient size draw up the earth for blanching, pressing with the hand to keep the leaf upright and banking up to the top on each side.

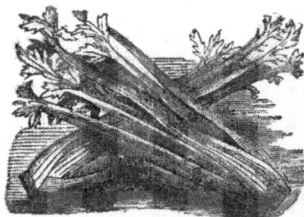

Henderson's White Plume. This requires less labor for blanching, is crisp, solid, and of nutty flavor and valuable for family use. (See Specials.)

Henderson's Half Dwarf. Solid, crisp, and nutty flavor and very desirable.

Boston Market Dwarf. Short, bushy, white, solid and excellent flavor.

Dwarf Golden Heart. The heart of this variety is waxy and showy, and for market use desirable. It is very solid and of excellent flavor, and a good keeper.

Giant White Solid.. Large size, solid, crisp, and good market variety.

Celeriac, or Turnip Rooted Celery. A variety with turnip shaped roots which may be cooked and sliced and used with vinegar, making an excellent salad. It is hardy and otherwise treated as other celery.

Giant White Solid

Soup Celery. Its seed is used for flavoring soups, stews, etc., and is sold for this purpose at a low price.

Self Blanching. See Specialties.

CARROT.

The Carrot like other root crops, delights in a sandy loam, richly tilled. For early crop sow in spring, as soon as the ground is in good working order; for later crops they may be sown any time until the middle of June. Sow in rows about fifteen inches apart, thinning out to three or four inches between the plants. In field culture, when grown for horses or cattle, the rows should be two feet apart, so that the crop can be worked by the Horse Cultivator. As Carrot seed is slow to germinate, all precautious must be taken.

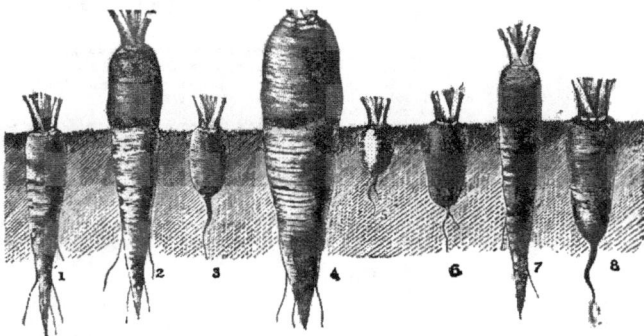

Early Scarlet Horn. A favorite sort for early crop, but not large enough for general culture. It is one of the varieties that is sold in the markets bunched up in the green state. It matures earlier than the Long Orange, and is some times need for forcing. No 3.

Half Long Red (Stump Rooted.) Largely grown for the market In size and time of maturity it is between the the Early Scarlet Horn and the Long Orange. No. 6.

Guerande, or Ox Heart. Intermediate in length, between the Early Horn and Half Long Varieties, and three to five inches in diameter. In quality it is extra good. Where other sorts require digging, Ox Heart can be easily pulled.

Large White Belgian. Grows one-third out of the ground; root pure white, green above ground, with small top; grows to a very large size and is easily gathered; flesh rather coarse, is raised exclusively for stock. No. 4.

Danvers. A very valuable sort; in form midway between the Long Orange and Early Horn class. It is of a rich shade of orange, growing very smooth and handsome. This variety will yield the greatest bulk with the smallest length of root of any now grown. Under the best cultivation it has yielded from twenty-five to thirty tons per acre. No. 8.

Improved Long Orange. The best late, deep orange colored variety, equally adapted for garden or farm culture. An improvement on the Long Orange, by careful selections of the best formed and deepest colored roots. No. 7.

Long Scarlet Altringham. A large, good flavored field variety, for table use or feeding stock. No. 2,

St Vallery or Intermediate. See Specialties.

Collard.

Is used in place of Cabbage, and grows where it is difficult to make Cabbage head. Cultivate same as Cabbage.

Chicory.

This is grown to mix with or as a substitute for coffee. It requires the same cultivation as Carrots.

Cress or Pepper Grass.

Well known as a pungent salad. It should be sown thickly and at frequent intervals for succession; it quickly runs to seeds. Cover very slightly in planting.

Double and Triple Curled. Is very fine and can be cut two or three times.

Water Cress. Is a perennial and will grow in and alongside of streams and ponds. It has a very pleasant-pungent taste.

CUCUMBER.

Cucumbers succeed best in warm, moist, rich loamy ground. They should not be planted in the open air until there is a prospect of settled warm weather. Plant in the hills about four feet apart each way. The hills should be previously prepared by mixing thoroughly with the soil of each a shovelful of well rotted manure. When all danger from insects is past, thin out the plants, leaving three or four of the strongest to each hill. The fruit should be plucked when large enough, as if left to ripen on the vines, it destroys their productiveness.

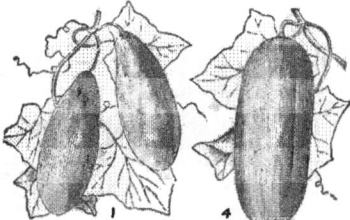

Early Russian.   Early Frame.

Improved Long Green.

Early Russian. Fruit three to four inches long, an inch an a half in diameter; generally produced in pairs; flesh tender, crisp and well flavored; comes into use about ten days earlier than any other variety, and makes a fine, small pickle.

Early Frame. Excellent variety for table use; tender and well flavored, and keeps green longer than any other variety; also makes splendid hard, green pickles, comes into use after the Early Cluster.

Extra Long White Spine. A variety used largely for forcing, by market gardeners. They grow ten to twelve inches long and very straight. They make fine, hard brittle pickles when four to five inches long; dark green and handsome.

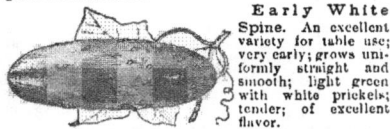

Early White Spine. An excellent variety for table use; very early; grows uniformly straight and smooth; light green with white prickels; tender; of excellent flavor.

Long Green Turkey. The leading long green variety for pickling, of excellent quality and productiveness, fruit dark green, firm and crisp.

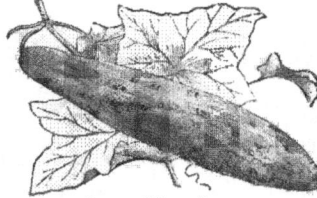

Improved Long Green. Undoubtedly the best variety in cultivation for table or pickling. About one foot in length, firm and crisp; this variety produces seeds sparingly.

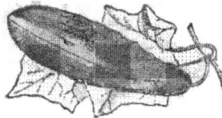

Nichol's Medium Green. For early forcing, late sewing for pickling, or for ordinary table use this variety will be found useful. It is of a dark green color, pleasant flavor, and very productive.

Early Cluster. Vines vigorous, producing the crop near the root and in clusters. Fruit short, dark green. Good for table use, but not adapted to pickling.

Boston Pickling, or Green Prolific. One of the best pickling varieties, dark green, tender, crisp, very productive, of fine flavor, uniform size, and good for table use.

Gherkin, for Pickling. A very small oval shaped, prickly variety. It is grown exclusively for pickling; is the smallest of all the varieties, and should always be pickled when young and tender. The seed is slow to germinate.

Giant Pera. }
Serpent.   } See Specialties.
Siberian. }

Corn—Sweet.

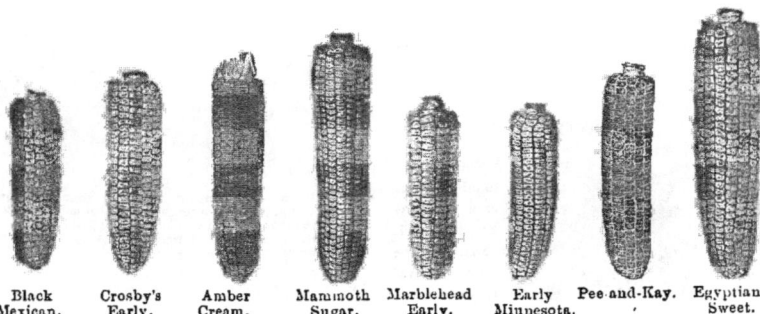

Black Mexican.   Crosby's Early.   Amber Cream.   Mammoth Sugar.   Marblehead Early.   Early Minnesota.   Pee-and-Kay.   Egyptian Sweet.

A rich, warm, alluvial soil is the best, and immediately before planting this should be as deeply and thoroughly worked as possible. Plant for a succession of crops every three weeks, in hills three feet apart each way, and six seeds in a hill. Cover about half an inch, thin out to three plants.

Pee and Kay. It has a very large, plump, sweet ear, and comes nearly as early as the Marblehead. The stalks are from six to seven feet high, with from two to three ears on the stalk, set well down, kernels large, plump, pearly white and sweet. We can recommend it highly.

Cory. The earliest of all sweet corns. It closely resembles the Early Marblehead, but earlier by at least a week. To market men, the Cory is a valuable variety, as the first sweet corn will bring double the price it commands when the supply becomes general.

Triumph. One of the earliest and best of the large varieties. The flavor is rich and sweet, kernels large and fine, and from 12 to 16 rows on each cob. One of the best for the market gardeners as well as for the family use.

Crosby's Early. Highly prized by market gardeners; very early; ears rather short, averaging from 12 to 16 rows; of a rich sugary flavor.

Amber Cream. 8-rowed; cream colored; height 4 feet; very sweet.

Marblehead Early. Larger than the Cory and a little later, it is a good early sort for the home garden and market gardeners.

Mammoth Sugar. Very large ears and very sweet.

Early Minnesota. Very early; a decidedly excellent variety; ears fair size and uniform; plant rather dwarf.

Black Mexican. Although the ripe grain is bluish-black, the corn, when in condition for the table, looks remarkably white, and is surpassed by none in tenderness. This by many, is considered the most desirable for family use of any of the second sorts.

Egyptian Sweet. Noted for its productiveness, large ears, and for sweetness and tenderness. It is peculiarly adapted for canning purposes. The superiority of often bringing a half more per can than other sorts. In rich ground the stalks will average 3 ears each. Its season is about the same as the Evergreen.

Stowell's Evergreen. The Standard late variety. If planted at the same time with earlier kinds, will keep the table supplied until October. It is hardy and productive, very tender and sugary, remaining a long time in a fresh condition, suitable for boiling.

Gold Coin.
Perry's Hybrid. } See Specialties.

Egg Plant.

New York Improved Egg Plant.

The Egg Plant will thrive well in any good garden soil; succeeds best in a deep, warm, rich soil and full exposure to the sun. Sow in hot bed very early in Spring; transplant two and one-half feet apart each way after weather becomes settled and warm. If no hot bed is at hand, plants may be started in pots or boxes.

New York Improved. The leading market sort, very large and smooth; fine dark color, very prolific and of excellent quality.

Early Long Purple. Much smaller than the New York Improved; very early and productive, fruit long, dark rich purple, good quality.

Black Pekin. The fruit of this variety is jet black, fine grain and delicate flavor; very prolific and desirable for market gardeners.

Endive.

One of the best salads for Fall and Winter use. Sow from late in the Spring to the middle of Summer, in shallow drills fourteen inches apart; thin the plants to one foot in drills, and when fully grown, tie over the outer leaves of a few plants every week or fortnight in dry weather, to blanch, which takes ten days in hot, and twenty days in cool weather. Draw up a little earth to the base of the plant. Rich, mellow soil, in an open situation is most suitable.

Green Curled Endive.

Green Curled. Is the hardiest variety, with beautifully curled dark green leaves, which blanch white, and are very crisp and tender.

Garlic.

This is extensively used for flavoring soups, stews, etc. The sets should be planted early in spring in rich soil in rows one foot apart, and from three to five inches apart in the rows. Cultivate like onions. When the tops die off the crop is ready to gather.

Kohl-Rabi.

This is an intermediate between the Cabbage and Turnip. For an early crop start in hot-bed and treat the same as early cabbage; if for late crop, sow in June or July. Remove the plants early in the Fall and store for Winter use, the same as turnips. This is a favorite with Europeans, and very superior for feeding cows for milk.

Early White Vienna. Best early variety for table; bulbs white, handsome, small, highly esteemed by market gardeners.

Early Purple. Very similar to the last, except in color, which is a bright **White Vienna Kohl Rabi.** purple, a desirable sort.

Kale or Borecole.

The Kales are more hardy than Cabbage, make excellent greens for winter and spring use, and are improved by frost. Sow from May to June, in well prepared soil, covering it thinly and evenly, and cultivate the same as Cabbage. Half an ounce will sow a bed of twenty square feet.

Green Curled Scotch. Very hardy, and is improved by a moderate frost. Leaves bright green and beautifully curled. It stands the winters in the Middle States without protection.

Dwarf Green Curled. This variety is extensively grown as Winter Greens, sown in the Fall, in rows one foot apart and treated in every way as Spinach, it is ready for use in early Spring.

Sea Kale. This is quite a favorite with many; its young shoots are blanched for use. It is trained and treated like the Cabbage.

Green Curled Scotch Kale, or Borecole.

Sea Kale.

Leek.

The Leek is very hardy and easily cultivated; it succeeds best in a light but well enriched soil. Sow as early in Spring as practicable, in drills one inch deep and one foot apart. When six or eight inches high, they may be transplanted in rows ten inches apart each way, as deep as possible, that the neck, being covered, may be blanched. If fine leeks are desired, the ground can hardly be made too rich.

London Flag. The variety most generally cultivated in this country, hardy, of good quality.

London Flag Leek.

Lettuce.

Lettuce thrives best in rich, moist ground. For successive crops, sowing may be made in the open ground as early as the spring opens, and continuing until July. Always thin out well or the plants will not be strong. When wanted as a cut salad, sow the seed thickly in rows or broadcast.

Early Curled Silesia. A fine early curled variety which does not head, leaves large, tender and of fine flavor.

Early Curled Simpson.

This does not head, but forms a close, compact mass of leaves; very early, excellent for forcing.

Early Curled Simpson.

Boston Curled

Of superior quality; does not form solid heads; fine for early use.

Boston Curled.

Early Prize Head. Forms a mammoth plant; in which even the outer leaves are crisp and tender, and remains so throughout the season. It is slow to run up to seed, of superb flavor and very hardy, one of the best varieties for family use, but for market gardens it is too tender to stand much handling

Hanson. The heads are of very large size, deliciously sweet, tender and crisp, even to the outer leaves. Color green outside and white within.

Black Seeded Simpson. Like the curled Simpson, this variety does not, properly, form a head; but it differs in the leaves being nearly white, and attaining nearly DOUBLE the size of the Curled Simpson. It stands the summer heat splendidly while it is equally suited for forcing.

Early Summer Cabbage.

One of the very best head Lettuces for the summer that we know of. The heads are of good size, close and well formed. It is a splendid market variety

Oak Leaved. A distinct variety due to the peculiar outline of the leaves, which are shaped like those of the oak. The heads are compact, crisp and tender, and it is largely free from that bitter taste peculiar to so many kinds of Lettuce. See specialties.

Tennis Ball. A favorite forcing variety. Well formed heads, hardy and crisp, of excellent quality. One of the earliest of the heading varieties.

Salamander. An excellent summer variety, forming good sized heads that stand drought and heat longer without injury than any other sort.

Salamander.

Phila. Butter or Cabbage.

Produces fine, greenish-white, large heads, of extra quality, remarkably crisp, and tender, sure to head, of quick growth. It is one of the best for forcing, and for summer use, as it is slow to shoot to seed, and resists heat well.

Phila. Butter or Cabbage.

Ice Drumhead. Produces a beautiful head, very firm, solid and compact. The head is of an attractive and silvery white, rich, buttery, and most delicious in flavor. It comes early and stands a long while before running to seed; excellent for early spring and summer use.

White Paris Cos. The heads are long, upright, with oblong leaves. It is very hardy, of large size, and long in running to seed; tender, brittle, and high flavored.

All the Year Round.

A hardy, crisp eating and compact growing variety, with small, close heads of a dark green color; an excellent summer Lettuce, and valuable for forcing.

White Paris Cos.

Strong's Perfection. See Specialties.

Martynia.

Used much for pickling, when gathered while green and tender.

Sow in open ground and transplant to two feet apart.

Musk Melons.

One oz. for 50 hills; three pounds for an acre.

Melons thrive best in good sandy loam. Plant as soon as the ground becomes warm, in hills six feet apart; a little well rotted manure in each hill will be of great benefit. Put twelve to fifteen seeds to a hill, and after they are up and all danger from bugs is over, thin out to three plants to the hill. If the growth is too rapid, pinch off the top and leading shoots, and thin out the fruit, which will increase the size of those remaining. Pumpkins, Squashes or Cucumbers should not be grown near them, as they would be apt to hybridize.

Emerald Gem Melon. This most excellent new musk melon originated in Michigan. It is of superior flavor and quality; the outside skin is an emerald green color and quite smooth; they ripen early and produce well; the flesh is light red or salmon, very thick, juicy and crystalline, and luscious in flavor. See specialties.

California Netted Cantaloupe. This is the most popular and best market variety grown in this State; large, deeply ribbed and netted; green flesh and of delicious flavor and a good keeper.

Montreal Improved Green Nutmeg. Nearly round, slightly flattened at the ends, with a densely netted green skin. They grow to a large, uniform size, averaging from fifteen to twenty pounds in weight, specimens often weighing twenty-five pounds. The flesh is remarkably thick and of good flavor. Owing to its large and handsome appearance, it sells rapidly in the market at very high prices.

Surprise. An excellent variety, having thin, cream-colored skin, thickly netted; of medium size and thick, salmon-colored flesh. The flavor is delicious, and they are very productive.

Surprise.

Champion Market Musk Melon. In shape is almost a perfect globe and densely netted; ripens early and grows to a very large, uniform size. The flesh is thick, light green in color, and of a rich, sweet flavor. Vines are vigorous and remarkably healthy. Very productive. See specialties.

Skillman's Fine Netted. This is a small, rough, netted variety, flattened at the ends; flesh green; very thick, firm, sugary, and of delicious flavor. Among the earliest of the green-fleshed melons.

Baltimore. A green-fleshed Melon, which should be largely grown. It is very productive; of good size, flesh thick and of delicious flavor, and is largely grown by leading market gardeners as being in every way a desirable sort.

Casaba, or Persian. Of good size, very delicious and fine flavor; usual weight from 10 to 15 pounds; the best prolific, late oval, netted green-fleshed variety.

Casaba, or Persian.

Large Hackensack. Very popular with market gardeners in the vicinity of large cities, being of a very large size; very prolific, rich in flavor, thick, juicy flesh, and always commands a ready sale.

Large Hackensack.

Bay View. A large oval Melon of the Persian type, of superior quality, thin rind, flesh green, firm and sugary.

Miller Cream Nutmeg Melon.

This splendid melon was thoroughly tested the past season by many of our best market gardeners and melon growers, and is pronounced by all one of the very best they have ever grown. The flesh is of a rich salmon color, very thick, sweet and melting in quality. The rind is very thin, slightly sutured and finely netted. Vines grow strong and are very productive, covering the ground with fruit. They retain their bright fresh appearance, and remain solid several days after being pulled. See Specialties.

Green Citron. A very desirable melon either for the table or market; very juicy; honey flavor; thick green flesh; a standard sort.

White Japan. Medium size; flesh thick, skin pale green; one of the earliest; worthy of a place in every family garden.

Green Citron.

Golden Gem. This valuable new cantaloupe, is admitted by prominent melon growers to be the very best early variety now grown. They grow very uniform in shape and size, weighing about two pounds each, skin green and thickly netted. They are very thick-meated, flesh of a light green color, the inside surface when cut open, being of a beautiful golden color. In quality and flavor they are *superior*, being uniformly *rich, sugary and luscious*. They are *extra early* in ripening, the vines keeping green longer and producing better than any variety we have ever known. They sell in markets, where known, right alongside of other good varieties, at double price.

Miller's Cream. See Specialties.
Emerald Gem. See Specialties.
Champion Market. See Specialties.

Watermelon.

One ounce to 50 hills, or about three pounds to an acre.

Mountain Sprout. A good market sort, fruit of large size; longish oval; skin dark green, marbled with light shades; red flesh of excellent quality.

Mountain Sprout.   Black Spanish.

Black Spanish. Fruit large, of a round shape, color a very dark green, and seeds black.

Mountain Sweet. Fruit oblong, dark green, rind thin, flesh red, solid and very sweet.

Ice Cream or Peerless. Fruit of medium size, nearly round; skin pale green, rind very thin, white seeds, flesh solid and delicious.

Ice Cream or Peerless.   Georgia Rattlesnake,

Georgia Rattlesnake. One of the largest varieties, and stands shipment long distances. Fruit cylindrical, square at the ends, smooth, distinctly striped and mottled light and dark green. Flesh bright scarlet, and very sweet.

Pride of Georgia. Originated in Monroe County, Georgia. The rind is dark green, shape nearly oval, and ridged like an orange; grows partly on one end, flesh rich scarlet, very sweet and crisp; attains a large size, and a good shipper.

Citron. For preserving; flesh white and solid; seed red.

Scaly Bark. An excellent variety; of great value to shippers; remains in choice eating condition from ten to fifteen days after being pulled. The flesh is light crimson; solid, tender and of fine flavor. Skin is almost smooth, looks as if covered with fish scales. Rind, though quite thin, is remarkably tough.

Cuban Queen. The largest and one of the best grown; an excellent keeper, skin beautifully striped dark and light green. The flesh is red, solid, delicate in flavor and very sweet; bears transit well.

Cuban Queen.

Orange. Flesh red, tender and sweet, separating from the rind like an orange.

Mammoth Ironclad.

Mammoth Ironclad. A variety of undoubted excellence, of large size and weight, crops of it averaging nearly 50 pounds each. The flesh is deep red and of a delicious rich flavor, holding its fine qualities very close to the skin. In outside appearance it is somewhat like the Gypsy. For shipping and keeping qualities the Ironclad is unsurpassed. The vines are strong growing, and altogether it is a most valuable acquisition.

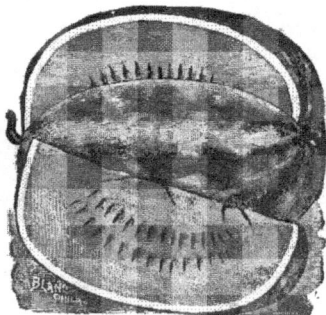

Kolb Gem.

Kolb Gem. This variety originated in Alabama three years ago, has proved to be a very valuable acquisition. It is uniformly round and grows to a good size, often attaining a weight of twenty-five or fifty pounds; the flesh is a bright red and flavor excellent, rind dark green, striped and very tough; It is unsurpassed as a shipping melon, retaining its freshness and sweetness for a long time after ripening. It is unusually productive and will mature as far north as Chicago.

Imperial Lodi. This is now the most popular of all the California grown varieties. Large, oblong, skin light pea-green in color, and thin. Red flesh, very sweet and fine in flavor, and one of the very best for cultivation for market sales.

Seminole.
Hungarian Honey.
The Volga.   } See Specialties.
Green and Gold.
Florida Favorite.

Mushroom Spawn.

The Mushroom is an edible fungus of a white color, changing to brown when old. The gills are loose, of a pinkish red, changing to liver color. It produces no seed, but instead, a white, fibrous substance in broken threads, called spawn, which is preserved in horse manure, being pressed in the form of bricks. Thus prepared it will retain its vitality for years.

CULTURE. Mushrooms can be grown in the cellar, in sheds, or in hot-beds in open air, on shelves, or out-of-the-way places. Fermenting horse manure, at a temperature of about 70 degrees, is made into beds the size required, eighteen inches deep. In this bed plant the broken pieces of spawn six inches apart, covering the whole with two inches of light soil, and protect from cold and severe rains. The mushrooms will appear in about six weeks. Water sparingly and with lukewarm water.

Mustard.

Makes a pungent salad. Sow thickly in rows and cut for use when two inches high. White London is the best for salads. The Brown or Black, is, however, more pungent.

Nasturtium.

The seeds, while young and succulent, are pickled for capers. The plants are quite ornamental and make excellent screens in the garden.

Okra, or Gumbo.

This vegetable is grown for its pods which are used in soups, stews, etc. It is very nutritious and of easy culture. Sow when the ground has become warm, three feet apart and one inch deep, and thin out to ten inches in the row. The pods are dried for winter use.

New Improved Dwarf. This new early variety, has long, green, slender pods, very productive, and grows fourteen inches high.

Long Green. Long ribbed erect pods, sharply tapering to a point; very productive.

Onion.

The value of this crop depends almost solely on the quality of the seed sown. Realizing this, we have taken the greatest care in selecting our stocks, and can confidently recommend them to all our customers, those who use large quantities, as well as those who use small, as being unsurpassed for quality, germination and trueness; being grown for us solely by men of years of experience in raising this important seed. Our seed will produce full-sized onions the first year of sowing, for which purpose sow four to five lbs. per acre. For growing small sets our seed is equally good, and should be sown for this purpose at the rate of about 60 lbs. to the acre.

Early Red Globe. A comparatively new variety, maturing as early as the flat sort. It is globe shaped; skin deep red; flesh mild and tender. Very handsome in appearance.

Extra Early Red. A medium sized, flat variety; an abundant producer, and very uniform in shape and size; moderately strong flavored, and comes into use nearly two weeks earlier than the Large Red Wethersfield; very desirable for early market use.

Large Red Wethersfield.

Large Red Wethersfie'd. This is a standard variety. Large size; skin deep purplish red; form round, somewhat flattened; flesh purplish white; moderately fine grained, and stronger flavored than any of the other kinds. Very productive, the best keeper, and one of the most popular for general cultivation.

Giant Rocca. An immense onion. Globular in form; skin tender. It will produce a large onion from seed the first season, but to attain the largest growth, the smallest bulbs should be set out the next spring, when they will continue increasing in size, instead of producing seed.

Giant White Italian Tripoli. A large, beautiful, pure white, flat onion of mild excellent flavor, and will produce a somewhat larger onion from seed than the White Portugal.

Giant Rocca.

Yellow Strasburg. (Yellow Dutch.) Later, flatter and larger than Yellow Danvers; good keeper.

Yellow Danvers.

Yellow Danvers. A fine variety of medium size, globular in form; skin yellowish brown; flesh white, comparatively mild and well flavored, and very productive; requires rich soil and good cultivation to produce heavy crops. By careful selection we have improved the original shape of this variety, so that many seedsmen catalogue it as Yellow Globe Danvers.

White Globe.

White Globe. Yields abundantly, producing handsome and uniformly globe shaped bulbs. The flesh is firm, fine grained, and of mild flavor. Sometimes called Southport White Globe.

White Portugal or Silver Skin. Mild flavor and handsome; much grown for pickling; poor keeper for market, but good for White Sets.

Queen. A silver skinned variety, of quick growth and remarkable keeping qualities. If sown in early spring it will produce onions one to two inches in diameter early in summer, and if sown in July, will with favorable weather be ready to pull late in autumn, and be sound and fit for use until the following summer.

Particularly valuable for pickles, and if sown thickly they will mature perfect hard onions from one-half to three-quarters of an inch in diameter.

Large Red Italian Tripoli. This has the same characteristics as the White Tripoli; except in color however.

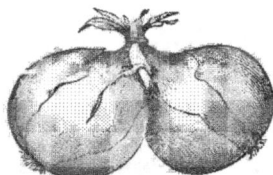

Bulbs.

Top Sets or Buttons. Produce on the top of the stalk instead of seed, a number of small bulbs or onions, about the size of acorns, which, if planted, will produce a large onion maturing earlier than from seed. The large onion produces the top onion, and the little top onion produces the large onion.

Bottom Sets. These are produced from seeds sown thickly in beds or drills. When the top dies down the small bulbs are gathered and spread out and kept in a cool dry place for future planting, and should be set, when the ground is in condition, in rows one foot apart and three or four inches distant.

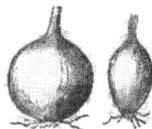

Parsnip.

The value of the Parsnip for the table depends solely on the careful selection of the best roots and most thorough cultivation. As the seed is slow to germinate, too much care cannot be taken with planting. The soil must be warm and mellow. The earth should be firmly pressed over the seed. It should be covered to the depth of half an inch. Sow in drills 15 to 18 inches apart and thin out to 6 inches in the row.

Hollow Crown or Long Smooth. Roots oblong, ending somewhat abruptly, with a small tap root; grows mostly below the surface; has a very smooth clean skin, and is easily distinguished by the leaves arising from a cavity on the top or crown of the root.

Student. A half long variety of delicious flavor.

Pepper.

Grown largely for pickles. Sown in hot bed early and transplanted to the open ground when the weather is favorable. They should be planted in warm, mellow soil, in rows eighteen inches apart. They may also be sown in the open ground when the danger of frost is past, and the soil is warm and weather settled.

Golden Dawn. In size and shape it resembles the Large Bell. It is very productive; color a bright golden yellow; excellent quality, being distinguished from all others, on account of its mild flavor and beautiful appearance.

Red Cayenne. A long, slim pod, rather pointed, and when ripe, of a bright red color. Extremely strong and pungent, and is the sort used for commercial purposes.

Sweet Mountain. Plants very vigorous and productive, growing upright with moderately large leaves. Fruit large, long, smooth and handsome, being when green of a bright deep green color, entirely free from purple tinge, and when mature of a rich red. Flesh thick, sweet and mild flavored. Well suited to use as a stuffed pickle.

Large Squash. Fruit large, flat, tomato shaped, more or less ribbed; skin smooth and glossy; flesh mild, thick meated, and pleasant to the taste, although possessing more pungency than the other large sorts; very productive, and the best variety for pickling.

Large Bell, or Bull Nose. A very large sort of inverted bell shape, suitable for filling with cabbage, etc., and for a mixed pickle. Flesh thick, hard and less pungent than most other sorts, and one of the earliest varieties.

Chili. Used in the manufacture of pepper sauce. Pods sharply conical, brilliant scarlet and exceedingly pungent when ripe. Requires a long, warm season, and plants should be started quite early in hot bed.

Large Bell, or Bull Nose.

Pars'ey.

Used for garnishing and seasoning soups, meats, etc. Succeeds best in a mellow, rich soil. Sow thickly, early, in rows 1 foot apart and ½ inch deep; thin out the plants to stand 6 inches apart in the rows. The seed is slow of germination, taking from three to four weeks to make its appearance, and often failing to come up in dry weather. To assist its coming up, soak the seed a few hours in warm water, or sprout in damp earth, and sow when it swells or bursts. For winter use protect in a frame or light cellar.

Fern Leaved. Nothing better for garnishing could be desired. As a garden decorative plant, it is very ornamental. It will stand the winter if covered before frost.

Dwarf Extra Curled. Leaves tender, crisp and very curly, of a beautiful bright green color, and ornamental; excellent for garnishing.

Champion Moss Curled. A very fine English sort; leaves beautifully curled and mossy; a handsome standard sort.

Pumpkin.

Sow in good soil, when the ground has become, warm, in hills 8 or 10 feet apart each way, or in fields or corn about every fourth hill; plant at the same time with the corn; always avoid planting near other vines, as they will hybridize. The Cashaw is generally preferred for cooking or making pies.

Mammoth Tours, or Jumbo. Grows to an enormous size, often weighing 150 pounds, very productive; flesh salmon color; good keeper; desirable for cooking purposes or for stock feeding.

Connecticut Field. One of the best for field culture; can be grown with corn; largely used for stock for winter feeding.

Cashaw. A very prolific variety, resembling in form the Winter-Crook-Neck Squash, although growing to a much larger size, frequently weighing 60 pounds and over; color light cream; flesh salmon color.

Large Cheese. About the most desirable variety for culinary purposes, light yellow, with very thick sweet, brittle flesh, and a most excellent keeper.

Large Cheese.

Sugar. This variety is smaller than the Large Field, but of finer grain, sweeter and very prolific. First rate either for table or for feeding to stock.

New Japanese Pie Pumpkin. See Specialties.

Tennessee Sweet Potato Pumpkin. See Specialties.

Etampes. See Specialties.

PEAS.

Peas mature earliest in a light, rich soil; for a general crop, a rich deep loam, or inclining to clay, is the best. When grown for a market crop sow in rows, 1 inch apart and 2 to 3 inches deep, the rows from 2 to 4 feet apart. according to the variety. When grown in gardens sow in double rows, 6 to 8 inches apart, the tall ones requiring brush. Commence sowing the extra early varieties as early as the ground can be worked. They should be kept clean, and earth up twice during growth. The wrinkled varieties are not as hardy as the small hard sorts, and if planted early should have a dry soil; they are, however, the sweetest and best flavored varieties. The dwarf varieties are best suited for small gardens and can be planted in rows 1 foot apart.

Cleveland's Alaska. This is considered to be the earliest, most prolific and finely flavored variety of pea grown. See cut. Specialties.

First and Best. This is one of the best extra early sorts for market planting, and is a very heavy and reliable yielder and of good quality.

Rural New Yorker. Early, productive, and uniform in ripening. It grows about 20 inches high, and is quite similar to Philadelphia Extra Early.

Royal Dwarf White Marrowfat. A large, delicious marrow pea, an excellent cropper, and a favorite with gardeners; Height, 2 feet.

American Wonder. It is best suited to the private gardens, as it is not productive enough as a market sort. It is very early, and requires no staking. The peas are wrinkled, and extreme dwarf growth, about 10 inches in hieght. It is of the finest quality.

Carter's Premium Gem.

Carter's Premium Gem. Pods long and of a dark green color. A type of and improvement on the Little Gem; very early and productive, height, 1 foot.

'Bliss's Ever-Bearing.

Bliss's Ever Bearing. Height, eighteen inches to 2 feet; foliage large. Pods, 3 to 4 inches in length, each producing 6 to 8 large wrinkled peas. Half an inch and over in diameter, and in quality unsurpassed. A continuous bearer, which gives it especial value. It should be sown thinner than any other kinds else the vines will become too crowded.

Champion of England. This is acknowleged to be the best of the late varieties. It is tall growing, attaining a height of 5 feet, and requires to be staked up. The pods and peas are of the largest size.

Telephone. A tall, wrinkled marrow, enormously productive, and of the best quality. Is a strong grower, averaging 18 pods to the stalk. The pods are of the largest size, and contain from 6 to 7 large peas. A desirable sort for the family garden.

Extra Early Tom Thumb. A remarkable early variety. Very dwarf, growing but nine inches. If planted early in the Spring, three crops can be obtained in a single season.

Bliss's Abundance. A second early variety, attaining a height of from 15 to 18 inches. Pods 3 to 3½ inches long, roundish and well filled, containing 6 to 8 large wrinkled peas of excellent quality. This variety branches directly from the roots forming a veritable bush, making it necessary to sow the seeds much thinner than usual. Six to eight inches apart in the rows is as near as the plants should stand; if the soil is very rich 8 inches is preferable.

Carter's Stratagem.

Carter's Stratagem. Seeds green, square wrinkled, height 2 feet, vigorous, branching habit; remarkably luxuriant foliage, leaves unusually large sized, under favorable conditions an enormous cropper; pods long, well filled with from seven to nine peas of the largest size, extra fine quality. One of the most elegant and showy peas in cultivation.

Yorkshire Hero. A splendid wrinkled green marrow pea of branching habit and abundant bearer. Seedsmen on both sides of the Atlantic find their sales for this variety constantly on the increase; 2½ feet.

Tall White Marrowfat. A favorite marrow sort; 6 feet. Mostly grown as a field pea, and very productive.

Black-Eyed Marrowfat. This is extensively grown as a field pea; hardy and productive, but not so fine flavored as most other varieties; 4 feet,

Tall Sugar. (Edible pods.) Can be used either shelled or cooked in the pods, which when young are very tender and sweet; 5 feet.

Dwarf Sugar. (Edible pods.) Similar to the last; height 3 feet.

Radish.

Radishes require a sandy loam, made rich and light.   A heavy clay soil will not produce good smooth roots. Sow in 12 inch drills as early as the ground will permit, and once in two weeks for succession.

French Breakfast

Early Scarlet Turnip.

French Breakfast. A very quick growing variety; brittle; crisp and tender; of oval form, bright scarlet, white tipped, and a very handsome sort.

Early Scarlet Turnip. A small, round, scarlet, turnip-shaped, small top variety, of quick growth, mild and crisp when young.

Early White Turnip. Like the above, except of a white color.

Olive-Shaped Scarlet. Very early; handsome rose color, oblong in shape; crisp and tender.

White Tipped Scarlet Turnip. An early variety of medium size and excellent flavor, and of very handsome appearance.

Long White Spanish. Roots long; skin white, slightly wrinkled; solid and pungent; somewhat milder than the Black Spanish.

White Strasburg. Though not a new variety, is one that should be more largely grown. The roots are oblong, of a pure white color, very brittle, and of a mild flavor. For summer and fall use this sort will be found very desirable.

White Strasburg.

Long Black Spanish.   Chinese Rose Winter.

Long Black Spanish. Black skin, white flesh, very firm, solid, good keeper, grows long and large.

Chinese Rose Winter. Bright rose color; excellent for winter use; white flesh.

Early Long Scarlet Short Top. A main variety for out door planting for market gardeners or family use; grows 6 to 8 inches long; very crisp and brittle; quick growth; uniformly straight.

Round Black Spanish. Globe-shaped, black skin, white flesh, very firm; the flavor is piquant and appetizing.

California White Winter. A mammoth variety, growing 12 inches long, white-fleshed, firm, and of excellent quality.

Beckert's Chartier. Decidedly distinct in appearance from any Radish in cultivation. The color at the top is crimson, running into pink downward it is pure, waxy white. It will attain a very large size before it becomes unfit for the table. (See specialties.)

Early Long Scarlet.

Earliest Carmine. See specialties.

RHUBARB.

One ounce will sow 50 feet of drill.

Rhubarb succeeds best in deep, rich loam; the richer the soil and the deeper, it is stirred the better, as it is scarcely possible to cultivate too deeply or to manure too highly. It is propagated by seeds, or by division of the roots—the latter being the usual method. Sow in drills eighteen inches apart, and thin out the plants to nine inches apart in the drills. When the plants are one year old transplant into beds, setting the plants five feet apart each way. Do not cut until the second year, and give a liberal dressing of manure every Fall.

We would advise, for small and family gardens, to procure the roots, which can be set out as desired.

Linnæus. An early and productive variety; skins thin; pulp highly flavored, possessing little acidity; one of the best sorts for family use.

Victoria Leaves large; skin thicker than above; pulp more acid, but a more productive variety; used largely for market.

Spinach.

One ounce will sow 100 feet of drill; ten pounds required for one acre.

Spinach is very hardy, extremely wholesome, and makes most delicious greens, and is of the easiest culture. Sow in drills one foot apart, and commence thinning out the plants as soon as the leaves are an inch wide. Cut before hot weather, or it will become tough and stringy. For early Spring use, the seed should be sown early in the Autumn; and the plants protected through the winter by a slight covering of leaves or straw.

Round Thick Leaved Leaves large, thick and fleshy; the variety generally grown for market, and equally good for Spring or Fall sowing.

Round Leaved Viroflay.

A splendid variety, with leaves long and broad, round, thick and fleshy, dark green. Young plants transplanted into a rich soil will grow to an enormous size.

Round Leaved Viroflay.

Prickly, or Fall. Best suited for Fall planting, as it is the hardiest variety and will withstand the severest weather with only a slight protection of leaves or straw. The seed is prickly, leaves triangular, oblong or arrow-shaped.

Long Standing Spinach.

Long Standing. An improved strain; stands three weeks longer without going to seed than any variety we know of. This valuable property will be appreciated by market gardeners.

Savoy Leaved. A very hardy and productive sort; leaves handsomely curled; a valuable variety for market or family use.

Salsify or Vegetable Oyster.

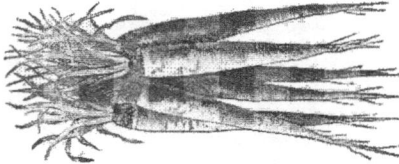

Salsify.

Long, white, tapering roots, resembling somewhat the small white parsnip, and when cooked, have a flavor similar to oysters. Cultivate same as Parsnips.

Large White. The standard variety; tender and very fine.

Scorzonera, or Black Oyster Plant. Similar to the White Salsify, save in color.

Squashes.

Squashes should be planted in a warm, light, rich soil, after the weather has become settled and warm. Plant in well-manured hills, in the same manner as Cucumbers and Melons—the bush varieties three or four feet apart each way, and the running kinds six to eight feet. Eight to ten seeds should be sown in each hill, thinning out, after they have attained their rough leaves and danger from bugs is over leaving three or four of the strongest plants per hill.

Early Yellow Bush Scallop. An early, flat, scallop-shaped variety; color yellow; flesh pale yellow and well flavored; very productive; used when young and tender.

Early White Bush Scallop. Similar to the preceding, except in color, which is white.

Summer Crookneck. One of the best; very early and productive. It is small, crooked neck, covered with warty excrescences; color bright yellow; shell very hard when ripe.

Boston Marrow.

Boston Marrow. A fall and winter variety, very popular. Of oval form; skin thin; when ripe, bright orange mottled with light cream color; flesh rich salmon yellow, dry, fine grained, and for sweetness and excellence, unsurpassed.

Cocoanut. Very prolific, producing six to twelve on a vine. Outer color light yellow, the bottom of the fruit being of a rich green hue. Quality first-class.

Hubbard Squash.

Hubbard. This is a superior variety, and the best winter squash known; flesh bright orange yellow, fine grained, very dry, sweet and rich flavored; keeps perfectly good throughout the winter; boils or bakes exceedingly dry, and is esteemed by many to be as good baked as the sweet potato.

Winter Crookneck. The most certain to produce a crop, the strong growing vines suffering less from insects than those of the other sorts. Color varying from dark green to clear yellow. Flesh variable, effected by soil and weather. If kept from cold and damp, they will keep the entire year.

Winter Crookneck.

Improved American Turban. (Essex Hybrid.) Developed by selection and crossing from the old American Turban, being of a richer color, having a hard shell and in its remarkable keeping qualities. It is of medium size, and the skin is a rich orange red. Flesh deep, rich color, very thick, and of excellent quality. The earliest of the winter varieties

Imp. Am. Turban.

Pine Apple. Vigorous and hardy, coming into bearing late in the season, and then producing fruit at nearly every joint, making it one of the most productive kinds grown. Skin creamy white; flesh very thick and with a peculiar flavor, on which account it is much liked for pies; it is also used green like the summer squashes, and baked or stewed like the winter kinds.

Pine Apple.

Perfect Gem. Vine coming into bearing late, but very productive. Fruit four inches in diameter, nearly round, ribbed white; flesh yellowish white and cooking, very sweet and well flavored. This is the best of the intermediate kinds, and many think it fully equal to the winter sorts.

Perfect Gem.

Mammoth Chili.

Mammoth Chili. Rich orange-yellow, flesh thick, and of good quality for making pies. They grow to an enormous size, specimens frequently attaining the weight of 200 lbs. Valuable sort for feeding stock.

Sibley. See Specialties.

Brazil Sugar. See Specialties.

Turnip.

One ounce for 150 feet of drill; or two pounds for an acre.

Turnips succeed best in highly enriched sandy or gravelly soil. Sow in drills 12 to 18 inches apart, cover half inch, and when plants are well up thin to 5 or 6 inches apart, for early kind, and Rutabaga and large sorts to 10 inches. Best always to sow just before a rain, or water well, as success depends upon quick germination and rapid growths.

Extra Early Purple Top Munich. This new variety is two weeks earlier than any other in cultivation. It is of a handsome appearance, somewhat flattened, white, with purplish top; flesh snow white, fine grained, and most delicate.

Extra Early Purple Top Munich.

Red Top Strap Leaf. Rapid grower and of mild flavor; the most popular variety for early use, either for the table or stock.

Early White Egg. A new egg-shaped variety, for Spring or Fall Sowing, flesh white, firm, fine grained, mild and sweet; au extra keeper, in every respect a first-classed table and market sort.

Yellow Globe. One of the best for a general crop; flesh firm and sweet; grows to a large size; excellent for table use or feeding stock, and keeps well until Spring.

Golden Ball. A rapid grower of excellent flavor; globe-shaped; bright yellow color; good keeper and a superior table variety.

Early White Flat Dutch. An early, white fleshed; strap-leaved variety, usually sown for early Summer use in the Spring; of quick growth, mild flavor and excellent quality; also grown for a Fall crop.

Early White Flat Dutch.

Yellow Aberdeen, or Scotch. Hardy, productive, and a good keeper; globe shaped; yellow; flesh firm; good for table use or feeding stock.

Long White, or Cow Horn. Grows very quickly partly above ground; very productive; flesh white, fine grained and sweet; of excellent quality.

Sweet Russian or White Ruta Baga. This is a most excellent kind, either for table or stock. It grows to a very large size, flesh white, solid, firm texture, sweet and rich, keeps well.

Skirving's Purple Top. Grows to a large size, yellow flesh, solid fine flavored, good keeper; good table or stock variety.

Early White Egg.   Long White, or Cow Horn.

Early Snowball. Small, solid, sweet and crisp, and also of remarkably quick growth.

Early White Stone. An English garden variety; round in shape; firm, of quick growth, medium size; very desirable.

Improved Purple Top Yellow Ruta Baga. The best variety of Swedish Turnip in cultivation; hardy and productive; flesh yellow, of solid texture; sweet and well flavored; shape slightly oblong, terminating abruptly, with no side or bottom roots; color, deep purple above, and bright yellow under the ground; leaves small, light green, with little or no neck, the most perfect in form, the richest in flavor, and the best in every respect.

Laing's Improved. One of the large sorts; productive and good size, sweet, firm, very hardy; excellent for table or stock feeding.

Sweet German. This variety is very popular in many sections. It partakes largely of the nature of the Ruta Baga, and should be sown a month earlier than the flat turnips. The flesh is white, hard, firm and sweet, and it keeps nearly as well as the Ruta Baga. Highly recommended for winter and spring use.

Tomatoes.

One ounce for 1,500 plants; ¼ lb. (to transplant) for an acre.

This vegetable is now one of the most important of garden and market products. The seed may be sown in a hot-bed, greenhouse, or where a temperature of not less than 60 degrees is kept. When the plants are about two inches high they should be set out in boxes three inches deep. When safe from frost, plants may be set in the open ground. They are planted for early crops on light, sandy soil, at a distance of 4 feet apart, in hills. Water freely at the time of transplanting, and shelter from the sun a few days until the plants are established. Tomatoes will always produce greater crops and be of better flavor when staked up or when trained against walls or fences.

General Grant. A very early sort; fair sized, but not as smooth as the later sorts.

Hathaway's Excelsior. Vines large and vigorous, fruit medium size, smooth, apple-shaped; dark, rich color when ripe; quite early, a favorite Southern sort.

Early Conqueror. A well-known standard sort, medium in size, irregular in shape, flattened and slightly corrugated; color scarlet-crimson.

Livingston's Perfection. Very large and early; blood-red; perfectly smooth; thick meat; few seeds; a good shipping sort; realy one of the best of all the Livingston tomatoes of which we now have so many strains.

Sacramento Favorite.

Sacramento Favorite. Is one of the very best; large size, smooth as an apple, firm and handsome; dark red and fine for market and shipping.

Optimus Tomato.

Optimus Tomato. A variety that should be placed in the front rank among early Tomatoes. In all trials it is found remarkably early, in that respect being fully the equal of or superior to the "Mikado." Optimus is a very smooth variety, uniform in size, and shape, ripens evenly, and is of a bright red color. The flesh is scarlet crimson, very solid, of good flavor and entirely free from core. The fruit is usually produced in clusters of five.

Mayflower. Very early and productive; very large; splendid shape; perfectly smooth; bright red; and ripens uniformly to the stem.

The Mikado. One of the earliest and of the largest size. Perfectly solid and of unsurpassed quality. The Mikado differs from all tomatoes in its immense size. They are produced in great clusters and are

Mikado.

perfectly solid, generally smooth, but occasionally irregular. The color, is purplish red, like that of the Acme; while it has all the solidity that characterizes the Trophy. It is not unusual for single fruit to weigh from one pound to one and a half pounds each. Its earliness is a remarkable feature in so large a tomato, and adds to its value. Whether for slicing or for cooking purposes the quality is excellent. The foliage of Mikado Tomato will show the distinctiveness of the variety.

Livingston's Favorite. One of the most perfect shaped tomatoes grown; very smooth; darker than the perfection; ripens evenly and quite early; is noted for its shipping qualities.

Acme. Very productive; form round; very smooth and uniform; delicious in flavor; possesses good shipping qualities.

Paragon. Medium size; color dark red; ripens evenly; very solid; largely used for canning.

Acme.

Cardinal. This is a beautiful tomato, being of a brilliant cardinal red, very glossy looking when ripe; the flesh of the same brilliant color; ripens evenly through, having no hard, green core, like many others; in shape it is round and smooth and solid.

Cardinal.

Early, Large, Smooth Red. Standard market variety; skin bright scarlet; good size, good quality, ripens early.

Yellow Plum. Bright yellow in color; round and regular in shape; useful for preserves.

Livingston's Beauty. It is extra early, growing in clusters of four or five; glossy crimson, partaking of some of the characteristics of the Acme; solid; retains its color and size until late in the season. See Specialties.

Trophy, selected.

Trophy, Selected. One of the best standard varieties; fruit large, smooth, bright red, solid and good flavor; unsurpassed for all purposes.

Strawberry also called Ground Cherry. Small fruit used for preserves. We can recommend this little favorite.

POT, SWEET, AND MEDICAL HERBS.

Herbs, in general, delight in rich, mellow soil. Sow the seeds early in the spring in shallow drills, 1 foot apart; when up a few inches, thin out at proper distances, or transplant. No garden is complete without a few sweet, aromatic or medical herbs for flavoring soups, meats, etc., and care should be taken to harvest them properly. This should be done on a dry day just before they come into full blossom; then dry quickly in the shade, pack close in dry boxes or vessels, so as to exclude the air.

Anise. Used for garnishing and flavoring.
Angelica, Garden. Supposed to have medical virtues.
Arnica. Has medical qualities.
Balm. Used for tea or balm wine; height, 1 foot.
Belladonna. Used in medicine.
Boneset. Has medical qualities.
Basil, Sweet. Used for soups, stews and sauces; 1 foot.
Bene. Used medicinally; 18 inches.
Borage. Excellent for bees, etc., 3 feet.
Caraway. For confectionery and medicine, also flavoring; 2 feet.
Catnip. Has medical qualities.
Coriander. Grown for its seed, also for garnishing; 2 feet.
Cumin. Good for pigeons, etc.
Dill. The leaves are used in soups, sauces and pickles; also the seed for flavoring; 3 feet.
Elecampane. Has tonic expectorant qualities.
Fennel Sweet. The leaves are ornamental; when boiled they are used in fish sauces; 6 feet.

Hoarhound. Used medicinally; 2 feet.
Lavender. An aromatic medicinal herb; 2 feet.
Marigold, Pot. For flavoring and medicine; 1 foot.
Opium Poppy. (White Seeded.) Used medicinally; 3 feet.
Pennyroyal. Has medicinal qualities.
Rosemary. Yields an aromatic oil and water, and largely in use.
Rue. Said to have medicinal qualities.
Saffron. Used in medicine and also in dyeing.
Sage. The tender leaves and tops are used in sausages, stuffing and sauces; 18 inches.
Savory, Summer. For seasoning purposes; 1 foot.
Savory, Winter. For same use as the above.
Tansy. For medicinal use; 3 feet.
Thyme. Broad-leaved English. Used as a seasoning.
Wormwood. Used medicinally, beneficial for poultry, and should be planted in poultry yards.

SEEDS FOR FAMILY GARDENS.

These are the choicest and best varieties for small gardens and home use.
30 packets (sold for $1 50) for $1 00, consisting of

2	best kinds	Snap Beans.	2	best kinds	Cabbage.
2	"	Beets.	1	"	Cauliflower.
2	"	Sweet Corn.	1	"	Celery.
1	"	Carrot.	2	"	Cucumbers.
2	"	Lettuce.	1	"	Muskmelon.
1	"	Onions.	1	"	Watermelon.
1	"	Pepper.	1	"	Pumpkins.
1	"	Parsnip.	1	"	Squash.
2	"	Peas.	3	"	Radish.
1	"	Tomatoes.	2	"	Turnips.

All for the small price of One Dollar.

LAWN GRASS, CLOVER AND OTHER FIELD SEEDS.

These we keep in very large stock, and of unsurpassed quality. We import heavily of Eastern and European varieties, and make a specialty of Alfalfa and other California grown Seed.

A Beautiful Lawn

Is the first thing that attracts one's attention on approaching a residence, consequently this is the first thing to look after, either in arranging a new place or an old established home. A beautiful grass plot is within the reach of every one, and the arrangement of the trees and flowers should be an after consideration, according to the tastes and means of the owner, but when possible, combine both,

How to Secure a Beautiful Lawn.

In establishing a new lawn great care should be taken in preparing the ground before sowing the seed. If at all inclined to be wet, the plot designed for the lawn should be most thoroughly underdrained and carefully graded, and the entire surface made rich and as fine as possible. Bone dust and super-phosphate are the most suitable for enriching a lawn, as they are free from the seed of the obnoxious weeds, which cannot be said of stable manure, unless it has been thoroughly composted with the utmost possible care. The ground being ready, sow the seed as early in the Spring as convenient, the earlier the better, if the soil is in good condition. No one kind of grass will make a lawn that will keep beautifully green all through the season, but a mixture of several is essential, as some varieties are most luxuriant in Spring, others in Summer, and again others in the Autumn, and a proper combination of these various sorts is required to create and maintain a perfect carpet-like lawn. Our Fancy Mixture is most admirably adapted to this purpose, and so near perfection as possible to attain.

All lawns will be greatly benefited, if as early in Spring as the weather will permit, they are carefully raked so as to remove the dead grass and leaves that may be on them; then sprinkle it with our Fancy Mixture, which will renew the thin places and spots that have been killed by the Winter or other causes then give it a thorough rolling with a heavy roller.

LAWN GRASS Fancy Mixture Is composed of a variety of fine dwarf, close growing grasses, which on properly prepared, finely pulverized ground, will produce a neat, velvety lawn and permanent sod 80 lbs. to the acre. 30 cts. per lb.

KENTUCKY BLUE GRASS Fancy Lawn Is the finest and best of all grasses when used separately or in mixtures for general lawn purposes; for this purpose 60 to 80 pounds are necessary. 30 cts. per lb. crop short.

SWEET-SCENTED VERNAL. One of the earliest Grasses in Spring and latest in Autumn and more fragrant than any other grass. Valuable to mix in pastures with other grasses on account of its earliness, and it exhales a delightful fragrance when in bloom. About 30 pounds to the acre. 50 cts. lb.

Kentucky Blue Grass.

ITALIAN RYE GRASS Is more of an annual, and is also good in mixtures for the lawn or for hay crop. It is of quick growth and valuable for sheep pasturage. 15 cts. per lb.

ORCHARD GRASS or COCK'S FOOT. One of the most valuable grasses on account of its quick growth and valuable aftermath. It is ready for grazing two weeks sooner than most grasses, and when fed off is again ready for grazing in a week, and will continue green when other grasses are withered by dry weather. It is palatable and nutritious, and stock eat it greedily when green. It has a tendency to grow in tufts, and so does better if sown with clovers, and as it ripens at the same time, the mixed hay is of the best quality. For grazing, it has no equal, and should be used more than it is. When sown alone, 25 lbs. per acre; if sown with clover, half that amount. It is perennial, and will last for years. 20 cts. per lb.

WATER MEADOW GRASS (*Poa aquatica*). This is an excellent pasture grass for very wet situations. Sow twenty pounds to the acre. 40 cts. per lb.

ROUGH STALKED MEADOW GRASS (*Poa trivialis*). This is one of the most valuable of grasses for moist, rich soils and sheltered situations. Sow twenty pounds to the acre. Per lb. 30 cts.

ENGLISH, or AUSTRALIAN RYE GRASS is a perennial, much like the English Blue Grass and is very valuable for either lawns, pasturage or for hay; and well adapted for moist land. Sow for lawns 60 pounds, hay 30 pounds per acre. 15 cts. per lb.

WOOD MEADOW GRASS Grows from one and a half to two feet high; has a perennial creeping root, and an erect, slender, smooth stem. Its chief value is in that it will produce a good crop of hay in moist, shady situations, where it frequently grows quite tall. Cattle are fond of it; it is succulent and nutritious, and is perhaps the best variety for sowing in orchards, under trees, and shaded situations, either for hay or pasturage, and for parks and pleasure grounds. About 25 pounds per acre. 40 cts. per lb.

JOHNSON GRASS. This is one of the most valuable forage plants, very popular in the Southern States, and will come into universal use in all parts of the United States when known. It is perennial, a rapid grower, very nutritious, being eagerly devoured by all kinds of stock. Comes early in spring, grows until the frost cuts it down in the fall, stands the drought better than any grass, and having long cane-like roots, which penetrate the soil for moisture; superior both as a grazing and hay grass. 30 pounds per acre. 20 cts. per lb.

MEADOW FOXTAIL. A valuable pasture grass of rapid growth and much relished by all kinds of stock. Adapted for rich, moist soils. Sow 20 pounds per acre. 40 cts. per lb.

BROMUS or RESCUE GRASS. This grass is recommended for its drouth-resisting quality. Will thrive on any soil where it is not too wet. Sow 35 pounds per acre. 40 cts. per lb.

TALL MEADOW OAT-GRASS. This grass is early and very luxuriant. It makes fine pasturage and good hay. Can be cut often. It is also valuable to plough under for soiling. Sow 30 to 40 pounds per acre. 30 cts. per lb.

MEADOW, or WOOLLY SOFT GRASS (*Holcus lanatus*) Has the merit of easy culture, and accommodates itself to all descriptions of soil, from the richest to the poorest. Sow 30 lbs. per acre. Weight, 8 pounds per bushel. 30 cts. per lb.

MEADOW FESCUE TRUE ENGLISH BLUE GRASS (*Festuca pratensis*)—One of the most valuable pasture grasses, its long and tender leaves are much relished by stock of all kinds. In some Southern States it is called RANDALL GRASS, sometimes EVERGREEN GRASS. Sow in spring or fall, at the rate of thirty to forty pounds per acre. 20c. per lb.

CRESTED DOGSTAIL GRASS. This grass may be sown on lawns and other places to be kept under by the scythe. The roots penetrate deeply, and remain longer green than any other variety. Sow twenty to twenty-four pounds to the acre. 50c. per lb.

HARD FESCUE is also noted for its drouth-resisting quality, and well adapted for lawn mixture and valuable for sheep pasture. Sow thirty pounds to the acre. 25c. per lb.

BERMUDA GRASS. The roots of this grass are very tenacious of life, outrooting other vegetation. It grows in almost any soil and spreads rapidly, making a good pasturage. The seed is hard to save and is worth $3 00 per pound. The roots can be furnished for $2 00 per barley sack or $3 00 per barrel. Cut up into short lengths and sown broadcast and cover with a roller. One barrel will thus plant an acre.

EGYPTIAN, OR PEARL MILLET Produces an enormous amount of green feed. It can be cut repeatedly, growing very rapidly after cutting, and is equal to Sweet Corn for feed. Sow in drills two or three feet apart; four pounds will sow an acre. 40c. per lb.

AFRICAN CANE, OR SORGHUM. Is also a fine forage plant, and in large demand for Spring planting. 10c. per lb.

HERD, RED TOP GRASS, (or BENT GRASS) Is most largely used for wet lands, but does well in almost any soil, moist or dry. It makes good hay or pasture and is much used in mixture with timothy and clover. Sow 30 pounds per acre. 15 cts. per lb.

TIMOTHY Is very largely grown for hay crop in northern climates, and is fine when sown with Red Top and Clover. Sow 15 pounds per acre. 10 cts. per lb.

Herd, Red Top Grass.

MESQUIT GRASS Is very desirable for dry lands. It resists the drought well and makes a good crop for hay or pasturage. Sow 30 pounds per acre. 15 cts. per lb.

SHEEP FESCUE GRASS (*Festuca ovina*)—This variety grows naturally on light, dry sandy soil, and on elevated mountain pastures. Timothy Sow twenty-five to thirty pounds to the acre. 30c. per lb.

COMMON MILLET Can be sown broadcast in the Spring of the year for hay; thirty to forty pounds per acre. If for seed, sow in drills twenty pounds to the acre. It produces largely as an annual early crop. 10c. per lb.

HUNGARIAN GRASS Is a very valuable forage plant for light dry soils. It withstands drouth and remains green when most vegetation is parched. Sow and cultivate as for Millet. 10c. per lb.

GERMAN GOLDEN MILLET. Is not quite as early as the above, but yields more largely. 10c. per lb.

WHITE MILLO MAIZE, OR BRANCHING DHOURA. Of South American origin. Valuable as a forge plant and for its grain, having great capacity to stand drought. It can be cut and fed at any stage, or cured when heading out, for fodder. It bears grain in erect full heads, and is equal to corn for feeding all sorts of stock; also makes excellent meal. It requires all summer to mature seed. Plant three to five seeds in a hill eighteen inches apart four foot rows, and thin to two plants and cultivate as corn. It shoots out greatly and makes a great amount of foliage. Three to five pounds per acre. Can be cut for green feed several times a season. 25c. per lb.

YELLOW MILLO MAIZE, OR YELLOW BRANCHING DHOURA. Tall, nine to ten feet stooling from the ground like the White Millo Maize, but not so much. The seed head grows to great size on good land. These heads are set close and solid, with a large plump grain, double the size of White Millo, and of deep golden yellow color. The Cultivation is like Corn. 10c. per lb.

AMBER CANE (SORGHUM.) Is the earliest variety, and being rich in saccharine matter is grown for making sugar and syrup. It makes a large amount of forage for stock feed. 10c. per lb.

EGYPTIAN CORN (White and Red Varieties.) Both produce an immense crop of both seed and stalks for forage to the acre and mature without rain. The white is more cultivated, and perhaps the earliest. The seed is quite valuable to feed stock or poultry. 5c. per lb.

KAFFIR CORN. A variety of Sorghum, cultivated for both forage and grain, growing from 4½ to 6 feet high, is stocky and erect, and has wide foliage. Kaffir Corn has the quality common to all Sorghums of resisting drought, and in this fact is to be found its peculiar value. It has yielded paying crops of grain and forage even in dry seasons, when corn has utterly failed. Sow in rows three feet apart, five to six pounds to the acre. 25c. per lb

CLOVER SEEDS.

There are no plants so valuable for fertilizers as the Clovers. They have the faculty of absorbing nitrogen from the air, and also of rendering available much of the inert plant food of the soil. Their long, powerful tap roots penetrate to a great depth, loosen the soil, admit air, and by their decay add immensely to the fertility of the soil. The seed may be sown in fall or spring; which is the best season will depend upon local climate, and method of culture. In any case, it should be evenly distributed on a mellow, well prepared soil. Plaster will increase the growth remarkably, and should be sown broadcast the season following the seeding.

RED CLOVER. Two varieties—large and medium. Both succeed well in California, especially in our bottom lands and deep soils; 25 pounds to the acre.

WHITE DUTCH CLOVER. Grows low, spreading and very fragrant, and is most excellent for lawns and lawn mixture; 10 pounds to the acre.

CRIMSON TREFOIL, OR SCARLET CLOVER. Grows about one foot high, dark roots, long leaves and blossoms of deep red. It makes good hay and will give four or five cuttings each season. Sow 15 pounds to the acre.

Red Clover.

ALSIKE, OR SWEDISH CLOVER. This variety is fast gaining great popularity. It is the most hardy of all the clovers; perennial. On rich, moist soils it yields an enormous quantity of hay or pasture, and may be cut several times in a season, but its greatest value is for sowing with other clovers and grasses, as it forms a thick bottom, and greatly increases the yield of hay, and cattle prefer it to any other forage. The heads are globular, very sweet and fragrant, and much liked by bees, who obtain a large amount of honey from them. Sow in spring or fall, at the rate of 10 pounds per acre, where used alone.

ALFALFA. Is cultivated above all other clover in California. It produces enormous crops, and is cut many times in the season for hay. It roots deeply, keeping fresh and green through our long dry season, and is the most valuable and profitable of all crops for abundance of feed. Sow 20 to 25 pounds to the acre. If in the fall sow early enough to get a little root before a frost, it can be sown again in February and Spring months.

Alfalfa.

BOKHARA CLOVER. This is a fall shrubbery plant, growing to a height of four to six feet. It produces an abundance of small white flowers of great fragrance. Sow 10 pounds to the acre. 25c. per lb.

ESPERSETTE. (French Sanfoin.) This plant is of a lignumivius character, having many stems two and three feet long. Smooth and tapering, with many long oblate leaflets in pairs, and spikes of variegated crimson flowers. The root is perennial of a hard, woody nature. The plant flowers early and can be repeatedly cut, thus furnishing a great abundance of most nutritious food through the long dry and heated seasons, and requiring no irrigation. Stock will eat it with impunity, without danger of bloat as in alfalfa. The seed and seed pods are said to be more nutritious than oats. The plant does best in calcareous and gravelly soils, and elevated slopes and arid regions, where other vegetation fails, it will not succeed in wet or low lands where there is no drainage. From 50 to 75 pounds are required for an acre. 12½c. per lb. $10 00 per 100 lbs.

MELILOTUS. This variety of clover grows on the banks of streams and among cobbles, gravel, slickens and sand. It yields an immense amount of feed for stock, who are very fond of it. The plant attains a height of 10 to 12 feet, keeping green the entire season, producing seed the second year and maturing in October. Price $12 50 per 100 lbs.

TEXAS BLUE GRASS. — "The Texas Blue Grass grows on the roadside, by fences and hedges; shade does not hurt it any more than Orchard Grass. It stands the hot and dry summers of the south very well, better than any other grass." Seed very scarce and difficult to obtain, and cannot be separated from the chaff. Per oz., 40c.; lb., $5 00.

CAROLINA. OR COW PEA. This makes a valuable fodder and is a good fertilizer. The pods can be harvested or all cut green for fodder, or it can be ploughed under for a fertilizer. $5 00 per 100 lbs.

VETCHES. Are much used for stock feed. Sow and cultivate same as for peas. 10 cts. per lb. $6 per 100 lbs.

LENTILS. Are similar to Vetches, and are cultivated in like manner. 15 cts. per lb. $10 00 per 100 lbs.

BROOM CORN. Many farmers make this a profitable crop, producing on an acre about 500 cwt. of broom and forty bushels of seed; plant and cultivate same as for corn.

BUCKWHEAT. Can be sown late as in July at the rate of 30 to 40 pounds per acre. It should be thrashed as soon as dry, as if left standing in mass it will quickly gather moist.

FIELD BEANS. Should be planted after all danger from frost is past. Does best in rich, dry, light soil. Hoe frequently while the plant is dry, but not otherwise. The Medium White, White Navy and the Bayo, or Chile varieties are mostly used for marketing in this country. Prices ou application.

FIELD PEAS. Should be sown on good cultivated soil at the rate of about one hundred and fifty pounds to the acre, in drills or broadcast. They are often sown in less quantity with oats and cut and cured together for hay, or threshed and bound together. Prices on application.

SUNFLOWER SEED. Is growing to be a valuable farm crop. The seed is very desirable for planting, while the leaves make excellent fodder. The plant is said to be an excellent protection from malaria, and should be grown for hedges about the house where this disease prevails.

ALL FIELD SEEDS, GRASS, CLOVER, ETC., when required in large quantity, will be sold at reduced rates, as market is variable, please write for special rates in quantity.

FIELD GRAIN.

☞ *Seed Wheat, Barley, Oats, Corn and other Grains, of every variety, will be furnished to our customers in quantities as may be desired; also Seed Potatoes at Lowest Market Rates. Prices given on application.*

TREE AND SHRUB SEEDS.

HOW TO GROW THEM.

THE growing of trees from seeds is in the case of some varieties a very simple and easy process, requiring but little care or skill on the part of the grower.

Some varieties require special treatment and great care and attention to insure success; others are very difficult to grow, and planters are not very likely to succeed until after having made repeated failures.

One important fact must be kept in view, and that is, IT TAKES TIME FOR THESE SEED TO GERMINATE, in some cases only a few days, in others, several weeks; while quite frequently they will lie dormant the whole season before commencing to grow. It often happens that seeds of a given variety, all taken from the tree at one time, sown together and subjected to the same treatment will show great irregularity in time of germinating, some coming up in a few days, others not until the next season, and still others not until the season following.

CONIFERS AND EVERGREEN TREE SEEDS should be kept in perfectly dry sand until the time of sowing; if this cannot be done readily, place them in a cool, dry spot, where mice will not eat them. CHESTNUTS and WALNUTS should be planted in the fall, or kept during the winter in sand or moss; they shrivel up by too long exposure to the air, and many of them lose their power of vegetating entirely APPLE, PEAR, QUINCE SEED, CHERRY PITS, PEACH PITS, also those with hard shells like the Locust, MAGNOLIAS, etc., should be placed in boxes with sand and exposed to frost before planting, otherwise they may not vegetate until a second year, but if too late in the spring to expose them to the action of the frost, they may be put into a vessel of hot water for an hour or so before planting. The seeds of DECIDUOUS TREES and SHRUBS, with few exceptions, can be planted from the end of March to the middle of May with success.

The soil should be deep, mellow and rich; if not so, make it so by deep spading and thoroughly pulverizing the ground. If not rich, apply a good liberal dressing of any old, well decomposed manure; mix thoroughly with the soil and raked down all smooth and level, and your seed-bed is ready. Now draw a line across one side of the plant, and with the hoe make a shallow trench from a half to one inch deep, according to the size of the seed to be sown; make the trench about six inches wide, scatter the seeds over the bottom, but not too thickly, then draw the soil back and cover to the depth of about the thickness of the seeds as evenly as possible, then press the beds gently with the back of the spade to make firm the earth around the seeds.

Great care must be taken not to give too much water, as the young plants imbibe moisture very easily. Water with a fine hose, but never so that the ground becomes soggy. Some shade must be used to protect the young plants from the hot, drying sun and winds, and also to keep the birds from destroying them.

The trenches or drills are to be two feet apart, so that the hoe or garden cultivator can be employed in cultivation. Keep the soil loose between the rows, and keep them well clear of the weeds. Seeds of the rarer sorts may be sown in cold-frames or in boxes; if in cold-frames, the sashes should be shaded and the frame raised at the corner three or four inches to allow the air to circulate freely.

Allow the young plants to remain from one to two years before transplanting.

CALIFORNIA TREE AND SHRUB SEEDS.

Abies Douglasii. Douglass Spruce. A very large timber tree, 200 to 300 feet high. of pyramidal shape. Found throughout the Rocky Mountains, from Oregon to Mexico. Very hardy. Oz. 50c.; lb., $5 00.

Abies Mertensiana. Tsuga M., Hemlock Spruce. A very large tree, 150 to 200 feet high, with rather thick, red-brown bark. Very hardy, ranging from California far into Alaska. Oz., 60c.; lb., $6 00.

Abies Menzeisii. Picea Sitchensis. Peculiar to the Northern Coast, found mostly in wet, sandy soil near the mouth of streams; the tallest spruce known; an excellent timber tree; pyramidal form. Very hardy. Oz. 60c.; lb., $6 00.

Cupressus Goveniana. Goven's Cypress. Thirty to forty feet high; very ornamental; found in the coast ranges of Monterey. Oz., 60c.; lb., $6 00.

Cupressus Macrocarpa. Monterey Cypress. A tree forty to sixty feet high, with rough bark, spreading, horizontal branches, with rich, green foliage; very ornamental for lawns or parks; also used extensively for hedges. Oz., 25c., lb., $2 50.

Cupressus McNabiana. McNab's Cypress. A small tree, six to ten feet high, found about Mt. Shasta, at 5,000 feet altitude. The leaves are small, and of a deep green. Oz. 40c.; lb., $4 00.

Cupressus Lawsoniana. Lawson's Cypress. A handsome tree, found in moist ground in the Shasta Mountains, and in the Coast ranges of Oregon. The wood is white, fragrant, fine and close grained, free from knots, easily worked, and very durable; also known as Oregon Cedar, White Cedar and Ginger Pine. Oz., 40c., lb., $4 00.

Cupressus Italian. A very erect, close-growing tree; fine for entrances and arches. Oz., 25c.; lb., $3 00.

Cupressus Guadalupensis. Blue Cypress. A new fast-growing variety with beautiful bluish foliage; very ornamental for lawns, parks and cemeteries. Oz., 25c.

Libocedrus decurrens. Thuya Craigiana. Found in the coast ranges, from Oregon to San Diego; grows from 100 to 150 feet high; fine, hardy timber tree; known as the White Cedar of California. Oz., 30c., lb., $3 00.

Madrona. A beautiful native tree of California; the foliage is of a deep green, and feathery; it attains a considerable size, flowers white. Oz., 25c.

Picea amabilis Silver Fir. Tall, symmetrical, valuable timber tree. Oz., 50c ; lb., $5 00.

Picea grandis. Balsam Fir. Grows 200 to 300 feet high, four to six feet in diameter; grows in rich, moist soils; valuable timber tree. Oz., 50c.; lb., $5 00.

Picea nobilis. California Red Fir. A magnificent tree, with thick, brown bark, making fine timber; forms large forests about the base of Mt. Shasta; timber said to be better than that of other firs. Oz., 50c.; lb., $5 00.

Picea Magnifica. 200 to 250 feet high. The Red Fir of the Sierras, found at an altitude of 7,000 feet. Very hardy. Oz., 60c.; lb., $6 00.

Picea Concolor. Abies lasiocarpa. A very ornamental tree; 100 to 200 feet high; very common throughout the Sierras, ranging into Oregon; also found in Arizona, Utah and Colorado. Oz., 50c.; lb., $5 00.

Pinus Benthamiana. A magnificent tree; grows from 200 to 300 feet high; fine timber. Very hardy. Oz., 50c.; lb., $5 00.

Pinus Coulteri. Great Coned Pine. Found in the coast ranges from Mt. Diablo to the southern part of this State. Oz., 35c.; lb., $3 50.

Pinus contorta. A low tree, five to fifteen feet high, found on the wet, sandy coast of the Pacific, from Mendocino to Alaska. Very hardy. Oz., 70c.; lb. $5 00.

Pinus Fremontiana. Pinus monophylla. A small tree, twenty to twenty-five feet high; frequent in the coast ranges in Nevada, Arizona and Utah; well known as the Nut Pine. Oz., 30c.; lb., $3 00.

Pinus insignis. Monterey Pine. A very ornamental tree for parks or lawns; grows from sixty to seventy feet high, of rapid growth, and has beautiful, green foliage. Oz., 25c., lb., $2 50.

Pinus Jeffreyi. A magnificent tree, from 100 to 200 feet high; usually found on our mountains at an elevation of 5,000 feet, ranging from California to Oregon. Very hardy. Oz., 35c.; lb., 3 50.

Pinus Lambertiana. Sugar pine. A hardy tree of gigantic dimensions, from 250 to 300 feet high, and from fifteen to twenty feet thick, with light brown, smoothish bark; found on both slopes of the Sierras. The wood is like that of the White Pine. Oz., 30c.; lb., $3 00.

Pinus monticola. From sixty to eighty feet high, and about three feet in diameter at the base. Found at an altitude from 7,000 to 10,000 feet, known as the white pine of California, and of the North. Oz., 60c.; lb., $6 00.

Pinus Parryana. A small tree, twenty to thirty feet high, found in the vicinity of San Diego, at an altitude of 2,000 feet. Oz., 50c.; lb., $5 00.

Pinus ponderosa. Yellow Pine. One of the largest pines known, 200 to 300 feet high, and twelve to fifteen feet in diameter, with very thick red-brown bark. Found in the Coast Range. Very hardy. Oz., 40c.; lb., $4 00.

Pinus tuberculata. California Scrub Pine. A small crooked tree, often found full of cones when only two or three feet high. Oz. 50c.; lb., $5 00.

Sequoia gigantea. Wellingtouia gigantea. The mammoth tree of California. This is the largest tree known to exist on the American continent, grows over 300 feet high. The bark is from one to two feet thick. Many of these California trees are over 90 feet in circumference. Oz., 60c., lb., $6 00.

Sequoia sempervirens. Known as the Redwood of California. The most valuable timber of the California forests. From 200 to 250 feet high, and from eight to twelve feet in diameter. The wood is of a rich, brownish red, light, but strong and durable, making excellent timber. Hardy. Oz., 50c., lb. $3 00.

Thuya gigantea. Giant Arbor Vitae. A tall graceful tree, 200 to 250 feet high, three to twelve feet thick, pyramidal form, with spreading and somewhat drooping branches, frequent in the coast ranges of Oregon. The wood is soft, fine-grained, and of light color. Oz., 60c., lb., $6 00.

Torreya Californica California Nutmeg. Found in the mountain districts. Grows to the hight of 60 feet the wood is light-colored, close-grained and small branches being redish. Oz., 25., lb., $2 00.

Arctostaphylos glauca. Great berried Manzanita. Oz., 50c., lb $2 00.

Mountain Laurel. Spice Tree. A handsome shrub or tree twenty to seventy feet high, the timber very handsome and valuable for ornamental wainscoting and finishing. Oz., 25c.. lb., $2 00.

Negundo Californicum, Box Elder. Usually a small tree, sometimes reaching a height of seventy feet. Oz., 25c., lb., $1 50.

Acer Macropyllum. Maple. A tree of 50 to 90 feet high, from coast ranges in California. The wood is white, hard, and takes a fine polish. Oz., 25c., lb., $2 50.

Cornus Nuttalli. Dogwood. A small showy tree, flowering in May, followed by large clusters of double berries, resembling the eastern Cornus. Wood close-grained and very hard. Oz., 50c., lb., $5 00.

Azalea occidentalis. Charming California Azalea, the ornament of the wooded districts. Flowers two to three inches long, white, pink variegated. Pkt. 25c.

Yellow or Black Locust. Robinia psuedo-accacia. This variety is noted for its rapid growth of hard and durable timber. It is hardy and succeeds well in most soils and climates. Oz., 10c ; lb., 60c.

Honey Locust. Gleditschia Triacanthos. This is a large and handsome tree. The trunk and branches generally beset with long and formidable spines, on which account it has been employed as a hedge. The wood is heavy and affords excellent fuel. Oz., 10c.; lb., 6 0c.

Osage Orange. Maclura Aurantiaca. One of the most valuable of hedge plants. The plants will also grow into fine trees, and the wood endures for centuries. Lb., 50c.

Hawthorn. Crataegus oxyacantha. A very handsome thorny hedge plant, which has been grown in various parts of the Northern and Middle States. Oz., 15.; lb., $1 50.

Buckthorn. Rhamnus catharticus. This makes a strong thorny hedge, adapted to the North and Middle States. Oz., 20c., lb., $2 00.

AUSTRALIAN TREE AND SHRUB SEEDS.

Eucalyptus globulous. Blue Gum. A very rapid growing tree, making valuable timber; height 200 feet. Oz., 50c.; lb., $3 00.

E. Rostrata. Red Gum. Oz , 50c.; lb., $6 00.

*E. bicolor. Black Box. A valuable timber tree; it is equal to the best Ironbark for all the purposes for which that wood is used, and is more easily wrought. It is sometimes called "Ironbark," 100 to 150 feet. Oz., 75c.

*E Citriodora. Lemon-scented Gum. A useful timber. The strong lemon scent which is emitted when the leaves are gently rubbed, is equally powerful and agreeable with that of the lemon-scented Verbena. Oz., 75c.

*E. hemipholia. Common Box. A hard but useful timber, strong, tough and durable, but will not last sunk in the ground. It is also a first-class fuel for domestic use or other industrial purposes. 100 to 150 feet.

*E longifolia. Woollybutt. An average sized tree. Fair timber for fencing and building purposes; it is a good fuel for domestic use; very durable. 100 to 120 feet. Oz., 75c.

*E leucoxylon. Crimson Flowered Eucalyptus. This is a very ornamental species of Eucalyptus; having large and very beautiful flowers, color crimson; and as the tree flowers while quite young, it is very desirable as an addition to the shrubbery or flower border. Oz., 75c.

*E obliqua. Stringybark. The best wood for flooring boards and rafters. It is of very quick growth, inferior fuel, but produces the best charcoal. 120 feet. Oz , 75c.

*E. paniculata. Common Ironbark. For most purposes is equal to the last species, and is more easily split into shingles or palings, it is as lasting and as good fuel as other Ironbarks; the wood is not so dark in color. 150 feet.

*E paniculata var., mycrophylla. Small-leaved Ironbark. The wood of this species is used for fencing and many purposes, the same as the other Ironbarks. But the wood being of a nature much more easy to work.

to which the hardness of the other sorts offers an obstacle, first-class fuel. 120 feet. Oz., 75c.

*E. robusta. Swamp Mahogany. A good lasting timber for house carpentry and many kinds of turnery, but not durable in the ground. 150 feet. Oz., 75c.

*E. siderophloia. Dark or broad-leaved Ironbark. The most valuable wood for piles, girders, railway sleepers; and for every purpose in which strength and durability are required. This specie is the strongest of all Australian timbers, and superior to most as fuel for steam engines, as it throws off more heat, etc. 150 feet. Oz., 75c.

Acacia decurrens. Black Wattle. Oz.. 50c., lb., $5 00

Acacia melanoxylon. Lightwood. Oz., 50c.

Acacia mollissima. Oz. 50c.

*Acacia pyenantha. Golden Wattle. Oz., 50c., lb., $5 00.

Acacia floribunda. Oz , 50c.

Acacia lopantha. Crested Wattle. Oz., 25c., lb., $2 00.

Dracena indivisa· A very desirable tree for a garden or a lawn, of graceful habit, makes rapid growth, very hardy, native of New Zealand. Oz., 50c., lb., $4 00.

Grevillea robusta· Silk Oak of East Australia. Beautiful fern-like foliage, attains a height of 100 feet, withstands drouth, of rapid growth, and flowers when about twenty feet in height, then it is a sight worth seeing, covered from top to bottom with bright orange scarlet flowers. Pkt. 50c., oz., $2 00.

Pittosporum eugenoides, nigrescens. and **undulatum.** Valuable evergreens; an ornamental shrub or tree from Southern Australia. Pkt., 25c.; oz., $1 00.

CONIFERS AND EVERGREEN TREE SEED.

Arbor Vitæ, American. Thuja occidentalis. Useful for hedges and wind breaks. Oz., 30c., lb., $3 00.

Chinese Arbor Vitæ. A small, elegant tree, with erect branches, and dense flat, light green foliage; becomes brown in winter. Oz., lb., 25c.; $2 50.

Golden Arbor Vitæ. A variety of the Chinese, nearly spherical in outline, with bright yellow tinged foliage. Beautiful. Oz , 50c., lb., $5 00.

Fir Balsam. Balsamea A small evergreen tree of symmetrical growth, and conical form when young. Of rapid growth, with rich, green foliage. Oz., 30c, lb., $3 00.

Fir Silver. A well known evergreen tree, tall symmetrical, very valuable. Oz., 15c., lb., $1 50.

Larch European. Larix Europœa. Valuable for forest planting. Oz.,15c., lb., $1 50.

Magnolia Grandiflora. The most majestic of all American trees, a native of the Southern States, perfectly hardy here. Oz., 25c,, lb., $2 50.

Pine, Scotch. Pinus Sylvestris. One of the most valuable of European varieties. It is hardy, of rapid growth, and adapted to a great variety of soil and climate. Oz , 20c., lb., $2 00.

Pine, White, or Weymouth. Pinus Strobus. An old, well known and useful tree. Of gigantic proportions and rapid growth. Oz., 30c. lb., $3 00.

Pepper Tree. Schinus molle. A handsome, ornamental evergreen tree, of graceful habit, light green foliage, and bright scarlet, berries; a desirable tree for parks and lawns. Oz., 25c., lb., $2 00.

Red Cedar. Juniperus Virginiana. Very valuable timber, and fine ornamental tree. It will stand the dry hot winds, and for wind-breaks, as well as for fence posts, the Red Cedar is invaluable, symmetrical in growth and readily shaped with the shears; it is one of the most useful trees. After properly planting, it will stand more neglect than any other evergreen. Oz, 15c., lb., $1 50.

Spruce Hemlock. Canadensis. A known evergreen tree of high latitudes. It is one of the most graceful of spruces, with a light and spreading, branches almost to the ground. It is a beautiful tree for the lawn and makes a highly ornamental hedge. Oz., 40c., lb., $4 00.

Spruce Norway. Abies Excelsa. A popular variety from Europe. Extensively planted for ornamental purposes, and for timber and wind-breaks. It is easily transplanted or grown from seed and succeeds in a great variety of soils and climate. Oz., 15c., lb., $1 50.

Brahea Filamamentosa. California Fan Palm, a hardy, vigorous growing plant; foliage very regular, of a bright green, deeply and regularly pinnated, the margins being covered with hair-like filaments, giving them a remarkable appearance. They are beautiful decorative plants in all respects, for in or outdoor use. Oz., 30c., lb, $3 00

FOREST AND DECIDUOUS TREE SEEDS.

Ash-American, White. Fraxinus American Americans. Prefers moist soil, but will grow almost anywhere; wood valuable for handles, in wagon-making, etc.; grows rapidly, one of the best of timbers; best when grown on dry land. Oz., 10c., lb., $1 00.

Ash-European. Fraxinus excelsior. Suitable for warm climates and dry loam soils, wood used in carriage-making. Oz., 10c., lb., $1 00.

Box Elder. Acer Negundo. Thrives on the western plains, grows rapidly, attaining 70 feet in height, excellent for planting along highways, endures drought. It sap yields sugar. Oz., 10c., lb., $1 00.

Catalpa Hardy. Catalpa Speciosa. An upright and rapid grower, the trees being remarkably straight and tall, so that even in mild climates, where hardiness is no object, the superior habit of growth of this variety is a matter of the utmost importance in its favor. Oz., 10c. lb., $1 00.

Elm-European. Ulmus Campestris. The best Elm for ornamental and for city planting. Oz., 10c., lb., $1 00.

Lime or Linden Sills Europma. Makes good paper pulp, the inner bark is used for cordage, matting, etc. Oz., 10c., lb , $1 00.

Norway Maple. Acer plantanoides. A well known ornamental tree. Oz., 10c., lb., $1 00.

Sugar Maple. Acer saccharinum. It succeeds well in all soils and locations, making a stout, vigorous, rapid growth of hard wood, most valuable for fuel and highly prized for manufacturing purposes. Oz., 10c., ¼ lb., 30c.; lb., $1 00.

Maple Soft, or Silver leaved. Acer dasycarpum. One of the most beautiful of Maples. Is being extensively planted on account of its extremely rapid growth. Its wood is soft and light, and the branches are often broken by the action of the wind and storm. Oz., 10c., lb., $1 00.

Mulberry White. Morus alba. Oz., 25c., lb., $2 50, **Mulberry Black.** Morus nigra. Oz., 25c., ¼ lb., 75c., lb., $2 50

Mulberry Russian. Valuable for its fruit, and its timber, which makes valuable posts and stakes, being hard elastic, close grained and susceptible of a fine polish. The Mulberry is also used for hedges, and the leaves for food for silk worms. The berries are often more than an inch long, and one-half inch or more in diameter. They are more acid and sprightly that our American Mulberries, and the fruit is prized by the Russians, for desert, and cooked in various ways, also made into wine. Oz., 40c., lb., $4 00.

Linden Silver or White-leaved European. A vigorous growing tree, of medium size and pyramidal form. It is noticeable among trees by its white appearance. Its handsome form, growth and foliage render it worthy to be classed among the finest of our ornamental trees. Oz., 25c., lb., $1 25.

Tree of Heaven. Ailanthus glandulosus. Quite extensively planted in some states, and is noted for its extremely rapid growth. It grows to a large size, and the foliage has a rich tropical appearance. Oz., 10c., lb., $1 00.

Virginia Creeper. American Ivy. Ampelopsis quinquefolia. This native vine is one of the most ornamental of the climbers, and is much cultivated for cover, ing walls and buildings. It is perfectly hardly, and give a dense mass of brilliant green throughout the summers which in the autumn changes to the richest shades of crimson and purple. Oz., 25c., lb., $2 50.

FRUIT TREE SEEDS.

Apple PyrusMalus Apple seeds do not reproduce the same variety. Upon the stock thus used for seed are grafted or budded the varieties desired. The seed can be planted in good soil, any time during the winter, or early in the spring, in rows eighteen inches apart. During their growth they should be well cultivated and kept free from weeds. ¼ lb., 20c.; lb., 50c.

Cherry Mahaleb. Cerasus Mahaleb. The remarks regarding apple seeds are applicable to cherries. This variety is considered the best stock upon which to graft the choicer sorts. ¼ lb., 20c.; lb., 60c.

Cherry Mazzard. Cerasus Communis. The common or ordinary variety of cherry is useful alone for grafting purposes. The stock is hardy, and if properly grafted, fine fruit can be relied on. ¼ lb., 20c.; lb., 50c.

Pear. Pyrus Communis. Sow the seed thickly in drills eighteen inches apart. The soil should be rich—a deep, moist loam is most suitable. The value of the stock depends largely on a rapid and vigorous growth the first season. Oz., 25c.; lb., $2 50.

Plum. Prunus Communis. The directions given for planting apples will also apply to plums, except the pits should be planted farther apart in the row. ¼ lb., 20c., lb., 50c.

Peach. Amygdalis Persica. Peach stocks are raised by planting the stones two or three inches deep. If the stones are cracked they are more sure to grow. The after treatment is about the same as for apples, though budding can be commenced sooner than grafting in apple stocks. Lb., 5c.; 100 lbs., $3 00.

Apricot Pits. Armenia Vulgaris. Planted and cultivated same as peach pits. Lb., 10c.; 100 lbs., $5 00.

Quince. Cydonia Communis. The culture for seed is the same as for apples. Oz., 25c.; lb., $2 50.

Texas Umbrella Tree. This is one of the finest ornamental and attractive trees known. It makes a spreading umbrella shape. Tip of very dense and beautiful foliage, will grow from 20 to 30 feet high. Oz., 30c.; lb., $3 00.

COLLECTION B. OF STRONG'S CHOICE
FLOWER SEEDS FOR 45 CTS VALUE 65 CTS.

No.1. Senecio elegans fl.pleno.
Tall Double Jacobaea. 5 cts.

No.2. Primula japonica var.
(Japanese Primrose). 15 cts.

No.3. Calendula „Meteor."
5 cts.

No.4. Bartonia aurea.
5 cts.

No.5. Myosotis alpestris.
(Alpine Forget-me-not). 10 cts.

No.6. Convolvulus tricolor (minor).
5 cts.

No.7. Penistemon gentianoides.
(Hartwegi hybridus). 10 cts.

No.8. Petunia hybrida Inimitable.
Striped and Blotched. 5 cts.

No.9. Lychnis chalcedonica.
5 cts.

FLOWER SEEDS

These require a good sandy soil, enriched with good fertilizers and well pulverized, loose and moderately moist. Sow the seed in usual way in boxes or warm seed bed, covering lightly, and keep in total darkness till the plant begins to show above ground, when gradually expose to the light. By pursuing this plan, uniform temperature and moisture is secured, and all seeds possessing life will be sure to grow. When the plants have grown to say to two inches in height, they are ready to transplant. Give plenty of room, according to habit of growth of the plant. Crowding destroys the vigor and beauty of the flower.

We offer the following liberal inducements to those who wish to purchase Fower Seeds in quantity. These rates apply only to seeds in packets, but the seeds will be sent by mail, post-paid.

Send us $1.00 and select Packets to value of $1.20.
Send us $2.00 and select Packets to value of $2.50.
Send us $3.00 and select Packets to value of $4.00.

ABBREVIATIONS MADE IN FLOWER SEED LIST.

A.—For Annuals that grow, bloom and die the first year. B.—For Biennials blooming and dying the second year. P.—For Perennials that usually bloom the first or second year from seed, but continue to grow and bloom for many years thereafter. H.—Indicates Hardy. H. H.—Half Hardy. T.—Tender.

The hardy can be sown in open ground early, or almost any time, not requiring protection. Half hardy cannot be sown in open ground until the weather becomes warm, unless sown in greenhouse or with good protection.

ABOBRA (Climber.) H. H. P., 10 feet.
Rapid growing, with dazzling scarlet fruit... 10c

ABRONIA. H. A. 9 to 18 in.
Trailing and prostrate habit, like the Verbena, and quite fragrant; natives of California.
Abronia Umbellata, rosy.................. 10c
" Arenaria, yellow................. 16c

ABUTILON. (Chinese Bellflower.)
H. H. A., 2 to 4 feet.
Flowers freely in house in Winter and Spring, and a good bedding Summer plant......... 15c
White, Yellow and Crimson mixed.......... 15c

ADLUMIA (Mountain Fringe.) H. B., 18 feet.
Climber, graceful foliage, light pink, tubular flowers.................................. 5c

ADONIS. (Pheasant's Eye.) H. A., 1 foot.
The Adonis has pretty, narrow leaves, and are very brilliant. It will flourish almost anywhere, in the shade or under trees.
Autumnalis. Autumn; blood red; 1 foot.... 5c
Vernalis. Yellow........................ 5c

AGERATUM. H. B.
Bears a great many flowers, and keeps in bloom a long time, and is, therefore, desirable for bouquet making. It is well to start the seed under glass transplant.
Ageratum Conspicum. White-flowered, blooms until frost, 18 inches............. 5c
Ageratum Lasseauxi. Very fine rose flowers, most valuable for cutting................ 10c
Ageratum Mexicanum. (Little Dorritt.) Azure blue, dwarf, splendid for bedding... 5c
Ageratum Mexicanum. (Little Dorritt.) Albiflorum, white....................... 5c

AGROSTEMMA (Rose Campion.)
H. P. 1 to 2 feet.
Annual, very pretty, free blooming and hardy; always makes desirable beds and useful for cutting; 12 inches in height.

Red and white........................... 5c
Atrosanguinea, dark blood-red.......... 5c
Alba; white............................. 5c
Finest mixed............................ 5c

ALYSSUM. H. A., 1 feet.

Pretty little white flowers, useful in making up all kinds of small bouquets. Its fragrance is very delicate. The Alyssum grows freely from seed and makes a pretty border.

Alyssum, Sweet, hardy annual, flowers small in clusters, 6 inches...................... 5c

Wierzbeckii, hardy perennials, yellow, 1 foot high.................................... 5c

Saxatile Compactum. Yellow compact for edgings................................. 5c

Serpyllifolium. Quite dwarf; yellow........ 5c

Procumbens. Very dwarf, white........... 5c

Compactum, Erectum. New, erect, flowering charming.................................. 5c

ALONSOA. H. H. A.

Young plants removed to the house or greenhouse in the autumn, will continue to flower during the winter, · The flowers are small but of remarkably brilliant colors.

Alonsoa Grandiflora. Large flowered, scarlet, 2 feet in height...................... 5c

Alonsoa Albiflora. White................. 5c

AMARANTHUS. H. H. A., 2 to 5 feet.

Valuable for their ornamental foliage, the leaves of most varieties being highly colored.

Tricolor (Joseph's Coat.) Red, yellow and green foliage............................. 5c

Melancholicus Ruber, of compact habit, with striking blood red foliage; 18 inches...... 5c

Caudatus (Love lies bleeding), long drooping "chains" of flowers, pretty for decoration.. 5c

Cruentus (Prince's Feather), flowers somewhat similar to A. Caudatus, but in erect masses.................................. 5c

Bicolor Ruber. Carmine scarlet; splendid.. 5c

Tricolor Splendens. Very beautiful; new.. 10c

Monstrosus. Blood red, flower spike........ 5c

Salicifolius. Highly decorative. Fountain plant.

AMMOBIUM (Everlasting Flower).

Ammobium Alatum Grandiflorum. A large flowered white, everlasting; fine for dried bouquets with fancy grasses, pick the flowers in the bud to dry................. 5c

AMPELOPSIS
(Vetchi, Japan Woodbine, Climber.)

Very hardy and rapid grower; attaches to buildings, fences, etc., as closely as English Ivy; leaves olive green, changing to scarlet. Easy to cultivate and ornamental; 50 feet. 10c

ANAGALLIS.

Anagallis is remarkable for the beauty of its flowers, useful for borders or baskets. Should be sown under glass; 6 inches.

Anagallis Grandiflora Superba, mixed colors 5c

ACROLINIUM (Everlasting). H. H. P., 1 foot.

Fine for Winter bouquets; pure white and rose colors............................... 5c

Acrolinium Flore Pleno. Fine double varieties, mixed.............................. 10c

ANTIRRHINUM MAJUS (Snapdragon.)
H. A., 2 to 3 ft.

One of the very best of our perennials, blooms abundantly the first Summer until after frost, and flowers well the second Summer and even longer. By removing a portion of the flowers, the plants will become strong.

Brilliant, scarlet, golden and white......... 5c
Luteum, yellow........................... 5c
Striatum, finest striped................... 5c
Majus, tall varieties; fine mixed............ 5c
Majus Album, pure white.................. 5c

Nanum (Dwarf varieties).

Album, pure white........................ 5c
Firefly, scarlet............................ 5c
Picturatum, new blotched................. 3c
Dwarf Varieties, fine mixed............... 5c

ARGEMONE. H. H. P.s 2 feet.

Handsome, large growing plant for flower-beds; white and yellow flowers resembling Poppies.

Hunnemanni, dark yellow flowers.......... 5c
Platyceras Grandiflora, large white flowers. 5c

AQUILEGIA.

Ornamental hardy plants known as (Columbine, or Wild Honeysuckle). Showy, and one of the best early bloomers; herbaceous; hardy perennial. Effective in rockeries.

Alpine, blue.............................. 5c
Artica, brick-red and green................ 10c
Chrysantha, golden spurred; beautiful, long yellow spurred flowers.................... 5c
Bicolor, fl. pl. Double blue and white...... 10c
Bicolor fl., pl., Rubra, double red.......... 10c
Vulgaris, fl. pl., fine double varieties, mixed. 10c
Vulgaris, fl. pl., Alba, double white........ 10c
Single varieties, mixed.................... 5c
Vervaeneana. Variegated foliage.......... 15c

ASPERULA.

A dwarf plant covered all summer with Cineraria-like blossoms; annual, blue, white and mixed colors.

Azurea Setosa, blue, free bloomer, sweet-scented................................. 5c
Odorata (Sweet Woodruff), white........... 5c

ASTERS.

Are one of the most popular and effective garden favorites, producing in abundance flowers of great richness and variety. They make elegant borders and showy beds; hardy annual.

Truffaut's Large Peony Flower. A favorite class, thrifty, upright growers; flowers large and almost perfectly round, with incurved petals; height 18 inches to 2 feet.... 10c
New Rose, 2 feet in height; robust, large flowers, petals finely imbricated; one of the very best; mixed colors.................. 10c
Imbricate Pompon, very perfect, almost a globe and beautifully imbricated; mixed colors.................................. 10c

Betteridge's Quilled. Plants strong and branching flowers composed of tube or quilled shaped petals, with a single row of outer flat petals, which are often a different color from the center. A very beautiful Aster. Mixed colors per pkt. 10c.

Cocardeau or New Crown, two colored flowers, the central petals being of pure white, sometimes small and quilled, surrounded with large, flat petals of a bright color, 18 inches, mixed colors; beautiful 10c

New Pæony-flowered Globe, the earliest of the Asters, flowers very large, plant branching and strong; does not require support.. 10c

Hedgehog or Needle. petals long, quilled and sharply pointed; 2 feet; mixed colors....... 10c

Chrysanthemum-flowered Dwarf White, a superb variety, every flower usually perfect; fine mixed varieties............ .... 10c

Dwarf Bouquet. splendid for edging and small beds................................ 10c

Dwarf Bouquet, pyramidal shaped.......... 10c

Dwarf Victoria, flowers very double and round; many extremely delicate, and some gorgeous shades, handsome varieties, mixed colors 10c

Mignon Aster, pure white flowers of beautiful form, resembling the Victoria race...... 15c

Alpinus, alpine aster, perennial, blue....... 5c

Alpinus Gymnocephalus, perennial, rose.. 5c

BALSAM.
(Lady Slipper or Touch-Me-Not).

This is one of the most beautiful and popular annuals. They are sown in beds or frames, and if growing too thick, thin out and prune as desired. They transplant readily. Among the many varieties we name:

Double Camelia-Flower, Double Rose-Flowered, Double Spotted and Carnation, striped.each 10c

Extra Double Mixed, of above and others.... 10c

BALLOON VINE (Cardiospermum).
H. A., 4 to 8 feet.

A half hardy, rapid growing, handsome climber, having small white flowers, which are followed by seed vessels shaped like balloons.................................... 5c

BELLIS (Double Daisy).
H. H. P., 6 inches.

Beautiful for edging, dwarf groups and beds; earliest and prettiest of the spring flowers.

Finest mixed and pure white............... 10c

Longfellow, new, large, double rose-colored flowers; fine............................ 15c

BEGONIA (Tuberous Rooted.)

Magnificent flowering plants for pots, and in Europe is extensively bedded out, flowering in the greatest profusion all Summer.

Single varieties........................... 15c

Double varieties........................... 25c

BARTONIA. H. A.

A succulent plant with large golden flowers expanding in the middle of the day.

Aurea or golden yellow; 2 feet 5c

BRACHYCOME (Swan River Daisy.)
H. A., ½ foot.

A dwarf plant covered all summer with Cineraria-like blossoms, annual; blue, white and mixed colors............................... 5c

BIDENS ATROSANGUINEA.
(Dahlia Zimapani)

A large showy free flowering plant, resembling single Dahlias; black purple flowers, fine... 10c

BROWALLIA. H. H. A.; 1½ feet.

The Browallias are excellent, free-flowering, and valuable for winter house-plants. When bedded out in Summer, are completely studded with bright, delicate flowers the whole season.

Czerwiakowski, deep blue, very fine........ 10c

Elata Alba, white.......................... 5c

Elata Nana, new, compact, very fine........ 10c

Elata Grandiflora, blue.................... 5c

Browallia abbreviata (pulchella,) deep rose pretty for pot culture...................... 10c

BRYONOPSIS (Ornamental Cucumber.)

A very beautiful climber, bearing green fruits, which change to bright scarlet striped with white; 8 to 10 feet....................... 5c

CACALIA. H. A., 1½ feet.

Pretty free-flowering plant, often called Flora's Paint Brush. Set plant six inches apart, They bloom early in summer until autumn; mixed colors............................... 5c

CALAMPELIS (Climber). H. H. A., 10 feet.

Scabra, blooms in racemes of bright orange flowers; one of the finest climbers........ 5c

CALANDRINIA. H. H. A., 1 foot.

Beautiful dwarf plant; succeed best in light rich soil. The sunshine causes the flowers to expand like portulaca, in a perfect blaze of beauty.

Mixed colors, large and showy.............. 5c

CALENDULA. H. A.

Remarkably free-flowering plants, producing a fine effect in beds and borders; succeeds in any garden soil; height 1 foot.

Officinalis, fl. pl., Le Proust; Nankeen colored, very fine; double, constant.............. 5c

Meteor, large doubled striped flowers of light orange.................................. 5c

Prince of Orange, similar to meteor but much darker; very beautiful................ 5c

CALCEOLARIA (Greenhouse Plant).
T. P., 1½ feet.

Gorgeous plants for greenhouse and window decoration; the large pocket-shaped flowers are borne in the greatest profusion through the Spring and Summer months; colors, yellow, maroon crimson, etc.; spotted and blotched in the most unique and beautiful fashion; height, 1½ feet.

Grandiflora, finest mixed.................. 25c

Pinnata California, yellow.................. 5c

Rugosa. Shrubby or bedding calceolarias, more hardy than the grandiflora variety is, bearing innumerable flowers; beautiful and small.. 25c

Striata, fine striped and mottled........... 25c

48 W. R. Strong Company, Sacramento, Cal.

CALLIOPSIS (Coreopsis.). H. A. 2 ft.

Showy, free-flowering and beautiful annual; the tall are fine for beds and mixed borders, and dwarf for bedding. Crimson, yellow, brown and marbled; mixed colors.

Atkinsoni, yellow and brown; biennial	5c
Cardaminifolia, of pyramidal habit	5c
Cornuta, yellow and large-flowered	5c
Longipes, yellow, perennial	5c
Fine mixture of tall sorts	5c
Fine mixture of dwarf sorts	5c

CALLIRHOE.

Beautiful annual; violet, purple and crimson flowers; white center; attractive, and blooms through the summer ... 5c

CAMPANULA (Canterbury Bell).

H. A. and P., 6 to 12 inches.

Well-known favorites; bearing large bell and saucer-shaped flowers in profusion.

Medium, fl. pl.; double blue, double white and double rose, each separate	10c
Medium, single, finest mixed	5c
Medium Striata, new; striped, very fine	10c
Calycanthema (Cup and Saucer). The flowers are large, resembling somewhat a cup and saucer; blue, white and lilac; fine mixed.	15c
Rosea, single rose	5c
Pyramidalis, very beautiful sorts, fine colors, mixed	5c
Speculum (Venus's Looking Glass). Single, finest mixed	5c
Speculum, double sorts, finest mixed	10c

CANARY BIRD FLOWER (Climber.)

H. H. A., 10 to 15 feet.

TROPŒOLUM.

Popular and pretty; rapid grower and abundant bloomer of rich yellow fringed flowers ... 10c

CANNA (Indian Shot). H. H. P.

Stately and ornamental plants, desirable in groups or background; soak seed in hot water 12 hours before sowing.

Extra choice mixed	5c
Dark leaved varieties	10c

CANDYTUFT. H. A. 6 to 12 inches.

Popular and useful, blooming long and freely and perfectly hardy. The flowers are quite a treasure for making bouquets and for massing or ribbon gardening. Varieties and shades are numerous.

Amara, pure white	5c
Coronaria "White Rocket;" large trusses of pure white flowers; much prized by the florists	
"Empress." A most beautiful Candytuft, being a series of Candellabra shaped branches each producing a large truss of white flowers, thus presenting a pyramid of bloom throughout the season	10c
"Carter's Carmine." This new variety is of a dwarf, compact habit, and bears a mass of fine Carmine bloom, true from seed	10c
Purpurea (Dark Crimson) beautiful	5c
Fine mixed, annual sorts	5c

Sempervirens Perennial. White, blooming and hardy, adapted for rockeries, baskets and etc ... 5c

CARNATION (Dianthus.)

H. H. P, 1 to 2 feet.

Magnificent and popular, very fragrant, and beautiful colors; hardy perennial.

Finest strains of German and Italian seed	25c
Good Mixed	10c
Grenadin. A new dwarf compact variety of great value to florists, producing a profusion of large double, brilliant scarlet flowers three weeks earlier than any other variety.	25c
Early Flowering Vienna. Extra fine	20c
Grenadin. White, new novelty	25c
German Perpetual or tree	25c

CASSIA.

Hardy perennial, with yellow flowers, 18 inches high; good border flower ... 5c

CATANANCHE COERULEA.

Coerulea, coerulea, fl. albo (bicolor). Fine everlastings.

Fine perennials, blue and white mixed ... 5c

CATCHFLY (Silene). H. A. 1½ feet.

Showy and great favorite; annual; bright dense heads of flowers; blooms freely and of easy culture; colors, red and white mixed double ... 5c

Pendula Carnea, double red, new and fine	5c
Compacta Alba, double white new and pretty	5c
Snow King, pure white Globular, new, and a fine novelty	10c
Orientalis Compacta, red compact	5c

CONVALLARIA MAJALIS (Lily of the Valley).

One of the most charming of our spring flowering plants, its slender stems set with tiny bells diffusing a delicious odor, have rendered it a universal favorite. They are very hardy, and require a shaded situation, soil rich sandy loam. Clean seed in berries ... 10c

Japonica, very fine ... 10c

CENTRANTHUS. H. A. 1½ feet.

Pretty, free flowering annual, effective in beds and borders; transparent stems and glaucous leaves; rose colored and white ... 5c

CENTAUREA. H. A.

Showy border plant, succeeding in almost any soil; hardy annual and perennial; varieties.

Bachelor's Button or Corn Bottle, 2 feet; quite showy	5c
Sweet Sultan, Hardy annual; 1 foot	5c

CLARKIA. H. A. 1 to 2 feet.

Hardy annual plant, blooming profusely with handsome flowers.

Double and single, mixed colors ... 5c

CINERARIA (Greenhouse Plant).

H. H. P., 1 foot.

Hybrida Grandiflora, a favorite attractive free flowering plant, blooming during the winter and early spring months. Mixed in Hot House or Conservatory.................. 25c

Plenissima, new, double, from finest double flowers. Beautiful........................ 40c

CHRYSANTHEMUM.

H. A. and P. 12 to 18 inches.

Very showy and effective favorites; colors have the appearance of being laid on with a brush; annual and perennial; varieties.

Chrysanthemum (Single Annual Varieties).

Tricolor Carinatum Album, white.......... 5c
Burridgi, (Lord Beaconsfield), white and rose. 5c
Coronarium, fl. pl., double yellow.......... 5c
Corocarium, fl. pl., double white............ 5c

Chrysanthemum, (Perennial varieties).

Indicum Majus, large flowering double varieties............................... 25c
Indicum, double pom pon mixed............ 25c
Japonicum, fl. pleno, Japannese............ 25c
Japonicum Nanum, fl. pl., dwarf double Japanese................................. 25c
Uliginosum, abundant, large white flowers, fine for cutting...................... 10c
Frutescens Grandiflorum, (Marguerite or Paris Daisy), H. P., now so fashionable and popular; large white star-like flowers, growing freely and profusely.................. 10c

COBŒA (Scandens).

H. H. P., 20 to 30 feet.

Climbing plant; rapid grower and large bell-shaped flowers; fine for Summer; plant seed edgewise............................... 10c
Scandens, fl. Alba, white.................. 20c

COLEUS.   T. P., 1 to 3 feet.

Ornamental foliage plant; leaves of all shapes and colors, of velvety appearance and great beauty. Splendid flower for garden decoration. Finest hybrid, mixed.............. 25c

COILINSIA.   H. H. A., 1 to 2 feet.

California annual; marbled or many colored, for beds and borders.................... 5c

COCKSCOMB (Celosia).

Annual plant, showy and attractive; half hardy
Cristata nana, dwarf, crimson, fine, variegata, new, brilliant, combs of crimson and gold..................................... 10c
Japan, branching variety of great beauty; scarlet and crimson combs, like ruffled lace, in pyramidal masses.
Tall and dwarf varieties mixed............. 10c
Pyramidalis Plumosa, fine feathered varieties, choice mixed...................... 10c

COSMOS.

This beautiful flower is a great favorite with all who have become acquainted with it. A showy graceful plant, bearing hundreds of flowers resembling Single Dahlias. For bouquets or flower pieces are unsurpassed, retaining their freshness for many days.
Cosmos, finest varieties mixed............. 10c

CONVOLVULUS MAJOR (Morning Glory).

H. A., 30 to 50 feet.

Varieties and colors too well known for description; white, dark blue, blood red, rose and striped, growing 20 feet high; nothing can equal them for rapidity of growth and profusion of bloom, thriving in almost any situation; tall mixed.................... 5c
Hederacia Grandiflora Superba. Large-flowering, mixed; white edged varieties. Many beautiful sorts..................... 10c
Hederacia Grandiflora Marmoratis. Large flowered variegated foliage, mixed......... 10c
Aureus Superbus. A smaller growing sort, with smaller flowers of golden yellow...... 10c
Mixed, mixed; including many varieties..... 5c

Bedding Varieties (C. Minor).

These grow only about 1 foot high; the flowers are freely borne and remain open all day; if pleasant; splendid for bedding.
Ipomœa Grandiflora. The Moon Flower, "Evening Glory" or "Good Night." Large pure white fragrant flowers in profusion, opening in the evening; rapid and luxuriant summer climber,........................ 10c
Cypress Vine (Ipomœa Quamaoclit). H. H. A., 15 feet.
Climbing Annual, popular, elegant and graceful; different colors, scarlet, white and rose; separate colors or mixed................. 5c
Rubro Coerulea Alba, fl, pl., new, beautiful white cyprus; choice novelty............. 10c

CREPIS (Hawkweed).

Annual of easy culture and abundant bloomer; red, white and yellow..................... 5c
Nana Compacta, dwarf, 18 inches.......... 5c

CYCIAMEN, PERSICUM.

Charming bulbons-rooted plants, with beautiful foliage, and rich-colored orchid-like fragrant flowers; universal favorites for winter and spring blooming. If seed is sown early they make flowering bulbs in one season; they require sandy loam; half hardy perennial; mixed; 6 inches............. 25c
Persicum gigantecum. This new large-flowering variety has beautiful mottled leaves, broad petals, and stout flower-stalks, throwing the flowers well above the foliage; 8 inches.................................. 40c

CYCLANTHERA.

A climbing plant of the gourd species, free-growing, handsome foliage and oval-shaped fruit; exploding loudly when ripe; half-hardy annual; explodens; 10 feet.......... 5c

DAHLIA.   H. H. P., 4 to 6 feet.

Tuberous root, hardy perennial; seed of finest single mixed colors.................... 10c
Extra choice double mixed, from named flowers...................................... 20c

DATURA (Trumpet Flower.)
H. A., 3 feet.

Strong growing plants known as "Angel's Trumpets," large showy flowers suitable for borders.

Datura Wrightii, large white and lilac flowers.   5c
Fastuosa, fl. pl., mixed; fine double varieties.   5c

DANTHUS (Pinks.)

A magnificent genus, embracing some of the most popular flowers in cultivation, producing a great variety of brilliant colors and profusion of bloom. The hardy biennials, or Chinese and Japanese varieties, bloom the first season, the same as hardy annuals, height, 1 foot.   The hardy perennial varieties are very fragrant, and of easy culture for the garden or greenhouse.

Chinensis (China or Indian Pink.)   Extra double, all colors mixed....................   5c
Heddewiggi. fl. pl. (Double Japan Pink.) Flowers very large and double, nearly three inches in diameter, of various shades of the most brilliant colors.....................   5c
Heddewiggi diadematus (Double Diadem Pink.) This is of denser growth than the Heddewiggi, and dwarfer habit. Very regular, densely double, and of all shades of color............ ....   5c
Laciniatus, fl. pl. (Double fringed Japan Pink.) Large double showy flowers with fringed edges, mixed, various colors and beautifully striped.....................   5c
Striata, fl. pl. Large double fringed flowers of crimson, rose, white, etc., all beautifully striped...................   10c
Laciniatus, very fine, large-flowered, single Japan Pink, mixed.....................   5c
Imperalis, fl. pl. (Double Imperial Pink.) A superb double variety, all colors mixed.....   5c
Pheasant's Eye (Plumaris Simptex.) A beautiful single variety, with fringe-edged white flowers, and a dark center; hardy perennial; 1 foot.....................   5c

DOLICHOS (Hyacinth Bean).
T. A., 10 feet.

A beautiful climber, flowers in clusters, purple and white, 10 feet.....................   5c
Giganteus, species from Texas..... ....   5c

DIGITALIS (Foxglove).
H. P., 3 to 4 feet.

Hardy perennials, three feet, handsome ornamental plant of stately growth and varied colors; mixed or separate colors...........   5c.
Monstrosa (Mammoth Foxglove.) The largest and best type; all colors mixed..........   10c

ERYSIMUM.   H. A., 1 foot

Annual, 1½ feet, free flowering and showy for beds or border, sulphur yellow and deeper orange shades.....................   5c

ESCHSCHOLTZIA (California Poppy).
H. A., 1 foot.

A hardy annual, profuse bloomer, with rich and beautiful colors; continues in bloom until frost; varieties.

Eschscholzia Californica. Sulphur yellow with orange center.....................   5c
Rose Cardinal. A charming new variety, producing freely beautiful large flowers of intense carmine.....................   10c
Crocea. fl. pl., mixed; a double-flowering, orange, scarlet and white.................   10c

EUPHORBIA (Snow on the Mountain).

Attractive foliage, with white and green bracts on the tips of each branch, veined and margined with white; 2 feet.
Variegata.....................   5c

EUTOCA.

Annual; desirable for cut flowers; blue and lilac; 6 inches.....................   5c

FENZLIA.

A charming little plant for carpet bedding or borders. Seed sown early in May will germinate quickly and begin blooming in a few weeks after starting. The plants do not grow over three inches high, but spread like portulaca, and all summer long are thickly covered with the beautiful blossoms of lovely colors.

Fenzila, finest mixed colors...............pkt. 10c

FUCHSIA.   T. P., 1 to 3 feet.

A beautiful plant blooming all the season; mixed; single and double.................   25c

FORGET-ME-NOT (Myosotis).
H. P., 6 to 12 inches.

Very popular and beautiful; will grow in any moist situation.

Alpestris, Forget-me-not.....................   5c
Dissitiflora, Large flowered species, beautiful and true.....................   15c
Palustris; the true Forget-me-not, blue, Alba, white.....................   10c
Azorica, flowers rich blue, shaded with purple.....................   10c
Myosotis (Alpestris Victoria).
Of stout and bushy habit of growth, bearing umbels of large bright azure-blue flowers with central double blooms. The plant attains a height of 5 to 7 inches, with a diameter of 8 to ten inches, and when fully grown is quite globular in shape, and perfectly covered with flowers. This beautiful Forget-me-not is the best for carpet bedding, edgings and masses, and for growing in pots for market.....................   20c
Eliza Fonrobert, New, large-flowering, bright blue, of pyramidal habit; remarkably fine and district.....................   15c
Eliza Fonrobert, Alba; white, beautiful......   15c

GAILLARDIA.

Splendid bedding plants, remarkable for the profusion, size, and brilliancy of their flowers, continuing in beauty during the summer and autumn; half-hardy annuals; 1½ feet.

Grandiflora, mixed single varieties; includes many sorts.....................   5c

Picta Lorenziana. A charming profuse flowering "so-called' double variety, entirely distinct from the single flowering. Fine for massing, and use as a bouquet flower, continuing in bloom until frost 10c

Amblyodon, fine red...................... 5c

GERANIUM. H. A. P.

A popular bedding plant for the house or garden, extensively used for massing; half-hardly perenuial; floweriug the first seasou; from 1 to 3 feet.

Zonale, Mixed, a superb straiu of the largest and finest varities; mixed colors.......... 25c

Variegated. Mixed, bronze, gold, and silver tri-colored foliage varieties.............. 25c

Double mixed. This seed will produce a large percentage of double flowers of extra fine colors............... .... 25c

Pelargonium, Mixed, (Lady Washiugton). From the finest fancy aud spotted large flowering...... .... 25c

Apple-Scented (Pelargoniumo doratissimum). This fragrant favorite variety can only bo grown from seed to form fine plants. Sow in light soil, aud keep moist until they germinate.................................. 25c

GLOXINIA HYBRIDA CRASSIFOLIA.

A bulbous-rooted plant, producing in great profusion, during the summer mouths, large bell-shaped flowers of the richest and most beautiful variety of brilliant colors; the bulbs must be kept warm and dry during the winter; 1 foot.

Grandiflora Erecta. Mixed, rich colored, erect flowers........................... 25c

Grandiflora, New French Tigred aud spotted varieties 25c

GLOBE AMARANTHA (Everlasting Flower).

"Bachelor's Buttons"; ornamental summer-blooming plants, aud fine for "Everlasting." H. A. 2 feet.

Globe Amaranth, white, purple, variegated and mixed.............................. 5c

Aurea Superba (Hangeana), fine orange.

Gillia. Low growing profuse blooming anuuals, borne in clusters, fine mixed........ 5c

GODETIA. H. A.

An attractive hardy annual, deserving more extensive cultivation. The plant blooms profusely, and bear showy flowers of rich and varied colors; 1½ feet.

Bijou, flowers splendid white, with a dark rose spot; very dwarf and dense growiug... 5c

Lady Abemarle, flowers large, of carmine crimson shade; the edges of the petals suffused with pale lilac.................... 5c

Grandiflora Macu'ata. Large white, flowers with crimson spots, fine.................. 5c

New Godetias (Rubicunda Splendeus). Double red very brilliant 10c

Lady Satin Rose, Deep rose pink, glossy and satiny, by some thought the most heautiful annual of recent introduction............. 10c

GOURD (Cucurbita). H. A.

Rapid growing, interesting plants with ornamental fringe, and varieties of singular shaped fruit; tender annuals; 15 to 20 feet.

Calabash, the dipper........................ 5c

Hercules' Club, club-shaped; 4 feet long..... 5c

Egg-shaped, fruit white like an egg......... 5c

Orange-Shaped, or Mock-Orange.......... 5c

Bottle-Shaped...... .... 5c

Turk's Turban, red striped................. 10c

Pear-Shaped, striped; very showy.......... 10c

Argyrosperma, Dish Rag, or (Bonnet Gourd). 10c

Angora, black-sceded white-spotted fruits, very useful for arbours etc................ 10c

Tricosanthes Colubrina True Serpent Gourd). Striped like a serpent, changiug to brilliant carmine when ripe; 5 feet in length....................... .... 10c

Powder Horn............................. 5c

Fine Mixed, from a large collectiou of large sorts.................................. 5c

Fine Mixed, small ornamental sorts.......... 5c

GYPSOPHILA, H. A. & H. P.

Delicate, free flowering little plants, covered with a profusion of tiny star-shaped, blossoms, valuable for making bouquets.

Acutifolia, rose-colored delicate and pretty.. 5c

Elegans, white a choice mixed.............. 5c

Paniculata Compacta, new dwarf compact variety, beautiful for bonquets............ 10c

Perennial Paniculate, tall, fine............. 5c

HELIOTROPE. H. H. P. 18 inches.

A deliciously fragrant plant, fine for bedding and pot culture; choice mixed...... ...... 10c

Fine mixture of dark flowering sorts......... 10c

HELIPTERUM.

One of the best everlastiugs neat foliage-flowers in clusters of bright yellow and white. They should be picked in the bud and hung in a shady place if wauted for dried bouquets. They will open more perfect and retain their color for years.

Helipterum Corymbiflorum, white......... 5c

Helipstæteaum Sanfordi, yellow........... 5c

HELICHRYSUM (Everlasting Flowers).

Very popular Everlastings with gobular flowers, useful for borders and beds. When used for dyeing, flowers should he picked before fully expanded. H. A.

H. Monstrosum fl. pl., a mixture of many varieties. 2 feet........................... 5c

HOLLYHOCK (Althaea Rosea). H. P.

Old fashioned favorites which should be in every garden. Seeds should he sown in June or July to have floweriug plauts the next summer or if sowu in the house early in the spring they will bloom the first year. Height 4 to 6 feet.

Hollyhock, white, red, yellow, each......... 10c

Fine Mixed, including many colors.. .... 10c

Extra Choice Mixed, From chaters unrivaled collection........ .... 15c

HIBISCUS,   II. A. 2 to 4 feet.

Hardy annual, showy and ornamental.
Africanus, rich; cream-brown center.......   5c
Coccineus Specibsus, scarlet; 1.ne........ .. 10c

HONESTY.   II. B., 2 feet.

Lunaria or Satan Flower, au intere 'ting
plant; seed vessel looks like transparent silver; handsome for bouquets or dried flowers:
hardy perennial..........................   5c

ICE PLANT (Mesembryanthemum).

II. R. A., 6 inches.

Dwarfer trailer, with thick fleshy leaves, having the appearance of being covered with ice
crystals...............................   5c
Tricolor, (dew plant)....................   5c
Album, White.............................   5e

IMPATIENS SULTANI.   H. T. A.

One of the most distinct and beautiful plants o
recent introduction for the warm greenhouse or
summer bedding; owing to its gorgeous coloring
and profuse and continuous flowering it is rapidly
becoming popular. This plant is of compact, neat
habit of growth, with good constitution, and almost a perpetual bloomer. Planted out in the open
ground at the end of June it grows luxuriantly,
flowers with the greatest profusion, and produce
an admirable effect until cut down by frost. The
flowers are of a brilliant rosy-scarlet color, about
1¼ inches in diameter.
Sultani................................... 25c

KAULFUSSIA.   II. A., 6 inches.

Dwarf annual, like an Aster; pretty branching
and free flowering; mixed colors.........   5c

LARKSPUR (Delphinum).

II. A. and perennial).

One of our most showy and useful plants, possessing almost every requisite for the adornment of
the garden; the hardy perennial producing splendid spikes of flowers in profusion throughout the
summer. If sown early they bloom the first year
from seed. The hardy annuals are profused
bloomers, and succeed best if sown in the autumn,
or very early in the spring.

Tall Rocket, Double Mixed, includes many
colors. 2½ feet.........................   5c
Mixed Dwarf Rocket Varieties, includes
many varieties..........................   5c
Double Stock Flower, a tall branching variety, with beautiful long spikes of flowers
of various colors; fine for cut-flowers; 2 feet.   5c
Larkspur (Delphinum), perennial varieties.
Nudicaule, Dwarf, of compact growth, with
spikes of bright scarlet flowers; 18 inches.. 10c
Cashmerianum, a beautiful dark blue, blooms
in corymbs of six or more; 15 inches....... 20c
Hybridum, many varieties extra fine mixed... 10c
Delphinium Zalil, a pure sulphur yellow flowering
perennial of a lovely and delicate shade, resembling in color the Marechal Neil Rose, a color unknown till now. The plant is of branching habit,
3½ to 4½ feet high, the branches ending in long-
spikes of 40 to 50 blossoms, which open almost at
the same time. The flowers are one inch in diameter, and last in flower from June till August.
Price per packet,.......................... 25c

LANTANA.   H. H. P.

A remarkably handsome free-flowering genus of
plants with brilliantly colored flowers, constantly
changing in hue, very effective either for pot culture cr bedding. Half-hardy perennial.
Finest varieties mixed.................... 10c

LINUM (Flowering Flax).   II. A., 1 foot.

Conspicuous for its brilliant colors.
Flavum, yellow; perennial........ ....   5e
Perennial sorts, fine mixed...................   5c

LINARIA.

Cymballaria (Kenilworth Ivy). A very pretty
climber...................................   5c

LEPTOSIPHON.   II. A., 8 inches.

Beautiful dwarf for lines and ribbon beds;
white and yellow; mixed, French..........   5c

LOBELIA.

Anuals. An elegant dwarf of easy culture; fine
for borders and ribbon beds and for vases and hanging baskets.

Erinus, Emperor William. A very compact
variety, with fine sky-blue flowers.......... 10c
Erinus, Crystal Palace Compact. A new
densely compact miniature variety, which,
during the summer months, is studded with
rich deep blue flowers.................... 10c
Erinus Speciosa, Crystal Palace. Of trailing growth; flowers of an ultra-marine blue.. 10c
Crystal Palace Oculata, dark stalks and dark
blue flowers, with a distinct white eye;
splendid.................................. 10c

LUPINUS (Sun Dials)   II. A. and P.

Desirable bedding plants with long, graceful
flower spikes, bearing richly colored, pea-shaped
flowers.
Mixed annual varieties; 1 to 3 feet.........   5c
Mixed perennial varieties. Hardy sorts........   5c

LAVENDER.   II. P., 1 to 2 feet.

Prized for its fragrant violet flowers; does best
in a dry, gravelly soil; hardy perennial.....   5c

LYCHNIS.

Showy flowering plants for shrubberies and
flower beds; flowers strikingly brilliant.
Chalcedonica, dazzling scarlet, hardy perennial; 1 to 3 feet...........................   5c
Haageana. Brilliant scarlet flowers, 2 inches
across; 1 foot............................. 10c
Mixed Haageana Hybrids. Shades of white
scarlet, flesh, pink, etc.; annual varieties; 1
foot...................................... 10c
Haageana Grandiflora Gigantea............ 10c

MARIGOLD. (Tagetes.)   H. H. A.

A class of showy and extremely effective plants
with fine double flowers of rich and beautiful colors,
very well adapted for large beds and bordering. No
garden should be without them.
Tall African. Many varieties mixed, 2 feet..   5c
Sulphurea, sulphur yellow, quilled double...   5c
Aurea Fistulosa Pl., quilled golden yellow..   5c

Dwarf French. A mixture of many shades;
1 foot.................................... 5c

Dwarf African, all colors mixed........... 5c

Signata Pumila. Splendid for edgings; dwarf
plants with fern-like foliage and small brilliant yellow cross-shaped flowers in profusion, which gives it a delicate, airy appearance, making beautiful borders for long
beds 5c

Signata Pumila (New Golden Ring.) Foliage
same as above; flowers have a deep golden
stripe across each petal, which forms a complete golden ring, very showy and pretty... 5c

Tall French, fine mixed, all shades........... 5c

MARVEL OF PERU (Four o'clock.)
H. H. P., 2 feet.

One of the most ornamental flowering plants;
they are quite fragrant, flowers expanding in the
evening; half hardy perenial; blooming the first
season from seed; the roots can be perserved in
winter like Dahlias.

Mixed; beautiful colors..................... 5c

Longiflora, long flower, pure white and fragrant...................................... 5c

Dwarf White Tom Thumb) When fully developed this variety does not exceed 10
inches in height, and forms a charming little
bush completely studded with pure white
flowers; new 10c

Multiflora, large umbels of dark lilac, red
flowers; perennial, fine ....

MARTYNIA. H. A., 3 to 4 feet.

Free flowering, of easy culture and hardy,
sweet-scented; yellow and purple......... 5c

MATRICARIA (Fever Few.)

Handsome free, flowering plants, good for
beds and pot culture.   · H. H. P.

Matricaria Eximia Crispa Fl. Pl. Lovely
little plants with double white flowers and
prettily curled foliage like parsley. 8 inches   10c

Capensis. Double white flowers; splendid
for bouquets etc. 5c

Grandiflora Fl. Pl. Large flowering double
white, beautiful........................... 15c

MAURANDIA (Climber.) T. A.
6 to 10 feet.

Very graceful for training on trellis work,
verandas, etc.; perennial, flowers the first
season from seed; violet pink, purple, white
and mixed................................. 10c

MIGNONETTE (Reseda Odorata.)

A well known annual with spike of deliciously
fragrant flowers. Indispensible in every garden.   H. A.

Grandiflora. Large flowered; per oz., 20c.... 5c

Ameliorata. Very sweet scented; per oz.,
15c...................................... 5c

Parsons' White. A distinct almost white variety, with long spikes........ 5c

Gabriele. New, red flowering; very sweet,
spikes very thick; one of the best for
florists' use.............................. 5c

New Hybird Spiral. It is a vigorous grower,
with spikes often attaining a length of 10
inches; delightfully fragrant............... 5c

Giant Pyramidal. Flowers reddish, sweetscented and very large..................... 10c

Machet. The plants are dwarf and vigorous,
of pyramidal growth. They throw up numerous long and broad spikes of deliciously
scented red flowers. Entirely distinct...... 10c

Crimson Queen. Very fine, robust, excellent
for pots, red flowered..................... 5c

Golden Queen. An entirely distinct sort,
with golden yellow flowers, which give it a
most attractive appearance; very fragrant... 10c

Victoria. New dark red, very fine.......... 10c

MIMULUS (Monkey Flower.) H. H. P.

A very interesting free-blooming genus of plants
with beautiful spotted and blotched flowers of brilliant colors. Perenuials in the green-house, annuals
in the open air.

Tigrinus Grandiflora. Very large flowering,
new tigred and spotted varieties, most beautiful; very showy as window plants........

Nanus. New dwarf varieties, spotted and
blotched, fine............................. 10c

Albus. White ground, handsome large-flowering varieties............................. 10c

Hose in Hose. Very curious and pretty, one
flower sitting in another; fine mixed........ 20c

Moschatus. (Musk Plant.) The thin delicate
leaves emit a delicate musk odor.......... 10c

MOMORDICA.

A curious annual climber, with yellow blossoms.
The fruit is the chief curiosity, is egg-shaped, and
covered with warty excrescences, which, when
ripe, bursts suddenly open, scattering its seed, and
showing a brilliant carmine interior. Fine for
trellises, fences, stumps, etc. Half hardy annua'.

Balsamina. (Balsam Apple.)............... 5c

Charantia. (Balsam Pear.) Golden yellow.. 5c

TALL NASTURTIUM (Tropæolum Major.)
H. H. A.

Elegant profuse flowering plants for verandas,
trellises, etc. The seed pods can be gathered while
green and tender, for pickling, hardy annuals; 10
feet.

Finest mixed. All colors, of Climbing Nasturtium 5c

Lobb's Nasturtium.   H. H. A., 4 to 6 feet.

Tropæolum Lobbianam, these are distinguished
from the Tall Nasturtiums above (Tropaeolum
Majus,) by their longer vines; their leaves and
flowers, however, are somewhat smaller, but their
greater profusion renders them superior for trellises, arbors, for hanging over vases, rock-work,
etc.; the flowers are of unusual brilliancy and richness, and they are also splendid for winter decoration in the green-house and conservatory.

Mixed, contains many beautiful sorts......... 10c

DWARF NASTURTIUM (Tropaeolum Minor.)
H. H. A.

The dwarf varieties are all desirable, and are among our most popular plants, standing any amount of heat and drought, growing vigorously and flowering freely all summer and fall; excellent for massing and ribboning, doing well even in poor soil, hardy annuals; 1 foot.

Empress of India, very dwarf habit; flowers brilliant crimson; abundant bloomer	10c
Lady Bird. Orange yellow, red spots	10c
Tom Thumb King Theodore, flowers almost black	5c
King of Tom Thumbs, crimson	5c
Coccineum, scarlet, fine	5c
Golden King, brilliant yellow	5c
Tom Thumb, mixed all colors	5c
Beauty, yellow and scarlet	5c

NEMOPHILA (Love Grove.)
H. A. 1 foot.

A charming dwarf California annual, neat, compact and of uniform growth, adapted for beds and borders, fine mixed varieties 5c

NIEREMBERGIA.   H. H. P.

A half hardy perennial, slender growing plant, perpetually in bloom, flowering the first year if sown early; desirable for the greenhouse, baskets, vases or bedding out; 1 foot   5c

NIGELLA.   H. A.
(Love in a Mist or Devil in a Bush.)

A compact, free flowering plant, with finely cut foliage, curious looking flowers and seed pods; of easy culture, growing in any garden soil; hardy annuals; 1 foot.

Damascena (Devil in a bush.) Double, blue and white	5c
Nana fl. pleno, double dwarf very beautiful, 6 to 8 inches high fine for edgings	10c

NOLANA.   H. A.

Very pretty annual of trailing habit, with Morning Glory-like flowers, well adapted to rock work. Height 6 inches.

Mixed. All varieties 5c

OENOTHERA (Evening Primrose.)
H. P. 1 to 2 feet.

Beautiful, free growing and useful, flowering in long spikes, fine for beds or borders.

Biennis (Evening Primrose) Yellow flowers opening in the evening and early morning..	5c
Acaulis alba, large white flowers, dwarf, showy and beautiful	5c
Taraxacifolia aurea, golden yellow, large flowered, very fine	5c
Rosea (Mexicana,) 6 inches high, extra fine, true rose colored flowers	10c

Passion Flower, (Climber.)   H. P.

Handsome rapid grower, fine for decoration and open ground.

Coerulea Grandiflora, large flowers, blue.... 10c

PERILLA.

The foliage of this plant is exceedingly elegant, of a very dark purple color, and produce a charming contrast with silver-leaved plants; growing freely in any soil; half-hardy annual; 1½ feet.

Nankinensis Atropurpureus Laciniatis, elegant...................................... 5c

PENTSTEMON.

One of our most beautiful and attractive herbaceous plants; bearing long, graceful spikes of rich-colored flowers; will bloom the first season if sown early in March, and planted out in May; half-hardy perennials; 2 feet.

Hartwegi. (gentianoides, hybridus), extra fine mixed, from the handsomest new sorts, which the seed reproduces in great variety. 10c

PANSIES.
Grandiflora Pansy (Viola Tricolor.)

This is a great favorite with all flower gardens. It is biennial and can be perpetuated by division of the roots. Seeds sown in autumn produce earlier and better flowers the coming season. They require good rich soil.

Pansies in Separate Colors.

Odier or Five Blotched. A beautiful strain, perfect in size and form of flowers, containing many beautiful colors; each of the 5 petals is marked with a large dark blotch; very effective	15c
Emperor William. Large handsome flowers borne in great profusion, well above the foliage, brilliant ultramarine blue with a purple violet eye	10c
Faust (King of the Blacks). Almost black, the darkest pansy known	10c
Lord Beaconsfield. A splendid sort; flowers deep purple violet, shading to white on the upper petals	10c
Snow Queen. Very large, satiny white, light yellow center	10c
Yellow Gem. Pure yellow, without eye	10c
"Non Plus Ultra," offered last year for the first time. Beautiful colors and large flowers. Highly affected, very choice mixed; pkt	25c
Cassier's. Very large-flowered. Seed saved from largest sized pansies, beautifully marked. A rich and showy strain; pkt....	25c
Bugnots Superb Blotched. Extra large flowers with very broad blotches, the two upper petals finely lined; refined shape and varied colors; pkt	25c
Trimardeau. An altogether distinct and beautiful new race, the flowers of which are larger than any hitherto produced. Each flower is marked with three large blotches or spots; and the plants produce an endless variety of beautiful shades	15c
White, pure black center	10c
Yellow, (golden,) pure black center, fine for bedding	10c
Azure Blue, bright sky blue	10c
Bronze, dark mahogany, shades fine	10c
German Finest Mixed, including many colors.	10c

PETUNIA T. P.

For out-door decoration or house culture few plants are equal to this class. They commence flowering early, and continue a mass of bloom throughout the whole season, until killed by frost; easily cultivated, requiring rich soil and a sunny situation. Of late years the single-triped, mottled and double varieties have been greatly improved.

Single Varieties.

Petunia, Hybrida, "Belle Etoile." Beautiful large flowered strain of striped and blotched................................ 15c

Grandiflora Venosa. Large flowering, finest shades of colors beautifully veined......... 10c

Finest Striped and Blotched. Seed saved from magnificent collections of striped and blotched varieties........................ 10c

Large Flowered Yellow Throat. These form a class of rare beauty, and come true from seed. The flowers are very large, and of perfect form, with a deep yellow throat, veined very much like the Salpiglossis..... 25c

Princess of Wurtemburg. Rose, beautiful.. 25c

Hybrida Grandiflora Fimbriata. Fringed varieties in splendid mixture.............. 25c

Marginata Maculata, green bordered and blotched varieties; single mixed; very rare 25c

Hybrida Grandiflora. Choicest mixed, seed saved from show flowers.................. 20c

Pure White, Single. Desirable for cemetery beds, or where large masses of white are wanted................................ 10c

Hybrida, finest mixed..................... 5c

Double Petunias.

Double Inimitable. Striped and blotched varieties; splendid mixed, per pkt........ 20c

Grandiflora "Double Inimitable." Striped and blotched varieties; splendid mixed, per pkt...................................... 20c

Double Large Flowering (Grandiflora Flore Pleno.) Extra fine mixed; choicest colors.... 25c

Double Fringed (Grandiflora Fimbriata Flore Pleno.) Charming Double Fringed Flowers 40c

Double Green-Edged Large Flowering (Grandiflora Marginata.) Flowers, very peculiar. A rare strain................. 40c

PYRETHRUM. H. P.

This family contains the well-known "Golden Feather," a low growing plant, with yellow foliage for ribbon beds, edgings, etc.; and also contains some of the handsomest flowering hardy plants for borders that are in cultivation.

Yellow Foliage Sorts For Ribboning.

Aureum. Bright yellow foliage; 1 foot...... 10c

Laciniatus. Yellow foliage, finely fringed; 1 foot................................... 10c

Selaginoides. Handsome fern-like foliage, ½ ft.................................... 15c

Hardy Flowering Varieties.

Showy, hardy, herbaceous perennials, with bright, beautiful flowers of many colors, which remain in bloom for a long time. Are invaluable as cut flowers for decorative purposes on account of their bright appearance and long duration. The single ones resemble our well known Margnerites and are very showy used in connection with them in floral pieces or bouquets.

Pyrethrum Roseum Hybridum Flore Pleno. Double Sorts, mixed...................... 25c

Pyrethrum Roseum Hybridum. Single sorts, finest mixed............................ 10c

RHODANTHE (Everlasting Flower.)
H. H. A. 1 foot.

Very valuable for winter bouquets, and also desirable for pot plants or for the garden; red, white and pink, finest mixed.......... 10c

RICINUS (Caster Oil Plants).
H. H. A., 6 to 15 feet.

This is a rapid grower with fine palm-like foliage, giving a fine effect on lawns or large beds.

Fine mixture of all varieties, foliage sorts.... 5c
"   "   "   dwarf sorts...... 5c

PRIMULA.

The "Chinese Primrose" is a great favorite for Winter and early Spring, blooming in the house or conservatory. The foliage is attractive, and the flowers borne in clusters; are perfectly charming. One of our best pot plants, of easy cultivation.

Chinensis. Fine mixed.................... 25c
"   Fimbriata. (finest fringed). Mixed.. 25c
"   "   Rubra, fringed, red......... 25c
"   "   Alba, Snow Queen, fringed, white.................................. 25c

Chinensis, Fimbriata. Coccinea, brilliant, new red................................ 25c

Chinensis, Fimbriata. Flore Pleno. Finest double fringed. Mixed.................... 40c

HARDY PRIMROSES.

Auricula. (Alpine Primrose). Beautiful colors. Mixed.......................... 10c

Japonica. (Japanese Primrose). One of the most beautiful. The flowers are larger than the common varieties, of shades of crimson, lilac, white, pink, etc. Fine mixed........ 15c

Primula Veris. Polyanthus. Choice mixed, 10c
"   "   Duplex. (Hose in Hose). Very curious and pretty; one flower set within another........................... 25c

PHLOX DRUMMONDI. H. A.

For beds and masses these beautiful annuals cannot be surpassed. They produce immense trusses of brilliant flowers of many hues. From early Spring until cut off by frost.

Finest Mixed............................ 15c

Grandiflora. Large-flowering varieties; choicest Mixed............................ 10c

Alba. Pure white, beautiful............... 10c

Coccinea. Brilliant. Scarlet. Splendid...... 15c

Stellata Splendens. With pure white stellated centers.......................... 10c

Rosea. Bright Rose..................... 10c

Rosea Alba-Oculato. Rose with white eye.. 10c

Leopoldi. Red with white eye............. 10c

Nana Compacta. Dwarf compact. Charming varieties for borders, bedding, etc 15c

Phlox Decussata. (Perennis). Perennial. Very hardy. Splendid sorts. Mixed...... 15c

POPPIES. Double.   II. A.

Double Carnation. Very double, with finely cut or fringed petals. Mixed colors........ 5c

Paeony Flowered. Splendid, large, double, mixed colors............................. 5c

Ranunculus Flowered. Small, double varieties...................................... 5c

Pavonium. New, single scarlet. Base, dark cherry red, encircled by jet black zone...... 10c

Single Perennial Varieties.

Oriental. (or Monarch Poppy). Will bloom the following Spring from seed grown in the Fall, foliage massive and beautiful; flowers simply grand, both in size and color. Rich scarlet, with black blotches at base.... 10c

Nudicaule. New yellow (Iceland Poppy). very graceful, with light green foliage and flowers of a bright yellow color............ 5c

Maculatum Superbum. With intense deep scarlet blotched flowers 5c

Romneya Coulteri. (Great White California Tree Poppy). A fine perennial of stately beauty, it is one of the best for yielding a succession of bloom from July until November. The flowers are large, 4 to 5 inches across, and are extremely delicate, with loose crumpled petals, resembling the single white paeony. Plant the seed in the Fall in a protected spot, and in the Spring you will have fine plants for transplanting., 25c

New Japanese Pompon Poppies. Small very double flowers produced in great profusion, Many lovely colors, mixed................. 25c

PORTULACA.

This is one of the most charming annuals of easy culture. Blooms best in a light sandy soil and will stand the hottest sun if well watered. Fine for bedding.

Grandiflora. Single mixed, many colors.... 5c
"   Double rose-flowered, extra mixed 10c

ROCKET (Hesperia).
H. P., 2 to 3 feet.

Well known, free-flowering and very fragrant; purple and white........................ 5c

SALPIGLOSSIS.   H. H. A.

Neat and beautiful ornamental autumn blooming plants, with curiously pencilled and marbled funnel-shaped flowers; suitable for the greenhouses or flower border; of easy culture, requiring a light, rich soil; half hardy annual, 1½ feet.

Grandiflora. Large flowered, all colors mixed. 10c

(SALVIA Flowering Sage).
H. H. P., 3 feet.

One of our handsomest summer and autumn flowering plants, when they are literally ablaze with brilliant flowers; very effective for massing on the lawn or for ribbon beds.

Splendens (Scarlet sage.) Beautiful, Fiery scarlet......................... 10c

---

Splendens Coccinea. Nana compacta, dwarf, compact, very free flowering............... 15c

SAPONARIA (Bouncing Bet.)   II. A.

Handsome dwarf growing plants, with pretty star-shaped flowers; excellent for massing and edging.

Multiflora compacta, new, compact, beautiful for borders planted in a sunny situation. 5c

Ocymoides. splendens. very brilliant red, fine 5c

SENSITIVE PLANT (Mimosa Pudica.)

A very interesting plant with fern-like foliage, which is so sensitive that the leaves close up immediately when touched or shaken; suitable for pots or borders   II. A., 1 foot.... 5c

SCHIZANTHUS (Butterfly Flower.)
H. H. A.

A splendid class of plants, combining elegance of growth and profusion of beautiful flowers, valuable in the garden and greenhouse. White, purple, yellow and crimson; half hardy annual; finest mixed colors.......... 5c

Papilionaceous. In this charming variety we have one of the finest annuals in cultivation. The flowers are handsome as some of the orchids................................ 5c

Papilionaceous Pyramidalis, compactus. New, compact, fine...................... 5c

Pinnatus, blue............................. 10c

STATICE (Everlasting).

An interesting free flowering plant of easy culture, long-blooming, and valuable for Winter bouquets, perennial, fine mixed..... 10c

Suworowi. The branching flower spikes of this new annual Statice are of a bright rose, shaded with crimson. Each plant produces from 10 to 15 spikes, measuring from 12 to 18 inches. One plant will last in flower more than two months, and if sown in succession it may be had in bloom throughout the whole summer and autumn................ 10c

SCABIOSA.   H. P.

The "Mourning Bride" or "Sweet Scabious" of our old garden, but much improved in size, colors and doubleness. They are very free bloomers, the colors white, carmine, lilac, maroon, etc., excellent for bouquets.

Nana· fl. pl., mixed dwarf, double. 1 foot.... 5c
Major fl. pleno Mixed. New, large flowering tall double sorts........................ 5c
Minor, fl. pl., cherry red, new.............. 5c
Candidissima. Double white flowers, useful for bouquets. 1 foot.................... 10c

SMILAX (Mendeola asparagoides.)
SMILAX (Myrsiphyllum.)
T. P. 6 feet.

This is the most popular and graceful evergreen vine in cultivation, adapted for hanging baskets and pot culture, floral wreaths, etc...................................... 10c

SUNFLOWER.   H. A.

Stately growing plants, with immense golden yellow flowers; the single varieties are well known, but the double sorts are not; they are perfectly magnificent.

DOUBLE SORTS.

Globosus Fistulosus. perfectly round flowers, very double, saffron; 6 feet................. 5c

Oculatus Viridis. double yellow flowers, with green center; 4 feet....................... 5c

Miniature Sunflower (Globe flowered.) Of dwarf branching habit, wearing many little flowers only 2 inches across; orange........ 5c

Nanum. fl. pl.. (Dwarf double.) Yel ow, quite dwarf, fine............................... 5c

Giant Russian. Flowers 18 to 20 inches across; grown principally for the seed of which it is very prolific................... 5c

JACOBÆA (Senicio.)

Remarkably pretty, free growing profuse flowering plants, almost unsurpassed for brilliancy and beauty. Grow freely from seed, and are easly propagated from cuttings, not one in fifty failing. The double are the only ones worth cultivating. Hardy annuals in open border, biennial in greenhouse. Sow in loam mixed with leaf mold. Purple, pink and white flowers.

Senecio Elegans. fl. pl. Tall double Jacobaea. Finest varieties........................... 5c

Nana fl. pl.. Double Dwarf sorts. Finest mixed, 8 inches...................... 5c

SWEET PEAS (Lathyrus Odoratus.)

Beautiful fragrant free flowering plants, thriving in any open situation; excellent for screening unsightly objects, will bloom all summer and autumn if the flowers are cut freely and the pods picked off as they appear. They may be sown in autumn in this section; early sowing is necessary, hardy annuals; 6 feet. No garden is complete without them................................. 5c

Queen of the Isles. Scarlet mottled with white and purple................................. 10c

Princess Beatrice. New Rose.................. 10c

Cardinal. New........................ . ... 10c

Blue Bird. Bright blue..................... 5c

Captain Clarke (Tricolor). White, rose and purple............................... 5c

Crown Princess, of Prussia. Bright blush, shading to rose............................. 5c

Invincible, scarlet. Bright scarlet flowers...... 5c

Fairy Queen. white and rose.................... 5c

Dark Red.................................... 5c

Purple Crown. purple........................... 5c

Snowflake. Pure white........................ 5c

Invincible Red-striped..................... 5c

Light Blue and Purple......................... 5c

Painted Lady. Red and white.................. 5c

Purple-Striped................................ 5c

Mixed, many colors........................... 5c

LATHYRUS (Everlasting Pea). ..

Showy, free flowering plants, growing in any common soil. A good climber for covering fences or walls. Hardy perennials.

Latifolius (Everlasting Pea). Red............. 10c

Albus, white, splendid climber.................. 10c

Rotundifolius. Copper Red fine 10c

Lathyrus. Mixed colors................. ...... 10c

TEN WEEKS STOCKS.

The Ten Weeks Stock, "Stock Gilly" or Gillyflower," as they are sometimes called, stands preeminent among annuals for either flower beds, pot culture, cut flowers, and delicious spicy perfume; they have been greatly improved in the past few years, and a large flowering strain has been originated which for size, doubleness and variety of exquisite shades of color is remarkable.

Large Flowering Dwarf Ten Week. The following are the best double varieties and most desirable colors for cultivation; mixed, all choice double large-flowering.......... 10c

Very Dwarf Snowflake. A beautiful smallgrowing variety, with vigorous main spike and numerous side shoots of very large double snow-white flowers; very early.......... 15c

Large Flowering Dwarf Ten Week. The following are the best double varieties and most desirable colors for cultivation; mixed, all choice double large-flowering...................... 10c

Very Dwarf Snowflake. A beautiful small-growing variety, with vigorous main spike and numerous side shoots of very large double snow-white flowers; very early.................... 15c

Dwarf Bouquet Ten-week Stock. Finest mixed............................... .... 10c

Large-flowering Pyramidal. This variety has compact flower spikes, and throws out many side shoots, excellent for pots..................... 10c

New Giant Perfection. This sort produces plants 2½ feet high, with long flower-spikes of extra double handsome flowers, and is extremely effective in beds and borders.................. 10c

White (Dresden perpetual), very beautiful, large spikes, splendid for cutting.................... 15c

Emperor, or Brompton (Winter or Bennial). These make very bushy and branching plants, with an abundance of choice double flowers. Sow in July or August. Will last several years when protected.

Many colors. In finest mixture................. 10c

Wallflower-leaved. Large flowering, choice mixed............................. 10c

The Wallflower-leaved Stocks have quite distinct dark glossy foliage.

Intermediate, or Autumnal. These are prized on account of their flowering late in Autumn or early in Spring. The seeds should be sown in July. Finest mixed...................... 10c

Perpetual Dwarf Ten-week Stock. mixed, (Semperflorens.) A double constant blooming sort, with fine double flowers of various colors; 15 inches... 10c

SWEET WILLIAM (Dianthus Barbatus.) H. P.

A well known attractive free-flowering plant, which has been greatly improved of late years, producing a splendid effect in beds and shrubbery with their rich and varied flowers; hardy perennial, 1½ feet.

Double. From choice collections................. 10c

Single. Choicest mixed....................... 5c

THUNBERGIA (Climber.)
H. H. A., 4 feet.

Very ornamental and rapid growth; the flowers are very much admired; colors red, white, buff and bright orange, with variously colored throats; choicest mixed.................................. 5c

VERBENA.

Georgeous for beds or massing, flowers of the most brilliant colors; flowering continually from Spring until late in the Autumn. Verbenas grown from seed are always thrifty and free bloomers, but flowering the first year from seed; HHP., 1 ft.

Hybrida, finest mixed varieties, from beautiful collection.. 10c
Defiance, scarlet, extra for bedding; beautiful..... 10c
Candidissima, with large trusses of flowers of the purest white.................................... 10c
Striata, Italian Carnation-like Striped, saved from a rich collection........................... 10c
Lutea, now yellow, distinct, new and pretty....... 15c
Venosa, blue fine for edging...................... 10c
Coccinea, fol. aureis, golden yellow foliage and dazzling scarlet flowers; strikingly beautiful, especially at the end of the summer............. 25c

VINCA (Madagascar Periwinkle.)　T. P.

Ornamental free-blooming plants; they flower from seed, if sown early, the first season, continuing until frost; or they may be potted and kept in bloom through the winter; 2 feet.

Vinca. Mixed colors............................... 10c

VIRGINIA STOCK.　H. A.
(Cheiranthus Maritimus.)

Beautiful free-flowering little plants, very effective in small beds, edging or baskets, growing in any soil; hardy annual.

Mixed. All colors, 3 inches...................... 5c

VIOLET (Viola Odorata.)　H. P.

Well known fragrant early spring blooming plants for edging, groups or borders; thriving best in summer in a shady situation, in a rich, deep soil; extensively used by florists for forcing for cut flowers during the fall and winter months; hardy perennials, 6 inches.

Single White (Odorata Semperflorens.) Very sweet-scented blue flowers............................. 10c
Single White (Odorata semperflorens.) Sweet Violet, very fragrant and free-flowering.......... 10c
The Czar, fl. albo, fine double white............. 20c
Lutea, Grandiflora, fine yellow.................. 10c
Viola, very fine mixed........................... 10c

WALLFLOWER (Cheiranthus Cheiri.)
H. H. P.

Well-known deliciously fragrant garden plants, blooming early in the spring, with large conspicuous spikes of beautiful flowers; they should be protected in a cold frame in the winter, and planted out in May; are much prized for boquet flowers; half-hardy perennials.

Single Mixed, all colors. 2½ feet................ 5c
Finest Double Mixed, all colors, 2 feet.......... 10c
Waltzia, (Everlasting.)
Yellow flowers, borne in clusters; fine for dried flowers.. 10c

WHITLAVIA.

Charming hardy annual, with delicate foliage and clusters of beautiful bell-shaped flowers, fine for ribbonning, mixed borders or shady spots; growing freely in any garden soil; also good for baskets, vases, etc.; 1 foot.

Grandiflora. Large, violet-blue................. 5c

ZINNIA ELEGANS. Fl. Pl.
(Youth and Old Age.)

Double Zinnias are in acquisition to our list of garden favorites; of branching habit and splendid brilliant colored double flowers, rivaling the Dahlia in beauty and form. The seed can be sown early in the hot-bed and transplanted, or sown later in the open ground; half-hardy annuals; 2 feet.

White. Pure white flowers, fine for florists....... 5c
Coccinea, Flore Pleno, fine double scarlet...... 5c
Kermesina Flore Pleno, bright crimson......... 5c
Alba, Fl. Pl., White.............................. 5c
Tall Double, finest mixed, splendid quality...... 5c
Grandiflora Robusta Plenissima (New Giant Zinnias.) A new very large flowering race, differing from the old varieties in their more luxuriant robust growth, and in the larger and more conical shape of the flowers, which have broader and many more petals. The plant forms a handsome bush, 3 feet in height, and the large perfectly formed double, measuring 5 to 6 inches across, are borne in profusion, lasting until killed by frost; splendid....... 10c
Pompone. Excellent Zinnias, differing from the the older ones in habit of growth and the immense size of their perfectly formed very double flowers of various striking colors. The plants are dwarf and bloom freely during a long period........... 10c
Zinnia Grandiflora. single, fine mixed.......... 5c

XERANTHEMUMS.

A showy class of everlastings; the flowers are white, purple and yellow, single and double. If gathered before fully opened and dried in the shade, they will retain their beauty for years. They make fine winter bouquets. Sow in Spring and thin out to one foot apart. Hardy annual. 1 foot.

Xeranthemum, mixed............................... 10c

ORNAMENTAL GRASSES.

Nearly all the ornamental grasses are very showy and beautiful, and when dried and tastefully arranged in connection with the Everlasting flowers, make exceedingly attractive winter bouquets.

Ornamental Grasses. A collection of eight different varieties, our own selection................ 30c
Agrostis Nebulosa. Light, feathery and graceful, fine for winter bouquets, hardy annual; 1 foot..... 5c
Briza Maxima (Large Quaking Grass.) Large pendent seeds, fine for clumps or bouquets, hardy annual; 1 foot....................................... 5c
Briza Gracilis (Small Quaking Grass.) Smaller graceful variety of above, hardy annual, 1 foot.... 5c
Bromus Brizæformis. Splendid variety, with drooping spikes of pendent seeds, hardy annual, 1 foot... 5c

Cryptopyrum Richardsoni, very fine and delicate for winter bouquets... .... 5c
Eragrostis Elegans (Love Grass.) Elegant and feathery foliage, hardy annual, 1 foot............. 5c
Gynerium Argenteum (True Pampas Grass.) Makes fine clumps for lawns, large silvery plumes, half-hardy perennial, 5 to 10 ft.................. 10c
Lagurus Ovatus (Hare's Tail Grass.) Woolly cone-shaped heads, fine for Winter bouquets, hardy annual, 1 foot................................... 5c
Stipa Pennata (Feather Grass.) Delicate long silvery feathers, fine for winter bouquets, hardy perennials, 2 ft................................ 10c
Tricholæna. Pretty Rose colored grass, hardy annual, 1 foot.................................. 10c
Pennisetum Longistylum. Graceful and interesting; admirable for the composition of bouquets....... 5c

Quantity of Seed Required to Sow an Acre of Ground.

	Pounds.		Pounds.
Grass, Timothy	20	Hamp—broadcast	40 to 50
Grass, Mesquit, in the chaff	35	Flax, when wanted for the seed	50
Grass, Hungarian	43	Flax, when wanted for the fiber	80
Grass, Millet	40	Beans, Dwarf or Bush—hills or drills	80
Grass, Mixed Lawn	75	Beans, tall or pole—hills	20
A much larger quantity of seed is required to make a close, fine lawn than for other purposes.		Beets—drills	5 to 6
		Broom Corn—drills	15
		Buckwheat—broadcast	45
Grass, mixture for mowing or grazing ⎱ Clover	8	Cabbage, in beds to cover an acre after transplanting	¼
Timothy	15	Carrots—drills	3 to 4
Redtop	15	Melon, Water—hills	2 to 3
Grass, Kentucky Blue, for pasture	30	Melon, Cantaloupe—hills	4
Grass, Kentucky Blue for lawn	75	Onions, black seed—drills	5 to 6
Grass, Orchard	40	Onions, top set—drills	200
Grass, English or Australian Rye, for meadow	50	Onions, black seed, for bottom sets	40
Grass, English or Australian Rye, for lawn	75	Parsnips—drills	6
Grass, Italian Rye	30 to 40	Peas—drills	100
Grass Redtop	80	Peas—broadcast	180
Alfalfa or Lucerne	20 to 25	Potatoes—hills	500 to 600
Clover, Red alone—broadcast	15 to 20	Pumpkins—hills	5
Clover, White alone—broadcast	12	Radishes—drills	8
Clover, Alsike—broadcast	10	Sage—drills	8
Barley—broadcast	125 to 150	Spinach—drills	15
Oats—broadcast	80	Squash, bush varieties—hills	5
Rye—broadcast	100	Squash, running varieties—hills	3
Wheat—broadcast	125	Tomato, in beds to transplant	¼
Wheat—drills	90	Turnip and Rutabaga—drills	1½
Corn, Sweet or Field—hills	15	Turnip and Rutabaga—broadcast	3
Corn, to cut green for fodder—drills or broadcast	150	Cucumber—hills	2
Vetches—broadcast	150		

Quantity of Seed Required to Produce a Given Number of Plants, or Sow Certain Quantity of Ground.

Artichoke	1 oz. to 500 plants	Lettuce	1 oz. to 3,000 plants
Asparagus	1 oz. to 60 feet of drill of 500 plants	Melon, Water	1 oz. to 50 hills
Beans, dwarf	1 lb. to 50 feet of drill	Melon, Musk	1 oz. to 50 hills
Beans, tall	1 lb. to 75 hills	Okra	1 oz. to 50 feet of drill
Beet	1 oz. to 50 feet of drill	Onion Seed	1 oz. to 100 feet of drill
Broccoli	1 oz. to 2,000 plants	Onion, top set	1 lb. to 20 feet of drill
Brussels Sprouts	1 oz. to 2,000 plants	Parsnips	1 oz. to 200 feet of drill
Cabbage	1 oz. to 2,000 plants	Parsley	1 oz. to 150 feet of drill
Carrots	1 oz. to 150 feet of drill	Peas	1 lb. to 50 feet of drill
Cauliflower	1 oz. to 2,000 plants	Pepper	1 oz. to 1,000 plants
Celery	1 oz. to 3,000 plants	Pumpkin	1 oz. to 40 hills
Chicory	1 oz. to 100 feet of drill	Radish	1 oz. to 100 feet of drill
Corn	1 lb. to 100 hills	Salsify	1 oz. to 70 feet of drill
Cress	1 oz. to 100 feet of drill	Sage	1 oz. to 150 feet of drill
Cucumber	1 oz. to 75 hills	Spinach	1 oz. to 100 feet of drill
Egg Plant	1 oz. to 1,000 plants	Squash, early	1 oz. to 50 hills
Endive	1 oz. to 150 feet of drill or 3,000 plants	Squash, winter	1 oz. to 10 hills
Kale	1 oz. to 2,000 plants	Tomato	1 oz. to 3,000 plants
Kohl Rabi	1 oz. to 2,000 plants	Tobacco	1 oz. to 10,000 plants
Leek	1 oz. to 150 feet of drill		

CATALOGUE OF TREES AND NURSERY STOCK

—OF—

W. R. Strong Company.

(INCORPORATED.)

1890=91.

To our Friends and Patrons.

We take pleasure in presenting a new edition of our descriptive Catalogue and Price List. The continued patronage of our friends, as shown by their frequent and increasing orders is very gratifying, and assures us that our efforts to please them are appreciated. ¶

Our facilities for growing and handling nursery stock are unsurpassed by any nursery on the Coast. Our main nursery, just outside the city limits of Sacramento, contains 210 acres; our branch at Acampo, 28 miles from Sacramento, on direct line of the Southern Pacific Railroad, contains 320 acres; also 60 acres at Penryn, Placer County; a tract at Woodland, Yolo County, and have lately purchased and added to our nurseries the entire plant, consisting of about 150,000 Citrus and Deciduous Trees, formerly owned and operated by the Palermo Citrus and Nursery Association, at Palermo, Butte County, making in all a total of over 600 acres devoted to the propagation of nursery stock, and testing new varieties of fruit.

In addition to these we have extensive nurseries in Florida, in which we grow all our orange and lemon trees, and from which this season we will have for sale about 150,000 orange and lemon trees of different varieties.

Our packing and shipping grounds are within fifty yards of the R. R. Passenger depot in Sacramento, and but five blocks from the freight depot, so that our trees can be delivered at shipping point within ten minutes after they are packed. Sacramento being a terminal point and a center where the principal railroads in the State with their branches concentrate, this with the shipping facilities of the Sacramento river, give us unequalled advantages in shipping and cost of freight. We can forward trees to almost any railroad town in California, without their having to be transferred.

Our trees are all packed with tule, wet straw and moss, and put up with the greatest care in neat, compact bales or bundles by aid of machinery, and almost invariably arrive at destination in first class condition.

Our stock this season is larger than ever before. Trees large, uniform in size, healthy and well grown; mostly trained low to protect them from the rays of the sun. Our buds and grafts are taken from bearing trees that have been fruited under our own observation, and can not help giving satisfaction when planted in the proper locality.

In the selection of varieties for propagating, we are governed largely by our extensive experience in fruit packing and shipping, and have endeavored to propagate only such varieties as are known to be the most profitable, and that are adapted to the climate and soil of California. We make it a point not to recommend or send out any new varieties until we have fully tested them ourselves, and proved them worthy of cultivation. Our Nurseries, have been kept clear of the Scale Bug pest, and we are determined by constant vigilance to keep them free from all scale and insect pests.

Read With Care the Following:

(1.) Persons planting should try to find out what succeeds best in their particular climate.

(2.) Different persons know fruits by different names, which sometimes causes planters to think they have been swindled, when they have actually got exactly what they ordered.

We regard fruit culture in California as being yet in its infancy; we think it is destined to become the paramount interest of the State. People generally are using more fruit than in former years, and as a proof of the success of the fruit interest in California, fruits of all kinds have brought better prices of late years than formerly. Our fruits are being sent to all parts of the world, and find a ready market. We are in the center of the commercial world, and from present indications we are to be the world's great fruit center. The low freights recently secured, and the lower rates which we still expect to get, will enable us to find market for all we can raise.

☞ Those varieties which we consider most valuable we have cultivated in larger quantities, and are——asterisk, thus (*).

Read Carefully the Terms of Sale.

☞ First—The articles in the following list will be furnished at the annexed prices only, when the quantities specified are taken. Moreover, these prices are intended for a reasonable assortment of varieties. When parties order long lists of only one or two trees of a kind, for such bills extra charge will be made.

☞ Second—When parties order specific varieties we will follow their instructions so far as practicable. But as it often occurs that we have run out of certain varieties, or may not have of the age and size ordered, we reserve the right to substitute in such cases other varieties equally good, unless positively instructed not to do so.

☞ Third—We will use every effort to avoid mistakes in varieties, for we fully realize that our success in the nursery business depends upon the reliability of our labels, but as there is such a margin for mistakes and misunderstanding (as above indicated), we will not warrant against errors or apparent mistakes in varieties, only to this extent, we will replace free of charge all trees that do not prove true to name, or we will refund in cash the original cost of such trees, with 10 per cent. interest per annum on said amount. (See fig. 2 on 1st page.)

☞ Fourth—All trees are carefully labeled and packed in the best manner for shipping, for which a charge will be made sufficient to cover the cost of material and labor. As trees are often delayed in transit and roughly handled, it is much better to pay a small sum to have them securely packed, than to have them poorly packed for nothing.

☞ Fifth—All orders should be made in a separate list, and not mixed up with the body of the letter. Write in a plain, legible hand, the name of the person and the place to which the goods are to go; also the route by which they are to be shipped. In the absence of such directions we will ship according to our best judgment, and will deliver to railroad or boat, all goods free of charge, but will not be responsible for accidents or delays which may occur in transit.

☞ Terms of Payment.—Cash, or sufficient guarantee that the money will be forwarded on receipt of trees.

For extra large trees and plants above the sizes mentioned, extra prices will be charged, and smaller ones lower in proportion.

Money may be sent by Express, Draft or Post-office Order, at our risk: but if sent in any other way, at sender's risk.

☞ Agents wanted in every community, to whom a liberal commission will be paid. Correspondence solicited.

☞ Any errors of ours in filling orders will be cheerfully rectified on receiving notice, PROVIDED SUCH NOTICE BE GIVEN WITHIN TEN DAYS FROM THE RECEIPT OF GOODS.

We desire to tender our thanks to the public for the liberal share of patronage they have extended us in the past, and we shall hope to merit a continuation of the same. We shall certainly try by strict integrity and prompt attention to business, to retain the public confidence so generously accorded us. Please advise us promptly of any errors or omission on our part, that we may have a chance to rectify.

APPLE TREES.

Apples are among our most profitable fruits, when proper varieties and locations are secured. Early and autumn varieties should be planted in the valleys and foothills, and winter varieties in the mountains and along the coast.

Our stock of trees comprises all the leading and popular sorts, and is unsurpassed in vigor, thrift and hardiness. There is so much variation in climate on this coast that the time of ripening of the several fruits can only be approximately named, and some apples that are classed as fall apples would be winter fruit in some localities. We would call special attention to our one-year extra apple trees; they are one year from bud, on strong roots, and are as large as two-year old trees. We should prefer them to two-year trees to plant. A one-year tree has buds all along the body, hence a good head can be secured at any desired height.

Apples—Leading Varieties.	Each	100	1000
1 year, No. 1—4 to 6 feet	$0 20	$15 00	$120
1 year, No. 2—3 to 4 feet	15	12 00	100
1 year, from bud—extra, 5 to 7 feet	25	20 00	150

APPLES.----Summer.

RED JUNE Small to medium, deep red, juicy and good. Ripens about the 20th of June.

EARLY HARVEST Large, pale yellow, mild, sub-acid. Ripens about the 20th of June.

*RED ASTRACHAN Large, roundish, striped with deep crimson, thick bloom, very juicy and acid, good bearer; ripens in June.

*WILLIAMS' Favorite Large, oblong, light red, juicy and good, ripens early in July.

APPLES.----Autumn.

*ALEXANDER Very large and beautiful, greenish yellow, striped with red, one of the best and most profitable market varieties. Ripens early in July.

WHITE ASTRACHAN Large, oblate, skin very smooth and white, with faint red stripes, juicy, acid, valuable for market; ripens 10th to 20th of July.

*GRAVENSTEIN Large, roundish, striped, very productive and good for market; ripens last of July to 1st of August.

*SANTA CLARA KING Large, roundish, skin yellow with red blush on exposed side, flesh crisp and juicy, good for all purpose; ripens 10th to 20th of August.

*YELLOW BELLFLOWER Large, oblong, pale yellow, flesh tender, sub-acid, very good; ripens in September.

*RHODE ISLAND GREENING Large, roundish, a little flattened, skin green, yellow flesh, tender, crisp, acid, juicy; ripens in October.

*KING of TOMPKINS COUNTY Large, conical shaped, skin yellowish, striped with red, flesh juicy, tender, vinous, flavor, very good; November to February.

APPLES.----WINTER.

*ESOPUS SPITZENBERG Large, oblong, skin smooth, yellowish, covered with red stripes, flesh crisp and juicy, one of the best keepers; November to March.

BALDWIN Beautiful, large red apple, flesh white, crisp, very good; October to February.

YELLOW NEWTON PIPPIN Medium size, skin greenish yellow, flesh crisp, sub-acid; one of the very best, but does best in the Coast Counties; November to March.

GREEN GENETING, OR VIRGINIA GREENING A large, late, green-colored apple, conical shape, smooth oil skin, flesh crisp and juicy, fine for cooking, a good shipper; October to March.

SWAAR Large, pale yellow, with exceedingly rich, aromatic flavor, good; November to March. Does best in the mountains.

*WINE SAP Medium, roundish, deep red, tree hardy and good bearer; November to March. One of the best for the mountains.

WHITE WINTER PEARMAIN Above medium size, skin pale yellow, flesh yellow, crisp and juicy, very good; ripens in October to February. Best in the Coast Counties.

*NICKAJACK Large, roundish, skin striped with crimson, flesh yellow, sub-acid flavor; November to February. A Southern Apple.

JONATHAN Above medium size, conical shape, red striped, sometimes quite red; a good keeper, especially in the Coast Counties.

HOOVER A large, deep red apple, good flavor, good bearer and fine keeper, one of the best; November to March. Does splendidly near the Coast.

TWENTY OUNCE PIPPIN A very large, conical shaped apple, covered with dull red stripes, has a fine crisp sub-acid flavor, will cook well when only half grown, a very profitable market kind, tree a strong vigorous grower with upright habit.

Crab Apples.

YELLOW SIBERIAN Fruit about an inch in diameter, fine rich yellow; good for jelly.
TRANSCENDENT A beautiful variety of large size, yellow flesh, with red cheek; very productive.
HYSLOP A large, beautiful red crab, one of the best.

Special Variety.

☞THE VIOLETT This is a new apple raised by J. W. Violett, of Ione. It is one of the largest apples grown, averaging nearly as large as the Gloria Monda; conical shape, a beautiful red nearly all over, solid, firm and crisp, good flavor, fine shipper; September to January. Tree strong grower with upright habit; bark, on new wood, smooth, glossy and light, chestnut color, leaves quite peculiar—a rich glossy green. 30 cts. each. $20 per 100.

PEARS.

We do not propagate a long list of pears. Our experience has been that only a few of the leading varieties are the most profitable. The following list includes most of the kinds that have proven valuable.

PRICE OF TREES—Leading sorts.

	each	100	1000
2 year, No. 1—4 o 6 feet, branched	$0 30	$25 00	$175
1 year, No. 1—4 to 6 feet	25	20	160
1 year, extra—5 to 8 feet	30	25	....
1 year—3 to 4 feet	20	15 00	....

PEARS—Summer.

MADELINE. Medium size, pale yellowish green, flesh white, melting, juicy; 20th of June.
DEARBORN'S SEEDLING. Small to medium, light yellow, flesh white, very juicy and melting; ripens 20th of June.
*BARTLETT. One of the most popular pears; large size, clear yellow skin; flesh fine grained, juicy, buttery and melting, with a rich, musky flavor; the best early pear, and has no competitor as a market and canning fruit. Tree vigorous, bearing early and abundantly. August.

PEARS—Autumn.

*KIEFER'S HYBRID. A large roundish pear, recommended highly, but we have not tested it sufficiently to judge of its merits.
*BEURRE HARDY. Fruit large, skin greenish, covered with light russet, flesh buttery, melting and juicy, one of the best, ships well; August.
SECKEL. Small to medium, skin dull yellowish brown, with russet red cheek, flesh white, very juicy, perfection of flavor; last of August.
BEURRE D'ANJO. Large round pear, one of the best, good shipper.
LOUIS BON DE JERSEY. A very sweet, delicious Autumn pear; shaped much like the Bartlett only more elongated, greenish yellow with bright red cheeks, flesh fine grained and exceedingly fine flavored, good for drying, canning or shipping.
CHINESE PEARS. Fruit large, flavor not good, but tree highly ornamental, foliage large, rich green till late in Fall, when they turn red and hang a long time. The Chinamen will pay 12 to 15 cents a pound for the fruit; trees 1 year, No. 1, $1 each.

PEARS—Winter.

BEURRE CLARGEAU. Fruit very large, skin yellow covered with russet dots, flesh yellowish, good flavor, good shipper; September to December.
EASMER BEURRE. Fruit large, skin yellowish green, with russety dots, flesh white, rich flavor, long keeper.
WINTER NELIS. Medium size, greenish, russet, melting and juicy, rich flavor, good shipper, October to December.
BEURRE BOSS. Large long russet pear, good flavor and good shipper, one of the very best, October to April.
WINTER SECKEL. Above the medium size, shaped much like the Bartlett and nearly as large, color and flavor much like the Fall Seckel, long keeper, good shipper.
P. BARRY. A California seedling, originated by the late B. S. Fox, of San Jose; a very large elongated russet pear, quite late, and a long keeper, can be kept till March; an excellent pear for Eastern shipping, fine texture and excellent flavor when fully ripe.

PEARS. Winter—Continued.

SANTA ANA. A new pear, originated at Santa Ana, in Los Angeles County. It is a large conical shaped pear, a bright golden yellow, covered with russet; it is an exceedingly handsome fruit, flesh fine grained and free from all woody substance, with a flavor equal to the finest Winter Nelis or the famous Seekel; it will eat well when picked from the tree, and yet will keep all Winter; it is a very remarkable pear in this respect; its shipping and keeping qualities cannot be excelled. We consider it a very valuable accession to our list of pears. The tree is a moderatly strong grower, with upright habit, forming a close, compact head, makes a very handsome tree. Price 35 cents each, $30 per 100.

PEACHES.

In order to secure healthy and vigorous trees it is necessary to prune severely. Their tendency in this State is to develop an immense number of fruit buds, and as they are not destroyed by frost, they produce more fruit than the tree can mature. The consequence is that it is small and inferior. The tree should be trained low and pruned regularly every year. By this practice the breaking of limbs is avoided, and the fruit grows much larger and finer. Many new varieties have been produced in the past few years, so that the fruiting season has been materially lengthened. The following list contains most of the valuable kinds, but the period of ripening varies so much in different localities that the time given can only be considered approximate.

We have the largest and finest stock of peaches on the Coast.

PRICE OF TREES—Leading Varieties.

	each	100	1000
1 year, No. 1—4 to 6 feet	$0 25	$20 00	$160
1 year, No. 2—4 to 6 feet	20	15 00	110
1 year, extra size trees	30	25 00	....

Freestone.

YELLOW ST. JOHN. A fine yellow freestone, very much like the Early Crawford, and ripens a little earlier. Shipping qualities good.

BRIGG'S RED MAY. Fruit medium to large, deep red cheek, flesh firm, good market variety; 1st of June.

GOV. GARLAND. Fruit large, bright red cheek, ripens with Alexander.

WATERLOO. Medium size, deep red, early.

ALEXANDER. Medium size, white flesh, with clear red cheek; ripens here 10th of June; the earliest shipping peach.

*HALE'S EARLY. An early and very profitable market peach; medium size, and nearly round; skin greenish, mostly covered with red when ripe; flesh white, melting, juicy, rich, sweet; 20th of June. Ships well.

*FOSTER. Very large yellow peach, red cheek, bears well, ripens about same time as Early Crawford.

*EARLY CRAWFORD. A magnificent large yellow peach, heavy bearer, one of the best for shipping and all purposes, ripens last of June.

*LATE CRAWFORD. Much the same as Early Crawford, but ripening two weeks later.

*WHEATLAND. A large yellow tree, bright red cheek, ripening a little later than Late Crawford, one of our most popular peaches.

*JONES' SEEDLING. Origin, Sacramento; large yellow flesh, with red cheek, excellent flavor, 10th of August.

*SUSQUEHANNA. Very large yellow peach, red cheek, of best quality; July. Ripens Aug. 1st.

KEYPORT WHITE. A large white peach, with red cheek, good for shipping, canning or drying, last of August.

WARD'S LATE FREE. Large white flesh peach, good for canning, September.

*SALWAY. Large yellow peach, dull red cheek, good flavor, superior market variety; 1st of September.

*BILYEU'S LATE OCTOBER. Large, white flesh, red cheek, very fine flavor, good shipper; ripens 20th of October, tree strong grower, doesn't curl, freestone, does best in foot-hills.

*PICQUET'S LATE. Very large, yellow, with a red cheek, flesh yellow, buttery, rich and sweet, and of the highest flavor.

*MUIR. Large, yellow peach, flesh very dry and sweet, pitt very small, one of the best for drying and canning, planted more for this purpose than any other peach.

WAGER. Almost a fac-simile of the Muir, and supposed by some to be the same.

*STILSON. (California Seedling.) A very large yellow fleshed peach, bright red cheeks, with dark crimson stripes, one of the very best market sorts, ripens two weeks later than the Late Crawford.

*LOVELL. Well recommended.

Clingstone.

*DAY'S YELLOW CLING. (California Seedling.) A very large, yellow flesh, with red cheek, good market variety; August.

*ORANGE CLING. A very large, yellow flesh, with red cheek, a well known variety. August.

*HEATH CLING. Large, white flesh, superior flavor; 1st of September.

*GEORGE'S LATE CLING. (California Seedling.) Very large, white flesh, with bright red cheek, superior quality; September.

LEMON CLING. Large, yellow, with bright red cheek, a fine market peach, good shipper.

*EDWARD'S CLING. (The same called by C. W. Reed, the California) A California Seedling, produced by the late Mr. Edwards, near this city. It is a large, yellow fleshed peach, highly colored, a fine market or shipping fruit.

*ALBRIGHT CLING. (California Seedling.) A very large, yellow peach, with bright red cheek. A fine shipper, and good peach in every particular.

*TUSCAN CLING. A very large, yellow cling, ripens same time as Early Crawford, a fine shipper, and its early ripening makes it very valuable.

*WINTER'S CLING. (A seedling from the Heath Cling.) Original tree raised by C. H. Wolfskill, of Winters. The old tree is now 32 years old and still bearing good crops of fruit, and Mr. Wolfskill says it has never curled or mildewed, while the Heath Cling does both. The Winters is almost a fac-simile of the Heath, except it is slightly larger, and much better shaped. It possesses all of the excellent qualities of the Heath, is larger, color a beautiful creamy white, with red blush on exposed side, is white to the pit, and therefore a fine canning peach. It is very solid and a fine shipper.

*McDEVIT CLING. (A California Seedling, raised by Neal McDevit, of Placer County.) This is one of the largest peaches we have ever seen, many of them weighing one pound each, peaches very uniform in size, rich golden yellow, becoming quite red when ripe, flesh very solid and firm, an excellent shipper, superior flavor; tree a good and regular bearer.

TUSCANY CLING. An exceedingly large yellow cling peach (from Italy,)· deep yellow with bright red cheek, very late good shipper, tree hardy and strong grower, don't curl or mildew, and consequently good for the Coast Counties.

McKEVITT'S CLING. A California seedling, very large, flesh white to the pit, firm and good, stands shipping well, good for canning and drying; 10th of September.

Peaches of Recent Introduction.—Special Varieties.

WILDER CLING. A new yellow, flesh cling. Fruit large uniform, flesh yellow; bright golden cheek, superior flavor, ripens with Salway, tree strong, vigorous grower, does not curl or mildew.

LEVI CLING. A large yellow cling, bright red cheek, resembles the McDevit, one of the best shipping varieties, its time of ripening, (after Salway is gone,) makes it very valuable.

PINE APPLE.
  BIDWELLS' EARLY.
    BIDWELLS' LATE.
      BIDWELLS' No. 7.   New varieties
        POOLS SEEDLING.   not tested,
          SEMINOLE.   said to be valuable.
            CHATMAN'S CLING.

NECTARINES.—Leading Varieties.

	each	100
1 year, No. 1—4 to 6 feet	$0 25	$20 00

NEW WHITE Large, creamy white, freestone, very superior for drying.

BOSTON Medium to large red freestone, fine flavor, good for drying.

CLEMENT'S NECTARINE A large red nectarine, good flavor, will make a good shipper, tree a good and regular bearer.

VICTORIA Large, red cling, good shipper.

APRICOTS.

A popular and profitable fruit, and though planted heavily it will always remain so, on account of the increasing demand. The soil and climate of California matures it to perfection. We have only propagated the best and most profitable varieties. Our customers will notice that we have placed the three last named varieties, Newcastle Early, French Apricot and McCormack at same price as all other Apricots. We do this because they are all really valuable varieties, and we want to introduce them. Royal Apricot are scarce this season, and we recommend the Newcastle Early as being its equal in every respect.

PRICE OF TREES -Leading Varieties.

	each	100	1000
1 year, No. 1—3 to 6 feet on peach root	$0 25	$20 00	$160
1 year, No. 1—4 to 6 feet, on Myrobolan	30	22 00	180

ROUTIER'S PEACH APRICOT   A new kind from Mr. Routier's orchard.   Large size, skin yellow in the shade, deep orange mottled, or splashed with red in the sun; flesh rich and juicy, very high flavor; good market variety.

EARLY ROYAL   Medium size, good color, very productive, a favorite for canning and drying.

HEMSKIRK   Very much like the Moorpark; one of the best; tree good bearer.

BLENHEIM   A good early variety, above medium oval; orange with deep yellow; juicy and tolerably rich flesh; vigorous grower and a regular prolific bearer.   Ripens with the Royal.

MOORPARK   Large, orange color, moderate early bearer, but of the highest flavor.

NEWCASTLE EARLY   A new variety originated by M. C. Silva & Son, of Newcastle, California. Medium size, round, well shaped, a shade smaller than the Royal; two weeks earlier than the Royal; very valuable on account of its earliness; tree a good and regular bearer, fruit ships well.

FRENCH APRICOT   Very large; good flavor; firm; ripens evenly on both sides; a good shipper, highly esteemed for canning and drying; a regular and prolific bearer; ripens with the Royal; very popular where it is known.

McCORMACK   Supposed to be a seedling of the Large Early, which it very much resembles, but ten days earlier.   Tree a strong grower and very productive, very showy, and fine for shipping.

PLUMS AND PRUNES.

The Plum and Prune succeeds admirably in this State, and we can and should not only produce for home consumption, but export large quantities instead of importing. Many varieties of Plums and Prunes have a tendency to over-bear, and, to secure a good article, the fruit should be carefully thinned out. This should be done when it is one-third or one-half grown. Those who are willing to take these pains will be amply repaid by a superior quality of fruit, and a more remunerative price.

PRICE OF TREES—Leading Varieties.

	each	100	1000
1 year, 6 to 7 feet, extra, on peach root	$0 25	$18 00	$150
1 year, No 1.—4 to 6 feet	20	15 00	135
1 year, 5 to 6 feet, extra, on Myrobolan Root	30	18 00	175
1 year, No. 1—4 to 5 feet, on Myrobolan Root	25	16 00	150

PEACH PLUM.   Fruit very large, round, greenish white, with red cheek; flesh yellow, sweet and firm; early; good for shipping.

*COLUMBIA.   Fruit large size; skin brownish purple, with fawn colored specks; flesh yellow, sugary, excellent; one of the best for shipping.

DUANE'S PURPLE.   Large, red-lish purple; flesh juicy and moderately sweet; good shipper.

VICTORIA (or Oakshade Prune.)   Medium size, beautiful red plum; good shipper, and superior for drying, being very free and quite a dry meated plum; very prolific.

COE'S GOLDEN DROP.   Fruit large, oval, flesh yellow, firm, rich and sweet; adheres to stone; good for canning and ships well.

*GROS PRUNE D'AGEN (Hungarian Prune.)   Very large, oval, violet red; very prolific, often growing double; good flavor; a valuable market kind, best shipper.

YELLOW EGG.   A very large elongated plum; golden yellow; adheres to the stone; quite juicy, rich sub-acid flavor; the best known canning variety and ships well.

WASHINGTON.   Large, round, greenish yellow; good for canning or drying.

KELSEY'S JAPAN PLUM.   Fruit very large, as large as an ordinary peach; roundish, or inclined to be conical; color greenish yellow, with faint red cheek; adheres closely to the pit, which is very small; flesh firm and juicy; it is the best keeper known

PLUMS AND PRUNES—Continued.

ROYAL NATIVE. Medium size, early, roundish, purple; flesh yellow amber, rich, good, high flavor; parts from the stone when ripe. A favorite in Vaca Valley, where its earliness makes it valuable.

BLOOD PLUM. A fine, handsome, strong growing tree; fruit above medium size, blood red both outside and inside, very handsome and fine flavor. Trees, 1 year, No. 1 (on Myrobolan), 50 cents each; $10 per 100.

ICKWORTH'S IMPERATRICE. Above medium size; purple, firm, sweet, rich, a valuable variety for market, bears transportation well, will keep a long time after being gathered. Clings to the stone; September to October.

SILVER PRUNE. Originated in Oregon. The fruit is a fac-smile of Coe's Golden Drop, except it is a darker green, and it is yet a question whether it should be called a prune or a plum. It is a very superior shipper, and it certainly makes an excellent dried fruit, either pitted or unpitted; makes a splendid prune.

PRUNIS PISSARDI. A medium size plum; red, fine flesh, good flavor, long keeper; the tree is very ornamental, foliage blood red.

PRUNIS SIMONI. Quite large, somewhat elongated, bright yellow, red cheek; very fine fruit; good for shipping or drying; tree a strong grower; bears heavily.

GERMAN PRUNE. A large purple prune, flesh greenish yellow, very sweet, always brings fancy prices as a fresh fruit; it is a good shipper and makes an excellent dried prune; tree a strong grower and a good and regular bearer.

PRUNES.

Our Stock of Prunes this season is unusually large and fine, both on Myrobolan and Peach Roots. As there is a large demand for Prune this season we advise our customers to place their orders at once.

Price of Trees.

PRUNES ON PEACH ROOTS.

	each	100	1000
1 year, No. 1—4 to 6 feet	$0 30	$25 00	$200
1 year, No. 2—2½ to 4 feet	20	15 00	
1 year, extra—5 to 8 feet	35	30 00	250

PRUNES ON MYROBOLAN ROOT.

	each	100	1000
1 year, No. 1—4 to 6 feet	30	$25 00	$225
1 year, No. 1—3 to 4 feet	20	18 00	150

*PETIT PRUNE D'AGEN. (French Prunes), the most popular drying Prune, small, reddish purple, very sweet, and takes the lead as a drying prune.

*BULGARIAN PRUNES. A very prolific, dark colored prune, larger than the French Prune, and by some considered a very valuable prune, but we have not yet tested it sufficiently to judge of its value.

*PRUNE D'AGEN (or Prune d'Ent). Very like the Petit or French Prune, only larger and more desirable. It is now demonstrated that this prune will bear as heavy crops as the French or Petit Prune, and as it is so much larger and of equally as good a quality, it is of course the most valuable of the two. There has been some fears that it might not be a good bearer, but that doubt has been dispelled. Many trees are now bearing heavy crops in this State. Price of trees same as the Petit Prune on Myrobolan root. It will not grow on peach root, but must be grown on plum root.

*TRAGEDY PRUNE. A new prune originated by Mr. Runyon, near Courtland, in this county. It would seem to be a cross between the German Prune and Purple Duane. Fruit medium size, nearly as large as the Duane Purple Plum; looks much like it, only it is more elongated; skin dark purple, flesh yellowish green, very rich and sweet, trees readily from the pit. Its early ripening (in June) makes it very valuable as a shipping fruit. Coming as it does before any other good plum, it will always bring fancy prices, both in the local and Eastern market. So far it has no rival. We believe we are the first to work it. The first to get orchards of this fruit will make fortunes out of it. We believe this Prune to ne almost equal to the French Prune for drying, though we have not tested it sufficiently as a drying prune, simply on account of its value as a shipping Prune, it has always brought a better price in the Eastern market than any other Prune or Plum.

CHERRIES.

As a pleasant and refreshing dessert fruit the cherry is everywhere highly esteemed. The early season at which it ripens, its juiciness, delicacy and richness render it always acceptable. It thrives best in rich dry loam. The trees should be trained low, that the foliage may protect the trunk, which should never be exposed to the sun. We cultivate only a few of the leading kinds, a brief description of which may be found below.

PRICE OF TREES.

	each	100	1000
2 year, No. 1—4 to 6 feet, branched	$0 35	$25 00	$200
1 year, No. 1—4 to 6 feet	30	20 00	160
1 year, No. 2—3 to 4 feet	20	15 00	125

Varieties.

EARLY PURPLE GUIGNE. Medium size, black; quite early.

*ROCHPORT BIGARREAU. A large, early, flesh colored cherry; valuable for canning or drying; it is also a good shipper; its very early ripening makes it very valuable; it will always command a good price.

KNIGHT'S EARLY BLACK. Large, black, tender, juicy, rich and high flavored; early. This is the earliest good variety.

*BLACK TARTARIAN. A very large, purplish black, rich and juicy; one of the best varieties.

GOVERNOR WOOD. A fine, early cherry, white, shaded with red, tender, juicy and delicious.

*ROYAL ANN (or Napoleau Bigarreau). Very large, pale yellow, with bright red cheek; flesh very firm, juicy and sweet; good shipper.

BLACK OREGON. Sometimes called Lewelling or Black Republican; a large, late black cherry; good flavor, long keeper and ships well.

CENTENNIAL. A new cherry, seedling from the Royal Ann, which it resembles; a little more oblate in form, and has a higher color; valuable for shipping, being a splendid keeper.

SCHMIDT'S BIGARREAU. Very large black cherry; moderate bearer; good shipper; late.

DEACON. A new, black, seedling cherry, very large, deep black, ripens with Black Tartarian. Its chief value being in its shipping qualities, as it is very hard and firm, sweet and good bearer.

QUINCE.

PRICE OF TREES.

	each	100
2 year, No. 1—4 to 6 feeet	$0 35	$25 00
1 year, No. 1—3 to 4 feet	30	20 00

ORANGE. Large, roundish; bright golden yellow; the best for geucial use.

EARLY GOODRICH. Very large, bright yellow; early; good flavor.

ALMONDS.

Nut growing should be carried on far more extensively in this state than it now is. Almonds are a sure grow over a large area of the state. They can be raised to profit at lower rates than the usual current prices. Our foothill lands seem to be peculiarly adapted for their culture. We know of no district in the state where they do better than in the foothills, at an altitude of from 600 to 2,000 feet above the sea level.

PRICE OF TREES.

1 year, No. 1—4 to 6 feet on peach	$0 20	18 00	150
1 year, No. 1—4 to 7 feet on almond	25	20 00	160
June Buds on almonds	20	15 00	125
June Buds on peach	15	12½	100

Varieties.

ROUTIER'S SOFT SHELL. A new seedling from the orchard of Hon. J. Routier; shell quite soft, good size, a regular and prolific bearer.

BLOWERS' LANGUEDOC. Originated and highly recommended by R. B. Blowers, of Woodland, a fine nut and good and regular bearer.

BYERS' LANGUEDOC. A new seedling, one of the best.

TWIN. A very large smooth nut, each nut containing a double kernel; shell soft, free, hardy and good bearer.

GOLDEN STATE. A large nut, soft shell, full smooth meat; parts readily from the hull; ripens early.

I X L. Nuts large, soft shell, good color; recommended by A. T. Hatch.

NONPARIEL. An extraordinarily heavy and regular bearer; shell very soft.

DRAKE'S SEEDLING. Originated by Mr. Drake Suisun, and recommended by him as being very prolific, and a regular and abundant bearer.

TEXAS PROLIFIC. A new seedling variety originated at Dallas, Texas. Nut fully as large as the Languedoc, but softer shell, very smooth and bright color, well filled with a very sweet meat; tree full as strong grower, and very much resembles the Languedoc tree. It is a very heavy and regular bearer. It is the only variety that will fruit well at Dallas, Texas. We consider it by all odds the finest and most desirable almond we have ever seen. **Price 50 cents each. $35 per 100, $250 per 1,000.**

FIGS.

It has been thoroughly demonstrated that the Fig will grow most luxuriantly, thrive and bear great crops from one end of the State to the other; the warm, dry alluvial soils, and the dry warm climate of the interior valleys, and foot-hills seem to be peculiarly adapted to its successful culture and earing: it will grow and do well on lands too dry to mature other fruits; it will do well on rich bottom lands, provided they are well drained, so that there is no Fruit that can be more generally grown all over the State; and no other with so little care and risk and that is more profitable in the end. At the same time there is no other Fruit that has been so generally neglected. It is only in the last few years, that the value of this fruit has been recognized. All of the common varieties can be made profitable, and with the varieties we are now introducing, there is no fruit that will be more desirable, or more profitable.

PRICE OF TREES.

	each	100	1000
2 year, No. 1—4 to 6 feet, branched (common kinds)	$0 25	$15 00	$120
1 year, No. 1—3 to 4 feet	15	12 00	100

WHITE ADRIATIC AND VERDONI.

	each	100	1000
2 year, 4 to 6 feet	$0 35	$25 00	$200
1 year, 3 to 4 feet	25	18 00	140

Varieties.

LARGE PURPLE. One of the most fruitful sorts; large size; dark purple, very sweet, good flavor; drys well.

BROWN ISCHIA. Very large, skin light or chestnut brown, very sweet and excellent.

PACIFIC WHITE. Fruit medium size, fine grained, very sweet, seeds very small; very white and exceedingly fine flavored when dry; but the skin when dry is thicker and more tough than the imported, that and its small size is the only objection to it. It never cracks and sours in drying. The tree is a strong grower, very hardy, and always good shaped, a fine shade or avenue tree. A good regular bearer.

SAN PEDRO (usually called WHITE SMYRNA). A very large, dirty, or rusty white fig; good flavor, one of the best as a green or fresh fruit; valuable for that purpose, but does not dry well if dried in the sun, as it cracks and sours in drying, but makes a very superior product when dried by artificial heat. We regard it as one of the best figs for profit we have, if properly handled; the tree is rather a slow grower, but a great bearer, exceedingly prolific.

VERDONI. Called by many White Adriatic, but it differs from the fig which is now generally called the White Adriatic in the color of the pulp or inside of the fruit. The Verdoni is white inside, while the other is red, otherwise they are very much alike. While they are both excellent figs, we are planting (in orchard) more largely of the Verdoni, mainly on account of its white flesh, but either of them will make a very superior dried product, that will equal if not surpass the best imported article, (where they are well grown and properly cured.)

WHITE ADRIATIC.

ORANGE and LEMON.

For the last four seasons we have been growing our Orange and Lemon trees in Florida, owing to the high prices of California grown trees, and the superiority of the Florida sour root over the sweet roots. In the spring of 1887, we sent buds of the leading varieties from trees in the best orchards in Riverside, Cal., to Florida and had them budded to our order, and have been propagating from these trees since, it is a thoroughly established and well-known fact that trees grown on the Florida Wild Orange Root are longer lived, more healthy and vigorous, stand our winters far better, can be transplanted with less loss, and are in every respect better than trees grown on sweet seedling roots. We can refer to all our customers, who have planted our stock, for the reliability of this statement. Out of 40,000 orange trees sold to one planter in 1887, less than 2 per cent failed to grow, a record that can not be equalled by any orchard planted with California grown trees.

Our Florida trees are grown for California trade.

We have this season 160,000 budded orange trees mostly Washington Navel, balance Lemon and assorted well-known varieties. We have had them all staked up and grown perfectly straight, most of them running in height from 3½ to 6 ft. They are clean, thrifty and free from all scale, and we can safely say that we will have this season the finest lot of trees ever brought into or grown in California, and we will sell them at prices that will defy competition.

In addition to this we saved out last season about 2,000 orange trees which we planted out in our nursery and salesyard. They are intended for early delivery before we can get trees out from Florida.

These trees have made a most remarkable growth and are especially adapted for yard planting.

We make a specialty of orders for car load lots, and will quote special low prices to any one wanting large orders.

See our trees and get our prices before buying elsewhere. Send for Orange Circulars.

PRICE OF BUDDED TREES.

	each	100	1000
4 to 6 ft. on 4 and 5 yr. roots	$1 50	$90 00	$750
3½ to 4 ft. on 3 and 4 yr. "	1 25	75 00	650
2 to 3 ft	75	50 00	350

Extra large trees, $2 00 each; $150 per 100.

Lemon, same sizes and prices of Orange trees.

Sweet (Indian River) seedlings, 4 to 5 years old, ¾ to 1¼ inch in diameter......60c each, $45 00 per 100
Sour orange trees for street planting, 4 to 7 years old, ¾ to 1½ inch in diameter......75c each; $50 00 per 100

We will give special rates to dealers, nurserymen or parties buying in large lots to plant.

Parties asking for special rates should state varieties and number of trees wanted.

Brief Description of Varieties. (All Hardy.)

WASHINGTON NAVEL. Acknowledged by all to be the leading orange; too well known to need any further description. ¾ of our trees are budded to this variety.

MEDT SWEET. A popular variety; medium size, very sweet, and good bearer; tree thornless.

NONPAREIL. A very handsome orange of most excellent quality, a popular sort in the market; tree a strong grower, hardy and a good bearer.

PARSON BROWN. Fruit medium size, oblong in shape, smooth high color, very sweet, ripens early, is sweet as soon as it begins to turn, grand bearer, tree has some thorns.

MAGNUM BONUM. A very large orange, a little flattened, skin smooth and glossy, fruit heavy and of excellent quality, ripens early, tree very prolific, thorny.

PEERLESS. Fruit large and round, smooth skin, one of the best market sorts, tree a heavy and regular bearer and strong grower.

ST. MICHAEL. Fruit medium size, very fine quality, a little flattened, thin skin, tree a good bearer, nearly thornless.

HART'S TARDIFF. A large round orange of good quality, its chief excellence consisting in its lateness; it does not ripen till May or June, and will hang on the tree in good eating condition until August; tree strong grower and good bearer.

JAFFA. Imported from the city of Joppa, in Syria, a very fine, medium size orange of superior quality, trees nearly thornless.

The VILLA FRAKA LEMON; the finest lemon ever introduced in California. This lemon has become the favorite in Florida; the fruit is of a very superior quality, tree a strong grower, heavy and regular bearer, excelling all other varieties in productiveness. The tree is exceedingly hardy; it withstood the heavy freeze in Florida in January, 1886, in the same orchards where all other kinds, and also orange trees, were killed. It ripens in July and August, thus coming in the hot season when lemons are most needed and when the market is bare of other citrus fruits. It is emphatically the lemon for profit.

MILAN LEMON Very similar to the Villa Franka.

EUREKA LEMON. A popular California variety.

WALNUTS.

EASTERN BLACK WALNUTS. A well known tree; valuable for timber, nut a little larger than the California walnut; price 2 year trees, 50 cents.

CALIFORNIA BLACK WALNUT. A native specie, valuable for shade and nuts. Very productive. 2 year trees, 5 to 7 feet, well branched, 30 cents each, per hundred $25. 1 year trees, 3 to 5 feet, 20 cents each, per hundred $15.

ENGLISH WALNUTS. Very popular and profitable nut, makes a very handsome shade, 2 year trees 5 to 8 feet, 50 cents each, $30 per hundred. 1 year 2 to 4 feet, 20 cents each, $15 per hundred. We have a large stock of these, and will quote special price on large lots.

PRAEPARTURIEN WALNUT. A very fine table nut, trees of dwarfish habit, bears quite young and heavy crop. Trees 2 to 3 feet, 25 cents each, $20 per hundred; 3 to 4 feet, 30 cents each, $25 per hundred. 4 to 5 feet, 50 cents each, $40 per hundred.

CHESTNUTS.

These nuts do well in the greater portion of the state, they are among our handsomest shade trees and the nuts bring a fancy price, they should be planted by every one.

Varieties.

ITALIAN CHESTNUT. A very large nut, sweet, bears well, tree very ornamental. Trees, 1 to 1½ feet, 15 cents each, $10 per hundred. 2 to 3 feet, 25 cents each, $20 per hundred. 3 to 4 feet, 40 cents each, $35 per hundred.

CHESTNUT (American Sweet). Same sizes, same prices as the Italian.

OLIVES

Olive culture in California has of late attracted much attention, and it is an established fact that a great many localities especially the foothills, are exactly suited to the successful growth of the olive, and the production of an Oil that will have no superior.

Olive growing in California is only in its infancy, but the flattering results that have been obtained, guarantees for Olive growing a perfect success and a most profitable future. There are a great many different varieties of the Olive now being propagated, most of them not yet thoroughly tested, and we only offer those varieties that have been tested and are known to be the most profitable.

PRICE OF MISSION OLIVE TREES.

	each	100
14 to 18 inches	$0 20	$15
18 to 24 inches	25	20
24 to 30 inches	30	25
PICHOLINE. 2 to 3 feet	25	20

Varieties.

MISSION. This we believe to be the best Olive for all purposes; it is good for both oil and pickles. PICHOLINE. A small olive used chiefly for oil; makes a fine grade of light oil. MANZANILLO (Queen Olive). Berries very large, highly prized for pickles; also good for oil. NEVADILLO. One of the finest olives for oil.

PRICE OF MANZANILLO AND NEVADILO.

	each	100
14 to 18 inches	$0 25	$20
18 " 24 "	30	25
24 " 30 "	35	30
2½ to 4 ft	50	40

GRAPES.

Grape growing in California is one of our leading industries, most all varieties thrive well, and produce abundant crops. We have endeavored to select out of the vast number of varieties such as have proved the most valuable. We have an extra large stock this season, and will quote special price on large orders.

We only quote prices on 1 year plants, as we find that 1 year vines give the best results. All our vines are extra well grown, well rooted and strictly first class in every respect.

PRICE.	Each	100	1000
1 year No. 1 (fine roots)...	$0 05	$2 50	$20

Varieties.

*WHITE MUSCAT. (Muscat of Alexandria). Fine, large, white grape, musk flavored, good market variety, either for shipping or raisins.

*MUSCATELLE GORDO BLANCO. Resembling the Muscat, berries large, less musky flavor, good raisin variety.

*FLAME TOKAY. A magnificient large, red grape, very firm, vigorous grower and productive, our most popular shipping grape.

*ZINFANDEL. A medium size, black grape, close compact bunches, very productive, valuable for wine.

SEEDLESS SULTANA. Small white grape, clusters large. It makes a fine raisin for culinary purposes, at the same time is a fine wine grape. It is the only grape we know of that is good for both raisins and wine.

EMPEROR. A large red grape, resembling the Tokay, ripens quite late, is an excellent shipper; its lateness and long keeping qualities make it a very valuable grape, does splendidly on our granite soils in the foothills, the vines of this variety should be staked up to get the best results.

CORNISCHON. The largest and latest grape we cultivate, berries quite elongated, firm, solid, and skin thick and tough, which will enable it to carry farther than any other grape. Sells well in the East.

ROSE PERU. Medium size black grape, ripens quite early, good bearer, one of our best early shipping grapes.

BLUE MALVOISE. Large, reddish black, oblong, with faint bloom, good early table grape.

BLACK FARURA. Large, oblong, firm black grape, good flavor, one of the best for shipping.

TROSSEAU. Bunches medium sized, cylindrical, berries black, covered with a thick bloom, yields a dark colored wine of the best quality for flavor and bouquet.

CARIGNAN. Bunches similiar to Mataro, berries oblong, black, produces heavy crops, and a highly colored good wine.

BERGER. A large white wine grape, very productive, makes an excellent wine, is a very profitable grape to raise.

MATTARO. A medium sized black grape, close compact bunches, an abundant bearer, makes a superior wine. This grape is always in good demand as a wine grape, brings good price, is a very profitable grape to grow.

PETITE BOUSCHET. Valuable as a coloring for wine.

*WHITE NIECE. Wine grapes.

*GRENACHE. Wine grapes.

Resistant Stock.

VITES CALIFORNIA. We have a fine stock of this valuable resistant stock. Grafts on these stocks make a stronger and more vigorous growth than on their own roots. Price 2 year, $10 per thousand.

CURRANTS.

PRICE.	Each.	Per 100
2 year—No. 1..	$0 12½	$10 00
1 year—No. 1..	8	6 00

CHERRY. Fruit of the largest size; bunches short; berries large, deep red; a valuable market sort.

WHITE DUTCH. Bunches long; berries yellowish white, nearly transparent; very sweet and agreeable; sometimes used for making currant wine.

GOOSEBERRIES.

PRICE.	Each	Per 100
American..	$0 20	$15 00
English..	25	20 00

BLACKBERRIES.

PRICE..............4 cents each | $3 00..............per 100 | $10 00..............per 1,000

WILSON'S EARLY. Fruit large, productive and early.

DORCHESTER. A fine sweet berry.

KITTATINNY. Good market variety; large and good flavor.

LAWTON. Good market variety for this locality; large and late.

CRANDALL'S EARLY. This berry was brought from Texas some years ago, and planted on the place of Dr. S. R. Crandall, of Auburn, Placer County. (The origin of this berry is not known to us). Here it was discovered that it was not only an excellent berry and prolific bearer, but was also found to ripen three weeks earlier than the Lawton, and continues to blossom and bear fruit until late in the Fall. We have often picked good, ripe, well developed berries as late as the last days of December. The wood of the vine is light colored, resembling the Wilson's Early, but is a much stronger grower, The berry is as large as the Lawton, fine flavor, firm and solid. It is an excellent shipper. Price $1 per dozen, $5 per 100, $15 per 1,000. Fifty plants at 100 rates; 500 at 1,000 rates.

RASPBERRIES.

PRICE..............5 cents each | $3 00...............per 100 | $15 00..............per 1,000

Leading Varieties.

HANSEL. Medium size berry, very early and firm; ships well.

BARTER. We have cultivated all of the leading varieties, and do not hesitate to recommend the Barter, as being the finest and most profitable berry we have ever seen, it is a very large bright red berry, bears very heavy crops, and frees easily from the stem; a splendid shipper, and has brought the highest price of any berry we ever handled

HERSTINE. Fine large market berry.

STRAWBERRIES.

PRICE.............50 cents per doz. | $1 00...............per 100 | $6 00.............per 1,000

Triomphe de Gand, Sharpless, Monarch of the West, Captain Jack, and many other new varieties not fully tested.

ESCULENT ROOTS.

Asparagus...2 cents each; $10 00 per 1,000

Rhubarb..1 year, 15c; 2 years, 25c.; extra large 4 years 50c. each

Hop Roots.. ..50c. per doz.; $1 50 per 100; $10 00 per 1,000

(Large lots at special rates, very low).

⤜⤜⤜Deciduous   Shade   and   Ornamental   Trees.⤛⤛⤛

POPLARS AND LOCUST.

	each	per 100
No. 1—2 to 2½ inches diameter......................................	$1 00	$60 00
No. 2—1½ to 2 inches diameter......................................	50	40 00
No. 3—1 to 1½ inches diameter......................................	25	20 00
No. 4—¾ to 1 inch diameter, 7 to 9 feet high.......................	15	10 00

(Large orders at special rates, very low).

CAROLINA POPLAR. A magnificent tree for street planting, forming a beautiful head; large leaf and spreading habit; rapid grower.

LOMBARDY POPLAR. Erect and upright grower.

BLACK LOCUST. Strong grower, valuable for timber; same price as poplar.

CORK BARK ELM. Rapid grower; symmetrical shape; 50 cents to $1 25 each.

AMERICAN ELM. A magnificent tree with drooping branches; 25 to 75 cents each.

SOFT OR SILVER MAPLE. Fine for street planting, handsome foliage; 25 to 50 cents each; large trees 75 cents to $1 each.

WEEPING WILLOW. A beautiful weeping tree, with slender drooping branches; 50 cents to $1 each. Our stock of both Maple and American Elm, is very large, and on large lots we will make very low prices.

UMBRELLA TREE. One of the most beautiful and ornamental trees grown. It naturally grows in the shape of an umbrella, and is a very rapid grower; makes a dense shade. Price 50 cents each; extra large trees 75 cents each.

MULBERRIES.

The Mulberry is a very valuable family of tree. Most of them make a beautiful, well shaped and clean shade tree. All make very valuable timber and make it very quick, being rapid growers. This fruit is excellent, and is recommended by some to plant in cherry orchards for the purpose of attracting the birds from the cherries, as they eat mulberries in preference to any other fruit.

PRICE OF TREES.

1 year, No. 1—5 to 8 feet...50 cents each

1 year, No. 2—3 to 5 feet...35 cents each

Varieties.

DOWNING'S EVERBEARING. A rapid growing tree, valuable for its fruit, as it remains in fruit for three months.

PERSIAN. Largest fruit, but slow grower.

NEW AMERICAN. This is a large, strong growing, beautiful shaped tree; one of the best shade trees that grows; it also produces large crops of very fine berries, very sweet and delicious. Fine.

RUSSIAN MULBERRY. This also makes a fine tree, and the fruit is said to be very large and fine; we have not fruited it yet.

CIRCASSIAN MULBERRY. This is a very fine, strong growing variety, makes a splendid shade tree; fruit of little value.

MORUS ALBA or WHITE MULBERRY. Fine shade tree, but fruit of no value.

MORUS MULTICOLUS. Only valuable for the foliage, which is used to feed silk worms; 10 to 25 cents. Large lots for silk culture very cheap.

DYOSPYROS KAKI, OR JAPANESE PERSIMMONS.

Hyakume, Kuro, Kume, Zemon, Dai Dai Maru, Zanji Maru Hachija, Tane Nashi. The two last named are nearly or quite seedless. We have several other varieties, but have not space to name or describe them. Most of our people are familiar with this fruit. Price 35 cents each.

ORNAMENTAL DEPARTMENT.

Our limited space will not admit of a full description of every shrub or flower, neither can we give the exact price for each particular size and style of plant. They vary so much in size, shape and condition that a minute description would occupy too much space. But we can guarantee satisfaction if you will, in ordering articles, where the price ranges from one figure to another, simply give the price you wish to pay, and we will send articles to correspond with the price given.

We do not grow Greenhouse Plants but carry them in stock during the selling season and can furnish anything in that line at regular florists' prices. So we can fill orders for anything in that line, though it may not be named in the Catalogue. In the item of Roses we can furnish over 100 varieties not mentioned in this Catalogue.

ROSES.

Price, in pots...60c. to $1 00 each.
Price, naked roots...30c. each.

CHOICE COLLECTION OF EVER-BLOOMING ROSES.

THE BRIDE. A pure, white rose, of large size and most perfect form. It is a sport from "Catharine Mermet," with which it is identical in growth and shape of flowers. The buds are pointed and the ends of petals are slightly curved back, giving it a most chaste and elegant appearance.

BON SILENE. Free bloomer and fine bedder; color brilliant carmine.

ANNA OLIVER. Creamy blush, shaded carmine.

ALINE SISLEY. Violet red, brightened with crimson Maroon.

BOUGERE. Beautiful dark pink; sweet fragrance.

BEAUTY OF STAPLEFORD. Flowers large, double and handsomely formed, color bright pink, shading gradually toward the center to deep rosy carmine, makes beautiful buds, and is a profuse bloomer.

CATHERINE MERMET. One of the finest roses grown. Bright rosy flesh, flowers of immense size and perfect form. One of the most popular roses for cut blooms.

CLOTH OF GOLD. Beautiful climber, flowers golden yellow; fragrant, large and beautiful.

GOLD OF OPHIR. (Climber). Very showy and delicate, flowers yellow, shaded with rose, a profuse bloomer.

MARECHAL NEIL. (Climber). Immense yellow roses, fragrant, well known to all.

COMTESSE RISA DU PARK. Bright coppery rose, shaded violet crimson. Very beautiful, a great favorite.

COMTESSE DE FRIGNEUSE. Long pointed buds of bright canary yellow.

CORNELIA COOK. Beautiful creamy white, buds of immense size and very double; when well grown is a magnificent flower.

COQUETTE DE LYON. A fine yellow rose, called the yellow Hermosa from its free flowering habit.

CAPTAIN CRISTY. Delicate pink, large, full and double, very profuse bloomer.

DEVONIENSIS. Often called the Magnolia rose. Creamy white, delicately flushed in the centre with pink. One of the most fragrant roses, and a favorite of long standing.

ROSES—Continued.

DUCHESS DE BRABANT. Few roses equal this in freedom of flowering; the flowers are rather loose when open, but are rich and peculiarly colored; color rose, heavily shaded with amber and salmon.

DUCHESS OF EDINBURGH. Very dark crimson; free flowering; large, fine form; beautiful in bud.

ETOILE DE LYON. A magnificent rose, color brilliant chrome yellow, deepening in the centre to pure golden yellow. Flowers large, very double and full and deliciously fragrant.

EXADELPHA. Beautiful yellow, large and full.

GRACE DARLING. Large, full, beautifully recurved petals; color, rosy pink, shaded yellow.

GENERAL DE TARTAS. Brilliant carmine shaded violet purple.

JULES FINGER. Brilliant rosy scarlet, shaded with crimson.

GENERAL JAQUIMINOT. Brilliant crimson; very large, of fine shape and exquisite fragrance. This grand old variety holds its own against all new comers, and is undoubtedly the finest hardy rose of its color.

LA FRANCE. Delicate silvery rose, shaded with cerise pink. Very large, and double flowering continuously throughout the season. One of the most fragrant roses grown. It stands first and foremost among roses.

NIPHETOS. Long buds of pure white; there is none equal it for cutting.

MADAM WELCHE. An extra fine variety; very large double, and of beautiful rounded form; color, Apricot yellow, very heavily shaded throughout the centre with dark orange red. One of the best Tea roses.

MARIE GUILLOT. Pure white, large, full and beautifully imbricated in form; one of the finest white Teas, highly fragrant.

MARIE VAN HOUTTE. Lovely creamy white, with outer petals suffused with bright pink. It grows vigorously; blooms freely and is most deliciously scented—no garden is complete without it.

PERLE DES JARDINS. Among tea roses, this still stands without a rival, in color, form, beauty of foliage and all that goes to make a perfect rose. Color, a rich shade of yellow, should be in every collection.

SOUV, DE GABRIEL DREVET. Salmon pink with center of coppery rose; of good size and fine form.

SOUV, DE MALMAISON. Known and prized by all; deep blush white, clear, full and distinct.

SAFRANO. This is the ideal Tea Rose; buff color, tinted Apricot yellow; exquisite fragance and splendid bud.

SOMBREUIL. Large, fine formed flowers; white tinged with delicate rose; blooms in clusters, constant.

MAD JOSEPH SCHWARTZ. A strong vigorous grower and one of the hardiest Tea roses. Color, white; beautifully flushed with pink.

EVERGREEN TREES.

EUCALYPTUS. Globulus (Blue Gum), in variety, in pots or bagged, 2½ to 10 feet, 20c to $1. Blue Gum and other varieties of Eucalyptus, in seed boxes. Transplanted in boxes so as to cut with balls of earth, 8 to 16 inches, $3 per 100.

☞ In large quantities for forest planting at special rates.

ACACIA. Native of Australia, rapid growth, beautiful foliage and masses of yellow and orange-colored flowers; in pots or bagged, 3 to 5 feet, 30 to 50 cents.

ACACIA MELONOXELON, or Blackwood Acacia, a very fine hardy kind.

ACACIA floribunda, or fragrans, long lance-like leaves.

ACACIA mollissima, fine elegant species; light green leaves.

PEPPER TREES (California Schinu Molle), 3 to 6 feet, 40 cents to $1.

PALMS, in variety, $1 to $5, as per size and variety,

CUPRESSUS (Cypress), most popular and very ornamental; perfectly hardy, and thrives well in most localities and soils.

CUPRESSUS LAWSONIANA (Port Orford Cedar) very fine; branches curve like green plums; 50c to $1.

CUPRESSUS FUNEBRUS, elegant drooping foliage, adapted for planting in cemeteries; 75cents to $1.

CUPRESSUS macrocarpa (Monterey Cypress), 15 cents to $1 each.

CUPRESSUS pyramidalias (Italian Cypress), very erect, close pressing branches; 50 cents to $1.

PINUS macrocarpa (Monterey Pine), 3 to 7 feet; 30 cents to 75 cents.

ARBOR VITÆ, golden, beautiful compact plants; 75 cents to $2.50.

SEQUOIA gigantea (California Mammoth Trees), $1 to $2.50.

LAUREL, English, good plants; 75 cents to $1.

MAGNOLIA GRANDIFLORA, 50 cents to $2.50.

☞ Surplus stock, which we will sell at special rates in quality. Price on application—

MISCELLANEOUS.

Pinks, in variety...........................35c each	Honeysuckle, in variety................35c each
Lillies (See Seed Catalogue for price of bulbs)	Ivy.....................................25c "
....25 to 75c "	Oleander...............................35c "
Chrysanthemums.....................25c "	Veronica...........................25 to 50c "
Fuchsia.................................35c "	English Box,.......................10 to 30c "
Heliotrope.............................35c "	Euonomous, plain....................40c "
Pampas Grass........................50c "	Euonomous, Varigated Golden..........50c "
Verbenas, per bunch.................20c "	Lauristinus..........................40c "
Pansies, per bunch..................10c "	Camelias, assorted............50c to $3 00 "
Violets, per bunch.............10 to 25c each	Geraniums....................25 to 75c "

Table Showing Number of Plants or Trees to the Acre at Given Distances.

Distance Apart.	No. Plants.	Distance Apart.	No. Plants.
3 in. x 3 in.................696,960		5 ft. x 4 ft.................2,178	
4 in. x 4 in.................392,040		5 ft. x 5 ft.................1,742	
6 in. x 6 in.................174,240		5½ ft. x 5½ ft.................1,417	
9 in. x 9 in.................77,440		6 ft. x 6 ft.................1,210	
1 ft. x 1 ft.................43,560		6½ ft. x 6½ ft.................1,031	
1½ ft. x 1½ ft.................19,360		7 ft. x 7 ft.................881	
2 ft. x 1 ft.................21,780		8 ft. x 8 ft.................680	
2 ft. x 2 ft.................10,890		9 ft. x 9 ft.................537	
2½ ft. x 2½ ft.................6,960		10 ft. x 10 ft.................435	
3 ft. x 1 ft.................14,520		11 ft. x 11 ft.................361	
3 ft. x 2 ft.................7,260		12 ft. x 12 ft.................302	
3 ft. x 3 ft.................4,840		13 ft. x 13 ft.................257	
3½ ft. x 3½ ft.................3,555		14 ft. x 14 ft.................222	
4 ft. x 1 ft.................10,890		15 ft. x 15 ft.................193	
4 ft. x 2 ft.................5,445		16 ft. x 16 ft.................170	
4 ft. x 3 ft.................3,630		16½ ft. x 16½ ft.................160	
4 ft. x 4 ft.................2,722		17 ft. x 17 ft.................150	
4½ ft. x 4½ ft.................2,151		18 ft. x 18 ft.................134	
5 ft. x 1 ft.................8,712		19 ft. x 19 ft.................120	
5 ft. x 2 ft.................4,356		20 ft. x 20 ft.................108	
5 ft. x 4 ft.................2,904		25 ft. x 25 ft.................69	
		30 ft. x 30 ft.................48	

Rule.—Multiply the distance in feet between the rows by the distance the plants are apart in the rows, and the product will be the number of square feet for each plant or hill, which, divided into the number of feet in an acre (43,560), will give the number of plants or trees to the acre.

Transplanting Trees.

In the first place see that the ground selected for orchard is thoroughly ploughed and well pulverized. Dig the holes large enough to allow all the roots to spread out in their natural shape, two feet wide and two feet deep will usually do, though the larger and deeper the hole is, the better, as you get the ground more thoroughly worked up. After the holes are all dug take the trees from the bale a few at a time, so that they will not be exposed. Do not expose roots to sun or frost, fill the hole with loose moist soil until the tree will stand about the same depth as it stood in the nursery, trim off all the bruised parts of the roots, place the tree in the hole so that the roots will spread out naturally, throw in moist earth and pack it solid around the roots, after the roots are covered, and the ground packed thoroughly it is an excellent thing to throw in a bucket of water, then fill up the hole. To preserve from borers and other injuries during the first summer, wrap the trunk with cloth, woolen preferred—but burlap will do.

Hints on Pruning.

☞The best dug tree loses more than half the fibrous roots that act as feeders. Shorten the top to correspond. Don't fail to cut back heavily when you transplant. Don't forget that a half root cannot support a whole top. Never neglect pruning. Trees trained low protect their own trunks from the sun's rays, are less liable to break with the weight of the fruit, and the fruit is easier gathered.

Transplanting Potted Plants.

In transplanting potted plants, lift the ball carefully out of the pot, then with a sharp knife cut the circle of roots that encompass the outside of the ball, so as to force a straight and not a crooked root from the plant into the ground, in order that, as the tree or plant increases in size, it will not be so liable to blow over. Thousands of trees are annually blown over and destroyed by reason of this circle of roots, for as the root is shaped when the plant is set, so it will continue to grow. Bagged plants should be placed with the bag on, only cutting the string at the collar or top of the bag.

Anything not mentioned in this Catalogue, or Greenhouse and Florists' specialties, will be furnished at regular florists' prices, provided it can be procured in the market.

Principal Office at Store, Nos. 102 to 110 J street, between Front and Second.

Principal Depot and Sales Yards, Second Streets, near Passenger Depot of C. P. R. R.

W. R. STRONG COMPANY, Proprietors

SACRAMENTO, CAL.

Fertilize Your Trees, Vines and Plants.

WE HAVE LATELY SECURED THE AGENCY FOR THE MEXICAN PHOSPHATE AND SULPHUR
COMPANY, MANUFACTURERS OF SUPERPHOSPHATE FERTILIZERS FROM GENUINE
GUANO OR PHOSPHATES IMPORTED FROM GULF OF CALIFORNIA AND
COAST OF MEXICO.

"He that maketh 2 blades of grass grow where but one grew before is a benefactor of mankind."

The Mexican Phosphate and Sulphur Company are the owners, under concession from the **Mexican Government** of deposits of Guano in the Gulf of California, and are engaged in shipping same to Europe, where it finds ready sale and has already taken front rank in the market. Over $250,000 worth of raw phosphates have been shipped, and demand is increasing.

Believing that the same might be introduced and used with profit by the cultivators of the soil in California, the company has commenced the manufacture of Nitrogenous Superphosphates at Sobrante Station, on the line of the Central and Southern Pacific Railroad, from Guano, imported from its deposits, and now offer to the public a genuine article in the way of a fertilizer for farms, orchards, vineyards, gardens of all kinds, such as has never been offered in California before.

A sample of this fertilizer has been submitted to Prof. E. W. Hilgard of the College of Agriculture in the University of California, with the following results:

UNIVERSITY OF CALIFORNIA, November 3, 1886.

DR. J. KOEBIG:

Dear Sir:—I have analyzed your sample of "Nitrogenous Super Phospate," with the following result:

Soluble Phosphoric Acid	12.00 per cent.
Reverted Phosphoric Acid	.95 "
Insoluble Phosporic Acid	2.83 "
Potash	2.23 "
Ammonia	1.67 "
Nitric Acid	2.95 "

The above amount of Nitric Acid is equal to 0.85 per cent. Ammonia, therefore total of Nitrogen calculated as Ammonia, 2.72 per cent.

This fertilizer is a valuable manure for vineyards, orchards, gardens, farms, and I recommend its use by the cultivators of the soil generally in California. Yours truly,

DR. E. A. SCHNEIDER.

—— o ——

UNIVERSITY OF CALIFORNIA, COLLEGE OF AGRICULTURE.

BERKELEY, November 20th, 1886.

DR. J. KOEBIG, San Francisco.

Dear Sir:—I take pleasure in adding my testimony to that of Dr. Schneider as to the high quality of the "Nitrogenous Phosphate" fertilizer, analyzed by him at your request. It is a high grade article, and as such returns the user a better money value than a low grade fertilizer. It is especially well adapted to use in California, on account of the predominence in it of Phosphoric Acid, which is generally in small supply in our soils. Yet it is desirable that complete fertilizers be used in our orchards and vineyards and yours is of that character in furnishing Potash and Nitrogen as well. Very Respectfully. E. W. HILGARD.

The value of this Fertilizer consists in the large percentage it contains of Phosphoric Acid—the chief element of all plant food—in combination with the necessary quantities of Potash and Ammonia, and the ease and cheapness with which it can be applied.

In ordinary soils the following quantities will be found sufficient:

For Wheat, Barley, Corn and Oats, 300 to 350 pounds per acre.
For Grass, Sugar Beets and Vegetables, 250 to 300 per acre.
For Young Vines, Fruit Trees, from ½ pound to 1 pound each.
For Old Vines, Fruit Trees, from 2 pounds to 5 pounds each.
For Flower Gardens, Lawns, House Plants, etc., a light top dressing, applied at any time, will be found very beneficial.

It is not claimed that this fertilizer is an absolute cure for Phylloxera, or the other evils which are incident to the cultivation of the soil; but it is confidently asserted that by enriching the soil and supplying the needs of plants they attain greater growth and are better able to withstand the attack of either animal pests or inclement seasons. This fertilizer is introduced to the people of California for this purpose and a critical test of its merits invited.

On our own and very poor land around the factory, at Sobrante Station, we sowed barley and oats; one-half of each was fertilized with 250 lbs. to the acre, as an experiment.

ACTUAL RESULT OBTAINED.

1 Acre.	Not Fertilized.	Fertilized.
Barley	1024 lbs., or 22 buhels	2364 lbs., or 51 bushels.
Oats	733 " or 23 "	1213 " or 39 "

Send all orders direct to

W. R. STRONG COMPANY, Sacramento, Cal.

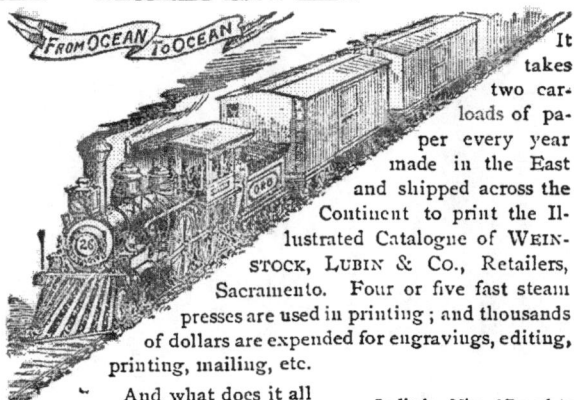

W. R. STRONG COMPANY TRACT, EAST SACRAMENTO.

The above is a cut of 130 acres of land we own and have been using in our Nursery Department for the growing of Fruit and Nursery Stock.

It has been planted in orchard trees, etc., most of which will be in full bearing the coming season, and are of the best and most marketable varieties. The soil is superior, and water for irrigation and domestic use abundant, and of best quality. The yield of fruit for market the coming season on some of the blocks, will nearly, if not quite, equal the valuation of the land. No property in the vicinity of Sacramento is more desirable for pleasant and healthy suburban homes, or that will grow into value faster.

This property is now surveyed and made into blocks corresponding with the streets of the city, containing from three and one-third to four and one-half acres, and will thus be sold in quantities to suit. Being just outside of Sacramento, it is free from City taxation, while enjoying all of its advantages. The S. P. and S. V. R. R. passes its whole length, with an R. R. Station within two minutes walk, and the Electric City Cars, are within ten minutes walk, and will doubtless, as population increases, be extended through its grand avenue.

A complete map and full particulars will be furnished on application to persons who wish to buy.

We have also for sale 50 acres, all in orchard, at Penryn, in Placer County's celebrated Fruit Belt, which will be sold in 10 and 20 acre lots if desired. Also 20 acres in Orange Vale Colony, mostly set in orange trees. Also 54 acres one mile from Sacramento City limits, one-half planted in Tokay Grapes and Figs, now two years old, besides other desirable property.

For further particulars apply to

W. R. STRONG COMPANY.

W.R. Strong Company

SACRAMENTO AND LOS ANGELES

CAPITAL NURSERIES

Wholesale Dealers, Packers & Shippers

of CALIFORNIA
Fruit & Produce

Car Load Lots our Specialty

1891

SEED, TREE & NURSERY STOCK

W.R. STRONG COMPANY

SACRAMENTO
CALA.

CATALOGUE

—— OF ——

W. R. Strong Co, Sacramento, Cal.

FOR 1892.

IT is with pleasure we again place before you this, our annual Catalogue of Seeds and Trees for the season of 1892, and in so doing we wish to thank our many friends and patrons for their liberal patronage and we trust that our dealings have been such that it will merit a continuance of the favors shown us. We shall use every effort in the future as we have in the past to give satisfaction, and with our increased facilities and thorough knowledge of the business we can assure our customers that their wants will be supplied promptly with the purest and best stock to be obtained on the most reasonable terms.

It is now a well known fact that California supplies a good portion of the Vegetable and Flower Seeds that are used in the United States and Europe. Owing to our long seasons we are enable to grow and mature most all varieties. Most all the large seedmen know this and are now handling California stock.

WARRANTY.

No honest seedsman can sell seeds and guarantee and be responsible for the growth thereof. For there are contingencies continually arising to prevent the very best seed from giving satisfaction, such as sowing too deep, too shallow, in too wet, or too dry soil, insects of all descriptions destroying the plants as soon as or before they appear, also other causes. We therefore do not guarantee, expressed or implied. We test our seeds before sending them out, and should they fail to grow we will cheerfully replace them or give other seeds to the same amount.

SUGGESTIONS.

Order early as possible while our stock is complete, then you will be sure of getting what you wish, besides having it handy when you are ready to plant.

Use our order sheets and envelopes when you have them; it will be more convenient and less danger of miscarrying or mistakes.

In ordering both Seeds and Trees please have them on separate sheets as the Nursery is a distinct branch.

IMPORTANT.

Be very careful to write your name and address plainly. We often receive orders without the name or address, and it is impossible to always trace them up. State the way you wish your order forwarded, otherwise we will be compelled to use our own judgment.

SEND CASH with your order(at our risk if sent by Postal or Express Order, or Draft on any good Banking House). Small sums may be sent in postage stamps if proper care is taken to prevent adhesion together.

W. R. STRONG CO'S

GENERAL PRICE LIST OF SEEDS

FOR 1891-92.

WE .WOULD ADVISE OUR CUSTOMERS to order their seeds in bulk or by weight, as it is cheaper and of more advantage to you to do so. But for the accommodation of small growers we put our Vegetable and Herb Seeds up in small and neat lithographic descriptive packets at five cents each, or fifty cents per dozen.

PEAS, BEANS and CORN in half-pound boxes at Ten Cents each, or One Dollar per dozen, and in one pound boxes at 15 cents each; $1 75 per dozen. These packets are of full weight, and contain more Seed than those offered by Seed Houses generally.

ALL SEEDS QUOTED BY THE OUNCE AND IN SMALL PACKETS WILL BE FORWARDED BY MAIL, POSTAGE PREPAID BY US.

· SEEDS QUOTED AT POUND RATES (if to be sent by mail), add TEN CENTS PER POUND TO COVER COST OF POSTAGE.

Assortments of Seeds for Family Garden.

To accommodate those not familiar with selection of the choicest varieties, we have prepared boxes of THOSE KINDS MOST DESIRABLE. Three sizes; price, one dollar, two dollars, and five dollars each, and which are at least one-fourth less than catalogue rates, and which we are sure will give satisfaction.

Peas.

EXTRA EARLY.

	Per hun.	Per lb.
Cleveland's Alaska, earliest of all, 20 inches	$9 00	$0 15
Cleveland's R. N. Y., 2 feet, prolific, ripens at one time, fine flavor	8 00	15
Extra Early, first and best, 2 feet	7 00	15
Premium Tom Thumb, 8 inches	8 00	15
Premium Gem, wrinkled, sweet, 12 inches	8 00	15
Carter's Stratagem	9 00	15
American Wonder, 10 inches	9 00	15
Laxton Alpha, 3 feet	8 00	15
Bliss Abundance, 18 inches	9 00	15
Bliss Everbearing, 24 inches	9 00	15
McLean's Advancer, 36 inches	8 00	15

GENERAL CROP.

	Per hun.	Per lb.
Pride of the Market	$8 00	15
Prince of Wales	8 00	15
Yorkshire Hero, 2 feet	8 00	15
Telephone, 3 feet	8 00	15
Champion of England, 5 feet	7 00	15
Royal Dwarf Marrow, 2 feet	6 00	10
Large White Marrowfat, 5 feet	5 00	10
Black Eye Marrowfat, 4 feet	5 00	10

EDIBLE PODS, SUGAR PEAS.

	Per hun.	Per lb.
Tall and Dwarf White Seed	$12 50	20
Tall and Dwarf Gray Seed	12 50	20

Field Peas in quantity and variety, at lowest market rates.

Beans.

DWARF SNAPS OR GREEN STRING.

	Per hun.	Per lb.
Early Refugee	$ 8 00	$0 15
Early Pinkeye China	8 00	15
Early Red Valentine	8 00	15
Cleveland's Round Pod, earliest, best and most prolific of all	9 00	15
Early White Valentine	9 00	15
Early Mohawk	8 00	15
Early Yellow Six Weeks	7 00	15
Green Flageolet, fine	10 00	15
Wax Flageolet, yellow pod, large, fine	10 00	15
Early Golden Wax, yellow pod	8 00	15
Wardell's Kidney Wax	10 00	15
Ivory Wax, yellow pod	10 00	15

	Per hun.	Per lb.
White Seeded Wax, yellow pod	10 00	15
Black Seeded Wax, " "	8 00	15
Dwarf White Kidney	6 00	15
Dwarf Cranberry	7 00	15
Broad Windsor	5 00	10
Dwarf Lima	15 00	25

POLE OR RUNNING.

	Per hun.	Per lb.
Southern Prolific	$ 8 00	15
London Horticulture	8 00	15
Large White Lima, Hand Picked	10 00	15
King of the Garden Lima	11 00	15
Giant Wax, red seed	10 00	15
Dutch Case-knife	8 00	15
Scarlet Runners	12 50	20
White Runners	12 50	20
Asparagus or Yard Long	15 00	25

All varieties of Field Beans in quantity at the very lowest market rates.

Sweet Corn, Etc.

	Per hun.	Per lb.
Triumph	$9 00	$0 15
Perry's Hybrid	9 00	15
Squantum	8 00	15
Extra Early Cory	9 00	15
Early Pee and Kay	9 00	15
Early Minnesota	8 00	15
Early Crosby, very early	8 00	15
Early Moore's Concord	8 00	15
Early Mammoth Sugar	8 00	15
Black Mexican	8 00	15
Stowell's Evergreen	8 00	15
Egyptian or Washington Market	8 00	15
Adam's Extra Early	7 00	15
Early Canada, Eastern grown	6 00	10
Early White Flint, Eastern grown	5 00	10
Large Yellow Eight-rowed, Eastern grown	5 00	10
Pop Corn (Rice and Common)		10

Sweet Corn for fodder and Common Yellow and White Field Corn, or any of the above in Quantity at lowest market rates.

Artichoke.

	Per oz.	Per lb.
Green Globe	$0 30	$3 00

Jerusalem Tubers, $5 00 per 100 pounds.

Two pounds for 25 cents of Peas, Beans and Corn, when quoted at 15 cents per single pound.

Twenty-five pounds and over will be sold at 100 pound rates.

Asparagus.

	Per oz.	Per lb.
Palmetto	$0 15	$1 25
Colossal, largest and best	10	60
Two-year-old roots, $1 50 per hundred.		

Beets.

	Per oz.	Per lb.
Edmond's Blood Turnip	$0 10	$0 60
Extra Early Eclipse, new and fine	10	60
Extra Early Egyptian	10	50
Extra Early Bassanno	10	50
Dewing's Early Blood Turnip	10	60
Early Blood Turnip	10	50
Early Long Dark Blood	10	50
Bastian's Half Long Dark Blood	10	60
Mangel Wurzel, or Stock Beet	10	25
Improved Long Red Mangel Wurzel	10	35
Norbiten Giant Mangel	10	35
Yellow Globe Mangel	10	35
Red Globe Mangel	10	35
Improved White Sugar	10	25
Swiss Chard	10	75

Brussels Sprouts

	Per oz.	Per lb.
Improved Dwarf	$0 15	$1 50

Brocoli.

	Per oz.
Early Purple Cape	$0 40
Early White Cape	40

Cabbage.

	Per oz.	Per lb.
New Express	$0 15	$1 50
Early Etampes	15	1 50
Early York Dwarf	15	1 00
Early Large York	15	1 00
Early Oxheart, finest	15	1 00
Henderson's Early Summer	15	2 00
Jersey Early Wakefield	15	2 00
Early Bloomsdale Market	15	2 00
Improved Early Winingstadt	15	2 00
Early Dwarf Dutch	15	1 50
Early Drumhead or Battersea	15	1 50
Premium Flat Dutch	15	2 00
Premium Drumhead	15	2 00
Stone Mason	15	2 00
Mammoth Marblehead	15	2 00
Improved Brunswick	15	1 50
German Filderkraut	15	1 50
Savoy Drumhead	15	1 50
Savoy Early Dutch	15	1 50
Red Dutch Pickling	15	1 50

Carrot.

	Per oz.	Per lb.
Early French Forcing	$0 10	$1 00
Early Scarlet Horn	10	1 00
Earliest Short Horn, for forcing	10	1 00
Danvers Orange, Half Long	10	75
Early Half Long Scarlet, Stump Rooted	10	75
Improved Long Orange	10	75
Large White Belgian	10	60
Large Red Altingham	10	60
St. Vallery or Intermediat	10	1 00
Guarande or Ox Heart	10	1 00

Cauliflower.

	Per oz.	Per lb.
Henderson's Early Snowball	$2 50	$....
Extra Early Dwarf Erfurt selected	1 00	....
Early London	60	6 00
Early Paris, best	75	7 00
Large White French	75	7 00
Lenormand's Short Stem	75	7 00
Large Asiatic	50	5 00
Veitch's Autumn Giant	50	5 00
Half Early Paris or Nonpareil	75	7 00
Large Late Algeriers	75	7 00

Celery.

	Per oz.	Per lb.
Self Blanching	$0 25	$3 00
Henderson's White Plume	25	3 00
Henderson's Dwarf	15	1 50

	Per oz.	Per lb.
Golden Heart	15	1 50
Large White Solid	15	1 25
Dwarf White Solid	15	1 50
Boston Market	15	1 50
Ocleriac or Turnip Rooted	15	1 50
Celery Seed, for flavoring	15	1 50
CHERVILL	$0 10	$1 00
COLLARDS	10	1 00
CHICURY (large rooted)	10	1 10
CORN SALAD	10	1 00

Cress or Peppergrass.

	Per oz.	Per lb.
Broad Leaf	$0 10	$0 75
Fine Curled	10	75
Fine Water Cress	40	....

Cucumbers.

	Per oz.	Per lb.
Extra Long White Spine	$0 10	$1 00
Early Russian	10	1 00
Improved Early White Spine	10	1 00
Early Frame	10	1 00
Early Short Green	10	1 00
Nichols' Medium Green	10	1 00
Early Green Cluster	10	1 00
Early Boston Pickling	10	1 00
Improved Long Green	10	1 00
Burr Small Gherkins	20	2 00
Giant Pera	15	1 25
Snake or Serpent	25	2 50
Siberian	25	3 00

Egg Plant.

	Per oz.	Per lb.
Early New York Purple	$0 50	$5 00
Early Long Purple	30	3 00
Early Black Peakin	50	5 00

Endive.

	Per oz.	Per lb.
Green Curled	$0 15	$1 50
Moss Curled	15	2 50

Garlic.

The Price of Garlic is variable.

Kale or Borecole.

	Per oz.	Per lb.
Green Curled Scotch	$0 10	$1 00
Dwf. German Green and Purple	10	1 00
Sea Kale	25	3 00

Kohl Rabi.

	Per oz.	Per lb.
Early White Vienna	$0 20	$2 00
Early Purple Vienna	20	2 00
Large Green	20	3 00

Leek.

	Per oz.	Per lb.
Best London Flag	$0 15	$2 50
Monstrous Carentan	15	2 50

Lettuce.

	Per oz.	Per lb.
Hanson	$0 10	$1 00
Simpson's Early Curled	10	1 00
Early Prize Head	10	1 00
White Paris Cos. Romaine Lettuce	10	1 00
Satisfaction	10	1 00
Philadelphia Butter	10	1 00
Early White Head Cabbage	10	1 00
Early Curled Silesia	10	1 00
Large Drumhead or Ice Cabbage	10	1 00
Simpson's Black Seeded	10	1 00
All the Year Round	10	1 00
Boston Market—for forcing	10	1 00
Tennis Ball, Black Seeded—for forcing	10	1 00
Salamander—for hot, dry weather	10	1 00
Deacon	10	1 00
Bird Lettuce		30

Martynia.

	Per oz.	Per lb.
For making Pickles	$0 25	$3 00

Half Pound and Over Will Be Sold at Pound Rates.

Mushroom Spawn.

One Pound Bricks...........................$0 25

Musk Melon.

	Per oz.	Per lb.
Surprise	$0 10	$1 00
California Large Netted	10	1 00
White Japan	10	1 00
Hackensack	10	1 00
Early Yellow Canteloupe	10	1 00
Golden Gem	10	1 00
Montreal Market very large	10	1 00
Bay View	10	1 00
Skillman's Fine Netted	10	1 00
Large Green Nutmeg Citron	10	1 00
Cassaba, or Green Persian	10	1 00
Miller's Cream	15	1 25
Emerald Gem	15	1 25
Champion Market	15	1 25
Osage	15	1 50

Watermelon.

	Per oz.	Per lb.
Mammoth Iron Clad	$0 10	$ 75
Kolb's Gem	10	75
Scaly Bark	10	75
Black Spanish	10	75
Icing, or Ice Cream, Peerless	10	75
Mountain Sweet, or Gray Seeded Ice Cream	10	75
Mountain Sprout	10	75
Cuban Queen	10	75
Imperial Lodi, or California	10	75
Gypsy, or Rattlesnake	10	75
Orange Rind	10	1 25
Citron Melon, for preserves	10	1 00
Pride of Georgia	10	75
Florida Favorite	10	1 00
Hungarian Honey	15	1 50
Seminole	15	1 50
Green and Gold	15	1 50
The Volga	15	1 25

Nasturtium.

	Per oz.	Per lb.
Tall Sorts	$0 15	$1 50
Dwarf	15	1 50

Okra, or Gumbo.

	Per oz.	Per lb.
Early Dwarf	$0 10	$1 00
Tall Green	10	1 00
White Velvet	15	1 50

Onions.

	Per oz.	Per lb.
Early Large Red	$0 15	$1 50
Large Red Wethersfield	15	1 50
Yellow Danvers	15	1 50
Yellow Dutch Strasburg	15	1 50
White Portugal, Silver Skin	25	2 50
White Globe	25	2 50
Tripoli, White and Red	20	2 00
Giant Yellow Rocca	20	2 00
Early Queen	20	2 00

ONION SETS—Prices variable; lowest market rates.

Parsnips.

	Per oz.	Per lb.
Hollow Crown	$0 10	$0 75
Half Long Student	10	75

Parsley.

	Per oz.	Per lb.
Triple Curled	$0 10	$0 75
Plain Curled	10	75
Fern Leaf	10	75
Moss Curled	10	75

Pepper.

	Per oz.	Per lb.
Golden Dawn	$0 25	$2 50
Long Red Cayenne	25	2 50
Chili, very small for pepper sauce	25	2 50
Cherry Red	25	2 50
Large Squash, or Tomato sh'p	25	2 50
Large Bell, or Bull-nose	25	2 50
Sweet Spanish, or Mountain	25	2 50

Pumpkin.

	Per oz.	Per lb.
Large Yellow, or Conn. F'ld	$0 10	$ 35
Large Cheese, for table use	10	50
Cashaw, or Crookneck	10	50
Mammoth Tours	15	1 00
Japanese Pie	15	1 50
Tennessee Sweet Potato	15	1 50
Mammoth Etampes	15	1 50

Radish.

	Per oz.	Per lb.
Early Long Scarlet	$0 10	$ 75
Early Scarlet Turnip rooted	10	75
Early Scarlet Turnip White tip	10	75
Early White Turnip rooted	10	75
Olive shaped, or Half-long Scarlet	10	75
French Breakfast, or Half-long Scarlet, White Tip	10	75
Beck's Chartier	10	75
Scarlet China Winter	10	75
Black Spanish, Fall or Winter	10	75
White Strasburg Radish	10	1 00
Mammoth White China, or California	10	1 00
Earliest Carmine	10	1 00

Rhubarb, or Pie Plant.

	Per oz.	Per lb.
Linnaeus, Giant	$0 20	$2 00
Victoria, Giant	20	2 00

Two year roots, $2 50 per dozen, 25 cents each; one-year roots, $1 50 per dozen, or 15 cents each.

Salsify, or Vegetable Oyster.

	Per oz.	Per lb.
Best White	$0 15	$1 50
Scorzonera, or Black Salsify	20	2 00
Sandwich Island	20	2 00

Squash.

	Per oz.	Per lb.
Pineapple	$0 10	$1 00
Perfect Gem	10	1 00
Early Yellow Bush Scallop	10	75
Early White Bush Scallop	10	75
Yellow Summer Crookneck	10	75
American Turban	10	75
Marblehead	10	75
Boston or Vegetable Marrow	10	75
Hubbard	10	75
Mammoth, Chili	10	75
Sibley	15	1 50
Brazil Sugar	10	1 00
Field Squash		35

Spinach.

	Per oz.	Per lb.
Round Summer, or Large Dutch	$0 10	$ 35
Extra Large Prickly, Winter	10	35
Improved Thick Leaved	10	35
Monstrous Viroflay, extra large	10	35
Long Standing, Late Seeding	10	35
Bloomsdale	10	85

Sunflower.

	Per oz.	Per lb.
Mammoth Russian	$0 10	$0 80

Tobacco.

	Per oz.	Per lb.
Connecticut Seed Leaf	$0 40	$4 00
Virginia	40	5 00
Havana	50	6 00

Tomato.

	Per oz.	Per lb.
Early Conqueror	$0 20	$2 00
Acme	20	2 00
Livingston's Perfection	20	2 00
Paragon	20	2 00
Hathaway's Excelsior	20	2 00
General Grant	20	2 00
Sacramento Favorite Improved	20	2 50
Mayflower	20	2 00
Trophy	20	2 00
Large Yellow	20	2 00
Red Cherry	20	2 00

Half Pound and Over Will Be Sold at Pound Rates.

Tomato.

	Per oz.	Per lb.
Strawberry, or Winter Cherry	$0 30	$4 00
Cardinal	20	2 00
Livingston's Favorite	20	2 00
Livingston's Beauty	20	2 00
Mikado	20	2 50
Optimus	20	2 50
Dwarf Champion	20	2 50

Ruta Baga Turnip.

	Per oz.	Per lb.
Large White French	$0 10	$0 60
Sweet Russian, White	10	60
Sweet German, White	10	60
Improved Purple Top Yellow	10	60
Skirving's Swede, Purple Top Yellow	10	60

	10	60
Laing's Improved Yellow Early	10	60
Improved American Yellow Purple Top	10	60

Turnip.

	Per oz.	Per lb.
Early Snowball	$0 10	$ 75
White Egg	10	75
Early Yellow Stone	10	60
Early White Flat Dutch, Strap Leaved	10	60
Early Purple Top, Strap Leaved	10	60
Early Purple Top, Munich	10	60
Large White Norfolk	10	60
Yellow Aberdeen Purple Top	10	60
Purple Top White Globe	10	60
Orange Yellow, or Golden Ball	10	60
Yellow or Amber Globe	10	60
Pomeranian White Globe	10	60
Long White or Cowhorn	10	60

Sweet and Medicinal Herbs, Etc.

A few herbs should have a place in every vegetable garden. A very small space will give all that are needed in any family. The culture is simple. Make a little seed-bed in the early spring, and set the plant out in a bed as soon as large enough.

	Oz.	Lb		Oz.	Lb.
Anise	$0 10	$1 00	Hyssop	$0 25	$3 00
Angelica	25	...	Horehound	30	...
Arnica	2 00	...	Lavender	25	2 50
Balm	50	...	Marjoram, Sweet	25	2 50
Belladonna	75	...	Marigold Pot	25	2 50
Basil (Sweet)	25	3 00	Opium Poppy	20	2 50
Bene	20	...	Pennyroyal	75	...
Caraway	10	30	Rosemary	40	...
Catnip	75	...	Rue	40	...
Coriander	10	30	Savory, Summer	25	2 50
Cumin	10	1 00	Savory, Winter	25	2 50
Dandelion	25	2 50	Saffron	15	1 50
Dill	10	50	Sage, Common	20	2 00
Elecampane	50	...	Tansy	50	...
Fennel, Large Sweet	10	50	Thyme, English	40	4 00.
Henbane	40	...	Wormwood	40	...

The above are also put up in Five Cent packages of Fifty Cents per dozen.

Grass and Clover Seeds.

When sold in quantity, at much reduced rates and being subject to market fluctuations. Prices given on application.

Express or Freight charges must be paid by the purchaser, and when small quantities are wanted to be forwarded by mail, be sure to send 10 cents per pound extra to cover postage.

Clover Seed.

	Per 100	Per lb		Per lb
Alfalfa	$0 10	12½	Alsyke, or Sweedish Clover	$0 25
Mammoth or Saplin Clover	12½	15	Crimson Trefoil	50
Common, or Red Clover	12½	15	Yellow Trefoil	50
White Dutch Clover		25	Sanfoin, or Esperaette	10

Grass Seed.

	Per 100	Per lb.		Per 100	Per lb.
Lawn Grass, Best Mixed	$25 00	$0 30	Timothy Grass Seeds	$ 7 00	$0 10
Lawn Grass, Extra Fancy Blue	25 00	30	Red Top Grass Seeds	9 00	15
Sweet Vernal Grass		50	Mesquite Grass Seeds	9 00	15
Perennial Rye Grass	11 00	15	Orchard Grass Seeds	15 00	20
Australian Grass	10 00	15	Evergreen Millet Grass	14 00	20
Italian Grass	10 00	15	German or Golden Millet Grass	6 00	10
Fine Fescue Grass		50	Egyptian or Pearl Millet		25
Meadow Fescue		50	Hungarian Grass	6 00	10

Miscellaneous and Field Seeds.

	Per 100	Per lb.		Per lb
Amber Sugar Cane Seed	$6 00	$0 10	Castor Oil Beans	25
African Seed	6 00	10	Hemp Seed	10
Egyptian Corn, White	2 50	5	Flax Seed	10
Egyptian Corn, Red	2 50	5	Canary Seed	10
Buckwheat	2 50	5	Mixed Bird Seed	10
Sun Flower Seed	16 00	30	Rape Seed	10
Vetches	6 00	10	Bird Lettuce	30
Lentils	6 00	10	Cuttle Fish Bone	75
Broom Corn	2 00	5	Maw, or Poppy Seed	30

Bird Seed.

Canary, Hemp, Rape, Millet and Mixed Bird Seeds, 6 pounds for 50 cents, 14 pounds for $1 00.

Twenty-five Pounds and Over Will Be Sold at 100 Pound Rates.

⚜ SEEDS OF SPECIAL MERIT. ⚜

---o---

New Bush Lima Beans.

HENDERSON'S DWARF LIMA.

No variety of Beans that has ever been sent out has received as wide distribution in so short a time as the Bush Lima. A few years ago this variety was unknown, but to-day it is known over most all this continent. This has been due to its great merit which the public were quick to recognize as soon as it was brought to their attention. One of the most valuable characteristics of the Bush Lima is its extreme earliness, as it comes in from two to three weeks ahead of any of the climbing Limas. The small size of the Bush Lima which at first was urged as an objection to it, has proved one of the strongest points in its favor, as the public, rightly enough, prefer small beans, always associating great size in peas or beans with coarser quality. The Bush Lima is enormously productive, bearing continuously through the summer until killed by the frost. Its greatest merit lies in its being a true bush variety, but the experience of all who have grown it has been that it excels as well in quality, quantity and earliness. Price, per lb. 25c.

---o---

Early Snowball
Cauliflower!

There is no vegetable in which the quality of the seed is of more vital importance than the Cauliflower, and none in which it is more difficult to secure the best. During the past years we have had samples from the best growers of this country and Europe planted on our trial grounds, and have carefully studied them, and as a result present our stock of Snowball Cauliflower as THE BEST IN EXISTENCE. The strain we have of this variety is without doubt the very best to be had. Our stock was grown from the very finest specimens, noted for their earliness, large size, uniform shape and compact growth. None of those we set out for seed failed to produce large, beautiful, smooth, and snow-white heads. For forcing under glass during winter and early spring in cold climates, or for planting later in the open ground, no stock of Snowball Cauliflower can surpass it. Pkt. 10c., oz. $2.50.

Gold Coin Sweet Corn.

We again offer this variety of Sweet Corn with confidence that it is worthy of even more extended cultivation than it had the last two seasons. It has given great satisfaction, and has been pronounced the sweetest and best flavored corn in existence. We have never seen a variety of corn that will approach it in evergreen properties, and its yield is simply immense. If the weather is at all favorable, the great bulk of the crop can be gathered at any time during a period of four weeks and be found in fit condition for table use. It almost always yields two and sometimes three mammoth ears to the stalk. The cob is snowy white, compactly covered with large and very long grains. It is not an old variety under a new name, but is remarkably distinct and handsome in appearance. It is bound to have another great run the coming season, as it has no rival in sweetness and delicacy of flavor. Price, per lb. 25c., ¼ lb. 15c.

———o———

Giant Pera Cucumber.

This is one of the largest and best long Cucumbers in cultivation. The skin is perfectly free from spines, flesh clear, crisp and white. They are of the most delicious flavor, no other cucumber we have ever eaten surpassing them. Another remarkable quality is that they are very crisp and tender at all stages, and can be eaten at any time during growth. They grow to an enormous size, frequently to one and a half feet in length and ten to eleven inches in round circumference; very smooth and straight, with a beautiful green skin. The vines grow vigorously, fruit sets near the hill and grows closely together, making them exceedingly prolific. The seed cavity is very small and the seeds are slow to form and few in number. Price, per oz. 15c., lb. $1 25.

Golden Self-Blanching Celery.

It is of very handsome form and even growth, reaching a very large size, but very stocky and robust. The stalks grow vigorously, with large ribs; very thickly and closely set. It is entirely self-blanching, without any banking up or covering whatever, even the outer ribs assuming a yellowish-white color of a very fresh and pleasing appearance. The heart is of a beautiful golden yellow color, very large, crisp and solid, and unsurpassed in delicious quality and flavor. It is unequalled in striking appearance on the table, and decidedly the best keeper of all the Self-Blanching varieties. Price, oz. 25c., lb. $3 00.

———o———

Serpent or Snake Cucumber.

A remarkable and very interesting curiosity. The Cucumbers grow curled up like a snake with the head protruding, and sometimes are six feet in length. The illustration will represent their shape, and although they attain great size, the quality is only fair, grown more as a curiosity than any thing else, and to exhibit at fairs. Can also be used for pickling. Per pkt. 10c., postpaid.

Siberian Cucumber.

Absolutely the EARLIEST Cucumber known, producing fruits five inches long, in the open ground, from seed in fifty-five days. It is without question a remarkable variety, and will be a surprise for market gardeners and truckers, who heretofore have grown the Early Russian for earliest. The past season it was distributed over a wide area of the country, and all reports received fully sustain all the claims we make for it; and it has come to stay. Size of the "new Siberian" MEDIUM, what a critical gardener would call JUST RIGHT. A splendid free bearer, fruits straight and smooth, flesh extraordinarily tender and crisp; and for early forcing purposes, or for slicing it is a most valuable addition to our list of cucumbers. Price per oz., 25c., per lb., $3 00.

St. Vallery or Intermediate Carrot.

The longer we grow and sell the seed of this variety, the stronger our original favorable opinion is confirmed in regard to its merits as a table or general crop variety. The size is about 12 inches long by 2¼ to 2¾ inches in diameter, a beautiful rich orange-red color; roots grow very smooth, and flesh even and fine. The shape is between the Long Orange and half-long varieties. The roots grow especially fine in a light soil. Price, oz. 10c., lb. $1 00.

———o———

The Osage Musk Melon.

The great popularity which this new Melon has attained is due mainly to its peculiar luscious, spicy flavor and its perfect shipping qualities. The skin is very thin, of a dark green color, and slightly netted. The flesh is of a salmon color, remarkably sweet, extremely thick, sweet and delicious to the rind. The seed cavity is remarkably small; the stock is very true, and seems always to produce uniform melons of good quality; and a great point of merit is that. no matter what the size of the melon, be it large or small, they are all sweet and delicious—which can not be said of any other melon. It is also very productive. It is a remarkable keeper, and will stand shipping better than any melon we ever saw. The extreme thickness and solidity of the flesh render it less liable to bruise or spoil in transportation than any other; and the skin is such a very dark, blackish green that spots which would render netted melons unsaleable, would not be noticed in the Osage, so that it always reaches market in splendid condition. Pkt. 10c., 1 oz, 15c., 1 lb, $1 50.

The flesh is solid, thick, a vivid, brilliant orange in color, and is possessed of rare edible qualities. The weight ranges from 8 to 11 pounds. It ripens its fruit simultaneously with the Hubbard. A good shipper and long keeper. It has a rich delicate flavor. It is very productive and ripens so evenly that nearly the whole crop can be gathered at one time. Price, per oz. 15c., lb. $1 25

Emerald Gem Musk Melon.

Few vegetables have proved as worthy as this, the Emerald Gem Musk Melon. It is certainly the most distinct and at the same time the most deliciously flavored Melon we ever came across. The flavor is delicious and sweet beyond description. It is so rich and juicy that it nearly drops to pieces and is best eaten with a spoon. It is a very early and prolific variety with a skin, which, while it is ribbed, is perfectly smooth and of a deep emerald color. The flesh which is thicker than in most other melons, is of a suffused salmon color, in fact, this variety is so thick meated that it yields but little seed. Those seeking a Musk Melon for quality alone, will find all they are looking for in the Emerald Gem. Price, per oz. 15c., per lb. $1 25.

---o---

Strong's Perfection Cabbage Lettuce.

We offered this valuable variety of Lettuce for the first time last season, and from the universal satisfaction it gave, we have no hesitation in again listing it among our Seeds of Special Merit. It is without doubt one of the best acquisitions of the Lettuce tribe. As we stated last year this Lettuce originated in one of the large vegetable gardens near this city. Being in the shipping business the shipment of winter and spring vegetables is a specialty with us. We therefore have ample opportunity to test the merit of all vegetables, and it is a matter of vast importance to us to secure the best. This new Lettuce was the largest, finest and best flavored we ever came across, measuring 13 inches in diameter, of which 8 inches is solid head. We secured a small quantity of the seed from our market gardener, and have propagated and improved the strain ourselves, and out of numerous standard varieties in our Test Gardens it has proven itself perfection, eclipsing all other varieties for its large size, solid crisp heads, delicate flavor, and beautiful light green color. Our supply of seed was quite limited last season, and only a few of our customers had the pleasure of testing its valuable qualities, but this year we saved a good quantity of the seed and having good, true stock we will be able to supply all at considerably lower prices, Price, per pkt. 15c , oz. 50c., lb. $6 00.

Champion Market Melon.

This is a fine green fleshed melon. They are just the right size for market, being neither too large for economical handling nor too small to bring a good price; globular in shape, closely netted, handsome in appearance and as its name indicates, it is the champion in any market. Is very productive, frequently bearing seven melons on a single vine, while on one vine we have counted five melons set within a length of 22 inches. The melons mature early. It is an excellent shipper, and we consider it, unquestionably, the most profitable variety that can be grown for market. Price, oz. 10c., lb. $1 00.

---o---

Hungarian Honey.

This variety has proved to be the richest and sweetest flavored of all Water Melons. The Melons ripen early, the vines are healthy and productive. It grows to weight from 8 to 10 pounds and almost globular in shape; the color of the skin is dark green. The flesh is deep red, stringless, and of the sweetest honey

flavor, richer than any other Water Melon grown. Pkt. 10c., oz. 15c., lb. $1 50.

Kentucky Wonder.

—o—

A melon that has sustained every claim made for it. Kentucky Wonder is oblong in shape, skin dark green, flesh a beautiful scarlet color, crisp and not tough, rich and sugary flavor, always firm, very solid and never mealy. Attains an average weight of forty to sixty pounds. Not a *mammoth variety*, but a real good, old-fashioned Kentucky melon, that has no equal for quality. The best all around melon for home or market yet introduced. Per oz. 15c.: lb. $1 50.

New Japanese Pie Pumpkin.

—o—

This remarkable variety is crooknecked, with an extremely small seed cavity. It is nearly all solid meat and the quality is extra fine. The seeds are distinct in appearance, being curiously sculptured in the manner of Chinese letters. It is very productive, ripens early, of medium size, good keepers and weigh 15 to 20 pounds each. The flesh is a rich salmon color, unusually fine grained, and when cooked or stewed, is almost as dry and mealy as a sweet potato. For making pies, custards, etc., they are hard to beat. Containing but little water, they are easily cut and dried, like dried apples, and make excellent pies or sauce for winter use. Price, per oz. 15c., lb. $1 25.

The Volga Water Melon

—o—

Is cultivated on the lower Volga, near the Caspian Sea, for shipment in barrels to St. Petersburg and Moscow. In solidity and hardness it is remarkable, and therefore carries well. In productiveness it surpasses most sorts, two melons being sometimes borne at adjacent joints of the same vine. In form it is nearly perfectly globular. In color it is so pale green as to be nearly white, with nearly imperceptible stripes. Although so solid and hard, the rind is not thick. The flesh is remarkably crisp, and when fully ripe, very sweet, luscious and red in color, very productive, attaining an average weight of 15 pounds. For private use it should be grown largely, as it is of fine flavor and attractive appearance. The seeds are very small and few in number. Price, per lb. $1 25.

Green and Gold.

Is the largest early variety in cultivation, melons ranging from 25 to 45 pounds, and its productiveness is equal to any of the red-fleshed sorts, while in delicious flavor it surpasses them all. The rind is the thinnest of any melon, the white being only 3-8 to 1-2 an inch in thickness. The flesh is a beautiful golden orange color, free from any tinge of white or other color, even immediately around the seeds. The flesh is beautifully granular in appearance, juicy and sweet, and as we have already stated, of unequalled flavor. Coupled with the delicious flavor of the Green and Gold Water Melon, its rich golden color will make it most desirable as an ornament for the table, especially if its golden slices are arranged in contrast with the crimson of the other sorts. Pkt. 10c.; oz. 15c., lb. $1 50.

Seminole Water Melon.

Oblong in shape, smooth and beautifully proportioned; it is of two colors, gray and light green, the gray greatly predominating. Melons of both colors are formed on the same vine, and are precisely the same in every respect except color. It is a perfect Melon and a decided addition to the list, being very early, large, enormously productive and of excellent flavor. This melon possesses four qualities which will make it the most popular ever offered to the public. It is **extra early, extra large, enormously productive, and of most delicious flavor.** Pkt. 10c., oz. 15c., lb. $1 50.

———o———

Brazil Sugar.

This variety, originally from South America has been thoroughly tested in the United States the past years, and is pronounced by critical growers a most valuable acquisition to our list of summer and autumn squashes. The flesh and skin are of a bright yellow color, slightly warted. As its name indicates, it is one of the sweetest of all squashes, the flesh being unusually fine-grained and tender, so much so that it is palatable even when eaten raw. They reach a weight of three to four pounds each, ripen early, and grow so vigorously that they are but little afflicted by the squash-bug. Pkt., 5c.; oz., 10c.; lb., $1 00.

———o———

Stratagem Pea.

A remarkable variety and claimed to be the finest dwarf wrinkled pea grown; in table quality none can surpass it; grows to a height of two feet; vines very strong and needing but a slight support; the strong sturdy haulm is literally covered with large pods, many of which measure five and one-half inches in length, and contain as many as ten large fine-flavored wrinkled peas. An excellent sort for the home table or the market.

Earliest Carmine Forcing Radish.

This Radish is, without doubt, the best forcing variety in existence. They will produce good roots in about twenty days from time of sowing. They can also be used to good advantage as a general crop. The color is a fine shade of carmine; flesh pure white, crisp, sweet and fresh to the taste. Price, per oz., 10c.; lb., $1 00.

———o———

Improved Sacramento Favorite Tomato.

This is not a new Tomato by any means, but we can say with pride that it is one of the finest table and shipping Tomatoes that has ever been introduced. It originated some ten to fifteen years ago by a Mr. Bascom, who kept it up to the standard until he died some five or six years after, when it was allowed to run down. The last four years we have grown and improved the strain so that it is now one of the finest Tomatoes grown. They are of large uniform size, smooth skin, thick flesh, a beautiful shade of bright red, and of unexcelled flavor. The vines are vigorous and productive, producing as much to the acre as any other variety. We are the only ones who have the true stock of this valuable Tomato. Parties wishing seeds or plants of this, the best Tomato grown, will do well to place their orders with us with the assurance that they are getting one of the best Tomatoes in existance. Price, per oz., 20c., per lb., $2 50.

Dwarf Champion Tomato.

This is without doubt ous of the beet Tomatoss for market gardeners. It ie also a good variety for family use. Its 'habit of growth is peculiar, for not only is it dwarf and compact, bnt the etem beiug thick, stiff and short jointed it is actually self-supportiug when laden with fruit—a characteristic ws have eeen in no other variety. The foliage is aleo distinct and pecnliar, being very dark greeu in color, thick and corrugated. Ite close upright growth enablee it to be planted much nearer together than any of the other eorte and the yield therefore is likely to bs mnch greater, for in productivsnese it ie nnsnrpassed. It is also very early. The fruit resembles the Acme, and ie of a purplish-pink color, and always smooth and symmetrical in form. It is medium size and attractive in appearance; the skin is tough, and the flesh eolid aud of fine quality. Altogsther the Dwarf Champion Tomato is a decided acquieition, whether wanted for market or private use.

—o—

Japan Clover. (*Lespedeza Striata*.) This highly appreciated species of clover ie by no means a new discovery, but it is only lately that the seed has been gathered in quantitiee for sale. It ranks far above red clover in nutritive value, aud is by analysis 72 per cent. Being of dwarfish habits on most eoils, yet on rich lands it reachee a height of two feet and makes ths best kind of hay. Also for the renovating of lands it equale the best of clovers. For live stock it is almost a complets food. The seed is yet scarce, thirty cents per pound in quantity. Ten pounds are sufficient for one acre, as it spreads very rapidly.

Yellow Millo Maize or Yellow Blanching Dhoura.

A variety of sorghum, valuabls for both forage and grain. Its growth is tall, nine to twelve feet, etooling from the gronud like the white Millo Maize. It eends out shoots also from the joints. The seed heads grow to great size, often weighing a full pouud after being fully ripe. The heads are eet close and solid, with a large plnmp grain, double ths size of White Millo, and of deep golden yellow color. In ehape, the seed head ie thick, well shouldered, solid, never long and narrow, and by reason of size and weight, each head ie the full equal iu grain to a fine ear of corn. The heade begin to turn down usually as soon as formed, and when rips hang on short goose-neck etems. The grain makee most excellent feed for horses, cattle, chickens or human food. It will mature its main head in 100 days and still go on maturing others until cut down by frost. It has been grown near Sacramento and from a single seed six and seven stalks have been produced, averaging four and five large heads sight inches long to each etalk loaded down with plump seed. If used for fodder it can be cut four and five times during the season. Stock raisers should have a number of acres of this valuable maize each season, five or ten pounds to the acrs. Price, per lb., 10c.; 100 lbs., $3 00.

CLEVELAND'S ALASKA

THE QUICKEST PEA ON RECORD.

Eckford's New Large Flowering Sweet Peas.

Sweet Peas are just becoming appreciated. They are now "the fashionable flower" for personal wear or table decoration. The waxy flowers and foliage make a lovely contrast and the perfume is deliciously delicate. Eckford's new varieties when properly grown are nearly double the size of the ordinary sweet peas. Cut the blooms off by the handful as fast as they develop, the plants will then continue to bloom all the summer, whereas if allowed to go to seed they will stop blooming. Plant early in a trench about five inches deep, making the ground rich with well rotted manure will insure large flowers. We find by experience here in California the peas are like the pansies—must be planted in the fall to insure a fine spring bloom. Pansies sow end of July to September and the Peas after the first rains in October or November. For a colder climate plant as early in the spring as possible. Finest mixed, per pkt., 10c.

———o———

Texas Bluegrass Seed. (*Poa Arachnifera*.) A new winter grass which is fast being introduced into the Southern States. It is much superior to the Kentucky Bluegrass because of its long roots, which will go four or five times as deep for moist ure. It makes a beautiful lawn for winter, and when grown with the Bermuda makes a lawn which lasts the whole year. It is hardy and can be planted at any time of the year, but midsummer. The price is 50cts. per oz., $5 per lb. Postage paid.

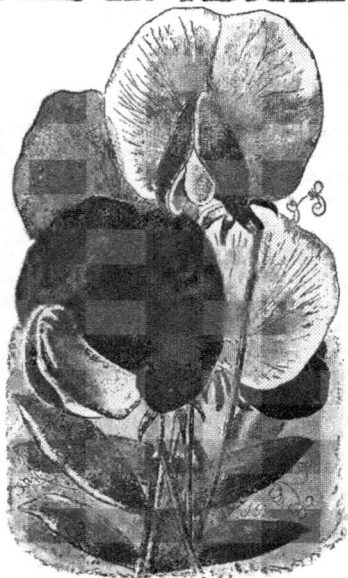

W. R. STRONG COMPANY'S

DESCRIPTIVE LIST OF

VEGETABLE SEEDS

We examine all new varieties of vegetables, etc., but do not include them in our list unless they are proved, after thorough test, to be of superior excellence. We have no hesitation in saying that our Seeds cannot be excelled in quality and freshness by any other collection.

The following list will cover all varieties needed for successful gardening:

Artichoke.

Culture.—Sow in seed bed early in spring, in drills twelve inches apart. When one year-old transplant to permanent bed spaded deep, and dressed with rotten manure, ashes and a little salt, then plant them about two feet apart. The edible portion is the undeveloped flower heads, which should be used before they begin to open, and then cut to the ground, for if the flowers expand they weaken the plants. In the fall cover with manure which should be spaded in the following spring, taking care not to injure the plants The crop is the largest and best the second year, after which the bed should be renewed by seed or suckers.

Globe Artichoke.

Large Globe. —the best sort for general use. Buds large nearly round; scales deep green, shading to purple, very thick and fleshy.

Jerusalem.—A hardy and productive plant, used for pickling and feeding stock. Strong tubers. Per 100 lbs. $5 00.

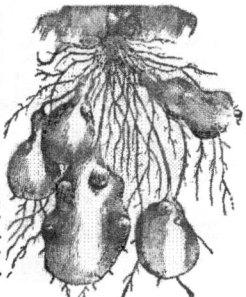

Jerusalem.

Asparagus.

Asparagus is one of the earliest spring vegetables and would be in universal use were it not for the prevalent idea that it is difficult to grow it. There is no vegetable on our list that can be produced so cheaply and easily. It delights in a moist, sandy soil, but can be grown in any garden by following the directions. A bed 12x40 feet requiring 75 to 100 plants, give an abundant supply for an ordinary family.

Culture.—Beds are usually formed by setting plants one or two years old, which can be procured of us. If you wish to grow them yourself, prepare a light, rich spot early in the spring, and after soaking the seed twenty-four hours in warm water, sow in drills one foot apart.

Giant Collossal Asparagus.

When the plants are well up, thin two or three inches in the row, and give frequent and thorough cultivation during the summer. The plants will be fit to set the next spring. The permanent beds should be prepared by deep spading, working in a large quantity of rotted manure. Dig trenches four feet apart and twelve to eighteen inches deep, and spade in at least four inches of well rotted manure in the bottom. Set the plants two feet apart in this trench and cover with two inches of fine soil. After the plants are well started give frequent and thorough cultivation, and draw a little earth in the trenches at each hoeing until they are filled. Early the next spring spade in a dressing of manure, and one quart of salt to each square rod, and cultivate well until the plant begins to die down. The bed may be cut one, two or three times, *all* the short shoots above the surface should be cut, and after final cutting, give a good dressing of manure, ashes and salt. Ever after that, the bed should give a full crop if annually dressed with manure, ashes and salt. As soon as the tops are ripe and yellow they should be cut and burned.

Conover's Colossal.—A mammoth sort frequently sending up fifteen to thirty sprouts from one to one and a half inches in diameter from a single plant, and spreading less than most sorts. Color deep green; quality good.

Palmetto.—It is of very large size, even and regular in growth and appearance. It is a very early sort and highly recommended by Southern men.

Broccoli

White Cape Broccoli.

Produces heads in autumn like a Cauliflower. Sow about the middle of April; transplant in rich soil and manage as winter Cabbage.

For an early crop sow in a hot-bed and cultivate as early Cauliflower. It succeeds best in a moist soil and cool climate; can be had in perfection from November to April.

Early Purple Cape.—This is the best for the Northern States, producing compact heads, of a brownish purple, and of good flavor.

White Cape.—Not as early as the above; heads large, creamy white; close and certain to head.

Brussels Sprouts.

This is one of the best vegetables for winter use, producing from the axils of the leaves an abundance of sprouts resembling small cabbages, of excellent mild flavor.

Brussels Sprouts.

Beans.

Dwarf Snaps or Stringless.—One pound will plant 50 feet of drill; 80 pounds one acre in drill.

All varieties of this class are tender, and do best in rather dry, light soil, and should not be planted till the ground is warm and can continue at intervals throughout the season. Plant three inches deep, in rows two feet apart. Keep well hoed, drawing the earth up to the stems while dry.

Wardells Kidney Wax. Beans white, with two shades of reddish purple more or less visible, and a distinct kidney snaps. Prepared for the table it has a fine buttery flavor, and is destined to become the leading snap bean, as well as a strongly endorsed winter shelled sort.

Cleveland's Improved Red Pod Valentine is ten days earlier than the Red Valentine and much more prolific and combines all its good qualities. One of the best for market and gardeners.

White Valentine is a good short snap, and also desirable as a shell bean.

Red Eye, or Early China is largely cultivated in California by market gardeners, and is good either as a snap or dry shell bean.

Early Mohawk is one of the hardiest varieties and will endure some frost. It is a good string bean, and is also desirable for pickling. (Fig. 4.)

Early Refugee is very productive and fine for spring snaps or for pickling. Used by market gardeners. (Fig. 2.)

Yellow Six Weeks.— Extra early, vines large, vigorous, branching and very productive. Pods straight and flat and of fair quality; beans long, kidney-shaped, yellow. with darker marks around the eye. Excellent variety for general crop.

White Kidney is an excellent green shell bean, and one of the best for baking. (Fig. 6.)

Golden Wax.—One of the best dwarf beans grown; pods are large, long, brittle and entirely stringless, of a rich golden wax color, and six days earlier than the ordinary wax; very fine both as a snap bean and a shell bean for winter use.

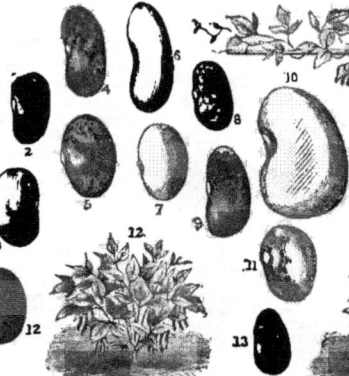

German or Black Wax is one of the best. Pods are of rich, waxy yellow when fit for use, and very tender and delicious. (Fig. 13.)

Ivory Pod Wax are a white bean and earlier than the Black Wax. Pods are tender and stringless, and of a rich creamy flavor, and are ivory white.

Crystal White Wax are similar to the above—crisp, tender, and of the richest flavor. The pods develop quickly and retain their tenderness longer than any other sorts.

English Dwarf or Broad Windsor is a very hardy kind and can be planted very early in the season, in good soil, in drills five feet apart. Pinch off tops as soon as the lower pods begin to fill. They are used only as shell beans.

Best of All Dwarf Beans.—A very popular variety in the South, and as its name indicates, one of the best and most valuable green-podded beans for market or family use. The pods are about six inches long, very fleshy, succulent, stringless and of good quality. Early and prolific.

BEANS. POLE OR RUNNING—One pound to 75 hills.

These are generally more tender than dwarf kinds, and should not be planted till the ground becomes warm. Set poles about four feet apart, and pinch off the tops when they grow higher than the poles. They succeed best in sandy loam mixed with well rotted compost to each hill.

Yellow Flageolet Wax.—The pods of this excellent variety are of very large size; sometimes 10 to 12 inches in length, entirely stringless, very fleshy and of the finest quality, being exceedingly tender and succulent. It is equally good as a Shell Bean.

King of the Garden Lima.—When green, much larger in pod and bean than the ordinary Large Lima; vigorous, productive, handsome, popular, excellent; two vines will be sufficient for each pole.

Large Lima are the most buttery and delicious of all, and are a universal favorite. green or dry. (Fig. 10.)

Giant Wax (Red Seed) make pods 6 to 9 inches long, thick and fleshy, of yellow waxy color, and is very productive and tender. (Fig. 12.)

Horticultural, or Speckled Cranberry is an old favorite and is equally good as a snap or as a shell bean, either green or dry. (Fig. 5.)

White Dutch Runners are very ornamental, large white seed, and beautiful clusters of white flowers, and is a good shell bean.

Scarlet Runners are a great favorite, producing clusters of beautiful scarlet flowers, which are very ornamental. This is very fine for use as a green shell bean. Fig. 14.

Dutch Case-Knife. A very productive variety, and one of the earliest; sometimes used as "snaps," but generally shelled. Next to the Lima the best market sort.

Southern Prolific. Desirable for snap beans, mature in seventy days. Bears its pods in clusters. Popular in the South.

Asparagus, or Yard Long. Pod sometimes grows from two to three feet long; very curious, succulent and tender.

Dwarf Lima } See Specialties.

Beets.

The soil best suited for Beet culture is that which is rather light and well enriched. Sow in drills one foot apart and 1 inch deep, as early as the ground can be worked; continue for a succession as late as the middle of July; when the plants are large enough thin out to stand 6 inches apart in the rows. The Sugar and Mangel Wurzel varieties are grown for feeding stock, and should be sown from April to June in drills 2 feet apart, and afterwards thinned out to stand 1 foot apart in the rows; keep well cultivated. One ounce will sow a drill fifty feet in length; five or six pounds are required for an acre.

Eclipse. A very early, smooth, globe-shaped beet with small top and thin root; its skin an intense deep red, its flesh of very fine texture, earliness and quality it is excelled by none. Many of our Market Gardeners prefer it to the Egyptian.

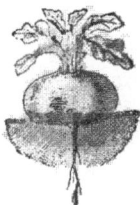

Early Blood Turnip. An old standard variety of fine form and flavor. Next to Eclipse in earliness.

Eclipse.

Dewing's Improved Blood Turnip. Roots deep blood-red, of fine form and flavor. Very early. An excellent market variety.

Long Dark Blood. Long, smooth, growing to good size; half out of the ground; color dark blood-red; top small, dark red, and of upright growth; keeps well. It is apt to be tough when sown too early.

Early Blood Turnip.

Dewing's Improved Blood Turnip.

Henderson's Pineapple

Long Blood.

Egyptian Blood Turnip.

Bassano.

Try a packet of our Perfection Cabbage Lettuce,

Edmund's Improved Blood Turnip. Of handsome turnip shape, skin deep blood-red, flesh also very dark, and exceedingly sweet and tender in quality; roots grow regularly of good marketable size, with a very small top and having but a single tap root, which allows their being grown very near together. They mature early and have given the best satisfaction as a bunch variety for market.

Egyptian Turnip. A standard sort, being from ten to twelve days earlier than the Blood Turnip. The roots are large in size, and of a rich, deep crimson color.

From the smallness of the tops of the Egyptian at least one-fourth more can be grown on the same space than any other variety.

Extra Early or Bassano. Turnip-shaped. An improved early kind, small top, round root, sweet and tender, attain a very large size.

Bastian's Half-Long Blood. Of bright color and excellent quality; a valuable variety to follow the early sorts. For winter use plant about the middle of July.

Mangel Wurtzel.—(For Field Culture.)

Four to six pounds to the acre. Extensively cultivated in all parts of the country as a field crop for feeding stork in the winter. When grown for this purpose, the distance between the rows should be from two to two and a half feet, so that the cultivation can be done with horse tools instead of with hand-hoes.

Norbiton Giant. One of the finest quality in cultivation; grows to an enormous size.

Golden Tankard Mangel. This is a distinct and superior strain of the Yellow or Golden fleshed Mangel, being much finer and firmer in the flesh, and containing more sugar. On account of its peculiar shape, enormous crops are grown when the plants are set out closer in the rows than in ordinary Mangel crops, it having yielded upwards of seventy-five tons per acre.

Red Globe Mangel.

Yellow Ovoid.

Imperial Sugar.

Long Red Mangel.

Orange Globe Mangel.   Golden Tankard Mangel

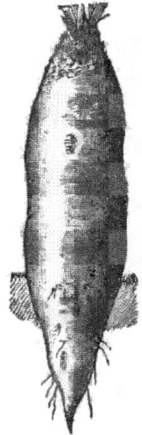

Yellow Ovoid. A very nutritious and valuable variety; bulb ovoid; intermediate between the long and globe varieties; flesh solid, vigorous and productive.

Red Globe Mangel. A large red oval variety, which keeps well, and produces better crops on shallow soil than the Long Red.

Orange Globe Mangel. The same as the above, only differing in color.

Mammoth Long Red. Grown extensively for agricultural purposes, producing large roots partly above the ground.

White Sugar Beet. The large amount of saccharine matter contained in this variety makes it very valuable for stock feeding purposes; grows to a large size.

Cabbage.

One ounce for about 2,000 plants.

Cabbages require a deep rich soil and thorough working. The seed for the early crops can be sown in hot beds. When of size to transplant, place the earlier kinds from 12 to 18 inches apart. The largest and later kinds 2 feet or more. The plants should be set down to first leaf, so that the stem is all below the surface of the ground, and hoe often. Our seed is from the finest and purest selected strains of American growth.

We would advise all those who wish Cabbage Seed to order early, as there is a shortage in the crop this season and prices will rule high as soon as sowing begins.

Express.—This valuable variety which was first introduced three years ago, is all that was claimed for it by the introducers. Excels in earliness all the sorts we have grown and has the shape of the Etampe cabbage, but is smaller and eight to ten days earlier; has few outside leaves and therefore may be planted very close. It makes a large, hard head, of very handsome appearance; cooking qualities are excellent.

Extra Early Etampe. A splendid early sort producing medium sized, conical shaped heads of the finest quality. Grows very quickly and is a most desirable sort either for private use or market gardeners.

Stone Mason.

Stone Mason.

Characterized for its sweetness and delicacy of flavor, and for its reliability for forming a large head. Very hardy, and will endure the cold of extreme Northern climates.

Improved Premium Late Flat Dutch. This is the best strain of this standard variety and more largely grown than any other for market and long-keeping quality. Short stem and large solid flat heads.

Red Dutch. Used almost exclusively for pickling. It is one of the hardiest of all Cabbages; will keep later in the season than any of them. Slow to mature, however, and requires a richer soil for its perfect development.

Henderson's Early Summer. Heads about ten days later than the Jersey Wakefield. It may be classed as the best *large early* Cabbage. In weight it is equal to most of the late varieties, its short outer leaves enable it to be planted as close as the Jersey Wakefield.

Red Dutch.

Early Jersey Wakefield. The *best early* Cabbage in cultivation. It possesses the merit of large size of head, small outside foliage, and uniformity in producing a crop.

All Seasons. Similar in form to the Stone Mason; solid, compact; claimed to be as early and larger than the Henderson's Summer; comparatively new; wherever tried has given surprising satisfaction.

"True" Jersey Early Wakefield.

Large Late Drumhead. A favorite winter variety with the market gardener. It bears extra large solid heads, and is a little later than the Flat Dutch.

Large Late Drumhead.

Early Winningstadt. A second early variety, coming in about three weeks later than the early varieties, it is an excellent sort, as it heads uniformly and is of large size, often weighing 20 lbs.; heads pyramidal, the outer leaves spiral and spreading, which necessitates planting it wider than the early sorts. One of the best for early shipments.

Mammoth Marblehead. One of the latest and largest of the Cabbage tribe. Solid, tender and free headed.

Drumhead Savoy. The Savoy Cabbages are the finest flavor of all; finely crimped and netted and yet makes a compact, solid head. Dark green.

Mammoth Marblehead.

Excelsior Flat Dutch. This is a California variety and we consider it one of the best late sorts grown. The heads are large and compact, of a light green foliage. Valuable as a Winter Cabbage, also for fall use by sowing early.

Filderkraut resembles the well known Winningstadt, but is larger, more pointed, and heads up with fewer outside leaves. Largely grown for making kraut.

Fottler's Improved Brunswick. A second early and late variety grown originally by the Boston gardeners, but which is now cultivated quite generally all over the country.

Early Dwarf Ulm Savoy. This is earlier and dwarfer than the Drumhead, and of very fine flavor.

Cauliflower.

CULTURE. Cauliflower ought to receive a similar treatment to Cabbage, except that it requires an extra rich soil, an occasional application of liquid manure and frequent watering, especially when heading. Early sorts are mostly sown in hot beds, and transplanted before setting out in open ground, and finally transplanted in rich deeply worked soil, two feet by fifteen inches apart. Late sorts are sown and cultivated like late Cabbage. When heading tie the top leaves together to protect from expose to the sun.

Early Dwarf Erfurt. Extra Early Dwarf, small leaf, solid, pure white heads, best quality.

Early Snowball. The earliest and best heading variety cultivated; dwarf habit and short outer leaves. (See among specials.)

Early Paris. A popular French variety, White and sure to head, and standard sort for early or late crop.

Late Asiatic. Large, white and compact, but later than the preceding.

Large White French. A superior late sort of fine quality, with short stem and large well-formed heads.

Large Late Algiers. New, and much prized for late sort.

Veitch's Autumn Giant. This is one of the best late varieties grown. Robust habit, large heads, compact and thoroughly protected by leaves.

Be Sure to Get Some of Our Seeds of Special Merit.

Celery.

One ounce will make about 2,000 plants.

Should he sown in open ground, as early as it will he fit to work, and he kept clear of weeds until ready for transplanting. Cut tops once or twice before to insure stocky plants. When ground is well prepared, set in rows three feet apart and six inches from each other, and see that the soil is well packed around the roots by pressing with the foot. Run the cultivator or hoe between the rows to destroy the weeds, and when grown to sufficient size draw up the earth for blanching, pressing with the hand to keep the leaf upright and banking up to the top on each side.

Henderson's White Plume. This requires less labor for blanching, is crisp, solid, and of nutty flavor and valuable for family use.

Henderson's Half Dwarf. Solid, crisp, and of nutty flavor and very desirable.

Boston Market Dwarf. Short, bushy, white, solid and excellent flavor.

Dwarf Golden Heart. The heart of this variety is waxy and showy, and for market use desirable. It is very solid and of excellent flavor, and a good keeper.

Giant White Solid. Large size, solid, crisp, and good market variety.

Celerio, or Turnip Rooted Celery. A variety with turnip-shaped roots which may he cooked and sliced and used with vinegar, making an excellent salad. It is hardy and otherwise treated as other celery.

Soup Celery. Its seed is used for flavoring soups, stews, etc., and

Giant White Solid.
is sold for this purpose at a low price.

Self Blanching. See Specialties.

Carrot.

The Carrot like other root crops, delights in a sandy loam, richly tilled. For early crop sow in spring, as soon as the ground is in good working order; for later crops they may he sown any time until the middle of June. Sow in rows about fifteen inches apart, thinning out to three or four inches between the plants. In field culture, when grown for horses or cattle, the rows should be two feet apart, so that the crop can be worked by the horse cultivator. As Carrot seed is slow to germinate, all precautions must be taken.

Early French Forcing Carrot. This variety has two things very much in its favor, namely: its extreme earliness and fine flavor; stump-rooted and grows about two inches in length. No. 5

Early Scarlet Horn A favorite sort for early crop but not large enough for general culture. It is one of the varieties that is sold in the markets bunched up in the green state. It matures earlier than the Long Orange, and is sometimes used for forcing. No. 3.

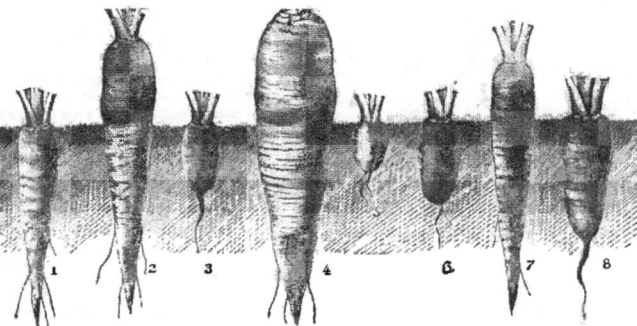

Half Long Red (Stump Rooted.) Largely grown for the market. In size and time of maturity it is between the Early Scarlet Horn and the Long Orange. No. 6.

Guerande, or Or Heart. Intermediate in length, between the Early Horn and Half Long Varieties, and three to five inches in diameter. In quality it is extra good. Where other sorts require digging, Ox Heart can be easily pulled.

Large White Belgian. Grows one-third out of the ground; root pure white, green above ground, with small top; grows to a very large size and is easily gathered; flesh rather coarse, is raised exclusively for stock. No. 4.

Danvers. A very valuable sort; in form midway between the Long Orange and Early Horn class. It is of a rich shade of orange, growing very smooth and handsome. This variety will yield the greatest bulk with the smallest length of root of any now grown. Under the

best cultivation it has yielded from twenty-five to thirty tons per acre. No. 8.

Improved Long Orange. The best late, deep orange colored variety, equally adapted for garden or farm culture. An improvement on the Long Orange, by careful selections of the best formed and deepest colored roots. No. 7.

Long Scarlet Altringham. A large, good-flavored field variety, for table use or feeding stock. No. 2.

Red Saint Vallery. This fine variety has now become more generally known, and with its handsome appearance and good quality, it combines the distinguishing properties of both good kitchen-garden and good field carrots—that is, great productiveness, and at the same time a fine regular shape, and thick, sweet, tender flesh. See Specialties.

Collard.

Is used in place of Cabbage, and grows where it is difficult to make Cabbage head. Cultivate same as Cabbage.

Chicory.

This is grown to mix with or as a substitute for Coffee. It requires the same cultivation as Carrots.

Cress or Pepper Grass.

Well known as a pungent salad. It should be sown thickly and at frequent intervals for succession. It quickly runs to seeds. Cover very lightly in planting.

Double and Triple Curled. Is very fine and can be cut two or three times.

Water Cress. Is a perennial and will grow in and alongside of streams and ponds. It has a very pleasant pungent taste.

Cucumber.

Cucumbers succeed best in warm, moist, rich, loamy ground. They should not be planted in the open air until there is a prospect of settled warm weather. Plant in the hills about four feet apart each way. The hills should be previously prepared by mixing thoroughly with the soil of each a shovelful of well rotted manure. When all danger from insects is past, thin out the plants, leaving three or four of the strongest to each hill. The fruit should be plucked when large enough, as if left to ripen on the vines, it destroys their productiveness.

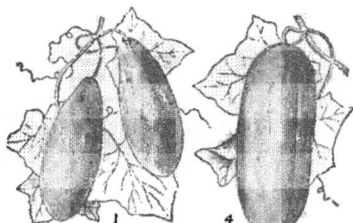

Early Russian.   Early Frame.

Early Russian. Fruit three to four inches long, an inch and a half in diameter; generally produced in pairs; flesh tender, crisp and well flavored; comes into use about ten days earlier than any other variety, and makes a fine, small pickle.

Early Frame. Excellent variety for table use; tender and well flavored, and keeps green longer than any other variety; also makes splendid hard, green pickles; comes into use after the Early Cluster.

Extra Long White Spine. A variety used largely for forcing, by market gardeners. They grow ten to twelve inches long and very straight. They make fine, hard brittle pickles when four or five inches long; dark green and handsome.

Early White Spine. An excellent variety for table use; very early; grows uniformly straight and smooth; light green with white prickles; tender; of excellent flavor.

Long Green Turkey. The leading long green variety for pickling, of excellent quality and productiveness, fruit dark green, firm and crisp.

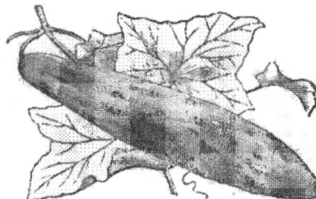

Improved Long Green.

Improved Long Green. Undoubtedly the best variety in cultivation for table or pickling. About one foot in length; firm and crisp; this variety produces seeds sparingly.

Nichol's Medium Green. For early forcing, late sowing for pickling, or for ordinary table use this variety will be found useful. It is of a dark green color, pleasant flavor, and very productive.

Early Cluster. Vines vigorous, producing the crop near the root and in clusters. Fruit short, dark green. Good for table use, but not adapted to pickling.

Boston Pickling, or Green Prolific. One of the best pickling varieties, dark green, tender, crisp, very productive, of fine flavor, uniform size, and good for table use.

Gherkin, for Pickling. A very small oval shaped, prickly variety. It is grown exclusively for pickling; is the smallest of all the varieties, and should always be pickled when young and tender. The seed is slow to germinate.

Giant Pera. }
Serpent.   } See Specialties.
Siberian.   }

Black Mexican.   Crosby's Early.   Amber Cream.   Mammoth Sugar.   Marblehead Early.   Early Minnesota.   Pee and-Kay.   Egyptian Sweet.

A rich, warm, alluvial soil is the best, and immediately before planting this should be as deeply and thoroughly worked as possible. Plant for a succession of crops every three weeks, in hills three feet apart each way, and six seeds in a hill. Cover about half an inch, thin out to three plants.

Perry's Hybrid.

A very fine, new, early variety, fully as early as the Minnesota, and ears much larger, each containing 12 or 14 rows of kernels, well filled to the end. The grains are very large and pure white, but the cob is red. The ears are about the same lengths as Crosby's, but larger round, and are ready to market fully a week earlier. The stalks grow 5½ feet high, and the ears (2 to a stalk) are set about 2 feet from the ground.

Corn—Sweet.

Pee and Kay. It has a very large, plump, sweet, ear, and comes nearly as early as the Marblehead. The stalks are from six to seven feet high, with from two to three ears on the stalk, set well down, kernels large, plump, pearly white and sweet. We can recommend it highly.

Cory. The earliest of all sweet corns. It closely resembles the Early Marblehead, but earlier by at least a week. To market men, the Cory is a valuable variety, as the first sweet corn will bring double the price it commands when the supply becomes general.

Triumph. One of the earliest and best of the large varieties. The flavor is rich and sweet, kernels large and fine, and from 12 to 16 rows on each cob. One of the best for the market gardeners as well as for the family use.

Crosby's Early. Highly prized by market gardeners; very early; ears rather short, averaging from 12 to 16 rows; of a rich sugary flavor.

Moore's Early Concord. Very early, with large ears, 12 rows; excellent in quality for table or market.

Squantum, or Potter's Excelsior. An excellent variety of the finest quality for table use and market; ripens early, with fine large ears and deep grain.

Mammoth Sugar. Very large ears and very sweet.

Early Minnesota. Very early; a decidedly excellent variety; ears fair size and uniform; plant rather dwarf.

Black Mexican. Although the ripe grain is bluish-black, the corn, when in condition for the table, looks remarkably white, and is surpassed by none in tenderness. This by many, is considered the most desirable for family use of any of the second sorts.

Egyptian Sweet. Noted for its productiveness, large ears, and for sweetness and tenderness. It is peculiarly adapted for canning purposes. The superiority of often bringing a half more per can than other sorts. In rich ground the stalks will average 3 ears each. Its season is about the same as the Evergreen.

Stowell's Evergreen. The standard late variety. If planted at the same time with earlier kinds, will keep the table supplied until October. It is hardy and productive, very tender and sugary, remaining a long time in a fresh condition, suitable for boiling.

Gold Coin. } See specialties.

Egg Plant.

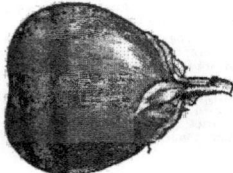

The Egg Plant will thrive well in any good garden soil; succeeds best in a deep, warm, rich soil and full exposure to the sun. Sow in hot bed very early in Spring; transplant two and one-half feet apart each way after weather becomes settled and warm. If no hot bed is at hand, plants may be started in pots or boxes.

New York Improved. The leading market sort, very large and smooth; fine dark color, very prolific and of excellent quality.

Early Long Purple. Much smaller than the New York Improved; very early and productive, fruit long, dark, rich purple, good quality.

New York Improved Egg Plant.   Black Perkin. The fruit of this variety is jet black, fine grain and delicate flavor, very prolific and desirable for market gardeners.

Endive.

One of the best Salade for fall and winter use. Sow from late in the spring to the middle of Summer, in shallow drills fourteen inches apart; thin the plants to one foot in drills, and when fully grown, tie over the outer leaves of a few plants every week or fortnight in dry weather, to blanch, which takes ten days in hot and twenty days in cool weather. Draw up a little earth to the base of the plant. Rich, mellow soil, in an open situation is most suitable.

Green Curled Endive.

Green Curled is the hardiest variety, with beautifully curled dark green leaves, which blanch white, and are very crisp and tender.

Garlic.

This is extensively used for flavoring soups, stews, etc. The sets should be planted early in spring in rich soil in rows one foot apart, and from three to fine inches apart in the rows. Cultivate like onions. When the tops die off the crop is ready to gather.

Kohl-Rabi.

This is an intermediate between the Cabbage and Turnip. For an early crop start in hot-bed and treat the same as early Cabbage; if for late crop, sow in June or July. Remove the plants early in the Fall and store for Winter use, the same as turnips. This is a favorite with Europeans, and very superior for feeding cows for milk.

Early White Vienna. Best early variety for table; bulbs white, handsome, small, highly esteemed by market gardeners.

Early Purple. Very similar to the last, except in color, which is a bright   White Vienna Kohl-Rabi.
purple, a desirable sort.

Kale or Borecole.

The Kales are more hardy than Cabbage, make excellent greens for winter and spring use, and are improved by frost. Sow from May to June, in well prepared soil, covering it thinly and evenly, and cultivate the same as Cabbage. Half an ounce will sow a bed of twenty square feet.

Green Curled Scotch. Very hardy, and is improved by a moderate frost. Leaves bright green and beautifully curled. It stands the winters in the Middle States without protection.

Dwarf Green Curled. This variety is extensively grown as Winter Greens, sown in the Fall, in rows one foot apart and treated in every way as Spinach, it is ready for use in early spring.

Sea Kale. This is quite a favorite with many; its young shoots are blanched for use. It is trained and treated like the Cabbage.

Green Curled Scotch Kale or Borecole.

Sea Kale.

Leek.

The Leek is very hardy and easily cultivated; it succeeds best in a light but well enriched soil. Sow as early in spring as practicable, in drills one inch deep and one foot apart. When six or eight inches high, they may be transplanted in rows ten inches apart each way, as deep as possible, that the neck, being covered may be blanched. If fine leeks are desired, the ground can hardly be made too rich.

London Flag. The variety most generally cultivated in this country, hardy, of good quality.

Carentan or Scotch Champion. An extra large variety from Scotland, growing rapidly, and very hardy.

London Flag Leek.

Lettuce.

Lettuce thrives best in rich, moist ground. For successive crops, sowing may be made in the open ground as early as the spring opens, and continuing until July. Always thin out well or the plants will not be strong. When wanted as a cut salad, sow the seed thickly in rows or broadcast.

Early Curled Silesia. A fine early curled variety which does not head, leaves large, tender and of fine flavor.

Early Curled Simpson. This does not head, but forms a close compact mass of leaves; very early, excellent for forcing.

Early Curled Simpson.

Boston Curled. Of superior quality; does not form solid heads; fine for early use.

Boston Curled.

Early Prize Head. Forms a mammoth plant; in which even the outer leaves are crisp and tender, and remains so throughout the season. It is slow to run up to seed, of superb flavor and very hardy, one of the best varieties for family use, but for market gardens it is too tender to stand much handling.

Hanson. The heads are of very large size, deliciously sweet, tender and crisp, even to the outer leaves. Color green outside and white within.

Black Seeded Simpson. Like the curled Simpson, this variety does not, properly, form a head; but it differs in the leaves being nearly white, and attaining nearly double the size of the Curled Simpson. It stands the summer heat splendidly while it is equally suited for forcing.

Early Summer Cabbage. One of the very best head Lettuces for the summer that we know of. The heads are of good size, close and well formed. It is a splendid market variety.

Oak Leaved. A distinct variety due to the peculiar outline of the leaves, which are shaped like those of the oak. The heads are compact, crisp and tender, and it is largely free from that bitter taste peculiar to so many kinds of Lettuce.

Oak Leaved.

Tennis Ball. A favorite forcing variety. Well formed heads, hardy and crisp, of excellent quality. One of the earliest of the heading varieties.

Salamander. An excellent summer variety, forming good sized heads that stand drought and heat longer without injury than any other sort.

Salamander.

Phila. Butter or Cabbage. Produces fine, greenish-white large heads, of extra quality, remarkably crisp and tender, sure to head, of quick growth. It is one of the best for forcing and for summer use, as it is slow to shoot to seed, and resists heat well.

Phila. Butter or Cabbage.

Ice Drumhead. Produces a beautiful head, very firm, solid and compact. The head is of an attractive and silvery white, rich, buttery, and most delicious in flavor. It comes early and stands a long while before running to seed; excellent for early spring and summer use.

The Deacon. This is one of the dark green, thick-leaved sorts, nearly all of which are of good quality. Head compact, roundish, or a little flattened when of full size; in some plants measuring fully five inches in diameter. Outer leaves few in number which, with the perfectly defined head, gives the plant a very distinct appearance. We have found this variety the slowest to run to seed, and one of the best heading kinds we have ever tested.

White Paris Cos. The heads are long, upright, with oblong leaves. It is very hardy, of large size, and long in running to seed; tender, brittle and high flavored.

All the Year Round. A hardy, crisp eating and compact growing variety, with small, close heads of a dark green color; an excellent summer Lettuce, and valuable for forcing.

White Paris Cos.

Strong's Perfection. See Specialties.

Martynia.

Used much for pickling, when gathered while green and tender.

Sow in open ground and transplant to two feet deep.

Musk Melons.

One oz. for 50 hills; 3 pounds for an acre.

Melons thrive best in good sandy loam. Plant as soon as the ground becomes warm, in hills six feet apart; a little well rotted manure in each hill will be of great benefit. Put 12 to 15 seeds to a hill, and after they are up and all danger from bugs is over, thin out to 3 plants to the hill. If the growth is too rapid, pinch off the top and leading shoots, and thin out the fruit, which will increase the size of those remaining. Pumpkins, Squashes or Cucumbers should not be grown near them, as they would be apt to hybridize.

Emerald Gem Melon. This most excellent new musk melon originated in Michigan. It is of superior flavor and quality; the outside skin is an emerald green color and quite smooth; they ripen early and produce well; the flesh is light red or salmon, very thick, juicy and crystalline, and luscious in flavor. See specialties.

California Netted Cantaloupe. This is the most popular and best market variety grown in this State; large, deeply ribbed and netted; green flesh and of delicious flavor and a good keeper.

Montreal Improved Green Nutmeg. Nearly round, slightly flattened at the ends, with a densely netted green skin. They grow to a large, uniform size, averaging from 15 to 20 pounds in weight, specimens often weighing 25 pounds. The flesh is remarkably thick and of good flavor. Owing to its large and handsome appearance, it sells rapidly in the market at very high prices.

Surprise. An excellent variety, having thin, cream-colored skin, thickly netted; of medium size and thick, salmon-colored flesh. The flavor is delicious, and they are very productive.

Champion Market Musk Melon. In shape is almost a perfect globe and densely netted; ripens early and grows to a very large, uniform size. The flesh is thick, light green in color, and of a rich, sweet flavor. Vines are vigorous and remarkably healthy. Very productive.

Surprise.

Skillman's Fine Netted. This is a small, rough, netted variety, flattened at the ends; flesh vrey thick, firm, sugary, and of delicious flavor. Among the earliest of the green-fleshed melons.

Baltimore. A green-fleshed melon, which should be largely grown. It is very productive; of good size, flesh thick and of delicious flavor, and is largely grown by leading market gardeners as being in every way a desirable sort.

Casaba, or Persian.

Casaba, or Persian. Of good size, very delicious and fine flavor; usual weight from 10 to 15 pounds; the best prolific, late oval, netted · green-fleshed variety.

Large Hackensack.

Large Hackensack. Very popular with market gardeners in the vicinity of large cities, being of a very large size; very prolific, rich in flavor, thick, juicy flesh, and always commands a ready sale.

Bay View. A large oval melon of the Persian type, of superior quality, thin rind, flesh green, firm and sugary.

Miller Cream Nutmeg Melon.

This splendid melon was thoroughly tested the past season by many of our best market gardeners and melon growers, and is pronounced by all one of the very best they have ever grown. The flesh is of a rich salmon color, very thick, sweet and melting in quality. The rind is very thin, slightly sutured and finely netted. Vines grow strong and are very productive, covering the ground with fruit. They retain their bright fresh appearance, and remain solid several days after being pulled.

Green Citron. A very desirable melon either for the table or market; very juicy; honey flavor; thick green flesh; a standard sort.

White Japan. Medium size; flesh thick, skin pale green; one of the earliest; worthy of a place in every family garden.

Green Citron.

Golden Gem. This valuable new cantaloupe is admitted by prominent melon growers to be the very best early variety now grown. They grow very uniform in shape and size, weighing about two pounds each, skin green and thickly netted. They are thick-meated, flesh of a light green color, the inside surface when cut open being of a beautiful golden color. In quality and flavor they are *superior*, being uniformly *rich, sugary and luscious*. They are *extra early* in ripening, the vines keeping green longer and producing better than any variety we have ever known. They sell in markets, where known, right alongside of other good varieties, at double price.

Emerald Gem. ⎫
The Osage. ⎬ See Specialties.
Champion Market. ⎭

Don't fail to read about our Specialties; there is sure to be something you will want.

Watermelon.

One ounce to 50 hills, or about three pounds to an acre.

Moun'ain Sprout. A good market sort, fruit of large size; longish oval; skin dark green, marbled with light shades; red flesh of excellent quality.

Mountain Sprout.   Black Spanish.

Black Spanish. Fruit large, of a round shape, color a very dark green, and seeds black.

Mountain Sweet. Fruit oblong, dark green, rind thin, flesh red, solid and very sweet.

Ice Cream or Peerless. Fruit of medium size, nearly round; skin pale green, rind very thin, white seeds, flesh solid and delicious.

Ice Cream or Peerless.   Georgia Rattlesnake.

Georgia Rattlesnake. One of the largest varieties, and stands shipment long distances. Fruit cylindrical, square at the ends, smooth, distinctly striped and mottled light and dark green. Flesh bright scarlet, and very sweet.

Pride of Georgia. Originated in Monroe County, Georgia. The rind is dark green, shape nearly oval, and ridged like an orange; grows partly on one end, flesh rich scarlet, very small and crisp; attains a large size, and a good shipper.

Citron. For preserving; flesh white and solid; seed red.

Scaly Bark. An excellent variety; of great value to shippers; remains in choice eating condition from ten to fifteen days after being pulled. The flesh is light crimson; solid, tender and of fine flavor. Skin is almost smooth, looks as if covered with fish scales. Rind, though quite thin, is remarkably tough.

Cuban Queen. The largest and one of the best grown; an excellent keeper, skin beautifully striped dark and light green. The flesh is red, solid, delicate in flavor and very sweet; bears transit well.

Orange. Flesh red, tender and sweet, separating from the rind like an orange.

Cuban Queen.

Mammoth Ironclad.

Mammoth Ironclad. A variety of undoubted excellence, of large size and weight, crops of it averaging nearly 50 pounds each. The flesh is deep red and of a delicious rich flavor, holding its fine qualities very close to the skin. In outside appearance it is somewhat like the Gypsy. For shipping and keeping qualities the Ironclad is unsurpassed. The vines are strong growing, and altogether it is a most valuable acquisition.

Florida Favorite Watermelon. Finest table melon extant; oblong in shape, growing to very large size; rind dark, with light-green stripes; flesh light crimson, very crisp and deliciously sweet; seed rather small and of light creamy white color. Ripened the past season 10 days earlier than the Kolb Gem, Ironclad or Rattlesnake. We offer seed grown by originator.

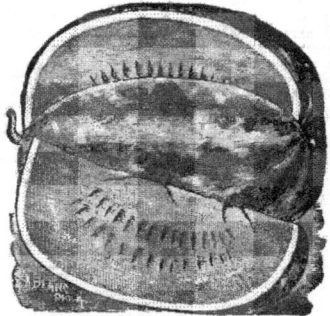

Kolb Gem.

Kolb Gem. This variety originated in Alabama three years ago, has proved to be a very valuable acquisition. It is uniformly round and grows to a good size, often attaining a weight of twenty-five to fifty pounds; the flesh is a bright red and flavor excellent, rind dark green, striped and very tough. It is unsurpassed as a shipping melon, retaining its freshness and sweetness for a long time after ripening. It is unusually productive and will mature as far north as Chicago.

Imperial Lodi. This is now the most popular of all the California grown varieties. Large, oblong, skin light pea-green in color, and thin. Red flesh, very sweet and fine in flavor, and one of the very best for cultivation for market sales.

Seminole.
Hungarian Honey.   } See Specialties.
The Volga.
Green and Gold.

Mushroom Spawn.

The Mushroom is an edible fungus of a white color, changing to brown when old. The gills are loose, of a pinkish red, changing to liver color. It produces no seed, but instead, a white, fibrous substance in broken threads, called spawn, which is preserved in horse manure, being pressed in the form of bricks. Thus prepared it will retain its vitality for years.

CULTURE. Mushrooms can be grown in the cellar, in sheds, or in hot beds in open air, on shelves, or out-of-the-way places. Fermenting horse manure, at a temperature of about 70 degrees, is made into beds the size required, eighteen inches deep. In this bed plant the broken pieces of spawn six inches apart, covering the whole with two inches of light soil, and protect from cold and severe rains. The mushrooms will appear in about six weeks. Water sparingly and with lukewarm water.

Mustard.

Makes a pungent salad. Sow thickly in rows and cut for use when two inches high. White London is the best for salads. The Brown or Black, is, however, more pungent.

Nasturtium.

The seeds, while young and succulent, are pickled for capers. The plants are quite ornamental, and make excellent screens in the garden.

Okra, or Gumbo.

This vegetable is grown for its pods, which are used in soups, stews, etc. It is very nutritious and of easy culture. Sow when the ground has become warm, three feet apart and one inch deep, and thin out to ten inches in the row. The pods are dried for winter use.

White Velvet Okra. Quite distinct from any other variety, the pods being round and smooth, while in the old sorts they are ridged or square-edged. It is the most tender and the finest flavored of any variety grown, the pods being very soft and velvety to the touch and are of a creamy white color. They grow to a larger size than any other Okra, are never prickly to the touch, and are produced in the greatest abundance.

New Improved Dwarf. This new early variety, has long, green, slender pods, very productive, and grows fourteen inches high.

Long Green. Long ribbed erect pods, sharply tapering to a point; very productive.

Onions.

The value of this crop depends almost solely on the quality of the seed sown. Realizing this, we have taken the greatest care in selecting our stocks, and can confidently recommend them to all our customers, those who use large quantities, as well as those who use small, as being unsurpassed for quality, germination and trueness; being grown for us solely by men of years of experience in raising this important seed. Our seed will produce full-sized onions the first year of sowing, for which purpose sow four or five lbs. per acre. For growing small sets our seed is equally good, and should be sown for this purpose at the rate of about 60 lbs. to the acre.

Early Red Globe. A variety maturing as early as the flat sort. It is globe shaped; skin deep red; flesh mild and tender. Very handsome in appearance.

Extra Early Red. A medium sized, flat variety; an abundant producer, and very uniform in shape and size; moderately strong flavored, and comes into use nearly two weeks earlier than the Large Red Wethersfield; very desirable for early market use.

Large Red Wethersfield.

Giant Rocca. An immense onion. Globular in form; skin tender. It will produce a large onion from seed the first season, but to attain the largest growth, the smallest bulbs should be set out the next spring, when they will continue increasing in size, instead of producing seed.

Great White Italian Tripoli.

A large, beautiful, pure white, flat onion, of mild, excellent flavor, and will produce a somewhat larger onion from seed than the White Portugal.

Giant Rocca.

Large Red Wethersfield. This is a standard variety. Large size; skin deep purplish red; form round, somewhat flattened; flesh purplish white; moderately fine grained, and stronger flavored than any of the other kinds. Very productive, the best keeper, and one of the most popular for general cultivation.

Yellow Strasburg. (Yellow Dutch.) Later, flatter and larger than Yellow Danvers; good keeper.

Yellow Danvers.

Yellow Danvers. A fine variety of medium size, globular in form; skin yellowish brown; flesh white, comparatively mild and well flavored, and very productive; requires rich soil and good cultivation to produce heavy crops. By careful selection we have improved the original shape of this variety, so that many seedsmen catalogue it as Yellow Globe Danvers.

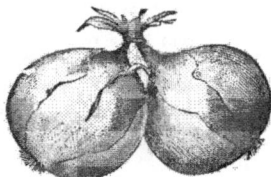

White Globe.

White Globe. Yields abundantly, producing handsome and uniformly globe shaped bulbs. The flesh is firm, fine grained, and of mild flavor. Sometimes called Southport White Globe.

White Portugal or Silver Skin. Mild flavor and handsome; much grown for pickling; poor keeper for market, but good for White Sets.

Queen. A silver skinned variety, of quick growth and remarkable keeping qualities. If sown in early spring it will produce onions one to two inches in diameter early in summer, and if sown in July, will with favorable weather be ready to pull late in autumn, and be sound and fit for use until the following summer. Particularly valuable for pickles, and if sown thickly they will mature perfect hard onions from one-half to three-quarters of an inch in diameter.

Large Red Italian Tripoli. This has the same characteristics as the White Tripoli; except in color however.

Bulbs.

Top Sets or Buttons. Produce on the top of the stalk instead of seed, a number of small bulbs or onions, about the size of acorns, which, if planted, will produce a large onion maturing earlier than from seed. The large onion produces the top onion, and the little top onion produces the large onion.

Bottom Sets. These are produced from seeds sown thickly in beds or drills. When the top dies down the small bulbs are gathered and spread out and kept in a cool dry place for future planting, and should be set, when the ground is in condition, in rows one foot apart and three or four inches distant.

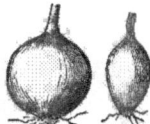

Parsnip.

The value of the Parsnip for the table depends solely on the careful selection of the best roots and most thorough cultivation. As the seed is slow to germinate, too much care cannot be taken with planting. The soil must be warm and mellow. The earth should be firmly pressed over the seed. It should be covered to the depth of half an inch. Sow in drills 15 to 18 inches apart and thin out to 6 inches in the row.

Hollow Crown or Long Smooth. Roots oblong, ending somewhat abruptly, with a small tap root; grows mostly below the surface; has a very smooth clean skin, and is easily distinguished by the leaves arising from a cavity on the top or crown of the root.

Student. A half long variety of delicious flavor.

Pepper.

Grown largely for pickles. Sown in hot bed early and transplanted to the open ground when the weather is favorable. They should be planted in warm, mellow soil, in rows eighteen inches apart. They may also be sown in the open ground when the danger of frost is past, and the soil is warm and weather settled.

Golden Dawn. In size and shape it resembles the Large Bell. It is very productive; color a bright golden yellow; excellent quality, being distinguished from all others, on account of its mild flavor and beautiful appearance.

Red Cayenne. A long, slim pod, rather pointed, and when ripe, of a bright red color. Extremely strong and pungent, and is the sort used for commercial purpose.

Sweet Mountain. Plants very vigorous and productive, growing upright with moderately large leaves. Fruit large, long, smooth and handsome, being when green of a bright deep green color, entirely free from purple tinge, and when mature of a rich red. Flesh thick, sweet and mild flavored. Well suited to use as a stuffed pickle.

Large Squash. Fruit large, flat, tomato shaped, more or less ribbed; skin smooth and glossy; flesh mild, thick meated, and pleasant to the taste, although possessing more pungency than the other large sorts; very productive, and the best variety for pickling.

Large Bell or Bull Nose. A very large sort of inverted bell shape, suitable for filling with cabbage, etc., and for a mixed pickle. Flesh thick, hard and less pungent than most other sorts, and one of the earliest varieties.

Large Bell or Bull Nose.

Chili. Used in the manufacture of pepper sauce. Pods sharply conical, brilliant scarlet and exceedingly pungent when ripe. Requires long, warm season, and plants should be started quite early in hot bed.

Pumpkin.

Sow in good soil when the ground has become warm, in hills 8 or 10 feet apart each way, or in fields of corn about every fourth hill; plant at the same time with the corn; always avoid planting near other vines, as they will hybridize. The Cashaw is generally preferred for cooking or making pies.

Mammoth Tours, or Jumbo. Grows to an enormous size, often weighing 150 pounds, very productive; flesh salmon color; good keeper; desirable for cooking purposes or for stock feeding.

Connecticut Field. One of the best for field culture; can be grown with corn; largely used for stock for winter feeding.

Cashaw. A very prolific variety, resembling in form the Winter-Crook-Neck Squash, although growing to a much larger size, frequently weighing 60 pounds and over, color light cream; flesh salmon color.

Sugar. This variety is smaller than the Large Field, but of finer grain, sweeter and very prolific. First rate either for table or for feeding to stock.

Large Cheese. About the most desirable variety for culinary purposes, light yellow, with very thick sweet, brittle flesh, and a most excellent keeper.

Tennessee Sweet Potato. There is no pumpkin in cultivation that has given such good satisfaction in all sections as this variety. Although comparatively new it has become a universal favorite. When cooked it has the appearance of a Sweet Potato, but is of finer flavor, and for pies, etc., it has no equal. Flesh thick, creamy white, and very fine grained. Hardy and productive.

Mammoth Red Etampes Pumpkin. This Mammoth, which has been raised to weigh over 150 pounds, has a brilliant, showy red skin. The flesh is very thick, and in quality is about equal to any of the Mammoth class of pumpkins, whose real value is for stock feed rather than for table use.

New Japanese Pie Pumpkin. See Specialties.

Etampes. See Specialties.

Parsley.

Used for garnishing and seasoning soups, meats, etc. Succeeds best in a mellow, rich soil. Sow thickly, early, in rows one foot apart and one half inch deep; thin out the plants to stand six inches apart in the rows. The seed is slow of germination, taking from three to four weeks to make its appearance, and often failing to come up in dry weather. To assist its coming up, soak the

seed a few hours in warm water, or sprout in damp earth, and sow when it swells or bursts. For winter use protect in a frame or light cellar.

Fern Leaved. Nothing better for garnishing could be desired. As a garden decorative plant, it is very ornamental. It will stand the winter if covered before frost.

Dwarf Extra Curled. Leaves tender, crisp and very curly, of a beautiful bright green color, and ornamental; excellent for garnishing.

Champion Moss Curled. A very fine English sort; leaves beautifully curled and mossy; a handsome standard sort.

PEAS.

Peas mature earliest in a light, rich soil; for a general crop, a rich deep loam, or inclining to clay, is the best. When grown for a market crop sow in rows, 1 inch apart and 2 to 3 inches deep, the rows from 2 to 4 feet apart, according to the variety. When grown in gardens sow in double rows, 6 to 8 inches apart, the tall ones requiring brush. Commence sowing the extra early varieties as early as the ground can be worked. They should be kept clean, and earth up twice during growth. The wrinkled varieties are not as hardy as the small hard sorts, and if planted early should have a dry soil; they are, however, the sweetest and best flavored varieties. The dwarf varieties are best suited for small gardens and can be planted in rows 1 foot apart.

Cleveland's Alaska. This is considered to be the earliest, most prolific and finely flavored variety of peas. See cut. Specialties.

First and Best. This is one of the best extra early sorts for market planting, and is a very heavy and reliable yielder and of good quality.

Rural New Yorker. Early, productive, and uniform in ripening. It grows about 20 inches high, and is quite similar to Philadelphia Extra Early.

Royal Dwarf White Marrowfat. A large, delicious marrow pea, an excellent cropper, and a favorite with gardeners; height, 2 feet.

American Wonder. It is best suited to the private gardens, as it is not productive enough as a market sort. It is very early and requires no staking. The peas are wrinkled, and extreme dwarf growth, about 10 inches in height. It is of the finest quality.

Pride of the Market. This is a new variety of robust, free branching habit. The peas have a most beautiful appearance and agreeable flavor. It bears pods from five to seven inches in length, and well filled. We recommend it to all for private or market use. Height 2 feet.

Prince of Wales. Seed white, wrinkled; height 2½ feet; vigorous growth, branching habit, prolific; pods large sized, well filled with large peas of first quality; time of ripening medium; in every respect firstclass.

Carter's Premium Gem.

Carter's Premium Gem. Pods long and of a dark green color. A type of and improvement on the Little Gem; very early and productive, height, 1 foot. One of the best for gardeners.

Blise's Ever Bearing.

Bliss's Ever Bearing. Height, eighteen inches to 2 feet; foliage large. Pods, 3 to 4 inches in length, each producing 6 to 8 large wrinkled peas. Half an inch and over in diameter, and in quality unsurpassed. A continuous bearer, which gives it especial value. It should be sown thinner than any other kinds, else the vines will become too crowded.

Champion of England. This is acknowledged to be the best of the late varieties. It is tall growing, attaining a height of 5 feet, and requires to be staked up. The pods and peas are of the largest size.

Telephone. A tall, wrink'ed marrow, enormously productive, and of the best quality. Is a strong grower, averaging 18 pods to the stalk. The pods are of the largest size, and contain from 6 to 7 large peas. A desirable sort for the family garden.

Extra Early Tom Thumb. A remarkably early variety. Very dwarf, growing but nine inches. If planted early in the Spring, three crops can be obtained in a single season.

Bliss's Abundance. A second early variety, attaining a height of from 15 to 18 inches. Pods 3 to 3½ inches long, roundish and well filled, containing 6 to 8 large wrinkled peas of excellent quality. This variety branches directly from the roots forming a veritable bush, making it necessary to sow the seeds much thinner than usual. Six to eight inches apart in the rows is as near as the plants should stand; if the soil is very rich 8 inches is preferable.

Carter's Stratagem. Seeds green, square wrinkled, height, 2 feet, vigorous, branching habit; remarkably luxuriant foliage, leaves unusually large sized, under favorable conditions an enormous cropper; pods long, well filled with from seven to nine peas of the largest size, extra fine quality. One of the most elegant and showy peas in cultivation.

Yorkshire Hero. A splendid wrinkled green marrow pea of branching habit and abundant bearer. Seedsmen on both sides of the Atlantic find their sales for this variety constantly on the increase; 2½ feet.

Tall White Marrowfat. A favorite marrow sort; 6 feet. Mostly grown as a field pea, and very productive.

Black-Eyed Marrowfat. This is extensively grown as a field pea; hardy and productive, but not so fine flavored as most other varieties; 4 feet.

Tall Sugar. (Edible pods.) Can be used either shelled or cooked in the pods, which when young are very tender and sweet; 5 feet.

Dwarf Sugar (Edible pods.) Similar to the last; height 3 feet.

Radish.

Radishes require a sandy loam, made rich and light. A heavy clay soil will not produce good smooth roots. Sow in twelve inch drills as early as the ground will permit, and once in two weeks for succession.

French Breakfast.   Early Scarlet Turnip.

French Breakfast. A very quick growing variety; brittle; crisp and tender, of oval form, bright scarlet, white tipped, and a very handsome sort.

Early Scarlet Turnip. A small, round, scarlet, turnip-shaped, small top variety, of quick growth, mild and crisp when young.

Early White Turnip. Like the above, except of a white color.

Olive-Shaped Scarlet. Very early; handsome rose color, oblong in shape; crisp and tender.

White Tipped Scarlet Turnip. An early variety of medium size and excellent flavor, and of very handsome appearance.

Long White Spanish. Roots long; skin white, slightly wrinkled; solid and pungent; somewhat milder than the Black Spanish.

White Strasburg. Though not a new variety, is one that should be more largely grown. The roots are oblong, of a pure white color, very brittle, and of a mild flavor. For summer and fall use this sort will be found very desirable.

White Strasburg

Long Black Spanish.   Chinese Rose Winter.

Long Black Spanish. Black skin, white flesh, very firm, solid, good keeper, grows long and large.

Round Black Spanish. Globe-shaped, black skin, white flesh, very firm; the flavor is piquant and appetizing.

Chinese Rose Winter. Bright rose color; excellent for winter use; white flesh.

Early Long Scarlet Short Top. A main variety for out-door planting for market gardeners or family use; grows six to eight inches long; very crisp and brittle; quick growth; uniformly straight.

California White Winter. A mammoth variety, growing twelve inches long, white fleshed, firm, and of an excellent quality.

Beckert's Chartier. Decidedly distinct in appearance from any Radish in cultivation. The color at the top is crimson, running into pink about the middle, and from thence downward it is pure, waxy white. It will attain a very large size before it becomes unfit for the table.

Earliest Carmine. See Specialties.

Early Long Scarlet.

Rhubarb.

One ounce will sow fifty feet of drill.

Rhubarb succeeds best in deep, rich loam; the richer the soil and the deeper it is stirred the better, as it is scarcely possible to cultivate too deeply or to manure too highly. It is propagated by seeds, or by division of the roots—the later being the usual method. Sow in drills eighteen inches apart, and thin out the plants to nine inches apart in the drills. When the plants are one year old transplant into beds, setting the plants five feet apart each way. Do not cut until the second year, and give a liberal dressing of manure every Fall.

We would advise, for small and family gardens, to procure the roots, which can be set out as desired.

Linnæus. An early and productive variety; skin thin; pulp highly flavored, possessing little acidity; one of the best sorts for family use.

Victoria. Leaves large; skin thicker than above, pulp more acid, but a more productive variety; used largely for market.

You are not in the swim if you do not get a Packet of Perfection Cabbage Lettuce.

Spinach.

One ounce will sow 100 feet of drill; ten pounds required for one acre.

Spinach is very hardy, extremely wholesome, and makes most delicious greens, and is of the easiest culture. Sow in drills one foot apart, and commence thinning out the plants as soon as the leaves are an inch wide. Cut before hot weather, or it will become tough and stringy. For early spring use, the seed should be sown early in the autumn; and the plants protected through the winter by a light covering of leaves or straw.

Round Thick Leaved. Leaves large, thick and fleshy; the variety generally grown for market, and equally good for spring or fall sowing.

Round Leaved Viroflay.

Round Leaved Viroflay. A splendid variety, with leaves long and broad, round, thick and fleshy, dark green. Young plants transplanted into a rich soil will grow to an enormous size.

Prickly or Fall. Best suited for fall planting, as it is the hardiest variety and will withstand the severest weather with only a slight protection of leaves or straw. The seed is prickly, leaves triangular, oblong or arrow-shaped.

Long Standing Spinach.

Long Standing. An improved strain; stands three weeks longer without going to seed than any variety we know of. This valuable property will be appreciated by market gardeners.

Savoy Leaved. A very hardy and productive sort; leaves handsomely curled; a valuable variety for market or family use.

Salsify or Vegetable Oysters.

Salsify.

Sandwich Island Mammoth. Grows uniformly to an extra large size, averaging fully double the size and weight of roots of the old variety. The roots notwithstanding their enormous size, are of very

superior quality and very delicate in flavor; it is such a decided improvement that we are quite sure all market gardeners who once try it will use it exclusively. The Salsify is one of the most delicious and nutritious of vegetables, and should be more generally cultivated for use in winter, when the supply of really good vegetables is so limited.

Long, white, tapering roots, resembling somewhat the small white parsnip, and when cooked, have a flavor similar to oysters. Cultivate same as parsnips.

Large White. The standard variety; tender and very fine.

Scorzonera or Black Oyster Plant. Similar to the White Salsify, save in color.

Squashes.

Squashes should be planted in a warm, light, rich soil, after the weather has become settled and warm. Plant in well-manured hills, in the same manner as Cucumbers and Melons—the bush varieties three or four feet apart each way, and the running kinds six or eight feet. Eight to ten seeds should be sown in each hill, thinning out, after they have attained their rough leaves and danger from bugs is over eaving three or four of the strongest plants per hill.

Early Yellow Bush Scallop. An early, flat, scallop-shaped variety; color yellow; flesh pale yellow and well flavored; very productive; used when young and tender.

Early White Bush Scallop. Similar to the preceding, except in color, which is white.

Summer Crookneck. One of the best; very early and productive. It is small, crooked neck, covered with warty excrescences; color bright yellow; shell very hard when ripe.

Boston Marrow.

Boston Marrow. A fall and winter variety very popular. Of oval form; skin thin; when ripe, bright orange mottled with light cream color; flesh rich salmon yellow, dry, fine grained, and for sweetness and excellence, unsurpassed.

Cocoanut. Very prolific, producing six to twelve on a vine. Outer color light yellow, the bottom of the fruit being of a rich green hue. Quality first-class.

Hubbard Squash.

Hubbard. This is a superior variety, and the best winter squash known; flesh bright orange yellow, fine grained, very dry sweet and rich flavored; keeps perfectly good throughout the winter; boils and bakes exceedingly dry, and is esteemed by many to be as good baked as the sweet potato.

We have a Fine Stock of Vegetable Plants—See the List of Varieties and Prices.

Winter Crookneck. The most certain to produce a crop, the strong growing vines suffering less from insects than those of the other sorts. Color varying from dark green to clear yellow. Flesh variable, effected by soil and weather. If kept from cold and damp, they will keep the entire year.

Winter Crookneck.

Improved American Turban. (Essex Hybrid.) Developed by selection and crossing from the old American Turban, being of a richer color, having a hard shell and in its remarkable keeping qualities. It is of medium size, and the skin is a rich orange red. Flesh deep, rich color, very thick, and of excellent quality. The earliest of the winter varieties

Imp. Am. Turban.

Pine Apple. Vigorous and hardy, coming into bearing late in the season, and then producing fruit at nearly every joint, making it one of the most productive kinds grown. Skin creamy white; flesh very thick and with a peculiar flavor, on which account it is much liked for pies; it is also used green like the summer squashes, and baked or stewed like the winter kinds.

Pine Apple.

Perfect Gem. Vine coming into bearing late, but very productive. Fruit four inches in diameter, nearly round, ribbed white; flesh yellowish white and cooking, very sweet and well flavored. This is the best of the intermediate kinds, and many think it fully equal to the winter sorts.

Perfect Gem.

Mammoth Chili.

Mammoth Chili. Rich orange-yellow, flesh thick, and of good quality for making pies. They grow to an enormous size, specimens frequently attaining the weight of 200 lbs. Valuable sort for feeding stock.

Sibley. See Specialties.

Brazil Sugar. See Specialties.

Turnip.

One ounce for 150 feet of drill; or two pounds for an acre.

Turnips succeed best in highly enriched sandy or gravelly soil. Sow in drills 12 to 18 inches apart, cover half inch, and when plants are well up thin to 5 or 6 inches apart, for early kind, and Rutabaga and large sorts to 10 inches. Best always to sow just before a rain, or water well, as success depends upon quick germination and rapid growths.

Extra Early Purple Top Munich. This new variety is two weeks earlier than any other in cultivation. It is of a handsome appearance, somewhat flattened, white, with purplish top; flesh snow white, fine grained, and most delicate.

Extra Early Purple Top Munich.

Red Top Strap Leaf. Rapid grower and of mild flavor; the most popular variety for early use, either for the table or stock.

Early White Egg. A new egg-shaped variety, for Spring or Fall Sowing, flesh white, firm, fine grained, mild and sweet; an extra keeper, in every respect a first-classed table and market sort.

Yellow Globe. One of the best for a general crop; flesh firm and sweet; grows to a large size; excellent for table use or feeding stock, and keeps well until Spring.

Golden Ball. A rapid grower of excellent flavor; globe-shaped; bright yellow color; good keeper and a superior table variety.

Early White Flat Dutch.

An early, white fleshed; strap-leaved variety, usually sown for early Summer use in the Spring; of quick growth, mild flavor and excellent quality; also grown for a Fall crop.

Early White Flat Dutch.

Yellow Aberdeen, or Scotch. Hardy, productive, and a good keeper; globe shaped; yellow; flesh firm; good for table use or feeding stock.

Long White, or Cow Horn. Grows very quickly partly above ground; very productive; flesh white, fine grained and sweet; of excellent quality.

Sweet Russian or White Ruta Baga. This is a most excellent kind, either for table or stock. It grows to a very large size, flesh white, solid, firm texture, sweet and rich, keeps well.

Skirving's Purple Top. Grows to a large size, yellow flesh, solid fine flavored, good keeper; good table or stock variety.

Early White Egg.   Long White, or Cow Horn.

Early Snowball. Small, solid, sweet and crisp, and also of remarkably quick growth.

Early White Stone. An English garden variety; round in shape; firm, of quick growth, medium size; very desirable.

Improved Purple Top Yellow Ruta Baga. The best variety of Swedish Turnip in cultivation; hardy and productive; flesh yellow, of solid texture; sweet and well flavored, shape slightly oblong, terminating abruptly, with no side or bottom roots; color, deep purple above, and bright yellow under the ground; leaves small, light green, with little or no neck, the most perfect in form, the richest in flavor, and the best in every respect.

Laing's Improved. One of the large sorts; productive and good size; sweet, firm, very hardy; excellent for table or stock feeding.

Sweet German. This variety is very popular in many sections. It partakes largely of the nature of the Ruta Baga, and should be sown a month earlier than the flat turnips. The flesh is white, hard, firm and sweet, and it keeps nearly as well as the Ruta Baga. Highly recommended for winter and spring use.

Tomatoes.

One ounce for 1,500 plants; ¼ lb. (to transplant) for an acre.

This vegetable is now one of the most important of garden and market products. The seed may be sown in a hot-bed, greenhouse, or where a temperature of not less than 60 degrees is kept. When the plants are about two inches high they should be set out in boxes three inches deep. When safe from frost, plants may be set in the open ground. They are planted for early crops on light, sandy soil, at a distance of 4 feet apart, in hills. Water freely at the time of transplanting, and shelter from the sun a few days until the plants are established. Tomatoes will always produce greater crops and be of better flavor when staked up or when trained against walls or fences.

General Grant. A very early sort; fair sized, but not as smooth as the later sorts.

Hathaway's Excelsior. Vines large and vigorous, fruit medium size, smooth, apple-shaped; dark, rich color when ripe; quite early, a favorite Southern sort.

Early Conqueror. A well-known standard sort, medium in size, irregular in shape, flattened and slightly corrugated; color scarlet-crimson.

Livingston's Perfection. Very large and early; blood-red; perfectly smooth; thick meat; few seeds; a good shipping sort; really one of the best of all the Livingston tomatoes, of which we now have so many strains.

Sacramento Favorite.

Sacramento Favorite. Is one of the very best; large size, smooth as an apple, firm and handsome; bright red and fine for market and shipping. See specialties.

Optimus Tomato. A variety that should be placed in the front rank among early tomatoes. In all trials it is found remarkably early, in that respect being fully the equal of or superior to the "Mikado." Optimus is a very smooth variety, uniform in size and shape, ripens evenly, and is of a bright red-color. The flesh is scarlet crimson, very solid, of good flavor and entirely free from core. The fruit is usually produced in clusters of five.

Mayflower. Very early and productive; very large; splendid shape; perfectly smooth; bright red, and ripens uniformly to the stem.

Mikado.

The Mikado. One of the earliest and of the largest size. Perfectly solid and of unsurpassed quality. The Mikado differs from all tomatoes in its immense size. They are produced in great clusters and are perfectly solid, generally smooth, but occasionally irregular. The color is purplish red, like that of the Acme; while it has all the solidity that characterizes the Trophy. It is not unusual for single fruit to weigh from one pound to one and a half pounds each. Its earliness is a remarkable feature in so large a tomato, and adds to its value. Whether for slicing or for cooking purposes the quality is excellent. The foliage of Mikado Tomato will show the distinctiveness of the variety.

Livingston's Favorite. One of the most perfect shaped tomatoes grown; very smooth; darker than the Perfection; ripens evenly and quite early; is noted for its shipping qualities.

Dwarf Champion Tomato. This is one of the most distinct and valuable Tomatoes of recent introduction. It resembles no other variety, being of dwarf, stiff habit, so much as to scarcely need any support. The foliage has a peculiar corrugated appearance, and is of a very dark green color. It is very early and wonderfully prolific. The fruit is a rich color and, while of medium size, is perfectly round and smooth, and contains so few seeds that it is really more "meaty" than many other Tomatoes twice the size.

Acme. Very productive; form round; very smooth and uniform; delicious in flavor, possesses good shipping qualities.

Paragon. Medium size; color dark red; ripens evenly; very solid largely used for canning.

Acme.

Cardinal. This is a beautiful tomato, being of a brilliant cardinal red; very glossy looking when ripe; the flesh of the same brilliant color; ripens evenly through, having no hard green core, like many others; in shape it is round, smooth and solid.

Cardinal.

Early, Large, Smooth Red. Standard market variety; skin bright scarlet; good size, good quality, ripens early.

Yellow Plum. Bright yellow in color; round and regular in shape; useful for preserves.

Livingston's Beauty. It is extra early, growing in clusters of four or five; glossy crimson, partaking of some of the characteristics of the Acme; solid; retains its color and size until late in the season.

Trophy Selected. One of the best standard varieties; fruit large, smooth, bright red, solid and good flavor; unsurpassed for all purposes.

Strawberry, or Ground Cherry This fruit has a pleasant strawberry-like flavor; grows enclosed in a husk and is much liked by many for preserves and sauce, also for pies. They grow well in almost any dry soil, are easier raised than the Tomato and are prolific bearers. They are excellent when dried in sugar, and will keep in the husk nearly all winter if stored in a cool dry place. No one after raising them once, will ever make a garden again without reserving a small space for a few of these plants.

POT, SWEET, AND MEDICAL HERBS.

Herbs, in general, delight in rich, mellow soil. Sow the seeds early in the spring in shallow drills, 1 foot apart; when up a few inches, thin out at proper distances, or transplant. No garden is complete without a few sweet, aromatic or medical herbs for flavoring soups, meats, etc., and care should be taken to harvest them properly. This should be done on a dry day just before they come into full blossom; then dry quickly in the shade, pack close in dry boxes or vessels, so as to exclude the air.

Anise. Used for garnishing and flavoring.
Angelica, Garden. Supposed to have medical virtues.
Arnica. Has medical qualities.
Balm. Used for tea or balm wine; height, 1 foot.
Belladonna. Used in medicine.
Basil, Sweet. Used for soups, stews and sauces; 1 foot.
Bene. Used medicinally; 18 inches.
Caraway. For confectionery and medicine, also flavoring; 2 feet.
Catnip. Has medical qualities.
Coriander. Grown for its seed, also for garnishing; 2 feet.
Cumin. Good for pigeons, etc.
Dill. The leaves are used in soups, sauces and pickles; also the seed for flavoring; 3 feet.
Elecampane. Has tonic expectorant qualities.
Fennel Sweet. The leaves are ornamental; when boiled they are used in fish sauces; 6 feet.

Horehound. Used medicinally; 2 feet.
Lavender. An aromatic medicinal herb; 2 feet.
Marigold, Pot. For flavoring and medicine; 1 foot.
Opium Poppy. (White Seeded.) Used medicinally; 3 feet.
Pennyroyal. Has medicinal qualities.
Rosemary. Yields an aromatic oil and water, and largely in use.
Rue. Said to have medicinal qualities.
Saffron. Used in medicine and also in dyeing.
Sage. The tender leaves and tops are used in sausages, stuffing and sauces; 18 inches.
Savory, Summer. For seasoning purposes; 1 foot.
Savory, Winter. For same use as the above.
Tansy. For medicinal use; 3 feet.
Thyme, Broad-leaved English. Used as a seasoning.
Wormwood. Used medicinally, beneficial for poultry, and should be planted in poultry yards.

SEEDS FOR FAMILY GARDENS.

These are the choicest and best varieties for small gardens and home use.
30 packets (sold for $1 50) for $1 00, consisting of

2	best kinds	Snap Beans.	2	best kinds	Cabbage.
2	"	Beets	1	"	Cauliflower.
2	"	Sweet Corn.	1	"	Celery.
1	"	Carrot.	2	"	Cucumbers.
2	"	Lettuce.	1	"	Muskmelon.
1	"	Onions.	1	"	Watermelon.
1	"	Pepper.	1	"	Pumpkins.
1	"	Parsnip.	1	"	Squash.
2	"	Peas.	3	"	Radish.
1	"	Tomatoes.	2	"	Turnips.

All for the small price of One Dollar.

LAWN GRASS, CLOVER AND OTHER FIELD SEEDS.

These we keep in very large stock, and of unsurpassed quality. We import heavily of Eastern and European varieties, and make a specialty of Alfalfa and other California grown Seed.

A Beautiful Lawn

Is the first thing that attracts one's attention on approaching a residence, consequently this is the first thing to look after, either in arranging a new place or an old established home. A beautiful grass plot is within the reach of every one, and the arrangement of the trees and flowers should be an after consideration, according to the tastes and means of the owner, but when possible, combine both,

How to Secure a Beautiful Lawn.

In establishing a new lawn great care should be taken in preparing the ground before sowing the seed. If at all inclined to be wet, the plot designed for the lawn should be most thoroughly underdrained and carefully graded, and the entire surface made rich and as fine as possible. Bone dust and super-phosphate are the most suitable for enriching a lawn, as they are free from the seed of the obnoxious weeds, which cannot be said of stable manure, unless it has been thoroughly composted with the utmost possible care. The ground being ready, sow the seed as early in the Spring as convenient, the earlier the better, if the soil is in good condition. No one kind of grass will make a lawn that will keep beautifully green all through the season, but a mixture of several is essential, as some varieties are most luxuriant in Spring, others in Summer, and again others in the Autumn, and a proper combination of these various sorts is required to create and maintain a perfect carpet-like lawn. Our Fancy Mixture is most admirably adapted to this purpose, and as near perfection as possible to attain.

All lawns will be greatly benefited, if as early in Spring as the weather will permit, they are carefully raked so as to remove the dead grass and leaves that may be on them; then sprinkle it with our Fancy Mixture, which will renew the thin places and spots that have been killed by the Winter or other causes then give it a thorough rolling with a heavy roller.

LAWN GRASS Fancy Mixture Is composed of a variety of fine dwarf, close growing grasses, which on properly prepared, finely pulverized ground, will produce a neat, velvety lawn and permanent sod. 80 lbs. to the acre.

KENTUCKY BLUE GRASS Fancy Lawn Is the finest and best of all grasses when used separately or in mixtures for general lawn purposes; for this purpose 80 to 100 pounds are necessary. Crop short.

SWEET-SCENTED VERNAL. One of the earliest Grasses in Spring and latest in Autumn and more fragrant than any other grass. Valuable to mix in pastures with other grasses on account of its earliness, and it exhales a delightful fragrance when in bloom. About 30 pounds to the acre. 50 cts. lb.

Kentucky Blue Grass

ITALIAN RYE GRASS Is more of an annual, and is also good in mixtures for the lawn or for hay crop. It is of quick growth and valuable for sheep pasturage. 15 cts. per lb.

ORCHARD GRASS or COCK'S FOOT. One of the most valuable grasses on account of its quick growth and valuable aftermath. It is ready for grazing two weeks sooner than most grasses, and when fed off is again ready for grazing in a week, and will continue green when other grasses are withered by dry weather. It is palatable and nutritious, and stock eat it greedily when green. It has a tendency to grow in tufts, and so does better if sown with clovers, and as it ripens at the same time, the mixed hay is of the best quality. For grazing, it has no equal, and should be used more than it is. When sown alone, 25 lbs. per acre; if sown with clover, half that amount. It is perennial, and will last for years. 20 cts. per lb.

WATER MEADOW GRASS *(Poa aquatica)*. This is an excellent pasture grass for very wet situations. Sow twenty pounds to the acre. 40 cts. per lb.

ROUGH STALKED MEADOW GRASS *(Poa trivialis)*. This is one of the most valuable of grasses for moist, rich soils and sheltered situations. Sow twenty pounds to the acre. Per lb. 30 cts.

ENGLISH, or AUSTRALIAN RYE GRASS is a perennial, much like the English Blue Grass and is very valuable for either lawns, pasturage or for hay; and well adapted for moist land. Sow for lawns 60 pounds, hay 30 pounds per acre. 15 cts. per lb.

PERENNIAL RYE GRASS. This is like the above variety, except that it has a finer leaf and is better adapted for lawns, although it makes a fine pasture. Sow 50 pounds to the acre. Price per pound, 15c. Per 100 lbs, $11.00.

WOOD MEADOW GRASS Grows from one and a half to two feet high; has a perennial creeping root, and an erect, slender, smooth stem. Its chief value is in that it will produce a good crop of hay in moist, shady situations, where it frequently grows quite tall. Cattle are fond of it; it is succulent and nutritious, and is perhaps the best variety for sowing in orchards, under trees, and shaded situations, either for hay or pasturage, and for parks and pleasure grounds. About 25 pounds per acre 40 cts. per lb.

JOHNSON GRASS. This is one of the most valuable forage plants, very popular in the Southern States, and will come into universal use in all parts of the United States when known. It is perennial, a rapid grower, very nutritious, being eagerly devoured by all kinds of stock. Comes early in spring, grows until the frost cuts it down in the fall, stands the drought better than any grass, and having long cane-like roots, which penetrate the soil for moisture; superior both as a grazing and hay grass. 30 pounds per acre. 20 cts. per lb.

MEADOW FOXTAIL. A valuable pasture grass of rapid growth and much relished by all kinds of stock. Adapted for rich, moist soils. Sow 20 pounds per acre. 40 cts. per lb.

BROMUS or RESCUE GRASS. This grass is recommended for its drouth resisting-quality. Will thrive on any soil where it is not too wet. Sow 35 pounds per acre. 40 cts. per lb.

TALL MEADOW OAT-GRASS. This grass is early and very luxuriant. It makes fine pasturage and good hay. Can be cut often. It is also valuable to plough under for soiling. Sow 30 to 40 pounds per acre. 30 cts. per lb.

MEADOW, or WOOLLY SOFT GRASS (Holcus Lanatus.) Has the merit of easy culture, and accommodates itself to all descriptions of soil, from the richest to the poorest. Sow 30 lbs. per acre. Weight, 8 pounds per bushel. 30 cts. per lb.

MEADOW FESCUE TRUE ENGLISH BLUE GRASS (Festuca pratensis)—One of the most valuable pasture grasses, its long and tender leaves are much relished by stock of all kinds. In some Southern States it is called RANDALL GRASS, sometimes EVERGREEN GRASS. Sow in spring or fall, at the rate of thirty to forty pounds per acre. 20c. per lb.

CRESTED DOGSTAIL GRASS. This grass may be sown on lawns and other places to be kept under by the scythe. The roots penetrate deeply, and remain longer green than any other variety. Sow twenty to twenty-four pounds to the acre, 50c. per lb.

HARD FESCUE Is also noted for its drouth-resisting quality, and well adapted for lawn mixture and valuable for sheep pasture. Sow thirty pounds to the acre. 25c. per lb.

BERMUDA GRASS. The roots of this grass are very tenacious of life, outrooting other vegetation. It grows in almost any soil and spreads rapidly, making a good pasturage. The seed is hard to save and is worth $2.50 per pound. The roots can be furnished for $2.00 per barley sack or $3.00 per barrel. Cut up into short lengths and sown broadcast and cover with a roller. One barrel will thus plant an acre.

EGYPTIAN, OR PEARL MILLET. Produces an enormous amount of green feed. It can be cut repeatedly, growing very rapidly after cutting, and is equal to Sweet Corn for feed. Sow in drills two or three feet apart; four pounds will sow an acre. 30c. per lb.

HERD, RED TOP GRASS (or BENT GRASS) Is most largely used for wet lands, but does well in almost any soil, moist or dry. It makes good hay or pasture and is much used in mixture with timothy and clover. Sow 30 pounds per acre. 15 cts. per lb.

TIMOTHY Is very largely grown for hay crop in northern climates, and is fine when sown with Red Top and Clover. Sow 15 pounds per acre. 10 cts. per lb.

Herd, Red Top Grass.

MESQUIT GRASS Is very desirable for dry land. It resists the drought well and makes a good crop for hay or pasturage. Sow 30 pounds per acre. 15 cts. per lb.

SHEEP FESCUE GRASS (Festuca ovina)— This variety grows naturally on light, dry sandy soil, and on elevated mountain pastures. Timothy Sow twenty-five to thirty pounds to the acre. 20c. per lb.

COMMON MILLET Can be sown broadcast in the Spring of the year for hay; forty pounds per acre. If for seed, sown in drills twenty pounds to the acre. It produces largely as an annual early crop. 10c. per lb.

GERMAN or GOLDEN MILLET. Is not quite as early as the above, but yields more largely. 10c. per lb.

HUNGARIAN GRASS Is a very valuable forage plant for light dry soils. It withstands drouth and remains green when most vegetation is parched. Sow and cultivate as for Millet, 10c. per lb.

WHITE MILLO MAIZE, OR BRANCHING DHOURA, Of South American origin. Valuable as a forage plant and for its grain, having great capacity to stand drought. It can be cut and fed at any stage, or cured when heading out, for fodder. It bears grain in erect full heads, and is equal to corn for feeding all sorts of stock; also makes excellent meal. It requires all summer to mature seed. Plant three to five seeds in a hill eighteen inches apart, four foot rows, and thin to two plants and cultivate as corn. It shoots out greatly and makes a great amount of foliage. Three to five pounds per acre. Can be cut for green feed several times a season. 25c. per lb.

YELLOW MILLO MAIZE, OR YELLOW BRANCHING DHOURA. Tall, nine to twelve feet stooling from the ground like the White Millo Maize. The seed head grows to great size on good land. These heads are set close and solid, with a large plump grain, double the size of White Millo, and of deep, golden yellow color. The cultivation is like Corn. 10c. per lb.

AMBER CANE (SORGHUM.) Is the earliest variety, and being rich in saccharine matter is grown for making sugar and syrup. Is also a fine forage plant and in large demand for spring planting. 10c. per lb.

EGYPTIAN CORN (White and Red Varieties.) Both produce an immense crop of both seed and stalks for forage to the acre and mature without rain. The Red is more cultivated, and perhaps the earliest. The seed is quite valuable to feed stock or poultry. 5c. per lb.

KAFFIR CORN. A variety of Sorghum, cultivated for both forage and grain, growing from 4½ to 6 feet high, is stocky and erect, and has wide foliage. Kaffir Corn has the quality common to all Sorghums of resisting drought, and in this fact is to be found its peculiar value. It has yielded paying crops of grain and forage even in dry seasons, when corn has utterly failed. Sow in rows three feet apart, five to six pounds to the acre. 25c. per lb.

CLOVER SEEDS.

There are no plants so valuable for fertilizers as the Clovers. They have the faculty of absorbing nitrogen from the air, and also of rendering available much of the inert plant food of the soil. Their long, powerful tap roots penetrate to a great depth, loosen the soil, admit air, and by their decay add immensely to the fertility of the soil. The seed may be sown in fall or spring; which is the best season will depend upon local climats, and method of culture. In any case, it should be evenly distributed on a mellow, well prepared soil. Plaster will increase the growth remarkably, and should be sown broadcast the season following the seeding.

RED CLOVER. Two varieties—large and medium. Both succeed well in California, especially in our bottom lands and deep soils; 25 pounds to the acre.

WHITE DUTCH CLOVER. Grows low, spreading and very fragrant, and is most excellent for lawns and lawn mixture; 10 pounds to the acre.

CRIMSON TREFOIL, OR SCARLET CLOVER. Grows about one foot high, dark roots, long leaves and blossoms of deep red. It makes good hay and will give four or five cuttings each season. Sow 15 pounds to the acre.

Red Clover.

ALSIKE, OR SWEDISH CLOVER. This variety is fast gaining great popularity. It is the most hardy of all the clovers; perennial. On rich, moist soils it yields an enormous quantity of hay or pasture, and may be cut several times in a season, but its greatest value is for sowing with other clovers and grasses, as it forms a thick bottom, and greatly increases the yield of hay, and cattle prefer it to any other forage. The heads are globular, very sweet and fragrant, and much liked by bees, who obtain a large amount of honey from them. Sow in spring or fall, at the rate of 10 pounds per acre, where used alone.

ALFALFA. Is cultivated above all other clover in California. It produces enormous crops, and is cut many times in the season for hay. It roots deeply, keeping fresh and green through our long dry season, and is the most valuable and profitable of all crops for abundance of feed. Sow 20 to 25 pounds to the acre. If in the fall sow early enough to get a little root before a frost, it can be sown again in February and Spring months.

Alfalfa.

BOKHARA CLOVER. This is a fall shrubbery plant, growing to a height of four to six feet. It produces an abundance of small white flowers of great fragrance. Sow 10 pounds to the acre. 25c. per lb.

ESPERSETTE. (French Sanfoin.) This plant is of a liguminous character, having many stems two and three feet long. Smooth and tapering, with many long oblate leaflets in pairs, and spikes of variegated crimson flowers. The root is perennial of a hard, woody nature. The plant flowers early and can be repeatedly cut, thus furnishing a great abundance of most nutritious food through the long dry and heated seasons, and requiring no irrigation. Stock will eat it with impunity, without danger of bloat as in alfalfa. The seed and seed pods are said to be more nutritious than oats. The plant does best in calcareous and gravelly soils, and elevated slopes and arid regions, where other vegetation fails. It will not succeed in wet or low lands where there is no drainage. From 50 to 75 pounds are required for an acre.

MELILOTUS. This variety of clover grows on the banks of streams and among cobbles, gravel, slickens and sand. It yields an immense amount of feed for stock, who are very fond of it. The plant attains a height of 10 to 12 feet, keeping green the entire season, producing seed the second year and maturing in October. Price $12 50 per 100 lbs.

TEXAS BLUE GRASS. — "The Texas Blue Grass grows on the roadside, by fences and hedges; shade does not hurt it any more than Orchard Grass. It stands the hot and dry summers of the south very well, better than any other grass." Seed very scarce and difficult to obtain, and cannot be separated from the chaff. Per oz., 40c.; lb., $5 00.

CAROLINA. OR COW PEA. This makes a valuable fodder and is a good fertilizer. The pods can be harvested or all cut green for fodder, or it can be ploughed under for a fertilizer. $5 00 per 100 lbs.

VETCHES. Are much used for stock feed. Sow and cultivate same as for peas. 10 cts. per lb. $6 per 100 lbs.

LENTILS. Are similar to Vetches, and are cultivated in like manner. 15 cts. per lb. $10 00 per 100 lbs.

BROOM CORN. Many farmers make this a profitable crop, producing on an acre about 500 cwt. of broom and forty bushels of seed; plant and cultivate same as for corn.

BUCKWHEAT. Can be sown late as in July at the rate of 30 to 40 pounds per acre. It should be thrashed as soon as dry, as if left standing in mass it will quickly gather moist.

FIELD BEANS. Should be planted after all danger from frost is past. Does best in rich, dry, light soil. Hoe frequently while the plant is dry, but not otherwise. The Medium White, White Navy and the Bayo, or Chile varieties are mostly used for marketing in this country. Prices on application.

FIELD PEAS. Should be sown on good cultivated soil at the rate of about one hundred and fifty pounds to the acre, in drills or broadcast. They are often sown in less quantity with oats and cut and cured together for hay, or threshed and bound together. Prices on application.

SUNFLOWER SEED. Is growing to be a valuable farm crop. The seed is very desirable for planting, while the leaves make excellent fodder. The plant is said to be an excellent protection from malaria, and should be grown for hedges about the house where this disease prevails.

ALL FIELD SEEDS, GRASS, CLOVER, ETC., when required in large quantity, will be sold at reduced rates, as market is variable, please write for special rates in quantity.

FIELD GRAIN.

☞ *Seed Wheat, Barley, Oats, Corn and other Grains, of every variety, will be furnished to our customers in quantities as may be desired; also Seed Potatoes at Lowest Market Rates. Prices given on application.*

TREE AND SHRUB SEEDS.

HOW TO GROW THEM.

THE growing of trees from seeds is in the case of some varieties a very simple and easy process, requiring but little care or skill on the part of the grower.

Some varieties require special treatment and great care and attention to insure success; others are very difficult to grow, and planters are not very likely to succeed until after having made repeated failures.

One important fact must be kept in view, and that is, IT TAKES TIME FOR THESE SEED TO GERMINATE, in some cases only a few days, in others, several weeks; while quite frequently they will lie dormant the whole season before commencing to grow. It often happens that seeds of a given variety, all taken from the tree at one time, sown together and subjectd to the same treatment will show great irregularity in time of germinating, some coming up in a few days, others not until the next season, and still others not until the season following.

CONIFERS AND EVERGREEN TREE SEEDS should be kept in perfectly dry sand until the time of sowing; if this cannot be done readily, place them in a cool, dry spot, where mice will not eat them. CHESTNUTS and WALNUTS should he planted in the fall, or kept during the winter in sand or moss; they shrivel up by too long exposure to the air, and many of them lose their power of vegetating entirely APPLE, PEAR, QUINCE SEED, CHERRY PITS, PEACH PITS, also those with hard shells like the LOCUST, MAGNOLIAS, etc., should be placed in boxes with sand and exposed to frost before planting, otherwise they may not vegetate until a second year, but if too late in the spring to expose them to the action of the frost, they may be put into a vessel of hot water for an hour or so before planting. The seeds of DECIDUOUS TREES and SHRUBS, with few exceptions, can be planted from the end of March to the middle of May with success.

The soil should be deep, mellow and rich; if not so, make it so by deep spading and thoroughly pulverizing the ground. If not rich, apply a good liberal dressing of any old, well decomposed manure; mix thoroughly with the soil and raked down all smooth and level, and your seed-bed is ready. Now draw a line across one side of the plant, and with the hoe make a shallow trench from a half to one inch deep, according to the size of the seed to be sown; make the trench about six inches wide, scatter the seeds over the bottom, but not too thickly, then draw the soil back and cover to the depth of about the thickness of the seeds as evenly as possible, then press the beds gently with the back of the spade to make firm the earth around the seeds.

Great care must be taken not to give too much water, as the young plants imbibe moisture very easily. Water with a fine hose, but never so that the ground becomes soggy. Some shade must be used to protect the young plants from the hot, drying sun and winds, and also to keep the birds from destroying them.

The trenches or drills are to be two feet apart, so that the hoe or garden cultivator can be employed in cultivation. Keep the soil loose between the rows, and keep them well clear of the weeds. Seeds of the rarer sorts may be sown in cold-frames or in boxes; if in cold-frame, the sashes should be shaded and the frame raised at the corner three or four inches to allow the air to circulate freely.

Allow the young plants to remain from one to two years before transplanting.

CALIFORNIA TREE AND SHRUB SEEDS.

Abies Douglasii. Douglass Spruce. A very large timber tree, 200 to 300 feet high, of pyramidal shape. Found throughout the Rocky Mountains, from Oregon to Mexico. Very hardy. Oz. 50c.; lb., $5 00.

Abies Mertensiana. Tsuga M., Hemlock Spruce. A very large tree, 150 to 200 feet high, with rather thick, red-brown bark. Very hardy, ranging from California far into Alaska. Oz., 60c.; lb., $6 00.

Abies Menzeisii. Picea Sitchensis. Peculiar to the Northern Coast, found mostly in wet, sandy soil near the mouth of streams; the tallest spruce known; an excellent timber tree; pyramidal form. Very hardy. Oz. 60c.; lb., $6 00.

Cupressus Goveniana. Goven's Cypress. Thirty to forty feet high; very ornamental; found in the coast ranges of Monterey. Oz., 60c.; lb., $6 00.

Cupressus Macrocarpa. Monterey Cypress. A tree forty to sixty feet high, with rough bark, spreading, horizontal branches, with rich, green foliage; very ornamental for lawns or parks; also used extensively for hedges. Oz., 25c., lb., $2 50.

Cupressus McNabiana. McNab's Cypress. A small tree, six to ten feet high, found about Mt. Shasta, at 5,000 feet altitude. The leaves are small, and of a deep green. Oz. 40c.; lb., $4 00.

Cupressus Lawsoniana. Lawson's Cypress. A handsome tree, found in moist ground in the Shasta Mountains, and in the Coast ranges of Oregon. The wood is white, fragrant, fine and close grained, free from knots, easily worked, and very durable; also known as Oregon Cedar, White Cedar and Ginger Pine. Oz., 40c., lb., $4 00.

Cupressus Italian. A very erect, close-growing tree; fine for entrances and arches. Oz., 25c.; lb., $3 00.

Cupressus Guadalupensis Blue Cypress. A new fast-growing variety with beautiful bluish foliage; very ornamental for lawns, parks and cemeteries. Oz., 25c.

Libocedrus decurrens. Thuya Craigiana. Found in the coast ranges, from Oregon to San Diego; grows from 100 to 150 feet high; fine, hardy timber tree; known as the White Cedar of California. Oz., 30c., lb., $3 00.

Madrone. A beautiful native tree of California; the foliage is of a deep green, and feathery; it attains a considerable size, flowers white. Oz., 25c.

Picea amabilis Silver Fir. Tall, symmetrical, valuable timber tree. Oz., 50c.; lb., $5 00.

Picea grandis. Balsam Fir. Grows 200 to 300 feet high, four to six feet in diameter; grows in rich, moist soils; valuable timber tree. Oz., 50c.; lb., $3 00.

Picea nobilis. California Red Fir. A magnificent tree, with thick, brown bark, making fine timber; forms large forests about the base of Mt. Shasta; timber said to be better than that of other firs. Oz., 50c.; lb., $5 00.

Picea Magnifica. 200 to 250 feet high. The Red Fir of the Sierras, found at an altitude of 7,000 feet. Very hardy. Oz., 60c.; lb., $6 00.

Picea Concolor. Abies lasiocarpa. A very ornamental tree; 100 to 200 feet high; very common throughout the Sierras, ranging into Oregon; also found in Arizona, Utah and Colorado. Oz., 50c.; lb., $5 00.

Pinus Benthamiana. A magnificent tree; grows from 200 to 300 feet high; fine timber. Very hardy. Oz., 50c.; lb., $5 00.

Pinus Coulteri. Great Coned Pine. Found in the coast ranges from Mt. Diablo to the southern part of this State. Oz., 35c.; lb., $3 50.

Pinus contorta. A low tree, five to fifteen feet high, found on the wet, sandy coast of the Pacific, from Mendocino to Alaska. Very hardy. Oz., 70c.; lb., $5 00.

Pinus Fremontiana. Pinus monophylla. A small tree, twenty to twenty-five feet high; frequent in the coast ranges in Nevada, Arizona and Utah; well known as the Nut Pine. Oz., 30c.; lb., $3 00.

Pinus insignis. Monterey Pine. A very ornamental tree for parks or lawns; grows from sixty to seventy feet high, of rapid growth, and has beautiful, green foliage. Oz.; 25c., lb, $2 50.

Pinus Jeffreyi. A magnificent tree, from 100 to 200 feet high; usually found on our mountains at an elevation of 5,000 feet, ranging from California to Oregon. Very hardy. Oz., 85c.; lb., $3 50.

Pinus Lambertiana. Sugar pine. A hardy tree of gigantic dimensions, from 250 to 300 feet high, and from fifteen to twenty feet thick, with light brown, smoothish bark; found on both slopes of the Sierras. The wood is like that of the White Pine. Oz., 30c.; lb., $3 00.

Pinus monticola. From sixty to eighty feet high, and about three feet in diameter at the base. Found at an altitude from 7,000 to 10,000 feet, known as the white pine of California, and of the North. Oz., 60c.; lb., $6 00.

Pinus Parryana. A small tree, twenty to thirty feet high, found in the vicinity of San Diego, at an altitude of 2,000 feet. Oz., 50c.; lb., $5 00.

Pinus ponderosa. Yellow Pine. One of the largest pines known, 200 to 300 feet high, and twelve to fifteen feet in diameter, with very thick red-brown bark. Found in the Coast Range. Very hardy Oz., 40c.; lb., $4 00.

Pinus tuberculata. California Scrub Pine. A small crooked tree, often found full of cones when only two or three feet high. Oz. 50c.; lb., $5 00.

Sequoia gigantea. Wellingtonia gigantea. The mammoth tree of California. This is the largest tree known to exist on the American continent, grows over 300 feet high. The bark is from one to two feet thick. Many of these California trees are over 90 feet in circumference. Oz., 60c., lb., $6 00.

Sequoia sempervirens. Known as the Redwood of California. The most valuable timber of the California forests. From 200 to 250 feet high, and from eight to twelve feet in diameter. The wood is of a rich, brownish red, light, but strong and durable, making excellent timber. Hardy. Oz., 50c., lb. $3 00.

Thuya gigantea. Giant Arbor Vitae. A tall graceful tree, 200 to 250 feet high, three to twelve feet thick, pyramidal form, with spreading and somewhat drooping branches, frequent in the coast ranges of Oregon. The wood is soft, fine-grained, and of light color. Oz., 60c., lb., $6 00.

Torreya Californica California Nutmeg. Found in the mountain districts. Grows to the hight of 60 feet the wood is light-colored, close-grained and small branches being reddish. Oz., 25., lb., $2 00.

Arctostaphylos glauca. Great berried Manzanita.. Oz., 50c., lb $2 00.

Mountain Laurel. Spice Tree. A handsome shrub or tree twenty to seventy feet high, the timber very handsome and valuable for ornamental wainscoting and finishing. Oz., 25c., lb., $2 00.

Negundo Californicum, Box Elder. Usually a small tree, sometimes reaching a height of seventy feet. Oz., 25c., lb., $1 50.

Acer Macropyllum. Maple. A tree of 50 to 90 feet high, from coast ranges in California. The wood is white, hard, and takes a fine polish. Oz., 25c., lb., $2 50.

Cornus Nuttallii. Dogwood. A small showy tree, flowering in May, followed by large clusters of double berries, resembling the eastern Cornus. Wood close-grained and very hard. Oz., 50c., lb., $5 00.

Azalea occidentalis. Charming California Azalea, the ornament of the wooded districts. Flowers two to three inches long, white, pink variegated. Pkt. 25c.

Yellow or Black Locust. Robinia pseudo acacia. This variety is noted for its rapid growth of hard and durable timber. It is hardy and succeeds well in most soils and climates. Oz., 10c.; lb., 60c.

Honey Locust. Gloditschia Triacanthos. This is a large and handsome tree. The trunk and branches generally beset with long and formidable spines, on which account it has been employed as a hedge. The wood is heavy and affords excellent fuel. Oz., 10c.; lb., 60c.

Osage Orange. Maclura Aurantiaca. One of the most valuable of hedge plants. The plants will also grow into fine trees, and the wood endures for centuries. Lb., 50c.

Buckthorn. Rhamnus catharticus. This makes a strong thorny hedge, adapted to the North and Middle States. Oz., 20c., lb., $2 00.

AUSTRALIAN TREE AND SHRUB SEEDS.

Eucalyptus globulous. Blue Gum. A very rapid growing tree, making valuable timber; height 200 feet. Oz., 50c.; lb., $5 00.

E. Rostrata. Red Gum. Oz , 50c.; lb., $6 00.

***E. bicolor.** Black Box. A valuable timber tree; it is equal to the best Ironbark for all the purposes for which that wood is used, and is more easily wrought. It is sometimes called "Ironbark," 100 to 150 feet. Oz., 75c.

***E Citriodora.** Lemon-scented Gum. A useful timber. The strong lemon scent which is emitted when the leaves are gently rubbed, is equally powerful and agreeable with that of the lemon-scented Verbena. Oz., 75c.

***E. hemipholia.** Common Box. A hard but useful timber, strong, tough and durable, but will not last sunk in the ground. It is also a first-class fuel for domestic use or other industrial purposes. 100 to 150 feet.

***E longifolia.** Woollybutt. An average sized tree. Fair timber for fencing and building purposes; it is a good fuel for domestic use; very durable. 100 to 120 feet. Oz., 75c.

***E leucoxylon.** Crimson Flowered Encalyptus. This is a very ornamental species of Eucalyptus; having large and very beautiful flowers, color crimson; and as the tree flowers while quite young, it is very desirable as an addition to the shrubbery or flower border. Oz., 75c.

***E obliqua.** Stringybark. The best wood for flooring boards and rafters. It is of very quick growth, inferior fuel, but produces the best charcoal. 120 feet. Oz , 75c.

***E. paniculata.** Common Ironbark. For most purposes is equal to the last species, and is more easily split into shingles or palings, it is as lasting and as good fuel as other Ironbarks; the wood is not so dark in color. 150 feet.

***E paniculata var.. mycrophylla.** Small-leaved Ironbark. The wood of this species is used for fencing and many purposes, the same as the other Ironbarks. But the wood being of a nature much more easy to work. to which the hardness of the other sorts offers an obstacle, first-class fuel. 120 feet. Oz., 75c.

***E. robusta.** Swamp Mahogany. A good lasting timber for house carpentry and many kinds of turnery, but not durable in the ground. 150 feet. Oz., 75c.

***E. siderophloia.** Dark or broad-leaved Ironbark. The most valuable wood for piles, girders, railway sleepers; and for every purpose in which strength and durability are required. This specie is the strongest of all Australian timbers, and superior to most as fuel for steam engines, as it throws off more heat, etc. 150 feet. Oz., 75c.

Acacia decurrens. Black Wattle. Oz.. 50c., lb., $5 00

Acacia melanoxylon. Lightwood. Oz., 50c.

Acacia mollissima. Oz. 50c.

***Acacia pyenantha.** Golden Wattle. Oz., 50c., lb., $5 00.

Acacia floribunda. Oz , 50c.

Acacia lopantha. Crested Wattle. Oz., 25c., lb., $2 00.

Dracena indivisa. A very desirable tree for a garden or a lawn, of graceful habit, makes rapid growth, very hardy, native of New Zealand. Oz., 50c., lb., $4 00.

Grevillea robusta. Silk Oak of East Australia. Beautiful fern-like foliage, attains a height of 100 feet, withstands drouth, of rapid growth, and flowers when about twenty feet in height, then it is a sight worth seeing, covered from top to bottom with bright orange scarlet flowers. Pkt. 50c., oz., $2 00.

Pittosporum eugenoides, nigrescens. and undulatum. Valuable evergreens; an ornamental shrub or tree from Southern Australia. Pkt., 25c.; oz., $1 00.

CONIFERS AND EVERGREEN TREE SEED.

Arbor Vitæ, American. Thuja occidentalis. Useful for hedges and wind breaks. Oz., 30c., lb., $3 00.

Chinese Arbor Vitæ. A small, elegant tree, with erect branches, and dense flat, light green foliage, becomes brown in winter. Oz., lb., 25c.; $2 50.

Golden Arbor Vitæ. A variety of the Chinese, nearly spherical in outline, with bright yellow tinged foliage. Beautiful. Oz 50c., lb., $5 00.

Fir Balsam. Balsamea A small evergreen tree of symmetrical growth, and conical form when young. Of rapid growth, with rich, green foliage. Oz., 30c , lb., $3 00.

Fir Silver. A well known evergreen tree, tall symmetrical, very valuable. Oz., 15c., lb., $1 50.

Larch European. Larix Europæa. Valuable for forest planting. Oz.,15c., lb., $1 50.

Magnolia Grandiflora. The most majestic of all American trees, a native of the Southern States perfectly hardy here. Oz., 25c,, lb., $2 50.

Pine, Scotch. Pinus Sylvestris. One of the most valuable of European varieties. It is hardy, of rapid growth, and adapted to a great variety of soil and climate. Oz., 20c., lb., $2 00.

Pine, White, or Weymouth. Pinus Strobus. An old, well known and useful tree. Of gigantic proportions and rapid growth. Oz., 30c. lb., $3 00.

Pepper Tree. Schinus molle. A handsome, ornamental evergreen tree, of graceful habit, light green foliage, and bright scarlet, berries; a desirable tree for parks and lawns. Oz., 25c., lb., $2 00.

Red Cedar. Juniperus Virginiana. Very valuable timber, and fine ornamental tree. It will stand the dry hot winds, and for wind-breaks, as well as for fence posts, the Red Cedar is invaluable, symmetrical in growth and readily shaped with the shears; it is one of the most useful trees. After properly planting, it will stand more neglect than any other evergreen. Oz., 15c., lb., $1 50.

Spruce Hemlock. Canadensis. A known evergreen tree of high latitudes. It is one of the most graceful of spruces, with light and spreading branches almost to the ground. It is a beautiful tree for the lawn and makes a highly ornamental hedge. Oz., 40c., lb., $4 00.

Spruce Norway. Abies Excelsa. A popular variety from Europe. Extensively planted for ornamental purposes, and for timber and wind-breaks. It is easily transplanted or grown from seed and succeeds in a great variety of soils and climate. Oz., 15c.; lb., $1 50.

Brahea Filamamentosa. California Fan Palm, a hardy, vigorous growing plant; foliage very regular, of a bright green, deeply and regularly pinnated, the margins being covered with hair-like filaments, giving them a remarkable appearance. They are beautiful decorative plants in all respects, for in or outdoor use. Oz., 30c., lb, $3 00

FOREST AND DECIDUOUS TREE SEEDS.

Ash-American, White. Fraxinus American Americans. Prefers moist soil, but will grow almost anywhere; wood valuable for handles, in wagon-making, etc.; grows rapidly, one of the best of timbers; best when grown on dry land. Oz., 10c., lb., $1 00.

Ash-European. Fraxinus excelsior. Suitable for warm climates and dry loam soils, wood used in carriage-making. Oz., 10c., lb., $1 00.

Box Elder. Acer Negundo. Thrives on the western plains, grows rapidly, attaining 70 feet in height, excelent for planting along highways, endures drought. Its sap yields sugar. Oz., 10c., lb., $1 00.

Catalpa Hardy. Catalpa Speciosa. An upright and rapid grower, the trees being remarkably straight and tall, so that even in mild climates, where hardiness is no object, the superior habit of growth of this variety is a matter of the utmost importance in its favor. Oz., 10c. lb., $1 00.

Elm-European. Ulmus Campestris. The best Elm for ornamental and for city planting. Oz., 10c., lb., $1 00.

Lime or Linden Silla Europæa. Makes good paper pulp, the inner bark is used for cordage, matting, etc. Oz., 10c., lb , $1 00.

Norway Maple. Acer plantanoides. A well known ornamental tree. Oz., 10c., lb., $1 00.

Sugar Maple. Acer saccharniam. It succeeds well in all soils and locations, making a stout, vigorous, rapid growth of hard wood, most valuable for fuel and highly prized for manufacturing purposes. Oz., 10c., ¼ lb., 30c.; lb., $1 00.

Maple Soft, or Silver leaved. Acer dasycarpum. One of the most beautiful of Maples. Is being extensively planted on account of its extremely rapid growth. Its wood is soft and light, and the branches are often broken by the action of the wind and storm. Oz., 10c., lb., $1 00.

Mulberry White. Morus alba. Oz., 25c., lb., $2 50, **Mulberry Black.** Morus nigra. Oz., 25c., ¼ lb., 75c., lb., $2 50

Mulberry Russian. Valuable for its fruit, and its timber, which makes valuable posts and stakes, being hard elastic, close grained and susceptible of a fine polish. The Mulberry is also used for hedges, and the leaves for food for silk worms. The berries are often more than an inch long, and one-half inch or more in diameter. They are more acid and sprightly than our American Mulberries, and the fruit is prized by the Russians, for dessert, and cooked in various ways, also made into wine. Oz., 40c., lb., $4 00.

Linden Silver or White-leaved European. A vigorous growing tree, of medium size and pyramidal form. It is noticeable among trees by its white appearance. Its handsome form, growth and foliage render it worthy to be classed among the finest of our ornamental trees Oz., 25c., lb., $1 25.

Tree of Heaven. Ailanthus glandulosus. Quite extensively planted in some states, and is noted for its extremely rapid growth. It grows to a large size, and the foliage has a rich tropical appearance. Oz., 10c., lb., $1 00.

Virginia Creeper. American Ivy. Ampelopsis quinquefolia. This native vine is one of the most ornamental of the climbers, and is much cultivated for covering walls and buildings. It is perfectly hardly, and gives a dense mass of brilliant green throughout the summer which in the autumn changes to the richest shades of crimson and purple. Oz , 25c., lb., $2 50.

FRUIT TREE SEEDS.

Apple Pyrus Malus. Apple seeds do not reproduce the same variety. Upon the stock thus used for seed are grafted or budded the varieties desired. The seed can be planted in good soil, any time during the winter, or early in the spring, in rows eighteen inches apart. During their growth they should be well cultivated and kept free from weeds. ¼ lb., 20c.; lb., 50c.

Cherry Mahaleb. Cerasus Mahaleb. The remarks regarding apple seeds are applicable to cherries. This variety is considered the best stock upon which to graft the choicer sorts. ¼ lb., 20c.; lb., 60c.

Cherry Mazzard. Cerasus Communis. The common or ordinary variety of cherry is useful alone for grafting purposes. The stock is hardy, and if properly grafted, fine fruit can be relied on. ¼ lb., 20c.; lb., 50c.

Pear. Pyrus Communis. Sow the seed thickly in drills eighteen inches apart. The soil should be rich—a deep, moist loam is most suitable. The value of the stock depends largely on a rapid and vigorous growth the first season. Oz., 25c.; lb., $2 50.

Plum. Prunus Communis. The directions given for planting apples will also apply to plums, except the pits should be planted farther apart in the row. ¼ lb., 20c., lb., 50c.

Peach. Amygdalis Persica. Peach stocks are raised by planting the stones two or three inches deep. If the stones are cracked they are more sure to grow. The after treatment is about the same as for apples, though budding can be commenced sooner than grafting in apple stocks. Lb., 5c.; 100 lbs., $3 00.

Apricot Pits. Armenia Vulgaris. Planted and cultivated same as peach pits. Lb., 10c.; 100 lbs., $5 00.

Quince. Cydonia Communis. The culture for seed is the same as for apples. Oz., 25c.; lb., $2 50.

Texas Umbrella Tree. This is one of the finest ornamental and attractive trees known. It makes a spreading umbrella shape. Tip of very dense and beautiful foliage, will grow from 20 to 30 feet high. Oz., 80c.; lb., $3 00.

W. R. STRONG COMPANY
GENERAL LIST OF VEGETABLE PLANTS.

Several seasons ago we added to our list of specialties, the growing of vegetable plants; with each season our demand has so increased that we have been obliged to put a larger area under glass for the purpose of forwarding the plants for the benefit of our customers wishing to plant early.

On most of the varieties listed below we have grown our own seeds realizing the importance to our customers of obtaining the very best to be had, many seeds have been greatly improved by saving seed from the finest specimens of vegetables. We can safely say our plant establishment is the most complete on the coast.

Early Winningstadt Cabbage.   Perfection Tomato.   Egg Plant.   Favorite Tomato.   Mammoth Marble-head Cabbage.

HENDERSON'S NO. 400

We offer for sale for the first time plants of Henderson's New No. 400 Tomato. Seed of this Tomato was offered for sale for the first time last season by Peter Henderson & Co. in small packets, and prize of $250 offered to the person that would select the most suitable name for it. We purchased some of the seed from original stock and have given the Tomato a thorough test along with many other varieties. Our opinion is, that it is the largest perfect shaped Tomato extant. Fruit is of immense size, symmetrical in shape, many specimens grown by us weighed nearly two pounds. In color it is of a handsome carmine when ripe; vines vigorous and enormously productive. This Tomato is a decided novelty and cannot fail to give entire satisfaction.

IMPROVED SACRAMENTO FAVORITE. Enough has been said of this Tomato in former catalogues issued by us, so that it will not be necessary for us to enter into details. While it is not a novelty by any means, we wish to call special attention to it. We have improved this Tomato by selecting the finest specimens each year for seed and our improved strain, offered this season is the finest we have ever grown. Fruit is blood red, thickly-meated, solid and perfectly smooth. This is the finest Tomato grown for canning or for general use. Henderson's $400, $2 00 per 100. Improved Sacramento Favorite, list prices.

Cabbage Plants.
Ready about December 1st.

	Per 100.	Per 1000.
Red Dutch	$0 40	$3 00
Early Winningstadt	40	3 00
Early Summer	40	3 00
Henderson's Succession	40	3 00
Large Flat Dutch	40	3 00
Large Late Drumhead	40	3 00
Savoy Drumhead	40	3 00

Cauliflower Plants.
Ready about December 1st.

	Per 100.
Early Snowball	$0 50
Early Paris	50
Late Dutch	50
Large Algiers	50

Sweet Potato Plants.
Ready March 1st.

	Per 100.	Per 1000.
Yellow Carolina	$0 50	$4 00

Egg Plants.
Ready in March and April.

	Per 100.	Per 100.
New York Purple	$0 25	$1 00
Black Pekin	25	1 25

Pepper Plants.
Ready in March and April.

	Per doz.	Per 100.
Large Bell	$0 25	$1 00
Sweet Mountain	25	1 00
Long Cayenne	25	1 00

Celery Plants.
Ready in March.

	Per doz	Per 100.
Large White Solid	$0 25	$1 00
White Plume	25	1 00

We grow immense quantities of these plants and shall be prepared to supply all orders at short notice.

Tomato Plants. Ready about March 1st.

Put up in boxes of 50 to 100 plants each. We make a specialty of tomato plants, and can always supply in their season well grown stalky plants of the best known variety.

All seed of Perfection, Sacramento Favorite, Livingston Beauty, Dwarf Champion, Mikado, New Boss, etc., grown by ourselves, and seed is of choicest selection.

Special New Kinds.

MIKADO, SELECTED, PERFECTION, NEW DWARF CHAMPION, NEW BOSS, IMPROVED SACRAMENTO FAVORITE AND HENDERSON'S NO. 400.

Per doz. 20 cents, Per 100 $1 00. Henderson's No. 400, Per doz. 40 cents, Per 100 $2 00.

Special Prices.

On all kinds of plants furnished on application on all orders aggregating from 1,000 to 10,000 plants. In all cases we will ship plants by express in small quantities, unless otherwise ordered.

Send for our special plant circular, issued Dec. 1st if you wish to set large quantities of plants.

W. R. STRONG COMPANY.

FLOWER SEEDS.

These require a good sandy soil, enriched with good fertilizers and well pulverized, loose and moderately moist. Sow the seed in usual way in boxes or warm seed bed, covering lightly, and keep in total darkness till the plant begins to show above ground, when gradually expose to the light. By pursuing this plan, uniform temperature and moisture is secured; and all seeds possessing life will be sure to grow. When the plants have grown to say to two inches in height, they are ready to transplant. Give plenty of room, according to habit of growth of the plant. Crowding destroys the vigor and beauty of the flower.

We offer the following liberal inducements to those who wish to purchase Flower Seeds in quantity. These rates apply only to seeds in packet, but the seeds will be sent by mail, post paid.

Send us $1.20 and select Packets to value of $1.00.
Send us $2.00 and select Packets to value of $2.50.
Send us $3.00 and select Packets to value of $4.00.

Abbreviations Made in Flower Seed List.

A.—For Annuals that grow, bloom and die the first year. B.—For Biennials blooming and dying second year. P.—For Perennials that usually bloom the first or second year from seed, but continue to grow and bloom for many years thereafter. H.—Indicates Hardy. H. H.—Half Hardy. T —Tender.

The hardy can be sown in open ground early, or almost any time, not requiring protection. Half hardy cannot be sown in open ground until the weather becomes warm, unless sown in greenhouse or with good protection.

ABOBRA (Climber.) H. H. P., 10 feet.
Rapid growing, with dazzling scarlet fruit... 10c

ABRONIA. H. A. 9 to 18 in.
Trailing and prostrate habit, like the Verbena, and quite fragrant; natives of California.
Abronia Umbellata, rosy.................... 10c
" Arenaria, yellow.................. 10c

ABUTILON, (Chinese Bellflower.)
H. H. P., 2 to 4 feet.

Flowers freely in house in winter and spring, and a good bedding Summer plant......
White, Yellow and Crimson mixed.......... 15c

ACHILLEA. H. P.
A charming plant 1½ foot high, bearing an abundance of small double white flowers through the summer and autumn; excellent for florists, pkt..................... 15c

ADLUMIA, (Mountain Fringe.) H. B., 18 feet.
Climber, graceful foliage, light pink, tubular flowers............................. 5c

ADONIS. (Pheasant's Eye.) H. A., 1 foot.
The Adonis has pretty, narrow leaves, and are very brilliant. It will flourish almost anywhere, in the shade or under trees.
Autumnalis. Autumn; blood red; 1 foot... 5c
Vernalis. Yellow......... .... 5c

AGERATUM H. B.

Bears a great many flowers, and keeps in bloom a long time, and is, therefore, desirable for bouquet making. It is well to start the seed under glass in order to transplant early in the spring.
Ageratum Conspicum. White-flowered, blooms until frost, 18 inches............ 5c
Ageratum Swanley. Blue, charming, large-flowered; most valuable for cutting...... 10c
Ageratum Mexicanum. (Little Dorritt.)
Azure blue, dwarf, splendid for bedding.. 5c
Ageratum Mexicanum. (Little Dorritt)
Albiflorum, white................. ..... 5c

AGROSTEMMA. (Rose Campion.)
H. P., 1 to 2 feet.
Perennial, very pretty, free blooming and hardy always makes desirable beds and is useful for cutting; 12 inches in height.

Coronaria................................... 5c
Atrosanguinea, dark blood-red............ 5c
Alba, white............................ .... 5c
Finest mixed 5c

ALYSSUM. H. A., 1 foot.

Pretty little white flowers, useful in making up all kinds of small bonqnets. Its fragrance is very delicate. Alyssum grows freely from seed and makes a pretty border. To keep it blooming the year round and make a compact roll or border, after each blooming, when the plants begin to look ragged and seed are forming, trim the border carefnlly and evenly. You will soon be repaid with another array of blossoms.

Alyssum, Sweet. Hardy annual, flowers small in clusters, 6 inches.............. 5c
Wierzbeckii. Hardy perennials, yellow, one foot high. These yellow varieties are trnly beautifnl dnring the spring months. The blossoms are a light cannary color and show to a good advantage among other flowers. When started they last for years.......... .... 5c
Saxatile Compactum. Yellow compact for edgings-............................... 5c
Serpyllifolium. Quite dwarf, yellow....... 5c
Procumbens. Very dwarf, white. The finest Dwarf Alyssum grown and adds a great deal to our list of border plants........ 5c
Compactum, Erectum. New, erect, flowering and charming..................... 5c

ALONSOA. H. H. A.

Yonng plants removed to the honse or greenhouse in the antumn, will continue to flower during the winter. The flowers are small but of remarkably brilliaut colors.
Alonsoa Grandiflora. Large flowered, scarlet, 2 feet in height.................. 5c
Alonsoa Albiflora. White...... ... . 5c

AMARANTHUS. H. H. A., 2 to 5 feet.

Valuable for their ornamental foliage, the leaves of most varieties being highly colored.
Tricolor (Joseph's Coat.) Red, yellow and green foliage....................... 5c
Melancholicus Ruber. Of compact habit, striking blood-red foliage; 18 inches..... 5c
Caudatus (Love lies bleeding.) Long drooping "chains" of flowers, pretty for decoration............................... 5c
Cruentus (Prince's Feather.) flowers somewhat similar to A. Candatus, but in erect masses.... .... 5c
Bicolor Ruber. Carmine scarlet; splendid.. 5c
Monstrosus. Blood red, flower spike....... 5c
Salicifolius. Highly decorative. Fountain Plant.

AMMOBIUM (Everlasting Flower). H. B.

Ammobium Alatum Grandiflorum. A large flowered white, everlasting; fino for dried bonquets with fancy grasses, pick the flowers in the bud to dry.................. 5c

AMPELOPSIS. H. P.

(Vetchi, Japan Woodbine, Climber.)

Very hardy and rapid grower; attaches to buildings, fences, etc., as closely as English Ivy; leaves olive green, changing to scarlet. Easy to cultivate and ornamental; 50 feet.................. 10c

ANAGALLIS. H. A.

Anagallis is remarkable for the beanty of its flowers; useful for borders or baskets. Succeeds best in light, sunny places.
Anagallis Grandiflora Superba. Mixed colors 5c

ACROLINIUM (Everlasting). H. H. P., 1 foot.

One of the most beantifnl and useful everlastings for winter bouquets. The flowers resemble the marguerite, with large yellow centres, and when used with fancy grasses make very showy and cheerful bonquets tc brighten up the home. Gather before fully opened and hang in a dark place to dry before using.
Acrolinium Album. Pure white.......... 5c
Acrolinium Roseum. Bright rose......... 5c
Acrolinium Florepleno Fine double varieties mixed........................... 10c

ANTIRRHINUM MAJUS (Snapdragon.)
H. A., 2 to 3 feet.

One of the very best of our perennials, blooms abuudantly the first summer until after frost, and flowers well the second summer and even longer. By removing a portion of the flowers, the plants will become strong.
Brilliant. Scarlet, golden and white........ 5c
Luteum. Yellow........................ 5c
Striatum. Finest striped................. 5c
Majus, Tall varieties; fine mixed.......... 5c
Majus Album. Pure white............... 5c
Majus Crescia. Fine deep scarlet.......... 5c

Nanum (Dwarf Varieties).

Album. Pure white....................... 5c
Firefly. Scarlet......................... 5c
Picturatum. New blotched...... .... 5c
Dwarf Varieties. Fine mixed............ . 5c

ARGEMONE. H. H. P., s 2 feet.

Handsome, large growing plant for flower-beds; white and yellow flowers resembling Poppies.
Hunnemanni. Dark yellow flowers........ 5c
Platyceras Grandiflora. Large white flowers. 5c

AQUILEGIA. H. P.

Ornamental hardy plants known as Columbine or Wild Honeysuckle. Showy, and one of the best carly bloomers; herbaceous hardy perennials. Effective in rockeries. Fine for bouquets.
Coerulea Hybrida (Haylodgensis). Large sulphur-yellow flowers, blue spnrs and sepals; fine.......................... 15c
Skinneri. Scarlet, tipped with yellow, very haudsome species...................... 20c
Arctica. Brick-red and green 10c
Chrysantha. Golden Spurred; beautiful, loug yellow spurred flowers............ 5c
Bicolor, fl. pl. Double blue and white...... 5c
Bicolor, fl. pl., Rubra. Double red........ 5c
Vulgaris, fl. pl. Fine double varieties, mixed. 5c
Vulgaris, fl. pl., Alba. Double white...... 5c
Single varieties, mixed.................. 5c
Vervaeneana. Variegated foliage.......... 10c

ASPERULA.

A dwarf plant covered all summer with clusters of charming fragrant flowers. Admirably adapted for bouquets.

Asperula Azurea Setosa. Sky-blue, H. A., one foot; pkt. 5c
Asperula Odorata (Sweet Woodruff). Flowers and leaves have a delicious odor when dried that imparts an agreeable perfume to clothes, etc., when kept among them. Flowers white; height 6 to 12 in., H. P... 10c

ASTERS.   H. A.

Are the most popular and effective garden favorites, producing in abundance flowers of great richness and variety. They make elegant borders and showy beds; hardy annual.

Trufflaut's Large Pæony Fower (Benary's Improved). A favorite class, thrifty, upright growers; flowers large and almost perfectly round, with incurved petals; height 18 inches to 2 feet.............. 10c
Dwarf Pæony Perfection. A dwarf class of great beauty........................... 10c
Large Globe-Flowered German. Many colors, mixed........................... 10c
New Rose. Two feet in height; robust, large flowers, petals finely imbricated; one of the very best; mixed colors............. 10c
Imbrique Pompon. Very perfect, almost a globe and beautifully imbricated; mixed colors 10c

Comet. Differing from all others in shape of flowers, its long, wavy and twisted petals, are formed into a dense half globe resembling the Japanese Chrysanthemums each petal a delicate pink margined with white. Pkt. 20 cts.

Betteridge's Quilled. Plants strong and branching flowers composed of tube or quilled shaped petals, with a single row of outer flat petals, which are often a different color

Comet.

from the center. A very beautiful Aster. Mixed colors per pkt. 10 cts.

Cocardeau or New Crown. Two colored flowers, the central petals being of pure white, sometimes small and quilled, surrounded with large, flat petals of a bright color, 18 inches, mixed colors; beautiful.. 10c
New Pæony-flowered Globe, or Uhland. The earliest of the Asters, flowers very large, plant branching and strong; does not require support...... .... 10c
Hedgehog, or Needle. Petals long, quilled and sharply pointed; 2 feet; mixed colors. 10c
Chrysanthemum-flowered Dwarf White. A superb variety, every flower usually perfect; fine mixed varieties............. 10c
Dwarf Bouquet. Splendid for edging and small beds............................. 10c
Dwarf Bouquet. Pyramidal shaped....... 10c
Victoria. Flowers very double and round; many extremely delicate, and some gorgeous shades, handsome varieties, mixed colors 10c

Mignon Aster. Pure white flowers of beautiful form, resembling the Victoria race... 15c
Alpinus. Alpine Aster, perennial, rose..... 5c
Alpinus Gymnocephalus. Perennial, rose.. 5c
"Crimson, Ball," or Jewel Aster. Petals incurved; new novelty, forming a crimson ball; beautiful........................... 25c
Prince of Wales. New crimson fine........ 20c
Victoria Asters. (Benary's Prize.) Remarkably handsome and large flowering; many colors mixed...... .... 15c
Victoria Needle. Entirely disti ct and beautiful; petals quilled; nine colors mixed............................... 10c
White Varieties. Choicest mixed.......... 15c

Harlequin. A peculiar variety with oddly spotted and striped flowers of striking beauty, entirely distinct from all others. Of upright habit. Medium height and profuse blooming. Price pkt. 15 cts.

Triumph. Deep scarlet changing to a lake crimson. This is without doubt the most beautiful and perfect of all Dwarf Asters. Each plant forms an elegant bouquet of itself. 7 to 8 inches high.   Triumph.
The flowers measure from 2½ to 3 inches in diameter, and are of faultless Pæony form. Pkt. 20 cts.

BALSAM.   H. H. A.

(Lady Slipper or Touch-Me-Not.)

This is one of the most beautiful and popular annuals. They are sown in beds or frames, and if growing too thick, thin out and prune as desired. They transplant readily. Among the many varieties we name:

Double White, Rose-Flowered, Double Camellia-Flower, Double Rose-Flowered, Double Spotted and Carnation, striped, each...................... 10c
Extra Double Mixed. Of above and others 10c

BALLOON VINE (Love in a Puff.)

H. A., 4 to 8 feet.

A half hardy, rapid growing, handsome climber, having small white flowers, which are followed by seed vessels shaped like balloons...... .... 5c

BELLIS (Double Daisy.)

H. H. P., 6 inches.

Beautiful for edging, dwarf groups and beds; earliest and prettiest of the spring flowers.

Finest Mixed............................. 10c
"Snow Ball" (Daisy.) New double white; beautiful............................. 15c
Longfellow. New, large, double, rose-colored flowers; fine...................... 15c
Double White............................. 10c

1 PANSY.   25
2 STAR PHLOX. 15
3 COSMOS.   10
4 SCABIOSA.   10
5 GAILLARDIA.   5
6 ZINNIA.   10
7 DATURA.   5

The Collection for 60 Cts.

BEGONIA (Tuberous Rooted.) T. P.

Begonia.

Magnificent flowering plants for pots, and in Europe is extensively bedded out, flowering in the greatest profusion all summer.

Single varieties....15c
Double varieties. .25c

Begonia Rex. Large, ornamental leaved plants......... 25c

BARTONIA. H. A.

B. Aurea (California Golden Bartonia.) Is a very showy annual. The leaves somewhat thistle-like in appearance, gray and downy. The flowers are of a bright, glossy yellow and exceedingly brilliant in the sunshine. It likes considerable moisture, and young plants sometimes suffer in a dry time. Sow seed where the plant is to flower, as it does not bear transplanting very well; height, 2 feet; pkt............ 5c

BRACHYCOME (Swan River Daisy). H. A., ¼ foot.

This beautiful annual is found on the banks of the Swan River in Australia, and has there the very appropriate name of Swan River Daisy. The plant grows from six to ten inches high and produces an abundance of Cineraria-like blossoms all summer. It is well adapted for small beds or rockeries. Mixed colors; pkt., 5c.

BROWALLIA. H. H. A., 1½ feet.

The Browallias are excellent, free-flowering, and valuable for winter house-plants. When bedded out in summer are completely studded with bright delicate flowers the whole season.
Czerwiakowski. Deep blue, very fine...... 5c
Elata Alba. White...................... 5c
Elata Nana. New, compact, very fine...... 10c
Elata Grandiflora. Blue; large flowered.... 5c

BRYONOPSIS (Ornamental Cucumber).

A very beautiful climber, bearing green fruits, which change to bright scarlet striped with white; 8 to 10 feet................. 5c

CACALIA. H. A., 1¼ feet.

Pretty free-flowering plant, often called Flora's Paint Brush. Set plants six inches apart. They bloom from early in summer until autumn; mixed colors................. 5c

CALAMPELIS (Climber). H. H. A., 10 feet.

Scabra. Blooms in racemes of bright orange flowers; one of the finest climbers....... 5c

CALANDRINIA. H. H. A., 1 foot.

Beautiful dwarf plant; succeeds best in light rich soil. The sunshine causes the flowers to expand like portulaca, in a perfect blaze of beauty.
Mixed colors, large and showy........... 5c

CALENDULA. H. A.

Remarkably free-flowering plants, producing a fine effect in beds and borders; succeeds in any garden soil; height 1 foot.
Officinalis, fl. pl. Le Proust; Nankeen colored, very fine; double, constant........ 5c
Meteor. Large double striped flowers of light orange...................... 5c
Prince of Orange. Similar to Meteor, but much darker; very beautiful...... ...... 5c
Grandiflora. Very handsome.............. 5c

CALCEOLARIA (Greenhouse Plant.) T. P., 1½ feet.

Calceolaria.

Gorgeous plants for greenhouse and window decoration; the large pocket-shaped flowers are borne in the greatest profusion through the Spring and Summer months; colors, yellow, maroon, crimson, etc. Spotted and blotched in the most unique and beautiful fashion; height, 1½ feet.

Grandiflora. Finest mixed....'............ 25c
Pinnata California. Yellow.............. 5c
Rugosa. Shrubby or bedding calceolarias, more hardy than the Grandiflora varieties, bearing innumerable flowers, beautiful but small............................. 20c
Striata. Fine striped and mottled......... 20c

CALLIOPSIS (Coreopsis). H. A., 2 ft.

Showy, free-flowering and beautiful annual, the tall are fine for beds and mixed borders, and dwarf for bedding. Crimson, yellow, brown and marbled, mixed colors.
Atkinsoni. Yellow and brown, biennial.... 5c
Cardaminifolia. Of pyramidal habit....... 5c
Coronata. Yellow and large-flowered...... 5c
Longipes. Yellow, perennial.............. 5c
Fine Mixture. Of tall sorts............... 5c
Fine Mixture. Of dwarf sorts............. 5c
Semiplena. New semi-double.............. 5c

CALLIRHOE.

Beautiful annual; violet, purple and crimson flowers; white center; attractive, and blooms through the summer........... 5c

CANNA (Indian Shot). H. H. P.

Stately and ornamental plants, desirable in groups or background; soak seek in hot water 12 hours before sowing.
Extra choice mixed...................... 5c
Dark leaved varieties...... .... 10c
Crozy's New Varieties. Most of them are dwarf in habit, early bloomers and very remarkable for beauty of both flower and foliage; are excellent too for pots; pkt.... 20c

CAMPANULA (Canterbury Bell).
H. A. and P., 5 to 12 inches.

Well-known favorites; bearing large bell and saucer-shaped flowers in profusion.

Medium, fl. pl. Double blue, double white and double rose, each separate; 10c.

Medium. Single, finest mixed; 5c.

Medium Striata. New; striped, very fine; 10c.

Calycanthema (Cup and Saucer). The flowers are large, resembling somewhat a cup and saucer; blue, white and lilac; fine mixed............ 10c

Rosea. Single rose...................... 5c

Pyramidalis. Very beautiful sorts, fine colors, mixed......................... 5c

Speculum (Venus's Looking Glass). Single, finest mixed 5c

Speculum. Double sorts, finest mixed...... 10c

CANARY BIRD FLOWERS (Climber).
H. H. A., 10 to 15 feet.
TROPÆOLUM.

Popular and pretty; rapid grower and abundant bloomer of rich yellow-fringed flowers 10c

CANDYTUFT. H. A., 6 to 12 inches.

Popular and useful, blooming long and freely and perfectly hardy. The flowers are quite a treasure for making bouquets and for massing or ribbon gardening. Varieties and shades are numerous.

Amara. Pure white...................... 5c

Coronaria (White Rocket). Large trusses of pure white flowers; much prized by the florists 5c

Empress. A most beautiful Candytuft, being a series of Candellabra shaped branches each producing a large truss of white flowers, thus presenting a pyramid of bloom throughout the season........... 10c

Carter's Carmine. This new variety is of a dwarf, compact habit, and bears a mass of fine Carmine bloom, true from seed..... 10c

Purpurea (Dark Crimson). Beautiful....... 5c

Fine mixed, annual sorts.................... 5c

Sempervirens Perennial. White, blooming and hardy, adapted for rockeries, baskets, etc.............................. 5c

CARNATION (Dianthus).
H. H. P., 1 to 2 feet.

Magnificent and popular, very fragrant and beautiful colors; hardy perennial.

Finest strains of German and Italian seed, 25c.

Good mixed, 10c.

Grenadin. A new dwarf compact variety of great value to florists, producing a profusion of large double brilliant scarlet flowers three weeks earlier than any other variety; 20c.

Early Flowering Vienna. Extra fine; 15c

Grenadin. White, new novelty............. 25c

German Perpetual or tree.... .... 25c

Riviera Market. This extra strain of Perpetual Carnation, we offer this year for the first time. The seed produces almost exclusively splendid double flowers, per pkt. 25c

CASSIA.

Hardy perennial, with yellow flowers 18 inches high; good border flowers.............. 5c

CATANANCHE COERULEA. H. P.

Catananche Coerulea. Fine everlastings; blue and white mixed.................... 5c

CATCHFLY (Silene). H. A., 1½ feet.

Showy and great favorite; annual; bright dense heads of flowers; blooms freely and of easy culture; colors, red and white mixed double... .... 5c

Pendula Carnea. Double red, new and fine. 5c

Compacta Alba. Double white new and pretty...................... 5c

Snow King. Pure white Globular, new, and a fine novelty........................... 5c

Orientalis Compacta. Red compact........ 5c

CONVALLARIA MAJALIS (Lily of the Valley).

One of the most charming of our spring flowering plants, its slender stems set with tiny bells diffusing a delicious odor, have rendered it a universal favorite. They are very hardy and require a shaded situation, soil rich sandy loam. Clean seed in berries. 10c

Japonica. Very fine...................... 10c

CENTRANTHUS. H. A., 1½ feet.

Pretty, free-flowering annual, effective in beds and borders; transparent stems and glaucous leaves; rose colored and white.. 5c

CENTAUREA. H. A.

Showy border plant, succeeding in almost any soil; hardy annual and perennial; varieties.

Batchelor's Button or Corn Bottle- Two feet; quite showy; old favorites.......... 5c

Sweet Sultan. Hardy annual; 1 foot...... 5c

Centaurea Cyanus, fl. pl. New double corn flower; produces double flowers of large size; very interesting and pretty; useful in floral work and bouquets; pkt.......... 10c

CLARKIA. H. A., 1 to 2 feet.

Hardy annual plant, blooming profusely with handsome flowers.

Double and single, mixed colors............. 5c

CINERARIA (Greenhouse Plant.)
H. H. P., 1 foot.

Hybrida Grandiflora. A favorite attractive free flowering plant, blooming during the winter and early spring months, in Hot House or Conservatory; mixed, per pkt. 25c.

Plenissima. New, double; from finest double flowers; beautiful; per pkt. 20c.

CHRYSANTHEMUM.
H. A. and P., 12 to 18 inches.

Very showy and effective favorites; colors have the appearance of being laid on with a brush; annual and perennial; varieties.

Chrysanthemum (Single Annual Varieties.)

Tricolor Carinatam Album. White........	5c
Burridgi (Lord Beaconsfield). White and rose	5c
Coronarium. Fl. pl., double yellow........	5c
Coronarium. Fl. pl., double white........	5c

Chrysanthemum (Perennial varieties.)

Indicum Majus. Large flowering double varieties.....	25c
Indicum. Double pom pon mixed..........	25c
Japenicum. Fl. pleno, Japanese...	25c
Japenicum Nanum. Fl. pl., dwarf double Japanese................................	25c
Uliginosum. Abundant large white flowers; fine for cutting........................	5c
Frutescens Grandiflorum (Marguerite or Paris Daisy.) H. P., now so fashionable and popular; large white star-like flowers, growing freely and profusely............	10c

COBŒA (Scandens.)
H. H. P., 20 to 30 feet.

Climbing plant; rapid grower and large bell-shaped flowers; fine for summer; plant

seed edgewise...................	10c
Scandens, fl. Alba. White.................	20c

COLEUS.   T. P., 1 to 3 feet.

Ornamental foliage plant; leaves of all shapes and colors, of velvety appearance and great beauty. Splendid flower for garden decoration. Finest hybrids, mixed, per pkt. 25c.

New large-leaved Coleus, mixed, choicest varieties per pkt. 40c.

Coleus.

COLLINSIA.   H. H. A., 1 to 2 feet.

California annual; marbled or many colored, for beds and borders...................	5c

COCKSCOMB (Celosia.)   T. A.

Annual plant, showy and attractive; half hardy.

Cristata nana. Dwarf, crimson, fine, variegated; new, brilliant combs of crimson and gold....................................	10c

Japan. Branching variety of great beauty; scarlet and crimson combs, like ruffled lace, in pyramidal masses.

Tall and dwarf varieties mixed..............	10c
Pyramidalis Plumosa. Fine feathered varieties, choice mixed.........	10c

CONVOLVULUS MAJOR (Morning Glory.)
H. A., 30 to 50 feet.

Varieties and colors too well known for description; white, dark blue, blood red, rose and striped, growing 20 feet high; nothing can equal them for rapidity of growth and profusion of bloom, thriving in almost any situation; tall mixed	5c

Hederacia Grandiflora Superba. Large-flowering, mixed; white edged varieties. Many beautiful sorts..................	10c
Hederacia Grandiflora Marmoratis. Large flowered variegated foliage, mixed.......	10c
Rubro Coerulea fl. Albo. Beautiful climber with large white flowers.....	10c
Rubro Coerulea (Violacea Vera.) Very large flowers of a bright sky blue.............	10c
Aureus Superbus. A smaller growing sort, with smaller flowers of golden yellow....	10c
Ipomœa Grandiflora. The Moon Flower, "Evening Glory" or "Good Night." Large white fragrant flowers in profusion, opening in the evening; rapid and luxuriant summer climber..............	10c
Limbata. Violet, margined with white; large and handsome....................	10c

Cypress Vine. (Ipomœa Quamoclit.)
H. H. A., 15 feet.

Climbing Annual. Popular, elegant and graceful; different colors, scarlet and white; separate colors or mixed..........	5c

CONVOLVULUS TRICOLOR (Minor.)
(Dwarf Bedding Varieties.)

These grow only about 1 foot high; the flowers are freely borne and remain open all day, if pleasant; splendid for bedding.

C. Minor. Choice mixed colors.............	5c

COSMOS.   H. A.

This beautiful flower is a great favorite with all who have become acquainted with it. A showy graceful plant, bearing hundreds of flowers resembling Single Dahlias. For bouquets or flower pieces are unsurpassed, retaining their freshness for many days.

Cosmos. Finest varieties mixed, 10c.	
Cosmos Grandiflora. Large white, 10c.	

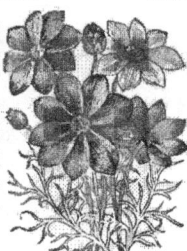

Cosmos.

CREPIS (Hawkweed.)

Annual of easy culture and abundant bloomer; red, white and yellow................	5c
Nana Compacta. Dwarf, 18 inches........	5c

CYCIAMEN PERSICUM.   T. P.

Charming bulbous-rooted plants, with beautiful foliage, and rich-colored orchid-like fragrant flowers; universal favorites for winter and spring blooming. If seed is sown early they make flowering bulbs in one season; they require sandy loam; half

hardy perennial; mixed; 6 inches........	20c
Persicum Giganticum. This new large-flowering variety has beautiful mottled leaves, broad petals and stout flower-stalks, throwing the flowers well above the foliage; 8 inches....................	30c

CYCLANTHERA.   H. A.

A climbing plant of the gourd species, free-growing, handsome foliage and oval-shaped fruit; exploding loudy when ripe; half-hardy annual; explodens; 10 feet........	5c

DAHLIA. H. H. P., 4 to 6 feet.

Dahlia.

When sown early Dahlias will bloom the first year from seed. The single varieties have become very popular within the last few years, and deservedly so, for in brilliancy of color and duration of flower they have hardly any equal. They are extensively used for cutting.

Best Single Dahlias. An extra fine mixture from named sorts of single hybrids, 10c.

Large Flowering Double. A mixture from prize flowers........................... 20c

Bidens Atrosanguinea.

Dahlia Zimapani, or Miniature Black Dahlia. A very little known variety from Mexico, which, owing to its merits, deserves a foremost place in the flower garden. The plants grow about 2 feet high and very bushy, and produce an abundance of the deepest crimson-maroon flowers of a velvety texture measuring 3 inches across. They are easily raised from seed.. 10c

DATURA (Trumpet Flower.)
H. A., 3 feet.

Strong growing plants known as Angel's Trumpets, large showy flowers suitable for borders.

Datura Wrightii. Large, white and lilac flowers.................................... 5c

Huberiana, fl. pl. Mixed; fine double varieties...................................... 5c

DIANTHUS (Pinks).

A magnificent genus, embracing some of the most popular flowers in cultivation, producing a great variety of brilliant colors and profusion of bloom. The hardy biennials, or Chinese and Japanese varieties, bloom the first season, the same as hardy annuals; height, 1 foot. The hardy perennial varieties are very fragrant, and of easy culture for the garden or green-house.

Chinensis (China or Indian Pink). Extra double, all colors mixed................. 5c

Heddewiggi, fl. pl., (Double Japan Pink). Flowers very large and double, nearly three inches in diameter, of various shades of the most brilliant colors.......... 5c

Heddewiggi Atropupureus, fl. pl. Dark blood-red; extra fine.................... 10c

The Bride. New, white with purple center.. 10c

Laciniatus, fl. pl. (Double-fringed Japan Pink). Large double showy flowers with fringed edges, mixed, various colors and beautifully striped.................... 5c

Striata, fl. pl. Large double-fringed flowers of crimson, rose, white, etc., all beautifully striped................................... 10c

Laciniatus. Very fine, large-flowered, single Japan Pink; mixed.................... 5c

Imperialis, fl. pl. (Double Imperial Pink). A superb double variety, all colors mixed... 5c

Pheasant's Eye (Plumaris Simplex). A beautiful single variety, with fringe-edged white flowers, and a dark center, hardy perennial; 1 foot...................... 5c

DOLICHOS (Hyacinth Bean.)
T. A., 10 feet.

A beautiful climber, flowers in clusters, purple and white, 10 feet....................... 5c

Giganteus. Species from Texas........... 5c

DIGITALIS (Foxglove).
H. P., 3 to 4 feet.

Hardy perennials, three feet handsome ornamental plant of stately growth and varied colors; mixed or separate colors......... 5c

Monstrosa (Mammoth Foxglove). The largest and best type; all colors mixed......... 10c

ERYSIMUM. H. A., 1 foot.

Annual, 1¼ feet, free-flowering and showy for beds or borders, sulphur yellow and deeper orange shades................................ 5c

ESCHSCHOLTZIA (California Poppy.) H. P., 1 ft

A hardy annual, profuse bloomer, with rich beautiful colors; continues in bloom until frost; single varieties, choice mixed...... 5c

Eschscholtzia Californica. Sulphur yellow with orange center..................... 5c

Rose Cardinal A charming new variety, producing freely beautiful large flowers of intense carmine........................ 10c

Crocea, fl. pl. Mixed; a double-flowering orange, scarlet and white............... 10c

EUPHORBIA. (Snow on the Mountain) T. A.

Attractive foliage, with white and green bracts on the tips of each branch veined and margined with white, 2 feet.

Variegata.................................. 5c

EUTOCA. H. A.

Annual; desirable for cut flowers; blue and lilac; 6 inches........................... 5c

FENZLIA. H. A.

A charming little plant for carpet bedding or borders. Seed sown early in May will germinate quickly and begin blooming in a few weeks after starting. The plants do not grow over three inches high but spread like portulaca, and all summer long are thickly covered with the beautiful blossoms of lovely colors.

Fenzlia. Finest mixed colors; pkt.......... 10c

FUCHSIA. T. P., 1 to 3 feet.

A beautiful plant blooming all the season; mixed; single and double............... 25c

FORGET-ME-NOT. (Myosotis).
H. P., 6 to 12 inches.

Very popular and beautiful; will grow in any moist situation.

Alpestris. Forget-me-not................. 5c

Disitiflora. Large-flowered species, beautiful and true; very scarce and high. 15c
Palustris. The true Forget-me-not, blue, Alba, white.............................. 10c
Azorica. Flowers rich blue, shaded with purple 10c
Myosotis (Alpestris Victoria). Of stout and bushy habit of growth, bearing umbels of large bright azure-blue flowers with central double blooms. The plant attains a height of 5 to 7 inches, with a diameter of 8 to 10 inches, and when fully grown is quite globular in shape, and perfectly covered with flowers. This beautiful Forget-me-not is the best for carpet bedding, edgings and masses, and for growing in pots for market................... 20c
Eliza Fonrobert. New, large-flowering, bright blue, of pyramidal habit; remarkably fine and distinct.................. 10c
Eliza Fonrobert, Alba. White, beautiful... 10c

GAILLARDIA. H. P.
Splendid bedding plants, remarkable for the profusion, size and brilliancy of their flowers, continuing in beauty during the summer and autumn; half-hardy annuals; 1½ feet.
Grandiflora. Mixed single varieties; includes many sorts............................ 5c
Gaillardia Picta Josephus. Broad yellow ribbons.............................. 5c
Gaillardia Picta Fistulosa. Quilled....... 5c
Picta Lorenziana. A charming profuse flowering "so-called" double variety, entirely distinct from the single flowering. Fine for massing, and use as a bouquet flower, continuing in bloom until frost........ 5c
Amblyodon. Rich blood red............... 5c

GERANIUM. H. H. P.

Geranium.

A popular bedding plant for the house or garden, extensively used for massing; half hardy perennial; from 1 to 3 feet.
Zonale, Mixed. A superb strain of the largest and finest varieties; mixed colors.
Zonale, Golden and **Bronze.** Choice mixed, 25c.
Zonale, Silverfoliaged-Varieties. Finest mixed, 25c.
Double mixed. This seed will produce a large percentage of double flowers of extra fine colors........ .... 25c
Pelargonium, mixed (Lady Washington.) From the finest fancy and spotted, large-flowering.............................. 25c
Apple-Scented (Pelargonium Odoratissimum) This fragrant favorite variety can only be grown from seed to form fine plants. Sow in light soil, and keep moist until they germinate........ .... 25c

GENTIANA.
One of the very best hardy plants. They are very sensitive about removal, hence the necessity of sowing the seed where they are to bloom.
G. Acaulis. Beautiful blue flowers, yellow throat; very rich; pkt................ .... 10c

GLOXINIA HYBRIDA CRASSIFOLIA.
A bulbous-rooted plant, producing in great profusion, during the summer months, large bell-shaped flowers of the richest and most beautiful variety of brilliant colors; the bulbs must be kept warm and dry during the winter; 1 foot.
Grandiflora Erecta, mixed. Rich colored, erect flowers.......... .... 25c
Grandiflora. New French Tigred and spotted varieties............ .... 25c

GLOBE AMARANTHA (Everlasting Flower.)
"Bachelor's Buttons;" ornamental summer-blooming plants, and fine for "Everlastings" H. A. 2 feet.
Globo Amarantha. White, purple and variegated mixed 5c

GILIA.
California Annual. Dwarf free flowering plants, with clusters of small delicate flowers, desirable for cutting; height 6 inches to 1 foot; tall mixed.............. 5c

GODETIA. H. A.
An attractive hardy annual, deserving more extensive cultivation. The plant blooms profusely, and bears showy flowers of rich and varied colors; 1½ feet.

Bijou. Flowers splendid white, with a dark rose spot; very dwarf and dense growing; 5c.

Lady Albemarie. Flowers large, of carmine crimson shade; the edges of the petals suffused with pale lilac; 5c.

Godetia.

Grandiflora Maculata. Large white flowers with crimson spots, fine. 5c
New Godetias (Rubicunda Splendens). Double red, very brilliant.................... 5c
Lady Satin Rose. Deep rose pink, glossy and satiny; by some thought the most beautiful annual of recent introduction.. 10c
"Duchess of Albany." Large satiny white flowers; beautiful and new 10c

GOURD. (Cucurbita). H. A.

Rapid growing, interesting plants with ornamental fruit, and varieties of singular shaped fruit, tender annuals; 15 to 20 feet.
Calabash. The dipper; 5c
Hercules' Club. Club-shaped; 4 feet long; 5c.
Egg-shaped. Fruit white like an egg; 5c.
Orange-shaped, or Mock Orange, 5c.
Bottled-shaped; 5c.
Turk's Turban, Red striped; 10c.
Pear-shaped. Striped; very showy......... 10c
Argyrosperma. Dish Rag, or (Bonnet Gourd). 10c
Angora. Black-seeded, white-spotted fruit, very useful for arbors, etc.............. 10c

Tricosanthes Colubrina (True Serpent Gourd. Striped like a serpent, changing to brilliant carmine when ripe; 5 feet in length ....　10c
Powder Horn............................　5c
Fine Mixed. From a large collection of large sorts...................................　5c
Fine Mixed. Small ornamental sorts.......　5c

GYPSOPHILA. H. A. & H. P.

Delicate, free-flowering little plants, covered with a profusion of tiny star-shaped blossoms, valuable for making bouquets.
Acutifolia. Rose-colored, delicate and pretty　5c
Elegant. White, a choice variety...........　5c
Paniculata Compacta. New, dwarf compact variety; beautiful for bouquets......　10c
Perennial Paniculata. Tall, fine...........　5c

HELIOTROPE. H. H. P., 18 inches.

A deliciously fragrant plant, fine for bedding and pot culture; choice mixed...........　10c
Fine mixture of dark flowering sorts.........　10c

HELIPTERUM.

One of the best everlasting neat foliage-flowers in clusters of bright yellow and white. They should be picked in the bud and hung in a shady place if wanted for dried bouquets. They will open more perfect and retain their color for years.
Helipterum Corymbiflorum. White........　5c
Sanfordi. Yellow.......................　5c

HELICHRYSUM. (Everlasting Flowers.) H. A.

Very popular Everlastings with globular flowers, useful for borders and beds. When used for dyeing, flowers should be picked before fully expanded; useful and ornamental in bouquets with dried grasses.
H. Monstrosum, fl. pl. A mixture of many varieties, 2 feet.......................　5c

HOLLYHOCK. (Althaea Rosea.) H. P.

Old-fashioned favorites which should be in every garden. Seeds should be sown in June or July to have flowering plants the next summer or if sown in the house early in the spring they will bloom the first year. Height 4 to 6 feet.
Hollyhock. White, red, yellow, each.......　10c
Fine mixed, including many colors ....　10c
Extra Choice Mixed, from Chater's unrivaled collection ....　15c

HIBISCUS. H. A., 2 to 4 feet.

Hardy annual, showy and ornamental.
Africanus. Rich; cream-brown center......　5c
Coccineus Speciosus. Scarlet; fine........　5c

HONESTY. H. B., 2 feet.

Lunaria or Satan Flower. An interesting plant; seed vessel looks like transparent silver; handsome for bouquets or dried flowers; hardy perennial................　5c

ICE PLANT (Mesembryanthemum.)
H. H. A., 6 inches.

Dwarf trailer, with thick fleshy leaves, having the appearance of being covered with ice crystals; fine for vases and baskets.......　5c
Tricolor (Dew Plant.) Finer crystals than the Ice Plant...........................　5c
Album. White................................　5c
M. Cordifolium Variegatum. With cream-colored foliage of a frosted wax-like appearance; fine for carpet bedding, borders, baskets, etc...............　10c

IMPATIENS SULTANI. H. T. A.

One of the most distinct and beautiful plants of recent introduction for the warm greenhouse or summer bedding; owing to its gorgeous coloring and profuse and continuous flowering it is rapidly becoming popular. This plant is of compact, neat habit of growth, with good constitution, and almost a perpetual bloomer. Planted out in the open ground at the end of June it grows luxuriantly, flowers with the greatest profusion, and produce an admirable effect until cut down by frost. The flowers are of a brilliant rosy-scarlet color, about 1¼ inches in diameter.
Sultani..... . ...　25c

KAULFUSSIA. H. A., 6 inches.

Dwarf annual, like an Aster; pretty branching and free flowering; mixed colors.........　5c

LARKSPUR (Delphinum.)
H. A. and perennial.

One of our most showy and useful plants, possessing almost every requisite for the adornment of the garden; the hardy perennial producing splendid spikes of flowers in profusion throughout the summer. If sown early they bloom the first year from seed. The hardy annuals are profuse bloomers and succeed best if sown in the autumn, or very early in the spring.
Tall Rocket, Double Mixed, includes many colors; 2½ feet.....................　5c
Mixed Dwarf Rocket Varieties, includes many varieties......................　5c
Double Stock Flower. A tall branching variety, with beautiful long spikes of flowers of various colors; fine for cut-flowers; 2 feet.......................　5c
Larkspur (Delphinum.) Perennial varieties.
Nudicaule. Dwarf, of compact growth, with spikes of bright scarlet flowers; 18 inches.　10c
Cashmerianum. A beautiful dark blue, blooms in corymbs of 6 or more; 15 inches　20c
Hybridum. Many varieties extra fine mixed.　10c
Delphinium Zalil. A pure sulphur yellow flowering perennial of a lovely and delicate shade, resembling in color the Marechal Neil Rose, a color unknown till now. The plant is of branching habit, 3½ to 4½ feet high, the branches ending in long spikes of 40 to 50 blossoms, which open almost at the same time. The flowers are 1 inch in diameter, and last in flower from June till August; price per pkt..........　25c

LANTANA. H. H. P.

A remarkably handsome free-flowering genus of plants with brilliantly colored flowers, constantly changing in hue, very effective either for pot culture or bedding. Half-hardy perennial.

Finest varieties mixed 10c

LINUM (Flowering Flax). H. A., 1 foot.

Conspicuous for its brilliant colors.

Flavum. Yellow; perennial 5c
Perennial sorts, fine mixed................. 5c

LINARIA.

Cymballaria (Kenilworth Ivy). A very pretty climber; fine for suspensions 5c

LEPTOSIPHON. H. A., 8 inches.

Beautiful dwarf for lines and ribbon beds; white and yellow; mixed, French........ 5c

LOBELIA.

Annuals. An elegant dwarf of easy culture; fine for borders and ribbon beds and for vases and hanging baskets.

Erinus, Emperor William. A very compact variety, with fine sky-blue flowers, 10c.

Erinus, Crystal Palace Compact. A new densely compact miniature variety, which, during the summer months, is studded with rich deep blue flowers, 10c.

Erinus Speciosa, Crystal Palace. Of trailing growth; flowers of an ultra-marine blue.. 10c
Crystal Palace Oculata. Dark stalks and dark blue flowers, with a distinct white eye; splendid........................... 10c

LUPINUS (Sun Dials). H. A. and P.

Desirable bedding plants with long graceful flower spikes, bearing richly colored, pea-shaped flowers; natives of California.

Mixed annual varieties, 1 to 3 feet........ 5c
Mixed perennial varieties; hardy sorts 5c
Arboreus (Yellow Tree Lupin).............. 10c

LAVENDER. H. P., 1 to 2 feet.

Prized for its fragrant violet flowers; does best in a dry gravelly soil; hardy perennial.... 5c

LYCHNIS.

Showy flowering plants for shrubberies and flower beds; flowers strikingly brilliant.

Chalcedonica. Dazzling scarlet; hardy perennial; 1 to 3 feet...................... 5c
Haageana. Brilliant scarlet flowers, 2 inches across; 1 foot........................... 10c
Haageana Grandiflora Gigantea. Fine.... 10c

MARIGOLD (Tagetes). H. H. A.

A class of showy and extremely effective plants with fine double flowers of rich and beautiful colors, very well adapted for large beds and bordering. No garden should be without them.

Tall African. Many varieties mixed, 2 feet... 5c
Sulphurea. Sulphur yellow, quilled double. 5c
Aurea Fistulosa Pl. Quilled golden yellow.. 5c
Dwarf French. A mixture of many shades; one foot. 5c
Dwarf African. All colors mixed.......... 5c

Signata Pumila. Splendid for edgings; dwarf plants with fern-like foliage and small brilliant yellow cross-shaped flowers in profusion, which gives it a delicate, airy appearance, making beautiful borders for long beds............................... 5c
Signata Pumila (New Golden Ring). Foliage same as above; flowers have a deep golden stripe across each petal, which forms a complete golden ring, very showy and pretty 5c
Tall French. Fine mixed, all shades........ 5c

MARVEL OF PERU (Four o'cock). H. H. P., 2 feet.

One of the most ornamental flowering plants; they are quite fragrant, flowers expanding in the evening; half hardy perennial; blooming the first season from seed; the roots can be preserved in winter like Dahlias.

Mixed; beautiful colors. 5c
Longiflora. Long flower, pure white and fragrant.................................. 5c
Dwarf White (Tom Thumb). When fully developed this variety does not exceed 10 inches in height, and forms a charming little bush completely studded with pure white flowers; new........................... 5c
Multiflora. Large umbels of dark lilac, red flowers; perennial, fine.................. 10c

MARTYNIA. H. A., 3 to 4 feet.

Free-flowering, of easy culture and hardy, sweet scented; yellow and purple........ 10c

MATRICARIA (Fever Few.) H. H. P.

Handsome free flowering plants, good for beds and pot culture.

Matricaria Eximia Crispa Fl. Pl. Lovely little plants with double white flowers and prettily curled foliage like parsley. 8 inches.................................. 5c
Capensis, Double white flowers; splendid for bonquets, etc....................... 5c
Grandiflora Fl. Pl. Large flowering double white, beautiful...................... 10c

MAURANDIA (Climber.) T. A. 6 to 10 feet.

Very graceful for training on trellis work, verandas, etc., perennial, flowers the first season from seed; violet pink, purple, white and red........................ 10c

MIGNONETTE (Reseda Odorata.) T. P.

A well-known annual with spike of deliciously fragrant flowers. Indispensible in every garden. H.A.

Grandiflora. Large flowered; per oz., 20c., 5c.

Ameliorata. Very sweet scented, red flowered; per oz., 15c. 5c.

Parson's White. A distinct almost white variety, with long spikes; 5c.

Gabriele. New, red flowering; robust spikes; very large; one of the best for florists' use 10c

Mignonette.

Miles' Hybrid Spiral. It is a vigorous grower, with spikes often attaining a length of 10 inches; delightfully fragrant.. 5c

Giant Pyramidal. Flowers reddish, sweet-scented and very large 5c

Machet. The plants are dwarf and vigorous, of pyramidal growth. They throw up numerous long and broad spikes of deliciously scented red flowers. Entirely distinct................................ 10c

Crimson Queen. Very fine, robust, excellent for pots, red flowered................... 5c

Golden Queen. An entirely distinct sort, with golden yellow flowers, which give it a most attractive appearance; very fragrant.............................. 10c

Victoria. Dark red; very fine............. 5c

MIMULUS. (Monkey Flower.) H. H. P.

A very interesting free blooming genus of plants with beautiful spotted and blotched flowers of brilliant colors. Succeeds best in shaded and damp situations. Perennials in the green-house, annuals in the open air.

Tigrinus Grandiflora. Very large flowering, new tigred and spotted varieties, most beautiful; very showy as window plants.. 15c

Nanus. New dwarf varieties, spotted and blotched, fine....................... .... 10c

Albus. White ground, handsome large flowering varieties........................ 10c

Hose in Hose. Very curious and pretty, one flower sitting in another; fine mixed..... 15c

Moschatus. (Musk Plant.) The thin delicate leaves emit a delicate musk odor......... 10c

MOMORDICA.   T. A.

A curious annual climber, with yellow blossoms. The fruit is the chief curiosity, is egg-shaped, and covered with warty excrescences, which, when ripe, bursts suddenly open, scattering its seeds, and showing a brilliant carmine interior. Fine for trellises, fences, stumps, etc. Half hardy annual.

Balsamina (Balsam Apple.)................ 5c

Charantia (Balsam Pear.) Golden yellow... 5c

TALL NASTURTIUM (Tropæolum Major.)
H. H. A.

Elegant profuse flowering plants for verandas, trellises, etc. The seed pods can be gathered while green and tender, for pickling, hardy annuals; 10 feet.

Finest mixed. All colors of Climbing Nasturtium.................................... 5c

Lobb's Nasturtium.   H. H. A., 4 to 6 feet.

Tropæolum Lobbianum. These are distinguished from the Tall Nasturtiums above (Tropaeolum Majus), by their longer vines; their leaves and flowers, however, are somewhat smaller, but their greater profusion renders them superior for trellises, arbors, for hanging over vases, rock-work, etc.; the flowers are of unusual brilliancy and richness, and they are also splendid for winter decoration in the green-house and conservatory.

Mixed. Contains many beautiful sorts 10c

Lucifer. Very dark scarlet................. 5c

Roi des Noirs. Black Brown...... .... 5c

TOM THUMB NASTURTIUMS. H. H. A.

The dwarf varieties are all desirable, and are among our most popular plants, standing any amount of heat and drought, growing vigorously and flowering freely all summer and fall; excellent for massing and ribboning, doing well even in poor soil, hardy annuals; 1 foot; mixed; many sorts; pkt 5c

Empress of India. Very dwarf habit; flowers brilliant crimson; abundant bloomer 10c

Lady Bird. Orange yellow, red spots....... 10c

Tom Thumb King Theodore. Flowers almost black................................. 5c

King of Tom Thumbs. Crimson.......... 5c

Coccineum. Scarlet, fine................. 5c

Golden King. Brilliant yellow............. 5c

Tom Thumb. Mixed all colors.............. 5c

Beauty. Yellow and scarlet................ 5c

Aurora. Very fine; new variety; beautiful pink 10c

NEMOPHILA (Love Grove). H. A., 1 ft.

A charming dwarf California annual, neat, compact and of uniform growth, adapted for beds and borders, fine mixed varieties. 5c

NIEREMBERGIA.   H. H. A.

A half hardy annual, slender growing plant, perpetually in bloom; desirable for the greenhouse, baskets, vases or bedding one foot.... ... . 5c

NIGELLA.   H. A.
(Love in a Mist or Devil in a Bush.)

A compact, free-flowering plant, with finely cut foliage, curious looking flowers and seed pods; of easy culture, growing in any garden soil; hardy annuals; 1 foot.

Damascena (Devil in a Bush). Double, blue and white............................. 5c

Nana, fl. pl. Double dwarf, very beautiful, 6 to 8 inches high; fine for edgings....... 5c

NOLANA.   H. A.

Very pretty annual of trailing habit, with Morning Glory-like flowers, well adapted to rock work. Height 6 inches.

Mixed. All varieties...................... 5c

OSTROWSKIA (Bokhara Bell Flower).
(Ostrowshia Magnificia.)

This new Bell Flower is a hardy perennial herbaceous plant; flowering the second season from seed; stately and beautiful. It forms a tall bush 3 to 5 feet high, surrounded with enormous bell-shaped flowers of an exquisite lavender shade, veined with purple. Every lover of flowers should have it. Pkt, 25c.

OENOTHERA (Evening Primrose).
H. P., 1 to 2 feet.

Beautiful, free growing and useful, flowering in long spikes, fine for beds or borders.

Biennis (Evening Primrose). Yellow flowers opening in the evening and early morning. 5c

Acaulis Alba. Large white flowers, dwarf, showy and beautiful....................... 5c

Taraxacifolia Aurea. Golden yellow, large flowered, very fine...................... 5c

Rosea (Mexicana). Six inches high, extra fine, true rose colored flowers........... 10c

PASSION Flower (Climber).   H. P.

Handsome rapid grower, fine for decoration and open ground.

Coerulea Grandiflora. Large flowers, blue.. 10c

PERILLA.

The foliage of this plant is exceedingly elegant, of a very dark purple color, and produce a charming contrast with silver-leaved plants; growing freely in any soil; half-hardy annual; 1½ feet.

Nankinensis Atropurpureus Laciniatis. Elegant 5c

PENTSTEMON.

One of our most beautiful and attractive herbaceous plants, bearing long, graceful spikes of rich-colored flowers; will bloom the first season if sown early in March, and planted out in May; half-hardy perennials; 2 feet.

Hartwegi (gentianoides, hybridus), extra fine mixed, from the handsomest new sorts, which the seed reproduces in great variety   10c

PANSIES.

Grandiflora Pansy (Viola Tricolor.)

This is a great favorite with all flower gardens. It is biennial and can be perpetuated by division of the roots. Seeds sown in autumn produce earlier and better flowers the coming season. They require good rich soil.

Pansies in Separate Colors.

Odier or Five Blotched. A beautiful strain, perfect in size and form of flowers, containing many beautiful colors; each of the 5 petals is marked with a large dark blotch; very effective 15c
Emperor William. Large handsome flowers borne in great profusion, well above the foliage, brilliant ultramarine blue with a purple violet eye 10c
Striped and Mottled. A very showy and rich strain; mixed colors, pkt............ 15c
"Fire King." A grand new novelty; golden yellow; the upper petals purple; very showy, pkt 15c
Faust (King of the Blacks.) Almost black, the darkest pansy known................ 10c
Lord Beaconsfield. A splendid sort; flowers deep purple violet, shading to white on the upper petals 10c
Snow Queen Very large, satiny white, light yellow center........................... 10c
Yellow Gem. Pure yellow, without eye..... 10c
"Non Plus Ultra." Offered last year for the first time. Beautiful colors and large flowers. Highly effective, very choice mixed; pkt....................... .... 25c
Cassier's. Very large-flowered. Seed saved from largest sized pansies, beautifully marked. A rich and showy strain; pkt.. 25c
Bugnots Superb Blotched. Extra large flowers with very broad blotches, the two upper petals finely lined; refined shape and varied colors; pkt.................... 25c
Trimardeau. An altogether distinct and beautiful new race, the flowers of which are larger than any hitherto produced. Each flower is marked with three large blotches or spots; and the plants produce an endless variety of beautiful shades.... 15c
Yellow Giant (Yellow Trimardeau.) New, with large black eye; remarkably showy; one of the best pansies................... 25c
White Giant (White Trimardeau.) With purple eye; very beautiful 25c

White. Pure black center................... 10c
Yellow (golden). Pure black center, fine for bedding............................ .... 10c
Azure Blue. Bright sky blue............. 10c
Bronze. Dark mahogany, shades fine 10c
Silver Edged................................. 10c
Gold Margined..... .... 10c
Havana Brown............................... 10c
Black with Bronzy Center................ 10c
German Finest Mixed.... .... 10c

PETUNIA.   T. P.

For out-door decoration or house culture few plants are equal to this class. They commence flowering early and continue a mass of bloom throughout the whole season, until killed by frost; easily cultivated, requiring rich soil and a sunny situation. Of late years the single-striped, mottled and double varieties have been greatly improved.

Single Varieties.

Petunia Hybrida, Belle Etoile. Beautiful large-flowered strain of striped and blotched............................. 10c
Grandiflora Venosa. Large flowering, finest shades of colors beautifully veined 10c
Finest Striped and Blotched. Seed saved from magnificent collections of striped and blotched varieties. 10c
Inimitable Dwarf (Nana Compacta Multiflora. Bushy; 5 to 8 inches high, with regularly striped flowers; exceedingly effective as borders or in plots; pkt................. 20c
Large Flowered Yellow Throat. These form a class of rare beauty, and come true from seed. The flowers are very large, and of perfect form, with a deep yellow throat, veined very much like the Salpiglossis................................. 25c
Princess of Wurtemburg. Rose, beautiful.. 25c
Hybrida Grandiflora Fimbriata. Fringed varieties in splendid mixture............ 25c
Marginata Maculata. Green bordered and blotched varieties; single mixed; very rare. 25c
Grandiflora Alba. A very beautiful large-flowered white Petunia; pkt.......... 20c
Pure White, Single. Desirable for cemetery beds, or where large masses of white are wanted 5c
Hybrida. Finest mixed.......... .... 5c

Double Petunias.

Double Inimitable. Striped and blotched varieties; splendid mixed; per pkt 20c
Double Large Fowering (Grandiflora, fl. pl.) Extra fine mixed; choicest colors......... 25c
Double Fringed (Grandiflora Fimbriata fl. pl). Charming double fringed flowers........ 40c
Lady of the Lake. A beautiful double white fringed Petunia; the seed will produce about 30 per cent. of plants with large double fringed pure white flowers; per pkt 30c

PYRETHRUM.   H. P.

This family contains the well-known Golden Feather, a low growing plant, with yellow foliage for ribbon beds, edgings, etc., and also contains some of the handsomest hardy plants for borders that are in Cultivation.

Yellow Foliage Sorts For Ribboning.

Aureum. Bright yellow foliage; 1 foot...... 10c
Laciniatus. Yellow foliage, finely fringed; 1 foot........................... 5c
Selaginoides. Handsome fern-like foliage; ½ foot.................. 15c
Golden Gem. Double white flowers and golden foliage. Beautiful for borders.pkt 10c

Hardy Flowering Varieties.

Showy, hardy, herbaceous perennials, with bright beautiful flowers of many colors, which remain in bloom for a long time. Are invaluable as cut flowers for decorative purposes on account of their bright appearance and long duration. The single ones resemble our well-known Marguerites and are very showy; used in connection with them in floral pieces or bouquets.

Pyrethrum Roseum Hybridum, fl. pl. Double sorts, mixed........................ 20c
Pyrethrum Roseum Hybridum. Single sorts, finest mixed........................... 10c

PHLOX DRUMMONDI.

For beds and masses these beautiful annuals cannot be surpassed. They produce immense trusses of brilliant flowers of many hues. From early Spring until cut off by frost.

Finest mixed, 15c.

Grandiflora. Large-flowering varieties; choicest mixed, 10c.

Alba. Pure white, beautiful, 10c.

Star of Quedlinburg.   Coccinea. Brilliant, scarlet, splendid.................... 15c
Stellata Splendens. With pure white stellated centers.................. 10c
Rosea. Bright Rose...................... 10c
Rosea Alba-Oculato. Rose with white eye.. 10c
Leopoldi. Red with white eye............. 10c
Nana Compacta. Dwarf compact; charming varieties for borders, bedding, etc........ 15c
Phlox Decussata (Perennis). Perennial; very hardy; splendid sorts; mixed........... 15c

Two New Varieties of Phlox.

Star of Quedlinburg and Fimbriata. These new Phloxes with their sharply fringed and toothed flowers are really great novelties. From the singularity and gracefulness of the flowers, they are ornaments in any garden. Of easy cultivation and beautiful as cut flowers. Both varieties including many colors mixed; per pkt., 15c.

PRIMULA.

The Chinese Primrose is a great favorite for Winter and early Spring, blooming in the house or conservatory. The foliage is attractive, and the flowers borne in clusters are perfectly charming. One of our best pot plants, of easy cultivation.

Chinensis. Fine mixed.......... .... 25c
Chinensis, Fimbriata (Finest fringed). Mixed 25c
Chinensis, Fimbriata Rubra. Fringed, red.. 25c
Chinensis, Fimbriata Alba. Snow Queen, fringed white........................... 25c
Chinensis, Fimbriata. Coccinea, brilliant, new red........................ 25c
Chinensis, Fimbriata, fl. pl. Finest double fringed; mixed 40c

HARDY PRIMROSES.

Primula Vulgaris. The true yellow Primrose (English) 15c
Auricula (Alpine Primrose). Beautiful colors; mixed................... 10c
Japonica (Japanese Primrose). One of the most beautiful. The flowers are larger than the common varieties, of shades of crimson, lilac, white, pink, etc. Finest mixed........................ 15c
Primula Veris (Polyanthus). Choice mixed. 10c
Primula Veris (Duplex, Hose in Hose). Very curious and pretty; one flower set within another...................... 25c

SINGLE AND DOUBLE POPPIES. II. A.

(Annual Varieties.)

Double Carnation. Very double, with finely cut or fringed petals; mixed colors....... 5c
Pæony Flowered. Splendid, large, double, mixed colors 5c
The Mikado. One of the most charming poppies. The petals at the base are pure white, while the fringed edges are of a brilliant crimson scarlet. This is undoubtedly one of the most effective annuals........................ 10c
Ranunculus Flowered. Small, double varieties...................... 5c
Umbrosum. Single flowers of glowing vermillion with a deep black spot on each petal. If sown in the Autumn will bloom very early in the Spring. They are extremely showy and well worthy a place in every garden.......................... 5c
Pavonium. New, single scarlet; base, dark cherry red, encircled by black zone...... 10c

Double and Single Perennial Varieties.

Orientale Hybridium. New, hybrids mixed. These are very choice and contain charming new colors........................ 25c
Orientale (or Monarch Poppy). Will bloom the following Spring from seed grown in the Fall, foliage massive and beautiful; flowers simply grand, both in size and color; the darkest red, fine............. 10c

Nudioaule (New Iceland Poppies). Very graceful with light green foliage and single flowers; many colors mixed........ 10c

Maculatum Superbum. With intense deep scarlet blotched flowers 5c

Papaver Creceum, fl. pl. New, double yellow perennial poppy................... 20c

Romneya Coulteri. (Great White California Tree Poppy). A fine perennial of stately beauty; it is one of the best for yielding a succession of bloom from July until November. The flowers are large 4 to 5 inches across, and are extremely delicate, with loose crumpled petals, resembling the single White Paeony. Plant the seed in the Fall in a protected spot, and in the Spring you will have fine plants for transplanting 25c

New Japanese Pompon Poppies. Small, very double flowers produced in great profusion; many lovely colors, mixed.... 15c

PARDANTHUS CHINESIS (Blackberry Lily).

Pardanthus Chinensis (Blackberry Lily). Small, lily-like flowers; orange, spotted with purple; hardy perennial............ 10c

PORTULACA.

This is one of the most charming annuals of easy culture. Blooms best in a light sandy soil and will stand the hottest sun if well watered. Fine for bedding.

Grandiflora. Single mixed, many colors.. 5c

Grandiflora. Double rose-flowered; extra mixed..................... ... . 10c

RHODANTHE (Everlasting Flower).

H. H. A., 1 foot.

Very valuable for Winter bouquets, and also desirable for pot plants or for garden; red, white and pink, finest mixed........ 5c

RICINUS (Castor Oil Plants).

H. H. A., 6 to 15 feet.

This is a rapid grower with fine palm-like foliage, giving a fine effect on lawns or large beds.

Fine mixture of all varieties, foliage sorts 5c

ROCKET (Hesperia).

H. P., 2 to 3 feet.

Well-known, free-flowering and very fragrant; purple and white..................... 5c

SALPIGLOSSIS.   H. H. A.

Neat and beautiful ornamental autumn blooming plants, with curiously pencilled and marbled funnel-shaped flowers; suitable for the greenhouses or flower border; of easy culture, requiring a light, rich soil; half hardy annual; 1½ feet.

Grandiflora. Large flowered; all colors mixed................................. 5c

SALVIA (Flowering Sage).

H. H. P., 3 feet.

One of our handsomest Summer and Autumn flowering plants, when they are literally ablaze with brilliant flowers; very effective for massing on the lawn or for ribbon beds.

Splendens (Scarlet Sage). Beautiful, fiery scarlet 5c

Splendens Coccinea, Nana Compacta. Dwarf, compact, very free flowering..... 10c

SAPONARIA (Bouncing Bet).   H. A.

Handsome dwarf growing plants, with pretty star-shaped flowers; excellent for massing and edging.

Multiflora Compacta, New, compact, beautiful for borders planted in a sunny situation 5c

Ocymoides, Splendens, very brilliant red, fine........ .... 5c

SENSITIVE PLANT (Mimosa Pudica).

A very interesting plant with fern-like foliage, which is so sensitive that the leaves close up immediately when touched or shaken; suitable for pots or borders; H. A., 1 foot.... 5c

SCHIZANTHUS (Butterfly Flower).

H. H. A.

A splendid class of plants, combining elegance of growth and profusion of beautiful flowers, valuable in the garden and greenhouse; white, purple, yellow and crimson; half hardy annuals....................

Papilionaceous. In this charming variety we have one of the finest annuals in cultivation. The flowers are handsome as some of the orchids................... 5c

Grandiflora Pyramidalis, Compactus. New compact, fine............................ 5c

Pinnatus. Blue............................ 5c

STATICE (Everlasting).

An interesting free flowering plant of easy culture, long-blooming and valuable for Winter bouquets, perennial, fine mixed.. 10c

SCABIOSA.   H. P.

The Mourning Bride or Sweet Scabious of our old garden, but much improved in size, colors and doubleness. They are very free bloomers; the colors white, carmine, lilac, maroon, etc., excellent for bouquets.

Nana, fl. pl. Mixed dwarf, double; 1 foot... 5c

Major, fl. pl. Mixed, new, large flowering, tall double sorts..... .... 5c

Minor, fl. pl. Rose color, new.............. 5c

Minor, fl. pl. Cherry red, new.............. 5c

Candidissima. Pure white flowers, useful for bouquets 5c

Scabiosa (Snowball). This new variety is a great addition to our gardens and is very valuable for floral work of every description. The flowers are pure white, very large and densely double............... 15c

SMILAX (Medeola Asparagoides).

SMILAX (Myrsiphyllum).

T. P. 6 feet.

This is the most popular and graceful evergreen vine in cultivation, adapted for hanging baskets and pot culture, floral wreaths, etc........................... 10c

SUNFLOWER.   H. A.

Stately growing plants, with immense golden yellow flowers; the single varieties are well known, but the double sorts are not; they are perfectly magnificent.

DOUBLE SORTS.

Globosus Fistulosus. Perfectly round flowers, very double, saffron; 6 feet.......... 5c

Oculatus Viridis. Double yellow flowers, with green center; 4 feet.............. 5c

Miniature Sunflower. (Globe flowered.) Of dwarf branching habit, bearing many little flowers only two inches across; orange.... 5c

Nanum, fl. pl. (Dwarf double.) Yellow, quite dwarf, fine........................... 5c

Giant Russian. Flowers 18 to 20 inches across; grown principally for the seed of which it is very prolific................ 5c

JACOBÆA (Senicio.)

Remarkably pretty, free growing profuse flowering plants, almost unsurpassed for brilliancy and beauty. Growing freely from seed, and are easily propagated from cuttings, not one in fifty failing. The double are the only ones worth cultivating. Hardy annuals in open border, biennial in greenhouse. Sow in loam mixed with leaf mold. Purple, pink and white flowers.

Senecio Elegans, fl. pl. (Tall double Jacobaea)

Finest varieties 5c

Nana, fl. pl. (Double Dwarf sorts.) Finest mixed, 8 inches...................... 5c

TEN WEEKS STOCKS.

The Ten Weeks Stock, Stock Gilly or Gilly-flower, as they are sometimes called, stands prominent among annuals for either flower beds, pot culture, cut flowers, and delicious spicy perfume; they have been greatly improved in the past few years, and a large flowering strain has been originated which for size, doubleness and variety of exquisite shades of color is remarkable.

Large Flowering Dwarf Ten Week. The following are the best double varieties and most desirable colors for cultivation; mixed, all choice double large-flowering, 10c.

Very Dwarf Snowflake. A beautiful small-growing variety, with vigorous main spike and numerous side shoots of very large double snow-white flowers; very early........................... .... 15c

Large-flowering Pyramidal. This variety has compact flower spikes, and throws out many side shoots; excellent for pots. 10c

New Giant Perfection This sort produces plants 2½ feet high, with long flower-spikes of extra double handsome flowers, and is extremely effective in beds and borders.................................. 10c

White (Dresden perpetual.) Very beautiful, large spikes, splendid for cutting........ 15c

Biennial Stock.

Brompton (Winter or Biennial.) Large flowering double; finest mixed.............. 10c

Brompton. Snow-white shining, large flowering................................... 15c

Emperor, or Perpetual. Large flowering. These make bushy and branching plants, with an abundance of choice double flowers. Sow in July or August. Will last several years when protected; many colors; finest mixed, pkt............ ...... 10c

Emperor. Pure white; large flowering...... 15c

Wallflower-Leaved. Large flowering, choice mixed............................ .... 10c

The Wallflower-Leaved Stocks have quite distinct dark glossy foliage.

Intermediate, or Autumnal. These are prized on account of their flowering late in Autumn or early in Spring. The seed should be sown in July and August for early spring flowering; finest mixed...... 10c

SWEET PEAS (Lathyrus Odoratus.)

Beautiful fragrant free flowering plants, thriving in any open situation; excellent for screening unsightly objects, will bloom all summer and autumn if the flowers are cut freely and the pods picked off as they appear. They may be sown in autumn in this section; early sowing is necessary, hardy annuals; 6 feet. No garden is complete without them.

Butterfly. White tinted lilac.............. 5c

Queen of the Isles. Scarlet mottled with white and purple 10c

Princess B atrice. New Rose.............. 10c

Princess of Wales. White, blue striped.... 10c

Apple Blossom. Bright rose; Wing's apple blossom. 10c

Violet Queen. The flowers range in colors from deep mauve to light violet.......... 10c

Queen of England. Extra large; pure white; very fine................................ 15c

Black Purple. Very dark; almost black.... 5c

Cardinal. New...................... ..... 10c

Blue Bird. Bright Blue.................... 5c

Captain Clarke. (Tricolor.) White, rose and purple...................... ..... 5c

Crown Princess, of Prussia. Bright blush, shading to rose........................ 5c

Invincible, scarlet. Bright scarlet flowers.. 5c

Fairy Queen. White and rose........... .. .. 5c

Dark Rod............................... 5c

Indigo King. Purple prince 5c

Snowflake. Pure white 5c

Invincible Red-striped.................... 5c

Light Blue and Purple.................... 5c

Painted Lady. Red and white............. 5c

Purple Striped..... .... 5c

Mixed. Many colors.................... 5c

LATHYRUS (Everlasting Pea.)

Showy, free flowering plants, growing in any common soil. A good climber for covering fences or walls. Hardy perennials.

Latifolius. (Everlasting Pea.) Red. 10c

Albus. White splendid climber............. 10c

Rotundifolius. Copper Red fine........... 10c

Lathyrus. Mixed colors................... 10c

SWEET WILLIAM (Dianthus Barbatus.) H. P.

A well known attractive free-flowering plant, which has been greatly improved of late years, producing a splendid effect in beds and shrubbery with their rich and varied flowers; hardy perennial, 1½ feet.

Double. From choice collections, 10c.

Single. Choicest mixed, 5c.

THUNBERGIA (Climber).

H. H. A., 4 feet.

Very ornamental and rapid growth; the flowers are very much admired; colors red, white, buff and bright orange, with various colored throats; choicest mixed........... 5c

AFRICAN GOLDEN VENIDIUM.

African Golden Venidium (Venidium Calendulaceum). This is an old but little known plant. It forms a compact bush only a few inches high; flowers bright yellow, shaded with orange, and are from four to five inches in circumference. The leaves are large and woolly, covering the ground and bringing out in strong contrast the flowers, which are borne profusely, nearly covering the plant. The plants remain in bloom throughout the Summer; are of easy culture, and exceedingly showy; they are also useful for rustic baskets and rock work.............. 10c

VERBENA.　H. H. P., 1 ft.

Georgeous for beds or massing, flowers of the most brilliant colors; flowering continually from Spring until late in the Autumn. Verbenas grown from seed are always thrifty and free bloomers; flowering the first year from seed. Soak the seed in tepid water an hour or two, and sow in a frame or shallow box filled with light, rich soil half an inch deep; water sparingly and keep in a light moderately warm situation. They germinate in two weeks. When an inch high, carefully lift them and pot in three-inch pots, shading from the sun for a few days; when started give plenty of light and air.

Hybrida. Finest marked varieties, from beautiful collection.................... 10c
Defiance. Scarlet, extra for bedding; beautiful 10c
Candidissima. With large trusses of flowers of the purest white 10c
Striata, Italian Carnation-like Striped. Saved from a rich collection........... 10c
Lutea. New yellow, distinct, new and pretty 10c
Venosa. Blue, fine for edging.............. 10c
Coccinea, fol. aureis. Golden yellow foliage and many colored flowers; strikingly beautiful, especially at the end of the Summer.
Verbena Hybr da Grandiflora. In our extra fine mixed Verbena we thought we had the finest Verbena seed known, but are free to admit that this new strain offered last year for the first time, is superior, both in size of flowers and cluster. In the Grandiflora the flowers are of unusual size, easily raised from seed that we are sure this new large, flowering strain will immediately become very popular. To place it within the reach of all, we offer it as low as it can be sold, and are sure that all purchasers will be delighted with it........................... ... 15c

VINCA (Madagascar Per.winkle).　T. P.

Ornamental free-blooming plants, they flower from seed, if sown early, the first season, continuing until frost, or they may be potted and kept in bloom through the Winter; 2 feet.
Vinca. Mixed colors...................... 10c

VIRGINIA STOCK.　H. A.
(Cheiranthus Maritimus.)

Beautiful free flowering little plants, very effective in small beds, edging or baskets, growing in any soil; hardy annual.
Mixed; all colors, 3 inches................. 5c

VIOLET (Viola Odorata).　H. P.

Well-known, fragrant, early, spring blooming plants for edging, groups or borders; thriving best in Summer in a shady situation, in a rich deep soil; extensively used by florists for forcing for cut flowers during the Fall and Winter months; hardy perennials, 6 inches.
Single Blue (Odorata Semperflorens). Very sweet-scented blue flowers 10c
Single White (Odorata Semperflorens). Sweet Violet, very fragrant and free-flowering.. 10c
The Czar, fl. albo. Fine white.............. 20c
Lutea, Grandiflora. Fine yellow........... 10c
Viola. Very fine mixed 10c

WALLFLOWER (Cheiranthus Cheiri).
H. H. P.

Well-known deliciously fragrant garden plants, blooming early in the Spring, with large conspicuous spikes of beautiful flowers; they should be protected in a cold frame in the Winter, and planted out in May; are much prized for bouquet flowers; half hardy perennials.
Single Mixed. All colors, 2½ feet............... 5c
Finest Double Mixed. All colors, 2 feet....... 10c

WAITZIA (Everlasting).

Waitzia Grandiflora. Yellow flowers, borne in clusters; fine for dried bouquets mixed with grasses............... .... 10c

WHITLAVIA.　H. A.

Charming hardy annual, with delicate foliage and clusters of beautiful bell-shaped flowers, fine for ribboning, mixed borders or shady spots; growing freely in any garden soil; also good for baskets, vases, etc.; 1 foot.
Grandiflora. Large, violet-blue............... 5c

ZINNIA ELEGANS, Fl. Pl.　H. A.
(Youth and Old Age.)

Double Zinnias are an acquisition to our list of garden favorites; of branching habits and splendid brilliant colored double flowers; rivaling the Dahlia in beauty and form. The seed can be sown early in the hot-bed and transplanted, or sown later in the open ground; half hardy annuals; 2 feet.

White. Pure white flowers; fine for florists, 5c.
Coccinea, fl. pl. Fine double scarlet, 5c.
Kermesina, fl. pl. Bright crimson, 5c.

Tall Double. Finest mixed: splendid quality.... 5c
Grandiflora Robusta Plenissima. (New Giant Zinnias). A new very large flowering race differing from the old varieties in their more luxuriant robust growth, and in the larger and more conical shape of the flowers, which have broader and many more petals. The plant forms a handsome bush, three feet in height, and the large perfectly formed double flowers, measuring 5 to 6 inches across, are borne in profusion, lasting until killed by frost; splendid.... 10c
Pompon. Excellent Zennias, differing from the older ones in habit of growth and the immense size of their perfectly formed very double flowers of various striking colors. The plants are dwarf and bloom freely during a long period 10c
Zinnia Grandiflora. Single, fine mixed.......... 5c
Tom Thumb Zinnias. Double mixed........... 5c

XERANTHEMUMS.

A showy class of everlastings, the flowers are white, purple and yellow, single and double. If gathered before fully opened and dried in the shade, they will retain their beauty for years. They make fine Winter bouquets. Sow in Spring and thin out to one foot apart. Hardy annual, 1 foot.
Xeranthemum. mixed...................... 5c

ORNAMENTAL GRASSES.

Nearly all the ornamental grasses are very showy and beautiful, and when dried and tastefully arranged in connection with the Everlasting flowers, make exceedingly attractive winter bouquets.

Ornamental Grasses. A collection of eight different varieties, our own selection............ 30c
Agrostis Minutiflora. New; very fine 10c
Agrostis Nebulosa. Light, feathery and graceful, fine for winter bouquets, hardy annual; 1 foot 5c
Briza Maxima (Large Quaking Grass.) Large pendent seeds, fine for clumps or bouquets, hardy annual; 1 foot.......................... 5c
Briza Geniculata. Graceful species for bouquets 5c
Bromus Brizæiormis. Splendid variety, with drooping spikes of pendent seeds, hardy annual, 1 foot.. 5c

Cynosurus Elegans. Fine for bouquets......... 5c
Eragrostis Maxima. Beautiful dancing spikelets for bouquets........................ 10c
Eragrostis Elegans (Love Grass.) Elegant and feathery foliage, hardy annual, 1 foot.......... 5c
Gynerium Argenteum (True Pampas Grass.) Makes fine clumps for lawns, large silvery plumes, half-hardy perennial, 6 to 10 feet...... 10c
Lagurus Ovatus (Hare's Tail Grass.) Woolly cone-shaped heads, fine for Winter bouquets, hardy annual, 1 foot........................... 5c
Stipa Pennata (Feather Grass.) Delicate long silvery feathers, fine for winter bouquets, hardy perennial, 2 feet......................... 10c
Tricholæna. Pretty rose-colored grass, hardy annual, 1 foot.............................. 10c
Poa Amabilis. Very fine for bouquets......... 10c

Quantity of Seed Required to Sow an Acre of Ground.

	Pounds.		Pounds.
Grass, Timothy........................	20	Hemp—broadcast....................	30 to 50
Grass, Mesquit, in the chaff........	35	Flax, when wanted for the seed..............	50
Grass, Hungarian........................	40	Flax, when wanted for the fiber..........	80
Grass, Millet............................	40	Beans, Dwarf or Bush—hills and drills........	80
Grass, Mixed Lawn......................	75	Beans, tall or pole—hills.................	20
A much larger quantity of seed is required		Beets, drills...........................	5 to 6
to make a close fine lawn than for other pur-		Broom Corn—hills.....................	15
poses.		Buckwheat—broadcast...................	45
Grass, mixed for mowing) Clover.....	8	Cabbage in beds to cover an acre after trans-	
or grazing >Timothy........	15	planting...........................	4½
) Redtop.........	15	Carrots—drills........................	3 to 4
Grass, Kentucky Blue, for pasture......	30	Melon, Water—hills...................	2 to 3
Grass, Kentucky Blue, for lawn...........	75	Melon, Cantaloupe—hills...............	4
Grass, Orchard.........................	40	Onions, black seed—drills.............	5 to 6
Grass, English or Australian Rye, for meadow.	50	Onions, top set—drills................	200
Grass, English or Australian Rye, for lawn....	75	Onions, black seeds, for bottom sets.......	40
Grass, Italian Rye.....................	30 to 40	Parsnips—drills......................	6
Grass, Redtop..........................	30	Peas—drills...........................	100
Alfalfa or Lucerne.....................	20 to 25	Peas—broadcast.......................	180
Clover, Red alone—broadcast...........	15 to 20	Potatoes—hills.......................	500 to 600
Clover, White alone—broadcast..........	12	Pumpkins—hills.......................	5
Clover, Alsike—broadcast..............	10	Radishes—drills......................	8
Barley—broadcast.....................	125 to 150	Sage—drills...........................	8
Oats—broadcast........................	80	Spinach—drills........................	15
Rye—broadcast.........................	100	Squash, bush varieties—hills...........	5
Wheat—broadcast......................	125	Squash, running varieties—hills.........	3
Wheat—drills..........................	90	Tomato, in beds to transplant...........	½
Corn, Sweet or Field—hills.............	15	Turnip and Rutabaga—drills............	1½
Corn, to cut green for fodder—drills or broad-		Turnip and Rutabaga—broadcast.........	3
cast.	150	Cucumber—hills.......................	2
Vetches—broadcast.....................	150		

Quantity of Seed Required to Produce a Given Number of Plants, or Sow Certain Quantity of Ground.

Artichoke....................1 oz. to 500 plants
Asparagus.... ......1 oz. to 60 feet of drill of 600 plants
Beans, dwarf................1 lb. to 50 feet of drill
Beans, tall.. . ...1 lb. to 75 hills
Beets......................1 oz. to 50 feet of drill
Broccoli....................1 oz. to 2,000 plants
Brussels Sprouts.............1 oz. to 2,000 plants
Cabbage....................1 oz. to 2,000 plants
Carrots.............. ....1 oz. to 150 feet of drill
Cauliflower.................1 oz. to 2,000 plants
Celery.....................1 oz. to 3,000 plants
Chicory....................1 oz. to 100 feet of drill
Corn..........................1 lb. to 100 hills
Cress......................1 oz. to 100 feet of drill
Cucumber.....................1 oz. to 75 hills
Egg Plant..................1 oz. to 1,600 plants
Endive... ....1 oz. to 150 feet of drill or 3,000 plants
Kale.......................1 oz. to 2,000 plants
Kohl Rabi..................1 oz. to 2,000 plants
Leek.......................1 oz. to 150 feet of drill

Lettuce.....................1 oz. to 3,000 plants
Melon, Water.................1 oz. to 50 hills
Melon, Musk..................1 oz. to 50 hills
Okra.......................1 oz. to 50 feet of drill
Onion Seed.... ....1 oz. to 100 feet of drill
Onion, top set..............1 lb. to 20 feet of drill
Parsnips...................1 oz. to 200 feet of drill
Parsley....................1 oz. to 150 feet of drill
Peas.......................1 lb. to 50 feet of drill
Pepper.....................1 oz. to 1,000 plants
Pumpkin....................1 oz. to 40 hills
Radish....................1 oz. to 100 feet of drill
Salsify....................1 oz to 70 feet of drill
Sage.......................1 oz. to 150 feet of drill
Spinach....................1 oz. to 100 feet of drill
Squash, early...............1 oz. to 50 hills
Squash, winter..............1 oz. to 10 hills
Tomato.....................1 oz. to 3,000 plants
Tobacco....................1 oz. to 10,000 plants

NURSERY DEPARTMENT.

W. R. STRONG COMPANY,

PROPRIETORS

Capital Nurseries

SACRAMENTO,

CAL.

ADDRESS ALL COMMUNICATIONS AS ABOVE.

SCHMIDT LABEL & LITHO. CO. S. F.

CATALOGUE OF
Trees and Nursery Stock.

IN PRESENTING this edition of our Catalogue and Price List we desire to thank our friends for past favors and solicit their orders for the coming season. We have an unusually large stock. Trees large, strong, uniform in size, and strictly first-class in every respect. We cordially invite a PERSONAL INSPECTION of our Nurseries. Correspondence solicited. All orders will receive prompt and careful attention. Satisfaction guaranteed. Varieties that we have in large quantities are marked with an asterisk, thus *

TERMS OF SALE.

FIRST. All articles in following list will be furnished at prices named ONLY when the quantities specified are taken.

SECOND. When particular varieties and sizes of trees are ordered, please state whether or not substitution will be allowed and to what extent, as it often happens with us as with all Nurseries, that we are out of some varieties and sizes, and unless otherwise instructed we will feel at liberty to substitute other similar varieties that are equally as good. When selection of varieties is left to us we will send the best in our judgment.

THIRD. All orders should be sent in as early as possible, as we endeavor to fill them in the order in which they are received.

FOURTH. All orders from unknown parties must be accompanied by cash, or satisfactory reference.

FIFTH. All orders to be sent C. O. D. must be accompanied by one-half the amount of bill. Money may be sent by Express, Draft or Money Order, at our risk.

SIXTH. All trees and plants are carefully labeled, graded and packed for shipment in the best possible manner, for which a reasonable charge sufficient to cover the cost of material only shall be charged. But we make no charge for delivering to the Railroad or Express Office at Sacramento.

SEVENTH, Orders should be written plainly on a separate sheet, and not be mixed up in the body of the letter. Give size and price of tree wanted, it will save us trouble and tend to prevent any mistakes.

EIGHTH. Be particular to give explicit marking and shipping instructions; when the route of shipment is left for us to choose we will use our best judgment, but in any case our responsibility ceases after delivery to Railroad Office here in good condition.

NINTH. Any errors in filling orders will be cheerfully rectified on receiving notice, provided, such notice be given within ten days from receipt of goods.

EXTENT OF GUARANTEE.

We fully realize that our success in the Nursery Business depends on the reliability of our labels, and we use every effort to avoid mistakes in varieties. But we will not warrant against errors or apparent mistakes in varieties, only to this extent: We will replace free of charge all trees that do not prove true to label, or will refund in cash the original cost of such trees, with ten per cent per annum, from time of purchase until trees begin bearing. But it must be mutually understood and agreed between purchasers and ourselves that in no case shall we be liable to any greater extent than above mentioned.

APPLE TREES.

Apples are among our most profitable fruits, when proper varieties and locations are secured. Early and autumn varieties should be planted in the valleys and foothills, and winter varieties in the mountains and along the coast.

☞ Our stock of trees comprises all the leading and popular sorts, and is unsurpassed in vigor, thrift and hardiness. There is so much variation in climate on this coast that the time of ripening of the several fruits can only be approximately named, and some apples that are classed as fall apples would be winter fruit in some localities. We would call special attention to our one-year extra apple trees; they are one year from bud, on strong roots, and are as large as two-year old trees. We should prefer them to two-year trees to plant. A one-year tree has buds all along the body, hence a good head can be secured at any desired height.

Apples—Leading Varieties.	Each	100	1000
1 year, No. 1—4 to 6 feet	$0 20	$15 00	$120
1 year, No. 2—3 to 4 feet	15	12 00	100
1 year, from bud—extra, 5 to 7 feet	25	20 00	150

APPLES.----Summer.

RED JUNE Small to medium, deep red, juicy and good. Ripens about the 20th of June.

EARLY HARVEST Large, pale yellow, mild, sub-acid. Ripens about the 20th of June.

*RED ASTRACHAN Large, roundish, striped with deep crimson, thick bloom, very juicy and acid, good bearer; ripens in June.

*WILLIAMS' Favorite Large, oblong, light red, juicy and good, ripens early in July.

APPLES.----Autumn.

*ALEXANDER Very large and beautiful, greenish yellow, striped with red, one of the best and most profitable market varieties. Ripens early in July.

*WHITE ASTRACHAN Large, oblate, skin very smooth and white, with faint red stripes, juicy, acid, valuable for market; ripens 10th to 20th of July.

*GRAVENSTEIN Large, roundish, striped, very productive and good for market; ripens last of July to 1st of August.

*SANTA CLARA KING Large, roundish, skin yellow with red blush on exposed side, flesh crisp and juicy, good for all purpose; ripens 10th to 20th of August.

*YELLOW BELLFLOWER Large, oblong, pale yellow, flesh tender, sub-acid, very good; ripens in September.

*RHODE ISLAND GREENING Large, roundish, a little flattened, skin green, yellow flesh, tender, crisp, acid, juicy; ripens in October.

*KING of TOMPKINS COUNTY Large, conical shaped, skin yellowish, striped with red, flesh juicy, tender, vinous, flavor, very good; November to February.

APPLES.----WINTER.

*ESOPUS SPITZENBERG Large, oblong, skin smooth, yellowish, covered with red stripes, flesh crisp and juicy, one of the best keepers; November to March.

BALDWIN Beautiful, large red apple, flesh white, crisp, very good; October to February.

YELLOW NEWTON PIPPIN Medium size, skin greenish yellow, flesh crisp, sub-acid; one of the very best, but does best in the Coast Counties; November to March.

GREEN GENETING, OR VIRGINIA GREENING A large, late, green-colored apple, conical shape, smooth oil skin, flesh crisp and juicy, fine for cooking, a good shipper; October to March.

SWAAR Large, pale yellow, with exceedingly rich, aromatic flavor, good; November to March. Does best in the mountains.

*WINE SAP Medium, roundish, deep red, tree hardy and good bearer; November to March. One of the best for the mountains.

WHITE WINTER PEARMAIN Above medium size, skin pale yellow, flesh yellow, crisp and juicy, very good; ripens in October to February. Best in the Coast Counties.

*NICKAJACK Large, roundish, skin striped with crimson, flesh yellow, sub-acid flavor; November to February. A Southern Apple.

JONATHAN Above medium size, conical shape, red striped, sometimes quite red; a good keeper, especially in the Coast Counties.

HOOVER A large, deep red apple, good flavor, good bearer and fine keeper, one of the best; November to March. Does splendidly near the Coast.

TWENTY OUNCE PIPPIN A very large, conical shaped apple, covered with dull red stripes, has a fine crisp sub-acid flavor, will cook well when only half grown, a very profitable market kind, tree a strong vigorous grower with upright habit.

Crab Apples.

YELLOW SIBERIAN Fruit about an inch in diameter, fine rich yellow; good for jelly.

TRANSCENDENT A beautiful variety of large size, yellow flesh, with red cheek; very productive.

HYSLOP A large, beautiful red crab, one of the best.

Special Variety.

☞ THE VIOLETT This is a new apple raised by J. W. Violett, of Ione. It is one of the largest apples grown, averaging nearly as large as the Gloria Mondo; conical shape, a beautiful red nearly all over, solid, firm and crisp, good flavor, fine shipper; September to January. Tree strong grower with upright habit; bark, on new wood, smooth, glossy and light, chestnut color, leaves quite peculiar—a rich glossy green. 30 cts. each. $20 per 100.

PEARS.

We do not propagate a long list of pears. Our experience has been that only a few of the leading varieties are the most profitable. The following list includes most of the kinds that have proven valuable.

PRICE OF TREES—Leading sorts.

	each	100	1000
2 year, No. 1—4 to 6 feet, branched	$0 30	$25 00	$175
1 year, No. 1—4 to 6 feet	25	20	160
1 year, extra—5 to 8 feet	30	25	....
1 year—3 to 4 feet	20	15 00	....

PEARS—Summer.

MADELINE. Medium size, pale yellowish green, flesh white, melting, juicy; 20th of June.

DEARBORN'S SEEDLING. Small to medium, light yellow, flesh white, very juicy and melting; ripens 20th of June.

'BARTLETT. One of the most popular pears; large size, clear yellow skin; flesh fine grained, juicy, buttery and melting, with a rich, musky flavor; the best early pear, and has no competitor as a market and canning fruit. Tree vigorous, bearing early and abundantly. August.

PEARS—Autumn.

*KIEFER'S HYBRID. A large roundish pear, recommended highly, but we have not tested it sufficiently to judge of its merits.

*BEURRE HARDY. Fruit large, skin greenish, covered with light russet, flesh buttery, melting and juicy, one of the best, ships well; August.

SECKEL. Small to medium, skin dull yellowish brown, with russet red cheek, flesh white, very juicy, perfection of flavor; last of August.

BEURRE D'ANJO. Large round pear, one of the best, good shipper.

LOUIS BON DE JERSEY. A very sweet, delicious Autumn pear; shaped much like the Bartlett only more elongated, greenish yellow with bright red cheeks, flesh fine grained and exceedingly fine flavored, good for drying, canning or shipping.

CHINESE PEARS. Fruit large, flavor not good, but tree highly ornamental, foliage large, rich green till late in Fall, when they turn red and hang a long time. The Chinamen will pay 12 to 15 cents a pound for the fruit; trees 1 year, No. 1, $1 each.

PEARS—Winter.

BEURRE CLARGEAU. Fruit very large, skin yellow covered with russet dots, flesh yellowish, good flavor, good shipper; September to December.

EASTER BEURRE. Fruit large, skin yellowish green, with russety dots, flesh white, rich flavor, long keeper.

WINTER NELIS. Medium size, greenish, russet, melting and juicy, rich flavor, good shipper, October to December.

BEURRE BOSS. Large long russet pear, good flavor and good shipper, one of the very best, October to April.

WINTER SECKEL. Above the medium size, shaped much like the Bartlett and nearly as large, color and flavor much like the Fall Seckel, long keeper, good shipper.

P. BARRY. A California seedling, originated by the late B. S. Fox, of San Jose; a very large elongated russet pear, quite late, and a long keeper, can be kept till March; an excellent pear for Eastern shipping, fine texture and excellent flavor when fully ripe.

PEARS. Winter—Continued.

SANTA ANA. A new pear, originated at Santa Ana, in Los Angeles County. It is a large conical shaped pear, a bright golden yellow, covered with russet; it is an exceedingly handsome fruit, flesh fine grained and free from all woody substance, with a flavor equal to the finest Winter Nelis or the famous Seckel; it will eat well when picked from the tree, and yet will keep all Winter; it is a very remarkable pear in this respect; its shipping and keeping qualities cannot be excelled. We consider it a very valuable accession to our list of pears. The tree is a moderatly strong grower, with upright habit, forming a close, compact head, makes a very handsome tree. Price 35 cents each, $30 per 100.

PEACHES.

In order to secure healthy and vigorous trees it is necessary to prune severely. Their tendency in this State is to develop an immense number of fruit buds, and as they are not destroyed by frost, they produce more fruit than the tree can mature. The consequence is that it is small and inferior. The tree should be trained low and pruned regularly every year. By this practice the breaking of limbs is avoided, and the fruit grows much larger and finer. Many new varieties have been produced in the past few years, so that the fruiting season has been materially lengthened. The following list contains most of the valuable kinds, but the period of ripening varies so much in different localities that the time given can only be considered approximate.

We have the largest and finest stock of peaches on the Coast.

PRICE OF TREES—Leading Varieties.

	each	100	1000
1 year, No. 1—4 to 6 feet	$0 25	$20 00	$160
1 year, No. 2— 2 to 3½ feet	20	15 00	110
1 year, extra size trees	30	25 00	....

Freestone.

YELLOW ST. JOHN. A fine yellow freestone, very much like the Early Crawford, and ripens a little earlier. Shipping qualities good.

BRIGG'S RED MAY. Fruit medium to large, deep red cheek, flesh firm, good market variety; 1st of June.

GOV. GARLAND. Fruit large, bright red cheek, ripens with Alexander.

WATERLOO. Medium size, deep red, early.

ALEXANDER. Medium size, white flesh, with clear red cheek; ripens here 10th of June; the earliest shipping peach.

*HALE'S EARLY. An early and very profitable market peach; medium size, and nearly round; skin greenish, mostly covered with red when ripe; flesh white, melting, juicy, rich, sweet; 20th of June. Ships well.

*FOSTER. Very large yellow peach, red cheek, bears well, ripens about same time as Early Crawford.

*EARLY CRAWFORD. A magnificent large yellow peach, heavy bearer, one of the best for shipping and all purposes, ripens last of June.

*LATE CRAWFORD. Much the same as Early Crawford, but ripening two weeks later.

*WHEATLAND. A large yellow free, bright red cheek, ripening a little later than Late Crawford, one of our most popular peaches.

*JONES' SEEDLING. Origin, Sacramento; large yellow flesh, with red cheek, excellent flavor, 10th of August.

*SUSQUEHANNA. Very large yellow peach, red cheek, of best quality; July. Ripens Aug. 1st.

KEYPORT WHITE. A large white peach, with red cheek, good for shipping, canning or drying, last of August.

WARD'S LATE FREE. Large white flesh peach, good for canning, September.

*SALWAY. Large yellow peach, dull red cheek, good flavor, superior market variety; 1st of September.

*BILYEU'S LATE OCTOBER. Large, white flesh, red cheek, very fine flavor, good shipper; ripens 20th of October, tree strong grower, doesn't curl, freestone, does best in foot-hills.

*PICQUET'S LATE. Very large, yellow, with a red cheek, flesh yellow, buttery, rich and sweet, and of the highest flavor.

*MUIR. Large, yellow peach, flesh very dry and sweet, pitt very small, one of the best for drying and canning, planted more for this purpose than any other peach.

WAGER. Almost a fac-simile of the Muir, and supposed by some to be the same.

*STILSON. (California Seedling.) A very large yellow fleshed peach, bright red cheeks, with dark crimson stripes, one of the very best market sorts, ripens two weeks later than the Late Crawford.

*LOVELL. Well recommended.

Clingstone.

*DAY'S YELLOW CLING. (California Seedling.) A very large, yellow flesh, with red cheek, good market variety; August.

*ORANGE CLING. A very large, yellow flesh, with red check, a well known variety. August.

*HEATH CLING. Large, white flesh, superior flavor; 1st of September.

*GEORGE'S LATE CLING. (California Seedling.) Very large, white flesh, with bright red check, superior quality; September.

LEMON CLING. Large, yellow, with bright red cheek, a fine market peach, good shipper.

*EDWARD'S CLING. (The same called by C. W. Reed, the California) A California Seedling, produced by the late Mr. Edwards, near this city. It is a large, yellow fleshed peach, highly colored, a fine market or shipping fruit.

*ALBRIGHT CLING. (California Seedling.) A very large, yellow peach, with bright red cheek. A fine shipper, and good peach in every particular.

*TUSCAN CLING. A very large, yellow cling, ripens same time as Early Crawford, a fine shipper, and its early ripening makes it very valuable.

*WINTER'S CLING. (A seedling from the Heath Cling.) Original tree raised by C. H. Wolfskill, of Winters. The old tree is now 32 years old and still bearing good crops of fruit, and Mr. Wolfskill says it has never curled or mildewed, while the Heath Cling does both. The Winters is almost a fac-simile of the Heath, except it is slightly larger, and much better shaped. It possesses all of the excellent qualities of the Heath, is larger, color a beautiful creamy white, with red blush on exposed side, is white to the pit, and therefore a fine canning peach. It is very solid and a fine shipper.

*McDEVIT CLING. (A California Seedling, raised by Neal McDevit, of Placer County.) This is one of the largest peaches we have ever seen, many of them weighing one pound each, peaches very uniform in size, rich golden yellow, becoming quite red when ripe, flesh very solid and firm, an excellent shipper, superior flavor; tree a good and regular bearer.

TUSCANY CLING. An exceedingly large yellow cling peach (from Italy,) deep yellow with bright red cheek, very late good shipper, tree hardy and strong grower, don't curl or mildew, and consequently good for the Coast Counties.

McKEVITT'S CLING. A California seedling, very large, flesh white to the pit, firm and good, stands shipping well, good for canning and drying; 10th of September.

Peaches of Recent Introduction.—Special Varieties.

WILDER CLING. A new yellow, flesh cling. Fruit large uniform, flesh yellow; bright golden check, superior flavor, ripens with Salway, tree strong, vigorous grower, bears regular, does not curl or mildew.

LEVI CLING. A large yellow cling, bright red cheek, resembles the McDevit, one of the best shipping varieties, its time of ripening, (after Salway is gone,) makes it very valuable.

BARTON CLING. New seedling; from Placer County. A very large bright yellow Cling. Flesh crisp, juicy; ripens about 15th of September; the finest peach of its season. Tree strong grower, and does not curl or mildew. Price of dormant buds, 50c each, $30 per 100.

BLOOD FREE. Large fancy peach. Flesh blood-red; very fine for preserving. We only have the dormant buds. Price, 25c each.

NECTARINES.—Leading Varieties.

	each	100
1 year, No. 1—4 to 6 feet	$0 25	$20 00

NEW WHITE Large, creamy white, freestone, very superior for drying.

BOSTON Medium to large red freestone, fine flavor, good for drying.

CLEMENT'S NECTARINE A large red nectarine, good flavor, will make a good shipper, tree a good and regular bearer.

VICTORIA Large, red cling, good shipper.

APRICOTS.

A popular and profitable fruit, and though planted heavily it will always remain so, on account of the increasing demand. The soil and climate of California matures it to perfection. We have only propagated the best and most profitable varieties. Our customers will notice that we have placed the three last named varieties, Newcastle Early, French Apricot and McCormack at same price as all other Apricots. We do this because they are all really valuable varieties, and we want to introduce them. Royal Apricot are scarce this season, and we recommend the Newcastle Early as being its equal in every respect.

PRICE OF TREES—Leading Varieties.

	each	100	1000
1 year, No. 1—3 to 6 feet on peach root	$0 25	$20 00	$160
1 year, No. 1—4 to 6 feet, on Myrobolan	30	22 00	180

ROUTIER'S PEACH APRICOT   A new kind from Mr. Routier's orchard.   Large size, skin yellow in the shade, deep orange mottled, or splashed with red in the sun; flesh rich and juicy, very high flavor; good market variety.

EARLY ROYAL   Medium size, good color, very productive, a favorite for canning and drying.

HEMSKIRK   Very much like the Moorpark; one of the best; tree good bearer.

BLENHEIM   A good early variety, above medium oval; orange with deep yellow; juicy and tolerably rich flesh; vigorous grower and a regular prolific bearer.   Ripens with the Royal.

MOORPARK   Large, orange color, moderate early bearer, but of the highest flavor.

NEWCASTLE EARLY   A new variety originated by M. C. Silva & Son, of Newcastle, California. Medium size, round, well shaped, a shade smaller than the Royal; two weeks earlier than the Royal; very valuable on account of its earliness; tree a good and regular bearer, fruit ships well.

FRENCH APRICOT   Very large; good flavor; firm; ripens evenly on both sides; a good shipper, highly esteemed for canning and drying; a regular and prolific bearer; ripens with the Royal; very popular where it is known.

McCORMACK   Supposed to be a seedling of the Large Early, which it very much resembles, but ten days earlier.   Tree a strong grower and very productive, very showy, and fine for shipping.

PLUMS AND PRUNES.

The Plum and Prune succeeds admirably in this State, and we can and should not only produce for home consumption, but export large quantities instead of importing. Many varieties of Plums and Prunes have a tendency to over-bear, and, to secure a good article, the fruit should be carefully thinned out. This should be done when it is one-third or one-half grown. Those who are willing to take these pains will be amply repaid by a superior quality of fruit, and a more remunerative price.

PRICE OF TREES—Leading Varieties.

	each	100	1000
1 year, 6 to 7 feet, extra, on peach root	$0 25	$18 00	$150
1 year, No 1.—4 to 6 feet	20	15 00	135
1 year, 5 to 6 feet, extra, on Myrobolan Root	30	18 00	175
1 year, No. 1—4 to 5 feet, on Myrobolan Root	25	16 00	150

PEACH PLUM.   Fruit very large, round, greenish white, with red cheek; flesh yellow, sweet and firm; early; good for shipping.

*COLUMBIA.   Fruit large size; skin brownish purple; with fawn colored specks; flesh yellow, sugary, excellent; one of the best for shipping.

DUANE'S PURPLE.   Large, reddish purple; flesh juicy and moderately sweet; good shipper.

VICTORIA (or Oakshade Prune.)   Medium size, beautiful red plum; good shipper, and superior for drying, being very free and quite a dry meated plum; very prolific.

COE'S GOLDEN DROP.   Fruit large, oval, flesh yellow, firm, rich and sweet; adheres to stone; good for canning and ships well.

*GROS PRUNE D'AGEN (Hungarian Prune.)   Very large, oval, violet red; very prolific, often growing double; good flavor; a valuable market kind, best shipper.

YELLOW EGG.   A very large elongated plum; golden yellow; adheres to the stone; quite juicy, rich sub-acid flavor; the best known canning variety and ships well.

WASHINGTON.   Large, round, greenish yellow; good for canning or drying.

KELSEY'S JAPAN PLUM.   Fruit very large, as large as an ordinary peach; roundish, or inclined to be conical; color greenish yellow, with faint red cheek; adheres closely to the pit, which is very small; flesh firm and juicy; it is the best keeper known.

PLUMS AND PRUNES—Continued.

ROYAL NATIVE. Medium size, early, roundish, purple; flesh yellow amber, rich, good, high flavor; parts from the stone when ripe. A favorite in Vaca Valley, where its earliness makes it valuable.

BLOOD PLUM. A fine, handsome, strong growing tree; fruit above medium size, blood red both outside and inside, very handsome and fine flavor. Trees, 1 year, No. 1 (on Myrobolan), 50 cents each; $40 per 100.

ICKWORTH'S IMPERATRICE. Above medium size; purple, firm, sweet, rich, a valuable variety for market, bears transportation well, will keep a long time after being gathered. Clings to the stone; September to October.

SILVER PRUNE. Originated in Oregon. The fruit is a fac-simile of Coe's Golden Drop, except it is a darker green, and it is yet a question whether it should be called a prune or a plum. It is a very superior shipper, and it certainly makes an excellent dried fruit, either pitted or unpitted; makes a splendid prune.

PRUNIS PISSARDI. A medium size plum; red, fine flesh, good flavor, long keeper; the tree is very ornamental, foliage blood red.

PRUNIS SIMONI. Quite large, somewhat elongated, bright yellow, red cheek; very fine fruit; good for shipping or drying; tree a strong grower; bears heavily.

GERMAN PRUNE. A large purple prune, flesh greenish yellow, very sweet, always brings fancy prices as a fresh fruit; it is a good shipper and makes an excellent dried prune; tree a strong grower and a good and regular bearer.

PRUNES.

Our Stock of Prunes this season is unusually large and fine, both on Myrobolan and Peach Roots. As there is a large demand for Prune this season we advise our customers to place their orders at once.

Price of Trees.

PRUNES ON PEACH ROOTS.

	each	100	1000
1 year, No. 1—4 to 6 feet	$0 30	$25 00	$200
1 year, No. 2—2½ to 4 feet	20	15 00	
1 year, extra—5 to 8 feet	35	30 00	250

PRUNES ON MYROBOLAN ROOT.

	each	100	1000
1 year, No. 1—4 to 6 feet	30	$25 00	$225
1 year, No. 1—3 to 4 feet	20	18 00	150

PETIT PRUNE D'AGEN. (French Prunes), the most popular drying Prune, small, reddish purple, very sweet, and takes the lead as a drying prune.

BULGARIAN PRUNES. A very prolific, dark colored prune, larger than the French Prune, and by some considered a very valuable prune, but we have not yet tested it sufficiently to judge of its value.

PRUNE D'AGEN (or Prune d'Ent). Very like the Petit or French Prune, only larger and more desirable. It is now demonstrated that this prune will bear as heavy crops as the French or Petit Prune, and as it is so much larger and of equally as good a quality, it is of course the most valuable of the two. There has been some fears that it might not be a good bearor, but that doubt has been dispelled. Many trees are now bearing heavy crops in this State. Price of trees same as the Petit Prune on Myrobolan root. It will not grow on peach root, but must be grown on plum root.

TRAGEDY PRUNE. A new prune originated by Mr. Runyon, near Courtland, in this county. It would seem to be a cross between the German Prune and Purple Duane. Fruit medium size, nearly as large as the Duane Purple Plum; looks much like it, only it is more elongated; skin dark purple, flesh yellowish green, very rich and sweet, frees readily from the pit. Its early ripening (in June) makes it very valuable as a shipping fruit. Coming as it does before any other good plum, it will always bring fancy prices, both in the local and Eastern market. So far it has no rival. We believe we are the first to work it. The first to get orchards of this fruit will make fortunes out of it. We believe this Prune to be almost equal to the French Prune for drying, though we have not tested it sufficiently as a drying prune, simply on account of its value as a shipping Prune, it has always brought a better price in the Eastern market than any other Prune or Plum.

CHERRIES.

As a pleasant and refreshing dessert fruit the cherry is everywhere highly esteemed. The early season at which it ripens, its juiciness, delicacy and richness render it always acceptable. It thrives best in rich dry loam. The trees should be trained low, that the foliage may protect the trunk, which should never be exposed to the sun. We cultivate only a few of the leading kinds, a brief description of which may be found below.

PRICE OF TREES.

	each	100	1000
2 year, No. 1—4 to 6 feet, branched	$0 35	$25 00	$200
1 year, No. 1—4 to 6 feet	30	20 00	160
1 year, No. 2—3 to 4 feet	20	15 00	125

Varieties.

EARLY PURPLE GUIGNE. Medium size, black; quite early.

'ROCHPORT BIGARREAU. A large, early, flesh colored cherry; valuable for canning or drying; it is also a good shipper; its very early ripening makes it very valuable; it will always command a good price.

KNIGHT'S EARLY BLACK. Large, black, tender, juicy, rich and high flavored; early. This is the earliest good variety.

*BLACK TARTARIAN. A very large, purplish black, rich and juicy; one of the best varieties.

GOVERNOR WOOD. A fine, early cherry, white, shaded with red, tender, juicy and delicious.

*ROYAL ANN (or Napolean Bigarreau). Very large, pale yellow, with bright red cheek; flesh very firm, juicy and sweet; good shipper.

BLACK OREGON. Sometimes called Lewelling or Black Republican; a large, late black cherry; good flavor, long keeper and ships well.

CENTENNIAL. A new cherry, seedling from the Royal Ann, which it resembles; a little more oblate in form, and has a higher color; valuable for shipping, being a splendid keeper.

SCHMIDT'S BIGARREAU. Very large black cherry; moderate bearer; good shipper; late.

DEACON. A new, black, seedling cherry, very large, deep black, ripens with Black Tartarian. Its chief value being in its shipping qualities, as it is very hard and firm, sweet and good bearer.

QUINCE.

PRICE OF TREES.

	each	100
2 year, No. 1—4 to 6 feet	$0 35	$25 00
1 year, No. 1—3 to 4 feet	30	20 00

ORANGE. Large, roundish; bright golden yellow; the best for general use.

EARLY GOODRICH. Very large, bright yellow; early; good flavor.

ALMONDS.

Nut growing should be carried on far more extensively in this state than it now is. Almonds are a sure grow over a large area of the state. They can be raised to profit at lower rates than the usual current prices. Our foothill lands seem to be peculiarly adapted for their culture. We know of no district in the state where they do better than in the foothills, at an altitude of from 600 to 2,000 feet above the sea level.

PRICE OF TREES.

1 year, No. 1—4 to 6 feet on peach	$0 20	18 00	150
1 year, No. 1—4 to 7 feet on almond	25	20 00	160
June Buds on almonds	20	15 00	125
June Buds on peach	15	12½	100

Varieties.

ROUTIER'S SOFT SHELL. A new seedling from the orchard of Hon. J. Routier; shell quite soft, good size, a regular and prolific bearer.

BLOWERS' LANGUEDOC. Originated and highly recommended by R. B. Blowers, of Woodland, a fine nut and good and regular bearer.

BYERS' LANGUEDOC. A new seedling, one of the best.

TWIN. A very large smooth nut, each nut containing a double kernel; shell soft, free, hardy and good bearer.

GOLDEN STATE. A large nut, soft shell, full smooth meat; parts readily from the hull; ripens early.

I X L. Nuts large, soft shell, good color; recommended by A. T. Hatch.

NONPARIEL. An extraordinarly heavy and regular bearer; shell very soft.

DRAKE'S SEEDLING. Originated by Mr. Drake Suisun, and recommended by him as being very prolific, and a regular and abundant bearer.

TEXAS PROLIFIC. A new seedling variety originated at Dallas, Texas. Nut fully as large as the Languedoc, but softer shell, very smooth and bright color, well filled with a very sweet meat; tree full as strong grower, and very much resembles the Languedoc tree. It is a very heavy and regular bearer. It is the only variety that will fruit well at Dallas, Texas. We consider it by all odds the finest and most desirable almond we have ever seen. Price 50 cents each. $35 per 100, $250 per 1,000.

FIGS.

It has been thoroughly demonstrated that the Fig will grow most luxuriantly, thrive and bear great crops from one end of the State to the other; the warm, dry alluvial soils, and the dry warm climate of the interior valleys, and foot-hills seem to be peculiarly adapted to its successful culture and caring; it will grow and do well on lands too dry to mature other fruits; it will do well on rich bottom lands, provided they are well drained, so that there is no Fruit that can be more generally grown all over the State; and no other with so little care and risk and that is more profitable in the end. At the same time there is no other Fruit that has been so generally neglected. It is only in the last few years, that the value of this fruit has been recognized. All of the common varieties can be made profitable, and with the varieties we are now introducing, there is no fruit that will be more desirable, or more profitable.

PRICE OF TREES.

	each	100	1000
2 year, No. 1—4 to 6 feet, branched (common kinds)	$0 25	$15 00	$120
1 year, No. 1—3 to 4 feet	15	12 00	100

WHITE ADRIATIC AND VERDONI.

	each	100	1000
2 year, 4 to 6 feet	$0 35	$25 00	$200
1 year, 3 to 4 feet	25	18 00	140

Varieties.

LARGE PURPLE. One of the most fruitful sorts; large size; dark purple, very sweet, good flavor; drys well.

BROWN ISCHIA. Very large, skin light or chestnut brown, very sweet and excellent.

PACIFIC WHITE. Fruit medium size, fine grained, very sweet, seeds very small; very white and exceedingly fine flavored when dry; but the skin when dry is thicker and more tough than the imported, that and its small size is the only objection to it. It never cracks and sours in drying. The tree is a strong grower, very hardy, and always good shaped, a fine shade or avenue tree. A good regular bearer.

SAN PEDRO (usually called WHITE SMYRNA). A very large, dirty, or rusty white fig; good flavor, one of the best as a green or fresh fruit; valuable for that purpose, but does not dry well if dried in the sun, as it cracks and sours in drying, but makes a very superior product when dried by artificial heat. We regard it as one of the best figs for profit we have, if properly handled; the tree is rather a slow grower, but a great bearer, exceedingly prolific.

VERDONI. Called by many White Adriatic, but it differs from the fig which is now generally called the White Adriatic in the color of the pulp or inside of the fruit. The Verdoni is white inside, while the other is red, otherwise they are very much alike. While they are both excellent figs, we are planting (in orchard) more largely of the Verdoni, mainly on account of its white flesh, but either of them will make a very superior dried product, that will equal if not surpass the best imported article, (where they are well grown and properly cured.)

WHITE ADRIATIC.

ORANGE AND LEMON.

In Orange and Lemon we offer the largest and finest Stock ever brought into or grown in the State. From reports received from our agent in Florida we will have this season over 180,000 Orange and Lemon, consisting of Villa Franka Lemon, Medt Sweet, Washington Navel, Hart's Tardiff Orange, and all the leading varieties of Orange and Lemon. These trees are grown in our own Nurseries especially for California trade. Every tree being staked and made to grow perfectly straight, until they are three to three and one-half feet high, when they are topped and made to branch out; they are strong, thrifty and free from scale, and all budded on the popular Sour Orange Stock.

The following is extract of report of *U. S. Department of Agriculture, Bulletin No. 4, page 15:*

CALIFORNIA.

The orange has held a leading place among the fruits of California ever since American occupation, but the question of stock has not been considered to be of particular importance. Within the past few years, however, the introduction and remarkable success of the wild sour orange stock (*C. bigaradia*) of Florida has opened up a discussion which will result in lasting benefit to the State. Certain nurserymen who have large interests in sweet stock at stake bitterly oppose the introduction of the sour orange, and endeavor to bias public opinion by making the term sour stock include all roots except that of the sweet orange, thus seeking to make the condemnation which all California growers award to the lemon, China lemon, lime, etc., as stocks cover also the sour orange stock. The injustice of this is manifest and can but work injury to those employing such means.

The deep, rich alluvium, formed from granite and limestone and underlaid with a retentive sub-soil and sufficient surface irrigation, form a combination of conditions to which the sour orange is peculiarly well suited.

From data sent this office by California orange growers who have tried the sweet and sour orange stocks side by side on a large scale it is safe to conclude:

1. That the sour stock trees make a more thrifty growth;
2. That they are more free from disease and are entirely resistant to Mal di Goma (foot rot or gum disease);
3. That they are less liable to be injured by cold while young;
4. That the quality of the fruit is not impaired.

We make a specialty of car-load lots, and will quote special low prices to nurserymen, dealers and planters wanting large orders. In writing for special quotations be particular to state size, varieties and number wanted.

The sizes given below are as the trees stood in the nursery.

See our trees and get our prices before buying elsewhere. Send for Orange Circulars.

PRICE OF BUDDED TREES.

	each	100	1000
4 to 6 ft. on 4 and 6 yr. roots	$1 50	$90 00	$750
3½ to 4 ft. on 3 and 4 yr. "	1 25	75 00	650
2 to 3 ft.	75	50 00	350

Extra large trees, $2 00 each; $150 per 100.

Lemon, same sizes and prices of Orange trees.

Sweet (Indian River) seedlings, 4 to 5 years old, ¾ to 1¼ inch in diameter......60c each, $45 00 per 100

Sour orange trees for street planting, 4 to 7 years old, ¾ to 1¼ inch in diameter..75c each; $50 00 per 100

Brief Description of Varieties. (All Hardy).

*WASHINGTON NAVEL, Acknowledged by all to be the leading orange; too well known to need any further description. ¼ of our trees are budded to this variety.

*MEDT SWEET. A popular variety; medium size, very sweet, and good bearer; tree thornless.

NONPAREIL. A very handsome orange of most excellent quality, a popular sort in the market; tree a strong grower, hardy and a good bearer.

PARSON BROWN. Fruit medium size, oblong in shape, smooth high color, very sweet, ripens early, is sweet as soon as it begins to turn, grand bearer, tree has some thorns.

MAGNUM BONUM. A very large orange, a little flattened, skin smooth and glossy, fruit heavy and of excellent quality, ripens early, tree very prolific, thorny.

PEERLESS. Fruit large and round, smooth skin, one of the best market sorts, tree a heavy and regular bearer and strong grower.

ST. MICHAEL. Fruit medium size, very fine quality, a little flattened, thin skin, tree a good bearer, nearly thornless.

*HART'S TARDIFF. A large round orange of good quality, its chief excellence consisting in its lateness; it does not ripen till May or June, and will hang on the tree in good eating condition until August; tree strong grower and good bearer.

JAFFA. Imported from the city of Joppa, in Syria, a very fine, medium size orange of superior quality, trees nearly thornless.

*The VILLA FRAKA LEMON; the finest lemon ever introduced in California. This lemon has become the favorite in Florida; the fruit is of a very superior quality, tree a strong grower, heavy and regular bearer, excelling all other varieties in productiveness. The tree is exceedingly hardy; it withstood the heavy freeze in Florida in January, 1886, in the same orchards where all other kinds, and also orange trees, were killed. It ripens in July and August, thus coming in the hot season when lemons are most needed and when the market is bare of other citrus fruits. It is emphatically the lemon for profit.

MILAN LEMON. Very similar to the Villa Franka.

EUREKA LEMON. A popular California variety.

WALNUTS.

EASTERN BLACK WALNUTS. A well known tree; valuable for timber, nut a little larger than the California walnut; price 2 year trees, 50 cents.

CALIFORNIA BLACK WALNUT. A native specie, valuable for shade and nuts. Very productive. 2 year trees, 5 to 7 feet, well branched, 30 cents each, per hundred $25. 1 year trees, 3 to 5 feet, 20 cents each, per hundred $15.

ENGLISH WALNUTS. Very popular and profitable nut, makes a very handsome shade, 2 year trees 5 to 8 feet, 50 cents each, $30 per hundred. 1 year 2 to 4 feet, 20 cents each, $15 per hundred. We have a large stock of these, and will quote special price on large lots.

PRAEPARTURIEN WALNUT. A very fine table nut, trees of dwarfish habit, bears quite young and heavy crop. Trees 2 to 3 feet, 25 cents each, $20 per hundred; 3 to 4 feet, 30 cents each, $25 per hundred. 4 to 5 feet, 50 cents each, $40 per hundred.

CHESTNUTS.

These nuts do well in the greater portion of the state, they are among our handsomest shade trees and the nuts bring a fancy price, they should be planted by every one.

Varieties.

ITALIAN CHESTNUT. A very large nut, sweet, bears well, tree very ornamental. Trees, 1 to 1¼ feet, 15 cents each, $10 per hundred. 2 to 3 feet, 25 cents each, $20 per hundred. 3 to 4 feet, 40 cents each, $35 per hundred.

CHESTNUT (American Sweet). Same sizes, same prices as the Italian.

OLIVES.

Olive culture in California has of late attracted much attention, and it is an established fact that a great many localities especially the foothills, are exactly suited to the successful growth of the olive, and the production of an Oil that will have no superior.

Olive growing in California is only in its infancy, but the flattering results that have been obtained, guarantees for Olive growing a perfect success and a most profitable future. There are a great many different varieties of the Olive now being propagated, most of them not yet thoroughly tested, and we only offer those varieties that have been tested and are known to be the most profitable.

PRICE OF MISSION OLIVE TREES.

	each	100
14 to 18 inches	$0 20	$15
18 to 24 inches	25	20
24 to 30 inches	30	25
PICHOLINE. 2 to 3 feet	25	20

Varieties.

MISSION. This we believe to be the best Olive for all purposes; it is good for both oil and pickles.
PICHOLINE. A small olive used chiefly for oil; makes a fine grade of light oil.
MANZANILLO (Queen Olive). Berries very large, highly prized for pickles; also good for oil.
NEVADILLO. One of the finest olives for oil.

PRICE OF MANZANILLO AND NEVADILO.

	each	100
14 to 18 inches	$0 25	$20
18 " 24 "	30	25
24 " 30 "	35	30
2½ to 4 ft	50	40

GRAPES.

Grape growing in California is one of our leading industries, most all varieties thrive well, and produce abundant crops. We have endeavored to select out of the vast number of varieties such as have proved the most valuable. We have an extra large stock this season, and will quote special price on large orders.

We only quote prices on 1 year plants, as we find that 1 year vines give the best results. All our vines are extra well grown, well rooted and strictly first class in every respect.

PRICE.	Each	100	1000
1 year No. 1 (fine roots)	$0 05	$2 50	$20

Varieties.

*WHITE MUSCAT. (Muscat of Alexandria). Fine, large, white grape, musk flavored, good market variety, either for shipping or raisins.

*MUSCATELLE GORDO BLANCO. Resembling the Muscat, berries large, less musky flavor, good raisin variety.

*FLAME TOKAY. A magnificient large, red grape, very firm, vigorous grower and productive, our most popular shipping grape.

*ZINFANDEL. A medium size, black grape, close compact bunches, very productive, valuable for wine.

SEEDLESS SULTANA. Small white grape, clusters large. It makes a fine raisin for culinary purposes, at the same time is a fine wine grape. It is the only grape we know of that is good for both raisins and wine.

EMPEROR. A large red grape, resembling the Tokay, ripens quite late, is an excellent shipper; its lateness and long keeping qualities make it a very valuable grape, does splendidly on our granite soils in the foothills, the vines of this variety should be staked up to get the best results.

CORNISCHON. The largest and latest grape we cultivate, berries quite elongated, firm, solid, and skin thick and tough, which will enable it to carry farther than any other grape. Sells well in the East.

ROSE PERU. Medium size black grape, ripens quite early, good bearer, one of our best early shipping grapes.

BLUE MALVOISE. Large, reddish black, oblong, with faint bloom, good early table grape.

BLACK FARURA. Large, oblong, firm black grape, good flavor, one of the best for shipping.

TROSSEAU. Bunches medium sized, cylindrical, berries black, covered with a thick bloom, yields a dark colored wine of the best quality for flavor and bouquet.

CARIGNAN. Bunches similiar to Mataro, berries oblong, black, produces heavy crops, and a highly colored good wine.

BERGER. A large white wine grape, very productive, makes an excellent wine, is a very profitable grape to raise.

MATTARO. A medium sized black grape, close compact bunches, an abundant bearer, makes a superior wine. This grape is always in good demand as a wine grape, brings good price, is a very profitable grape to grow.

PETITE BOUSCHET. Valuable as a coloring for wine.

*WHITE NIECE. Wine grapes.

*GRENACHE. Wine grapes.

Resistant Stock.

VITES CALIFORNIA. We have a fine stock of this valuable resistant stock. Grafts on these stocks make a stronger and more vigorous growth than on their own roots. Price 2 year, $10 per thousand.

CURRANTS.

PRICE.	Each.	Per 100
2 year—No. 1	$0 12½	$10 00
1 year—No. 1	8	6 00

CHERRY. Fruit of the largest size; bunches short; berries large, deep red; a valuable market sort.

WHITE DUTCH. Bunches long; berries yellowish white, nearly transparent; very sweet and agreeable; sometimes used for making currant wine.

GOOSEBERRIES.

PRICE.	Each	Per 100
American	$0 20	$15 00
English	25	20 00

BLACKBERRIES.

PRICE............4 cents each | $3 00..............per 100 | $10 00..............per 1,000

WILSON'S EARLY. Fruit large, productive and early.

DORCHESTER. A fine sweet berry.

KITTATINNY. Good market variety; large and good flavor.

LAWTON. Good market variety for this locality; large and late.

CRANDALL'S EARLY. This berry was brought from Texas some years ago, and planted on the place of Dr. S. R. Crandall, of Auburn, Placer County. (The origin of this berry is not known to us). Here it was discovered that it was not only an excellent berry and prolific bearer, but was also found to ripen three weeks earlier than the Lawton, and continues to blossom and bear fruit until late in the Fall. We have often picked good, ripe, well developed berries as late as the last days of December. The wood of the vine is light colored, resembling the Wilson's Early, but is a much stronger grower. The berry is as large as the Lawton, fine flavor, firm and solid. It is an excellent shipper. Price $1 per dozen, $5 per 100, $15 per 1,000. Fifty plants at 100 rates; 500 at 1,000 rates.

RASPBERRIES.

PRICE..............5 cents each | $3 00..............per 100 | $15 00..............per 1,000

Leading Varieties.

HANSEL. Medium size berry, very early and firm; ships well.

BARTER. We have cultivated all of the leading varieties, and do not hesitate to recommend the Barter, as being the finest and most profitable berry we have ever seen, it is a very large bright red berry, bears very heavy crops, and frees easily from the stem; a splendid shipper, and has brought the highest price of any berry we ever handled

HERSTINE. Fine large market berry.

STRAWBERRIES.

PRICE..............50 cents per doz. | $1 00..............per 100 | $6 00..............per 1,000

Triomphe de Gand, Sharpless, Monarch of the West, Captain Jack, and many other new varieties not fully tested.

ESCULENT ROOTS.

Asparagus...2 cents each; $10 00 per 1,000
Rhubarb....................................1 year, 15c; 2 years, 25c.; extra large 4 years 50c. each
Hop Roots..50c. per doz.; $1 50 per 100; $10 00 per 1,000

(Large lots at special rates, very low).

Deciduous Shade and Ornamental Trees.

POPLARS AND LOCUST.

	each	per 100
No. 1—2 to 2½ inches diameter...	$1 00	$60 00
No. 2—1½ to 2 inches diameter...	50	40 00
No. 3—1 to 1½ inches diameter...	25	20 00
No. 4—¾ to 1 inch diameter, 7 to 9 feet high.................................	15	10 00

(Large orders at special rates, very low).

CAROLINA POPLAR. A magnificent tree for street planting, forming a beautiful head; large leaf and spreading habit; rapid grower.

LOMBARDY POPLAR. Erect and upright grower.

BLACK LOCUST. Strong grower, valuable for timber; same price as poplar.

CORK BARK ELM. Rapid grower; symmetrical shape; 50 cents to $1 25 each.

AMERICAN ELM. A magnificent tree with drooping branches; 25 to 75 cents each.

SOFT OR SILVER MAPLE. Fine for street planting, handsome foliage; 25 to 50 cents each; large trees 75 cents to $1 each.

WEEPING WILLOW. A beautiful weeping tree, with slender drooping branches; 50 cents to $1 each. Our stock of both Maple and American Elm, is very large, and on large lots we will make very low prices.

UMBRELLA TREE. One of the most beautiful and ornamental trees grown. It naturally grows in the shape of an umbrella, and is a very rapid grower; makes a dense shade. Price 50 cents each; extra large trees 75 cents each.

MULBERRIES.

The Mulberry is a very valuable family of tree. Most of them make a beautiful, well shaped and clean shade tree. All make very valuable timber and make it very quick, being rapid growers. This fruit is excellent, and is recommended by some to plant in cherry orchards for the purpose of attracting the birds from the cherries, as they eat mulberries in preference to any other fruit.

PRICE OF TREES.

1 year, No. 1—5 to 8 feet...50 cents each
1 year, No. 2—3 to 5 feet...35 cents each

Varieties.

DOWNING'S EVERBEARING. A rapid growing tree, valuable for its fruit, as it remains in fruit for three months.

PERSIAN. Largest fruit, but slow grower.

NEW AMERICAN. This is a large, strong growing, beautiful shaped tree; one of the best shade trees that grows; it also produces large crops of very fine berries, very sweet and delicious. Fine.

RUSSIAN MULBERRY. This also makes a fine tree, and the fruit is said to be very large and fine; we have not fruited it yet.

CIRCASSIAN MULBERRY. This is a very fine, strong growing variety, makes a splendid shade tree; fruit of little value.

MORUS ALBA or WHITE MULBERRY. Fine shade tree, but fruit of no value.

MORUS MULTICOLUS. Only valuable for the foliage, which is used to feed silk worms; 10 to 25 cents. Large lots for silk culture very cheap.

DYOSPYROS KAKI, OR JAPANESE PERSIMMONS.

Hyakume, Kuro, Kume, Zemon, Dai Dai Maru, Zanji Maru Hachija, Tane Nashi. The two last named are nearly or quite seedless. We have several other varieties, but have not space to name or describe them. Most of our people are familiar with this fruit. Price 35 cents each.

ORNAMENTAL DEPARTMENT.

☞ Our limited space will not admit of a full description of every shrub or flower, neither can we give the exact price for each particular size and style of plant. They vary so much in size, shape and condition that a minute description would occupy too much space. But we can guarantee satisfaction if you will, in ordering articles, where the price ranges from one figure to another, simply give the price you wish to pay, and we will send articles to correspond with the price given.

☞ We do not grow Greenhouse Plants but carry them in stock during the selling season and can furnish anything in that line at regular florists' prices. So we can fill orders for anything in that line, though it may not be named in the Catalogue. In the item of Roses we can furnish over 100 varieties not mentioned in this Catalogue.

ROSES.

Price, in pots..60c. to $1 00 each.
Price, naked roots...30c. each.

CHOICE COLLECTION OF EVER-BLOOMING ROSES.

THE BRIDE. A pure, white rose, of large size and most perfect form. It is a sport from "Catharine Mermet," with which it is identical in growth and shape of flowers. The buds are pointed and the ends of petals are slightly curved back, giving it a most chaste and elegant appearance.

BON SILENE. Free bloomer and fine bedder,; color brilliant carmine.

ANNA OLIVER. Creamy blush, shaded carmine.

ALINE SISLEY. Violet red, brightened with crimson Maroon.

BOUGERE. Beautiful dark pink; sweet fragrance,

BEAUTY OF STAPLEFORD. Flowers large, double and handsomely formed, color bright pink, shading gradually toward the center to deep rosy carmine, makes beautiful buds, and is a profuse bloomer.

CATHERINE MERMET. One of the finest roses grown. Bright rosy flesh, flowers of immense size and perfect form. One of the most popular roses for cut blooms.

CLOTH OF GOLD. Beautiful climber, flowers golden yellow; fragrant, large and beautiful.

GOLD OF OPHIR. (Climber). Very showy and delicate, flowers yellow, shaded with rose, a profuse bloomer.

MARECHAL NEIL. (Climber). Immense yellow roses, fragrant, well known to all.

COMTESSE RISA DU PARK. Bright coppery rose, shaded violet crimson. Very beautiful, a great favorite.

COMTESSE DE FRIGNEUSE. Long pointed buds of bright canary yellow.

CORNELIA COOK. Beautiful creamy white, buds of immense size and very double; when well grown is a magnificent flower.

COQUETTE DE LYON. A fine yellow rose, called the yellow Hermosa from its free flowering habit.

CAPTAIN CRISTY. Delicate pink, large, full and double, very profuse bloomer.

DEVONIENSIS. Often called the Magnolia rose. Creamy white, delicately flushed in the centre with pink. One of the most fragrant roses, and a favorite of long standing.

ROSES—Continued.

DUCHESS DE BRABANT. Few roses equal this in freedom of flowering; the flowers are rather loose when open, but are rich and peculiarly colored; color rose, heavily shaded with amber and salmon.

DUCHESS OF EDINBURGH. Very dark crimson; free flowering; large, fine form; beautiful in bud.

ETOILE DE LYON. A magnificent rose, color brilliant chrome yellow, deepening in the centre to pure golden yellow. Flowers large, very double and full and deliciously fragrant.

EXADELPHA. Beautiful yellow, large and full.

GRACE DARLING. Large, full, beautifully recurved petals; color, rosy pink, shaded yellow.

GENERAL DE TARTAS. Brilliant carmine shaded violet purple.

JULES FINGER. Brilliant rosy scarlet, shaded with crimson.

GENERAL JAQUIMINOT. Brilliant crimson; very large, of fine shape and exquisite fragrance. This grand old variety holds its own against all new comers, and is undoubtedly the finest hardy rose of its color.

LA FRANCE. Delicate silvery rose, shaded with cerise pink. Very large, and double flowering continuously throughout the season. One of the most fragrant roses grown. It stands first and foremost among roses.

NIPHETOS. Long buds of pure white; there is none equal it for cutting.

MADAM WELCHE. An extra fine variety; very large double, and of beautiful rounded form; color, Apricot yellow, very heavily shaded throughout the centre with dark orange red. One of the best Tea roses.

MARIE GUILLOT. Pure white, large, full and beautifully imbricated in form; one of the finest white Teas, highly fragrant.

MARIE VAN HOUTTE. Lovely creamy white, with outer petals suffused with bright pink. It grows vigorously; blooms freely and is most deliciously scented—no garden is complete without it.

PERLE DES JARDINS. Among tea roses, this still stands without a rival, in color, form, beauty of foliage and all that goes to make a perfect rose. Color, a rich shade of yellow, should be in every collection.

SOUV. DE GABRIEL DREVET. Salmon pink with center of coppery rose; of good size and fine form.

SOUV. DE MALMAISON. Known and prized by all; deep blush white, clear, full and distinct.

SAFRANO. This is the ideal Tea Rose; buff color, tinted Apricot yellow; exquisite fragance and splendid bud.

SOMBREUIL. Large, fine formed flowers; white tinged with delicate rose; blooms in clusters, constant.

MAD JOSEPH SCHWARTZ. A strong vigorous grower and one of the hardiest Tea roses. Color, white; beautifully flushed with pink.

EVERGREEN TREES.

EUCALYPTUS. Globulus (Blue Gum), in variety, in pots or bagged, 2½ to 10 feet, 20c to $1. Blue Gum and other varieties of Eucalyptus, in seed boxes. Transplanted in boxes so as to cut with balls of earth, 8 to 16 inches, $3 per 100.

☞ In large quantities for forest planting at special rates.

ACACIA. Native of Australia, rapid growth, beautiful foliage and masses of yellow and orange-colored flowers; in pots or bagged, 3 to 5 feet, 30 to 50 cents.

ACACIA MELONOXELON, or Blackwood Acacia, a very fine hardy kind.

ACACIA floribunda, or fragrans, long lance-like leaves.

ACACIA molissima, fine elegant species; light green leaves.

PEPPER TREES (California Schinn Molle), 3 to 6 feet, 40 cents to $1.

PALMS, in variety, $1 to $5, as per size and variety,

CUPRESSUS (Cypress), most popular and very ornamental; perfectly hardy, and thrives well in most localities and soils.

CUPRESSUS LAWSONIANA (Port Orford Cedar) very fine; branches curve like green plums; 50c to $1.

CUPRESSUS FUNEBRUS, elegant drooping foliage, adapted for planting in cemeteries; 75cents to $1.

CUPRESSUS macrocarpa (Monterey Cypress), 15 cents to $1 each.

CUPRESSUS pyramidalias (Italian Cypress), very erect, close pressing branches; 50 cents to $1.

PINUS macrocarpa (Monterey Pine), 3 to 7 feet; 30 cents to 75 cents.

ARBOR VITÆ, golden, beautiful compact plants; 75 cents to $2.50.

SEQUOIA gigantea (California Mammoth Trees), $1 to $2.50.

LAUREL, English, good plants; 75 cents to $1.

MAGNOLIA GRANDIFLORA, 50 cents to $2.50.

☞ Surplus stock, which we will sell at special rates in quality. Price on application—

MISCELLANEOUS.

Pinks, in variety.........................35c each
Lillies (See Seed Catalogue for price of bulbs)
   ....25 to 75c "
Chrysanthemums..................25c "
Fuchsia................................35c "
Heliotrope.............................35c "
Pampas Grass..........................50c "
Verbenas, per bunch..................20c "
Pansies, per bunch....................10c "
Violets, per bunch.............10 to 25c each

Honeysuckle, in variety...............35c each
Ivy.....................................25c "
Olrander.............................35c "
Veronica.......................25 to 50c "
English Box...................10 to 30c "
Euonomous, plain......................40c "
Euonomous, Varigated Golden..........50c "
Lauristimus..........................40c "
Camelias, assorted............50c to $3 00 "
Geraniums.......................25 to 75c "

Table Showing Number of Plants or Trees to the Acre at Given Distances.

Distance Apart.	No. Plants.	Distance Apart.	No. Plants.
3 in. x 3 in.	696,960	5 ft. x 4 ft.	2,178
4 in. x 4 in.	392,040	5 ft. x 5 ft.	1,742
6 in. x 6 in.	174,240	5½ ft. x 5½ ft.	1,417
9 in. x 9 in.	77,440	6 ft. x 6 ft.	1,210
1 ft. x 1 ft.	43,560	6½ ft. x 6½ ft.	1,031
1½ ft. x 1½ ft.	19,360	7 ft. x 7 ft.	881
2 ft. x 1 ft.	21,780	8 ft. x 8 ft.	680
2 ft. x 2 ft.	10,890	9 ft. x 9 ft.	537
2½ ft. x 2½ ft.	6,960	10 ft. x 10 ft.	435
3 ft. x 1 ft.	14,520	11 ft. x 11 ft.	361
3 ft. x 2 ft.	7,260	12 ft. x 12 ft.	302
3 ft. x 3 ft.	4,840	13 ft. x 13 ft.	257
3½ ft. x 3½ ft.	3,555	14 ft. x 14 ft.	222
4 ft. x 1 ft.	10,890	15 ft. x 15 ft.	193
4 ft. x 2 ft.	5,445	16 ft. x 16 ft.	170
4 ft. x 3 ft.	3,680	16½ ft. x 16½ ft.	160
4 ft. x 4 ft.	2,722	17 ft. x 17 ft.	150
4½ ft. x 4½ ft.	2,151	18 ft. x 18 ft.	134
5 ft. x 1 ft.	8,712	19 ft. x 19 ft.	120
5 ft. x 2 ft.	4,356	20 ft. x 20 ft.	108
5 ft. x 4 ft.	2,904	25 ft. x 25 ft.	69
		30 ft. x 30 ft.	48

RULE.—Multiply the distance in feet between the rows by the distance the plants are apart in the rows, and the product will be the number of square feet for each plant or hill, which, divided into the number of feet in an acre (43,560), will give the number of plants or trees to the acre.

Transplanting Trees.

In the first place see that the ground selected for orchard is thoroughly ploughed and well pulverized. Dig the holes large enough to allow all the roots to spread out in their natural shape, two feet wide and two feet deep will usually do, though the larger and deeper the hole is, the better, as you get the ground more thoroughly worked up. After the holes are all dug take the trees from the bale a few at a time, so that they will not be exposed. Do not expose roots to sun or frost, fill the hole with loose moist soil until the tree will stand about the same depth as it stood in the nursery, trim off all the bruised parts of the roots, place the tree in the hole so that the roots will spread out naturally, throw in moist earth and pack it solid around the roots, after the roots are covered, and the ground packed thoroughly if is an excellent thing to throw in a bucket of water, then fill up the hole. To preserve from borers and other injuries during the first summer, wrap the trunk with cloth, woolen preferred—but burlap will do.

Hints on Pruning.

The best dug tree loses more than half the fibrous roots that act as feeders. Shorten the top to correspond. Don't fail to cut back heavily when you transplant. Don't forget that a half root cannot support a whole top. Never neglect pruning. Trees trained low protect their own trunks from the sun's rays, are less liable to break with the weight of the fruit, and the fruit is easier gathered.

Transplanting Potted Plants.

In transplanting potted plants, lift the ball carefully out of the pot, then with a sharp knife cut the circle of roots that encompass the outside of the ball, so as to force a straight and not a crooked root from the plant into the ground, in order that, as the tree or plant increases in size, it will not be so liable to blow over. Thousands of trees are annually blown over and destroyed by reason of this circle of roots, for as the root is shaped when the plant is set, so it will continue to grow. Bagged plants should be placed with the bag on, only cutting the string at the collar or top of the bag.

Anything not mentioned in this Catalogue, or Greenhouse and Florists' specialties, will be furnished at regular florists' prices, provided it can be procured in the market.

Principal Office at Store, Nos. 102 to 110 J street, between Front and Second.

Principal Depot and Sales Yards, Second Streets, near Passenger Depot of C. P. R. R.

W. R. STRONG COMPANY, PROPRIETORS

SACRAMENTO, CAL.

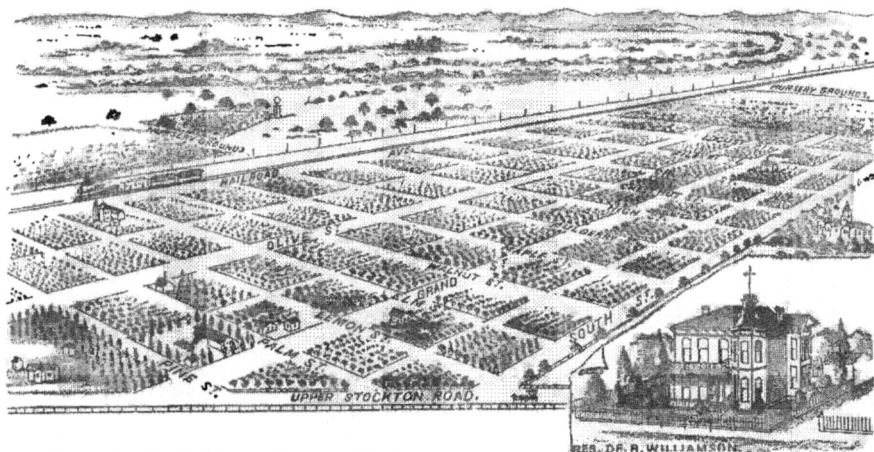

Cut of the W. R. Strong Company Tract.

A GRAND OPPORTUNITY

—TO—

Get Beautiful Suburban Homes Cheap, and on Easy Terms.

We have decided to subdivide and sell in small tracts our beautiful orchard and nursery grounds, just outside the city limits of Sacramento. This property is in bearing fruit orchard, AND WILL PAY A HANDSOME REVENUE FROM THE START. The soil is very superior, and the land lays beautifully, and all under a system of irrigation.

A STREET CAR LINE

is contemplated, to run to the property. There is NO HEALTHIER LOCATION IN THE SACRAMENTO VALLEY than this. The water is superb. It is from this Ranch that the Sacramento Board of Health urged the City to get its supply of water—and they still advocate it.

It will be only a short time when this property will be wanted for BUILDING LOTS. It lies east of the City, and the City is extending in that direction faster than in any other. To see it is to be convinced of the truth of the above assertion.

Those who wish property near the City should not miss this golden opportunity.

We also have other lands for sale in this County, and in other Counties in this State, which we will sell either in large or small tracts at a bargain. Most of it is improved and productive property, although we have some unimproved cheap lands for sale.

For further information, call on or write to

W. R. STRONG COMPANY,

Sept. 1, 1891.   SACRAMENTO, CAL.

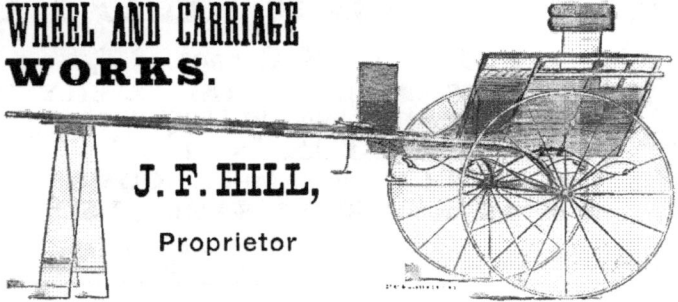

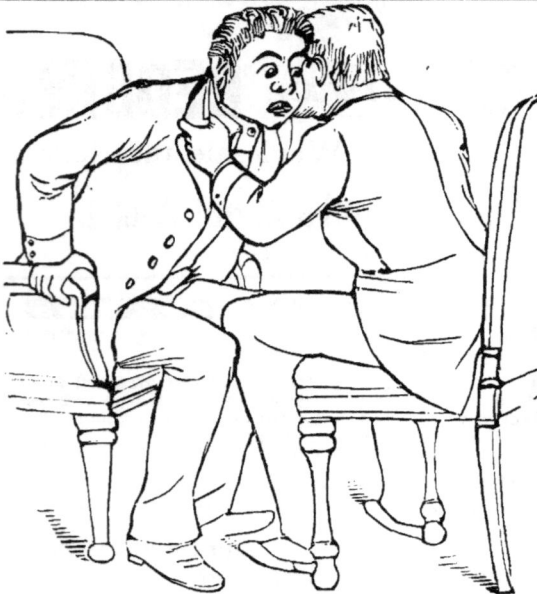

Description of Flowers on Front Page of Cover.

No. 1. Fuchsias—T. P. The Fuchsias are general favorites both for out door and window decoration. They require a light, rich, sandy soil. Sprinkle often and give plenty of light and air. With care they are easily raised from seed. The north side of a house or fence being the best situation. We offer seed of finest double; also double and single choicest mixed varieties.

No. 2. New Margaret Carnation. This new class has justified the highest expectations. The plants are of dwarf, compact habit, branching close to the ground, therefore do not require any support. Seedlings begin blooming the fourth month from the time of coming up, and bloom most abundantly, 80 per cent of the flowers being double and never burst. Packet embracing many colors. 25c. (See cut on outside of cover.]

Eschscholtzia (California Poppy.) This plant so well known here in California, is the favorite wild flower of the State. Also gives great satisfaction as a cultivated flower in our gardens with other flowers. These are easily grown in almost any situation, bearing a profusion of delicate satiny flowers, of brilliant colors.

No. 4. Hollyhock—H. B. One of our grandest Summer and Autumn flowering plants, bearing long spikes of double flowers 3 to 4 inches across. (See cut.) The seed we offer has been saved from the choicest improved double varieties.

Description of Vegetables on Back Page of Cover.

No. 1. Wardell's Kidney Wax Beans. This is one of the finest Wax Beans grown. The most valuable point in its favor is that it has NOT YET SHOWN THE SLIGHTEST INDICATION OF RUST OR SPOT no matter where or under what condition grown.

No. 2. Earliest Carmine Radish. Valuable for forcing. Tender, crisp and fresh to the taste. Color a beautiful shade of carmine.

No. 3. Saint Vallery Carrot. This splendid variety originated in France near the city of Saint Vallery, from whence it takes its name. It grows to uniform size, intermediate in shape, between the Half Long and Long Orange. The roots are straight and smooth, broad at the top, measuring about two and one-half inches, with a length of about eleven inches. The color is a rich orange red; its table qualities are faultless. It will be found a most excellent variety for either garden or field culture.

No. 4. Improved White Spine Cucumber. An excellent variety for the table, grows uniformly straight and smooth, measuring about ten inches long. They make fine, hard brittle pickles when four to five inches long.

No. 5. Edmond's Blood Turnip Beet. We can recommend this variety for both family and market use. The skin is a deep blood red, flesh very dark and exceedingly sweet and tender. Grows regularly of good market size, not over large and coarse as many sorts of Turnip Beets when they have plenty of room. They mature early and give the very best satisfaction as a bunch beet in the market. They remain sweet and tender longer than other sorts.

No. 6. Improved Sacramento Favorite Tomato. One of the best large size Tomatoes grown, smooth as an apple, flesh thick and firm, color bright red. A splendid shipper.

No. 7. Snowball Cauliflower. The earliest and best heading variety in cultivation; dwarf, with short outer leaves.

No. 8. Strong's Perfection Cabbage Lettuce. Without doubt the finest Lettuce grown. For further description see among Specialties.

No. 9. Monstrous Carentan Leek. A very choice variety of extra large size, rapid growth, and very hardy. The leaves are fan shape, of a dark green color; the edible stem is six to eight inches long and three inches in diameter.

W. R. Strong Company
Sacramento
Cal.

Cor. Front & J Street

STRONG'S PERFECTIO
CABBAGE. LETTUC

www.ingramcontent.com/pod-product-compliance
Lightning Source LLC
Chambersburg PA
CBHW021118270326
41929CB00009B/940